TAMMANY HALL

Books by M. R. Werner

———◆———

BARNUM
BRIGHAM YOUNG
TAMMANY HALL

The "Wigwam," Broad Street,
1789—1790

The "Wigwam" and Museum of
Tammany Society, Broad Street,
1790—1798

TAMMANY HALL

THE WIGWAM FROM 1790
TO THE PRESENT DAY

The "Wigwam" from 1812 to
1868. The first Tammany Hall.

Tammany Hall today

The "Wigwam," corner of Nassau
and Spruce Streets, 1798—1812

From the collection of Mr. Edwin P. Kilroe
Tammany Hall, 1830

TAMMANY
HALL

BY M. R. WERNER

"Tammany, Tammany
Swamp 'em, swamp 'em
Get the wampum
Taammanee!"

—*Old Song*

But do you not admire, I said, the coolness and dexterity of t
ready ministers of political corruption?

Yes, he said, I do; but not of all of them, for there are some w
the applause of the multitude has deluded into the belief that
are really statesmen, and these are not much to be admired.

What do you mean? I said; you should have more feeling for th
When a man can not measure, and a great many others who can
measure declare that he is four cubits high, can he help believing w
they say?

PLATO, *The Republi*

GARDEN CITY   NEW YO
DOUBLEDAY, DORAN & COMPANY,
1928

ACKNOWLEDGMENT

My thanks are due to Mr. Bernard O'Donohoe for invaluable assistance, to the staff of the New York Public Library for unlimited courtesy and aid, and to Mr. Edwin P. Kilroe for kind permission to use illustrations from his excellent collection of Tammany Hall material.

The "Wigwam," Broad Street,
1789—1790

The "Wigwam" and Museum of
Tammany Society, Broad Street,
1790—1798

TAMMANY HALL

THE WIGWAM FROM 1790
TO THE PRESENT DAY

The "Wigwam" from 1812 to
1868. The first Tammany Hall.

Tammany Hall today

The "Wigwam," corner of Nassau
and Spruce Streets, 1798—1812

From the collection of Mr. Edwin P. Kilroe
Tammany Hall, 1830

TAMMANY HALL

BY M. R. WERNER

"Tammany, Tammany
Swamp 'em, swamp 'em
Get the wampum
Taammanee! "

— *Old Song*

But do you not admire, I said, the coolness and dexterity of these ready ministers of political corruption?

Yes, he said, I do; but not of all of them, for there are some whom the applause of the multitude has deluded into the belief that they are really statesmen, and these are not much to be admired.

What do you mean? I said; you should have more feeling for them. When a man can not measure, and a great many others who can not measure declare that he is four cubits high, can he help believing what they say?

PLATO, *The Republic*

GARDEN CITY   NEW YORK
DOUBLEDAY, DORAN & COMPANY, INC.
1928

PREFACE

TAMMANY HALL is the oldest and the most powerful institution of a political and sociological nature in America. The span of its existence and the strength that it has so constantly exhibited make it interesting to inquire into the sources of its power, the details of its daily life, and the character of the men who have made it what it has been and what it is, and who were themselves shaped by the machine with which their fortunes were so inextricably involved.

Besides being an association and a building where men whose interests are common congregate for the purpose of making their efforts effective, Tammany Hall is a symbol. The Tammany concept is one of crass reality in contradistinction to the unduly fanciful optimism of its opponents, for the Tammany idea is and always has been based firmly and soundly on the notion that everyone is working for his pocket and his vanity all the time. Tammany Hall has always catered to both the pockets and the vanity of its members, and the members have always seen to it that they got their shares of money and prestige from the institution. It is futile to designate Tammany Hall in the abstract by such terms as "good" or "bad"; Tammany is an entity whos epurpose is the complete satisfaction of two fundamental passions of mankind. Its history is the story of men striving ruthlessly and successfully for the attainment of those ends which seem at the moment most desirable. Wherever men may happen to live, they will often be corrupt, if thereby they can make money and feed their appetite for power without being killed or placed in solitary confinement. Tammany Hall has represented the complete organization of those endeavours, and its history is more picturesque than that of any other similar congregation in the United States, because the institution has been more continuously powerful than any other group of men organized in this country for the purposes of aggrandizement.

Other cities and other countries have had and still have their political groups, with their attendant political and social

corruption, but they come and they go and they change their
names. Tammany Hall remains constant as an hereditary
monarchy, with only the changes that hereditary monarchies
always experience in the process of the growth and multiplica-
tion of their subjects. Philadelphia had its Gas Ring; St. Louis
had its garbage deals and traction conspiracies; Cincinnati had
George B. Cox; San Francisco had "Blind Boss" Buckley and
Abe Ruef; Minneapolis had "Doc" Ames; but, ever since
three weeks after the Constitution of the United States went
into effect, New York has had its Tammany Hall, which it has
sometimes worshipped and sometimes whipped, and whose
members have always been devoted to turning the manifold
resources of the metropolis to their personal use. Tammany
Hall has always been distinctive from its contemporaries and
its rivals, because it has carefully guarded its permanence as
an institution, even at the expense of individual members. It
has its history and its traditions, but its spirit is by no means
confined to the City of New York or to the United States of
America. Its methods and its principles could probably be
found among the monks of the Thebaid and in the council
chambers of Canaan, if only the records were available. Vis-
count Bryce wrote that "the dynasty of bosses who during
eighty years have reigned [in New York] purely by the gifts of
political leadership may be compared with that line of monarchs, neither hereditary nor elective, but most of them rising
by their military talents, which ruled the Roman Empire from
Nero down to Constantine."

The permanence of Tammany Hall in our civilization does
not seem in danger. As George Washington Plunkitt, one of
the most picturesque of its latter-day district leaders, remarked:
"Tammany's like the everlastin' rocks, the eternal hills, and
the blockades on the 'L' road—it goes on forever." Tammany
has been caught, exposed, and discredited many times during
its career; some of the leaders have been jailed; but the resilience
of the institution has always amazed its opponents. Two years
after the startling Tweed Ring exposures Tammany Hall,
under the leadership of "Honest John" Kelly, was once more
in power. Several revealing legislative investigations could
not break the autocracy of Richard Croker. The reason may be
the fact that men have always been more interested in par-

ticular jobs and specific sums of money than in such abstract
questions as good government. Socrates and Thrasymachus
took up the matter many years ago in this conversation:

"When we had got to this point in the argument, and everyone
saw that the definition of justice had been completely upset,
Thrasymachus, instead of replying to me, said: Tell me,
Socrates, have you got a nurse?

"Why do you ask such a question, I said, when you ought
rather to be answering?

"Because she leaves you to snivel, and never wipes your nose:
she has not even taught you to know the shepherd from the
sheep.

"What makes you say that? I replied.

"Because you fancy that the shepherd or neatherd fattens
or tends the sheep or oxen with a view to their own good and
not to the good of himself or his master; and you further
imagine that the rulers of states, if they are true rulers, never
think of their subjects as sheep, and that they are not studying
their own advantage day and night. . . . Observe also what happens when they take an office; there is the just man neglecting
his affairs and perhaps suffering other losses, and getting nothing out of the public, because he is just; moreover, he is hated by
his friends and acquaintances for refusing to serve them in unlawful ways. But all this is reversed in the case of the unjust
man. I am speaking, as before, of injustice on a large scale in
which the advantage of the unjust is most apparent; and my
meaning will be most clearly seen if we turn to that highest
form of injustice in which the criminal is the happiest of men,
and the sufferers or those who refuse to do injustice are the
most miserable—that is to say tyranny, which by fraud and
force takes away the property of others, not little by little
but wholesale; comprehending in one, things sacred as well as
profane, private and public; for which acts of wrong, if he
were detected perpetrating any of them singly, he would be
punished and incur great disgrace—they who do such wrong in
particular cases are called robbers of temples, and man-stealers
and burglars and swindlers and thieves. But when a man besides taking away the money of the citizens has made slaves of
them, then, instead of these names of reproach, he is termed

happy and blessed, not only by the citizens but by all who hear
of his having achieved the consummation of injustice. For
mankind censure injustice, fearing that they may be victims
of it and not because they shrink from committing it."[1]

Socrates succeeded finally in convincing Thrasymachus that
justice was good for the soul, that the just man was therefore
happy, that happiness was more profitable than misery, and
that accordingly justice was more profitable than injustice.
The difference, however, between Socrates and Charles F.
Murphy was that Murphy was interested in money and in
power, and Socrates was interested in happiness and in the
soul. William M. Tweed may have had moments when he
thought of his own soul and of the welfare of his fellow men, but
the complications that developed from the vast amount of
money he was accumulating and the enormous power he was
amassing occupied most of his twenty-four hours each day.

Big John Kennedy, the Tammany leader in Alfred Henry
Lewis's novel *The Boss*, as he was about to go into the retirement of death, said to his protégé: "Think first, last, an' all th'
time of yourself. You may not be of account to others, but
you're the whole box of tricks to yourself. Don't give a man
more than he gives you. Folks who don't stick to that steer
land either in bankruptcy or Bloomin'dale." That has always
been the pragmatic creed of Tammany Hall. George Washington Plunkitt, the Tammany district leader who dispensed his
philosophy daily from the bootblack stand in front of the
New York County Court House during the early years of the
twentieth century, said:

"You can't be patriotic on a salary that just keeps the wolf
from the door. Any man who pretends he can will bear watchin'.
. . . But when a man has a good fat salary, he finds himself
hummin' 'Hail Columbia,' all unconscious, and he fancies, when
he's ridin' in a trolley car, that the wheels are always sayin':
'Yankee Doodle Came to Town.' I know how it is myself. When
I got my first good job from the city I bought up all the fire-
crackers in my district to salute this glorious country. I couldn't
wait for the Fourth of July. I got the boys on the block to fire

---

[1]Plato, *The Republic*, Book I, Jowett translation.

them off for me, and I felt, proud of bein' an American. For a long time after that I use to wake up nights singin' the 'Star-Spangled Banner.'"[1]

Mr. H. G. Wells made a survey of the United States in 1910. In the book which resulted, *The Future in America*, he asked: "Is the average citizen fundamentally dishonest? Is he a rascal in humbug and grain? If he is, the future can needs be no more than a monstrous social disorganization in the face of divine opportunities." Whatever the future may have in store for us, Mr. Wells's phrase is an accurate description of large portions of the past as seen with Tammany Hall as a focus. When one sets out to write the history of Tammany Hall, one soon finds that the story is concerned more than anything else with the history of corruption, political and social, legislative and personal, in the City of New York.

A writer in the *North American Review* of October, 1866, re-marked:

"We have undertaken to write something about the government of the City of New York, and yet we have fallen into a discourse on stealing. The reason is, that, after having spent several weeks in investigating our subject, we find that we have been employed in nothing else but discovering in how many ways, and under what a variety of names and pretexts, immature and greedy men steal from that fruitful and ill-fenced orchard, the city treasury."

Tammany Hall has been the watchman of that orchard more often than any other organization, and greedy as well as immature men have usually been assigned to the outposts.

Big John Kennedy told his protégé:

"A man who can take care of himself with his hands, an' who never lets whiskey fool him or steal his head can go far in this game of politics. An' it's a pretty good game at that, is politics, and can be brought to pay like a bank."

There is nothing that Tammany men have resented more than being called thieves, and they have never been able to

---

[1] *Plunkitt of Tammany Hall*, by William L. Riordan, pp. 104–105.

understand the justice of the epithet; they themselves have always preferred to call it business. It was George Washington Plunkitt who made the famous distinction between honest graft and dishonest graft. He delivered this speech one day to his Boswell, Mr. Riordan:

"Everybody is talkin' these days about Tammany men growin' rich on graft, but nobody thinks of drawin' the distinction between honest graft and dishonest graft. . . . Yes, many of our men have grown rich in politics. I have myself. I've made a big fortune out of the game, and I'm gettin' richer every day, but I've not gone in for dishonest graft—blackmailin' gamblers, saloon-keepers, disorderly people, etc. —and neither has any of the men who have made big fortunes in politics.

"There's an honest graft, and I'm an example of how it works. I might sum up the whole thing by sayin': 'I seen my opportunities and I took 'em.'

"Just let me explain by examples. My party's in power in the city, and it's goin' to undertake a lot of public improvements. Well, I'm tipped off, say, that they're going to lay out a new park at a certain place.

"I see my opportunity and I take it. I go to that place and I buy up all the land I can in the neighbourhood. Then the board of this or that makes its plan public, and there is a rush to get my land, which nobody cared particular for before.

"Ain't it perfectly honest to charge a good price and make a profit on my investment and foresight? Of course it is. Well, that's honest graft. . . .

"It's just like lookin' ahead in Wall Street or in the coffee or cotton market. . . .

"For instance, the city is repavin' a street and has several hundred thousand old granite blocks to sell. I am on hand to buy, and I know just what they are worth.

"How? Never mind that. I had a sort of monopoly of this business for a while, but once a newspaper tried to do me. It got some outside men to come over from Brooklyn and New Jersey to bid against me.

"Was I done? Not much. I went to each of the men and said: 'How many of these 250,000 stones do you want?' One said

20,000, and another wanted 15,000, and another wanted 10,000. I said: 'All right, let me bid for the lot, and I'll give each of you all you want for nothin'.'

"They agreed, of course. Then the auctioneer yelled: 'How much am I bid for these 250,000 fine pavin' stones?'

"'Two dollars and fifty cents,' says I.

"'Two dollars and fifty cents!' screamed the auctioneer. 'Oh, that's a joke! Give me a real bid.'

"He found the bid was real enough. My rivals stood silent. I got the lot for $2.50 and gave them their share. . . .

"Tammany was beat in 1901 because the people were deceived into believin' that it worked dishonest graft. They didn't draw a distinction between dishonest and honest graft, but they saw that some Tammany men grew rich, and supposed they had been robbin' the city treasury or levyin' blackmail on disorderly houses, or workin' in with the gamblers and lawbreakers.

"As a matter of policy, if nothing else, why should the Tammany leaders go into such dirty business, when there is so much honest graft lyin' around when they are in power? Did you ever consider that?

"Now, in conclusion, I want to say that I don't own a dishonest dollar. If my worst enemy was given the job of writin' my epitaph when I'm gone, he couldn't do more than write:

"'George W. Plunkitt. He Seen His Opportunities, and He Took 'Em.'"[1]

The Rev. Dr. Charles H. Parkhurst presented a somewhat different version of the business of Tammany Hall one Sunday morning in March, 1892, at the Madison Square Church, and his sermon startled New York:

"Tammany Hall," said Dr. Parkhurst, "is not a political party but purely a business enterprise, as much so as Standard Oil or the Western Union Telegraph, and superior to any other company of which I have knowledge, in respect to the perfection of its organization. The material in which it deals and from which it draws prolific dividends is crime and vice, such as flourish in gambling resorts, disorderly houses and corner groceries. The

[1]*Plunkitt of Tammany Hall*, by William L. Riordan, pp. 3–10.

more material it can handle the larger its profits and therefore the policy which it steadfastly pursues is to foster crimes and exercise guardianship over the criminals.

"And not only does the organization stand as the organization of crime, but it embodies the tyranny of crime. There are citizens in this town abominating the whole existing system that do not dare to stand up and be counted. . . .

"Men of tainted reputation cannot occupy positions of high municipal authority without that fact operating to the discouragement of virtue and the lowering of moral standards. It is a trying condition of affairs for such as are attempting to improve the moral state of our young men, to have men exalted to positions of distinguished authority against whom the most damning charge that can be made is to publish their history."[1]

As we progress through the history of Tammany Hall—which is the history of the government of the City of New York—we shall see that Dr. Parkhurst was not exaggerating.

After he had visited some American political saloons in Chicago with the boss of that city, Alderman Kenna, better known as "Hinky-Dink," Mr. H. G. Wells wrote: "It struck me that I would as soon go to live in a pen in a stockyard as into American politics." And that is the conclusion that thousands of American citizens have also reached as a result of their experience with or their observation of the game which "can be brought to pay like a bank." Except in times of great financial distress, or when revelations have indicated that politicians were getting too gay, it has been found practically impossible to interest the citizen in such sordid details as the business of his government. He prefers to leave it in the hands of such organizations as Tammany Hall, and to take what they give him, unless perchance it proves too rotten. Professor William Bennett Munro observed: "Sound democracy is predicated upon the interest, the alert and sustained interest of the individual citizen. That ought to be a commonplace of action— but in America it is only a commonplace of speech." And the leaders of Tammany Hall and similar organizations have always been careful to bring it about that government should

[1] *My Forty Years in New York*, by Rev. Charles H. Parkhurst, pp. 127–129.

remain so complicated as to prove continuously distracting to
people who have other business to attend to, should they wish
to turn their attention to everybody's business. George William
Curtis once told an audience that a machine politician had
said to him: "This is a nasty state and it takes a great deal of
nasty work to carry it, and I trust we have nasty agents enough
to do it." "So far as I have observed," remarked Mr. Curtis,
"his confidence was well founded." In the face of the difficulties
that Tammany Hall has placed in their way, the best people,
even when they have stopped long enough in their individual
pursuits to give their attention to the community, have become discouraged rapidly and sometimes permanently disheartened.

But then, too, Tammany Hall has used for its purposes
innumerable people who, because of the possession of large
sums of money or because of their hereditary positions in society,
have been regarded by themselves and some of their contemporaries as superior to their fellow men. An analyst of Tammany
Hall wrote: "It is not at ease with unsullied reputations; it is
not altogether happy with convicts." Tammany Hall's most
reputable associates have always been members of that vast
class between the definite criminal and the impeccable gentleman which was so happily described by Job Hedges when
he wrote: "Between 'Thou shalt not steal' and 'Honesty is the
best policy' lies the history of unindicted men." New York
under Tammany Hall's domination has usually been a good
example of what Lincoln Steffens called, "the government of
the people, by the rascals, for the rich."

It has pleased the politicians' vanity to have associated with
them a few rich men of important social position with whom
the political leaders could feel on friendly terms, and such men
have been invaluable for Tammany's show window. It has always flattered the vanity of rich men to feel that they were a
part of the most powerful political organization of their city,
and then, too, rich men are subject to heavy taxation, which
can be made less burdensome if the assessor is friendly rather
than impartial or hostile. Rich men also deal in railroads, street
cars, gas, water, electricity, and sundry other community commodities, and Tammany men, by virtue of their positions of
rulership, have been the dispensers of those commodities. Thus

arose a mutual admiration which operated to the satisfaction of the social and financial desires of both classes of society.

"They all are," wrote Lincoln Steffens, "according to their light, honorable men and patriotic citizens. They simply do not know what patriotism is. They know what treason is in war: it is going over to the enemy, like Benedict Arnold, and fighting in the open against your country. In peace and in secret to seize, not forts but cities and States, and destroy, not buildings and men, but the fundamental institutions of your country and the saving character of American manhood—that is not treason, that is politics, and politics is business, and business, you know, is business.

"'Do you really call it wrong to buy a switch?' asked a St. Louis business man. 'Even if it is necessary to your business?'

"'Say,' said a politician, 'if a rich mogul comes along and shakes his swag in your face and asks for a switch that he has a right to get, because he needs it in his business, wouldn't you grab off a piece? On the level, now, wouldn't you?'"[1]

In an article headed "A Century of Tammany, the Inherited Spirit of Graft," the New York *Press* published the following statement on October 12, 1903:

"It is more than Croker; it is Croker preceded by Kelly; it is Kelly preceded by Tweed; it is Tweed preceded by Wood; it is Wood preceded by the Forty Thieves; it is the Forty Thieves preceded by the Land Grafters; it is the Land Grafters preceded by scores of earlier grafters; it is that set of earlier grafters preceded by Aaron Burr—the first leader of Tammany, the first great grafter of a hundred years ago."

This was the house that Jack built according to one who did not like its design. George Washington Plunkitt, one of the labourers on the edifice, remarked:

"Look at the bosses of Tammany Hall in the last twenty years. What magnificent men! To them New York City owes pretty much all it is to-day. John Kelly, Richard Croker, and Charles F. Murphy—what names in American history com-

---

[1] *The Struggle for Self-Government*, by Lincoln Steffens, pp. 37–38.

pare with them, except Washington and Lincoln? They built up the grand Tammany organization, and the organization built up New York."

On another occasion Plunkitt said:

"The papers and some people are always ready to find wrong motives in what us statesmen do. If we bring about some big improvement that benefits the city and it just happens, as a sort of coincidence, that we make a few dollars out of the improvement, they say we are grafters. But we are used to this kind of ingratitude. It falls to the lot of all statesmen, especially Tammany statesmen. All we can do is to bow our heads in silence and wait till time has cleared our memories."

The history of Tammany Hall includes the biography of many men who managed its affairs and those of the government. These men devoted their lives to the organization and also used the organization to contribute to the comfort of their personal lives. Most of them were extraordinary men in the sense that they were shrewder than the men they dominated and the men they used. So many of the Tammany leaders, like John Kelly, Charles F. Murphy, "Big Tim" Sullivan, and the most powerful of them all, Richard Croker, were in one respect like the personalities of the keepers of houses of prostitution with whom their representatives were always in such intimate contact—they sold vice or pleasure, but they were generally credited with rarely taking any of it themselves. It was frequently said in praise of Sullivan, Murphy, and others that, while they owned and operated saloons themselves, liquor had not passed their lips in many years. Richard Croker once remarked that he knew that liquor was bad for horses, and that he didn't suppose it was very much better for men. "Big Tim" Sullivan, whose business interests were connected with liquor, once said: "I advocate Ingersoll's famous saying. You know it—that a man who don't chew, smoke, or drink ought to be shot. I'm that fellow, and I know I ought to be shot. The only thing I can say in my behalf is that I don't interfere with the other fellow's rights to do all three." In fact, Sullivan and his Tammany associates have always used to great advantage the other fellow's interest in liquor, and the saloon, besides being a great source of personal profit for many Tammany leaders, was in its social aspects a great help to the organization in marshalling votes on election day. And, as we shall see, some men needed only a few drinks to enable them to vote seventeen times.

The personalities of the various Tammany bosses form a peculiar study in American characteristics, and I shall try to supply in the course of this story of Tammany Hall complete details of their special traits, wherever the material is available. They furnish some contrasts—from the ribald Tweed to the grim Croker, including the sunny Sullivan and the glum Murphy. Both Richard Croker and Charles F. Murphy gained great repute in this country for wisdom, because they were both silent men, one of them gruff and the other sullen. It was assumed that they knew a lot which they did not wish to say; that was true; there was much in their minds which they could not have wished to reveal, but there was also much incoherent fumbling going on in the chaos of their brains. That they were not always the Masters they were so generally credited with being by the vast numbers of inferior men who hung on their lack of words, we shall perhaps see in the course of their histories. Croker was often stubborn, and Murphy was sometimes unreasonable. They went down to defeat occasionally because of overindulgence in those traits. Their silence must not always be interpreted as the taciturnity of the sage, for, while there is an old proverb that "Silence is golden," there is a more recent saying that "Silence reigned, and everybody got wet."

This taciturnity is, however, important from the historical point of view, for it indicates the limitations of the materials available. Politics is so much an inside story, and there are more things in conventions, candidates, bosses, primaries, and elections than are dreamed of in the imaginations of newspaper readers. It might almost be safe to say that imagination cannot go too far, and that anything is credible, for, as we shall see, the history of Tammany Hall is a long series of almost incredible men and almost incredible incidents, which, fortunately, are sometimes made vivid, and even startling, by legislative investigations and other spotlights. William Travers Jerome, in one of the speeches he made during his campaign for dis-

trict attorney of New York in 1901, gave a striking illustration
of the fantastic in political truth:

"Yes," said Mr. Jerome, "if you want it, I will tell you the
lemon story. It came about this way: there are a number of very
earnest and enthusiastic men with New England consciences,
who live in Litchfield County, Connecticut. They formed the
Litchfield County Universal Club; they built a clubhouse, and
last summer they asked me to come up there. It wasn't far
from a little place I have in the country. I talked with them
after dinner, and the toast—there was nothing but Apollinaris
at that dinner; it was in New England—and the toast that they
gave me to respond to, and that I was presumably to occupy
about five minutes in responding to, was 'Municipal Problems
and Their Solution.' . . . Well, I was up against it, and I had to
speak succinctly upon municipal problems and their solution.
And I gave a story by way of illustration. I told them it was
purely imaginary and symbolic, and this was the case that I
imagined: that there was a scarcity of lemons in the New York
market, and that a merchant in the city of New York, seeing
the situation, cabled to his agents on the Mediterranean, 'Ship
me so many thousand lemons by first steamer.' The scarcity of
lemons at once caused other shipments, but this merchant, by
his willingness to spend money, and by reason of his connections
abroad, got his five thousand dollars' worth of lemons on the
first steamer, which meant probably a gain of thirty-six hours.
There was such a scarcity of lemons when the steamer reached
the dock that, before the next steamer arrived, it would enable
him to make a profit of at least a dollar a box, which he was
fairly entitled to because of his sagacity in foreseeing the conditions of the market, and his readiness in meeting those conditions. When the ship arrived, he rushed up to the Custom
House, feeling perfectly delighted. When he had paid his
duties at the Custom House, he went down on the dock, and
a fellow came up and said, 'Are you the man that brought
these lemons over?' 'I am.' The fellow threw back his coat and
disclosed the shield of an inspector of the Board of Health. He
said, 'I think these lemons will have to be hand-picked.' Hand-
picking five thousand boxes of lemons meant simply that the
merchant would lose his market, because other steam shipments

of lemons would arrive before the hand-picking could be finished. He said, 'What is it worth?' 'Well, two hundred and fifty will do this time.' He had to pay it. He was simply trying to carry on his honest, legitimate business, and so, rather than lose his profit, he paid. Now, this was the story that I told up on the Litchfield Hills. It was a Friday night, and somebody telegraphed to the New York papers enough of the story to show what I was driving at, but not enough to show that I had stated it as a purely imaginary case. Now comes the point. On Monday morning, in my chambers in the Criminal Court Building, I had a visit from a certain person, who, after beating around the bush and lingering a long time, came out at last with the purpose of his errand. He had been directed, he said, by an official of the Health Department, to find out how—well, how—'Say, Judge, who put you next about those lemons?' When fairy tales like these come true, what must we not conclude concerning the plain facts of every day?"[1]

This story delighted Mr. Jerome's audiences. They asked for it at his meetings again and again; they never seemed to tire of hearing it, for there is no one who delights the public more than its plunderers, which is one reason why Tammany leaders have always been such popular men personally. The public in New York City is like the English Duke quoted in a speech by Gladstone. The Duke's son was leading a fast life and spending very large sums of money. His Grace's steward thought it only his duty to inform His Grace of his son's disgraceful conduct. "Indeed," replied the Duke with dignity, "there is a great deal to spend." New York has always felt the same about the problem, and the reason, perhaps, is found in this observation by E. L. Godkin: "New York is too rich to be brought to insolvency. Great cities, when badly administered, cannot be sold and abolished; they simply become dirty, unhealthy, unsafe, disgraceful, and expensive."

The boss who gets away with it is considered a remarkably clever fellow. The public never tires of accounts of his antics, and the more disreputable he is the more fascinating his biography appears to the constituents whom he has robbed. The

---

[1]*A Fight for the City*, by Alfred Hodder, pp. 142–145.

reason may perhaps be found in the fact that America has
never had any kings and queens to play with, nor has she had
any very great artists to amuse her. The only refuge for diversion is in the lives of her political conquerors and of her millionaires.

How completely we surrender ourselves to our political
bosses is revealed somewhat in the history of Tammany Hall,
and I shall endeavour to portray as impartially as possible
the story of that surrender. "The present actual fact is,"
wrote one political observer, "that, at the dictate of leaders
whom we have not chosen, we vote for candidates whom we
do not know, to discharge duties that we cannot understand."

E. L. Godkin once concluded that, "The three things a
Tammany leader most dreaded were in the ascending order of
repulsiveness, the penitentiary, honest industry, and biography." I shall attempt to give him in each case honest biography.

M. R. W.

CONTENTS

LIST OF ILLUSTRATIONS

LIST OF TEXT ILLUSTRATIONS

TEXT ILLUSTRATIONS

SAINT TAMMANY

TAMMANY HALL

CHAPTER I

SAINT TAMMANY

"No puny saint was he, with fasting pale,
He climbed the mountains, and swept the vale;
Rushed through the torrent with unequalled might;—
Your ancient saints would tremble at the sight—
Caught the swift boar, the swifter deer with ease,
And worked a thousand miracles like these.
To public views, he added private ends,
And loved his country most, and next his friends."
— *Anonymous eulogy of Saint Tammany.*

I

ONCE upon a time there was an Indian chief. His name was
Tammany, and his deeds were legend. He was sachem of the
tribe of Delaware Indians known as the Lenni-Lenape. His
birth, his accomplishments, and his death are matter of myth
rather than of record, but his admirers, who were numerous in
the later colonial period of American history, have built around
the little knowledge that we have concerning him stories of
extraordinary deeds and exceptional sagacity.

Dr. Samuel L. Mitchill, Professor of Chemistry, Natural
History, and Agriculture in the College of New York during
the first years of the nineteenth century, and also one time
United States Senator from New York, author of *Epistles to
His Lady Love*, a book of poems, and the first man in New York
State to talk by signs with deaf mutes, wrote in 1795 *The Life
Exploits and Precepts of Tammany; The Famous Indian Chief;
Being the Anniversary Oration Pronounced Before the Tammany
Society or Columbian Order.* In this pleasant oration, Dr. Mit-

chill, whose versatility also included a knowledge of Indian ethnology and "speculations on the phosphorescence of the waters of the ocean, on the fecundity of fish, on the decortication of fruit trees, on the anatomy and physiology of the shark," said of Tammany:

"Let Asia extoll her Zamolxis, Confucius, and Zoroaster; let Africa be proud of her Dido, Ptolemy, and Barbarossa; let Europe applaud her numberless worthies, who from Romulus to Charlemagne, and from Charlemagne down to the present day, have founded, conquered, inherited, or governed states; and where, among them all, will you find coercion so tempered by gentleness, influence so coöperative with legal authority, and speculation so happily connected with practice as in the Institutions of Tammany? Avaunt then ye boasters! Cease too your prating about your St. Patrick, St. George, and St. Louis; and be silent concerning your St. Andrew and St. David. Tammany, though no Saint, was, you see, as valorous, intrepid and heroic as the best of them; and besides that, did a thousand times more good."

During his moments of leisure from the intricate business of ruling the Lenni-Lenape, Tammany was alleged to have found time to discover corn, beans, and tobacco, which last commodity he used only to destroy fleas and to drive away mosquitoes. He was also said to have discovered the crab apple and to have invented the canoe. "In his hazardous excursions," wrote Dr. Mitchill, "he laboured with extraordinary zeal to subdue the monsters of the forest, and the Grecian Hercules himself does not appear to have achieved greater exploits." Tammany was invariably victorious in the end, but the battle was not easy. "He was supposed," wrote another admirer, "to have had an intercourse with the Great Spirit, for he was a stranger to every thing that is bad." But, like all those who have intercourse with the Great Spirit, he had the Evil Spirit, otherwise known as the Devil, against him. And Tammany and the Evil Spirit fought out their grievances many times. When the Evil Spirit, according to Dr. Mitchill, "caused poison sumach and stinging-nettles to grow so thick in the land, that they almost choaked every other vegetable" and

Tammany's people were "poisoned and punctured by them whenever they went forth to hunt," Tammany burned the ground, "which burned with such rapidity, that the Evil Spirit Himself who happened to be skulking about the spot, was sorely singed by the flames." When the Devil tried to flood Tammany's territory by damming up lakes Erie, Huron, and Michigan, Tammany calmly drained them off. "The lakes by degrees subsided," said Dr. Mitchill, "but the rapids of Detroit and the falls of Niagara, remain to this day, monuments of the astonishing event." Finally, the annoyances became too great, and Tammany and the Evil Spirit fought a personal wrestling match. "At length," said Dr. Mitchill, "after unceasing exertions for fifty days, Tammany skilfully taking advantage of the hip-lock, threw him head and shoulders to the ground, and endeavored to roll him into the Ohio, and drown him, but an immense rock standing in the way, he could not effect it." After this fierce combat was over, "for the space of more than a league square, not a tree of any size was left standing." It was only fitting and proper that, in view of this reputation, the following toast should have been offered on the 4th of July, 1812, in Tammany Hall: "The illustrious Tammany—Blush ye schools of Art for Tammany was the Child of Nature."

But Tammany's strength was not only physical. So great was his fame as a sage and a Solon that Manco Capac, Inca of Peru, invited him to meet him at a place in Mexico, halfway between their respective homes, and advise as to the best form of government for Peru. Tammany was generous, and he kept the appointment. A form of government was worked out, mutual compliments were exchanged, and each monarch returned home, "well pleased to have met," according to Mrs. Euphemia Vale Blake, historian of the Tammany Society. But, while Tammany was away helping the Inca Manco Capac, his own Lenni-Lenape fell into evil ways. They became lazy, then wicked, and finally diseased; when their benevolent chief returned home, he had to cure his people of ague and syphilis before he could do anything else with them, and he accomplished this by the use of dogwood and lobelia, according to Dr. Mitchill. After he had cured his people of the results of their dissipation, Tammany turned his attention to the better organization and discipline of the nation. He divided the people into thirteen tribes, and he gave each tribe an animal fetish as a symbol worthy of emulation. Tammany recommended to one of his tribes the agility of the Tiger, to another the industry of the Beaver, to a third the foresight of the Squirrel, who collects his nuts in his hole in the fall and enjoys them in the winter, and to another the Tortoise, whose benevolence holds up the world, and who is hurt very much when the inhabitants of his back behave badly.

The original Tammany could have learned much from his descendants, at least in the matter of bargaining, for he was not so shrewd in land deals as many of those who have since worked in his name. It is the tradition that Tammany was the first Indian chief to welcome William Penn to this country on October 27, 1682. Tammany and his relatives gave William Penn and his heirs three hundred square miles of valuable real estate with all the privileges that go with full ownership and received in return:

"5	p. Stockings	28 yds. Duffills
20	Barrs Lead	16 Knives
10	Tobacco Boxes	10 pr. Sissors
6	Coates 2 Guns	2 Blankets
8	Shirts 2 Kettles	20 Handfuls of Wampum
12	Awles	10 Glasses
10	Tobacco Tongs	5 Capps
6	Axes	15 Combs
4	yds. Stroud Water	5 Hoes
100	needles	9 Gimbletts
5	Hatts	20 Fishhooks
25	lbs powder	7 Half Gills
1	Peck Pipes	4 Handfull Bells."[1]

From 1698, when his various real estate negotiations with William Penn were completed, nothing further is heard of Tammany until 1771, when he suddenly appears in American daily life as a full-fledged saint instead of a hardy Indian chief. How

[1]This list is taken from the *Pennsylvania Archives*, Vol. I, p. 64. Quoted by Francis von A. Cabeen in his article, "The Society of the Sons of Saint Tammany of Philadelphia," *Pennsylvania Magazine of History and Biography*, Vols. XXV and XXVI, 1901, 1902.

this transformation came about is still unknown, but we next learn of Tammany as Saint Tammany in the City of Philadelphia in 1771, and he had by this time acquired a regular name day, which was the first day of May, and was later changed to the twelfth of that month. In less than two years, he was generally accepted as the patron saint of the entire province of Pennsylvania. During the Revolutionary War, Saint Tammany was chosen by the Pennsylvania troops in Washington's command as their patron, and his day, now May 12th, was celebrated with elaborate Indian ritual. The rest of the army quickly took up Tammany, and before long he was celebrated by civilians as well. At one time it was seriously feared that May 12th would supplant the Fourth of July as the day we celebrate.[1]

It was said that the Sons of Liberty and other patriotic Americans, when they began to agitate for their independence, wished a saint to represent their cause. It was not considered fitting to borrow an effete saint from monarchical Europe, and it was quite natural that the minds of the founders of the legend should turn to a 100-per-cent. American. As it was early in the history of immigration, the only American who could be considered 100 per cent. without rivalry was an American Indian. The determination of Americans to have a saint of their own was expressed thus by an anonymous poet:

"Celestial maid! shall Europe boast
The saints her nations feign,
And o'er thy best, thy favourite coast,
No sacred guardian reign?
Not so, blest Freedom! whilst thy rays
Illume our vast domain—
Not whilst Columbia's Order blaze
Effulgent in thy train!"

In the early years of his sainthood, Tammany's day was celebrated with considerable fervour. A buck tail, the Tammany symbol generally adopted, was worn in the hat, and during the course of the entertainment men dressed as Indians usually

---

[1]For accounts of the origin of Saint Tammany and his day see E. P. Kilroe's *Saint Tammany and the Origin of the Society of Tammany*, and *Harper's Magazine*, 1872, p. 689: Rufus Home's *The Story of Tammany*.

rushed into the scene with loud war whoops and performed an Indian dance. A collection frequently followed, and the purpose of this may be indicated by the statement in a letter Ebenezer Hazard of Philadelphia wrote to his friend Dr. Jeremy Belknap on June 14, 1784. "I apprehend," he said, "anybody might be admitted who would pay his club towards a good time and liquors to get drunk with." One of those who were opposed to the pastimes of the common people wrote to a Philadelphia newspaper after the celebration of 1786:

"This entertainment ends as all such entertainments do with us, in drunkenness and disorder, which are afterwards printed in their newspapers in the most agreeable colors, as constituting the utmost festivity and joy. But the principal end of this annual feast is to destroy the force of the Christian religion. For this religion you know forbids self-murder and drunkenness. Now by honouring and celebrating the name of Tammany who killed himself by burning his cabin over his head in a drunken frolic, they take away all infamy from these crimes and even place them among the number of virtues."[1]

This writer referred to the legend of the death of Tammany, according to which, when the Chief had accomplished all that he could in the way of wisdom for his tribe and happiness for himself, he wrapped himself up and burned himself alive.

Whatever may have been the moral tone of his sainthood, the fact remains that, from 1773 until 1789, Tammany's achievements were celebrated widely in the colonies in song and story. One of these songs is well worth reprinting. A comedy attributed to John Leacock was published in Philadelphia in 1776, entitled *The Fall of British Tyranny; or, American Liberty Triumphant*. Mr. Peter Buckstail, a character supposed to represent by his name a Son of Saint Tammany, speaks a prologue, and two other characters, Roger and Dick, are introduced on a plain near Lexington. They hold the following conversation:

"*Dick*—Roger, methinks I hear the sound of melody warbling through the grove. Let's sit awhile and partake of it unseen.

---

[1] *Pennsylvania Magazine of History and Biography*, Vol. XXVI, p. 447.

"*Roger*—With all my heart! Most delightful harmony! This is the First of May! Our shepherds and Nymphs are celebrating our glorious St. Tammany's Day: we'll hear the song out, and then join in the frolick, and chorus it o'er and o'er again. This day shall be devoted to joy and festivity."

The song follows:

THE FIRST OF MAY, A NEW SONG, IN PRAISE OF ST. TAMMANY,
THE AMERICAN SAINT

(*Tune*, The Hounds are all out, etc.)

Of St. George, or St. Bute, let the poet Laureat sing,
Of Pharoah or Pluto of old,
While he rhimes forth their praise, in false, flattering lays,
I'll sing of St. Tamm'ny the bold, my brave boys.

Let Hibernia's sons boast, make Patrick their toast,
And Scots Andrew's fame spread abroad,
Potatoes and oats, and Welch leeks for Welch goats,
Was never St. Tammany's food, my brave boys.

In freedom's bright cause, Tamm'ny pled with applause,
And reason'd most justly from nature;
For this, this was his song, all, all, the day long;
Liberty's the right of each creature, brave boys.

Whilst under an oak his great parliament sat,
His throne was the crotch of the tree,
With Solomon's look, without statutes or book,
He wisely sent forth his decree, my brave boys.

His subjects stood round, not the least noise or sound,
Whilst freedom blaz'd full in each face;
So plain were the laws, and each pleaded his cause,
That might Bute, North and Mansfield disgrace, my brave
    boys.

No duties nor stamps, their blest liberty cramps,
A King, tho' no tyrant was he;
He did oft' times declare, nay sometimes would swear,
The least of his subjects were free, my brave boys.

He, as King of the woods, of the rivers and floods,
Had a right all beasts to control;
Yet content with a few, to give nature her due,
So gen'rous was Tammany's soul! my brave boys.

In the morn he arose, and a-hunting he goes,
Bold Nimrod his second, was he;
For his breakfast he'd take a large venison stake,
And despis'd your flip-flops and tea, my brave boys.

While all in a row, with squaw, dog and bow,
Vermillion adorning his face;
With feathery head he rang'd the woods wide,
Sure St. George had never such grace, my brave boys:

His jetty black hair, such as Buckskin saints wear,
Perfumed with bear's grease well smear'd,
Which illum'd the saint's face, and ran down apace,
Like the oil from off Aaron's beard, my brave boys.

The strong nervous deer, with amazing career,
In swiftness he'd fairly run down,
And, like Sampson, wou'd tear wolf, lion, or bear;
Ne'er was such a saint as our own, my brave boys.

When he'd run down a stag, he behind him wou'd lag,
For so noble a soul had he!
He'd stop, tho' he lost it, tradition reports it,
To give him fresh chance to get free, my brave boys.

From his quiver he drew forth an arrow so keen,
And seiz'd fast his imperial bow;
It flew straight to the heart, like an Israelite dart;
Could St. Andrew ever do so, my brave boys?

With a mighty strong aim, and a masculine bow,
His arrow he drew to the head,
And as sure as he shot, it was ever his lot,
His prey it fell instantly dead, my brave boys.

His table he spread, where the venison bled;
Be thankful, he used to say;
He'd laugh and he'd sing, tho' a saint and a king,
And sumptuously dine on his prey, my brave boys.

Then over the hills, o'er the mountains and rills,
He'd caper, such was his delight;
And ne'er in his days, Indian history says,
Did lack a good Supper at night, my brave boys.

On an old stump he sat, without cap or hat,
When Supper was ready to eat;
Snap his dog, he stood by, and cast a sheep's eye,
For venison's the king of all meat, my brave boys.

Like Isaac of old, and both cast in one mould,
Tho' a wigwam was Tamm'ny's cottage,
He lov'd sav'ry meat, such that patriarchs eat;
Of ven'son and squirrel made pottage, my brave boys.

When four score years old, as I've oft' times been told,
To doubt it, sure, would not be right,
With pipe in his jaw, he'd buss his old squaw,
And get a young saint ev'ry night, my brave boys.

As old age came on, he grew blind, deaf and dumb,
Tho' his sport, t'were hard to keep from it,
Quite tired of life, bid adieu to his wife,
And blaz'd like the tail of a comit, my brave boys.

What country on earth, then did ever give birth,
To such a magnanimous saint?
His acts far excel all that history tell,
And language too feeble to paint, my brave boys.

Now to finish my song, a full flowing bowl;
I'll quaff and sing the long day,
And with punch and wine paint my cheeks for my saint,
And hail ev'ry first of Sweet May, my brave boys.[1]

---
[1]*Pennsylvania Magazine of History and Biography*, Vol. XXVI, pp. 14-16.

II

William Mooney was a paper hanger, upholsterer, and furniture dealer who lived and worked in New York City during the period of the Revolutionary War. He was a soldier in that war, but it has been charged that he deserted the American forces and joined the King's army. Whatever the truth of this charge may be, it is a fact that after the United States had won the war, Mooney became intensely patriotic. He attended meetings, and he took part in parades. In the great Constitutional Parade held in New York City on July 23, 1788, to celebrate the ratification by the states of the Constitution, William Mooney represented Upholstery, and he appeared on a float, posed in the act of preparing the chair of the first President of the United States. A few weeks after the Constitution went into effect, Mooney organized in New York the Society of St. Tammany, or Columbian Order.

Mooney's original idea appears to have been to make Columbus a co-saint with Tammany. He and his associates in the enterprise wished to take advantage of both the well-established name of Tammany as an American saint and the well-established prestige of Columbus as discoverer of America. The transactions of the New York Society were to be dated from the year of the discovery. The original Tammany Society which Mooney organized was "founded on the true and genuine principles of republicanism, and holds out as its objects the smile of charity, the chain of friendship, and the flame of liberty; and in general, whatever may tend to perpetuate the *love of freedom*, or the political advantages of this Country."[1]

The main purpose for which the Tammany Society was founded was rather vague in the minds of those who were conscious of its existence. The Society was not political, but it was patriotic; it was not partisan, but it was democratic. It was also intended to be charitable, social, benevolent, and fraternal. One of the principal objects for which the Society was founded seems to have been to combat the aristocrats, who, under Alexander Hamilton and his associates, had succeeded in gaining control of the new government. They had

---

[1] *New York Directory and Register*, 1790.

their social organization, the Society of the Cincinnati, the members of which all belonged to the best families; the eldest son of each member inherited membership in the Society. The Cincinnati had been formed by officers of the Continental Army before it disbanded. The Tammany Society was opposed to hereditary distinctions, and its members came from the class of enlisted men in the Revolutionary War rather than from among the officers. The struggle for supremacy between the aristocrats, known as Federalists, and the democrats, known as Republicans, had begun almost immediately after the actual fighting of the Revolutionary War ceased, and it continued vigorously for many years under the leadership throughout the nation of Alexander Hamilton, for the Federalists, and of Thomas Jefferson, for the democratic Republicans. After the Revolutionary War, the wealthy Tories, who had taken the side of Great Britain during the war, had been excluded from holding political or public offices. But soon after President George Washington was inaugurated, these disabilities were removed, and the Tories were forgiven their sins against their countrymen. This action caused great indignation in the ranks of the democrats, and it has been given as one reason for the founding of the Society of St. Tammany in New York.

One of the favourite toasts at the early dinners of the Tammany Society was: "May the industry of the Beaver, the Frugality of the Ant, and the constancy of the Dove perpetually distinguish the Sons of St. Tammany." It is obvious that those attributes have never been aristocratic ambitions. One reason given for the origin of the Indian ritual nomenclature and symbols adopted by the Tammany Society was that the members purposed to caricature the foreign manners of the Cincinnati and other aristocratic associations.

The members of the Society were divided into sachems, warriors, and hunters. There were thirteen sachems, one for each tribe of Tammany, representing the original thirteen states of the United States; their function was the same as that of the trustees of a college or a bank. A Grand Sachem was at their head, and William Mooney occupied that position. The President of the United States, in the early days of the Society, was always made Great Grand Sachem, or, as the ritualists preferred to call it, Kitchi Okemaw. There was also a Sagamore, the master of ceremonies, and a doorkeeper, known by the name of Wiskinskie, invented, perhaps, to compensate him for his otherwise menial position.

All the transactions of the Tammany Society were dated from three great eras: the day of its own organization, the day of the declaration of independence of the United States, and the date of the discovery of America by Columbus. The year was divided into four seasons: the Season of Snows, the Season of Blossoms, the Season of Fruits, and the Season of Hunting. The months were not called months, but moons. Thus, if an event was to be chronicled, it would be dated in this manner: "Manhattan, Season of Fruits, 17th day of the 7th Moon, Year of Discovery 361st, of Independence 78th, and of the Institution the 65th."

At the initiation of the Grand Sachem the "Et-hoh" song was sung, beginning, "Brothers, our council-fire shines bright, Et-hoh!" When mere members were being initiated a different stanza was sung, and one verse of that song was:

"Sacred's the ground where Freedom's found,
    And Virtue stamps her name;
    Our hearts entwine at Friendship's shrine,
    And Union fans the flame:
        Our hearts sincere
        Shall greet you here,
        With joyful voice
        Confirm your choice.
        Et-hoh! Et-hoh! Et-hoh!"

In their early processions, which were numerous, the members of the Tammany Society walked through the streets of New York in Indian file; many of them were dressed as Indians, with their faces painted, and they carried bows, arrows, tomahawks, and calumets; some wore tight-fitting bladders on their heads, in order to give the effect of "a proper depilous Indian skull." Those who were too self-conscious to dress as Indians placed a buck's tail in their hats and left their faces white. Tammany's main function in its early days was to celebrate Tammany Day, May 12th, and the Fourth of July. There was always a parade on May 12th, and one year the celebration included the performance of Mrs. Ann Julia Hatton's play, *Tammany; or, the Indian Chief*. Mrs. Hatton was a sister of Mrs. Siddons and a member of the famous Kemble family. When she came to this country, she championed republicanism, and she was soon taken up by the Tammany Society, whose members arranged for the production of her play. The work was said to be "seasoned high with spices hot from Paris," which then meant revolutionary fervour and nothing else, for the French were very busy at the time having their revolution.

The May 12th celebrations and the Fourth of July celebrations usually ended with a midnight revel in City Hall Park, where the young boys and the "wilder spirits" participated in the burning in effigy of Benedict Arnold, accompanied by a war dance. These Indian revels received the contempt of the more sedate families of the community, which was reflected in the editorials of their newspapers. *The American Citizen and General Advertiser*, for instance, said on July 6, 1809:

"It is painful to observe the ridicule which is annually thrown upon this glorious event by some semi-barbarians calling themselves the Tammany Society. Instead of commemorating the birth of the nation with that manliness and dignity which the occasion calls for and inspires, we see them with pain and disgust daubing their faces with paint, crowding their heavy heads with feathers; making savages in appearance more savage; representing as they term it, the genius of the nation in the person of some one who has no genius, and playing such tricks and exhibiting such figures as showmen would despise and be ashamed of. We derive, however, from the late commemoration a consolation of no trifling magnitude; we see that the Society is rapidly diminishing, and that the more civilized of the savages are beginning to associate with tamed and tutored men."

It is interesting that during every period of Tammany Hall's existence some newspapers have always seen the Society "rapidly diminishing," but the wish being father to the thought, the writers did not see the facts clearly.

Tammany was forced to abandon its Indian ceremonies be-

fore many years, because, during the War of 1812, there was
great popular indignation against the Indians; they were
charged with aiding the British and committing horrible atro-
cities. The older members of the Tammany Society resisted
vigorously the abandonment of the Indian traditional ceremonies, and some of them felt so strongly on the subject that
they resigned.

Tammany's Indian ritual served one very useful purpose,
and was of assistance to President Washington and his government. After the Revolutionary War there had been periodic
Indian disorders, particularly by the Creeks, who occupied
large tracts of land in Georgia and Florida. The government
was anxious to settle its disputes and to sign a favourable treaty
of peace with the Creeks. "In 1790," wrote Mrs. Euphemia
Vale Blake, the authorized historian of the Tammany Society,
"a plan was devised to get the chief of this tribe, or nation,
who was an educated half-breed, to come to New York with
some of his people, in the expectation that the sights of civilization and of permanent substantial cities would make the red
men feel their weakness, and the impossibility of resisting the
supremacy of the 'pale-faces.'" Colonel Marinus Willett, a
Revolutionary War hero and a member of the Tammany Society, was sent to negotiate the visit with the chief of the Creek
nation, whose name was Colonel Alexander McGillivray, a half-
breed, whose father had been a Scotch trader, and whose mother
was a Creek Indian. Fisher Ames, the Federalist, said of
McGillivray, "He is decent and not very black." In July,
1790, Willett started north with Big Chief McGillivray and
twenty-eight warriors of the Creek nation. The members of
the Tammany Society made vast preparations to receive their
fellow Indians. They brushed their Indian costumes, painted
their faces, and pitched tents on the banks of the Hudson River.
The Creek Indians, it was said, "were wonderfully surprised
and overjoyed, thinking they had found a new tribe of red
men, giving vent to their excitement in loud whoops, which
greatly startled, if they did not frighten, the Tammany braves."
The "Et-hoh" song was sung, and then the Grand Sachem of
Tammany, William Pitt Smith, assured the Indians in a speech
that, "though dead, the spirits of the two great chiefs, Tammany and Columbus, were walking backward and forward

in the wigwam." In the evening the Indians went to the theatre. For several days, "long talks" and sightseeing were resorted to for the entertainment of the terrifying guests, who appeared to be as terrified as their hosts. The Creeks dined one day with President Washington, and after dinner Washington wished to see the effect on their "untutored minds" of the new portrait which John Trumbull had painted of the President. They were very much surprised that one Great Father could stand before them and another, looking exactly the same, could appear in another part of the room. They touched the canvas to test its reality and exclaimed "Ugh!" in traditional Indian fashion.

The Indians were so pleased with their entertainment that a few days after their arrival in New York they signed a treaty of peace with Secretary of War Knox; the boundaries of their territory were fixed, and the border warfare ceased.

Tammany's next great activity was the celebration of the tercentenary of the discovery of America by Columbus, which occurred on October 12, 1792. In the evening, a monument to Columbus was unveiled. It was in the shape of an obelisk, "upward of fourteen feet in height," and it was ornamented with transparencies. In the course of the celebration attending the unveiling of the monument by the Tammany Society, fourteen toasts were drunk, including one to the memory of Christopher Columbus, one to Thomas Paine, another to the Rights of Man, and others to Lafayette and the French nation, "A Burgoyning to the Duke of Brunswick," the Genius of Liberty, the Day We Celebrate, and Washington, the Deliverer of the New World.

After this celebration in honour of Columbus, the elegant monument was placed in the Tammany Museum, which had already been founded by the Society. Annually on the 12th of October Columbus's monument was illuminated. The Tammany Museum was the first to be established in the City of New York, and its collections were kept in an upper room of the City Hall. The Museum was founded for the purpose of preserving Indian relics, but it was not very prosperous, and the Tammany Society turned it over to Gardiner Baker, its "snub-nosed, pock-pitted, bandy-legged, fussy, good-natured little" curator, with the provision that it should always be called the Tammany Museum, and that each member of the Society and the members of his family should be admitted free forever. Baker died in 1800, and the Museum collections were sold. Eventually, they became a part of the famous American Museum operated in New York by P. T. Barnum.

The most important attraction of the Tammany Society in the early years of its existence and an attraction that has remained important throughout its history, was its social features. When the Tammany Society was founded, there were practically no social clubs in New York City, and none where members of the middle class and workingmen could congregate. The place, which has since been filled by fraternal orders and benevolent institutions, was first occupied in New York by Tammany Hall, and it soon happened, almost imperceptibly, that men whose political views were the same because their social and economic status was about the same gathered together at Tammany's meetings. The early meetings were held in public houses, and it became a habit for members of Tammany to meet at "Brom" Martling's tavern in Nassau Street, where the Society's assembly room soon became known as the "Long Room." Abraham Martling himself believed firmly in the assumption that all men were created free and equal, which at that time was considered somewhat radical. He became a sachem of Tammany, and when he grew old, the organization appointed him to the position of Keeper of the City Hall. Those who did not believe with the members of the Tammany Society that all men were created free and equal took to sneering at the Tammany meeting place and called it "The Pig Pen," "by reason of its general unsightliness." After the regular business of the meetings was finished, the members "were disposed to make a night of it," "by calling some brother of recognized and tried social endurance to the chair," and spending "what remained of the 'evening'—which frequently lasted until morning—in drinking toasts, singing songs, and telling stories of the narrators' own exploits by field and flood." One can almost hear the ancestors of the Elks modestly remarking to one another, "Stop me, if you've heard this one."

The Tammany Society soon decided that it needed a hall of its own, and money was raised by a tontine consociation and a lottery. The early efforts were unsuccessful, but finally, in

1811, enough money was raised to build the first Tammany Hall at Nassau and Frankfort streets. One room was reserved for the meetings of the Society on certain evenings, and the rest of the building was rented out as an hotel.

It is the tendency of men of similar social standing, political opinions, and economic aspirations to gather together for the purpose of giving vent to the opinions and making something tangible of the aspirations. When the Tammany Society came into existence, the United States of America were just beginning to feel their freedom and to endeavour to express it. There were those who looked upon themselves as gentlemen and their neighbours as freemen, but there were also those who believed that both classes were entitled to the same privileges, even if they could not obtain the same emoluments. All, however, united in one solemn conviction, and that was that they the inhabitants of the United States of America were more advanced than any other group of people anywhere else in the world. "Behold the universe," demanded the historian of Congress in 1802. "See its four quarters filled with savages or slaves. Out of nine hundred millions of human beings but four millions are free." And none of his readers doubted for a moment that they were members of the chosen four million. "Yet at that time in America," wrote Albert J. Beveridge, "manhood suffrage did not exist excepting in three States, a large part of the people could not read or write, imprisonment for debt was universal, convicted persons were sentenced to be whipped in public and subjected to other cruel and disgraceful punishments. Hardly a protest against slavery was made, and human rights as we now know them were in embryo, so far as the practice of them was concerned."[1]

There had been upon the part of the founders of the United States government a unanimous distrust of political parties, and these organizations were not considered in the formation of the government. But, as the universal freemen could not all shout at once and assemble together in one hall, the four millions of them had to meet in their clubs and their houses, their taverns and their restaurants, in order to express themselves effectively. Thus political associations became neces-

---

[1] *Life of John Marshall*, Vol. III, p. 13.

sary, and Tammany Hall soon grew by a natural process of social development to be one of the leading organizations of this kind. Before it had been in existence as a benevolent society for more than ten years, Tammany became the principal political faction of New York City.

CHAPTER II

I

AARON BURR, whose virtues and vices have so often been exaggerated by his admirers and detractors, has been accused also of being the first person to use the Tammany Society for political purposes. Mooney was fond of display, and to him has been attributed the origin of Sachems, Sagamores, and Wiskinskies. Aaron Burr was a friend of Mooney's, or, rather, he patronized him in a business way, for when Mooney died his estate included a large number of unsatisfied claims against Aaron Burr for upholstery. Burr's most intimate friends, Matthew L. Davis and the Swartwout brothers, were among the early members of the Tammany Society, and they soon controlled the organization. Whatever the connection between Tammany and Burr or his friends, it is historical fact that Burr used the Tammany Society in the campaign by which he was elected Vice President of the United States and almost elected President.

Burr and his associates realized cunningly the power of what Alexander Hamilton and his associates called "the mob." Burr never painted his face, nor did he join in the energetic parades of the Tammany Society, but he was well aware of the number of votes that a parade could develop, and through his capable lieutenants he used those votes. Alexander Hamilton, in one of the statements concerning Aaron Burr which led to the famous duel between them, wrote to Gouverneur Morris that Aaron Burr "has no principles, public or private, could be bound by no argument; will listen to no monitor but his ambition; and for this purpose will use the worst portion of the community as a ladder to climb to permanent power, and an instrument to crush the better part. He is sanguine enough to hope everything, daring enough to attempt everything, wicked enough to scruple nothing." That was an excellent definition of the typical political boss, as we shall see by the histories of the later Tammany leaders. Hamilton, however, did not seem to realize that he himself was always using the so-called better part of the community as an instrument to crush the aspirations of the lower.

Matthew L. Davis, who, as Burr's literary executor, deserves the contempt of posterity because he burned so much of his hero's correspondence, was during Burr's lifetime his closest friend. Davis was, perhaps, our first great manufacturer of public opinion. During one political campaign in New York City meetings were held on different nights in every ward in the City; strong resolutions were passed and stirring addresses were made; both resolutions and addresses were published immediately afterward in the leading newspapers of the town, and they influenced not only the City but the entire country. It was only some time later that it was discovered that at each of these enthusiastic meetings only three persons were present —Davis and two friends. Some have it that Davis was taught these political methods by his leader, Aaron Burr.

The first important election at which such tactics were used by Davis, who was then a sachem of the Tammany Society, and Burr, who was then a candidate, was the exciting Presidential election of 1800. New York held the balance of power in this election. Presidential electors were then chosen by the legislature of each state, and they had more arbitrary powers than they possess to-day. It was important, therefore, that the candidate should control the Legislature, and Aaron Burr succeeded in capturing the electoral votes of New York State by the aid of members of the Tammany Society. The right to vote was highly restricted at that time by the qualification that a man had to possess a certain amount of property before he was fit to elect representatives of his opinions. As late as 1790 only 1,303 of the 13,330 male residents of New York City possessed sufficient property to entitle them to vote for Governor.

The real issue behind almost all the elections of this early period of American history was that between the men who believed in the privileges of property and those who believed in the rights of man. Tammany, of course, stood always with the latter, for the very good reason that most of its members possessed very little property.

Men were divided much more rigidly into definite classes than they were later and than they are to-day, and the obstacles placed in the way of the lower classes acquiring possessions sufficiently extensive to make them *haut ton*, or even middle class, were very great. A gentleman in the early days of Tammany Hall wore something of a uniform that there might be no mistake about his being one. His coat was blue, or green, or scarlet, and his long hair was tied in a queue and thickly powdered; his breeches were short and buckled at the knee; and his shirt was carefully ruffled. Trade, and especially banking, was almost entirely controlled by the gentry, and they clung to their privileges with that fervour with which men usually cling to that which does not naturally belong to them.

"A president of a bank," wrote a man who lived at the time, "was a grandee of the first order, and a cashier ranked with the ancient order or priesthood. A mechanic never ventured to ask for a discount in those days without some merchant as a patron and friend, and then the loan was obtained as a special favour." The value of this commercial control was obvious, and those who exercised it perpetuated their power by seeing to it that no other banks were chartered by the state legislatures. Burr played one of his most effective tricks on the moneyed class when he chartered the Manhattan Company, ostensibly a corporation designed to supply abundant fresh water to the inhabitants of New York City. An obscure clause in the charter of the Manhattan Company, however, enabled it to carry on banking activities as part of its privileges.

Because of the hampering class distinctions, the lower classes were beginning to get restless. The French Revolution had just happened, and such words as liberty, equality, and fraternity were frequently being used in America to express the idealism of discontent. In New York City Tammany Hall rapidly became the nucleus for these democratic aspirations, for, as we have seen, it was practically the only place democrats and workingmen could go and find men of similar opinions. Thomas Jefferson, who was by nature and principles fitted to be the national leader of the democratic Republicans, watched the development of the Tammany Society with intense interest, though he took no part in its organization nor in its deliberations.

During the Presidential election of 1800, when Thomas Jefferson became President of the United States and Aaron Burr Vice-President, Tammany Hall's activities were almost exactly the same as those which we shall see were so characteristic of the organization during every period of its career. Men who intended to vote the opposition ticket were brought into the Wigwam, entertained and persuaded, and, if there was doubt of their conviction, escorted to the polls by committees, who were appointed to see that they remained true to their promises.[1] At the election of 1801, thirty-nine young men, members of the Tammany Society, students of Columbia College, and mechanics, encouraged by the Tammany leaders, and, it was said, with money furnished by Tammany, bought together a piece of real estate with a house on it, so that they might have sufficient property to entitle them to vote. Their votes carried their ward election, but the courts decided that the scheme was illegal.

After Thomas Jefferson had been inaugurated President of the United States, Matthew L. Davis, sachem of Tammany, called on the President in Washington and spoke of the great influence which New York, through Tammany, had exercised in the election of 1800; he ventured to believe, he said, that Jefferson's election had been brought about entirely by the efforts of the Tammany Society in his behalf. Jefferson listened, and when Davis had finished, he reached out and caught a fly. He asked Mr. Davis to note the remarkable disproportion between one part of the insect and its entire body.[2] Mr. Davis got the point, and he returned to New York empty-handed, and with the impression that Mr. Jefferson suffered from ingratitude.

Alexander Hamilton was the author of the first draft of George Washington's Farewell Address, which was made public in 1796. With the growing power of the Tammany Society as a political organization in mind, he inserted in that address a passage decrying the dangerous and corrupting tendency of political combinations and associations. As soon as Washing-

[1]*Harper's Magazine*, 1872, p. 694.

[2]*The History of Tammany Hall*, by Gustavus Myers, 1917 edition, p. 15, footnote.

ton's Address appeared in the newspapers, Hamilton and his associates made it perfectly clear that Washington was referring in that passage to the Tammany Society. The result was that some Federalists, and others who worshipped Washington, resigned from Tammany, and only three persons attended the next celebration of Saint Tammany's Day.

Hamilton had learned a valuable lesson from the election of 1800, which was so disastrous to the party of which he was the recognized leader, the Federalists. He saw in the Tammany Society an engine that was powerful, and he urged on his associates the creation of a similar organization which would work for their cause. In a letter to Senator Bayard of Delaware, Hamilton wrote in April, 1802:

"Nothing is more fallacious than to expect to produce any valuable or permanent results in political projects by relying merely on the reason of men. Men are rather reasoning than reasonable animals, for the most part governed by the impulses of passion. This is a truth well understood by our adversaries, who have practised upon it with no small benefit to their cause; for at the very moment that they are eulogizing the reason of men, and professing to appeal only to that faculty, they are courting the strongest and most active passion of the human heart, *vanity!* It is no less true that the federalists seem not to have attended to the fact sufficiently; and that they erred in relying so much on the rectitude and utility of their measures as to have neglected the cultivation of popular favor, by fair and justifiable expedients. The observation has been repeatedly made by me to individuals with whom I particularly conversed, and expedients suggested, for gaining good will, which were never adopted. Unluckily, however, for us, in the competition for the passions of the people, our opponents have great advantages over us; for the plain reason that the vicious are far more active than the good passions; and that, to win the latter to our side, we must renounce our principles and our objects, and unite in corrupting public opinion, till it becomes fit for nothing but mischief. Yet, unless we can contrive to take hold of, and carry along with us some strong feelings of the mind, we shall in vain calculate upon any substantial or durable results. Whatever plan we may adopt, to be successful, must be founded on the truth of this proposition. And perhaps it is not very easy for us to give it full effects; especially not without some deviations from what, on other occasions, we have maintained to be right. But in determining upon the propriety of the deviations, we must consider whether it be possible for us to succeed, without, in some degree, employing the weapons which have been employed against us, and whether the actual state and future prospect of things, be not such as to justify the reciprocal use of them. I need not tell you that I do not mean to countenance the imitation of things intrinsically unworthy, but only of such as may be denominated irregular; such as, in a sound and stable order of things, ought not to exist."[1]

Hamilton then went on to suggest the organization of what he called "The Christian Constitutional Society," the objects of which were to be the support of the Christian religion and the Constitution of the United States. Its council was to consist of a president and twelve members, the same number as the number of sachems of the Tammany Society. Each state was to have its own subcouncil with the same number of members. The main activity was to be propaganda, or, as Hamilton preferred to call it, "the diffusion of information," via the newspapers and pamphlets. Another object was to be charity, and the Christian Constitutional Society was to maintain associations for the relief of immigrants and academies for the instruction of mechanics in their trades and in chemistry. Senator Bayard answered that the scheme was ingenious, but that he did not think that it would work. "Such an association," he wrote, "must be bottomed upon a stronger and more active principle than reason, or even a sense of common interest, to render it successful. There is more material for such an association upon the other side than upon ours. We have the greater number of political calculators, and they of political fanatics."

Hamilton and the Federalists, Seth Low and the Fusionists, and similar combinations against Tammany Hall that arose in the course of its history, never seemed to realize fully that the main reason for the success of Jefferson and the Democrats,

---

[1] *Works of Alexander Hamilton*, Vol. VI, pp. 540–543.

and Croker and Tweed and Kelly and Wood, was that the public believed more in the diffusion of economic advantages than in the diffusion of information of a Christian Constitutional character. Tammany Hall, even during its early years, shared its spoils with its supporters, while Hamilton and his class were under the delusion that the common people would remain perfectly happy so long as they saw their obvious betters enjoying prosperity which, by a slow, but sure, process of filtration would come down to them eventually. Tammany Hall interested the people, not because it believed in liberty, but because it gave them jobs as street cleaners and made them feel like sovereigns.

Senator Bayard assured Hamilton: "Let us not be too impatient, and our adversaries will soon demonstrate to the world the soundness of our doctrines, and the imbecility and folly of their own. Without any exertion upon our part, in the course of two or three years they will render every honest man in the country our proselyte." Senator Bayard did not appreciate the enduring qualities of a system by which large numbers of people are placed in the position to take their own advantages according to their own tastes, rather than to have them ladled out by ever so benevolent cooks.

The battle was the eternal one between those who have and those who want, and it sometimes became a bitter personal combat. The struggle of principles and personal ambitions led to the most famous duel in American history, as a result of which Alexander Hamilton lost his life. Tammany Hall was interested vitally in that duel, and several of its leading members were concerned in the details. When Aaron Burr shot and killed Alexander Hamilton at Weehawken in the early morning of July 11, 1804, two Tammany sachems were with Burr and one of them was his second; they were William P. Van Ness and Matthew L. Davis; another Tammany sachem, John Swartwout, was at Burr's house awaiting his return, and Tammany enthusiasts were said to have been waiting at different points along the route of the return journey to learn the result of the duel. That night, while Hamilton was dying, there was a celebration in Martling's Long Room. Toasts were drunk to Aaron Burr, the victor. But the next morning the Tammany Society prudently mourned the loss of Hamilton. It was one thing for individuals to rejoice at Hamilton's final defeat, but it was another for the organization to appear before public opinion as the defender of such an unpopular thing as violent death. The newspapers of the day after Hamilton's death contained this notice:

BROTHERS,—Your attendance is earnestly requested at an extra meeting of the tribes, in the Great Wigwam, precisely at the setting of the sun this evening, to make arrangements for joining our fellow-citizens and soldiers in a procession, in order to pay the last tribute of national respect due to the manes of our departed fellow-citizen and soldier, General Alexander Hamilton. By order of the Grand Sachem.

JAMES B. BISSET, *Secretary.*

Season of Fruits, in the Year of Discovery Three Hundred and Twelve, and of the Institution the Fifteenth, July the 13th.

II

In the early years of its career Tammany Hall was a strictly 100-per-cent. American organization, and it was particularly bitter in its opposition to the Irish. The Constitution of the Tammany Society adopted in 1789 provided that, "No person shall be eligible to the office of Sachem, unless a native of this Country." The only offices that could be held by persons who were so unfortunate as not to have been born in the United States of America were the purely honorary offices of Warrior and Hunter. Tammany refused absolutely to permit an Irish Catholic to run for office on its ticket, and it was not until 1809 that one Patrick McKay was permitted to be a Tammany candidate for the Assembly.

The Irish resented this prejudice, and more than two hundred of them assembled on the night of April 24, 1817, in Dooley's Long Room. They marched to Tammany Hall and urged on the party leaders the nomination for Congress of Thomas Addis Emmett, the Irish orator and patriot. There was some disagreement; eyes were blackened and noses battered in the course of the argument. The Irish invaders broke up the furniture and used the pieces as bludgeons with which to impress the Tammany men. Windows were smashed, and Tammany

Hall was in danger of being razed when Tammany reinforce-
ments arrived and drove the Irish back to Dooley's.

The attitude of the Tammany Society was at this time generally anti-foreign. In 1817, Tammany issued an address in
the course of which the Society deplored the spreading popularity of that foreign game known as billiards. Two years later
Tammany recommended that its members should buy only
articles manufactured by Americans in America, and it maintained that inferior articles were manufactured in perfidious
Europe specially for the American market.

Tammany had its first real opportunity to demonstrate its
100-per-cent. Americanism during the War of 1812. The Society
requested its members to work with their hands on the fortifi-
cations and defences of New York and Brooklyn. Members of
Tammany and other New Yorkers sang at this time:

> "Old England is trying to kick up a muss,
> I think she'd better not interfere with us.
> If she wants to fight us, she'll find it no fun,
> She'll git what she got from General Washington."

Shortly before the War of 1812 the Tammany Society demonstrated its formal patriotism when it carried on a campaign
for the interment of the bones of the 11,500 martyrs who had
died on British prison ships near New York during the Revolutionary War. The bones of these martyrs were found by John
Jackson on the property he had bought in the Wallabout Bay
section of Brooklyn. Jackson was a sachem of the Tammany
Society, and he thought that occasion for a grand celebration
to great political effect would be offered by the erection of a
tomb and a monument for those bones under the auspices of
the Tammany Society. He presented Tammany with a portion
of his Wallabout property as a site for the monument, but he
was determined that he would not be cheated out of the political effect of the interment, for, when the citizens of Brooklyn at a town meeting offered to bury the bones of the patriots
in the Reformed Dutch Church graveyard, and also offered
to erect a monument over them, Jackson indignantly refused
to give up the patriotic bones he had found. Meanwhile, the
rain and winter weather were uncovering the bones disgrace-

fully, and a benevolent gentleman who happened to be taking a walk with his wife in the neighbourhood thought that something should be done about it. He was Mr. Benjamin Aycrigg, and he entered into the following agreement with Mr. Amos Cheney:

"Wallabout, Long Island, Aug. 24, 1805.

"I do hereby agree to collect all the human bones as far as may be without digging, about the shore and banks of this place, (buried from on board the Prison Ship Jersey during the Revolution of America) and deliver the same to Benjm. Aycrigg, at this place, at one cent per pound, within one year from this date."

The Tammany Society appointed a committee to do something about the bones of the 11,500 martyrs, and the committee reported the accusation against the United States of America of "that most odious of vices and worst of crimes—Ingratitude!" During the years of neglect, twenty hogsheads filled with these bones of patriots had been collected by John Jackson, Benjamin Aycrigg, and the Tammany Society. Money for a tomb had not yet been raised, but it was thought that the grandeur of a procession might help the financial drive, and accordingly, on April 13, 1808, the ceremony of laying the corner stone for the patriots' tomb was performed. A procession formed at Tammany Hall and crossed the river to Brooklyn in thirteen large open boats. A huge pedestal monument in black marble was borne on a truck carriage, and, walking in front of it, Mr. Josiah Falconer, a watchmaker and a member of the Tammany Society, represented the "Genius of America." He was "adorned with the most elegant feathers which could be obtained, all in the Mexican style." Surrounding the "Genius of America" were nine young men, representing Patriotism, Honour, Virtue, Patience, Fortitude, Merit, Courage, Perseverance, and Science. However, the enthusiasm which expressed itself in parade and procession soon died out in committee and subscription campaign, and no monument appeared.

One can see in all the early Tammany celebrations the intense effort to express 100-per-cent. Americanism. But famine and political troubles in Ireland soon led to increased immi-

gration to New York and other cities of the United States, and
Tammany Hall was quick to appreciate the value of these newcomers in votes. One newspaper writer of the period remarked:
"Patriots who had avowedly fled their native soil to find safety
in this, and who proposed to return to their homes when it
should no longer be a hanging matter, were, by virtue of
the tomahawk, dubb'd savages of the first order." This large
Irish immigration had a most important effect on the political
history of New York City and on the history of Tammany
Hall. The Irish who came here were usually, unlike the German immigrants, without trades; they had experience in the
machinery of politics, but they had never been permitted political responsibility in their home country; they knew English; and they could not naturally feel any sense of loyalty or
public spirit toward the community which was too new to them
to command any respect from them. But they enjoyed a ready
personal adaptability to their new surroundings, and they
made themselves singularly at home soon after their arrival
in New York. One commentator, inspired by the sight of
40,000 Irishmen marching all day and drinking all night on St.
Patrick's Day, 1870, declaimed:

"God help the poor Exiles in Ireland,
     As they sit by the wild ocean's foam,
For, 'tis they that are Exiles entirely,
     While we are here more than at home!"

Forced finally to receive the Irish because of the potential
numbers of their votes, it was not long before Tammany Hall
was dominated by them. "Ask an Irishman," remarked one
writer, "and he will probably tell you that St. Tammany was
a younger brother of St. Patrick who emigrated to America for
the purpose of taking a city contract to drive all Republican
reptiles out of New York."

One of the factors that led to the increased influence of the
Irish in New York politics was the success of the movement for
universal manhood suffrage. Tammany Hall's early leaders
recognized that if they were to gain power and money, they
must first break the political control of the wealthy classes by
the strength of numbers, and this could be accomplished only

when every citizen in New York could vote, regardless of his property qualifications. A general meeting in Tammany Hall started the movement for manhood suffrage which led to the debate of that question in the Constitutional Convention of 1821. There were those who saw danger in the new proposal. Chancellor Kent, the leading legal authority of the day, said on the floor of the convention:

"By the report before us we propose to annihilate, at one stroke, all property distinctions, and to bow before the idol of universal suffrage. That extreme democratic principle has been regarded with terror by the wise men of every age, because in every European republic, ancient and modern, in which it has been tried, it has terminated disastrously, and been productive of corruption, injustice, violence, and tyranny. And dare we flatter ourselves that we are a peculiar people, who can run the career of history exempted from the passions which have disturbed and corrupted the rest of mankind? If we are like other races of men, with similar follies and vices, then I greatly fear that our posterity will have reason to deplore in sackcloth and ashes the delusion of the day."[1]

That Chancellor Kent's fears were only too well grounded was illustrated vividly during several phases of the subsequent history of Tammany Hall; but the Constitutional Convention of 1821, no matter how much its members respected the learning of Chancellor Kent, was not particularly interested in posterity, for it was controlled politically by Tammany Hall, and the amendment bestowing the right to vote on every white man in New York State was passed.

Many years later, in 1890, E. L. Godkin wrote:

"There is no doubt that universal suffrage has added to the difficulties of city government, and has lowered the standard of official purity and fitness; but, to use the slang phrase, it has so plainly 'come to stay,' and is so firmly lodged in the political arrangements of most civilized nations, that it is a mere waste of time to declaim against it. Complaining of it as an obstacle to good government is like complaining of a stormy sea as a reason for giving up navigation."

[1]Alexander, *Political History of the State of New York*, Vol. I, p. 301.

It is also useless to set up the possession of property as a standard for the right to vote, because in the subsequent history of the United States, and of New York particularly, men of property have proved to be most unfit guardians of public virtue, and frequently have been caught in the act of debauchery.

III

One circumstance which contributed greatly to the advantage of Tammany Hall from the beginning of its political career was the theory of the state with regard to elections. When this government of the United States was founded, a vote was entirely an individual matter, and the government had neither the desire nor the power to regulate its manner of expression. Political parties developed, and it was to the party that the government always intrusted the development of machinery for the expression of the will of the people. The state always disclaimed practically all responsibility for the one check that the citizen had on it, the casting of the ballot, and with some slight limitations it still disclaims such responsibility. Unless corruption can be proved, the state does not bother much with the business of the ballot.

The result of this system was that for many years there was not even a secret ballot. The voter was handed a ticket outside the polling place by the representative of Tammany Hall for the Democrats, or by the Republican representative, depending upon which he demanded. The political parties paid the expenses of printing and distributing the ballots. Tammany Hall did not mind the cost, for this consideration made it too expensive for most independent candidates to run for office, and the money needed for elections was collected by contributions from the candidates themselves, by contributions from office-holders, and later by blackmail of prostitutes and corporations, saloon-keepers and gamblers, business men and gunmen. As nothing was ever given for nothing, it was understood that the office-holders would make the most of their offices, and that corporations and individuals would obtain in return for their money protection from the rigidity of laws already on the statute books and the enactment of new laws which they required in their business.

Early in the career of the organization, the members of the Tammany Hall political association developed an efficient technique for the control of public offices and for the manipulation of the funds of those offices for their personal advantage. In 1806, Benjamin Romaine, who had been one of the leaders in the movement for the burial of the bones of the 11,500 martyrs, was removed from the office of City Comptroller, because he acquired land from the City without paying for it. In the following year, the City's inspector of bread, who was also a sachem of the Tammany Society, resigned because his threat to take one third of his subordinates' fees had been made public. William Mooney, the illustrious founder of Tammany Hall, was superintendent of the City's almshouse. He had intended that Tammany should be a benevolent institution, but he had no such intentions with regard to the almshouse, and it became necessary to remove him in 1809 for malfeasance in office. His salary was supposed to be $1,000 a year, with $500 for family expenses; when it was called to Mooney's attention that his expenses had been credited on the books with $4,000 for one year and that an additional $1,000 had been credited for supplies, he explained that the amounts were paid out in "trifles for Mrs. Mooney." A committee of the Common Council reported that during Mooney's administration the consumption of rum in the almshouse had been more than double, and that the consumption of gin was six times and that of brandy four times the quantities used in former years.

The system by which a politician was expected to receive office as reward for his campaign efforts and to make the most of the office above and beyond his salary, got the name by which it has since been generally known—the spoils system—from a speech in the Senate of the United States by the Senator from New York, William L. Marcy. Senator Marcy was defending the New York politicians against the attack of Henry Clay. He said:

"It may be that the politicians of New York are not so fastidious as some gentlemen are. They boldly preach what they practise. When they are contending for victory, they avow their intention of enjoying the fruits of it. If they fail, they will not murmur. If they win, they expect to reap all the advantages. They see nothing wrong in the rule, that to the victors belong the spoils of the enemy."

This would be all very well if the spoils were limited to the legitimate salaries of office, but it did not appear to be in human nature to limit them. The situation can be summed up, perhaps, in a joke quoted by Ostrogorski: "Tommy: 'Pa, what is human nature?' Mr. Figg: 'Human nature, my son, is the excuse generally offered by a man who has been acting like a hog.'"

The first sachems of Tammany Hall did not limit themselves to the legitimate spoils of their offices. That there were other sources of revenue for them is established by an abundance of incidents. "We have seen a statement published in 1838," wrote Gustavus Myers, "setting forth that $600,000 a year was collected from dives, gambling houses, unfortunate women of the streets, and in extortions from prisoners in the Tombs and the police courts, and even then it was referred to as 'an established custom.'"[1]

How firmly established this custom became in every period of Tammany rule, which was the practical expression of the spoils system, we shall see as we progress through the history of the organization.

Two outstanding examples of fraud by Tammany office-holders were revealed in 1837. Samuel Swartwout, a Tammany politician and collector of the port of New York, hurried to Europe when his accounts showed that he had borrowed from the government's funds, of which he was supposed to be the custodian, the sum of $1,225,705.69. William M. Price, United States District Attorney for the Southern District of New York, also a Tammany man, joined Swartwout in Europe when the accounts of his office indicated that he had stolen $72,124.06. These thefts were so large that they were officially known as defalcations. The public, with that charming levity which has always characterized its attitude toward wholesale plunder, made the best of a bad situation by coining a new word. For many years after the Swartwout episode, when a man put the government's money into his own pocket, it was said with a smile that he had "Swartwouted."

---

[1] "Tammany and Vice," *The Independent*, Vol. LII, p. 2924, 1900.

The report of the committee appointed by Congress in 1838 to investigate the Swartwout and Price defalcations illustrated the perfection that the political system in New York had already attained. Arent S. De Peyster, a weigher in the Custom House, testified that he was compelled to pay $15 of his salary of $1,500 at election time. When he was approached for this sum, he declined to pay it. "Mr. Vanderpoel, the deputy surveyor, observed," Mr. De Peyster testified, "that I ought to consider whether my $1,500 per annum was not worth paying fifteen dollars for. Under the impression that it was the price of my situation, I paid it." The direct connection of Tammany Hall with this system was illustrated by the testimony of David S. Lyon, deputy collector of the port under Swartwout:

"I have frequently been called on to contribute to political objects while I was deputy collector, as an officer of the Custom House. The amount was from twenty to one hundred dollars. The tax was *pro rata*, according to salary. It bore a proportion from one to six per cent. I frequently paid a part of the amount. When it was too high, and more than I could afford, I urged them to reduce it. In one instance, when I was assessed twenty dollars, Mr. Swartwout told the collector of the tax that ten dollars was enough for me to pay. For a few years back I have not paid anything to the general committee, because I could not afford to pay the amount assessed, and because I could not conscientiously longer sustain the party. The collectors of the Tammany Hall general committee, one of whom was John Becker, called on me several times. . . . I believe that nearly *all* the officers of the Custom House, indoors and out, and the clerks, were similarly taxed, and generally paid what they were assessed. It was assessed by the general committee of Tammany Hall, and for the support of the party denominated the Tammany Hall party. If the individual did not pay the amount he was taxed with, the collector would remark, 'You will be reported to the general committee'—and everybody well understood that proscription would follow. The collector of the general committee has an alphabetical book, which contains the names of persons taxed, and the amount each individual is required to pay."[1]

[1] *Report of the Committee of Investigation on the Subject of the Defalcations of Samuel Swartwout and Others.* 25th Congress, 3d Session, House of Representatives, 1839, p. 250.

The methods used at elections in the effort to gain the spoils of the enemy are illustrated by the somewhat extraordinary election of 1834, when the people of New York were electing a mayor for the first time by direct popular ballot. Previously, the Mayor had been appointed by the New York State authorities. The day of the election, Tuesday, April 8, 1834, was stormy, but the rain which came down heavily all day did not calm the excitement of the crowds of men who went about the City's streets. Stores were closed, and men stood in long lines waiting to vote. Tammany Hall favoured President Andrew Jackson, who was the real issue of the campaign, for gratitude with General Jackson amounted to a whim, and it was during his first administration that the spoils system originated. Tammany Hall sent strong men to the polling places to prevent any but its friends from voting. In wards where Tammany was in complete control this method was effective, but the Sixth Ward, already known as the "Bloody Sixth," was the scene of trouble. Men fought with knives and clubs in the polling places. The mobs of Tammany adherents tore down banners, destroyed ballots, and wrecked furniture. The election was to last three days, and on the second day the Whigs organized bands of men to fight the Tammany rioters. One man was stabbed to death; paving stones were hurled about with great effect in the "Bloody Sixth." The Mayor, Gideon Lee, arrived at Masonic Hall, the Whig headquarters and the scene of great disorder; he stood on the steps, held up his staff of office, and commanded peace. The mob threw stones at him, and the Mayor and more than ten of the city watch were wounded. Then a detachment of infantry and two squadrons of cavalry were called to keep the mob of 15,000 in order. The rioters respected the shining bayonets and the horses' hoofs. The ballot boxes of the Sixth Ward were taken to the City Hall under guard, and the votes were counted. Men remained in the streets until three o'clock in the morning to hear the result of the election. It was finally announced that C. W. Lawrence, the Tammany candidate, was elected Mayor by a small majority, and that the Whigs had carried the Common Council.[1]

Four years later, both parties imported men from Phila-

[1] *The Great Riots of New York*, by J. T. Headley, Chapter V.

delphia to vote in many wards in New York, for there was as yet no registration law, and fraudulent voting was simple of accomplishment. The hired Whig voters, who were brought from Philadelphia at $30 a head, wore pins on their left sleeves so that the watchers at the polls would not challenge their own men. The Democrats put ink marks on the ears of their men, so that they could be identified by Tammany Hall's watchers at the polls. The High Constable of Philadelphia furnished the voters, and he was employed because his official position brought him into intimate contact with the leading criminals of Pennsylvania, who made vigorous repeating voters. It was also said that during this election the inmates of the City Prison were released for the day on condition that they would vote the anti-Tammany ticket.[1]

IV

It must not be supposed that Tammany Hall's early activities were confined solely to ceremony and to fraud. Ceremony was used whenever the occasion offered for its effective display, and fraud was used only when it was a certain means of winning an election or of gaining money. During the rest of their time, the members of Tammany took active part in the controversies over the leading issues of the day, for those issues were the raw material of Tammany Hall's popularity with its public. However reluctant it sometimes was to do so, the organization, like every political organization, found it necessary upon occasion to commit itself on the principal questions of the day that it might thereby obtain votes with which to win offices, with which to gain money and prestige.

Tammany Hall's first great political antagonist was De Witt Clinton, and for many years they fought a vigorous battle. During the first twenty-five years of the nineteenth century De Witt Clinton was the most important politician and statesman of New York City and New York State. Clinton was more than six feet tall, strong, honest, conscientious, a scholar, and a member of one of the leading families of the State. He was also brusque, sometimes haughty, and inclined to lose patience

---

[1] *Testimony Relating to the Great Election Frauds of 1838, Taken in the Recorder's Court, New York, in October, 1840.*

with those who disagreed with him on abstract questions. In general character he resembled greatly the late Theodore Roosevelt. He could never endure a rival, and he frequently lost his temper when the designs of his opponents were successful. Clinton's invective power was famous during the period of his career.

De Witt Clinton had been one of the first members of the Tammany Society, and at one time he held the position of Scribe. He soon left Tammany Hall, however, for he quarrelled with his associates, and it was said that the cause of the quarrel was the influence in the Society of Aaron Burr, who was Clinton's strongest rival for the political control of New York City and of New York State. De Witt Clinton held simultaneously the offices of Mayor of New York City and State Senator of New York State. It was his lifelong ambition to become President of the United States, and Tammany was instrumental several times in preventing the consummation of that ambition. If he could not be President himself, Clinton wanted his aged uncle, the head of his illustrious family, George Clinton, to be chosen, but he was defeated in his purposes by Thomas Jefferson, who used Tammany Hall to break Clinton's power in New York.

By calling meetings for days when they knew Clinton was to be absent from the City and then accusing him publicly of neglecting to attend and by other similar tactics Tammany tried its best to discredit De Witt Clinton. In 1811, he lost his seat in the State Senate, and this was important, for it meant the loss of his patronage in the country districts. But just then the Lieutenant Governor of the state died. Clinton sought the office, which carried with it the power of presiding over the Senate, and in spite of Tammany's violent opposition, which included rioting, he was elected. Soon afterward, however, Tammany succeeded in defeating Clinton's reëlection as Mayor of New York City, and he was refused both a nomination for Governor and a nomination to succeed himself as Lieutenant Governor.

It looked as if Tammany Hall had finished De Witt Clinton's career. He had no money, for he had not used his political offices to make money; he had no business connections; and he had no political party, for he had quarrelled with both his

Tammany associates and with the Federalists. Tammany Hall rejoiced. But Clinton was not so destitute as Tammany Hall hoped. He still had in his mind the scheme for which his name is remembered. He had always wanted to build a canal across New York State, and everybody except a few friends had always laughed at the impracticability of his dream. Tammany Hall led the public laughter. The projected Erie Canal was called a "big ditch," and when the newspapers had said that, they thought they had said all that was necessary on the subject. In 1812, a Tammany newspaper printed this doggerel:

> "Oh, a ditch he would dig from the lakes to the sea,
> The Eighth of the world's matchless Wonders to be,
> Good land! how absurd! But why should you grin?
> It will do to bury its mad author in."

When Clinton's political ambitions were defeated, he was bitterly disappointed, and he retired to his farm at Newton, Long Island, where he would see no one and took consolation only in large quantities of liquor. He soon grew weary of sulking, however, and he began to write letters to men with influence and to men with money, with the object of interesting them in his Erie Canal. He was not in politics, and people did not therefore suspect him of partisan designs. He held public meetings, at which he spoke in favour of the Canal, and people now began to listen to him impartially. Soon his scheme became so popular that the Democratic-Republican Party, in spite of the opposition of Tammany Hall, was forced to nominate De Witt Clinton for Governor, and he was elected by a large majority. One of the poets of the day remarked:

> "Witt Clinton is dead, St. Tammany said,
> And all the papooses with laughter were weeping;
> But Clinton arose and confounded his foes—
> The cunning old fox had only been sleeping."

Tammany Hall continued to fight Clinton after he was elected Governor, but it was unsuccessful until aided by natural causes. On the 11th of February, 1828, De Witt Clinton had spent an unusually busy day, and he was resting and talking with his family when he fell back in his chair and died.

AN EARLY TAMMANY CARICATURE

It was during these years of its struggle with De Witt Clinton that Tammany Hall came out frankly as a political organization. The Society itself was not supposed to be political, and when it was incorporated in 1805 by the State of New York, the charter stated that the purpose of the incorporation was to enable its members "the better to carry into effect the benevolent purpose of affording relief to the indigent and distressed." We have seen how Tammany naturally grew into a political association, and in order to take a more open and more effective part in politics, the members of the Tammany Society organized the General Committee of Tammany Hall, as part of the Democratic-Republican Party. To this General Committee men were chosen by ward committees, but the members of the Tammany Society managed to control the elections in the wards, and they therefore always controlled the General Committee, which recommended candidates for public offices. A finance committee was also organized, and the sachems of the Tammany Society always managed to be members of this important committee, which raised the campaign funds. After nominations for office were made, they were ratified in a great popular meeting, but the principal members of the Tammany Society made this meeting one of enthusiastic approval of their choices rather than an open forum. Thus the members of the Tammany Society built up an organization for the control of New York City's Democratic politics, and at the same time made it appear that the Society itself had nothing whatever to do with politics, such things being managed by the General Committee of the Democratic-Republican Party, which happened to meet in Tammany Hall. But as the sachems of the Society were also the leaders of the General Committee, there was merely an effective confusion of names instead of a real difference in purpose. And confusion of the public mind has always been an asset to Tammany Hall.

v

The leaders of Tammany Hall had now become rich men, some through fraud, and some by means of the opportunities for business which their government connections afforded them. They were dependent upon the common people for their power, but they found it necessary only to flatter the common people in order to retain their support. The interests of the leaders of Tammany Hall were now the interests of rich men, and they were no more in accord with the civic wishes of their followers than Alexander Hamilton and the Federalists had been in accord with the workingmen of their time. This discord led to interesting difficulties between the people and their political potentates, for, by reason of their control of nominations and appointments to offices, the leaders of Tammany Hall had become the rulers of the people. To be sure, there were other political groups, but none so closely organized and none so effective as Tammany Hall. Signs of revolt, however, were abundant, and one of the most interesting of these was the movement started by Fanny Wright, the first woman agitator of importance in America.

Frances Wright came to New York from England in 1829 to lecture on her ideas of economic equality, religion, and the relationship of the sexes. Her ideas were simple, but, at the time, startling. She believed in a communist state, or at least, if she could not obtain her ideal, a larger share of the proceeds of labour for the labouring man; she thought that the state had no concern with religion, and that it should by no means encourage it; and she felt that marriage was not absolutely necessary to the consummation of true love.

Miss Wright was received with great enthusiasm at first by some people in the City who regarded themselves as liberal thinkers. But at her third lecture she announced her intention of establishing a free-thought newspaper in New York, and then both the press and the clergy became frightened and abusive, as was their wont whenever they sensed dangerous competition. The *Commercial Advertiser* called Miss Wright "a bold blasphemer and a voluptuous preacher of licentiousness." It remarked incidentally that she was "impervious to the voice of virtue and case-hardened against shame." The New York *Observer*, a weekly religious paper, described Miss Wright as "Infidelity in an Angel's garb."

Such talk led to active preparations to break up Miss Wright's meetings by people who were always ready to break up meetings for the fun of it at the instigation of people who were frightened at the spread of different ideas. Some gentlemen tried to smoke out the speaker and her audience in Masonic Hall by placing a barrel of combustibles covered with turpentine in the doorway and setting fire to it. A few days later, in the middle of Miss Wright's lecture, someone turned off the gas, and an audience of 2,000 was left in darkness. In order to make her more colloquial, and thereby more contemptuous, the newspapers always referred to Frances Wright as Fanny Wright.

Fanny Wright's doctrines won some support from workingmen and mechanics, and a political party known as the Workingmen's Party was organized in New York City. It polled 6,000 of the 20,000 votes at the election of 1829 and elected a member of the Legislature, defeating the Tammany Hall candidate. The newspapers were furious at this small sign of success, and William Cullen Bryant, editor of the *Evening Post*, turned to his poetry for the occasion. He published an ode, in the course of which he spoke of Miss Wright as

> "Thou in whose eloquence and bloom
> The age beholds a new Aspasia!"

The *Post* also feared that because of the strength which the new party had exhibited, and the character of its principles, reputable people would hesitate to make investments in the City of New York or to become residents there. The *Courier and Enquirer* took out its resentment this way: "There is a scandalous report about town, that Miss Epicene Wright has abstracted, or rather Agrarianized, a pair of Mr. Jennings's inexpressibles, and means to appear in them at her next lecture, which report says is to be delivered at the sign of 'All Things in Common,' Five Points." The *Courier and Enquirer* also invented a song to be sung on the departure of Fanny Wright for Europe to the tune of "Oh! Put the Onion to Your Eye." Among the verses was this one:

> "And if you want to raise the wind,
> Or breed a moral storm
> You must have one bold lady-man
> To prate about reform."

When Fanny Wright preached economic freedom and unrestricted sexual intercourse, she included the Negro slaves, who should not, she considered, be deprived because of their colour of the benefits enjoyed by their contemporaries. It was therefore not at all surprising that some Southern gentlemen intimated to Miss Mary Carroll, who in 1828 gave up a millinery business in New Orleans to start "a philosophical bookshop," that they would not be surprised if Miss Wright should, one of these mornings, find her throat cut.

Fanny Wright's movement accomplished a great deal. The agitation for equal rights which she had precipitated caused Tammany Hall to put through the Legislature a mechanics' lien law for the protection of workingmen, and it also led to the abolition of imprisonment for debt and the reform of the system of compulsory service in the State militia.[1]

The internal changes in Tammany Hall which the movement for greater equality brought about led to the origin of the Loco-Foco Party and to a strange scene in Tammany Hall on the night of October 29, 1835. A meeting was called for seven o'clock on that evening, and the Tammany leaders attempted to jam through their nominations, as usual, but the men who believed in the rights of workingmen protested against the candidates, whom they designated as monopolists. The regular Tammany Hall men found it impossible to read their nominations, because of the disturbance created by the Equal Rights, Anti-Monopolist adherents. They left the hall to the workingmen's orators, went into the cellar, and turned off the gas. "It is half-past seven, and the darkness of midnight is in Tammany Hall," wrote a contemporary observer. "Nothing but the demon spirit of monopoly, in its war upon humanity, could have been wicked enough to involve such an excited throng in total darkness." But some men had the newly invented loco-foco matches and cigars in their pockets. These were lighted, and the meeting continued with greater fervour than ever. Resolutions were passed denouncing monopoly, the United States Bank, and all other banks and bankers, and declaring in favour of equal rights, a sound currency and strict construction of the Constitution of the United States. The next morning the *Courier and Enquirer* called the anti-monopolist faction of Tammany Hall Loco-Focos, and the name remained a party name for

---

[1] The Frances Wright movement is covered completely in *Frances Wright*, by William Randall Waterman.

many years. There had been a slightly less disorderly meeting in Tammany Hall a short time before, when Gideon Lee, a banker, had attempted to make Preserved Fish chairman. Preserved Fish was compelled to retire.[1] After the second disorderly meeting the Equal Rights faction separated from their Tammany brethren and nominated candidates of their own, who were defeated at the election. Some of the dissenters hurried back to the Tammany fold, and a reconciliation took place in 1837, when most of the radicals returned.

Mrs. Euphemia Vale Blake, Tammany's official historian, pointed out that "it never shuts the door in the face of returning prodigals." This has usually been true, for Tammany Hall's leaders have always been wise enough to realize that there was no profit in resentment. Frequently, after serious dissensions, the organization has forgiven all, and the opponents have been received cordially.

By acting as the friend of the common people as long as it was necessary to gain their votes, and by using the power conferred by those votes in the interests of the rich and the privileged classes, Tammany Hall was able to remain powerful. In times of general prosperity Tammany Hall's problem was easy, but turbulent economic conditions created difficulties, because then Tammany Hall's opponents could gain the attention of the people, who never cared much who ruled them so long as they could enjoy their own necessities.

The period of which we are now treating was not one of prosperity. New York had experienced in 1835 the most colossal fire in its history. Insurance companies had been unable to meet their obligations, and over-speculation had caused a financial panic. Bread was expensive, and the cost of coal was beyond the means of the workingman. It was felt that bankers and large merchants had profited unduly at the expense of workingmen and shopkeepers, and resentment was high. At a mass meeting in City Hall Park in 1837 someone shouted, "Hart's flour store," and several hundred people

---

[1]Mr. Fish had been christened with his curious name when a New Bedford fisherman found him, an unknown baby, floating like Moses on the waters. The New Bedford native commemorated the rescue in the child's name, and, after all, he could not be expected to foresee that Preserved Fish would grow up to be one of New York City's leading merchants.

rushed for the wholesale flour establishment of Eli Hart in Washington Street. The doors were broken down, and about five hundred barrels of flour and one thousand bushels of wheat were emptied into the streets.

Tammany Hall's leaders realized the danger to their power in the state of mind behind such action, and they catered immediately to the workingmen and to the Equal Rights Party. The ward committees of Tammany Hall began practical work toward the alleviation of suffering. John M. Bloodgood, a Tammany leader, went among the poor with a large basket filled with cakes, pies, and meat, and he gave them out to those who asked for them. The ward politicians began to furnish their constituents with clothing, fuel, food, and even money. These methods were immediately effective; it was discovered shortly afterward that the benevolent Bloodgood, who held the office of Police Justice, gained his money by extorting it from the counterfeiters, thieves, and prostitutes who were brought into his court.

The eternal struggle between the poor and the rich went on, and Tammany Hall, which was sometimes on one side and sometimes on the other, depending upon the economic weather, found a formidable and picturesque opponent in the Hon. Mike Walsh. Michael Walsh was born in Ireland in 1815, and he came to the United States with his parents when he was a child. His father owned a mahogany yard in New York City, and he entertained special opinions of his own concerning the proper form of republican government. These prevented him from accepting that of the United States of America, and the elder Walsh refused to become a naturalized citizen. The son inherited his father's independence, at least, for it was one of his *mots* that, "Any dead fish can swim with the stream, but it takes a real live one to go against the current." During the summer months Mike Walsh slept in one or another of the City's parks, because he believed that the night air hardened his constitution, and for the same reason he refused to wear an overcoat in winter. When he was a boy, Walsh was apprenticed to a lithographer; he then became a journalist and a political agitator. With George Wilkes, the most eminent blackmailer of his day, and later founder of the *Police Gazette*, Mike Walsh founded a newspaper called *The Subterranean*, in which he expressed his political views with amazing vigour and with considerable intelligence. In the following speech, which he delivered at Tammany Hall in 1841, Mike Walsh set forth his views of the politics of the period and of Tammany Hall politicians in particular:

"I know perfectly well, and no man who knows anything about the matter will dare question the truth of the statement, that the delegates to nominating committees are chosen not by the electors of each ward, but generally by a few unprincipled blackguards, usually office-holders or office-seekers, who meet in the back room of some low groggery, where they place upon a ticket for the support of their fellow-citizens a number of wretches of their own moral calibre, whose characters and consciences have been so long buried that they have become putrid.

"The formal ceremony of electing these delegates is always a most ridiculous and insulting farce. 'A meeting of the democratic electors of the ward' is called—a number of fellows who either hold or expect office go round amongst the lowest rum holes in the ward—treat the 'setters', in addition to which, they give the ringleaders a few dollars apiece, to insure the presence of their gangs. Every contractor brings a number of poor men whose spirits have been broken, and whose frames have been withered and bowed down by that worst form of slavery—*the slavery of poverty*, and out of whose sorrowing sighs, sweat and blood, this same bloated *brute* has distilled a fortune, and they are compelled when at the meeting, by the wretchedness and degradation of their condition to respond with counterfeit sincerity, to each mandate of their LABOR'S PLUNDERER, even though it were to violate, stifle, and trample upon a man who had sacrificed himself and family in vainly attempting to redeem them; those, with the city watchmen, lamplighters, police officers and a number of selected or favoured *thieves*, who receive indulgences from the police judges and officers to commit a certain number of crimes without molestation, in consideration of the *valuable political* services which they render on those and various other occasions, assemble half an hour before the time specified in the call—arrange the meeting, cry out 'aye,' when the names are called—give three cheers before the 'noes' can be taken, after which the 'contractor' who acts as chairman pronounces everything 'carried unanimously'—then a motion to adjourn is passed, all hands go down and drink, and thus are made nearly all our *honorable* nominating committees. (Tremendous cheers and hisses, mingled with cries of 'go it Mike, go it my hero, give it to 'em,' with counter cries of 'turn him out, throw him out of the window, pull him off the stand,' etc.)

"Come up; come up here, you craven cowardly scoundrels, you that are hallooing I mean, and pull me off yourselves. Is not this a pretty scene, there now are a parcel of watchmen, lamplighters, hirelings, menials, police officers and their companions—the very stool pigeons and thieves I have just been describing! . . . You have *men* to contend with here! not poor destitute and forlorn wretches. . . . But I come here determined to reduce the county meeting to its legitimate purposes—to appeal from the decision of a corrupt committee, who dispose of nominations to the highest bidder, as the hireling soldiery of Rome used to sell the imperial diadem. . . . And why do you consider a manly proper and patriotic act a dangerous innovation? Because you are slaves? (Terrific uproar.) Yes, abject, willing slaves—slaves by choice, while you foolishly flatter yourselves that you are democrats. (Cries of 'pull him down, pull him down, this is no place for such remarks.') Keep still gentlemen—don't worry yourselves—*this is just the place for such remarks;* but you have acted so long like automatons, that to act like men seems to you to be a new state of being. (Then turning round to Slamm, Ming, Riel and others, who were hissing.) . . . But I wish you to distinctly understand me when I tell you that Tammany Hall belongs to us—we being the only honest, virtuous portion of the democratic party, and I wish you also to distinctly understand that we are determined to keep possession of it until you are able to dispossess us—and that I believe is as good as a lease for life, isn't it boys? (Terrific cheering, hisses and cries of 'yes,' mingled with 'go it Mike,' 'turn him out, etc.', which finally ended in two or three beautiful fights. The uproar was here so great, that the reporters were unable to note a word for several minutes.)"[1]

---

[1]*Sketches of the Speeches and Writings of Michael Walsh*, pp. 21–32.

AN EARLY TAMMANY CARICATURE

Walsh's newspaper, *The Subterranean*, had for its slogan, "Through Ages Thou Hast Slept in Chains and Night—Arise, Now, Man, and Vindicate Thy Right," and for its motto, "Independent in everything—Neutral in nothing." On October 25, 1845, Mike Walsh expressed in this newspaper the following opinion of Tammany Hall and its occupants:

"Tammany Hall, after all, is a great crib about election times. During the balance of the year, its large bar-rooms and entries are exclusively occupied by well-dressed boarders and visitors, and if a ragged or illy-dressed member of the *unterrified* should chance to intrude, he would excite of much seeming curiosity and astonishment amongst the regular visiters, as a wild Winnebago would in the streets of Constantinople. On ordinary occasions, it is the *genteel* hotel, and any boisterous conduct would be considered by the landlord and his attendants in the light of gross violation of the established rules. But how striking is the change during the excitement of elections. Then the idle dandies and wealthy Spanish cloak gentry are entirely lost in the Goth and Vandal-like eruption of the shirtless and unwashed democracy. Short pipes and mortar-stained hats are in great abundance, and applicants for office seem to vie with each other in their unqualified admiration of men with patched clothes and empty stomachs. How sudden—how palpable is the condescension of pompous, arrogant nabobs on these periodical occasions. It always affords me alternate feelings of heart-felt humor and intense mortification, to look on unperceived at the varied scenes of one of those curious dramas. Who can resist the irresistible ludicrousness of seeing a number of fat, purse-proud officials, half pulverized and dancing 'strait-fours' with clam-boys and ashes venders, to whom they would scorn to speak to at any other time? I dropped in a few evenings since, when I discovered Matsell [Chief of Police at the time], two Aldermen and an ex-Mayor, dancing to the tune of 'The devil among the tailors,' which old Nexan was playing pretty correctly for a man so far gone in liquor, on a second handed jewsharp, with which George Rice presented him: in another corner five or six slabbering hunkers of great pretended dignity, were hugging each other as though they were so many pious professors of opposite sexes in a love feast. Then a jolly old captain connected with the Custom House was standing on a chair, blowing out 'Starm along, O starmy,' at the extreme top of his voice, in the chorus of which some twenty or thirty motley spirits joined with great apparent éclat. Now and then some chap with a very bad hat, but in great apparent glee, would jump up as tho' he was made of India rubber, and with a significant flourish of one leg and one hand, would yelp out, 'No sociability or excitement without liquor!—you hear that, eh? Who objects to that 'ere sentiment?' This generally had the effect of eliciting an invitation to drink from some avaricious office holder, who was fearful his liberality might be questioned.

"There is something even to a rigidly temperate individual like myself,[1] truly exhilarating in these scenes of jovial and glorious equality, which is only marred by reflecting on the shortness of its duration. I sometimes almost wish that I could take a glass or two of wine so as to take a hand in the game occasionally. The gloomy, churlish, money-worshipping, all-pervading spirit of the age has swept nearly all the poetry of life out of the poor man's sphere, so that little is left him during the sad interims which occur in his life of toil, beyond an opportunity of pondering on his little wrongs. Ballad-singing, street dancing, tumbling, public games, all are either prohibited or discountenanced, so that Fourth of July and election sports alone remain. No wonder then, that thousands of poor men flock to Old Tammany and the neighbouring houses on such occasions to get a taste of the equality which they hear so much preached, but never, save there, see even partially practised."

In one of his speeches to the working men, Mike Walsh remarked: "There are many men in the party who fawn upon us and call us the bone and sinew of the country, upon this platform, and who would use us until there was nothing but bone and sinews left of us." When Walsh described so eloquently to the people the wrongs that the politicians had inflicted upon them, some shouted, "We've stood it too long." "All I'm afraid

---

[1]Mike Walsh was found dead many years later in the area of a public house on Eighth Avenue, where it was said he had been drinking the night before. His periodic drunkenness was one of the favourite accusations of his enemies.

of is that you'll stand it too much longer," Mike Walsh answered. The popular demand for Walsh became so great that Tammany Hall was compelled to nominate him for the Assembly in place of the Hon. Samuel J. Tilden, subsequently Governor of New York and candidate for the Presidency of the United States. This is Walsh's own account of the glorious occasion as he published it in *The Subterranean* for November 1, 1845:

"About seven o'clock P. M. I stepped into my residence— I'm never ahead of time, though always on hand—washed my face—put on a clean shirt—blacked my old boots—brushed the professor's hat, and slipped into Johnny Brighton's little summer coat, and started for Tammany Hall in company with myself. Here I arrived a short time after the meeting was organized, found some six or seven thousand persons at least, all of whom were roaring out all sorts of noises at the top of their voices, and pulling, hauling, and fighting as hard as they could. I pushed through the tumultuous crowd as fast as I was able, and was greeted at every step by some warm-hearted and enthusiastic disciple.—It seemed like the meeting between Napoleon and his faithful adherents on his way from Rochefort to Paris, after returning from Elba. As soon as I reached the stand I was hailed by the assembled thousands beneath, with a deafening, soul-cheering round of applause, such as Tammany Hall or no other Hall ever rang with before. In wild, frantic, and electric enthusiasm, it far transcended even all that had been hitherto bestowed upon me. . . . From the moment I was first seen upon the stand they would hear nobody nor listen to anything but 'Walsh,' 'Walsh,' 'Mike,' 'Mike.' Not being in any great hurry, I permitted a few office-holders to make harlequins of themselves for the sport of the assembled multitude who were 'bahing' at them, and ridiculing them with every species of contemptuous and ludicrous remark, 'No Custom House dictation,' 'Go lay down,' 'Get a substitute,' 'Go learn to spell before you attempt to read,' 'I move we pass everything without hearing it at all,' 'I second the motion,' 'Carried,' 'Hurrah,' etc., etc.—'Walsh, Walsh,' 'Nobody but Mike, the poor man's well-tried friend,' 'Mike, they can't buy you from us,' 'You're the only man amongst them we've got confidence in, and you're the only one we'll listen to,' and a thousand similar declarations were heard from all parts of the room. Seeing I had everything my own way, I magnanimously stepped forward several times and requested the multitude to listen to the office-holding simpletons and blowers, who were endeavoring to make some little show, in the hope of retaining the fat situations to which they have no claim, beyond servile subserviency and shameless impudence. . . .

"The calls for me now became truly terrific and thinking it about time I should put a stop to the insulting mummery, I stepped forward, and after ordering a mock auctioneer from the Seventeenth Ward, named Bob something, and one or two other loafers out of the road, so as to have plenty of elbow room, I commenced a speech which was listened to with the most breathless attention for an hour or two, unbroken by any interruptions save the thundergusts of applause with which the close of every paragraph was hailed. Every now and then three vociferous cheers for 'Mike Walsh' would burst in earthquake tones from the thousands of working men present, the misery and depredation of whose condition I brought so vividly before them, that it was impossible to repress them. Scarcely a man amongst them but would willingly have faced a cannon's mouth at any moment during the whole time to redress the bitter and accursed wrongs to which the laboring poor are so shamefully subjected by the plundering drones who roll in luxury on the proceeds of the poor man's toil. At the conclusion of the speech, which had to be prolonged much longer than I intended, in consequence of the repeated, deafening, and irresistible cries of 'go on,' 'go on,' nine tremendous cheers were given for 'Mike Walsh, the poor man's friend,' and 'Champion of the Young Democracy.'"

Walsh was then nominated. The account in the New York *Herald* of the same meeting proves that Walsh was not unduly exaggerating his own importance to the assembled multitude, and the *Herald* gives additional details:

"The Chairman, amid great confusion and uproar, proceeded to state the object of the meeting to be, to respond to the nominations of Edward Sanford for Senator, and the members of the Assembly.

"The reading of the call was on motion dispensed with. Here a low, ruffianly looking individual pushed himself forward on the platform, and took his seat beside the Chairman.

"Capt. Rynders immediately seized the offender, and in the true democratic spirit, coolly knocked him down. (Great confusion, hisses and yells.) The used-up man shouted that he was a full-blooded democrat.

"Capt. Rynders.—Well, then, behave like one—that's all we want. (Hurrahs, shouts and deafening cheers. 'Go it, Rynders—show your authority—hit him again, old boy'—were among the exclamations which his patriotic sentiment called forth.)

"Voice in the Crowd.—I move that Captain Rynders make a speech.

"Capt. Rynders.—Shut up; I shan't. . . .

"Here a very fat, greasy-looking fellow, with well plastered soap locks, called for three cheers for Mike Walsh. . . .

"The nomination of Edward Sandford for Senator was now cordially responded to. Samuel Osgood for Register, was then proposed, and called forth three hearty cheers. Capt. Rynders waved his hat, and seemed likely to go into hysterics. . . .

"A fight now took place on the platform—several men got on the reporters' table, and their object seemed to be to ascertain who could yell the loudest.

"Three groans for Tilden was then called for and given. The vast hall was in a state of commotion—rows, fights and yells, the order of the night. Hats were knocked off and crushed—noses smashed—eyes blackened, and shins bruised.

"A man in a blue coat on the stand, now cried, 'Tilden's nomination's carried.'

"Fat Man in the Crowd.—You be damned—you're a custom house officer—go to h—ll. . . .

"The meeting now became very uproarious—cries for 'Walsh, Walsh,' were heard in various directions.

"Captain Rynders again attempted to make a speech, but failing to obtain a hearing, said 'he didn't care a damn for anybody.'"

Mike Walsh was elected to the Assembly, and the day after election he became seriously ill. It was charged that an attempt had been made to poison him, but he recovered, and *The Sub-terranean's* leading editorial on Saturday, November 21, 1846, was headed "The late Cowardly and Infamous attempt to Murder me." Walsh remarked that he would take his seat in the Assembly if he had "a spoonful of breath left," and that, "it would be utterly impossible to induce me to die under any circumstances until I take my seat as a member of that body."

Mike Walsh's comments on the habits as well as the opinions of his contemporaries were vigorous. This note appeared on the editorial page of *The Subterranean* one day:

"Accident.—Pierre Young, the well known smoucher, met with a very serious accident at the late dinner and debauch given by that incorrigible set of loafers known as the Tammany Society. It appears, as near as I can gather, that on rising to give a toast, toward the close of the performance, he pulled out his handkerchief to wipe the grease and slabber from his face, when some six or eight pounds of ham and other eatables dropped upon the floor. The accident, which, in consequence of the beastly state of intoxication in which his associates were, passed off almost unperceived, might, under other circum-stances, have subjected him to a good deal of merriment and ridicule. Pierre! when you try such games in future, you should keep a little more sober, and have your eye about."

Commenting on the electioneering methods of an alderman of the period, Walsh wrote:

". . . Mann Hart, the Alderman was electioneering for himself with a huge bundle of very old clothes under his arm, with which he bought up the votes of many honest, but ragged and shivering *freemen*. This licentious Israelite played his part with a skill as depraved, as it was consummate. . . . Having taken the precaution to fortify himself against the cold by swallowing ten or a dozen 'hot doctors,' and enveloping himself in a stout overcoat and large camblet cloak, he took up his stand on the shady side of the way where the wind was most pinchingly cold, and there made his mercenary appeals to the chilling, pinching necessities of the hungry and half-clad por-tion of the houseless democracy. With one hand he held out the obnoxious ticket, and with the other, the well worn garment, with which he hoped to stifle the conscientious scruples of the wavering voter. This degrading and humiliating inducement, I regret to say, had the desired effect in too many instances. . . .

"Mann-Manessa—or whatever the devil it is—Hart,the wandering Jew who formerly speculated in the cast-off garments of Congressmen, and who is now Alderman of the Fifth Ward, and a pretended broker, shaver, or bogus money dealer in Wall street, takes pretty extensive airs upon himself since he got into the Common Council. What right has he to be Alderman of the Fifth Ward when he sleeps in the Eighth Ward? Why does he sneak out of that house in Broome street every morning as if he had been committing a burglary during the night? A pretty pup truly to go round arresting every poor unfortunate female who evinces a holy horror towards the unchristian embraces of old clo' dealers. How would a full expose of his position and business in the Broome street house set upon his pork-hating stomach? It may not be generally known to the bigoted portion of the Fifth Ward Christians that this fellow is a lineal descendant of Mordecai Hart, the fellow that pressed the crown of thorns on Christ's head. Such however is the fact, and I regret to say that he resembles his dastardly and brutal ancestor in many things besides name. Let me hear no more of your impertinence, or I shall light on you in earnest."

There was considerable prejudice against Jews during the period. Mordecai M. Noah, the editor of the Tammany newspaper, the *National Advocate*, was put up by Tammany Hall as candidate for sheriff. When it was objected that a Jew ought not to be permitted to hang a Christian, which as sheriff he would most likely be compelled to do, Noah replied: "Pretty Christians to require hanging at all." He got the job.

It was not long before Mike Walsh's criticisms of his contemporaries resulted in suits against him for criminal libel. He was sentenced to Blackwell's Island. David C. Broderick, a friend of Walsh's, and later United States Senator from California, thought it a disgraceful violation of the freedom of the press that Walsh should be jailed, and he urged his friend to show his contempt for the world in general and his enemies in particular by making a first-class martyr of himself. Broderick insisted that the best way to accomplish this was for Walsh

to commit suicide by throwing himself into the East River as
the prison boat was taking him to Blackwell's Island. Walsh
and Broderick said their sad farewells on the dock. "Hero!
patriot! martyr! farewell forever," remarked Broderick, as he
shook Walsh's hand. "I will remain behind to see that posterity
does you justice." But Mike Walsh decided to remain behind
also. Broderick never forgave him.[1]

Mike Walsh's associate in the editorship of *The Subterranean*,
George Wilkes, was also put in jail for criminal libel, and after
he was released, Wilkes published the diary of his prison term,
which he called *The Mysteries of the Tombs*, and which was a
best-seller in 1844. In the course of this work he offered the following revelations of the system by which the police and the
politicians of the period extorted money from those they arrested and sentenced:

"The simple and unsuspecting, who only look upon a police
officer as a minister of justice and on a magistrate as the pure
and dignified dispenser of the law, imagine that the former
thrive simply upon six shilling fees for every arrest they make;
and are by no means aware that a large number of them
are the pensioners of brothels and derive four-fifths of their
income either directly or indirectly from female prostitution.
In their ignorance of this, they are also strangers to the luxury
of laughing at the ridiculous spectacle of these fellows pretending to be arrayed against a class which puts clothes upon their
backs, money in their pockets and furnishes them with their
bread and butter. This revenue is collected in different ways.
One prostitute may have a difference with another which results in blows. An officer arrests each party at the complaint
of the other and each pays five or ten dollars to be released. A
landlady retains the clothes of a delinquent for board. An
officer recovers them and receives in pay a liberal fee and perhaps a *tender favor* in addition. Balls are given in palaces of
pleasure and two officers receive five dollars each, for maintaining peace and protecting the filles des joies in the quiet
enjoyment of licentiousness.

"But the most lucrative depredations which are made upon
this unhappy class, are obtained by foray; or, in other words,

---
[1] *Thirty Years of New York Politics*, by Matthew P. Breen, pp. 305–306.

MIKE WALSH

a general descent of the magistrate and a posse of officers upon a house, and a sweep of all of its inmates into the Tombs. This is done on pretext of the aforesaid house being 'disorderly,' and some familiar devil of the Tombs is made to previously swear out a complaint to that effect as a sort of justification of the outrage. The women are then seized and dragged rudely to prison and locked up. On their way, each officer who has one in charge, pledges his victim his eternal friendship, and receives in lieu all the money she has about her as an earnest for his good offices with the magistrate in getting her discharged. In the morning, the terrors of her confinement has rendered her willing to any sacrifice, and she then takes out her ear rings and strips her fingers to urge his aid again. The officer pockets this lawful plunder, but still makes no effort to release her, for there is yet another source which will yield a tribute, if she is kept a little longer. She has a *cher ami* outside who is interested in her fate and he will come down handsomely for the deliverance of his lady-love. The lover found and sounded, there is no further reason for her detention, and she is accordingly discharged on sham bail, with an admonition, which, if meant, would be suicidal to the interests of him who gives it, to 'never do so again.' Sometimes one of these poor victims of official tyranny will be betrayed into an outburst of indignation, and if this should happen to be accompanied with a refusal, or inability to pay, she is sent to Blackwell's Island by the indignant magistrate as a vagrant, and then, good night to her forever.

"I know a most aggravated case of this kind of extortion. A party of French girls, the mistresses of some military officers at Quebec, came on to this city on a frolic. Two of them were only sixteen years of age, and knew nothing of the world beyond what they had gained through their connection with the officers who had seduced them. All put up together in a house somewhere up town, but had been there only four days, when word reached the police officer that a party of French girls, with plenty of money, had just arrived and stopped at such a number in such a street. The magistrate to whom it was told was in extasies. It was a pecuniary godsend, which would enable him to pay a shortly coming bill, and he fervently thanked Providence for the blessing. A complaint against them was sworn out at once, for fear some other magistrate should get the start of him, and about five o'clock in the afternoon the descent made. Almost ignorant of our language, trembling and terrified, the wretched girls were seized unceremoniously and marched, shivering in their gossamer indoor dresses, through the chill of a bleak October day, to the Tombs. They were thrust all together into a cold, damp cell, ignorant of their offence, and left to the terrors of an imagination which had never yet conceived a scene so horrible as this. The magistrate who committed them went home to a comfortable supper and snored sonorously between the softest blankets; the poor girls, who were his superiors in everything, who had been reared in luxury and always had been the object of tenderest solicitude, wept in a shivering circle upon a dungeon floor. . . . They ate no breakfast, but at breakfast time received the visits of the officers who arrested them—tempted them to humanity with all the money and valuables in their persons, and informed them of the names of some who might interest themselves in their release. This necessarily delayed matters until a late hour in the afternoon, when all the strings having been pulled and all the contributions being in, the magistrate wiped the recent traces of venison steak and Scotch ale from his lips, and called them out for examination. He took them into a privy chamber, one by one, and there, in the widest sense of the term, examined them. As the public may have some curiosity as to the nature of Star Chamber examinations in such cases as these, I will describe this one for their especial edification.

"The magistrate approached the trembling girl, with his arms clasped magisterially behind him and his brows bent upon her in a most magisterial manner. He asked her her name, age, place of birth and business, and after receiving answers to these questions, relaxed a little, and in a softer tone inquired who seduced her. He relaxed a little more, made his tone softer still, and then asked her *how?*

"She blushed, hung down her head and made no answer.

"The representative of justice laid his hand softly on her shoulder with the insinuation of a cat, and relaxing his countenance still further, till he became positively amiable, remarked, as he slightly compressed his fingers in the moulded beauty between them—'You are very pretty.'

"'Oh, sir!'

"'Indeed you are!' (Another amorous compression with a slight change of latitude.) 'Why, what a pretty foot you have! What a pretty ankle, too, and——'

"'For shame, sir!' cried the outraged girl, coloring scarlet and repulsing him with indignation.

"'Come, come!' said his honor, resuming his sternness and adding to it with a most formidable frown, 'recollect where you are, and who I am! I am informed that you have been engaged in passing counterfeit money.'

"'Oh, *mon Dieu!*'

"'Yes; I have been informed that you have been engaged in passing counterfeit money, and I intended to search you in as delicate and gentlemanly a manner as possible.'

"'Counterfeit money!' exclaimed the astonished girl in surprise, and forgetting her delicacy in her terror at the charge, told his honor he might search her and see; and in the impulse of unthinking innocence, pulled forward her dress and revealed to him the treasures of her bosom.

"His honor peeped into it, as eager as a Turk would into the seventh heaven, and inspired by this into extraordinary diligence, (though he found no spurious indications there,) he continued his search in a most faithful manner.

"She hoped his honor was satisfied.

"Not quite; French women were very adroit in concealing their money; they did not only trust to the intricacies of their *clothes*, but sometimes——

* * * * * * *

"The magistrate continued his search, and after protracting it for several minutes, Justice was satisfied. Hard luck if it wasn't! I might attempt and succeed in getting up an indignation on this subject, but I suppose it was all meant in a joke, and so we might as well laugh it off.

"After his honor was through, he discharged the prisoner on condition that she should not repeat the circumstances of her examination, and that she should leave the city within three days. The same ceremony was then performed, in detail, with the other three, and they were released upon the like condition.

"These magistrates have fine opportunities for studying human nature, but they sometimes carry their researches to extremes."[1]

In 1844, Wilkes was describing with poetic license a system which prevailed throughout most of the history of Tammany Hall as a political institution. Tammany Hall nominated or appointed the police magistrates, and its leaders were the men for policemen to see when they wanted jobs or promotion. They were usually expected to pay for these favours, and at election time they were all expected to offer campaign contributions and to work personally for the success of the Tammany Hall ticket. What they did in their jobs was considered their own business. George Wilkes knew whereof he spoke, for his associations were the same as those of the men he was writing about. Some years later Wilkes sued John Chamberlin for defamation of character because Chamberlin had stated that Wilkes "acted like the son of a prostitute, and lived like one brought up in a brothel, and had been supported by the wages of prostitution." Chamberlin's affidavit asserted: "That the said George Wilkes, plaintiff herein, filled that rôle with the said Kate, and, as her 'fancy man,' frequented her house, took her money, gratified her lusts, eating the bread that had been won, and wearing the clothes that had been bought by the wages of prostitutes." Wilkes did not recover damages. It may be objected that the evidence submitted by a man of Wilkes's reputation and activities is not worthy of consideration. But, it must be remembered that information of this kind of activity is not usually obtainable in the theses of doctors of philosophy, where it is customary to give authority for every statement.

That there was general political and personal corruption during the period is clear not only from such sources as the writings of Mike Walsh and George Wilkes, but also from the *Documents of the Board of Aldermen*. Prisoners whose terms had expired were kept in jail until election day for the value of their votes, and convicts were permitted to escape on condition that they voted properly.[2] Office holders were expected to make money out of prisoners, if their jobs concerned prisoners, and out of real estate if their jobs were connected with the City's

[1]*The Mysteries of the Tombs*, by George Wilkes, pp. 39, ff., 1844.
[2]*Documents of the Board of Aldermen*, Vol. XI, No. 40.

land. Mike Walsh, addressing a meeting of Democrats, asserted: "I tell you now, and I say it boldly, that in this body politic of New York, there is not political or personal honesty enough left to drive a nail into to hang a hat upon."

It was in 1846, just at this period of rampant Tammany corruption, which was beginning to become somewhat too obvious, that Washington Irving returned to New York from Spain, where he had been Minister of the United States. He was received enthusiastically by the populace of New York, and Tammany joined vigorously in the welcome, for Tammany Hall needed a reputable man. The leaders of Tammany Hall offered Washington Irving the nomination for Mayor of New York. "It was not as a literary man especially that they desired to honor Irving," wrote Mrs. Euphemia Vale Blake, "for they had always plenty of literary timber at hand, but partly for old association's sake, and from their natural instinct to honor any man who had brought honor to America." Irving declined, and Tammany Hall nominated instead Andrew H. Mickle, who was born in a hut in the "Bloody Sixth" Ward; it was said by his opponents that no less than a dozen pigs were present at the birth and lived with the family for many years. Mickle had married the daughter of a wealthy tobacco merchant. He was elected Mayor of New York, and when he died, he left an estate valued at more than a million dollars.

Mrs. Euphemia Vale Blake wrote in her *History of the Tammany Society*:

"We have elsewhere called attention to the fact that the Tammany Society was never without a supply of oratorical and poetical talent more than sufficient to embellish with appropriate poems and songs the ceremonies of its anniversaries and other festal occasions; indeed, it may truthfully be said that for the first eighty years of Tammany's existence all the best poetry of New York was Democratic; and nearly all the well-known poets were Tammany men."

And Mrs. Euphemia Vale Blake knew, for, besides being the historian of the Tammany Society, she was the editor of an anthology, *The Universal Name; or One Hundred Songs to Mary*.

CHAPTER III

I

THE early career of Tammany Hall did not furnish any protagonist for the political drama of New York, because in the first period of its history—with the exception of the short time when Aaron Burr and Matthew L. Davis were in partial control—the Society and the organization were never dominated completely by any one strong man; during this same period the public officials of New York City were most of them undistinguished personalities, whose effect on the people and on the issues of their time was negative and limited by their almost complete lack of distinctive qualities of leadership.

Beginning, however, with the rise to political prominence of Fernando Wood, Tammany Hall developed a series of personalities who were to have a greater effect upon the Society and upon the government of the City of New York than any men of their time. From about 1850 until the death of Charles F. Murphy in 1924, except for a few short intervals, Tammany Hall and the City were under the domination of absolute monarchs, and the first person to attain this commanding position was Fernando Wood.

Fernando Wood was born in Philadelphia on June 14, 1812, when his father, a wholesale dry-goods merchant, had just been made bankrupt by the War of 1812. Henry, Isaac, Zachariah, and Benjamin were the names of his brothers, but when Fernando was born, instead of reading the Bible, Mrs. Wood was reading the most popular novel of the time, *The Three Spaniards*, of which a bold fellow named Fernando was the hero, and his mother named her son after the character she so much admired. Fernando Wood first brought himself into minor notice at the age of seventeen, when he knocked down a Pennsylvania state senator with a chair, after the senator had drawn a bowie knife in answer to a biting comment by the young Fernando on one of the senator's remarks. The next exploit with which the energetic young man was credited by his admirers was saving the lives of three beautiful maidens in a runaway stagecoach which the driver was too drunk to control. Wood was about to become an actor in New York City, when he received a job as manager of a tobacco factory in Richmond, Virginia. Returning to New York City some months later, he opened a tobacco shop in Pearl Street, where, it was said, he heroically served survivors of the great cholera epidemic of 1832.

Fernando Wood's enthusiasm for General Andrew Jackson and his interest in Democratic politics caused him to neglect the demands of the tobacco trade, and he became bankrupt. After this disaster he paid attention to his business exclusively for a period, and at the end of that time he had some money. There were those who said that his business transactions were not entirely honest, and among these was his former partner, Edward E. Marvine, who sued Wood for $8,000 which he claimed that the bold Fernando had obtained on false representations. Wood escaped trial by one day under the Statute of Limitations, for the Recorder of New York was one of his political friends.

Meanwhile, Fernando Wood had found time from his business manipulations to win an election to Congress. He was a handsome man, six feet tall, and he aimed to please his neighbours by his manners; he carefully cultivated friends and managed to make himself pleasant to stevedores, shipbuilders, immigrants, mechanics, labourers, and shopkeepers; he also mastered the technique of primary elections in New York. He was twenty-eight years old when he was sent to Congress, and his campaign biographer, Donald MacLeod, assured his readers: "The veteran legislators in some sort made a pet of the young Representative. When he had made his fiscal speech, John Quincy Adams grasped him by the hand, and said: 'Young man, when I am gone, you will be one of the foremost men in this country.'"

When his term in the House of Representatives expired, Fernando Wood returned to the shipping business in New York. In September, 1848, he heard of the discovery of gold in California, and he fitted out a ship with supplies to sell to the hordes of people he foresaw would rush there. It was said that

Wood's barque, the *John W. Cater*, was the first supply ship to reach California after the news of the discovery, and the cargo was sold at an immense profit; it was also said that Wood cheated his partner in the enterprise of his legitimate share in that immense profit. Wood now had enough money to retire from business and apply himself "to study, to supply the defects of his imperfect early education," as one newspaper writer put it. However, the studies to which Fernando Wood applied himself were not concerned with pure science or abstract thought. He studied the character of New York in 1850 and learned how to use the engines of his environment for his personal advantage.

Between 1840 and 1850 New York City expanded more rapidly in population than at any previous time in its history, and the growth attendant upon the increase in the number of its inhabitants created difficult problems. In the decade from 1830 to 1840, more than five hundred thousand immigrants had landed at New York, but in the years between 1840 and 1850 more than one million five hundred thousand persons arrived from Europe at that port. Because of the discovery of gold in California and the political revolutions all over Europe in 1848, immigrants kept pouring into the City. Many of these new arrivals were Irish members of the Roman Catholic Church, and those native Americans who spent some of their non-working hours viewing with alarm the tendencies of the times, saw in this large influx of foreign Catholics a huge conspiracy upon the part of Mother Church to conquer the New World.

"There is a disposition in the United States," wrote James Bryce, "to use the immigrants, and especially the Irish, much as the cat is used in the kitchen to account for broken plates and food which disappears. The cities have no doubt suffered from the immigrant vote. But New York was not an Eden before the Irish came; and would not become an Eden were they all to move on to San Francisco."

It is true that the immigrants did complicate the political problems of New York City, and there was one type of immigrant Irishman, the saloon keeper, who had an especially powerful effect on the political complexion of the city. The distillers, brewers, and manufacturers of bar room fixtures were always willing to extend credit to an Irishman who aspired to be a saloon keeper, and it was easy to obtain a license. Not only did the Irish immigrant who became a saloon keeper find himself in a profitable business, but he soon found that his social position was of considerable prominence. Because of this social position, he rapidly became of political importance in his ward, and men in high political positions found it worth while to flatter and to aid him. Theodore Roosevelt once wrote:

"Bartenders form perhaps the nearest approach to a leisure class that we have at present on this side of the water. Naturally they are on semi-intimate terms with all who frequent their houses. There is no place where more gossip is talked than in bar rooms, and much of this gossip is about politics—that is, the politics of the ward, not of the nation."

It was not long before the saloon keeper, whose social position made him so familiar with the intricacies of organization politics, took to holding public office himself. He had friends who would vote for him, and who would get their friends to vote for him, and the salaries and perquisites of public office were tempting. Office holding also placed him in a position to help the neighbours by jobs and privileges, which in turn increased the patronage of his saloon and also increased his political prestige. The circle of circumstances which was thus formed was almost unbreakable.

Fernando Wood's day was the day of "Bill" Poole, "Yankee" Sullivan, "Tom" Hyer, "Dutch" Charlie, and John Morrissey, who were the leading pugilists of the time, and who controlled saloons and took part in local politics. Captain Isaiah Rynders, the leader of a band known as the Empire Club, was prominent in the saloons and in Tammany Hall. The men of the Empire Club, the Dead Rabbits,[1] and Mike Walsh's Spartan Band loved to fight and to go to fires. Their leaders were all prominent in Tammany Hall or in the opposition to it, and the public

---

[1] The Dead Rabbits got their name when a gang known as the Roach Guards, called after a prominent liquor dealer of the period, split into two factions. At one of their argumentative meetings some one threw a dead rabbit into the room, and one faction decided to assume that totem.

business of the club members was largely training immigrants to vote and commanding the approaches to the polls on election day.

The methods used by some of the men who acted as tally clerks and watchers at the polls on election days are illustrated by the testimony of Quincy Stowell, an inspector of elections, before a special committee of the Board of Aldermen. The hearing was concerned with the contest over the seat in the Board of Aldermen of Dennis Mullins, Democrat, elected, it was alleged, by illegal counting. Quincy Stowell testified:

"... Mullins came in the room; he said he wanted a majority of six or seven in that district; Sullivan and Bickford kept the tally when they were counting the tickets; ... when the votes were counted the Inspectors said there was a majority of nine or twelve for Mullins; when the time came for counting the tickets, Sullivan appeared to be very much under the influence of liquor; so much so that the others laughed at him; the result was declared without the tickets in the hat or under the box being produced; I acted as challenger on the part of Mr. Egan; I drink some every day; do not know that I drank five or ten glasses; I might have drank as many as ten times, of strong liquor; I did not drink so much as to be drunk; I might have vomited that day; do not know that I did; it was not from liquor; I did not go home at three o'clock; I did not lie down or fall down; I was so sober that day as to know everything that was going on under my observation; ... Mullins stood up beside Austin, and said there was a majority of five against him in the other districts, and he wanted six or nine in that district; it was spoken so that all in the room could hear it; ... I am turnkey at the penitentiary; ..."[1]

Captain Isaiah Rynders and the members of the Empire Club met immigrants at the steamers, found them places to live, got them jobs, or started them in the liquor business. Through the efforts of their self-appointed guardians, the immigrants were naturalized long before the period required by law, and their votes were marshalled in favour of the Tammany Hall tickets. When he was a boy, Captain Rynders had worked

---

[1] *Documents of the Board of Aldermen*, No. 13, Sept. 17, 1849, pp. 144–148.

on Hudson River lumber boats, where he learned to box and to wrestle. He cast his first vote for General Andrew Jackson, and he once boasted that in all his life he had never voted for any but the Democratic ticket. His tastes were what were known as "sporting," and his interests ran largely to horses and prize fights. His business was politics and saloon keeping. When he first came to live in New York City, Captain Rynders, who earned his title on Mississippi River steamboats, took up with the sporting men of the town, "all lovers of good dinners and handsome women," as the *Herald* remarked upon the occasion of Captain Rynders's death. In 1844, Captain Rynders became a member of the General Committee of Tammany Hall, and his language, which was known as "homely," was attractive to the men who frequented political meetings. Rynders kept a saloon at 28 Park Row, known as The Arena, where he formed the Empire Club. He himself, it was said, never drank liquor. The members of the Club devoted themselves around election time to breaking up the meetings of the Whigs, the anti-Tammany party, and this they usually accomplished by the use of carrots and catcalls, cabbages and hisses. They especially enjoyed breaking up the meetings of the Abolitionists, for Captain Isaiah Rynders believed that Negro slavery was a divine institution. It was said that he quoted Scripture to support slavery and followed his quotations immediately with the most vivid oaths against the opponents of that institution. Upon one occasion Rynders and his crowd invaded a meeting against slavery held by William Lloyd Garrison. They forced the audience to listen to a man who Rynders insisted was a medical doctor. The doctor submitted that Negroes were not men because the Negro's facial line was not at a right angle to the general surface of the ground, but, like that of most animals, at a much smaller angle. Park Godwin, one of the editors of the *Evening Post*, denounced the obstreperousness of Captain Rynders and of Tammany Hall in that paper. Captain Isaiah Rynders and the members of the Empire Club decided to kill Mr. Godwin. This, according to a writer in *McClure's Magazine*, is what happened:

"One afternoon, having left his office to go home, Mr. Godwin stopped, as was his custom, in Florence's restaurant for some oysters. As he stood at the oyster-stand, he saw in the remote part of the room Rynders and some of his men. He at once suspected that they proposed to assault him before he could leave the building. He realized that it would not do for him to run, however; so he began to eat his oysters, while deliberating upon his course in case he should be attacked. Suddenly he noticed that a man stood beside him, and looking up he saw 'Mike' Walsh, who said to him: 'Go on eating your oysters, Mr. Godwin, but do it as quickly as you can, and then go away. Rynders and his men have been waiting here for you and intend to kill you, but they won't attack you as long as I am by your side.'

"The advice was followed. After Mr. Godwin, having finished his oysters, had gone out, Rynders stepped up to Walsh and said: 'What do you mean by interfering in this matter? It is none of your affair.'

"'Well, Godwin did me a good turn once, and I don't purpose to see him stabbed in the back. You were going to do a sneaking thing; you were going to assassinate him, and any man who will do that is a coward.'

"'No man ever called me a coward, Mike Walsh, and you can't.'

"'But I do, and I will prove that you are a coward. If you are not one, come upstairs with me now. We will lock ourselves into a room; I will take a knife and you take one; and the man who is alive after we have got through, will unlock the door and go out.'

"Rynders accepted the challenge. They went to an upper room. Walsh locked the door, gave Rynders a large bowie-knife, took one himself, and said: 'You stand in that corner, and I'll stand in this. Then we will walk toward the centre of the room, and we won't stop until one or the other of us is finished.'

"Each took his corner. Then Walsh turned and approached the centre of the room. But Rynders did not stir. 'Why don't you come out?' said Walsh. Rynders, turning in his corner, faced his antagonist, and said: 'Mike you and I have always been friends; what is the use of our fighting now? If we get at it, we shall both be killed, and there is no good in that.' Walsh for a moment said not a word; but his lip curled, and he looked upon Rynders with an expression of utter contempt. Then he said: 'I told you you were a coward, and now I prove it. Never speak to me again.'"[1]

Another man who was destined to become an important figure in the pugilistic and political circles of New York for many years made his social début in Captain Isaiah Rynders's Arena saloon. John Morrissey, born in Ireland, and resident of Troy, New York, learned to fight in bar rooms and on Hudson River boats. He heard in Troy that "Dutch" Charlie had laughed contemptuously when he was approached with a proposal for a match with young Morrissey. Working as a deck hand on the Hudson River steamer of which his future father-in-law was captain, John Morrissey, then eighteen years old, arrived in New York City and went immediately to 28 Park Row to inquire for "Dutch" Charlie. Captain Rynders and other members of the Empire Club were in the bar room. He asked for "Dutch" Charlie and was told that he had gone to see Lady Suffolk trot. Whereupon young Morrissey asked if any prize fighters were present, took off his cap, and remarked, "I can lick any man here." Tom Burns, Mike Murray, and about six others grabbed clubs, pitchers, chairs, bottles, and other handy utensils and rushed at Morrissey. He kept his feet for a long time, but was finally floored when one of his assailants hit him under the ear with an earthenware spittoon. Captain Isaiah Rynders admired Morrissey's nerve, and he was carefully nursed until he was able to go back to Troy. Soon afterward Morrissey returned to New York and became an immigrant runner. When Big Tom Burns and General Billy Wilson attempted to drive him away from a ship, a fight started in which belaying pins were used instead of fists, and Morrissey cleared the decks, chasing both Burns and Wilson. This fight made him famous among political leaders, and he was used extensively in the election campaigns of the 'forties.[2]

Morrissey's leading exploit of this period, however, was his famous battle with Tom McCann. This is the account of it as it was given by a sporting editor of the *Police Gazette*:

---

[1]"Tammany," by E. J. Edwards, *McClure's Magazine*, Vol. IV, 1894–1895, pp. 575–580.

[2]*John Morrissey, His Life, Battles, and Wrangles, from His Birth in Ireland until He Died a State Senator*, compiled by William E. Harding, sporting editor of *Police Gazette*, 1881.

Contemporary woodcut from New York Daily Graphic

"THE HONORABLE GENTLEMAN FROM SARATOGA
JOHN MORRISSEY"

"Morrissey, during his visits to New York, became infatuated with a noted cyprian, Kate Ridgely, who was a mistress of Tom McCann, a noted rough-and-tumble fighter. . . . Kate Ridgely, at that time, kept a fashionable bagnio at 74 Duane street.

"Although devotedly attached to McCann, Kate coquettishly pretended to think highly of Morrissey. This inflamed McCann's jealousy, and when he met his rival in Sandy Lawrence's house proposed to fight him for an undivided share in Kate's affections. . . .

"At the commencement of the fight McCann was successful, and threw Morrissey heavily. As he fell a stove was overturned, a bushel of red-hot coals rolled out, and Morrissey was forced on them. McCann held him there until the smell of burning flesh filled the room. The bystanders threw water on the coals, and the gas and steam arose in McCann's face and choked and exhausted him. Morrissey then had his own way, and bucked and pounded McCann into insensibility. From that time until the day of his death Morrissey was called 'Old Smoke.'"

Such a man was useful in the politics of the period, and, as we shall see, Morrissey became a member of Congress from New York and served several terms in the State Senate.

It was with a knowledge of these conditions of the period in which Fernando Wood became the leading political figure, that the editor of the New York *Herald* wrote a few years later:

"Our city legislators, with but few exceptions, are an unprincipled, illiterate, scheming set of cormorants, foisted upon the community through the machinery of primary elections, bribed election inspectors, ballot box stuffing, and numerous other illegal means. . . . The consequence is that we have a class of municipal legislators forced upon us who have been educated in barrooms, brothels, and political societies; and whose only aim in attaining power is to consummate schemes for their own aggrandizement and pecuniary gain."

II

Fernando Wood received the Tammany Hall nomination for Mayor of New York in 1850; the nomination, however, was not granted without difficulty. Tammany Hall was split into two factions, one known as the "Barnburners" and the other called the "Hunkers." The "Barnburners" were radical Democrats who believed that slavery should not be permitted to extend further in the United States than it had already spread, and they were also opposed to monopolies and excessive rents for property. The origin of the name "Barnburners" was attributed to a Democratic contractor, who remarked of the radicals: "These men are incendiaries; they are mad; they are like the farmer, who, to get the rats out of his granary, sets fire to his own barn." The "Hunkers" were so called because they were the conservative men of the party, who thought that slavery should be unrestricted, and who believed firmly in the economic policy of *laissez faire*. There is a Dutch word, hunker, which is defined by Webster: "To squat so as to be supported on the fore part of the feet."

Fernando Wood carefully rode between the two factions; he was suspected by the "Barnburners" of being a "Hunker," for he believed politically in slavery, and he was also accused by the "Hunkers" of catering to the "Barnburners." An ineffective compromise was arranged between the two groups, and they united on Wood's nomination, but he was defeated in the election. The New York *Herald* attributed Fernando Wood's defeat to an indignant reaction upon the part of the respectable adherents of the Democratic Party against the obvious corruption practised by the leaders of Tammany Hall and their rank and file. And the *Herald* was not unduly biased, for it favoured the election of Fernando Wood and usually supported Tammany Hall.

Corruption in public life, a direct result of the disreputable character of the men nominated to public office by the leaders of Tammany Hall, had caused the business men of the community, who ordinarily were rather too content to mind their own particular businesses, to awaken to the fact that it was their money which was being stolen, and, as always happened when business men had this unpleasantly vivid revelation, Tammany Hall was defeated.

It was at this period that the Board of Aldermen of New York City was known popularly as "The Forty Thieves," of which notorious body William M. Tweed was a member.

"The Forty Thieves" sold the City's ferry leases and street railway franchises to the highest bidders as part of their regular aldermanic business. Besides their deals in street railways and ferries, "The Forty Thieves" took financial advantage of the citizens' interest in patriotic display and in death. They robbed the City on the Fourth of July, 1852, by raising the bills for fireworks to $4,100. And when the body of Henry Clay, which was lying in state in the New York City Hall, had to be sent to Albany, the City paid large bills for the undertaking, including one for $1,400 for cigars and liquors used on the boat. The City was charged by "The Forty Thieves" $100,000 for land to be used as a paupers' burial ground; it was estimated that the land was actually worth $30,000.

There was at that time a Board of Assistant Aldermen as well as a Board of Aldermen. James W. Flynn, an official of the newly organized Third Avenue Railroad Company, which wished a franchise to run street cars along Third Avenue, testified that his company paid ten thousand dollars to get the franchise passed through the Board of Assistant Aldermen and between seven and eight thousand dollars to receive the approval of the Board of Aldermen. The Aldermen and the officials of the Third Avenue Railroad Company sometimes met in Tammany Hall to discuss terms.[1]

Horace M. Dewey, a member of the firm of Dewey, Dingeldein & Co., which operated stage coaches in New York City, testified to the following relations with "The Forty Thieves":

"Q. Had you business transactions with Alderman Tweed, of the Seventh Ward, prior to that time?

"A. I don't know that I had business transactions with him; that is I never traded with him. . . . I let him have money a great many different times, sometimes in checks and sometimes in money, not over a thousand dollars at any one time, and down to two hundred dollars. . . .

"Q. On what security did you furnish these moneys to Alderman Tweed?

"A. On the security of his promise to pay it, or his checks, dated ahead.

---

[1] *Documents of the Board of Aldermen*, Vol. XXI, Part II, 1854, No. 55, p. 1337.

"Q. Can you assign any reason why Alderman Tweed applied to you or your firm to loan him money?

"A. He said he was short; that is the only reason I know.

"Q. Not having any business transactions with him, did you not think it strange that he should make this application to you?

"A. I did not think anything strange of it, at the time. . . .

"Q. How often were they made?

"A. Almost as often as I met him, sometimes once a week and sometimes once a fortnight; it ran for a long period of time. . . .

"Q. Do you remember a pair of horses, owned by your firm, finding their way into the possession of one of the Aldermen of the city?

"A. I never knew of any, and never heard of any.

"Q. Have all these moneys been returned to you, that were loaned to the various parties?

"A. I believe not.

"Q. How much remains outstanding?

"A. I believe somewhere between one and two thousand dollars; Francis owes me two hundred dollars; Tweed owes me a thousand dollars now.

"Q. How long has Alderman Tweed owed you a thousand dollars?

"A. I let him have it last Tuesday. . . . Alderman Tweed did not owe me anything until Tuesday last; for some time I had been sick, and out of town for some time; during that time he owed me nothing; Alderman Francis owed me the two hundred dollars some six weeks. . . .

"Q. Before the passage of the Third Avenue railroad, did you have any interview with any of the Aldermen or Assistant Aldermen upon the subject of the passage of that grant?

"A. I did.

"Q. With which of them?

"A. With nearly all of them. . . ."[1]

This condition of affairs became too public, and Fernando Wood was defeated by the votes of men who broke from the Tammany Hall ticket as a protest. The breach between

[1] *Documents of the Board of Aldermen*, Vol. XXI, Part II, No. 55, pp. 1350–1356.

the factions of Tammany Hall also widened and resulted in the division into "Hardshells" and "Softshells." These two groups fought vigorous battles with each other for the control of Tammany Hall as a meeting place and for the political control of New York City. The arguments sometimes ended only when members of both sides had suffered fractured skulls, and when some of the doors of Tammany Hall had been smashed down.

The "Softshells," some of whom had been "Barnburners," got their name because they believed in compromise when necessary; the "Hardshells" steadfastly refused to deviate from their uncompromising conservative principles. A meeting was held in Tammany Hall on December 2, 1852, at which the claims of the rival committees were being discussed. While the committee members were arguing in the committee room, some of the less important Tammany followers were in the bar room playing a game known as Father Simon. The game consisted in one of the players making a series of motions with his hands, and if the other players did not make precisely the same motions as the leader, who was called Father Simon, they were compelled to buy drinks for the entire party. The game had lasted a long time, and the forfeits had been so many that the players were quite drunk. Rumours of dissension in the committee room reached the bar room, and the players decided to settle the committee's questions with their fists. They rushed into the committee room, where a motion for changing the time of primary elections was being discussed. Chairs were thrown about, and tables were upset. The terrified committee members attempted to get out of the room by any means; some rushed through windows which they did not stop to open, and several were badly injured. One of the drunken men hit the chairman, Mr. Schell, over the head with a chair and opened his skull several inches.

Other meetings at which blows were threatened but avoided resulted in the victory of the "Softshells" for the control of Tammany Hall. The sachems of the Tammany Society had maintained that the Society was still not a political organization, and that the Hall itself was leased to a hotel proprietor; but they saw to it that the "Softshell" faction only was permitted to hold political conferences in Tammany Hall. The

"Hardshells" talked of hiring another hall and starting a second Tammany organization, but nothing was done about it, for Tammany Hall now had its traditions and its history, and the publicity value of these was enjoyed by the party which controlled the building. Some playful members of both factions represented themselves as Hard or Soft by distributing hard-shell almonds and soft-shell almonds.

In the election of 1854 Fernando Wood was again the Tammany Hall candidate for Mayor, the "Softshells" and the "Hardshells" uniting in a more or less loose bond for the occasion; they realized that the only chance of victory over their Whig opponents was by some sort of concerted action in the Democratic Party. The campaign was virulent, and one of the main issues was the antagonism between the native-born citizens of the United States and the naturalized foreigners, which had been smouldering for so long, and which broke out in this campaign because of the part played by the Know Nothing Party. The *Morning Courier and Enquirer*, which was opposed to Fernando Wood and the foreign vote, estimated "that foreigners cast two fifths of the entire vote of the city."

Fernando Wood's past business transactions were published in the newspapers, and Wood's only reply was: "The People will elect me Mayor though I should commit a murder in my family between this and the Election." Fernando Wood was elected by 1,456 votes, and 10,000 people assembled in a mass meeting in the City Hall Park to discuss the alleged frauds by which the election was won. It was said that the "Bloody Sixth" had cast 400 more votes than it had voters. Joseph Souder, an anti-Tammany representative of that ward, said in a public meeting that fraud had been committed everywhere in his ward by Irish inspectors of election, and that the people were being ruled by Rum and Romanism. Tammany Hall, he maintained, had succumbed to the influence of Rome, was ruled by it, and would soon be buried by it.

The anti-foreign, and particularly anti-Catholic, sentiment which had played such an important part in the election of 1854 was part of a national movement started by what was called the Native American Party, which had previously been a secret order. It received the name of the Know Nothing Party, because, whenever a member was asked any questions, he answered that he knew nothing. The order had held its meetings in secret places, and one of the passwords was, "Have you seen Sam?" The Star-Spangled Banner was its emblem, America for the Americans its slogan, and Washington its patron saint. The secrecy of the order had been penetrated when the members began to take part in politics and then the organization came out frankly as a political party. A Know Nothing almanac of 1855 declared the principles of the party to include: "Anti-Romanism, Anti-Bedinism, Anti-Papistalism, Anti-Nunneryism, Anti-Winking-Virginism, Anti-Jesuitism." One Know Nothing, who called himself the Angel Gabriel, preached against foreigners from the steps of the New York City Hall every Sunday, until the authorities thought it wise to expel him from the City. The author of a long epic called "Know Nothing" sang concerning foreigners:

> "Their customs, laws, and language are not ours;
> Their bigotry sticks by them like their brogue.
> As full-blown sunflowers turn toward the sun,
> Their hearts turn to the cross upon the church.
> Our young Republic will be ruled by Rome,
> While nunneries will be strung upon our streets
> As thick as beads upon a rosary,
> Unless we watch our native country's weal
> With vigilance—a plant which blooms in votes.
> For shameless demagogues, on supple knees,
> Bow to the dust before the foreign power."

It was said that Fernando Wood had been a Know Nothing in the early years of his political career. Abijah Ingraham, the author of a pamphlet called *A Biography of Fernando Wood, A History of the Forgeries, Perjuries, and Other Crimes of Our "Model" Mayor*, wrote:

"We have in our possession two affidavits from highly respectable citizens, members of the Know-Nothing order, from which it appears that our Mayor was quite a 'spouter,' at the meetings of the order, and from his first attendance seemed to be particularly desirous to show his utter contempt for the Irish, and more specially for the Catholic priesthood. He invented, no doubt, a vulgar story, describing a dirty trick he once played upon a Catholic priest in the interior of Pennsylvania, and upon a poor Irish lady who gave him shelter for the night.

"It appears from this story, that our 'model' Mayor was travelling on foot in the interior of Pennsylvania, and had become much fatigued, as night approached. In this condition he visited the humble cottage of an Irish woman, at whose house there lodged for that night a Catholic priest. . . . Her humanity finally induced her to say to Mr. Wood, that if he would occupy the same bed as the priest, he might be accommodated. He very cheerfully consented, and entered the humble dwelling of the Catholic Irish woman. . . .

"He relates what then happened, what is entirely too disgusting for publication. Our Mayor says he had an urgent call to get up and go out in the night, and did not like to crawl down the ladder, or to alarm the woman of the house. So he quietly relieved himself by drawing towards him the under garment of the priest. In the morning he says he complained bitterly to the priest, of the disagreeable condition of the bed. Appearances indicated that the priest had been unfortunate, and he begged of his companion Wood, to make no remarks to the landlady, but leave that to him, and he would make it all right.

"This disgusting story, purely and wholly manufactured, an impudent falsehood no doubt, Wood related with such embellishments as he was capable of, at nearly all the meetings of the Know-Nothings he attended. He told the story from the Battery to Harlem, and in presence of hundreds of persons. We have the affidavits of two respectable persons, that they heard him tell the story repeatedly. There are hundreds who could make a similar affidavit. The fact is indisputable. His object was to show his detestation of the religion of the Catholics, and show, if he was elected Mayor, the earnestness of his convictions of the truth of the Know-Nothing principles."

Whatever of truth there may have been in the biased hyperbole of the Know Nothings, it was true that the Catholic Church exercised considerable influence in New York City, but usually it was applied directly for its own benefit and not directly in the general political situation. The Catholic Church in New York City received from the city government in 1850 or thereabouts a lease to the whole block of ground from Fiftieth to Fifty-first streets from Fifth to Madison avenues, the present site of St. Patrick's Cathedral, and in 1852 it received another lease to the block for $83.33; this lease gave the Church complete title to the property. A few years later, the city government paid the Church $24,000 for permission to extend Madison Avenue through this property, and the taxes on the increased value of the property, amounting to $8,928.84 due to this extension were paid by the city government and not by the Church.[1]

The Archbishop of New York wrote this unctuous letter to Fernando Wood during one of his terms as Mayor:

New York, Dec. 16/59.

DEAR SIR:

My agreeable, but in view of recent circumstances, perhaps unseasonable interview with you last night, has only increased my respect for your independent and dignified perseverance, in carrying out what you believed to be right and just.

You will permit me to explain in brief the reasons which prompted me to intrude on your privacy.

Looking at the whole question from the point of view in which I think it must strike your own mind, I cannot imagine any step more calculated on the one hand to do honor to your administration, and on the other, to pay a high, independent, and voluntary tribute to the class of people referred to in our conversation, than that, which, in my own name, and with a full knowledge of all the circumstances present and prospective, I have taken the liberty to recommend.

The appointment is one in which, apart from low and bigoted prejudices here and there, will be sustained much to your honor, by the great body of the people of New York. But in addition, it will have a private and inappreciably delicate value in the estimation of those who consider themselves your personal and political friends. To myself, it will be a personal compliment which I shall never forget.

In all views of the case, if I were your confidential adviser, I could not in a fair upright exercise of my judgment, give any

[1] *New York City Council of Political Reform, Five Reports*, by Dexter A. Hawkins, 1873, pp. 4–5.

other advice. I will only add one word more, that if it were a
matter solicited by petition, you could have a catalogue of
twenty or twenty-five thousand names. But, under the actual
circumstances, I would consider the appointment as much more
honorable to all parties if you deemed it consistent with your
duty to make the nomination and stand by it; just as General
Jackson nominated Mr. Taney to Supreme Judgeship—many
years ago—and which appointment, neither he—nor his successors in the Presidency—nor the country—has ever had any
reason to repent.

If the person named by me were of doubtful character or
responsibility, there might be an apprehension that the public
might censure you for his appointment. But this is not the case.
And his appointment to a position not so much of emolument
as of distinction, will catch and fill with admiration the eyes
of those who have honestly, I am sure, labored in their efforts
to elevate you to your present position, in accordance with the
immense consciousness and display of energy manifested by
yourself.

I have the honor to Remain,
Very Respectfully,
Your Obedient Servant,
✠ JOHN, *Archbishop of New York.*

HON. FERNANDO WOOD
Mayor Elect.[1]

III

"Well it now appears that Mr. Wood is Mayor," wrote the
editor of the *Morning Courier and Enquirer* in his issue of
November 9, 1854. "With a majority of 17,366 against him,
Mr. Wood is Mayor. Supported by none but ignorant foreigners
and the most degraded class of Americans Mr. Wood is Mayor.
In spite of the most overwhelming proofs that he is a base
defrauder, Mr. Wood is Mayor. Contrary to every precedent
in the allotment of honor through a municipal history of nearly
two hundred years, Mr. Wood is Mayor. His assertion to us
that a murder by his own hands could not prevent his election,
had reason in it; Fernando Wood is Mayor. On New Year's

---

[1]From the original letter in the Manuscript Collections of the New York Public
Library.

Day he will go to City Hall, and he will go there to give the lie, in the face of every man woman and child in this city, to the maxim—That honesty is the best Policy. Have things indeed come to this? We will not yet believe it. We cannot believe it."

But, there was more subtlety in Fernando Wood than the *Courier and Enquirer* credited him with. He was too capable a politician to give the lie to anything "in the face of every man, woman and child," for he preferred working behind their backs. For the first six months of his term Fernando Wood enforced the laws as they had never been enforced before, and he culti-vated cannily a personal reputation for integrity. When the proprietor of a line of omnibuses sent the Mayor elect a season pass, Wood sent it back with attendant publicity. As soon as he became Mayor, Fernando Wood issued a righteous proclama-tion against selling liquor on Sunday, and within two weeks there were less than twenty saloons open on Sunday, whereas there had been 2,300 operating on that day. Mayor Wood also saw to it that rowdyism was suppressed, that hackmen did not charge exorbitant fares, that pickpockets were arrested, that brothels and gambling houses were closed, and that the streets were kept cleaner. In the Mayor's office Wood kept a public complaint book, where any citizen might enter a com-plaint, and frequently the Mayor investigated these personally. Fernando Wood's reputation for civic virtue became so great that the temperance advocates urged that he be nominated for Governor, and a pious delegation from Iowa made a pilgrimage to New York to ask him to be a candidate for President of the United States. His reputation for suppressing crime became national, and the story was told that, when a passenger threw a pickpocket off a train in Michigan, though the pickpocket had threatened to cut the passenger's throat, the other passengers shouted in their enthusiasm, "That must be Mayor Wood."[1]

By virtue of his reputation, Fernando Wood received a re-nomination to the Mayor's office in 1856, and after his reëlec-tion he began the deals that made his administration notorious for corruption. The election itself had been gained by corrupt manipulation of the primaries, and by the use of the City's police at the polls to prevent anti-Wood voters from expressing

[1] *Sunshine and Shadow in New York*, by Matthew Hale Smith, p. 269.

themselves by means of their votes. Street fights took place, and ballot boxes were smashed. The saloon keepers of the City worked industriously for the Mayor, and in return for their services they were permitted to remain open on Sunday. It was stated by the opposition that 10,000 fraudulent votes had been cast for Fernando Wood.

During his second administration Fernando Wood began to profit personally by his office, and his friends profited as well.[1] One of the most lucrative sources of corrupt profit was the sale of public offices to the highest bidder, with the unmentioned understanding that the buyer was to get his money back in whatever way he could at the expense of the City. In one case Fernando Wood broke faith with one man and sold the office to another after he had promised it to the first. John K. Hackett wished to be Corporation Counsel of New York, and Fernando Wood promised to appoint him to that office, but he changed his mind when John E. Devlin, a Tammany sachem, offered Wood a high price for it. According to one of Fernando Wood's unfriendly biographers, the following scene resulted:

"In order to appease John K. Hackett for having sold him out of the Corporation Counsel's office, Wood promised to insert his name in the blank of the appointment he held of Corporation Attorney, but afterwards appointed to that position N. Hill Fowler. Indignant at the treatment he had received, Hackett proceeded to Wood's residence, was shown into the parlor, and as soon as ex-Mayor Wood entered, Hackett said, 'Mr. Wood, I called to say to you, personally, that you are a scoundrel, a rascal, and a perjured villain.' Wood then threatened to put him out, and rang the bell for a servant, and the latter was about entering when Mr. Hackett drew a revolver from his pocket, and continued: 'If that man comes between us I shall blow out his brains and cut off your ears. So you may as well listen. On a certain night, at a room in the Astor House, were four persons: Mr. D., Mr. ——, Mr. ——, and yourself. One of these four is a scoundrel, a rascal, a perjured villain, and a hound. It is not Mr. D., nor Mr. ——, nor Mr. ——. Who he is

---

[1] It is confusing to keep Fernando Wood's deals in their chronological order, but the main point is to give an idea of the methods he used, and instances are therefore offered from several periods of his career as Mayor of New York.

I leave you to imagine.' Hackett, a few years after this scene transpired, was nominated for Recorder, and Fernando Wood supported him—so devoid of shame and every manly instinct is he."[1]

N. Hill Fowler, who was Corporation Attorney under Mayor Wood, testified in the Supreme Court some years later to his transactions with Fernando Wood:

"Q. You was once, Mr. Fowler, Corporation Attorney for the city of New York?

"A. Yes, sir.

"Q. Who appointed you?

"A. Fernando Wood. . . .

"Q. When was your name put in?

"A. Not until after I had partly fulfilled my contract with Mr. Wood. . . .

"Q. What was the contract?

"A. I was to give Fernando Wood $5,000 in cash, my first year's salary and divide the perquisites of the office for the balance of the time.

"Q. What did you do in pursuance of this contract?

"A. I gave him $4,000 the night he gave me the appointment. . . .

"Q. How about fulfilling the rest of the contract?

"A. I drew my salary each month; I paid it over to him at his office; I continued to do so for one year, according to agreement.

"Q. What about the perquisites?

"A. The amount of perquisites for the term was $10,408, and this sum I divided equally with him.

"Q. Did you give Mr. Wood any other moneys in pursuance of that contract?

"A. I have loaned him money. . . . He sent down to my office and wanted to borrow $1,000, and said he would hand it to me within a week; I said I was not in any hurry for the amount, and he gave me a due bill for the amount; I kept the due bill until a little while before he was going to Europe, when he told

[1] *A Condensed Biography of a Candidate for Speaker: Fernando Wood, His Forgeries and Other Crimes*, p. 15.

me that he was going to Europe, and he didn't like to have this thing standing in this way; he said, 'You have not made anything out of this office, and I want to give you a chance'; I was not Corporation Attorney at that time; he said 'Make Shea, who is now Corporation Attorney, give you the judgments against the city in favor of the Corporation Attorney; they will amount to about $6,000; you may collect them, and all that you receive you may retain.' . . . I said I didn't know much about them, but I could ascertain; he said he supposed about half of the judgments were good; I told him I supposed they were not good for anything; he said, 'Well, Fowler, we have had so many transactions I don't think there will be anything wrong in the matter, and on my return from Europe I will give you a check for the balance. . . . When he returned, I wrote him a note asking him if he would please send me up a check for $1,000, borrowed money; he wrote back that he guessed he didn't owe me anything; he told me that if I had any demand against him and could show any document for it, he was ready to pay it, but if I could not do that, he would not pay it; we had some sharp words; I have never received from him anything in consideration of the contract."[1]

The important offices in the gift of the Mayor were not only bought and paid for in this manner during Fernando Wood's reign, but even minor jobs were purchased by subordinates from their department heads. This system was made plain by the testimony before a committee of the State Senate of two street-cleaning inspectors.

Charles Ciese, being duly sworn, testified:

"Q. Did you get an appointment as special inspector?
"A. Yes, sir.
"Q. How did you get it and what did you pay for it?
"A. Mr. Dorhwent [a saloon keeper] came to my house and told me, 'Ciese, you are an old man, and you need very badly an office, and I can help you to an office if you can pay $200.' I told him 'I am not able to give $200, that I got it not.' Then he said, 'Never mind, you are an old friend to me and if you cannot pay $200 you pay $125.' I said, 'What kind of office?'

---

[1]New York *Herald*, May 20, 1871.

He said, 'In the City Inspector's office, where you have nothing to do, but you go around the streets sometimes and look for dead cattles and dead animals, and you make a reports.' I say, 'I cannot speak English well enough.' He says, 'Never mind, you get instructions from the superintendent, he is German.' I said, 'I am willing,' and I went down and paid Mr. Dorhwent $100 cash, and I got my books and I got my shield. Then I came down one day to Mr. Dorhwent's and he showed me a gentleman and said this was my superintendent, Mr. Wiegand. 'You have to report to him every week, every day.'"[1]

John F. Siegmann, being duly sworn, testified:

"Q. Did you get an appointment as special inspector in the City Inspector's department?

"A. Yes, sir. . . .

"Q. How did you get your appointment?

"A. I was up in Dorhwent's [a saloon at Fifty-ninth Street between Third and Lexington avenues], and Mr. Wiegand was there. I had been trying to get a place as interpreter in the court last winter, and so Wiegand says to me: 'Siegmann, if you spend some money—if you pay me some money, I'll get you a place so better as interpreter, where you can make $2 every day.' 'What is that?' I said. He says, 'One of the special street inspectors.' I said, 'How much will it cost?' He said, 'About $200.' I told him I had not got so much money as that, that I had not $100, and could not afford it. He said, 'You give me $100. I paid him $90, and he was satisfied. (Laughter.) He asked me when I would pay the rest. I told him from the first payment I got I would give him the other $10. In a couple of days he took me along to the City Inspector's office and introduced me to a gentleman who he said was Mr. Boole's brother; he says, 'This is Mr. Siegmann, one of my special inspectors who I have under me.' 'Very good'; then he says, 'What is your name, sir?' I said, 'John F. Siegmann.' . . . Then he gave me a book, and he said, 'I will send you up a shield in two or three days.' I got it; here it is. (The witness produced

---

[1]*Proceedings of a Select Committee of the Senate of the State of New York, Appointed to Investigate Various Departments of the Government of the City of New York.* Senate Document No. 38, 88th Session, 1865, Vol. II, p. 170.

a German silver shield, having on it the words "Special Inspector City Inspector's Department.") . . .

"Q. What occurred next?

"A. Well, sir, he told me next I had to make returns, and to go around the streets and see if I could find any dead animals, and so—— (Laughter.)

"Q. So—what?

"A. So I did. (Laughter.)

"Q. And you made your returns?

"A. Yes, sir, I made returns of so many as I see. I reported that to him and then he paid me my money—$2 for a day. . . .

"Q. How long did he pay you?

"A. He paid me from December, when I began, to the 21st of February, 1864, $12 a week.

"Q. What then occurred?

"A. Afterwards, when I made my return, he said, 'We have not got any more money now. Mr. Boole has gone to Albany to have the Legislature pass a bill. They will pass a bill and then you get paid.' (Laughter.) . . .

"Q. You never got any pay after that?

"A. No, sir.

"Q. What did you do after that?

"A. I stopped walking in the streets. (Laughter.)"[1]

The cleaning of New York City's streets was always a valuable source of profit to Tammany politicians, and one of Fernando Wood's most notorious and most profitable deals was in connection with the street-cleaning contract awarded to Andrew J. Hackley. Hackley was to be paid $279,000 a year for cleaning all of New York City's streets, although a responsible bidder had offered to do the same work for $84,000 a year less. When Hackley had applied for the street-cleaning contract in the regular way, he found it impossible to get his bid approved, but when he put $40,000 in a certain place in a room in the City Hall, the Common Council approved the bid. Then it was necessary to give Fernando Wood's brother Benjamin one quarter of the profits before the contract for cleaning the streets was signed by the Mayor, and this one quarter interest was worth $69,750 a year to the Wood family. Benjamin Wood

[1] *Op. cit.*, pp. 165–168.

was the editor and owner of the New York *Daily News,* a newspaper that he used actively in the interests of his brother's politics; it was he who, some years later, broke the bank at the Hon. John Morrissey's gambling house at Saratoga, when he won $124,000 in one night. Morrissey kept special cigars which cost one dollar each for his customers, and Ben Wood was credited with having smoked ninety of them on that historic occasion.

It was during Fernando Wood's administration that the City Hall of New York was sold at auction to satisfy a judgment of $196,000 which Robert W. Lowber obtained fraudulently against the City for a plot of ground that was estimated to be worth only $60,000. Lowber demanded that the City Hall with all its furniture and paintings must be sold to satisfy his judgment. Daniel F. Tiemann, later Mayor of New York, bought in the City Hall for $50,000 and was reimbursed by the City.

Some people were beginning to realize that the man who had gained a reputation during his first six months in office as a "Model Mayor" was not quite that. One of Fernando Wood's opponents described the situation when he said that Wood's adherents had "strangely fallen into the error of mistaking a pirate for a Puritan." Among his other beliefs, Fernando Wood cherished a firm belief in New York real estate, and William M. Tweed once remarked: "I never yet went to get a corner lot that I didn't find Wood had got in ahead of me." Wood's position as Mayor enabled him to purchase corner lots from the City at unusually reasonable rates.

Fernando Wood's life as Mayor was not one of contracts alone. He was compelled to fight several tense battles for the control of the police and of the other departments which he required in his and the City's business. During Mayor Wood's second administration the State Legislature created the Metropolitan Police Force, which was under the control of the New York State government and not under that of the City. Mayor Wood insisted that this act was illegal, and he retained the old police force, which was completely under his control, and which had been catering to criminals rather than hampering them. The Legislature also took the profitable power over the Street Cleaning Department away from the Mayor, and this act he also declared to be illegal. A crisis arose when one of the street commissioners died, and the question came up whether Mayor Wood or Governor King had the power to appoint his successor.

Each faction had its own police force, and crowds gathered at the Street Cleaning Department to see which would win the battle. Governor King had appointed Daniel D. Conover to be Street Commissioner, and Mayor Wood had instructed Deputy Street Commissioner Turner to retain that office. When Conover and his clerks were forcibly put out of the offices by Mayor Wood's police, an order was issued for the Mayor's arrest on the charge that he had incited a riot. When Captain Walling of the Metropolitan Police, the State force, went to the City Hall to arrest the Mayor, Fernando Wood turned to his Municipal Police and said, "Men, put that man out." They obeyed. Another order was issued, declaring that Mayor Wood had resisted arrest and that any policeman or constable was authorized to apprehend him on sight, but Coroner Perry, who attempted to arrest the Mayor, reported that the Mayor's office was "surrounded by the most desperate characters in the city." He was instructed to take a force of men and try again. Meanwhile, people gathered in windows and on roofs to watch the scene. There was no cheering, but instead a tense stillness as the crowd waited to see the result. Mayor Wood's Municipal Police filled the City Hall, and all the entrances were closed and guarded. When the detachment of Metropolitan Police arrived to enforce the arrest of the Mayor, the crowd shouted and hissed. As the State police started up the steps of the City Hall the battle began. Clubs, sticks, and every other available weapon were used by the Mayor's men, and their numbers being greater, the State police were forced to retreat. They formed again, however, and rushed the entrance of the City Hall. "The scene was a terrible one," wrote the reporter of the New York *Times*. "Blows upon naked heads fell thick and fast, and men rolled helpless down the steps, to be leaped upon and beaten until life seemed extinct." Then the crowd attacked the State police from the rear, and some of them who had fallen were kicked in the heads by Mayor Wood's supporters, while cheers and oaths in strangely accented English resounded.

The issue now before the Country is Peace & Constitutional Government looking to REUNION or War & military Despotism with certain DISUNION"

MAYOR FERNANDO WOOD

The Seventh Regiment of National Guards happened to be marching down Broadway at this moment to embark for Boston. General Sandford was summoned by the Recorder, and the situation was explained to him. The National Guards were turned toward the City Hall. Mayor Wood saw that it would be both dangerous and futile to resist further, and when the sheriff appeared he consented to be arrested. The New York *Times* remarked parenthetically the next day: "A volley from the Seventh Regiment, situated as it was, would not have been attended with very fatal consequences, for it is doubtful if the entire body possessed a single ball cartridge at the moment of its grand demonstration in front of the City Hall."

The next morning the legal battle took place, and among the participants were A. Oakey Hall, then the District Attorney of New York, whom we shall hear of soon again, and George G. Barnard, one of Fernando Wood's counsel, who also reappears presently in another rôle. Although now opposed to each other, they were soon to be too close friends for the good of the community.

There followed a period in which both sides tried to save face. The two police departments functioned for a month, and then the courts recognized the State forces officially and the State street commissioner as the legal officer. Those policemen who were injured in the riots sued Mayor Wood, and they were awarded $13,000, which Wood never paid. The amount was finally put in the tax levy and paid by the people of the City.

This controversy and his other personal actions caused the defeat of Fernando Wood for reëlection in 1856. The fight, however, was a close one. The reformers in Tammany Hall, who included Samuel J. Tilden, Peter B. Sweeny, Isaac V. Fowler, and John McKeon, nominated Daniel F. Tiemann for Mayor, and while Mayor Wood received the regular Tammany Hall nomination, he was defeated by 2,330 votes. Fernando Wood then left Tammany Hall and formed his own political organization, which he called Mozart Hall, because that was the name of its meeting place.

As frequently happened in the history of the City of New York, the reformers proved as unsatisfactory to the people as those they had endeavoured to reform. When the reform Mayor, Daniel F. Tiemann, who was personally an honest man,

FRANK LESLIE'S
ILLUSTRATED

NEWSPAPER

[No. 48.—Vol. II.]   NEW YORK, SATURDAY, NOVEMBER 8, 1856.   [Price Ten Cents.

TAMMANY HALL—ST. TAMMANY SOCIETY.

TAMMANY was one of those traditionary braves who inhabited in old times a very pleasant valley somewhere hidden away among the Alleghany Mountains. He was famous for hospitality, good sense, and, compared with his people, was remarkable for his advanced civilization. Tamanend lived to an advanced age, and was still remembered at the commencement of our revolution with love and veneration by the Indian tribes which existed in the north-west. Soon after General Washington was inaugurated, a number of our revolutionary patriots, in consideration that there were St. George's, St. David's, and other saintly christened societies, concluded that they would fashionize an American saint, and they commenced the order now known as St. Tammany, christened thus, more particularly at the instigation of the poet, patriot, and satirist, John Trumbull, who took a deep interest in the early organization of the order. Tammany Society was not originally commenced as a party institution, as it had for its original members, the moderate men

TAMMANY HALL DECORATED FOR MAYOR FERNANDO WOOD'S
CAMPAIGN OF 1856

but politically an incapable one, had served one term, Wood was
reëlected Mayor in 1858 by the combined votes of the disreputable classes, the regular Tammany Hall organization, and of
those who were dissatisfied with reform. Wood's Mozart Hall
had been turned into an efficient vote-getting institution by the
energetic efforts of Fernando Wood and his brother Benjamin.

Soon after his election to the office of Mayor, Fernando
Wood, who was then nearing fifty years old, married the
sixteen-year-old daughter of Drake Mills, one of the most
prosperous merchants of the city. This marriage—the Mayor's
third—strengthened considerably Wood's position with the
old merchants of New York, and it was said that Drake Mills
hoped to see his daughter become the First Lady of the Land
when Fernando Wood should become President of the United
States. But whatever Mr. Drake Mills may have been dreaming, he had a sharp sense of reality, for he stipulated that his
son-in-law the Mayor should invest $100,000 in Croton Water
stock for his young bride, and in case of her death the principal
was to revert to her parents.

IV

The Civil War was now imminent and the attitude of both
Tammany Hall and Fernando Wood toward the issues that
brought it about was characteristic. Tammany Hall had always
been opposed to the abolition of Negro slavery, and it was
especially active in its denunciation of and interference with
the abolitionists, for those who disbelieved in slavery believed
thereby in an idea, and Tammany men never forgave the
crime of individuality in defence of sentiments or ideals. The
whole Tammany idea was one of regularity, and because the
Democratic Party found it expedient to oppose the abolition
of Negro slavery, Tammany Hall's members, who were part of
the Democratic Party, broke up abolition meetings. On October 19, 1859, Fernando Wood delivered a speech at a mass
meeting in New Rochelle, and he then expressed his own attitude and that of the members of Tammany Hall toward the
abolition of Negro slavery:

"And what, in the meanwhile," said Fernando Wood, "will
become of our great commercial interests so closely interwoven

with Southern prosperity? The hundreds of millions of Northern capital invested in Southern productions—the wealth which is now annually accumulated by the people of the North, and especially New York, out of the labor of slavery— the profit, the luxury, the comforts, the necessity, nay, even the very physical existence depending upon products only to be obtained by the continuance of slave labor and the prosperity of the slave master?"[1]

This character of argument, which emanated from the minds of men who would do and did do anything for money, was popular in Tammany Hall. The attitude of so many members of Tammany Hall toward men whose colour happened to be brown was described broadly in a satire published as a broadside by the Philadelphia *Bulletin*. The orator was supposed to be Congressman John Morrissey, whose pugilistic exploits we have already related:

"40TH CONGRESS, 1ST SESSION
(From the Philadelphia *Bulletin*.)

A SPECIAL REPORT

"Evening Session—Mr. Wood of New York, in the Chair
"The appropriation for the Freedman's Bureau being under discussion, Mr. Elliott, of Massachusetts, having concluded his remarks, Mr. Morrissey, of New York, obtained the floor.
"MR. MORRISSEY (Dem. N. Y.)—Mr. Speaker, I arise on the present occasion, Sir, to say my say with regard to this Bureau concern, about which we have already heard so much from the other side. I think it is high time that our side of the House should be heard upon this subject, and all I want you to do, Sir, is to keep them fellers quiet, and don't let them come the gag over me with their 'orders' and 'previous questions.' I don't ask no odds from no one. This is a free fight, I take it—give us a fair show, and the devil take the hindmost. I can charge around in my own high grass, and fight my own flies. D——n a nigger!
"Mr. Speaker, the glorious charter of our liberties, the

---

[1] *Speech of Hon. Fernando Wood, Delivered at a Mass Meeting at New Rochelle, Westchester County, October 19, 1859.* A pamphlet.

Constitution of the United States, says that all men are created equal, and now, Sir, I should like to know where in that document you can find one word about the nigger. *D——n a nigger!* Just tell me that, will you? Is the nigger mentioned at all? and wouldn't our forefathers have said something about him, if they thought he was worth mentioning at all? *D——n a nigger!* Mr. Speaker, was GEO. WASHINGTON a nigger? Was General PUTNAM, or any hero of the Revolution, except BENEDICT ARNOLD, who ought to have been one? And anybody who says the CZAR OF RUSSIA or QUEEN VICTORIA is a nigger, lies, and he knows it. *D——n a nigger!* (Cries of 'Order.')

MR. MORRISSEY—"If that red-headed cuss from Wisconsin don't stop his jaw, I'll catch him some night in Shad's Oyster Cellar, and spread his nose over his face. *D——n a nigger!* I ain't afraid of no man in this House. I have reached the height of my ambition. I have been a wharf rat, chicken thief, prize fighter, gambler, and a Member of Congress. I have gone round the circle and left the Constitution and the flag with my constituents, and *D——n a nigger!* (Small Boy in the gallery— 'Hail Columbia.')

"Someone said that FRED DOUGLASS was fitter for this position than I am. I can lick the abolition cuss that said that and get backers a hundred to one. You can't come the guy gugles over me, so you needn't try it on. I am a free American citizen, and I'll bust the head of that grinning chap from Iowa, if he don't shut up his fly-trap. *D——n a nigger!* Mr. Speaker, I believe in the American eagle, the glorious feathered songster, who rises on pinions of fire, from lofty mountain top, and, piercing the sky, soars among the bannery stars—and d——n the bird; I've got him up there and can't get him down—anyhow, *D——n a nigger!*

"Why don't them as loves the nigger so much go to Africa? They can enjoy their society there. We can spare them; Andy says so, and he speaks by the book. The pure Democracy, undefiled, can take care of the country without their help. FERNANDY WOOD and I could run the machine better than five hundred nigger-loving, humanitarian, free-loving, bloomerite d——n Abolitionists, with their infernal Bureaus and Civil Rights Bills.

"If any gentleman on the other side wants his constitution amended, just let him step into the redundy, and I'll give him ten articles that'll give him the dyspepsy the rest of his natural life. D——n a nigger!

"The man from Massachusetts trots out his Latin. That don't skeer me. I ain't such a fool as some people think. Eplursy niuman zenith et broadaxe, et tu brute, nule prosequi, rombusque et diaphram! No use trying to come the school learning dodge over me. D——n a nigger!

"Mr. Speaker, we, as Democrats, are sick and tired of hearing about the nigger. Why don't they say something about the white man? I am a white man and so are my constituents. D——n a nigger!

"Mr. Speaker, them are my sentiments as a Democrat, Mr. Speaker.

"The allotted fifteen minutes being expended, the hammer fell and Mr. M. resumed his seat."

Tammany Hall made special efforts to defeat Abraham Lincoln in the campaign of 1860. Fictitious names were registered and voted upon by gangs of repeaters, and the result was that in New York City Stephen A. Douglas received 62,611 votes and Abraham Lincoln 33,311. When, after Lincoln's election, it seemed certain that the Southern states would secede from the United States, Mayor Fernando Wood sent a message to the Common Council of New York City that was the most extraordinary message even that eccentric body ever received. Mayor Wood suggested that the City of New York secede from the United States and establish Manhattan Island as a free and independent city state after the fashion of the mediæval city states. His message read in part:

To the Honorable the Common Council:

"Gentlemen:

"We are entering upon the public duties of the year, under circumstances as unprecedented as they are gloomy and painful to contemplate. The great trading and producing interests of not only the city of New York, but of the entire country, are prostrated by a monetary crisis; and though similar calamities have before befallen us, it is the first time that they have emanated from causes having no other origin than that which may be traced to political disturbances. . . .

"It would seem that a dissolution of the Federal Union is inevitable. Having been formed originally upon a basis of general and mutual protection, but separate local independence, each State reserving the entire and absolute control of its own domestic affairs, it is evidently impossible to keep them together longer than they deem themselves fairly treated by each other, or longer than the interests, honor, and fraternity of the people of the several States are satisfied. Being a government created by *opinion*, its continuance is dependent upon the continuance of the sentiment which formed it. It cannot be preserved by coercion or held together by force. A resort to this last dreadful alternative would of itself destroy not only the government, but the lives and property of the people.

"If these forebodings shall be realized, and a separation of the States shall occur, momentous considerations will be presented to the corporate authorities of this city. We must provide for the new relations which will necessarily grow out of the new condition of public affairs. . . .

"Being the child of the Union—having drawn our sustenance from its bosom, and arisen to our present power and strength through the vigor of our mother—when deprived of her maternal advantages, we must rely upon our own resources, and assume a position predicated upon the new phase which public affairs will present, and upon the inherent strength which our geographical, commercial, political, and financial preëminence imparts to us.

"With our aggrieved brethren of the Slave States we have friendly relations and a common sympathy. . . . Our ships have penetrated to every clime, and so have New York capital, energy, and enterprise found their way to almost every county and town of the American Union. If we have derived sustenance from the Union, so have we, in return, disseminated blessings for the common benefit of all. Therefore, New York has a right to expect, and should endeavor to preserve, a continuance of uninterrupted intercourse with every section. . . ."

Mayor Wood then went on to say how much New York City had suffered in the past five years from the encroachments and usurpations of the state Legislature. He told in detail of the state's interference with every phase of the city's corporate life. Now, he maintained, when the community of the United States was breaking into pieces, was the time for New York City to strike and to establish its independence, peaceably, if possible, forcibly, if necessary. He continued:

"Much no doubt can be said in favor of the justice and policy of a separation. It may be said that secession or revolution in any of the United States would be a subversion of all Federal authority, and, so far as the Central Government is concerned, the resolving of the community into its original elements—that if part of the States form new combinations and governments, other states may do the same. California and her sisters of the Pacific will no doubt set up an independent republic, and husband their own rich mineral resources. The Western States, equally rich in cereals and other agricultural products, will probably do the same. Then it may be said— Why should not New York City, instead of supporting by her contributions in revenue two thirds of the expenses of the United States, become also equally independent? As a free city, with but a nominal duty on imports, her local government could be supported without taxation upon her people. Thus we could live free from taxes, and have cheap goods nearly duty free. In this she would have the whole and united support of the Southern States, as well as of all other States to whose interests and rights under the Constitution she has always been true.

"It is well for individuals or communities to look every danger square in the face, and to meet it calmly and bravely. . . . If the Confederacy is broken up, the Government is dissolved; and it behooves every distinct community, as well as every individual, to take care of themselves.

"When disunion has become a fixed and certain fact, why may not New York disrupt the bands which bind her to a venal and corrupt master—to a people and a party that have plundered her revenues, attempted to ruin her commerce, taken away the power of self-government, and destroyed the Confederacy of which she was the proud Empire City? Amid the gloom which the present and prospective condition of things must cast over the country, New York, as a *Free City*, may shed the only light and hope for a future reconstruction of our once blessed Confederacy.

"Yet I am not prepared to recommend the violence implied in these views. In stating this argument in favor of freedom, 'peaceably, if we can; forcibly, if we must,' let me not be misunderstood. The redress can be found only in appeals to the magnanimity of the people of the whole state. The events of the past two months have no doubt effected a change in the popular sentiment of the State on national politics. This change may bring us the desired relief, and thus we may be able to obtain a repeal of the laws to which I have referred, and a consequent restoration of our corporate rights.

"FERNANDO WOOD,
"*Mayor.*"[1]

And in his daydream of imperial independence, Fernando Wood may have anticipated with glee the immense treasure which would fall under the control of the Democratic Party in New York City if it could only capture from the national government the huge customs duties that flowed with such enticing regularity into the port of New York from all over the world.

Fernando Wood's message did not meet with a favourable reception even among the members of his own party, who hated anti-slavery as much as he did. Two weeks later, arms consigned to the State of Georgia were seized in New York by the State of New York police. Mayor Wood telegraphed Governor Grown, of Georgia, in reply to the Governor's query, that the arms had been seized by police over whom he had no control, and that he did not approve of the seizure. If he had the power, he said, he would punish the police. The publication of this reply created popular indignation, for war spirit was beginning to become popular. When Southern men fired on Fort Sumter, and the Civil War began, Mayor Wood hurriedly got upon the band wagon, and in public he waved flags more excitedly than any of his neighbours, for he was too good a politician to remain a traitor after treason meant political death, at least. At the celebration of the 130th anniversary of

---

[1] *Documents of the Board of Aldermen*, Vol. XXVIII, 1861, Doc. No. 1.

George Washington's birth, on February 22, 1862, Fernando Wood delivered the following speech at Scranton, Pennsylvania:

"Indeed, I go further, and say that the world has had three, and but three, epochs, and these are: the Flood, the birth of Christ, and the American Revolution. The first alike destroyed and renewed the world, the second established the Christian Era and brought salvation to a ruined race, and the third proclaimed and vindicated the right of man to self-government."

And then he climbed upon the band wagon:

"And now, let me invoke my countrymen to a study of the example of Washington. We are in the midst of a revolution, more momentous, and yet not unlike that in which his glorious services were active. He fought to create a Republic; let us die, if need be, to maintain it. . . . And would to God that the whole people—the men of every section which has derived so much advantage from the Union—could present but one front in this, the trying hour of its peril. Would that all could elevate themselves to the emergency of the occasion, and that, with one voice, spoken through one great phalanx, we could send forth thunder tones to the North and the South. Would that personal and political prejudices were for once laid aside, that all could combine in one common effort to defend and maintain the Government—stand by her with our blood and with our treasure and to avert the blow which a foul conspiracy has leveled against it."[1]

This about-face was not so difficult for Mayor Fernando Wood to make, for apparently the political about-face was his most habitual motion. In 1839 Fernando Wood had been a leader in the abolitionists' tabernacle, established on Broadway by Arthur and Lewis Tappan, New York merchants, whose fanatic interest in Negro emancipation did not prevent them from insisting that all their clerks must abstain from liquor, shun the theatre, attend prayer meetings twice a week as well

---

[1] *Oration Delivered by Hon. Fernando Wood, on the Anniversary of Washington's Birthday, February 22, 1862, Scranton, Pa.* A Pamphlet. Pp. 7-8, 11.

as on Sundays, and arrive at work at half-past seven in the morning and leave late at night; but before commencing their work the Tappan clerks were all compelled to offer up prayers for the emancipation of the slaves. Fernando Wood spoke vigorously in favour of emancipation of the Negroes at the tabernacle of the Tappans and their friend David Hale, owner of the *Journal of Commerce*, in return for which he received the valuable support of this wealthy faction when as a young man he was first a candidate for the nomination to Congress.[1]

Tammany Hall, as soon as its leaders realized that the Civil War was inevitable, issued proclamations of loyalty, although it had a short time before declared in public resolutions that it was unalterably opposed to any quarrel with the Southern states. It was further resolved that until the war was over a banner should hang outside the Wigwam proclaiming Andrew Jackson's words: "The Union must and shall be preserved." Tammany Hall also sent a Tammany regiment to the front. Fernando Wood and his Mozart Hall, not to be outdone in new-found patriotism by Tammany Hall, also began to raise a regiment.

Tammany Hall's leaders saw in patriotism a useful means of putting Mozart Hall out of business, for the regular Tammany organization and Fernando Wood were now enemies. Tammany Hall declared publicly that its own loyal attitude was directly opposite to that of Mozart Hall, whose leader had proclaimed himself so openly disloyal. Tammany Hall also declined to participate in a State Democratic convention at which delegates from Mozart Hall were present, and the Mozart Hall faction was compelled to retire from the convention.

The election for Mayor of New York in 1861 was exciting. Tammany Hall and Mozart Hall had come to an agreement on State nominations, but they could not agree concerning the candidate for Mayor, because Fernando Wood insisted on running again for that office, and Tammany Hall would have none of him. Tammany Hall nominated C. Godfrey Gunther, a reputable fur merchant. The Republicans, in alliance with some dissatisfied Democrats, nominated George P. Opdyke, another reputable merchant. Opdyke was elected by a plurality

---

[1] *The Old Merchants of New York City*, by Walter Barrett, Vol. I, p. 233, 1889 edition.

of 1,000 votes, in spite of attempts upon the part of the Board of Aldermen to count him out. There was a wild scene at Tammany Hall on election night. Jimmy Nesbit, a Sixth Ward Tammany worker, was trying to arouse enthusiasm for Gunther, when someone shouted "Three cheers for Fernando Wood." Nesbit threw a water pitcher at the enthusiast's head, and he was about to follow it with a pewter mug when someone grabbed his arm. Then Mr. Chauncey Shaeffer told the audience that he had received his first meal, with liquor, from Tammany Hall, sixteen years previously, and that he would never desert her. Shaeffer also said that he had just called on President Lincoln and had urged him to give the contract for putting down the rebellion to Tammany Hall. Then someone shouted, "Shaeffer, you're drunk," and, "You're a disgrace to Tammany Hall," and Shaeffer stumbled off the platform.[1]

The celebration of the Fourth of July, 1862, was a grand occasion in Tammany Hall. At noon, a Sicilian brass band played American national airs from a balcony. Tammany Hall was covered with red, white, and blue streamers and Irish flags; a large transparency representing General Andrew Jackson, a good patriot, but also a good Democrat, hung in one of the front windows. The Grand Sachem, Nelson J. Waterbury, delivered an address to more than two thousand people; Mrs. Euphemia Vale Blake wrote that it was "steeped with patriotism." "Twenty-four picked boys, with piano accompaniment," sang "My Country 'Tis of Thee." The next number on the programme was to be the recitation of the "Ode to Washington," by Eliza Cook, who was also the authoress of "Lines Appended to a Bunch of Dried Grasses," "The Life-Boat Is a Gallant Bark," "The Mother to Her Deaf and Dumb Child," "On Seeing Some Agricultural Emigrants Embark," "On Hearing a Wounded Bird Singing in a Tree," "Garibaldi the True," and *The Glass of Gin*, a temperance novel. But, for some unexplained reason, Mrs. Cook's ode was not delivered, and Mr. Hosea B. Perkins recited one of his own compositions instead. The Tammany poets were there in abundance, and Mr. Henry Morford, whose poem, "Almost," was considered at the moment to be immortal,

---

[1] *The History of Tammany Hall*, by Gustavus Myers, 1917 edition, pp. 201–202.

recited the poem which he had been hired to write especially
for the occasion, entitled "Tammany and Union":

"In this hall so old and honored—filled with purpose proud and
    high,
Stood we, friends of the republic, on the Fourth of last July. . . .
Twelve short months—a year of changes such as ne'er the na-
    tions saw
Since creation sprung from chaos at the great primeval law.
One year past—and wide around us cannons roar and thunder
    drums,
For once more the Nation's Birth-day to a patriot people comes.
Flags are waving, voices bursting into words of deafening cheer,
For the nation lives—God bless it!—and its natal day is
    here! . . .

"But the year has other omens, quite as pregnant and as true
With the Sons of the Great Wigwam, more than all, *they* have
    to do.
And on this the nation's birth day, we must pause and look
    behind,
Measuring with a will determined and with patriotic mind
What have been the true relations, since this struggle first be-
    gan,
Borne by every true and loyal honest democratic man?
What has Tammany, the ancient, done to aid the holy cause—
Done to free the land from treason and to win the world's
    applause?
Ribald tongues have dared to utter words that should be
    stamped at once
As the falsehood of the liar or the drivelling of the dunce,
Placing in a false position those who bear your honored name,
While for 'wide-awakes' and negroes they demand the world's
    acclaim!
Is this just? Will you permit it on our history's page to stand
Without rising to efface it with a bold, determined hand?
Will you leave the blatant falsehood on the future's page to
    show?
Sure I hear the Great Tribe thunder, through their lips of war-
    paint, 'No!' . . .

"Oh, the very *doubt* was shameful! doubt like that which oft for
    life
Some half crazed and jealous husband throws upon a faithful
    wife!
What for years had stood a bulwark 'tween the ruin threatened
    wide
By the sectional disturbers swarming thick on every side—
But *Democracy, the faithful?* What, without its earnest aid,
Years ago had saved the nation being low in ruin laid?
When had Tammany once faltered when the *Union* was at
    stake,
From which faithless side soever waves of fear might upward
    break?
Where among the nation's records figured men of truer soul
Than the scribes of the Old Wigwam had inscribed upon its
    roll?
Who could doubt that in their coffins would rebel its honored
    dead,
When around the council fire one word of treason should be
    said?
Who could doubt its true men living would cast off the very
    name,
If to bear it would be linking hands with Burr and Arnold's
    shame?

"Hark, a sound even then was uttered that should chase one
    lingering doubt,
Thrilling all the nation's pulses as its fiery words rung out:
'Who dares touch the nation's banner, be the traitor's doom his
    lot!
Give him neither grace nor mercy—shoot him dead upon the
    spot!'
Who spoke out those words of truth that with no traitor thought
    would mix?
Who but Tammany's first Sachem—ever honored—John A.
    Dix! . . .

"Honor be to ABRAHAM LINCOLN, that thus far his course is
    true,
Doing for the nation's welfare all an honest man can do!

Honor to his name forever, that no Abolition force
Seems to have the power to move him far from safety's middle
    course!
Long ago he learned the lesson that they all must learn at
    length—
That the black Chicago platform had no element of strength—
That republican support at best must prove a rope of sand—
That democracy must aid him if he wished to save the land.

"He has erred—for man is mortal—but few men of any age
Could have walked so well and nobly on his racked, distracted
    stage.
He will save the perilled nation if his better sense he heeds,
Listens to that voice of warning that the best of rulers needs,
Puts his foot down till it crushes all fanaticism flat,
And becomes what all can welcome—*a full-blooded democrat.* . . .

"Victories yet shall crown the standard—victories scattered
    far and wide,
Like the long, bright roll of battles won on Mississippi's side!
Not even blunders like Manassas—like Ball's Bluff, and
    Charleston fight,
Where the gallant Seventy-ninth were mowed like grass, dis-
    daining flight,
Not even these can stop the torrent, or can keep it long delayed
While the boys can use the bayonet in *Dan Sickles's brigade!*
While the Irish legions struggle, with the bravest deeds of man,
To revenge their fallen comrades and release MIKE COR-
    CORAN! . . ."

After this poem, several partisan and patriotic orations were
delivered, and then the company adjourned to the Banquet
Room, where, as the programme put it, "The Waters of the
Great Spring" flowed "profusely."

Tammany Hall and Fernando Wood gave reluctant support
to the Civil War and to President Lincoln, but they both opposed bitterly the emancipation of the Negroes, and they
criticized Lincoln for listening to the hated abolitionists and
for curtailing the rights of free speech and the freedom of the
press. Fernando Wood remained loyal only so long as loyalty
was required for the acquisition of votes. "Loyalty," he re-

marked in a speech, "is a monarchical derivative. What means it? The King can do no wrong. No loyalty for me." He also said that the North could not beat the South, and that it might as well admit it at once and stop fighting. He was again playing an astute political game, for the Civil War was not entirely popular in New York City, where the draft law was being opposed with violence, and Wood realized that it was to his advantage to cater to the votes of those who did not wish to fight personally.

Tammany Hall was at this time gradually falling into the control of a group of men who had been quietly increasing their power at the expense of Fernando Wood's. The leaders of this group were William M. Tweed and Peter B. Sweeny. By astute political manipulation Sweeny had obtained almost complete control of the General Committee of Tammany Hall, and that gave him and his associates the dictatorship of the nominations to public office in New York City by the dominant Democratic Party. It also gave them influence in the appointments and nominations to State offices and to judicial positions.

Tweed was made permanent chairman of the Tammany Society on January 1, 1863. A new set of sachems was elected at the same time, and they were all henchmen of Tweed's and Sweeny's. The Tweed faction decided that it was time, as they put it, for the old warriors to give up their warm seats beside the council fires to the young braves. In April, 1863, Tweed became Grand Sachem of the Tammany Society when Elijah F. Purdy retired from that position.

It was necessary to reunite Tammany Hall after the many splits into "Barnburners" and "Hunkers," "Softshells" and "Hardshells," Tammany men and Mozart men, and the first step in this reorganization involved the elimination of Fernando Wood and his friends. The attempt was made to discredit Wood publicly by branding him as unpatriotic, although the fires of patriotism, as we have seen, did not burn very brightly in Tammany Hall itself until there was danger in disloyalty. But both factions soon decided that compromise was wiser than political warfare. Fernando Wood realized that he had lost control in New York City, and he consented to give in to the new Tammany leaders if some persons he wanted nominated, and to whom, it was said, he had already sold the nominations for between $100,000 and $200,000, received the approval of Tammany Hall, and if he himself were given a nomination to Congress. This compromise was agreed to.

When Tweed and Sweeny gained control of Tammany Hall, they began to place their henchmen carefully in positions of power and usefulness. John T. Hoffman was made Recorder. A. Oakey Hall, who had been a Republican and a Mozart Hall Democrat at various times, joined the new Tammany group and was made District Attorney. Albert Cardozo and George G. Barnard were made judges of the Supreme Court. Henry W. Genet was made County Clerk of New York County. Tweed himself had already been an alderman, a member of the Board of Supervisors, and a Congressman, and he was now content to take for himself the apparently obscure position of Deputy Street Cleaning Commissioner, which was in reality a most valuable post, because it enabled Tweed to appoint thousands of voters to small jobs on the streets.

The Tammany Ring which ruled New York and plundered it on the most colossal scale in its history was thus fortified in an almost impregnable position, and Fernando Wood was relegated to Congress for the rest of his life.

When Fernando Wood died in 1881, Mr. Covert, member of Congress from New York, rose in his seat in the House of Representatives, and in the course of a long eulogy, after many other long eulogies interlarded with indiscriminate poetic selections, said:

"What shall I say of him whose presence was so familiar to us all in this chamber? Of him, who, after nearly twenty years of faithful service in this House, has made his last appeal to us, has answered his last roll-call, and has passed out from this Chamber, never again to enter its portals?

"'You knew—who knew not Astrophel?
    Alas! that I should say I knew,
And have not in possession still!
    Things known permit me to renew.
Of him, you know his merit such
    I cannot say—you hear—too much.'"

Fernando Wood's estate was valued at more than half a million dollars.

CHAPTER IV

I

DURING their reign in Tammany Hall, William M. Tweed and his associates contributed more of significance and of colour to the history of the institution and to the government of New York City than any of their precursors. Tammany Hall in this period received a lesson in organization for plunder on a scale undreamed of before, and the Tweed group also contributed their modicum of morality, for they taught their successors the dangers of theft unlimited by discreet legal expedients.

William Marcy Tweed was born in Cherry Street, New York City, in 1823. His father was a chair maker who had emigrated from Ireland. William did not remain long in school; he became an apprentice in his father's workshop, where, it was said, he found great difficulty working efficiently with his hands. He left his father's shop to become a clerk for a saddler and hardware dealer, and, being ambitious to become a bookkeeper, he went to a private academy in Elizabeth, New Jersey. He was quick at figures, and especially at mental arithmetic, if we can believe those who remembered his accomplishments after he had demonstrated them so notoriously in practice. Tweed worked for a firm of brushmakers in which his father was a partner, and when his father retired, William and his brother Richard became chair manufacturers. Tweed was then twenty-eight years old. The elder Tweed aided his sons with his credit, but the firm finally failed, with a deficit of $200,000, and this loss, according to one account, forced Tweed's father, who was now an old man, to return to chair making. "The shock of this calamity," declared one writer, "broke his heart, and it was not long before he fell dead in a fit of apoplexy in his own house. He had never forgiven his sons for their conduct, and was alienated from both of them at the time of his death."[1] The reason for the failure of the Tweed fortunes was said to be that Richard Tweed gambled too much, and that William Tweed devoted too much of his time to the affairs of the volunteer fire department and to the intricacies of New York ward politics.

Until 1866, New York City's Fire Department was a volunteer organization, and citizens of all classes belonged to it. Most of the young boys of certain districts of the city ran with the engines because of their admiration for the life of a fireman. Before he was twenty-one years old, Tweed was a runner with Engine Company No. 12 in the Fourth Ward, and afterward he joined the company known as Americus, or Big Six. Of this company, the most famous in the City, he became foreman after he had been a member for six months.

There was bitter rivalry between the various volunteer fire companies, and frequently they were so anxious to get to fires ahead of each other that they stopped to fight for supremacy and forgot about the blazing buildings. When a down-town fire alarm was sent in, crowds gathered at the junction of East Broadway and the Bowery to watch Tweed's Big Six race with Engine Company No. 8, and the people cheered the contestants as if they were athletic teams rather than fire fighters. Tweed, corpulent even at that period, was better suited to be foreman than an active runner. His company was divided into two groups, known respectively as the "Quills" and the "Roughs," because the former consisted of cautious clerks, and the latter of men and boys whose occupations were varied and usually temporary. Tweed was once called before the fire commissioner to answer the charge of throwing an obstacle in front of the rival engine company so that it might not reach the fire as fast as his own men; he was threatened with removal. This rivalry between the members of the fire companies is illustrated by the case history of a fellow prisoner given by George Wilkes in his *The Mysteries of the Tombs:*

"Peter or Pete Williams, the fire boy, who a few nights ago stabbed a volunteer named Stanley, belonging to another engine, is one. A quarrel had previously existed between him and the deceased, and broke out anew in a discussion of

[1]*North American Review,* Vol. CXIX, pp. 361–362.

merits of the respective machines. A threatening demonstration was made upon Williams by his antagonist and the former fled. He was pursued by Stanley and a number of his associates, with threats of violence. Williams took refuge in a public house, and his pursuers gathered about the door and demanded the landlord to turn him out. He did so, and Williams attempted again to fly. He was unsuccessful, however, being opposed by Stanley; whereupon he drew a knife and stabbed him in the shoulder near the collar bone. He was immediately arrested and when told that Stanley was like to die, exclaimed that 'he had intended to kill the d——d son of a b—— and hoped he would die.' In the morning, or in the course of the night, Stanley expired. Williams, when he heard it, expressed his gratification at the result, and said that 'they could no more than hang him and he hoped they would do that as soon as possible.' He still remains dogged and sullen and expresses no degree of remorse. He is indicted for wilful murder. . . .

"Isinprince, next door to him, is also indicted for manslaughter. He too killed a rival fireman, by stabbing him in an engine quarrel. The fire department will earn the name of the war department by-and-bye."[1]

The head of a tiger with a circle around it was the symbol painted on the Big Six engine, and a few years later Thomas Nast chose the tiger to denote in his extraordinary caricatures the ferocity of Tammany Hall and Tweed toward their prey, the people of the City of New York. The symbol stuck to Tammany Hall, and it has been adopted by the organization as part of its charm.

At this time Tweed was described as "a tall overgrown man, full of animal spirits," with "a swaggering gait, free-and-easy manners, the constant use of slang, and the display of a coarse humor greatly in vogue among his firemen associates." "He talked much and with a spluttering volubility that made it hard to understand him." "He at one period was a deep drinker, but by the positive order of his physician he had stopped his excesses in this respect, and with fatherly interest advised young men of his acquaintance to be temperate and virtuous." "Nevertheless, with too common inconsistency, he was notori-

[1]*The Mysteries of the Tombs*, p. 14.

ous, even from his youth, for licentious excesses, which were a scandal to the neighborhood in which he dwelt, and which grew upon him in after years."[1]

The volunteer fire department, consisting of a compact group of men whose opinions and tastes were similar, naturally developed into an organization of considerable local political influence. The members could be persuaded to vote solidly on election days for a specific candidate, and to work for political organizations during the rest of the year; Tweed, as foreman of his company, was soon able to control their political usefulness. Upon one occasion in his early career Tweed presided at a meeting in Tammany Hall at the request of Elijah Purdy, a sachem, and this was Tweed's own recollection of the event:

"So I went that night, and behold! no Purdy came. 'Come on,' said I, 'I'll preside! So I took the chair, and wasn't very comfortable in it, either. A man from California, by the name of Doyle, was running for Recorder against Barnard. . . . I saw, as the roll call proceeded, that Doyle had the majority of delegates. Said I to a secretary, 'Have a motion made to dispense with calling the roll!' It was done. 'All in favor of Mr. Barnard as the nominee of this body say aye. Carried! The meeting is adjourned!' Well, there was a riot and I was driven into one corner; Isaiah Rynders had a pistol as long as my arm drawn and cocked. Said he, 'I'll pay you for this!' I was scared, but I didn't say so. 'I'm not afraid of a whole ward of you fighting villains,' said I, and we all got out."[2]

Tweed was first a candidate for office in 1850, when he contested a seat from the Seventh Ward in the Board of Assistant Aldermen. He was defeated by John H. Webb, a reputable shipbuilder, and it was said that Tweed became conscious of the fact that his position as foreman of a fire company did not carry with it a reputation which begot votes. He resigned the foremanship and was a candidate for alderman in 1851. He was elected, and he served in the notorious "Forty Thieves" Board of Aldermen during the years 1852 and 1853. When an investigation, which we have already noted, was held, into the

[1] *North American Review*, Vol. CXIX, pp. 363-364.
[2] New York *Herald*, April 13, 1878.

franchise activities of this board, Tweed denied in an affidavit that he had ever received any money from the Third Avenue Railroad Company, and he ended his affidavit with the following statement: "I have no knowledge that any member of the late Common Council or officer of the city government, had received any money whatever to influence his official action; in my own proceedings, I have been influenced only from a sense of duty." But many years later, in 1877, Tweed told a reporter for the New York *Herald*: "There never was a time when you couldn't buy the Board of Aldermen, except now. If it wasn't for John Kelly's severity, you could buy them now." The attitude of the Board of Aldermen at the period when Tweed was a member of it was made clear in the cynical remark of one of the aldermen in the course of debate on a petition to the Legislature urging that no franchises should be awarded except after public auction, and then only to the highest bidder. "Does anybody suppose," asked the alderman, "that this body of statesmen would give anything away without being paid for it?"[1]

A writer in the *North American Review*, commenting on the personnel of the New York City government at about this time, said: "The absolute exclusion of all honest men from any practical control of affairs in that city, and the supremacy in the Common Council of pickpockets, prize fighters, emigrant runners, pimps, and the lowest class of liquor-dealers, are facts which admit of no question." Apparently, conditions had changed merely in detail since Mike Walsh was a critic of municipal affairs. It was said that during the period shortly after Tweed was an alderman, a practical joker hired a newsboy to rush into the Council chamber where the City Fathers were in session and shout, "Mister, your liquor store is on fire!" All the members of the Board were alleged to have jumped to their feet and rushed to the door.[2]

In 1853, Tweed was elected to Congress, where he served from the fourth of March, 1853, until the fourth of March, 1855. But, like most Tammany Hall men, he did not care for Washington life. Some years later, when he was asked by a news-

---

[1] *History of Public Franchises in New York City*, by Gustavus Myers, p. 138, footnote 3.
[2] *Thirty Years of New York Politics*, by Matthew P. Breen, p. 250.

paper reporter if it was true that he had ambitions to be a United States Senator, Tweed answered: "If I wanted to go to the Senate, I'd go; but what for? I can't talk, and I know it. As to spending my time in hearing a lot of snoozers discuss the tariff and the particulars of a contract to carry the mails from Paducah to Schoharie, I don't think I'm doing that just now." The *North American Review*, which did not admire Tweed, wrote of his Washington career: "If common report is to be believed, Tweed more than occasionally sought relief from the cares of public life in the somewhat coarse dissipations of Washington, and even allowed himself to be fleeced by sharpers."

Tweed was defeated for reëlection to Congress by the candidate of the Know Nothing Party. In 1855, he was elected to the Board of Education of the City. This public body was at that period making money for its members by the sale of textbooks to the City and of positions to teachers. A few years later, a special committee of the Board of Education, appointed to investigate rumours of graft in the appointment of teachers in the Fourth Ward, gave in its report a picture of conditions that were also prevalent when Tweed belonged to the Board. A member of the investigating committee said in the course of one of the hearings:

"One poor little girl came upon the stand on crutches. That lame girl was taxed $75 for a paltry situation of $300 a year. I would ask, What could be more infamous? The man who divides the earnings of the common prostitute is superior to the man who would take blackmail for the position of a teacher. It is the most astounding thing that I ever heard of. . . . But we are told by the gentleman from the Fourth, that these things are organized all over the city, and that every one has his friends, and looks after their interests."[1]

In 1857 Tweed was elected to the Board of Supervisors, the position which he held until 1870, when the Board was abolished, and the post from which he developed his system for the

---

[1] *Wholesale Corruption! Sale of Situations in Fourth Ward Schools. Report of the Committee Appointed by the Board of Education. Published by the Citizens' Association of New York*, pp. 6–8.

corruption and the government of the City of New York. The power of the Board of Supervisors corresponded somewhat to the power exercised by the present Board of Estimate and Apportionment. It had charge of public improvements, taxation, and the various departments of the City's government which involved its income and expenditure. A position on this board was a golden opportunity for a crafty man who was furthering his own financial interests at all costs, and it had the added advantage that it was never in the limelight. A supervisor was not like a mayor, for, in the first place, there were twelve of them, six from the Democratic Party and six from the Republican Party. Then, too, a supervisor dealt in matters so complicated as municipal finance, which were both uninteresting and unintelligible to the common people. It was no wonder that Tweed clung to this strategic position, and he was content to add to it several other unobtrusive, but tactical, posts in the campaign which he waged to make the most of his opportunities for himself and his confederates.

Some years later Tweed testified before an investigating committee of the Board of Aldermen that the original ring which developed into the notorious Tweed Ring was formed while he was a member of the Board of Supervisors. The first combination was made for the purpose of controlling the board, which was supposed to be a bi-partisan organization. The Board of Supervisors had the power to appoint the inspectors of elections, and these positions were of the utmost importance to the politicians who wished to control the vote when they could not gain it. Tweed testified that the Democrats of Tammany Hall, of which he was one, were anxious to control absolutely these appointments of election inspectors instead of sharing them with the Republicans, and that they paid Peter P. Voorhis, one of the Republican members of the Board, $2,500 to stay away on the day the appointments of election inspectors were to be considered. "From that time out," Tweed testified, "it was all combination on every subject, most, that came up."[1]

---

[1] *Report of the Special Committee of the Board of Aldermen Appointed to Investigate the "Ring" Frauds, Together with the Testimony Elicited During the Investigation. Board of Aldermen, January 4, 1878.* Document No. 8, pp. 14, 16. Hereafter this document will be referred to in footnotes as Tweed Ring Investigation.

Tweed, examined by Hugh L. Cole concerning this phase of his activities, testified further:

"Q. By Ring, I mean a combination of men to do any improper thing; now, was there any other combination of members of the Board of Supervisors while you were a member of it?

"A. There was; John R. Briggs, Walter Roche and myself always went together for anything.

"Q. Did you three agree to do any acts whereby money was improperly diverted from the Treasury of the County, and received by you, or any of you?

"A. We did. . . . Mr. Briggs, Mr. Roche and myself used to meet together nearly every day, at my office in 95 Duane street; I had an office there; we were all members of the various committees before which bills were brought, and all knew the bills before the different committees, and we agreed what bill we would go for; there was hardly a time when our three votes wouldn't carry 'most anything. . . . We passed bills excessive in amount.

"Q. Did you have any understanding, you three, or any of you, to share with the claimants against the county treasury?

"A. In some instances some of them did, or were presumed to have; in other instances others did. In some I did myself.

"Q. Well, how were these agreements with the claimants made?

"A. Generally for a percentage of the bills."[1]

This combination for the purpose of dividing the spoils from New York City's income and expenditures continued until 1870, when the Board was abolished. New conspirators were added from time to time, but the system remained the same. By 1870 Tweed and his Tammany asscociates no longer needed the old Board of Supervisors, for they had developed more efficient machinery for their purposes of control and plunder, and therefore they preferred to abolish the Board by their own initiative rather than to permit their opponents to do so. By that time Tweed personally had acquired the positions of State Senator and Deputy Street Commissioner as well as

---

[1] Tweed Ring Investigation, pp. 19–20.

Supervisor; he had also accumulated some millions of dollars; the *Tribune* could refer with truthful satire to him as "Mr. Supervisor-Senator-Street-Commissioner Tweed." How he and his associates gained their power and money we can now indicate.

Tweed was asked by the counsel for the investigating committee:

"Q. Will you please state to the Committee how the Ring which, for convenience sake, I will call the Tweed Ring, was first formed?

"A. What you now call the Tweed Ring was formed during the administration of Mayor Hoffman; during his administration the Street Commissioner, Mr. Cornell, myself, the Deputy Street Commissioner, and Mr. Brennan, who was then Comptroller, used to take our dinners every day in this building with the keeper of the hall; we paid him so much a month for it, and for three or four years this was kept up socially, and finally it formed itself into a political organization for politics entirely; . . . that was all politics; no money was ever mentioned there; after a while Cornell's term of office expired, and he went out; Hoffman's term of office expired, and he went out, and Brennan went out, I was about the only one left of the original organization; then there came a new mayor; I forget who succeeded Hoffman—Hall, wasn't it? Connolly succeeded Brennan, and Mr. McLean succeeded Cornell, we used to meet every day together; once in a while Mr. Sweeny [Peter B. Sweeny] would come in and dine with us; then I was elected to the State Senate; I found it was impossible to do anything there without paying for it, and money had to be raised for the passage of bills up there; that was the way the Ring first became organized, to pay for bills to protect ourselves in the city."[1]

The leading members of what was popularly known as the Tweed Ring were four men: William M. Tweed, Peter B. Sweeny, Richard Connolly, and A. Oakey Hall. In describing later to his lawyer, John D. Townsend, the division of labour among members of the Ring, Tweed said that Sweeny took

---

[1]Tweed Ring Investigation, pp. 28–29.

care mainly of the election of candidates for judicial positions; Connolly was the financier, and became Comptroller of the City; Hall was adviser on all legislation and legal matters, for he was a trained lawyer, a member of the prominent law firm of Brown, Vanderpoel & Hall, and had been District Attorney; and that Tweed himself had general charge of all matters. The members of the Ring, however, were not rigidly circumscribed in their individual activities, for each contributed whatever was in his character and personality to contribute. Sweeny was astute, keen, cunning, and calculating, and he was the silent adviser and manipulator concerned with political deals of all kinds. Hall was a pseudo-playwright, poet, after-dinner speaker, and punster, and in addition to his duties as Mayor of New York he acted as a mountebank before the public. Tweed was lavish, generous, and boisterous, and his love of entertainment contributed to the popularity of the Ring with its followers. Then there were minor personalities who worked with Tweed and his three associates and they were rewarded with sums of money or with jobs. Among these were John T. Hoffman, Hall's predecessor as Mayor of New York, who was made Governor of New York by Tweed; Judge Albert Cardozo and Judge George G. Barnard, who owed their positions on the Supreme Court bench to Tweed and his associates, and who worked for them loyally and illegally; Senators Henry W. Genet, "Mike" Norton, and Thomas J. Creamer; City Auditor James Watson, the Ring's paymaster, and others whom we shall meet in the course of our inquiries. The anonymous writer of *The Copperhead Catechism* asked, "What is a Ring?" and he answered himself: "A hard band in which there is gold all round and without end."

We have already seen something of William M. Tweed in his youth. When he took command of New York in the 'sixties, Tweed was tall and corpulent, weighing almost three hundred pounds, and measuring five feet eleven inches. His complexion was florid, and his features large, and the hair that remained round the sides of his head was a reddish brown. A short beard and moustache of the same colour covered his chin and mouth. It was said that when he took his seat in the State Senate, the chair usually provided for senators was too small to hold his bulk, and that for the time being he held a levee in the cloakroom, while the clerk ordered a chair of sufficient proportions. His disposition was jovial, and many men took advantage of his good nature. Upon the occasion of his death, the *Sun* remarked among other things that Tweed "had a fund of stories not found in Rabelais." Tweed's reputation for licentiousness was perhaps exaggerated by the desires of contemporary commentators, but it was general.

Peter B. Sweeny, whom Thomas Nast usually portrayed in his amazing caricatures of the time with a tag reading Peter "Brains" Sweeny and whom other newspaper writers and artists sometimes called Peter "Bismarck" Sweeny, was the brains of the Tweed Ring and the most important member of it next to Tweed himself. Sweeny was the opposite of Tweed in almost every respect. He was of medium height and slight of build. His features were heavy, his forehead low, his eyes deep, and his hair and moustache coarse, black, and bristly. He was quiet, and he hated publicity or display. His methods were secret and his manner reserved.

Sweeny was born in New York City one year after Tweed, in 1824, of Irish parents. It was said that members of the family had been Catholic priests, and it was also said that his mother kept a liquor store in the "Bloody Sixth" Ward when he was a baby. Sweeny's father later kept a saloon in Jersey City, where Sweeny acted as a waiter. The rest of the family seem to have had livery-stable connections. Sweeny was educated at St. Peter's Roman Catholic parochial school and later at Columbia College. He studied law and entered the offices of James T. Brady, one of the leading attorneys of his day. Early in his career he turned his attention to politics, though he was also credited with extensive knowledge of the law. His first political endeavours were in the interest of his uncle, Thomas J. Barr, who was elected a State Senator in 1854, and who took his nephew with him to Albany, where young Sweeny acted as lobbyist for the principal stage-coach companies and opposed the granting of street railway franchises that would interfere with their business. It was as a lobbyist that Sweeny learned the art of manipulating men and measures for political and financial effect.

Sweeny could never appear to advantage in public, and when

he was chosen District Attorney of New York in 1858, he broke down during the trial of his first case. His humiliation was so great that he resigned the office immediately. The only other public offices he consented to hold during the reign of his confederates were those of City Chamberlain and Commissioner for Central Park, which did not bring him personally before the public. As City Chamberlain he gained a useful reputation for honesty when he turned over to the City the interest on the public funds, which former city chamberlains had considered their own perquisite. In this he was clever, for the reputation so gained enabled him to take larger sums from the city funds unperceived. Sweeny once described his own place in New York politics:

"I am not," he said, "and never claimed to be, a leader. Tweed . . . Mayor Hall, Comptroller Connolly, and others I might name, are more leaders than I am. I am a sort of adviser; I try to harmonize the interest of the party, and endeavor to secure good nominations and sound principles, as I understand them. But I do not aspire to the position of a leader. I am simply a passenger in a ship, with the privilege of going ashore if I do not like its management or its course."

However, he had a great deal to do with steering the course of that ship to his liking. His work was done in caucuses and in private offices, and his ability at estimating the exact strength of a candidate was famous in Tammany Hall. His own share in the proceeds of deals was always paid for him to his brother James M. Sweeny. Sweeny was a great admirer of Napoleon the Third, whom he had met once in Paris, and whom it was said he resembled in character.

Sweeny was familiar with law, history, political science, and general literature, and he had a passion for engravings and other *objets d'art*. He was also interested in a woman who had been a rubber in a Turkish bath, with whom he was alleged to have lived for many years and by whom he was said to have had a child. One writer maintained that it was only after there was talk of him as a prospective candidate for President of the United States, "that he performed the tardy act of justice of legalizing the relations existing between this woman and himself, and of removing in some measure the stain of bastardy from the brow of their child."[1]

A. Oakey Hall, whose political and social accomplishments aided him to become Mayor of New York during the reign of the Tweed Ring, had in his character elements which both Tweed and Sweeny lacked and needed for their crafty business. The New York *Times* published an editorial headed, "We Keeps a Hartist," which described the position of A. Oakey Hall in the Tweed Ring:

"It was a London barber, we believe," said the *Times*, "who, inspired by a noble ambition to distinguish himself from the vulgar herd of his fellow-craftsmen, announced to the genteel world that—using the royal pronoun—'in our establishment for the prosecution of the tonsorial art we keeps a hartist.' . . . Outside the honest, but humble, callings, too, the need has been acknowledged of someone who could throw over unpleasant details and ugly facts the charm of manners, who could keep clean hands while doing dirty work, who could give fine names to foul things, and use the grand old name of gentleman as a mask, behind which to do most ungentlemanly deeds.

"Just as the fops had their Pelham, the murderers their Eugene Aram, the 'gentlemen of the road' their Claude Duval, the seducers their Lovelace, so the Ring of New-York has its Oakey Hall. He is the 'artist' of the great organization of swindlers that has the honest hard-working citizens of New York under its heel. His companions in crime are a low set—mere jail-birds on a bender—who have no other thought than how to get the greatest possible amount of animal enjoyment out of their ill-gotten swag. They are men who make no pretension to respectability, who never knew what it is to be respectable, and never had a desire to know; who only wish to be, and to be thought, rich, and who live for no other end than to get as much

---

[1] *The Frauds of the New York City Government Exposed. Sketches of the Members of the Ring and Their Confederates*, by Abram Polhemus Genung, p. 40. Other information concerning Sweeny from "An Episode in Municipal Government, The Tweed Ring," by Charles F. Wingate, *North American Review*, Vols. CXIX, CXX, CXXI; Vol. CXIX, pp. 368–371.

champagne, and oysters, and women, and horses, for their money as it will buy. . . .

"But Oakey Hall looks higher than the men he has so long made his bed with. As the Turveydrop of the Ring, he must turn his attention to other things. . . . To the other members of the firm—the right to keep racers and trotters, the strong food of the harem, the relaxation of champagne suppers and euchre after the arduous labour of pocketing and investing their stealings; but to Oakey, the duty of amusing the elegant society of Shoddyville with conversation on Shakespeare and the musical glasses, while his industrious friends were making way with the cash-boxes of his refined victims. His part was to play at the gentleman and scholar. He has written books, so the trunk-makers say. And plays, too, 'Humpty Dumpty,' among others, or so 'tis whispered in 'the fust colored suckles.'. . .

"How admirably the Ring understand the distribution of labor! While the Boss keeps the 'gentlemen' of the Democratic Party in order—snubs Seymour's nose, tweaks Tilden's ear, treads on Hoffman's toes, and bullyrags the rank and file; while Sweeny does his best to keep the laborers in a riotous frame of mind, and having got the quiet citizens into a big scare, rouses his serfs into new enthusiasm by doling out, with a great show of magnanimity, a modicum of the money he has himself robbed them of; while Hilton is manœuvring to get his lots cleared of stone at the City's expense, and Barnard, for his part, look you, is gone to pray; and Vanderbilt is sitting, a while after dinner, on one of his ferry-boat boilers, picking his teeth for recreation; and while the whole foul, noisy crowd of sinecure vultures are fattening at their ease on the fair body of our City, the elegant posture-maker of the Ring endeavors to divert the public attention from the doings of his mates, by dressing himself up —now in a suit of green, now in a suit of check; by going round to seven theatres in a night, to show 'his friends, the people,' that there is no truth in the newspaper story that he had run away from the City; . . .

"Oakey Hall plays well his part. He is a shallow-pated charlatan, 'tis true, but he has wit enough to serve his masters, and impudence enough, insolence enough, and shamelessness enough to keep the easy-going, average New Yorker at bay. . . . As the 'Honorable' Oakey Hall—they are all honorable men—

as 'our worthy Mayor,' he will long keep his place in the new Rogues' Calendar. He will soon take his leave of us—and there's nothing that we would more willingly part withal—but will he be forgotten? We trust not. The *World* will write his eulogy in very choice Italian, and future Rings will learn by his splendid example how useful it is for a gang of thieves, no less than for a mere barber, to keep one member of the fraternity to do the ornamental while they do the useful, to cover their swindling with his suavity, and, like another Claude Duval, to lead the fine people gracefully from the coach to dance a corranto upon the heath while the ruder villains search the baggage for plunder at their ease."[1]

Abraham Oakey Hall was born in New York City, and he claimed descent from one of Cromwell's colonels. He was graduated from New York University and then entered the Harvard Law School, but he left there to go with his family to New Orleans, where he became a newspaper reporter. Hall abandoned newspaper work to enter the law office of Mr. Slidell, who is known in American history for his part in the *Trent* affair. Returning to New York from New Orleans, Oakey Hall tried authorship again, but soon he realized that the prizes in politics were larger than those offered by anything he had theretofore undertaken, and in about 1854, he suddenly appeared as a lobbyist in Albany. At this time Hall was a Republican and opposed to Tammany Hall. He was appointed Assistant District Attorney by Nathaniel B. Blunt, and upon the death of Blunt became Acting District Attorney of New York County. In 1862, he was elected to the office of District Attorney as the candidate of a combination of the Republicans and Fernando Wood's Mozart Hall Democracy. It was said that he used his office to build up his friendships, and he himself revealed the secret of his early success in these words: "Few persons have so many *tried* friends as I have, and tried friends are always magnanimous." It was one of his hallmarks that he never could resist a pun even when it made obvious his neglect of official duty. It was publicly charged, but never proved, that under Hall's administration as District Attorney of New York more than ten thousand indictments against various persons were

[1]New York *Times*, October 9, 1871.

From the collection of Edwin P. Kilroe. Copyrighted   © Harper & Bros.

A. OAKEY HALL   PETER B. SWEENY   RICHARD B. CONNOLLY

"pigeonholed." As District Attorney he gained notoriety when he made himself prominent during the popular murder trial of the day, that of Mrs. Cunningham for the murder of Dr. Burdell.

Hall soon realized that the dominant power in New York politics was Tammany Hall, and, with characteristic foresight and inconstancy, he forsook his former associations and joined that institution. Each member of Tammany Hall signs the book in which is written the constitution of the Tammany Society, and Abraham Oakey Hall signed on February 1, 1864, adding under his signature:

"Whilst Council fires hold out to burn,
The vilest sinner may return.

"OK."[1]

Tammany saw the potential value of Hall, and Sweeny and Tweed made him candidate for Mayor to succeed John T. Hoffman, whom they made Governor of New York at the same time. In his speech of acceptance of the nomination at Tammany Hall, Oakey Hall ended with: "I would not take the office if I did not take it as the trustee of the Democracy, and be able to do in the new office what I always did in the old—to take care of my friends, and to ask my friends to take care of me." Politicians in Tweed's time had the charm of frankness. In the same speech Hall remarked: "But somehow or other the press of business in my office [District Attorney] has been so great that I have never yet found time to prosecute a man for taking a drink after 12 o'clock at night. (Prolonged cheering and considerable merriment.)" Oakey Hall was elected by a large majority.

While he was Mayor, the Olympic Theatre produced his extravaganza, *Loyalina, Brigadier General Fortunio and His Seven Gifted Aides-de-Camp*. The Mayor was also the author of *Humpty Dumpty*, a burletta, a play called *Fernande*, and another called *Let Me Kiss Him for His Mother*. The Mayor loved more than anything to appear on the stage, and while he was District Attorney he gave a Humorous

---

[1]Photostat reproduction of Tammany Society Constitution and register in Manuscript Division of New York Public Library.

Dramatic Reading, entitled *Dido versus Æneas, an ancient breach of promise trial*. He also delivered a lecture called "An Evening in Crime-Land," which was received with great enthusiasm in both New York and Albany. But the Mayor's favourite diversion was making puns, and the newspapers delighted to publish his efforts. In his letter of appointment of his friend Thomas J. Barr as Police Commissioner, which he sent to the newspapers as well as to Mr. Barr, Oakey Hall referred to Mr. Barr's great "ancillary qualities." It was the Mayor's habit sometimes to use words without due respect for their previous condition of servitude, and when the newspapers insistently demanded to know what Mr. Barr's "ancillary qualities" were or possibly could be, Mayor Hall in the newspaper which he owned and edited, the *Leader*, turned off the joke on himself by writing that the word was derived from Ann-sillery, and referred to "a species of Sillery champagne much liked by Ann of Austria." In a speech on the Chinese question before a mass meeting of citizens Mayor Hall remarked daringly: "If this was a question one would feel disposed to joke about, we could very well say to-night—on this hot night of June, that the coolie question was a very good one to talk about." In the middle of his lecture before the New York University students on "Law in New York," when the gas suddenly went out, Mayor Hall remarked that there seemed to be a conflict of one gas with another. All these demonstrations did not decrease his popularity. But one newspaper writer turned this passion for playing on words against the Mayor when he remarked that "New York City is now governed by Oakey Hall, Tammany Hall, and Alcohol." Mayor Hall's monogram, which he designed himself, was formed of the letter O encircling a golden Key, which, being laid across two awls formed the letter H.

When Hall was a candidate for Mayor, the *Herald*, for Oakey Hall was a personal friend of James Gordon Bennett, the elder and the younger, wrote:

"It will be a refreshing novelty to have for Mayor of New York a strictly upright, honorable, capable man, and at the same time one who writes a drama or a farce with equal success, acts a part as well as most professionals on the stage, conducts the most difficult cases on the calendar, sings a good song, composes poetry by the yard, makes an effective stump-speech, responds to a toast with remarkable eloquence and taste, mixes a lobster salad as well as Delmonico's head cook, smokes the best cigar in New York, respects old age, and admires youth, as poets and orators invariably do."

A newspaper also remarked of the Mayor: "Oakey Hall is the best dressed man in the annals of Mayordom. He wears a different necktie every day." The Mayor outdid himself in dress and in catering to his constituents on St. Patrick's Day, 1870. Other mayors had reviewed the St. Patrick's Day parade for years, but Mayor Hall was not content to wear the traditional shamrock. He stood on a raised platform in front of the City Hall dressed in a green coat and also wore a pair of green kid gloves and a bright cravat of the same colour. This caused so much ridicule in the newspapers that on the following St. Patrick's Day this was what the men were wearing, according to a contemporary newspaper account:

"The Mayor was dressed in a new suit of green and black stripe cassimere. He wore an invisible green neck tie, from which shone a brilliant horse shoe; his gloves were the color of the shamrock and in his button-hole was an immense bouquet. Assistant Alderman Costello wore an old-fashioned vest of bright green satin covered with three-leafed shamrock worked in blue silk. All the members of the Common Council wore green kid gloves and sprigs of shamrock in their button-holes."

The *Sun* remarked after the Mayor's first appearance in green:

"Mayor O'Hall is said to have solemnly assured a committee of Germans that if the French get beaten during the present war, he will come out immediately in a full suit of Prussian blue. Meanwhile, he is having a tri-colored suit made, in case of another contingency. As for the famous green suit, with the shamrock buttons, it is laid for the present on the shelf."

Because of his obvious catering to both the Irish and the Germans, who controlled the largest numbers of votes, one newspaper referred constantly to A. Oakey Hall as "Mayor

Von O'Hall." The Mayor received on New Year's Day at the City Hall, where he provided a dozen kegs of beer. A German newspaper wrote:

"The Mayor wore the colors of the Nord German Bund, a ribbon of green Erin and gaiters à la Knickerbocker, thus uniting the mightiest elements governing this mighty metropolis. In acknowledging the victory [of Lager beer] the brewers of New York ought to provide the Mayor for life with free Lager."

The Mayor's office, according to his own newspaper, the *Leader*, was "carpeted with the softest Brussels," and had "exquisite engravings and photographs hanging on its walls." Among these were two portraits of Boss Tweed—Tweed was the first man in politics in New York City to earn and to receive the title "Boss." One of these portraits in the Mayor's office, according to the *Leader*, was "a life-like, porcelain affair," and the other "a steel engraving."

"Other faces," said the *Leader*, "smile on the blithe Mayor as he sits at his elegant desk, notably Comptroller Connolly, poor dead-and-gone James T. Brady, Governor Hoffman, Hugh Smith, Peter B. Sweeny, and an ancestor of Mayor Hall, one Colonel Okey, who was hanged by Charles II for assisting at the execution of Charles I."

The Mayor's manner of conducting business was genial. When he wished to call the attention of the Street Commissioner, George W. McLean, to a rotted tree concerning which he had received complaints, he wrote:

DEAR SIR:

I am told that many sentimental appeals have been made to you in behalf of the grand old tree fronting Broadway, just above the St. James Hotel, and which (the tree, not the hotel), was once a sapling upon the Varian farm; all "once upon a time," when there existed a morass where now stands the bronze statue of Vanderbilt. Most people have forgotten the song of "Woodman, Spare that Tree," but they have not forgotten General Morris, its author, nor Henry Russell, who so generally sung it thirty years ago. Let us also forget the sentiment implied in that lyric, and cut the tree down. Age has withered it, and custom has staled its infinite variety of "interviewing" with busy Broadway. A very excellent arborist informs me, as some of the neighbors fear, that the tree is in danger of unexpectedly falling over upon the adjoining buildings, or into the crowded thoroughfare during the "wild chilly blasts of December."

I shall hope to meet you at the next dinner of the St. Nicholas Society, and hear you or Richard Mount discourse upon the associations connected with or sprung from the aforesaid tree, which has already been embalmed in David Valentine's Manual. But, meanwhile cry aloud to your Inspector of Street Incumbrances, and spare not.

Very truly, your obedient servant.

A. OAKEY HALL.[1]

Responding to the toast, "The City of New York," at the dinner of the New England Society, Mayor A. Oakey Hall said in the course of a long speech in which he indulged freely in his favourite pastime of quoting Latin:

"And especially do we admire the taste you have displayed in quitting that part of the United States, where, as we Knickerbockers believe, New Englanders continue to persecute each other for opinion's sake. Here you enjoy extensive freedom—freedom in newspaper abuse; freedom to gamble in Wall Street; freedom in marriage; freedom in divorce; free lager; free fights; free voting: free love!"

A newspaper the next day speculated upon the number of glasses of champagne the Mayor had drunk before rising to his feet.

"Hall's all right," Tweed once said. "All he needs is ballast. If Oakey had had ballast enough to hold him down in the District Attorney's chair, he would have become a great man in time. Now he won't. Politics are too deep for him. They are for me, and I can wade long after Oakey has to float. He's light-headed."

Hall was a small man, with a heavy dark moustache and a

[1] *A. Oakey Hall Scrap Books*, Vol. III, New York Public Library collections.

scrubby black beard. He wore *pince-nez* glasses on a black string.

Tweed's other leading associate, Richard B. Connolly, was a weak, unscrupulous person who was exceptionally good at figures. He was always willing to do anything for money, and his knowledge of finance made him an apt person for the position of Comptroller, so far as the purposes of the Ring were concerned, at least. Connolly was born at Banta, near Cork, Ireland, and when he was a young man he emigrated to Philadelphia, where he worked as an auctioneer's clerk. He removed to New York. Charles F. Wingate wrote in the *North American Review* that "Connolly left Philadelphia owing to a low intrigue with a market-woman." In New York Connolly obtained an appointment in the Custom House, where he remained for some years and practised the politics necessary for Custom House employees to practise in order to retain their jobs. He then became discount clerk in the Bank of North America, where his ability as an accountant proved valuable to him. Connolly gradually gained local political influence in the Seventh Ward, and he became secretary of one of the ward committees. It was said that, while his neat penmanship was much admired, he could not be trusted to count votes correctly. In 1851 Connolly was made County Clerk of New York, and he was reëlected to that position three years later. It was charged that until the time of his reëlection to this office, Connolly had never troubled to become a naturalized citizen of the United States but had voted and held office in spite of that obvious disqualification. In November, 1859, Connolly was elected a State Senator and served two years, but he retired from that position to become general manager of the Central National Bank. Meanwhile, he remained active in the affairs of Tammany Hall, and in 1868 when Tweed and Sweeny were all powerful in the organization, they chose Connolly for the important post of the City's Comptroller.

Connolly was said to be obsequious to Tweed and Sweeny and arrogant to his clerks. His manner was crafty, insinuating, but somewhat cowardly, and he was popularly known to his friends as well as to his enemies by the sobriquet of "Slippery Dick."

The other most important friend of the Tweed group was Judge George G. Barnard, who did the bidding of Tweed and

Sweeny in the courts. It was in the time of Tweed that the
saying originated, "It is better to know the Judge than to know
the law," and the New York *Times* remarked concerning the
judiciary of the period:

"We are accustomed in this City to strange scenes in Courts
of Justice. We have Judges who make up for their deficiency
in learning by an abundance of bawdy jests and filthy oaths.
We have others who are the bosom friends of pimps and thieves,
and take care to be on the bench whenever any of their 'chums'
are in 'trouble.' We have others who try to win public confidence by loud protestations of their desire to do their duty,
while having a secret understanding with the knaves brought
before them."

Without the connivance of members of the judiciary Tweed
and his associates could not have accomplished the colossal
frauds which we shall soon observe them committing.

Judge Barnard was born in Poughkeepsie, New York, and
was graduated from Yale College. He went to California, where,
it was said, he was a "stool-pigeon" in a gambling house and
a performer with a Negro minstrel troupe. Returning to New
York, he entered politics, and by associating himself with the
Tammany Hall group he became Recorder in 1858. By packing
a primary meeting over which he presided, Tweed succeeded in
nominating Barnard for the Supreme Court. Judge Barnard's
brother is credited with the remark, "George knows about as
much law as a yellow dog."

Barnard was the judge who issued most of the injunctions
that enabled James Fisk, Jr., Jay Gould, and Daniel Drew to
perpetrate their amazing frauds in connection with their ownership and debauchery of the Erie Railroad. Tweed later testified
that it was he who introduced Jim Fisk to George Barnard. On
the witness stand Tweed said:

"Shortly after that, I introduced Mr. Fisk to Mr. Barnard,
and he became as intimate as I was with him, and attended to
that part of the business himself. He had more time to waste on
him than I did, and Barnard was a man who needed that kind
of thing.

"What do you mean by 'Wasting time on him'?" "Oh! well,

you had to waste much time with him—be around with him a
good deal, coax him, and make him believe he was a great man
—pat him on his back."[1]

Barnard enjoyed the company of Jim Fisk, who was the
greatest roisterer of the period, and whose boisterous career
came to a close a few years later when Edward S. Stokes shot
him after a quarrel which originated in rivalry for the affections
of Fisk's mistress, Josie Mansfield, who was called by one commentator, "the Cleopatra of Twenty-third Street." Fisk had
built her a house in that popular thoroughfare, where he had
also set up the Grand Opera House for the offices of the Erie
Railroad and the entertainment of his friends, as well as the
employment of his large acquaintance of ballet girls. Tweed was
one of those called to Fisk's bedside when he lay dying.

Judge Barnard's habits on the bench of the Supreme Court
were eccentric. He had a passion for whittling, and it was one of
the functions of the court attendant in his court to keep on the
bench an abundant supply of pine sticks of the proper size and
shape for the Judge. While listening to the droning arguments of
the attorneys, Judge Barnard whittled, and when the Court
adjourned there was always a large pile of shavings on the floor
beneath the Judge's chair. The Judge's language and manners
on the Bench were also peculiar.

Mr. Lucien Birdseye, a New York attorney, testified before
the legislative committee appointed to hear the charges brought
against Judge Barnard by the Bar Association:

"Q. Will you state if you remember any other particular
remarks that you have heard Judge Barnard make while he was
sitting on the bench? . . .

"A. As I recollect the transaction it was this: I was waiting
for a motion when the calendar of the special term was being
called, and some case arose which was a case for divorce. . . . A
gentleman was on the floor urging the hearing of a motion who
I recollect to have been counsel for the defendant, the wife, and
he said in the course of his remarks that his client denied that
she had been guilty of adultery, and was in court—he had
brought her into court—and the remark which attracted my

[1] Tweed Ring Investigation, p. 147.

attention was from Judge Barnard substantially to this effect:
'What of that, do you think I can tell whether she has committed adultery by looking at her?'

"Q. Were those the words?

"A. Those were not the precise words."

Further questioning of Mr. Birdseye revealed that instead of
the expression "commit adultery" His Honour had used a
more colloquial and a more vivid word.[1]

While the Erie Railroad fight with the Albany and Susquehanna
Railroad was going on, and when Judge Barnard was granting
injunctions almost daily for the benefit of his good friends Jim
Fisk and Jay Gould, Henry J. Raymond, editor of the New
York *Times* and opponent of Judge Barnard's methods and
habits, died, and Dorman B. Eaton, a lawyer opposed to
Barnard, was assaulted on the street in New York. Arthur
Johnes, a newspaper reporter, testified in the impeachment
proceedings which were subsequently brought against Judge
Barnard that he was present in court when the Judge remarked
casually from the bench: "My enemies are very unfortunate; one
of them went home from his woman and fell down dead in his
house; another tried to make a little capital by getting himself
knocked on the head, but got hit a little too hard."[2] When the
charges concerning Judge Barnard's language on the bench
were read during the impeachment proceedings which were held
in 1872 at Saratoga, a large number of ladies were seen to rise
hurriedly and leave the courtroom for the more congenial
atmosphere of the springs.

Judge Barnard's own attorney, William H. Beach, gave the
Court of Impeachment this estimate of his client's character:

"I am frank to say I do not approve all the acts of this
respondent. I think, sir, bad mannered as I am, I might be
able to improve him in dignity of demeanor and suavity of
address. He has been educated, as have been many of our sons,
in a rude school. He is a man of action, bold in his convictions,
fearless in their expression. He is not the kind of metal of which

[1] *Charges Against Justice George G. Barnard, and Testimony Thereunder, Before the
Judiciary Committee of the Assembly*, pp. 554-555.

[2] *Proceedings of the Court of Impeachment in the Matter of George G. Barnard*, Vol. I,
pp. 537 ff.

tools and instruments are made. He might become a daring leader of bold adventurers, were he not well grounded upon principle. But never, sir, could he be made the petty and insignificant puppet of meaner men. If he descends to crime, it will be with a bravery which sometimes adds dignity to its commission."[1]

It was just such a man whom Tweed and Sweeny needed for their plans, and, whether or not they can be termed dignified, the crimes of this band were committed with an audacity that by some might be called bravery.

Barnard was a tall, handsome man, whose hair was slightly tinged with gray, and whose moustache was jet-black, with a suggestion of dye. His eyes were shiny, and his complexion olive. In his dress he maintained the proper eccentricity to satisfy his peculiar sense of notoriety, and on occasions of state as well as relaxation he always wore an extraordinary white felt hat.

The other Tweed Ring judge, Albert Cardozo, was a man of more dignity and reserve than Judge Barnard, but he was ambitious. One of his bitter opponents said of him at the time that "he had the eyes of a serpent looking from the face of a corpse."

Tweed not only made his own judges, but he also manufactured lawyers of young men who desired to be made such. It was required by law that a candidate for admission to the bar must take an examination in open court of the General Term of the Supreme Court. The rules of admission were under the control of the three judges of this court, Barnard, Cardozo, and Ingraham. Matthew P. Breen, who had a contemporary knowledge of the politics of the period, gave an account of the special examination to which fourteen candidates approved by Tweed were treated. Breen wrote:

"As there is no official record of the facts, I cannot vouch for the authenticity of the following account of the examination, which was current at the time. But many well-known citizens living to-day remember the incident of which I write.

"Knowing that the applicants for admission were waiting for

---
[1]*Op. Cit.*, Vol. III, p. 1857.

the magician's wand to transform them into lawyers, Judge Barnard said to one of his associates on the Bench that he was 'going to have some fun with the boys.' On behalf of the General Term he conducted the 'special' examination. With mock gravity he put them through a catechism of which, it is said, the subjoined is a specimen:

"Q. 'Senator,' (addressing one of them) 'do you know there is such a thing as the State Constitution?'

"A. 'Yes, sir.'

"Q. 'If a proposed bill came up for consideration, which you knew was in violation of the Constitution, what would you do?'

"A. 'I would move to suspend the Constitution; same as we sometimes suspend the Rules of the Senate to pass a bill.'

"'Stand aside,' said the Judge with a smile, 'you will make a profound lawyer.'

"'Now, sir,' said the Judge, addressing Mr. Daniel Breezy, 'if you had a claim for a client of $50,000 against the City, what would be the first step you would take to recover it?'

"'I would go and see Bill Tweed,' was the sagacious answer.

"'You will make your mark as a Corporation lawyer,' said the Judge, amidst great merriment.

"The examinations of the other applicants were of a character somewhat similar to the foregoing."[1]

II

We have already noted that Tweed and Sweeny gained control of Tammany Hall and sent Fernando Wood to Congress. This ascendancy gave them the dictatorship of nominations to municipal offices, and what they needed after that was control of elections, so that their candidates might be assured of election to those offices where they were so badly needed if the machinations of the Ring were to be successful. They managed this by means of wholesale and open fraud. New York had suffered from rowdy and corrupt elections before Tweed and his associates were born, but the elections held under their auspices were corrupt on an unprecedented scale and frankly dishonest.

[1] *Thirty Years of New York Politics*, by Matthew P. Breen, pp. 157–159.

Tweed testified before the Board of Aldermen concerning election frauds during his reign:

"Q. Now, Mr. Tweed with regard to elections—to the management of the elections for the city and county officers— and generally, the elections for the city and county: When you were in office, did the Ring control the elections in this city at that time?

"A. They did, sir; absolutely.

"Q. Please tell me what the *modus operandi* of that was. How did you control the election?

"A. Well, each ward had a representative man, who would control matters in his own ward, and whom the various members of the general committee were to look up to for advice how to control the elections.

"Q. The General Committee of Tammany Hall?

"A. Of the regular organization. . . .

"Q. What were they to do, in case you wanted a particular man elected over another?

"A. Count the ballots in bulk, or without counting them announce the result in bulk, or change from one to the other, as the case may have been.

"Q. Then these elections really were no elections at all? The ballots were made to bring about any result that you determined upon beforehand?

"A. The ballots made no result; the counters made the result. . . . That was generally done in every ward by the gentleman who had charge of the ward. . . .

"Mr. Cole: Mr. Tweed, did you ever give any directions to any persons, to falsify or change the result of the actual *bona fide* ballots cast in any election?

"A. More in the nature of a request than a direction."[1]

During the Civil War elections had been held in New York City with great difficulty and with much attendant corruption. At the time of the election of 1862, the War Department commanded marshals to guard each polling place in the City, with orders to arrest any person who might attempt to vote and who had previously declined military service on the grounds that he

---

[1] Tweed Ring Investigation, pp. 133–137.

was not a citizen of the United States. Tammany Hall resented this serious interference with its business, and at a public mass meeting held the day before the election Tammany leaders announced that protection against such arrest would be provided for voters. Tammany Hall insisted that the Republican national administration under Lincoln was attempting to intimidate Democratic voters by threats of arrest. It was also announced in Tammany Hall that the organization had engaged the best lawyers to defend its voters, and that Judge Barnard and Recorder Hoffman would be in attendance all day to issue writs of *habeas corpus* for any Democrats who were arrested.

Two years later, in 1864, when Abraham Lincoln was a candidate for reëlection, General Benjamin F. Butler was sent to New York City with six thousand soldiers, for it had been rumoured that the election would be highly disorderly and that the Confederate government had its agents in New York and in Canada fomenting this disorder. At the time the City was filled with persons who were taking advantage of the conditions created by the Civil War to earn their livings by various forms of swindling and rowdyism. "Men who would enlist, receive bounty, desert, reënlist and redesert a half score of times or more," wrote John I. Davenport, "plundering the nation, state and city each time, would not and did not hesitate to perpetrate any fraud upon the ballot box which their recklessness or ingenuity could devise."[1]

In 1865, a stricter registration law was passed in the effort to curb the frauds of Tweed and his associates, who in that year intended to elect John T. Hoffman Mayor of New York. In spite of the strict law, men were registered in hordes from false addresses, and ballot boxes were smashed to pieces in districts hostile to the interests of the Tweed Ring.

The election of the following year, 1866, was preceded by a riotous meeting in City Hall Park. Tammany Hall was attempting to force the election of Mayor Hoffman as Governor. Three days before election the opposition to Tammany Hall organized a mass meeting in City Hall Park at which General Benjamin F. Butler, Horace Greeley, and Governor Curtin of Pennsylvania were to speak. A mob of Tammany men, supporters of Mayor Hoffman for Governor, mixed with the

[1] *The Election and Naturalization Frauds in New York City*, 1860–1870, p. 70.

crowd, and their leaders directed them in remarks that were intended to interfere with the speakers. When General Butler began his address, he was hooted vehemently; an apple was thrown at him and struck him in the breast. He picked it up, took out his pocket knife and began to cut the apple and to eat it. The crowd was captivated for a few minutes by this gesture, but the leaders continued to foment trouble, and finally General Butler lost patience and told the mob what he thought of them in the following words:

"I have hung your betters (cheers), and if you do not behave I shall get the chance to do the same to you. (Three cheers for Butler.) I have seen many more than you with arms in their hands, with minie rifles and muskets and bayonets, and I did not flinch from them. Do you suppose I shall flinch from onion-stinking breaths? (Laughter, groans and cheers.) You, the hooters here, think you are the equal of the negro, oh! no! (Tremendous cheers and groans.) The negro is as much, as immeasurably your superior, as heaven is above the hell where you are going. (Cheers and groans.) I do not respect you, and I certainly do not want your respect. You may be sure I do not fear you. You are not to overpower free speech and free thought, and insane howlings will not take the place of argument. Now then, men of the Five Points (laughter and cheers), bullies of the bawdy house! thieves of the lobby! and burglars of the Tombs (laughter, cheers, groans and howls, resembling a chorus of pandemonium), I simply declare here, as the voice of this nation, that you are not fit for the exercise of the elective franchise (great excitement), and in no better way than this could you demonstrate the fact."[1]

It was, however, at the election of 1868, when A. Oakey Hall was running for Mayor, that Tammany and the Tweed Ring practised their frauds on the largest scale. Tweed was questioned some years later concerning this election, and testified as follows:

"Q. Can you state now, at this time, whether the election which took place in the City of New York at that time [1868] was a fair and honest election?

"A. I have not the details in my memory.

[1]Davenport, p. 89.

THE GREEK SLAVE.

THE SLAVE DRIVERS.

"Q. What is your best impression?

"A. I don't think there is ever a fair or honest election in the City of New York. . . . I think that was the year in which a great many people were naturalized. . . .

"Q. Was that the year the Inspectors of Election lumped the votes and declared them without counting the vote?

"A. I shouldn't be surprised if it was . . . . I think it was. . . .

"Q. What I desire to find out is whether or not the vote which was given in the City of New York wasn't made so as to get some way or other of offsetting the vote which was given from the rest of the State?

"A. I do not know that. I know we took means to prevent them from doing what they wanted to do. . . . Well, one of the means, I know, was to get entire possession of the telegraph wires and keep them busy, one of us proposed to telegraph the whole Bible over them, if it was necessary."[1]

The success of the Tweed Ring depended largely upon their absolute control of the foreign vote, which consisted of about one half the entire vote of the City. According to the census returns of 1870, four ninths of the population of the City at the time the Tweed Ring was in power were foreign born. This condition made naturalization a most important factor in the control of elections, and it was in the process of naturalization that Tammany Hall, under the leadership of the Tweed group, perpetrated its greatest election frauds. The committee of the House of Representatives which investigated the fraudulent election of 1868 took testimony that revealed clearly the methods used to obtain fraudulent naturalization. As the New York *Tribune* remarked at the time, citizens were made "at the rate of a thousand per day with no more solemnity than, and quite as much celerity as is displayed in converting swine into pork in a Cincinnati packing house." Judge Barnard worked hard for his Tammany friends in the few weeks before the election of 1868. Charles E. Loew, clerk of the County of New York at the time, testified reluctantly that from October 6th to October 23rd Judge Barnard remained in the Supreme Court from six o'clock at night until midnight issuing naturali-

[1]Tweed Ring Investigation, p. 225.

zation papers, which were designed for use in the coming election. In the fourteen days from the 8th of October to the 23rd of that month Judge Barnard naturalized 10,093 men.

Tammany Hall established offices in the City where foreigners could obtain naturalization papers and witnesses who would swear that they had been in the country long enough to become citizens. Henry Butts, who worked for the United States marshals engaged in investigating naturalization frauds, and who himself obtained naturalization papers at the rate of three for five dollars, testified: "There are men in New York whom you can buy to make a false oath for a glass of beer. These men hang around such places, and are always ready to go into court to represent parties; one assuming such a name, the other assuming such a name." Tammany Hall engaged the New York Printing Company, which Tweed owned, to print 105,000 blank applications and 69,000 certificates of naturalization. Tammany Hall also paid the fees required by the clerk of the court for naturalization papers and gave foreigners red tickets which entitled them to their papers free; more than 40,000 such tickets were issued in 1868.[1]

The Republican Party in New York was also in the business of naturalization, and it gave different-coloured tickets to its adherents, but as the party appealed less to foreigners, the Republican trade was not so extensive as Tammany Hall's.

Theodore Allen testified before the Congressional Committee:

"I keep a public house, and a man by the name of James Goff and his brother, who were engaged in procuring naturalization certificates, used to come to my house a great deal. I saw a number of papers that were sent to Connecticut. I saw the two Goffs have 500 naturalization papers that they had sold for 50 cents apiece to send to Connecticut. I suppose 1,000 were sent to Brooklyn that I saw them have. They contracted for these papers, they said, at 50 cents a head. They were to send them to Brooklyn and Hartford, I believe. . . .

"I have lived in New York for 32 years. I have had my public house about a year. . . . 'St. Bernard' is the name of the hotel. The Goffs have always resided, I think, in Thompson

---

[1]House Report No. 41 on Election Frauds in New York, 1868, pp. 12–13, 20.

street; they are kept by girls. I was married, but my wife is dead. No girls keep me, but my bank is always open when the girls come after me. I will say this, however, that while I have lived in New York for 32 years, and while I know more women than any other man, yet I never was in a whorehouse but once in my life; I have been there on business, but just to go in and come right out. Whenever any of them get arrested I am very apt to be called on to get some of them out, and I also have to help the fellows out sometimes. I associate with any one who comes in my house and takes a drink and goes out and behaves himself. I do not allow any women in my house. . . . I voted the republican ticket last fall, but I was not in the employ of the party. I have a brother in New York named John Allen, but he is not the one known as the 'wickedest man' in New York.

"I did not count the papers that the Goffs had, but I counted some that the police came and took out of my house when they left there; that was between 50 and 60. Goff was not stopping at my house then, but his girl lived in Thompson street. I think I saw Goff have over 4,000 naturalization papers last fall, and over 10,000 during the last three years. These papers were all signed and sealed, ready for sale. They were gotten in all the courts that issued naturalization papers. . . . I think at one time they got as many as 500, and at other times as many as 100, 200 and 300, without producing any men at all. . . . They told me they got them from a clerk named McKean. . . . They had almost all the business that was done over here at court. . . . I have myself seen them getting papers in all the courts. They would often have 10 or 15 men, whom they would pass through and have sworn some 20 or 30 times under different names. They could thus grind out a great deal of corn in a very little while. There are a great many other parties whom I know to have been engaged in this business, but I would rather not mention names. As it is insisted on I will name them: Patrick McCaffrey, Moran, McCay, John Norton, Dougherty, Heffron, Mitchell, and O'Brien. I know a great many others, but I cannot now recall their names."[1]

A man named Rosenberg sold naturalization papers for Tammany Hall at an office in a saloon at No. 6 Centre Street.

[1]House Report No. 41, pp. 824–825.

He agreed to furnish blank naturalization papers to be filled in with anyone's name for two dollars each. Robert Murray, United States Marshal at New York, talked with Rosenberg after he was caught by the authorities. "Said I," Murray testified, "'Rosenberg, what possessed you to go into this business?' Said he, 'Mr. Murray, every certificate that you have purchased from me is genuine, and came out of the court room. I am at work for the democratic party, and paid for this thing. I get but very little of the $2 that is paid for these certificates.'"

Maximilian Boeck, a native of Bavaria, testified concerning his experience when he went to the City Hall to get naturalized:

"Q. Was there any man in the City Hall that proposed to be a witness for you for $5?

"A. No; he asked me for $2.

"Q. Did you go out in the hall and ask the man if he would be a witness for you?

"A. No; he came up and told me, 'You have got a witness?' I say, 'Well, no, I have not got a witness here, but my boarding-house boss will be here; I had not time to go up and fetch him.' The man that gave me the papers I gave $2. He asked me, 'Do you want a large or a small paper,' and he showed me one for $3, one for $2, and one for 50 cents, and I said, 'I like better this'; and he gave me this for $2."[1]

Election inspectors testified to their experiences with foreigners who attempted to register on false naturalization papers that they had purchased. When some of them were closely questioned at the polls on registration day, they forgot themselves and admitted they had obtained their naturalization papers at Tammany Hall. At one polling place nine men were waiting in line to be registered. The inspector of elections remarked, "We are acting altogether too lenient in this matter; the next man who offers a fraudulent paper I shall order his arrest." The nine men picked up their naturalization papers and walked hurriedly out of the polling place.

John McArthur, Jr., a member of the New York Police Board, testified:

[1]House Report No. 41, p. 138.

"Denis Fitzpatrick came to the 27th election district of the 19th ward, situated on Third avenue, between Eighty-third and Eighty-fourth streets, and wanted his name registered; one of the inspectors, Mr. Reed, asked him how long he had that paper; he said about two weeks; I then asked him if he had appeared in any court to get that paper; he said he had not; I asked him where he got it, and he said that he got it at McGinnis's porter house, in Eighty-seventh street, in Third avenue; I asked him who gave it to him, and he said he did not know; that it was a little fellow, about my size; I then took him to the station-house."[1]

Tweed and his associates were not satisfied merely with naturalizing hordes of men who had not been in the country long enough and then voting them for the Tammany Hall candidates, but they also organized wholesale repeating at the polls in 1868. The committee of the House of Representatives investigating these frauds reported:

"On the 30th and 31st of October, when only two days intervened until the day of the election, gangs or bodies of men hired for the purpose, assembled at these headquarters where they were furnished with names and numbers, and under a leader or captain, they went out in ones and twos and threes and tens and dozens, in nearly every part of the city, registering many times each, and when the day of election came these repeaters, supplied abundantly with intoxicating drinks, and changing coats, hats, or caps, as occasion required to avoid recognition or detection, commenced the work of 'voting early and often,' and this was carried on by these vagabonds until, wearied and drunken, night closed on the stupendous fraud which their depravity had perpetrated.

"With all the concealment which cunning could invent, or perjury secure, or bribery purchase, or the fear of punishment inspire, or the dread of violence from bands of conspirators and democratic desperadoes could command, or the blandishment of more accomplished knaves could entice, or the hopes of office could buy, or fear of the loss of place could bring, all of which would naturally conspire to throw obstacles in the way

[1]House Report No. 41, pp. 28, 40, 41.

of or defeat the investigation of the committee, it is by no means possible that the extent of these frauds has been revealed even in any one ward."[1]

John J. Mullen testified to his experience as a repeater for the Tammany Hall Democrats:

"Q. State what you know of persons registering on false names prior to the last presidential election in this city.

"A. On the first registering day I was going down Cortlandt street, near the corner of Washington, when I met a young man, whom I recognized as Matthew Strip; he keeps a grocery store in Albany street. He requested me to go in and register. I stated that I did not belong in that district. He said it made no difference. I went in and registered under the name of J. J. Mullen, of 156 Greenwich street. The registering clerk knew me, and knew that I did not reside there. He gave me a wink that it was all right. . . . While I was in there, some 18 or 20 persons came in with papers and registered from 41 Vesey street. The other clerk, who was opposed to it, passed an insinuation that it must be a very large house as some 40 had already registered from there. I came out from there about 6 o'clock in the evening, and was requested to go down to Washington street, near Albany, where they were registering. There I registered again. I met Strip again there, and Dennis Hogan, brother of the Police Justice Edward Hogan; they asked me if I had registered there yet. I told them no; they told me to go in. . . . I went in and registered, and then Hogan said it was all right. From there I went with Strip and Hogan to 34 Greenwich street and registered there, giving my residence as No. 12 Washington Street. Then I went to Patrick Moore's, brother of Alderman John Moore, and had a drink. I had to write there the names and places that I had registered under, and gave the memorandum to the bartender and he put it behind the bar for future reference. Then I started up town, and informed Captain Pettit, of the fifth precinct, that Alderman Moore was issuing naturalization papers, and requested him to send Detective Field to seize them. Alderman Moore

---

[1]House Report No. 41. Report of Majority, pp. 40-45.

in my presence issued out, I suppose, over 200 naturalization papers, taking them two by two out of a cigar box. . . .

"Q. How many persons were engaged in registering at the time you speak of?

"A. The street was crowded with men waiting for their turn to come in, long-shore men, steamboat men, farmers and greenhorns. They got a few glasses of drink and were instructed that on election day they were to get $2 a piece for every time they voted. . . .

"Q. What are the politics of Matthew Strip, Denis Hogan, Police Justice Hogan, Patrick Moore, and Alderman Moore?

"A. They are democrats.

"Q. In the interest of which political party was this registration being made?

"A. The democratic party.

"Q. State if any violence has been threatened to you by reason of your having communicated these facts to police headquarters?

"A. Not many nights ago my wife and I were walking along near Sullivan street, in Broome street, and I got a blow that knocked me senseless. I heard a voice singing out: 'That is the son of a bitch who sold us! Kill him! Kill him!' My wife screeched 'Murder!' Two colored women threw themselves on the top of me, and two colored boys shouted 'Murder!' I do not know where the police were. When I came to I ran to the station-house. My wife lost her hat and cloak. They knocked her down for howling, and it appeared that these colored women were the only persons to save me. I went up in the morning and made a complaint against Higgins and his brother, and several other persons whose faces I recognized. I thought I saw a knife, but I have been since informed it was a revolver. I know there is a hole in my hat; but whether it was made by a bullet, or by a knife, I do not know. I went to Police Justice Dodge in the morning, and stated the case to him just as it occurred. He told me to go to Judge Dowling, at the Tombs, as I lived in the 5th precinct. I went to Judge Dowling, and he told me to clear out.

"Q. What are his politics?

"A. He is a democrat; so is Dodge. Then I went down to the district attorney's office. There were two clerks in there and Mr. Gunning S. Bedford, now city judge. I stated the case to them, and they told me that if Dodge and Dowling took no notice of it they would not. I told them that I would appeal to the public for protection. I came up and went into the *News* office to have a statement written out, but they would not publish it, and would not have anything to do with it. . . ."

Cross-examined by Mr. Ross, Mullen said:

"Q. What is your business?

"A. I am a canvasser for Mr. Purrington, 28 Barclay street, for a patent carpet sweeper. . . .

"Q. Did you know it was unlawful to register in that way?

"A. Yes.

"Q. What made you do it?

"A. To get in with these parties, and to find out what kind of a swindle was going on, in order that I might expose them.

"Q. Who put you up to do this?

"A. Superintendent of Police John A. Kennedy; he told me to find out all that I could. . . .

"Q. How did you come here?

"A. I read an account in the New York *Herald* the other day about the investigation of this committee, and I came to Marshal Murray and asked him if he did not recollect when I came to him and offered to work this thing up for a little money. As I was a canvasser I could get into the confidence of longshore men by giving them a few glasses of rot-gut, and could coax them and ascertain where the papers were [false naturalization papers] . . .

"Q. How many times have you been convicted of criminal offence?

"A. I have been convicted twice; that is all I recollect.

"Q. No more than twice?

"A. I have been convicted twice for assault and battery and twice for petty larceny. . . .

"Q. When were you convicted first of larceny?

"A. In 1866.

"Q. What did you steal that time?

"A. I did not steal anything. I was a city messenger, and got a package to deliver; I lost my receipt-book, and got intoxicated, and was brought to the Tombs. They tried me seven different times in the court, and each time remanded me. I told the judge at last that if I was innocent he should discharge me, and if I was guilty he should punish me, and he gave me six months in the penitentiary for my impudence.

"Q. What did you steal the other time?

"A. There was a poor girl in Hudson street living a life of prostitution, and she applied to me to get her clothes from the washwoman to go home. When I went for them the wash-woman was out; and I shoved the door in and took the girl's clothes and went and pawned them, and then started with my wife to give the girl the $2 I had raised in the pawn office. It was for stealing these clothes I was convicted; it was the wrong clothes I took. My wife was arrested for it, and I went up and said it was I who took the goods, and they let my wife go and held on to me. . . .

"Q. What was your sentence?

"A. Six months' imprisonment and $100 fine. . . .

"Q. After you had been registered in the way you have stated, you saw Superintendent Kennedy?

"A. Yes.

"Q. How did you happen to see him after you registered?

"A. I went first to the 5th ward station-house, and told Captain Pettit how these parties were working. He told me to wait till Detective Field would come in, and he would send him with me. I waited for a whole day, but Field did not come. Then I went to the 3d ward station-house and notified Captain Ullmann. He told me I had better start up to police headquarters, and notify Superintendent Kennedy. Then I went to police headquarters. I started down to Moore's and had a drink there. While I was in there, Alderman Moore, brother to Patrick Moore, came running in and said, 'Some God damned son of a bitch has been up and told Captain Ull-mann that we were issuing papers by the hundreds to all who came along.' The alderman then rushed in behind the bar and grabbed hold of a cigar box where the papers were kept. I was sitting at a round table in the back room, where I suppose there were over 200 of us. He upset a table in his haste to get up stairs with these naturalization papers, and ran up stairs, and I immediately sneaked. The alderman's brother said, 'If I knew the son of a bitch who did that he would not leave the ward with his life.' I knew then it was Captain Ullman who gave me away. I went up to accuse him to his face. I said to the officers there, 'He has been down there and betrayed the whole secret, and I am going up to police headquarters to make a complaint against him. I started to the Eighth ward station-house, but I could get nobody to assist me. I then went up to police headquarters and saw Superintendent Kennedy, and a reporter wrote down my statement, and I swore to it."[1]

Police Justice Edward Hogan, a Tammany official, testified concerning Mullen's character:

"Q. Was this man, Mullen, ever brought before you for any criminal offence?

"A. My best recollection now is that he was brought before me four or five times for stealing, and for assaulting his wife at a house of prostitution; she being the complainant. He beat her there because she would not give him the money which she earned by prostituting her person. That was the charge."[2]

After the Tammany organization had registered hundreds of names at different polling places, and after careful mémoranda of these names were collected, as in Patrick Moore's cigar box behind his bar, on the day of election gangs of men were organized and taken to the polls to vote the Democratic ticket on those names. Unfortunately for the leaders of Tammany, however, many of the men who repeated for them were cheated out of their promised rewards, and it was these men who revealed the process before the Congressional Committee. The system was to get the men drunk, so that they did not care how many times they voted, and then to take them about the City to various polling places, giving them pieces of paper with the names on which they were to vote. William Wilson, a hat and bonnet presser, testified:

"I voted a good many times myself at that election; I cannot tell how many times; I voted once in Canal street; I was in-

---

[1]House Report No. 41., pp. 642–648.
[2]Ibid., p. 666.

toxicated most of the day and could not recollect where I voted.

"Q. Can you remember whether you voted more than once?

"A. I could not exactly say whether I did nor not; I got pretty drunk after I voted the first time. . . .

"Q. Who made you drunk?

"A. A lot of men that were with me; and I made a darned fool of myself. . . .

"Q. What did you get for voting?

"A. Nothing at all.

"Q. What were you promised?

"A. I supposed I should get $5 or $6.

"Q. Did you get it?

"A. No, sir.

"Q. Who promised you the $5 or $6?

"A. A whole lot of men; I do not know any of them from a bunch of beets."[1]

Groups of repeaters were organized in lodging houses and cheap hotels for men only, some of which were owned by prominent Tammany district workers. One of these Tammany hotel proprietors and district workers was Florence Scannell. William A. Jenner, an election inspector, testified:

"At the elections in November there were from 30 to 50 persons registered from the Compton House. Most of them were young men, ranging from 21 to 25 years of age. They used to come in late in the evening, in groups of four or five. With most groups Florence Scannell came. Each of these young men was challenged by me, and the oath administered. On each occasion Scannell prompted them to answer correctly the questions. Each of them said that he lived at the Compton House, and on my attempting to inquire what they understood as a residence at the Compton House, they would in some cases say that they paid their board by the day; in some cases by the week. That they slept there two or three nights out of the week, and the rest of the time they slept with their mistresses.

"Q. And Scannell used to come all the time?

"A. Not all the time; I think about half the time.

[1]House Report No. 41, pp. 512–514.

"Q. How many of these groups told you that they slept with their mistresses?

"A. I think they told that in about a dozen instances. . . .

"Q. Where does this man Scannell live now?

"A. He is one of the proprietors of the Compton House, corner of Twenty-third street and Fourth avenue."[1]

George Hill, an unemployed man, testified:

"Q. How often did you vote that day?

"A. I voted 9 or 10 times in different election districts in this city, mostly in the 8th ward. . . . The crowd went around with me and voted at the same time, so far as I know. When we met at the corner of Hester and Wooster streets a man, whose name I don't know, said to me if I would vote for him he would get me employment, or something to do. I said, 'All right, I will vote for you.' . . .

"Q. What ticket did you vote?

"A. The Democratic ticket right clean through. We voted in the first place in Green street, near Spring. We voted there three times each. . . . I was pretty full all day, and I cannot recollect how many times I voted at each place. . . .

"Q. I suppose these parties with you thought they were doing perfectly right in doing this way.

"A. I suppose they were hard up, as I was. I don't think there was any harm in it. I was very hard up and I had to steal, or do something to get a living.

"Q. You do not think it was wrong, then?

"A. I do not know as it is; even if I did I would have done it.

"Q. Who was this man that employed you?

"A. I do not know. . . .

"Q. Did he pay you for your services?

"A. Not much of anything. He gave me something to drink and something to eat. I did not see any money.

"Q. What else did he give you?

"A. He gave me some stamps and agreed to give me a good deal more. He promised me more, but did not fulfil his promise.

"Q. You think you were cheated, then?

"A. I think so."[2]

---

[1] House Report No. 41, pp. 50–51.

[2] *Ibid.*, pp. 482–483.

Edward Clark testified:

"I live at 46 Essex street, with George Hyam, a soap manufacturer. My business is card writing. I voted at the last election 15 or 18 times. . . . I voted the democratic ticket—the
Seymour ticket. The evening previous to the election I was met
by two men, who asked me if I wanted to make a few dollars.
They said there was no risk in it. They furnished drink and
liquor, and cigars. . . . We had drinks between each voting. I
put in two votes at the next place, changing my hat and coat
after all the rest had voted. Then we came to East Broadway,
and I put one vote in there. They promised to give me $10 for
each vote; but they got me so drunk that I did not know what
I was about. I found them next morning in the bar-room of the
New England Hotel, and asked why they did not pay me. They
said, 'You have put in 28 votes, and we have paid you $28.' I
am a native of Prussia. I cannot tell the names of any of the
gang. I know one or two by sight. There were five besides myself in voting. . . .

"When I asked for money for voting they licked me. That
is the reason I make this statement. I want satisfaction. I
got nothing for repeating except what I had to eat and drink.
My politics are republican. I do not like the democrats much.
I have got a grudge against them. I have been in the army, and
fought for a different party altogether than the party I voted
for."[1]

Francis Murray, a longshoreman, gave the following testimony:

"I voted three times, I believe. I was pretty full. . . .
"Q. In what districts?
"A. I could not tell you as to that. I was pretty full of whiskey
to tell the truth about it.
"Q. Where did you procure the names and numbers to vote
upon?
"A. They came to my house, a party of them. . . . I could not
give their names. There were about fifteen of them, I should
think. They wanted me to go out with them. I was pretty full,

[1] House Report No. 41, pp. 626-627.

and went along with them, and I could not tell you where it was—betwixt what streets I voted—to save my soul from the gallows; and I don't want to tell any lies about it. . . . There was a slip of paper handed me; I could not tell the name or the number; I was under the influence of liquor. . . . I was to have some money—five dollars.

"Q. Who proposed to pay that?

"A. I could not tell you; it was betwixt the party; they were to make it up betwixt them. They got me pretty well liquored up. That is something I am not in the habit of doing; I am a poor boy and have got a mother and two sisters to support, and work pretty hard to support them.

"Q. You were pretty drunk, were you?

"A. Yes, sir, I was pretty full, to tell the truth and no lie whatever.

"Q. What time in the day did you get drunk?

"A. I got drunk early in the morning. I was drunk all day. . . . I am pretty certain I voted three times.

"Q. Still you were not sober enough to know certainly whether you did or not?

"A. No, sir; I would not swear to a thing I am not positive of.

"Q. After the second time you were so drunk you cannot recollect anything about it?

"A. No, sir; I was pretty drunk.

"Q. You have no knowledge of what ticket you voted?

"A. I voted the democratic ticket. I would not vote the republican ticket, I never did and never would. I am democratic to the back-bone. . . .

"Q. Did you get the $5?

"A. I did, sir; it was made up betwixt the party, and a fellow came and slipped it in my hand. . . .

"Q. What business are you in?

"A. I work on the docks; anything that I can get hold of. . . .

"Q. Did you know it was wrong to vote more than once?

"A. Well, I don't know that I could say I knew it was wrong, because I cannot read or write; I always had to work hard for what I got.

"Q. Were you willing to commit a criminal offence for the sake of getting five dollars?

"A. No, sir; I would never have done it if I had not done it under the influence of liquor. . . .

"Q. Whom do you work for?

"A. I work for anybody I have to work for.

"Q. How long have you been out of employment, if at all?

"A. I could get work to-day, but I left it to come up here; on the pier, 47 East River.

"Q. What were you to have for your day's work?

"A. I was to have two dollars, that is if I was to work on the dock.

"Q. What were you to have for coming here?

"A. Nothing said about it.

"Q. Nothing said about five dollars, or about pay

"A. Nothing whatever to me."[1]

Many of the men used by Tweed and Tammany as repeaters were, like Francis Murray, unable to read and write, and some of them even forgot the names they were supposed to be assuming for the occasion. In one of the districts, it was said, an Irishman came in to vote. "What name?" asked the inspector. "Michael Murray, sir," he answered. "Michael Murray? No such name on the list," the inspector said. "There's a Michael Murphy." "Hould on, gintlemen, hould on, gintlemen," said the voter, "hould on," and he pulled a piece of paper from his pocket. "Sure and it *is* Michael Murphy, instid of Michael Murray!"[2]

Tammany also employed criminals to do the repeating. William H. Greene, a patrolman on the New York City police force, was stationed at the registry booth in the Seventh Ward in 1868 from eight o'clock in the morning until one o'clock in the afternoon. He testified:

". . . During that time a gang came there from the Bowery; I knew several of them personally by name; I knew that they did not live in the ward, much less in the district; there were some twenty or twenty-one of them. . . .

"I knew the best portion of these men. There are several of

---

[1]House Report No. 41, pp. 605–608.

[2]*The Election and Naturalization Frauds in New York City*, by J. I. Davenport. pp. 95–96.

them who have got several *aliases*. None of them live in the
district where they were registered. Here is a photograph of
one of them who gave the name of Henry Lawrence. He has
an *alias* of Charles Williams, and an *alias* of 'Nipsey.' He was
the leader of the gang. I got this picture at the station-house,
where they have got pictures of all of these celebrated men who
live by their wits.

"Q. State how this picture was taken.

"A. 'Nipsey' objected to having his likeness taken and made
all kinds of faces, and two men had to hold him, so as to get
his likeness as accurate as possible. He registered from 169
Henry street, Coroner Keenan's house. He is a celebrated pickpocket. He has stolen fortunes, and has been arrested several
times, but somehow or other he always slips through and is
never prosecuted.

"Q. Do you know the political party he acts with?

"A. Yes, sir, the democratic. . . .

"The registrars did not know these men at all, until I pointed
them out. The thing went so far that I said to the registrars,
'Now this thing is played out. Here, by George, are thieves
from the Bowery coming to register from houses where they
do not live and I think you ought to put a stop to it.' One of
the registrars spoke up and said, 'We'll lay for them on election day.' There is always a proclamation issued by the mayor,
offering $100 for the apprehension of illegal voters, and the
registrars thought they would 'lay' for these men until election
day. . . . A few days after that I was notified to go down into
the sixth ward to do duty. I did not know what I had done to
be changed; I had done nothing wrong, but the thought struck
me that it was for being a little efficient about the registry.

"Q. Do you know whether you were transferred at the instance of Police Justice Shandley?

"A. I do know perfectly well, because I was told so by Commissioner Acton and by Shandley himself. Shandley came down
and said he would get me off the police, and would kick my
damned head off, calling me a damned big bull-head."[1]

Many of the election inspectors were threatened with violence when they attempted to interfere with false registration

---

[1] House Report No. 41, p. 315.

and voting, which was the function they were supposed to serve. Abraham De Voursney, who acted as an inspector of elections in the Sixth Ward during this election, testified:

"At that time there was a string of voters probably thirty to forty in length, and Haggerty said he would advise any one to chuck us over the counter if we challenged another one of them. . . . I think it next to impossible for any man to go down and get a square vote at that precinct unless he had a regiment of soldiers with fixed bayonets. I think it is the next thing to impossible. That is my opinion, based on my experience as an inspector, and on my having served eight years in the police department."[1]

Abraham Baker, another election inspector, testified:

"About 4 o'clock in the afternoon the crowd got around me and threatened my life, so that I was advised I had better leave, and did so, as I did not want to be killed. . . ."[2]

Tammany Hall wished to discredit this testimony concerning its methods by proving that the Republicans also employed repeaters. How some of this counter testimony was obtained was illustrated by the testimony of William Davison:

"I went down last evening to get something to eat in a basement in Thompson street, between Spring and Prince. There came down a party of about six. One of them was Charles McCarthy, and another Pete Loftus. One of them came to me, and said he: 'Scotty, do you want to make five dollars?' (That is a kind of name that I am known by among them.) Said I: 'What with?' Said he: 'Go before the committee to-morrow, and I will get five dollars into your hand.' Said I: 'What have I got to say?' Said he: 'All you have got to do is to go before the committee and tell them how many times you repeated last election for the republican party, that you voted five or six times for Grant, and that you got five dollars each time; that is all you have got to do.' I said I could not say that. McCarthy,

---

[1] House Report No. 41, pp. 272–273.
[2] Ibid., pp. 304–305.

I believe, was here yesterday afternoon, and so was Pete Loftus, and I believe they got five dollars apiece.

"Q. Did they tell you that?

"A. Yes, sir. They got five dollars apiece. They said it was
a gift, in their strange way of talking. . . .

"Q. What are these men called?

"A. They have nicknames; one of them is Skid, and another
is. Slips. They have a good many nicknames. We never think
of hearing right names anywhere. . . .

"Q. What is the character of these men?

"A. When they get any work, they work; I know them to
run around from one night to the other, loafing here and
there. . . .

"By Mr. Ross [Democratic member of the Committee]:

"Q. What is your business?

"A. I am a boatman, and I sometimes go to sea. . . .

"Q. How long is it since you went to sea?

"A. I quit going to sea two years ago.

"Q. What have you been doing since?

"A. I had the chills and fever last summer.

"Q. Is that all you have been doing?

"A. I have been attending bar once in awhile in the 4th ward
for Ed. Flynn. He keeps a sailors' boarding house. I attended
bar for him about 18 months. . . .

"Q. Who brought you here to impeach those witnesses?

"A. I came myself. I told a friend who got licked the other
night, and he told me to come up here.

"Q. State whether you do not make your living by stealing.

"A. I do not.

"Q. Would you be willing that the police should see you and
say whether you are a thief or not?

"A. Yes, sir."[1]

Several witnesses testified that they repeated at the polls for
the Republican party. Cornelius Doherty testified:

"I voted eight or nine times at the last presidential election.
. . . I voted the full republican ticket; I guess there were 20 or
22 in the gang; they all voted the same ticket; some of them

[1]House Report No. 41, pp. 656–657.

voted 18 or 20 times; I left in the afternoon at 2 o'clock; I voted once under the name of Williams; that is the only name I can recollect; I was promised $25 for voting, but I did not get it. I was not summoned to come here; I came of my own accord; I saw in the *Herald* that the committee was sitting here; I cannot name any prominent republican who knew that repeating was going on; I am an iron moulder by trade, but I have been out of business since last winter; I have attended bar since then for Jacob Rome, 87 Mercer street; he has been sergeant-at-arms for the common council of the city; he will not speak to me because I acted with the republican party.

"Q. Is not Rome a democrat?

"A. So they say; but he has got a brother-in-law a republican. I know that Rome voted the republican ticket for sheriff last year. There are girls at his place. He keeps a dancing-house. I live there with a girl.

"Q. Is she a prostitute?

"A. Yes, sir.

"Q. You are one of that sort of men?

"A. I live with her for my pleasure."[1]

The methods used in the election of 1868 were typical of the methods used by Tammany to win elections before and since. More attention has been placed upon them because of the fact that there is in existence a mass of testimony revealing completely the tactics of the Democrats at this time. None of these things could have been accomplished without the aid and coöperation of the police force, but this was a simple problem, for Tammany always had the foresight to control the police. Perhaps no one single factor was more contributory to the continued success of Tammany Hall than its absolute control of the New York police. We have seen how Fernando Wood fought when the State took the police out of his power, but his successors managed to control the new police force that the Legislature established. Robert Murray, United States Marshal for the southern district of New York, testified before the Congressional Committee that of the 2,300 men on the police force in New York at least 80 per cent. belonged to the Democratic Party. The testimony of the policeman who

[1] House Report No. 41, pp. 632–633.

was zealous on election day has already been quoted, and it will be remembered that he was transferred from his post by Tammany Police Justice Shandley, who also threatened to remove him and to "kick his damned head off."

Tammany also controlled at this time every other department of the city government, and there was only one Republican ward in the entire City in 1868. The men Tammany Hall nominated and elected to public office were corrupt and incompetent. The result was that the physical condition of New York at this time was wretched. Situated as it was on an island, it remained without bridges. The vast produce which came to the City from everywhere in the world was landed on rotten wharves. There was no adequate means of transportation. Thieves ran riot through the streets. The public buildings were dilapidated, and the public places were uncared for. Because of defective sewage and unclean streets, the death rate was abnormal.

The *Times* remarked concerning the dirt in the City's streets: "Hercules would scarcely undertake to remove such an appalling accumulation unless he held a Tammany contract under a ten years' lease. In that event, the Herculean problem, very likely, would be not how to do it, but how not to do it." The Health Department was in an appalling condition. The head of that department in 1864 was Francis I. A. Boole, who appointed as city inspectors the men whose testimony has already been given in another place. Andrew D. White, who was then a member of the legislative committee appointed to investigate the Health Department, wrote in his autobiography that entire districts of the City were "in the worst possible sanitary condition. There was probably at that time nothing to approach it in any city in Christendom save, possibly, Naples."

White quoted the testimony of one of Boole's health inspectors concerning a case of smallpox in his district. He was asked:

"Q. Did you visit this sick person?
"A. No, sir.
"Q. Why did you not?
"A. For the same reason that you would not.
"Q. What was that reason?

"A. I didn't want to catch the disease myself.
"Q. Did the family have any sort of medical aid?
"A. Yes.
"Q. From whom did they have it?
"A. From themselves; they was 'highjinnicks' (hygienics).
"Q. What do you mean by 'highjinnicks'?
"A. I mean persons who doctor themselves."

Judge Whiting, counsel to the investigating committee, asked the other inspectors whether they had any "highjinnicks" in their districts.

"Some answered that they had them somewhat; some thought that they had them 'pretty bad,' others thought that there was 'not much of it,' others claimed that they were 'quite serious'; and finally, in the examination of a certain health officer who was very anxious to show he had done his best, there occurred the following dialogue which brought down the house:

"'Q. (By Judge Whiting) Mr. Health Officer, have you had any "highjinnicks" in your district?'
"'A. Yes, sir.'
"'Q. Much?'
"'A. Yes, sir, quite a good deal.'
"'Q. Have you done anything in regard to them?'
"'A. Yes, sir; I have done all that I could.'
"'Q. Witness, now, on your oath, do you know what the word "highjinnicks" means?'
"'A. Yes, sir.'
"'Q. What does it mean?'
"'A. It means the bad smells that arise from standing water.'"[1]

Not only did the politicians of the period and their henchmen in office neglect the condition of the streets, protect crime, and ignore the requirements of health, but they also actively encouraged robbery by means of prostitution, for it was at the period when Tweed reigned in New York that the panel-house game flourished as it never flourished before or since. In a contemporary book called *The Mysteries and Miseries of the*

---

[1] *Autobiography* of Andrew D. White, Vol. I, pp. 107–110.

Great Metropolis with Some Adventures in the Country, Being the Disguises and Surprises of a New-York Journalist, there is this first-hand description of the panel-house system:

"I determined to strike at once into Mercer Street, the heart of the panel-house district of the Eighth Ward, and where a man, known as the King of the Badger-Pullers, holds his regal sway in more than one house of this class. This man has followed this infamous mode of making money since the bounty business came to an end in 1865. He then opened a panel-house in the eighth precinct, but was driven out of it by Captain Mills. Migrating to the Fourteenth Ward, he was, for a time, very successful in his robberies. But Captain Walsh at last arrested him, his pimps, and his girls, and they were all shipped off to Blackwell's Island for change of air. On gaining his release, this scoundrel betook himself to his old business and has now no less than five houses in full blast, and has acquired his very unenviable title in consequence. He is reported to be worth at least $150,000. Two years ago he was a candidate for the office of assistant alderman on the Democratic ticket; an office for which he had a very good show of election, as he is captain of a very strong political organization, to which all the leading Tammany Hall politicians belong, including the present police-captain of the precinct in which he runs his panel-houses. . . .

"After the exercise for many days of the most delicate and, I flatter myself, skillful diplomacy, we succeeded in worming ourselves into the confidence of the keepers of one of these houses. Through the assistance of a private detective, we discovered a panel-house, the proprietor of which was anxious to retire from the neighbourhood. He had taken a house in Twenty-seventh Street, and did not think he could run two. We soon secured an interview with him, with the ostensible purpose of taking the house off his hands, and on two occasions we passed some time in his private apartments and actually succeeded in witnessing the whole operation of panel-thieving. We carefully inspected all the arrangements and contrivances of the house, with which we expressed our entire satisfaction, and we were as much behind the scenes as the conjurer's assistant or a theatrical machinist at Niblo's Garden. We soon came to the conclusion that no possible precaution on the part of men entering such houses can prevent their being robbed. At each visit we passed an hour in the private room from which the keeper of the house operates, through the panel-door, on the pockets of his victims. On our first gaining admission to the house, the proprietor proceeded to show us over it, criticizing with professional pride, its various arrangements as he went along. 'Perfect! They haven't a chance, sir!' he would constantly remark, and then he would chuckle and rub his hands together with delight at the thought of the ease with which he robbed his victims. This man was apparently about thirty years of age, strongly built, good looking, and well dressed. He certainly did not look like a panel-thief. His assistant was a thin, spare man, some five years older. He moved about with the soft tread and ever-watchful glance of a cat, and with a nervous quickness which at once proclaimed him a skillful operator. He also seemed to enjoy showing the house. The description of the ground-floor will suffice.

"The back-room, in which the panel-worker waits his opportunity, is almost unfurnished, containing only a lounge, two or three common chairs, and a small stove. The door of this room opens on to a private staircase, which leads down to the back basement and into an underground passage, which communicates with the street by a cellar-door. The front-room is a very comfortably furnished apartment, about 18 x 20, with a large fire burning in an open grate, and separated from the back-room by folding doors. The room-door leading into the entrance-passage is close to these doors, and can *apparently* be fastened by a large sliding bolt. This bolt is a false one. The head of the bed, unusually high, is placed edgewise against the wall, to face the windows, with a couch behind it, just clear of the entrance-door. Thus, the victim, when in bed, can neither see the door by which he entered nor the folding-doors. Against the folding-doors, covering the ordinary opening, stands a heavy, marble-topped wash-stand. A large, ponderous looking-glass hangs immediately over it, and two chairs are placed on either side. Between the windows there is a dressing-table, also with a chair on either side. The folding-doors apparently cannot be opened because of the wash-stand and looking-glass and two big bolts. But this is not so. The left-hand door, instead of being hung on hinges from the ordinary casing, has its hinges on the other door, in the centre of the room, and is kept closed by a large, common wooden button-bolt on the other side, in the room in which the panel-thief is concealed.

"Having thoroughly inspected the house, we returned to the back-room, and, with well-assumed ease, and having been posted by the detective in panel-house slang, we threw our-selves on the lounge, lit cigars, and opened a desultory conversa-tion with our host.

"'Staked the captain?'

"'No. We're on the break-up.'

"'Staked the beat?'

"'Yes.'

"'Heavy?'

"'Five dollars a night.'

"For the information of the uninitiated, I will explain the meaning of this conversation; the thieves had not bribed the captain of the precinct, preferring to run the risk of being broken up, but they paid the patrolmen five dollars a night.

"At this moment steps were heard in the passage; the gas was hastily turned down, and all kept breathless silence. An elderly man entered the front-room with a woman, and im-mediately all eyes were eagerly watching through the little peep-holes bored through the wall and doors, and into which pegs are inserted the moment the eye is withdrawn, to prevent the light showing through. The 'sucker', however, as the victim is termed, became alarmed at something, and began to parley with his companion. 'I have been into two houses already, this evening, and have been "rapped out" of each,' he said, 'for what reason I don't know. But, if I'm to be rapped out again, I won't stay.'

"'That sucker,' whispered the proprietor to his assistant, 'has been beat out of his money, and hasn't found it out yet. Don't let him squeal here. Rap him out at once.'

"The elderly gentleman was accordingly rapped out, and all again assumed their seats and cigars. At this moment the assistant discovered that the panel creaked a little, and sug-gested more grease on the hinges.

"'Oh,' replied the head, 'that won't be noticed by the sucker if the girl does her part well.'

"The assistant was about to say something more, when he was seized with a fit of coughing. When it had subsided he laughingly remarked: 'It's very strange, but when there's a sucker in that front-room I couldn't cough to save my life.' The conversation then turned on the number of girls and their lovers who are connected with the house. The rent and other matters were then discussed, and we were beginning to wonder what we could say or do next, when the negro servant, who had been out on an errand, came back in a hurry, and whispered that one of the girls had just passed the house with a sucker.

"'She's that new girl who only came to-night,' said the proprietor to his assistant. 'You had better hop out and work them in. She probably don't know the house in the dark.'

"The assistant kicked off his list slippers, drew on his boots, and was in the act of putting on his coat, when the noise of the opening of the street-door arrested his preparations, the gas was again hurriedly turned down, smoking was forbidden, and the peep-holes again resorted to. A German, about thirty years of age, entered the room with a dark-haired, flashily dressed woman, who immediately requested him to bolt the door. This he did, but he might have saved himself the trouble, for the door was no more closed then than it was before. These bolts are very ingenious. The catch on the jamb of the door, in which the bolt slides, has three false screw-heads in it. In reality, it is not attached to the door-casing at all, but is fastened to the body of the bolt by an unseen plate. Consequently, when the door is opened, the catch goes forward with the remainder of the bolt. This, of course, was not noticed by the man, as the gas was not turned up by the woman till after the door was closed. While the man was bolting the door, the woman hurried to the dressing-table, and hastily laid her hat on one chair and her cloak on the other. This action compelled the man to place his clothes on the couch or on one of the chairs by the folding-doors. Unless this arrangement is carried out, no robbery can be consummated. When all was ready, one of the operators scratched lightly on the door with his finger-nail, to warn the woman he was about to enter the room. The next moment the button was slipped, the man boldly opened the door wide, removed the chair out of his way, and glided rapidly to

the other chair, on which the man's clothes lay. At this moment
the woman redoubled her fascinations, for the purpose of distracting the attention of her victim, in which purpose she was
eminently successful. The work of going through the man's
pockets and what is technically known as 'weeding' his pocketbook, was quickly over, the chair was quietly replaced, the
panel-door closed, and the thief appeared with a roll of bills
in his hand. The whole thing was done in from twenty to
twenty-five seconds. Immediately after the closing of the door,
the second man went outside, and knocking on the passage-
door of the bedroom, said, in a loud whisper:

"'Jenny, here's Joe; hurry up.'

"'My God!' exclaimed the girl, jumping up, 'you must get
away as fast as you can. That's my lover. He's dreadful jealous,
and would shoot you as soon as look at you!'

"It is needless to say that the victim required no pressing
to do as required. He jumps into his clothes as fast as possible,
only too glad to get out of the way before the appearance of
the imaginary terrible lover, and apparently without the
slightest notion that he has been robbed. The panel-men had a
good laugh, in which, as a matter of course, we joined; and
then, thinking we had seen all we wanted to see, we soon after
took our leave, promising to return the following evening to
talk business. We were to pay nine hundred dollars for the
balance of their lease.

"The reader may judge of the risk we ran while in this den
from a remark made by the keeper of it when he read this article: 'If I'd known who that —— —— —— was when he was
in my place he'd have gone out of it in a deal packing-case with
two or three hundred weight of coal around him and been
dumped into the East River!' Our private detective was
present in the bar-room which this thief patronizes when he
thus unbosomed himself."[1]

III

Tweed and his associates, after they had gained control of
Tammany Hall, and, using that as an instrument, had elected
their candidates by means of fraud, took the important strategic
posts in the City's government for themselves. Tweed was now

[1]*Mysteries and Miseries of the Great Metropolis*, pp. 48–62.

Grand Sachem of Tammany Hall and Deputy Street Commissioner of the City of New York; Sweeny was a sachem of
Tammany Hall and City Chamberlain; A. Oakey Hall was
Mayor of New York; and Richard B. Connolly was the City's
comptroller. These four men, with the aid of the judges and
the minor officials whom they purchased, were now in a position to engage in positive stealing on a large scale at the expense
of the people of the City of New York. Previously members of
the Ring had taken money which belonged to the City, but
only indirectly through franchises and contracts and by purchasing real estate where they knew streets were about to be
opened and selling it back again to the City at exorbitant rates.
But now that their oligarchy was completely organized, they
helped themselves to the money in the City's treasury.

The extent of their thefts never has been accurately estimated, and it never can be, for it was so widespread that
all the data for an exact accounting were never available. Estimates of the amount stolen vary from more than $30,000,000
to $75,000,000. Henry M. Taintor, who was employed as a
special accountant for more than six years after the Tweed
Ring frauds were discovered, testified before the investigating
committee of the Board of Aldermen that he had been unable
to trace all the sources of fraud in that time, but that he was
sure it amounted to more than $30,000,000. Matthew J.
O'Rourke, who was instrumental in the discovery of the Tweed
Ring frauds, told Gustavus Myers that "from 1869 to 1871,
the 'Ring' stole about $75,000,000 and that he thought the total
stealings from about 1865 to 1871, counting vast issues of
fraudulent bonds, amounted to $200,000,000."[1]

Some estimate of the extent of the thefts committed by the
Tweed Ring is gained from the increase in the City's debt during
their period of power. An investigating committee of citizens
and aldermen, the Booth Committee, reported in 1871 that the
City debt on January 1, 1869, was $36,293,929.59 and that on
September 4, 1871, it had increased to $97,287,525.03. The New
York *Times* estimated that in the twenty-eight months from
December 31, 1869, to April 30, 1871, the debt of the City had
increased by $50,134,139.

The Tweed Ring made money for its members in a manner so

[1]*History of Tammany Hall*, by Gustavus Myers, revised edition, pp. 248–249.

simple as to require no unusual talents. Every person who received a contract for supplies from the City, or who did work on city buildings and public works, was instructed to raise his bills before submitting them to the City, at first by 55 per cent., later by 60 per cent., and finally by 65 per cent. The face amount of each bill was paid to the contractor by the City Auditor, James Watson, who received back at the time of payment from the contractor or merchant 60 or 65 per cent. of the bill in cash. Watson then acted as paymaster and distributed the share in the plunder to the various members of the Tweed Ring.

Watson, who owed his appointment as City Auditor to Tweed and his associates, had run away from New York in 1850 without paying his debts. He was brought back from California in the custody of a deputy sheriff and placed in Ludlow Street Jail, where he won the admiration of the warden because his penmanship was so neat. The warden placed him in charge of the prison records and then aided him to obtain his discharge. After he was released, he was appointed a collector in the Sheriff's office, at the suggestion of the warden of Ludlow Street Jail. He held that position under three sheriffs, and then he was appointed City Auditor at a salary of $1,500 a year. While Watson was in that office, it became almost a slogan among contractors that, "You must do just as Jimmy tells you, and you will get your money." Jimmy got his share, but he lived with ostentatious modesty in order not to create suspicion. He was fond of gambling, but he always stopped when he began to lose too much, on the grounds that his salary of $1,500 would not permit him to continue. His one luxury was trotting horses, and he owned several that were famous in his day; if James Watson had not loved horses so much, the Tweed Ring might have lasted a few years longer, as we shall see.

One of the Ring's aides-de-camp was Andrew J. Garvey, a plasterer. Garvey did all the plastering for the City of New York, and his bills for this work were so high that he might have done much of the plastering for the world at the same price and still have made a profit. In the month of July, 1869, Garvey's total receipts for plastering were $153,755.14, as recorded in the City's books. In the month of May, 1870, his bills were $394,614.57, and in the following months of June and July he received $945,715.11. For two days' repair work, alleged to have been performed on December 20 and December 21, 1869, Garvey was paid $133,187.20. The New York *Times*, commenting on these figures, said: "A plasterer who can earn $133,187 in two days, and that in the depth of Winter, need never be poor. Altogether Mr. Andrew J. Garvey received in two years—or someone received in his name—the sum of $2,870,464.06. He could certainly afford to give away the odd six cents in charity." Andrew J. Garvey, whom the *Times* always called the Prince of Plasterers, also acted as Grand Marshal at the Fourth of July celebrations in Tammany Hall, and he attended to all the decoration, which he could well afford to do for nothing. He also did plastering work free of charge for various members of the Tweed Ring in their own homes and then charged the work to the City. Before the Ring was organized completely, Garvey was in the habit of calling at Tweed's office in the Street Department and handing him money for his share of the exorbitant bills. But one day Tweed was sitting in the office of the Street Commissioner, George W. McLean, who did not share in the spoils. Garvey entered and handed Tweed a package wrapped loosely in newspaper. It fell to the floor, and Tweed quickly kicked it under the desk. After that embarrassing incident, Tweed instructed Garvey never to bring money to his office again but to deal with Watson or with Woodward, the Ring's assistant paymaster.

Colossal frauds were committed in collusion with Edward E. Jones & Company, stationers to the City. For a period of two years the stationery bills of the City were $2,272,643.39. When Tweed was asked on the witness stand whether there was any corrupt agreement between Jones & Company and any city official, he answered that Jones always paid back a percentage on all the work he received.

"Now, Mr. Tweed," the examining counsel asked, "do you think that two hundred and sixty-eight thousand four hundred and ninety dollars' worth of stationery could be used by the Common Council in a year?

"That is a good deal of money," Tweed answered. . . . "My idea is that no bill of Jones' was ever a legitimate bill. . . . I don't know anything of this particular bill, but I know when anyone from any of the city departments called on Jones & Company with a requisition for stationery for any of the different city or county departments they would make them presents for such requisition—blankets, saddles, jewelry, crockery, harness, and trunks, and everything they wished in that line. There used to be a store three or four doors below Mr. Jones'. It was a fancy goods store—crockery and fancy goods— I can't think of the very firm. Jones used to take persons who called with requisitions for stationery or supplies into this place and make these presents to them, and that was all charged in the bills for stationery, I suppose. . . . I know Jones would often take me—or Rogers or any of them—and buy anything in the way of fancy goods I wanted—Russian leather. . . . Robes for carriages, and sleighs and everything—fancy writing desks. . . . I can't name anything man would require that he wouldn't furnish if they asked him for it. . . .

"Q. And they were inserted in his bills for stationery?

"A. That was the understanding; they were to be. Fine pictures, and—oh, I can't name them. Almost everything. . . .

"Mr. Connolly received a good many little favors of that kind, and I guess pretty much everybody who went there with a requisition. . . . For instance, any department in the city, say your department, required stationery; a requisition would be made. Some young man from your department would go over to them and deliver the requisition. Jones would say, 'Well, this is a very nice requisition,' and then he would try if possible to have a larger requisition made out; and whether or not, he would invite this young man to go in, and show him a lot of fancy goods and make him presents of them and enlarge the requisition that way, or else not furnish the full amounts of the requisitions. I think Mr. Rogers and Jones were about the departments all the time, and called upon everybody. . . . I may say that everybody who furnished requisitions to Jones & Company for stationery and supplies received such presents. Received furniture, bridles, saddles, and everything. I think I would be right in saying everybody. . . .

"Q. I turn at random in one of these complaints to this item: '1869, November 19th; fifteen reams of official note-paper—$210'; that is how much?

"A. Fourteen dollars a ream.

"Q. Is it your idea that in making such an enormous and palpably erroneous charge, that they did it in that way?

"A. That is my idea. . . .

"Q. Their bills were not only tainted by this arrangement of fifteen per cent., but were also absolutely false as to quantities, amounts and prices?

"A. Yes, sir. . . . Mr. Rogers and Mr. Jones both told me they did it . . . for I know persons, bringing requisitions, got what they desired in that line—books and everything. When I say books, I mean novels—libraries."[1]

Tweed profited personally by all the printing which was done for the City. He was part owner of the New York Printing Company and the *Transcript*, an obscure newspaper. The *Transcript* received as advertising all the municipal and legal announcements. Tweed testified later that all the bills of the New York Printing Company were 25 per cent. higher than they should have been. "We got very heavy dividends," he added, "probably fifty or sixty or seventy thousand dollars a year, for some years." The capital of the company was $10,000.[2] Tweed's company also received more than $300,000 from the City for printing in book form the records of the City from 1675 to 1776. During the Civil War Tweed's influence obtained national printing contracts for the New York Printing Company. It was also said that Tweed forced large corporations that for reasons of their own could not afford his disfavour to buy their printing from his firm at exorbitant prices.

Tweed and his associates were getting so rich that they organized their own bank, the Tenth National Bank, which, of course, became a depository for city funds, and it was also the bank used by the Ring in all its financial transactions. Tweed, Hall, Connolly, James Fisk, Jr., and Ingersoll, a city contractor, were directors.

Through Ingersoll, who was his partner in the chair business, Tweed operated an arms company, and its weapons were sold to the National Guard. Vast sums of money were also made by Tweed and his associates on contracts for renting, repairing, and fitting up armouries for the National Guard.

---

[1] Tweed Ring Investigation, pp. 191–199.

[2] *Ibid.*, pp. 157–161.

A number of lofts, stables, and rooms which were never used for any purpose were rented to the City as armouries at the rate of $85,500. The armouries which were used by the National Guard cost the City $109,600 a year, and it was estimated that the same places could have been rented by a private party for $46,600. One of the armouries rented to the City consisted of the top floor of Tammany Hall. It was estimated that the available drill space in this room was 100 by 40 feet. Other rooms in Tammany Hall were also rented to the City ostensibly for officers' rooms and company meeting rooms. Tammany thus received $36,000 a year in rents for these rooms, which, it was estimated, were worth $3,000 a year.

Even greater amounts than those paid for rent were charged to the City for keeping ten armouries in repair for nine months. During that period Andrew J. Garvey was paid $197,330.24 for plastering work in armouries, and John H. Keyser, another Ring contractor, was paid $142,329.71 in the same period for plumbing. G. S. Miller, the Ring's carpenter, received $434,064.31 for work on ten armouries. James H. Ingersoll, Tweed's partner, was paid $170,729.60 for chairs supplied to armouries. The *Times* remarked concerning this item: "Thirty-five or forty chairs and three or four tables cost the City $170,729.60." The *Public School Journal* estimated that at five dollars each this would entitle the City to 34,145 chairs, "and as there are only about 10,000 militiamen in this city, each man must have been supplied with *three* chairs whereon to spread himself. If these chairs were placed side by side in a straight line they would extend a distance of *four miles and a half*, or from the City Hall to the old arsenal in the Central Park!"

The greatest frauds of all were practised by the Ring in connection with the construction of the New York County Court House, which still stands in the City Hall Park as a memorial to their methods. In 1858 the original law authorizing the construction of a County Court House was passed, and it provided for an expenditure of $250,000. In 1862 work was begun, and two years later the Board of Supervisors, of which Tweed was then a member, obtained authorization to raise an additional $800,000 for completion of the work. Apparently, however, this was not enough, for in the following year the Legislature authorized the Supervisors to spend an additional $600,000, and the Court House was then said to be nearer completion. But in 1870 another $600,000 was required, and still the building was not finished. The next year the Tweed Ring received $750,000 for the Court House. The entire amount appropriated was $6,200,000, but an additional $6,000,000 was paid out of the City's treasury for the Court House. The *North American Review* estimated that the final cost of this drab, ungainly building exceeded by more than four times the cost of construction of the Houses of Parliament in London.

Curiously enough, the Court House needed many repairs before it was finished, and several hundred thousand dollars were paid for repairs before the building was open or occupied. Some of the individual items charged to the City for work and supplies in connection with the County Court House were rather startling. The City was charged $675,534.44 for carpets, shades, and curtains. Perhaps the most flippant item was the bill for thermometers, which came to an even $7,500. J. McBride Davidson charged the City $404,347.72 for safes in the County Court House. Mr. Davidson kept a private bar in the rear of his safe supply office in Duane Street, where members of the Tweed Ring were treated to the best vintages of wines.

The bill for carpets, which amounted to $221,799.48 for the County Court House and to $343,931.91 for other city offices, led to entertaining speculations on the part of citizens and newspapers. One of the favourite pastimes in the City of New York after the exposures of the Tweed Ring frauds was calculating how far, placed end to end, the materials charged to the City would reach, and some ingenious mathematicians arrived in China before their calculations were completed. "Supposing," said the *Times*, "that carpets cost $5 a yard, this sum would suffice to cover 113,147 square yards." The *Times* then estimated that the Ring officials had charged the City for enough carpets to cover the eight and one quarter acres of the City Hall Park three times over.

Awnings for the Court House were sold to the City for $41,746.83, and "brooms, etc.," cost $41,190.95. There were $2,676.75 worth of locks on the various doors of the judges' chambers. Mr. Garvey's plastering work was said by the accounts to be worth $531,594.22, but the same plastering needed $1,294,684.13 worth of repairs before it was finished. Repairs to the woodwork required an expenditure of $750,071.92. The total expenditures in items like these totalled $8,223,979.89, but when they decided that the Court House could bear no more items without suspicion, the Ring charged other amounts to the general heading of county buildings, and the expert accountant who studied six years to find the extent of the frauds testified that these two general items of the Court House and County Buildings amounted to more than $13,000,000. Whether or not the contractor did Cheops out of several millions, as Mr. Kipling has surmised, at least Cheops got a Pyramid. But the City of New York for this enormous sum of money got a gloomy, meandering mess of unattractive rooms designed in the worst taste and executed with ugly materials.

The contractors who worked for the City and the Ring were not content with charging exorbitant sums of money for their work and their materials; they also did not live up to their contracts. The workmen at James H. Keyser's foundry told a reporter for the *Times* that when the iron chimney tops on the City Hall were condemned and removed, Keyser ordered them to repaint them black and put them back on top of the City Hall instead of supplying new ones. Upon another occasion, one hundred revolving chimney caps or swivel heads were ordered for city buildings, and they were made by Keyser out of condemned and worn-out stoves instead of from galvanized iron, which the contract called for.

Of course, the City was charged for much work that was never done, and sometimes the Ring used fictitious names when entering these items on the books. On December 28, 1869, a check for $33,283 was drawn to the order of Fillippo Donaruma. This check was endorsed, "Phillip F. Dummey." Three days later another check for $33,129.89 was made out to the order of Donaruma, and this time it was endorsed "Fillip Dummin." The Ring was careless, but it made no difference to its members, for both these checks were also endorsed by Andrew J. Garvey.

Some of the city departments were much more expensive than they were worth. The Permit Bureau, which was under the direct management of Mayor Hall, spent $2,842.64 in April, 1871, to collect $6 for permits, and in March of that year the Bureau spent $2,843.70 in order to collect $145. The previous month it cost the City $2,840.66 to collect $194.

One of the most valuable sources of plunder for the members of the Tweed Ring was the City's pay roll. This served the double function of taking care of the four leaders' friends, relatives, and political adherents and also of swelling their own pocket-books. The New York *Times* finally obtained access to these pay rolls and published the contents. Cornelius Corson, who was Tweed's partner in the New York Printing Company, drew from the City $10,000 a year as clerk to the commissioners for the building of the Ninth District Court House, $5,000 a year as chief of the Bureau of Elections, $2,500 a year as clerk to the Board of County Canvassers, $2,000 a year for preparing the proceedings of the Board of Supervisors, $2,500 as official reporter to the Board of Aldermen, and $2,500 as stenographer to one of the courts. He also received various sums of money for copying services. Mr. Cornelius Corson must have been a very busy man, especially collecting his various salaries, which amounted in all to $24,500 each year. Mayor Hall's nephew, Thomas Whitley Hall, received $1,200 a year for doing nothing as messenger to the President of the Board of Supervisors, his uncle. Another nephew, Edward J. Hall, received $5,000 a year as "Fifth Marshal" to his uncle the Mayor. James M. Sweeny, Peter B. Sweeny's brother, received $400 a month for acting as clerk of the Superior Court, and besides he was deputy chamberlain to his brother, the Chamberlain. Michael Coleman, who handled Tweed's personal real estate interests, received $333.33 each month from the City as "temporary clerk" in the office of the Commissioner of Taxes. Tweed's brother, brother-in-law, and one of his sons were on the City's pay rolls. Governor Hoffman's father-in-law and brother-in-law drew salaries from the City, and Sweeny provided for his brother-in-law and an uncle as well as his brother by giving them city salaries.

English Cabinet Ministers were in the habit of aiding their literary friends by giving them offices under the government which did not take much of their time from their historical or literary labours. Edward Gibbon enjoyed such a position on the Board of Trade while he was working on *The Decline and Fall of the Roman Empire*. But Mr. Tweed and Mr. Sweeny did not travel much in literary circles, and therefore sinecures were distributed by them to men of a somewhat different character. There was, for example, Mr. G. A. Phillips, better known in his time as "Oofty Gooft," a comic performer. He was appointed by the Tweed Ring as sixth clerk to the Water Register at a salary of $166.66 a month. Mr. Timothy Donovan, of the Nineteenth Ward, was deputy clerk of Fulton Market, at a salary of $1,000 a year, but he was never seen in the vicinity of Fulton Market. Donovan's main interest was prize fighting, and one of his claims to fame was the act of "biting off one of the ears of the late Alderman, Thomas Connor," who was credited himself on the City pay rolls with $1,200 a year, though he had been dead for many months. Other men on the City's pay rolls died, but the Tweed Ring did not seem to be aware of it, for their salaries continued to be received by someone for them. William Runnett, a minstrel performer, drew $106 a month as a water policeman even after he was dead. One of the Tweed Ring's friends was Micky Fay, who held four sinecures and owned two rum shops. He also was supposed to be a clerk in the Fulton Market, but he never visited there, for his avocation was dog and cat fighting. "He used to kill rats with his teeth in former years, but gave up the practice when he became an Assistant Alderman," recorded the historian of the New York *Times*. Tweed became a dog fancier and established a valuable kennel. William Long, *alias* Pudding Long, who aired the Tweed pups, was made an interpreter in the Fifth District Court at a salary of $100 per month, although it was said that he could neither read nor write any language.[1]

Tweed also kept public officials happy by making personal presentations to them. Police Justice Shandley received an elegant "gold hunting case watch, chain and locket of the value of $1,000 and a check for the same amount." He was overcome with emotion when the boss made the presentation. After the ceremony, which took place at the residence of Mrs. Maurice J. Walsh, the hostess "advanced and gave Boss

[1]Information concerning sinecures from New York *Times*, October 2, 1871, October 4, 1871, and October 5, 1871.

Tweed a rare bouquet." Tweed presented the retiring president of the Board of Assistant Aldermen with a diamond stud costing $1,500 on January 1, 1870, and the *Sun* said that it was the largest diamond stud ever presented to a retiring official of that board. These men who held sinecures and received presents from Boss Tweed were known as the "Shiny Hat Brigade," and they could be seen on fair afternoons—for they never rose early—on the sunny side of Broadway or Fifth Avenue, smoking their cigars and discussing horses, women, politics, and prize fighting. It was said by a contemporary observer, Matthew P. Breen, that from twelve to fifteen thousand of these men occupied the street corners of New York during the reign of Tweed.

Tweed testified concerning sinecures before the investigating committee of the Board of Aldermen:

"Q. During the existence of the Ring, were there not quite a number of persons upon the pay-rolls, who were regularly paid as if they were doing service to the city in one capacity or another, who actually didn't do any service at all?

"A. Or very little. . . . In my time, I also had a private payroll of my own—some forty or fifty or sixty thousand dollars paid out of my own pocket, but letting them think that they were paid by the city. Disbecker, who used to be a Police Commissioner, I paid forty or fifty dollars a month, out of my own pocket, for a year or two. He thought it came from the department. . . . He was appointed inspector of something or other, he thought—something that didn't exist at all. All the work he did was to get his pay every month.

"Q. Where did you get the money to pay that?

"A. From the City. . . . I had Mr. E. K. Apgar, I think, the Assistant Secretary of State. He didn't do anything but stump the State. . . .

"Q. What were these men on there for?

"A. Because they were electioneering for us.

"Q. For the Democratic Party or for the Ring?

"A. Apgar was on the State.

"Q. Well, what work was he doing?

"A. Spouting—talking—making speeches."[1]

---

[1] Tweed Ring Investigation, pp. 208–209.

IV

Tweed had great need in 1870 of "spouters" and other political henchmen, for he was engaged in vast deals with the New York State Legislature, which required all the oratorical and financial resources he could muster.

It was of the utmost importance to the members of the Tweed Ring that the Comptroller's office should never get out of their hands, for it was in that office that the records of their thefts were available. The office of Comptroller of New York had been elective, and the occupant held that position for four years. For three years, the Ring had been doing an enormous business, as we have just seen, and its financial operations all passed through the Comptroller's office, of which the City Auditor was a subordinate. The Ring controlled the nominations of Tammany Hall and controlled elections, but, even so, the members realized that they could scarcely afford to take the risk of a reform Comptroller, obtaining by some miracle the office which held the secrets of their success. In order to insure the safety of this office, Tweed, who was a State Senator, inserted a "joker" in the Tax Levy bill of 1870. It provided that the Comptroller of the City of New York was thereafter to be appointed by the Mayor and to hold office for four years. But the first person to be appointed to the office was to hold it until January 1, 1875. The Mayor was authorized to make the appointment five days after the Tax Levy bill passed. Mayor Hall immediately reappointed "Slippery Dick" Connolly, and the Ring felt safe until 1875 at least.

In order to maintain their power, the Ring now carried on negotiations with the Legislature for a new charter for New York City. Tweed explained on the witness stand that many Democrats in New York had become dissatisfied and were planning to oust him and his associates from the city offices. For that purpose, under the leadership of Senators "Mike" Norton, Thomas Creamer, Henry Genet, and L. D. Kiernan, the group which was known as the Young Democracy introduced a new charter into the Legislature early in the session. In order to combat this danger, Tweed and his associates wrote their own charter, which was devised, it was said, by the wily Peter Sweeny—and was rushed to Albany, where Assemblyman Frear, one of Tweed's political henchmen, took charge of its introduction. Tweed also obtained an endorsement of the new charter from the leading merchants and financiers of New York, who were his friends.

By this charter, Mayor A. Oakey Hall was given the absolute and unlimited power to appoint every important city official without the approval of anyone. The officials of the courts were to be appointed by the Comptroller, whose own appointment, as we have just seen, was also controlled by the Mayor. The heads of departments were to report to the Mayor alone and only at his request, so that no one except the Mayor could know the condition of the City's affairs. The Mayor and the Comptroller were also authorized to fix the amount of the salaries of all civil judges and all court attendants at any sum they might see fit, not exceeding $10,000 a year. The Ring guarded against the exercise of these vast powers by anyone except their own A. Oakey Hall, by providing in their charter that these powers were conferred only on the then incumbent of the Mayor's office, and in case of his removal by death, disability or resignation, the same powers were to be exercised by the Comptroller, who would succeed him in office.

The charter also created a Board of Audit consisting of the Mayor, A. Oakey Hall, the Comptroller, Richard B. Connolly, the Commissioner of Public Works, William M. Tweed, and the President of the Board of Parks, Peter B. Sweeny. This board was to audit all claims against the City and by this right it controlled all municipal expenditures. At its first meeting, the Board passed $6,312,000 worth of bills against the City, of which sum, it was subsequently discovered, 10 per cent. were legitimate. It was said that $15,750,000 worth of fraudulent bills were approved by this omnipotent board of directors. Henry L. Clinton said in a speech concerning this board, "Not an official—not a man in the whole city—can draw a dollar, not even his honor upon the bench, or the judges in any of our courts, except by the permission of these four individuals, chief among whom is the Mayor."

Tweed and Sweeny devised their charter cleverly. It was their *chef d'œuvre;* it provided the very thing reformers had been demanding for years: concentrated power in the hands of the Mayor so that he might be held responsible for the city

administration. The charter immediately won the admiration
of Horace Greeley and other reformers, who saw in it a step in
the right direction, although they knew their Tweed and their
Hall. On the other hand, the Tweed group had every reason to
expect that they would be able to keep either their Mayor or
their Comptroller alive and out of jail indefinitely, and therefore they were in favour of concentration of power in the hands
of those officials.

In order to pass this charter through the New York State
Legislature, Tweed had to use all his influence and huge sums
of money. As a State Senator, Tweed was in a position to direct
the campaign personally. He was a member of the important
committees of the Senate on Finance and Internal Affairs,
and his friends were on the other leading committees. He had
also arranged with the Speaker of the Assembly the appointments to all the leading committees in that body.

Tweed had a luxurious suite of rooms at the Delavan House
in Albany, and here he was visited by the most important
legislators of the capital. There was a private exit from No. 450,
Tweed's suite, so that senators and assemblymen should not
be embarrassed by meeting each other coming in and going out.
George William Curtis wrote of Tweed as a legislator:

"In Albany he had the finest quarters at the Delavan, and
when he came into the great dining-room at dinner-time, and
looked at all the tables thronged with members of the Legislature and the lobby, he had a benignant, paternal expression, as
of a patriarch pleased to see his retainers happy. It was a
magnificent rendering of Fagin and his pupils. You could
imagine him trotting up and down in the character of an un-
suspicious old gentleman with his handkerchief hanging out of
his pocket, that his scholars might show their skill in prigging a
wipe. He knew which of that cheerful company was the Artful
Dodger and which Charley Bates. And he never doubted that
he could buy every man in the room if he were willing to pay the
price."[1]

Tweed himself in his testimony described fully conditions
at Albany:

---

[1] *Other Essays from the Easy Chair*, by George William Curtis, p. 49.

"Q. Was it common report around the State house, and in Albany generally, that certain men made it their special vocation to see members, and to control their votes by giving them money?

"A. Yes, sir; and it was understood in the Lower House that there was an organization formed of men of both parties, Republicans and Democrats, called the Black Horse Cavalry, composed of twenty-eight or thirty persons, who would all be controlled by one man, and vote as he directed them. Sometimes they would be paid for not voting against a bill, and sometimes they would not be desired, if their votes were not necessary. When the vote was called, they would step into the anteroom of the lobby, and if their vote was required, someone would step out, and have them vote; if they wasn't, they wouldn't come in at all.

"Q. Do you know who composed that brigade—that Black Horse Cavalry?

"A. No; they kept changing all the time; every year they had a new leader. They generally quarrelled at the end of the session, and started the new year fresh.

"Q. If this was a matter of public repute, how could it possibly go on so long? What did you do to keep public sentiment suppressed?

"A. Well, we used money wherever it was necessary.

"Q. But you couldn't buy all the people of the State?

"A. Buy the representatives up there, as a general thing.

"Q. Well, now, how about the public press? Were they with you or against you?

"A. Well, they were generally against us in private, and with us in public.

"Q. What do you mean by that?

"A. I mean that we had to subsidize them. I mean the press at Albany when I speak now of the press. The *Argus* was with the Democrats, as a general thing. We used to have inserted in the tax-levy what was called a budget—what they required to have paid for printing. The *Albany Evening Journal*, which was a Republican paper, and run in the interest of the Republican party, and controlled by a gentleman named George W. Demers, was opposed to us, and had to be subsidized. . . .

"Q. What do you mean by 'subsidizing' those papers?

"A. Giving them money. . . . For articles we desired to have put in the paper. Sometimes they would bring us an article which was very strong against us, and containing some things we wouldn't very much care to have made public, and we would pay to have them stricken out, and they would be stricken out. . . . My relations with the *Albany Evening Journal* continued all the while I was there. . . .

"Q. Well, now, you say you paid money; did you pay any large sums of money?

"A. Oh, sometimes $5,000, sometimes $1,000, sometimes $500. It was a general dribble all the time. . . .

"When I first went to Albany as a Senator—it was 1868. In that year the fight came up between the Erie and the Hudson River Railroad Company in which I was retained by the Erie, and acquired rather a notoriety, that brought men who were looking after money to me. Among others who came there was a Mr. S. C. Hutchings, who was then an associate editor or reporter for the *Albany Evening Journal*. That was the Republican organ for the State, as it had been for many years. That paper was attacking me, and Mr. Hutchings came to me and told me he could have those attacks much modified—have them smoothed down, and that the paper could finally be brought round to support me politically, and enter into all my measures, which were not entirely political, and that I would never be attacked in that paper in a way that would amount to anything. I thought to myself that was a very good thing—a very desirable arrangement, and I asked him in what manner that could be done. He said he would bring me in communication with Mr. Demers, who was then living in Troy, and who was then the responsible editor of the *Evening Journal*. . . . After that I frequently saw Mr. Demers, and had interviews with him. He came to my rooms sometimes, but that was very seldom. He was an invalid, and didn't go out much. He was a man who had one foot in the grave already, and, in fact, did die shortly after. . . . Frequently Mr. Hutchings would bring me articles in my private room—I had a private room up there in the Delavan House—articles in proof, against us, prepared for the newspaper. I would talk them over with Mr. Hutchings and Mr. Sweeny, or Mr. Hall and others, and show them the articles and we would talk it over and fix it to suit ourselves, and it would appear as we altered it, either that day or the next day, as the case might be. We would fix them so that they wouldn't appear as an attack against us; or, even if it did attack us, it would attack us in such a way that we could answer and disprove it. It was really our own article. . . . I paid for it as I went along—sometimes $5,000, sometimes $1,000, sometimes less, as the necessities were. . . . I might mention, in this connection, that when I kept the Police Commissioner, Mr. Disbecker, on my pay roll, it was for services he rendered me at Albany. He was correspondent of the *World* and the *Staats Zeitung*, part of the time.

"Q. Can you give any idea of the amount of money that was put into the tax levies during your time, in behalf of the Albany *Argus?*

"A. I couldn't, and, if I could, I wouldn't dare to. It would be a frightful amount."[1]

Tweed, a few days later, computed the amount paid to the Albany *Argus*. He testified:

"The amount paid the *Argus* Company for printing (not including advertising), as shown by the Comptroller's books, was as follows:

1868	$ 5,000
1869	80,500
1870	176,600
1871	207,900
1872	136,400
1873	138,850
1874	23,200
1875	10,000
"Total	$778,450

"You will perceive how the bills drop off as soon as I left the Senate. The bills for 1872 and 1873 were the dribblings of the big years."[2]

---

[1]Tweed Ring Investigation, pp. 212–219.

[2]*Ibid.*, p. 239.

The method of the Black Horse Cavalry at Albany was to introduce a bill which struck at the interests of some large corporation, or the Tweed combine, and which was known as "strike" legislation. The bill progressed in the Committee of the Whole, and indications were that it was likely to pass. Then the Cavalry waited, and if the agents of the corporation, or the agents of Tweed, or Tweed himself did not pay the amount they wanted, the bill was advanced further. The corporation paid and the bill was never heard of again.

Lobbying on a colossal scale began at Albany with the railroad war between Commodore Vanderbilt on the one side and the Erie Railroad group, consisting of James Fisk, Jr., Jay Gould, and Daniel Drew on the other. One of Tweed's lawyers remarked concerning this historic battle of corruption: "The contest over the road ruined more reputations, destroyed more fortunes, and developed more rascality than any one enterprise in this country." Never before had the members of the New York Legislature seen such sums of money as were handed to them by the representatives of these two factions. Tweed testified that he was the agent of the Erie Railroad.

The session of 1868 was a stirring one, for a bill proposing to legalize $10,000,000 worth of Erie stock was up for consideration, an act which Judge Barnard, in one of his quaint moods, described as a bill legalizing counterfeit money. The hungry members of the Legislature, who received only $300 salary for each session they attended, scented plunder. Hotel keepers and boarding-house mistresses extended credit to members they had intended to dispossess; poker games flourished every night, and saloon keepers looked happier. There was a general air of optimism in Albany and the prevailing opinion was that an era of good feeling was about to set in. Some legislators clubbed together for the protection of their interests in the prospective bribery. All ordinary business of the Legislature was at a standstill, and men gathered in the lobbies of the hotels and in the lobby of the legislative chambers to discuss the coming event. Most of these discussions were concerned with relative opinions of members as to how much they ought to charge. Some men suggested $1,000 a legislator, but others laughed at them for their naïveté. The rate fluctuated between $2,000 and $3,000 a vote for either side, while some men, who were said by an ob-

server to be Sunday-school superintendents in the country districts during the months of the year when the Legislature was
not in session, insisted on nothing less than $5,000. The Erie
group offered in the beginning $1,000 a vote—$500 down and
$500 after their bill became a law, but this was viewed with con-
tempt, because it was considered that Commodore Vanderbilt,
who was now a wealthy man, and whose interests the passage of
this bill would affect greatly, would pay much more to have it
defeated. Tweed's advice to the New York Assemblymen,
it was said, was to "stand firm and not commit themselves."

Suddenly the rumour spread through the legislative halls
that Vanderbilt and the Erie had compromised their difficulties
privately. "The observer," wrote Charles Francis Adams,
"was reminded of the dark days of the war, when tidings
came of some great defeat, as that on the Chickahominy or at
Fredericksburg." Some members rushed to the lobbyists and
offered to close for $500 cash down, but their votes were now
worth nothing. The anger of the ravenous legislators was
terrible, and the bill, which had been thrown out of the Assembly a few days before by a vote of 83 to 32, now passed by a
vote of 101 to 6. The legislators were particularly angry at
Vanderbilt for what they chose to regard as treachery in settling
his disputes privately instead of paying for a war. The same
night they passed the *pro rata* freight bill and the bill compelling
the sale of through tickets by competing lines, because it was
thought that they were harmful to Vanderbilt's interests. The
fight then shifted from the Legislature to the courts, and
Judges Barnard and Cardozo issued injunctions and writs at
the request of Fisk, Gould, Drew, and Tweed, who were at the
moment trying to gain control of the Albany & Susquehanna
Railroad. The president of this road received subpoenas commanding Fisk and Gould to answer for contempt of court, but
he found it impossible to serve them on them by ordinary process servers. He sent his son to New York to serve the papers,
and the next day after the young man's arrival from Albany his
dead body was found floating on the Hudson River.[1]

Charles Francis Adams wrote that the inquirer after truth
must come to this inevitable conclusion concerning state legis-

---

[1] *Thirty Years of New York Politics*, by Matthew P. Breen, pp. 143-146.

latures at this period: "The weight of opinion and of evidence
gradually becomes irresistible, until his mind settles down into a
sad belief that probably no representative bodies were ever
more thoroughly venal, more shamelessly corrupt, or more
hopelessly beyond the reach of public opinion, than are certain
of those bodies which legislate for republican America in this
latter half of the nineteenth century."[1]

It was into a legislature of this character that Tweed's
charter was introduced in March, 1870. "We had arranged it,"
Tweed testified later, "so as to have no difficulty to pass it
in the lower house." These arrangements were carried on for
Tweed in the Assembly by A. D. Barber, the most eminent
lobbyist in Albany during the period. Tweed was asked, "What
is understood to be Mr. Barber's business in Albany?" "I
believe he has sworn there," Tweed answered, "that his business is to walk up and down the hill and talk to members. Mr.
Barber is a very smart man, very well posted, and very con-
versant with matters of legislation, and is very valuable for
advice in those matters. He has spent a great many years there,
knows a great many members, and his advice is sound, generally."[2]

The Albany correspondent of the New York *Sun* gave this
account of the scenes attending the passage of Tweed's charter
through the Assembly:

"Telegrams were received announcing that a horde of desperadoes and bruisers from the metropolis were *en route* to the
Capital, for the purpose of intimidating and terrifying the
Democrats of the rural districts into compliance with their
demands. No sooner was this known than counter telegrams
were sent summoning more desperadoes and bruisers, for the
purpose of holding in check those who had already appeared
upon the scene. Such a swarm of politicians, pimps, pugilists,
and roughs was never before seen in Albany. The hotels were
never so crowded, the barrooms never so well patronized.
Delavan Leland disposed of fifteen barrels of the poorest
whiskey ever manufactured, which it is said he purchased
for a mere song from the fugitive Collector Bailey. But very

---

[1]*Chapters of Erie*, by Charles Francis Adams, pp. 44–45.

[2]Tweed Ring Investigation, pp. 73–74.

few politicians closed their eyes last night. Grand Sachem Tweed kept open house all night, and so did Machiavelli Husted, of Westchester. The former attended to the Democrats, while the rooms of the latter were visited by Hamilton Harris and other leading Republicans. . . .

"At an early hour this morning the corridors and lobbies of the hotels and the rooms of the members were excessively thronged. The absorbing topic of conversation was the probable action of the Assembly on the charter. . . . Shortly before ten o'clock every inch of space within and without the Assembly Chamber was packed as tight as a box of plug tobacco.

"In the cloak rooms could be noticed the figure of Mr. A. D. Barber, the king of the lobby, and the proprietor of the Legislature. He carried his indispensable yellow stick. He was surrounded by his coadjutors, Geo. O. Jones, Abe Van Vechten, Smith Weed, and Hamilton Harris. Three pages stood near by, and throughout the proceedings that followed were kept running to and from the Chamber, bringing Mr. Barber messages and the result of the several votes. Mr. Barber would occasionally sail for a member and whisper something hurriedly in his ear. In one word the gentlemanly Barber had the entire outside direction of the proceedings. Grand Sachem Tweed was on the floor at an early hour, and moved about with the agility of the Americus Club tiger. . . ."

Various votes on various motions were taken, and Tweed's forces won every time. The *Sun* reporter continued:

"Grand Mogul Tweed all this time was posted in the rear of the Chamber, like a general marshaling his army. Victorious, he was all smiles, and spent most of the time in talking to some lady friends who sat on the sofas in the rear of the Chamber."[1]

In the galleries, watching the proceedings eagerly, were several New York Aldermen, whose power was about to be taken away from them by the new charter. Among these was Mr. Richard Croker, then a quiet young man who had just been elected to the Board of Aldermen. He must have watched the fantastic scene thoughtfully, for he learned then a great deal

[1] The *Sun*, March 31, 1870.

concerning what to do and what not to do when it came his turn to rule New York.

The charter passed the Assembly by a vote of 116 to 5, and the *Herald* reported, "the gallery audience cleared out as quickly as if the drop of the Bowery theatre had fallen upon the last scene of *Jack Sheppard*."

The next step in Tweed's campaign for his charter of omnipotence was the battle to force it through the State Senate. Tweed himself described the preliminary skirmishes of bribery in his testimony:

"'I saw,' he said, 'a number of Senators, more particularly Senators Norris Winslow, William Woodin, Bowen, Minier, and Senator James Wood. . . . I didn't know how to reach Winslow particularly, although he had been hanging around my room a good deal, being a member of a Committee of which I was chairman. He was said to be a wealthy man; president of a bank where he lived; president of an insurance company. I guess, in the county he came from, he was the most living of all the living men there; he was looked up to a great deal, and was a very active and energetic man. I didn't know just how to tackle him. . . . I talked the matter over with Mr. Winslow, and he thought they ought to have $50,000 apiece. I said we would pay for it, but I said we couldn't afford to pay that; finally we talked the matter over, and, in one or two days, Hastings suggested that if I got Woodin it would be well for me, as he was an influential man, a powerful speaker, and stood very high in his party.'

"Q. What Hastings do you mean?

"A. Hugh Hastings, here, of the *Commercial Advertiser;* I think I met him [Senator Woodin] in the library-hall of the Senate Chamber. I said to him, 'I hope that you are not going against me in this matter; it is a personal fight against me.' He said no, he wasn't. I said, 'They have threatened to remove me from my position as Deputy Street Commissioner; I feel it as a personal fight,' and that I felt bound to win, and I felt sure that I should win. . . . I said, 'Don't you want to help me? It has become a personal fight against me, and I would rather lose my life than lose a fight.' He said, 'You take it very earnest.' I said, 'Yes, I take it very earnest, and I will do almost anything a man can do to prevent myself being beaten. I was always earnest in everything I undertook, but I was particularly so in this matter, which I regard as having taken the form of a personal fight against me.' He said, 'I haven't got anything against you; I don't want to injure you in any way.' 'Well,' I said, 'this is injuring me.' Then he spoke about my position and so forth; that it ought to be worth a great deal of money to me, and I said it was, and I was willing to pay for it. I don't know who brought in money first, but money came up in the course of our conversation. . . . I reported that meeting to Winslow and Hastings separately, and they said, 'I guess you can get the old man; stick to him'; and I did stick to him. Next place I met him I talked to him again. He said he would come to my room and see me that night; then I felt pretty sure of him. . . . Then I suggested the caucus, and suggested that the Republicans should resolve in the caucus to support me in this measure. I said, 'Here is a way of getting over it, if money matters are mentioned: If you go in caucus, and if the resolution is arrived at, you can say, "I was governed by the caucus, and had to do it because the caucus did, and I personally went against it."' . . . I had an interview with Mr. Woodin the next day, and I said the same thing to him that I had said to Winslow in the course of conversation, that I was to give each of them forty thousand dollars; he wanted to know if I wouldn't give fifty.

"Mr. Cole: Who asked that?

"A. Mr. Woodin. I said I didn't propose to give more—I couldn't afford it; finally he consented to go with the others. I said, 'Shall I hand you $40,000?' He said, 'Do the same with this as you are doing with the rest.' I said, 'I am going to hand the rest to Mr. Winslow.' The Republicans held their caucus, and resolved to stand by the charter . . . when the bill came up every Republican voted for it except Mr. Thayer, and every Democrat voted for it except Mr. Genet. . . .

"Q. Were these the only Senators whom you had dealings with in connection with this matter?

"A. No, sir; I bought some of the others also. . . . I bought some of the Democrats by giving them places. . . . Places— employment of men in the department, where they put their name on the pay-roll, and drew their money once a month. . . Samuel H. Frost, in the First District, I gave places to—places

to his friends, you know—appointments. . . . I appointed quite a
number of men for him in different positions—small positions,
$2.50 or $3 a day—who did no work, but their name was on the
pay-roll, and they drew their pay every month. . . . I agreed to
do that, and he agreed to vote for the bill. . . . Senator Michael
Norton I agreed to help in his business matters in New York.
. . . Senator Cauldwell—I gave a place to his partner, Mr.
Whitney, to be not less than $20,000 a year; if it was less, I was
to make it up. He was appointed Deputy Collector of Assess-
ments, a place worth fifteen thousand and some hundred dollars; I did make up the rest of it at the end of the year. William
M. Graham I gave money to. . . . I was giving him money all the
time. It was $1,000 to-day, $500 to-morrow, $10,000 the next
day, to get him out of business difficulties. He was in trouble
with his bank matters, and borrowed money from me to help
himself out; but that didn't help him. He lost his money and
mine too. . . . Augustus Elwood, I think, I gave money to him
for that—for something else, if not for that. . . .

"Q. Well, Mr. Tweed, I want you to be precise about this
thing, because you are now dealing with reputations of honorable men.

"A. I am, except in the case of one man, and if I didn't
pay him for that, I did for other work of the kind. I don't
want to do the slightest injustice to any man. . . .

"Q. Did you carry this large amount up there in money?

"A. Some was carried up by me and some by different parties.

"Q. Name all the parties that took it up to you.

"A. Garvey's brother brought me up one hundred and odd
thousand dollars at one time. . . .

"Q. Did you ever have any conversation with Mr. Senator
Minier about his vote?

"A. I talked positively and directly with him about it. We
met, and the understanding was I was very anxious to pass
this charter. He said: 'It ought to be worth a good farm to do
that; you are all rich down in New York, and all getting rich,
and you have all got plenty of money, and you ought to pay
well to have anybody stand by you.' I told him I would stand
well by him; I said I would give him $10,000; he said $10,000
wouldn't do. Then I offered twenty, and that wouldn't do
either. 'Well,' he said, 'how would twenty-five thousand do?'

'Well, all right,' I said, 'twenty-five.' 'Well,' said he, 'I will see you again about it.' He did see me again, and it got up to fifty, and finally we settled upon forty thousand. . . .

"Senator Wood and I had had dealings before. . . . He kept talking about how poor he was; he said if I would take some interest in a rectifying distillery—he had an interest in some establishment for making new whiskey old, or old whiskey new, or something of that kind, and he wanted me to buy it. I said no, I didn't want to; I didn't know anything about the business, and I didn't want to put any money into a business I didn't understand. I told him I had secured others, as I told them all, for $40,000, and that was all I was willing to give. He finally consented."[1]

Tweed was asked how much the passage of his charter had finally cost him. "I have no idea," he answered; "hundreds of thousands of dollars." "As much as two hundred thousand dollars?" asked the counsel. "Just about three times that—about six hundred thousand dollars, I think, sir," Tweed answered.[2] Some of this money Tweed paid out of his own pocket, but part of it was paid by Jim Fisk, Jay Gould, and the Erie Railroad. The Tweed Ring contractors who profited so much from city jobs also were assessed for the bribery fund. Andrew J. Garvey, the Prince of Plasterers, and James H. Ingersoll, the Chief of Chair Makers, contributed $50,000 each; Keyser and Miller gave $25,000, and Mayor Hall also gave $25,000.

Tweed bribed his principal opponents, the leaders of the Young Democracy movement, Senators Norton and Creamer. He found it impossible, however, to purchase Senator Henry Genet at the time, but perhaps he did not try, for he was very angry with Genet for leading the revolt against his power. Creamer received not only money, but also a seat in Congress. The chairman of the Republican State Committee, Cornell, discovered that 75 per cent. of the officers of the Republican County Committee and 75 per cent. of the Republican district leaders were either in the pay of the Democrats or held sinecures from Tweed and Tammany Hall.[3] We have already seen from

---

[1] Tweed Ring Investigation, pp. 83-97.

[2] Ibid., pp. 73-74.

[3] Autobiography of Thomas C. Platt, p. 56.

Tweed's testimony how he purchased five Republican senators for $40,000 each.

When the charter came up for consideration in the Senate, Senator Genet, Tweed's leading opponent at this time, though he had been a henchman of Tweed's for many years, wished to offer twenty to thirty amendments, and he therefore asked for delay in the consideration of the charter. Tweed answered from his seat that the Senator could offer his amendments then, and he said, "I have declared by the Almighty that I will press this bill to a vote by all the energy and ability that I possess." "I don't see any necessity," said Senator Genet, "to call upon the Almighty about it." Perhaps he realized then that the Almighty was powerless in opposition to $40,000. Genet offered his amendments, and they were all promptly voted down.

The charter was passed in the Senate on the afternoon of April 5, 1870, and Governor Hoffman, Tweed's man, signed it immediately. "After Governor Hoffman put his name to the instrument," wrote the correspondent of the *World*, "he presented the pen with which he signed it to Tweed, and Tweed spent the rest of the night in showing it to the thirsty crowd that swallowed the basket of champagne he opened immediately after the bill passed the Senate."

The Tweed charter was *carte blanche* for the members of the Ring to enter the city treasury with shovels and load their wagons with gold. Tweed himself described the process of stealing and the division of the spoils which followed the passage of his charter:

"Q. After the legislation which placed the power to audit the bills in this Board of Audit, composed of yourself, Mayor Hall, and Mr. Connolly, did you three men have any understanding with each other as to how you were to make money out of that legislation?

"A. We did. . . . The understanding was that the parties to whom we advanced money, and whom we had confidence in, should, through our influence, advance bills for work purporting to be done for the county or the city; more particularly for the county, and they should receive only fifty per cent. of the amount of their bills.

"SENATOR TWEED IN A NEW RÔLE"

"Q. Well, this plan didn't necessarily contemplate that the bills should be *bona fide* at all?

"A. Well, we presumed that they would be, of course; any supposition was that they would have some basis, however slight. . . . Connolly had in his office a very confidential man at that time; one who had his utmost confidence, Mr. Watson; and he also had my confidence to the utmost limit; he had done a great deal of business for both of us in other matters. Mr. Woodward was a very active energetic young man in the Board of Supervisors, whose fidelity was undoubted. I proposed that these two should prepare the bills, and present them, and Connolly should pay them. . . . They were to give ten per cent. to me, ten per cent. to Mr. Connolly, ten per cent. to Mr. James Sweeny, for Mr. Peter B. Sweeny, and ten per cent. to Mr. Sweeny or Mr. Smith for Mr. Hall; and of the other ten per cent. they were to retain five themselves, two-and-a-half for each of them . . . and the other five per cent. was to be put back as a sinking fund for other expenses.

"Q. What do you mean by 'other expenses'?

"A. The obtaining of legislation, or other expenses which might be necessary. . . . I think before any bills were paid, but if not before, after payment of the first batch of bills, or some of them, Watson came to see me, and said that Connolly wasn't satisfied with the ten per cent.; he wanted twenty. I asked him what was the reason of that. He said that Connolly said that he had to take all the responsibility and the risk, and the thing couldn't be done without him. I said: 'It couldn't be done without me either.' I asked how he could do it that way anyhow. He said: 'The way we can do it is this: These people would be satisfied with less percentage; I think they would take one third, instead of one half, because they are giving nothing for it; I can make that arrangement with them, I know.' [Watson was referring to the contractors and manufacturers who were supposed to be working for the City on contracts.] 'Well, very well,' I said, 'go on and make the arrangement, if you can, and I am willing. Give Connolly twenty, and you must give me twenty-five, and give Mr. Sweeny ten per cent. 'That would make fifty-five,' he said: 'Then if I give Hall his ten per cent., where would we be?' I said: 'That's so; see Hall and tell him that expenses are "so heavy we can't afford to give him but five."' He said he would, and so it was arranged that way."[1]

There is an adage concerning honour among thieves, but obviously it did not apply to the members of the Tweed Ring.

v

The Tweed group were now in a position to enjoy themselves merrily. Their tastes ran to fat oysters and sleek trotting horses, large, shiny diamonds and magnums of champagne, brownstone mansions and gaudy women. It was said at the time that a politician who did not have a large diamond on his bosom was considered to have neglected his opportunities shamefully. One of the contemporary newspapers recorded that Tweed "wore a diamond like a planet in his shirt front." A big diamond was the badge of solidity in politics, and an alderman's constituents never could believe that he was in right with Tammany Hall and the powers of that institution unless he wore this insigne. The *Sun* published the following sketch, which, in the form of burlesque, gives an accurate picture of the luxury which attended the exercise of the Ring's power·

"At 9 o'clock on Sunday evening, a crimson-cushioned clarence was drawn over the snow in West Thirty-sixth Street. Its driver was muffled to his ears. The carriage stopped at No. 41. No. 41 is a palatial mansion, with a brown stone front, an aristocratic flight of stone steps, and a front door buried in gorgeous mouldings and carvings of mahogany and rosewood. The rich parlors of the dwelling were warm with luxurious gaslights, which danced within their figured shades. The ruddy light passed through the cream-coloured lace curtains dropping over the elegant windows, and stained the slippery sidewalk with a glow like that of Sauterne wine. This was the residence of the Hon. William Marcy Tweed.

"The occupant of the carriage was a young man of singular beauty. He was faultlessly attired, and wore magnificent diamonds. He is a brother-in-law of Mr. Peter Barr Sweeny, and a State Senator. He passed up the stairs with an air of con-

---

[1]Tweed Ring Investigation, pp. 74 ff.

summate self-possession, pulled the tiny china bell-knob sleeping at the side of the door, and was ushered into the magnificent hall of Senator Tweed's palace.

"Hardly had Senator Bradley's expensive clarence rolled away from Street Commissioner Tweed's residence when a lumbering old hack, drawn by a pair of bony livery nags, took its place. A man of magnificent presence, built like a Hercules, crawled out of the hack. He was dressed like a contractor, and had an air of quiet dignity about him. Throwing away the butt of a fragrant cigar, he stamped his feet on the icy pavement, walked up the granite steps, and disappeared within the mahogany door. This was Prince Harry Genet, of the Twelfth Ward.

"Five minutes passed. A second hack rolled over the snow to Supervisor Tweed's door. Its occupant was a tall gentleman with keen blue eyes, sharp features, and a brown spring overcoat. He wore diamonds, but they were very small. He oozed out of the carriage, and drifted up the steps within the mahogany door, where a warm welcome awaited him. This was the Ulysses of the Seventeenth Ward, the Hon. Thomas J. Creamer.

"The carriages had all disappeared. A broad-shouldered gentleman, clad in a rough tan-colored overcoat and wearing a black felt hat, walked up the street in the direction of the East River. He wore three studs in his shirt bosom. The top stud was a diamond worth at least $500; the others were of gold, about the size of the eyes of a canary. The broad-shouldered gentleman closely scanned the numbers of the various houses. Meeting a police-officer, he asked him where No. 41 was.

"'That's Bill Tweed's house,' said the officer, pointing to No. 41.

"The broad-shouldered gentleman looked at the house in amazement, saying, 'What, Tweedy living in nothing but a brown-stone front! Why, they told me his house was made of marble, and roofed with gold, and that the windows were set with split diamonds. Nothing but a brown-stone front, eh?'

"The broad-shouldered gentleman then walked up the steps and rang the bell. Within thirteen seconds his fat, chubby face, glowing with good humor, disappeared. This was the far-famed Thunderbolt of the Eighth Ward. [Senator Mike Norton.] . . .

"The caucus closed at midnight. The courtly Tweed opened

some superb old champagne, and distributed dollar cigars among his friends. . . . As the party passed out of Supervisor Tweed's mahogany door, one clarence and two hacks were ranged in front.

"'Where's your carriage, Mike?' asked Mr. Tweed of the Thunderbolt.

"'Coming down the avenue,' replied the good-natured Norton. 'I came up in a Sixth avenue car. It's too cold for a carriage.'

"Senator Tweed kindly offered to send the Thunderbolt home in his costliest carriage, but Senator Norton declined the honor, saying that it would ruin him to be seen in the Eighth Ward with Tweedy's diamond-handled whip."[1]

Tweed now lived in appropriate luxury. The tile-lined, immaculate stables in the rear of his house were frequently compared by naïve newspaper writers to the simple dwellings of the poor.

The greatest event of the social seasons during the reign of the Tweed Ring was the marriage of Miss Mary Amelia Tweed, daughter of Mr. and Mrs. William Marcy Tweed, to Mr. Arthur Ambrose Maginnis, of New Orleans. The ceremony took place at seven o'clock on the evening of May 31, 1871, in Trinity Chapel. Long before the appointed hour, the chapel "was crowded with a richly dressed audience, who awaited, in speechless expectation, the advent of the bridal party." The ladies were "aglow with rich silks and satins and flashing with diamonds," and "the confusion of white arms and shoulders, elegant laces and valuable jewelry was perfectly bewildering." When the bridal cortège arrived, "the whole audience rose and leaned over to catch a sight of the bridal magnificence." The bride, a young lady of twenty-one years, was surrounded by her bridesmaids, Miss Josie Tweed, a sister, and Miss Maginnis, a sister of the groom. As they marched up to the chancel, the organ, played by "the fine musician, Mr. E. A. Gilbert," rendered Mendelssohn's Wedding March. The bride was now leaning on the arm of her portly father, while the groom escorted Mrs. Supervisor-Senator-Commissioner Tweed, who was "richly attired in salmon-coloured silk, elegantly

[1]The Sun, March 15, 1870.

trimmed with deep *point aiguille* lace. She wore splendid diamonds." "Mr. Tweed himself," reported the *Sun*, "wore black evening dress, and a magnificent diamond flashed in his bosom." The bride "was dressed in white corded silk, *décolleté*, with demi-sleeves, and immense court train." Orange blossoms ran down her waist, and there was abundance of *point aiguille* lace; her sleeves were made of three rows of this costly fabric and were "wide at the bottom, *à la Marie Antoinette*." "On the bride's bosom flashed a brooch of immense diamonds, and long pendants, set with three large solitaire diamonds, sparkled in her ears." "Her shoes were of white satin with diamond buttons." The Rev. Dr. Joseph H. Price, who had married Miss Tweed's father and mother, officiated.

After the ceremony the bridal party drove to Mr. Tweed's mansion, which was then located at the corner of Fifth Avenue and Forty-third Street. A blue and white awning covered the entrance to the mansion, and a wide Brussels carpet extended from the curb to the door. The whole house was "a blaze of light." "The fountain at the side played merrily in the twilight and the flowers in the garden diffused a delicate perfume on the night air." A huge crowd of the people of the City of New York clustered closely around the canopy to catch sight of the party, and a strong force of policemen was needed to keep the curious within proper bounds.

Inside, from hallway to roof, the house was one mass of flowers, "'all from my own place at Greenwich,' said Mr. Tweed to the *Sun* reporter in accents of honest pride." "The musicians, who sat in a semicircle between the stairways in the hall, were partly hidden from view by a great harp of green and white, edged inside and out with white roses." "Even the grate," reported the *Times*, "was a solid bed of exotics." "The parlor," said the *Sun*, "beggared description." "Imagine all this," the fascinated reporter demanded, "lighted up with the utmost brilliancy, and hundreds of ladies and gentlemen in all the gorgeousness of full dress and flashing with diamonds, listen to the delicious strains of the band and inhale in spirit the sweet perfume which filled the atmosphere, and some inadequate notion can be formed of the magnificence of the scene."

The guests included Mr. Peter B. Sweeny, Mr. Comptroller

Connolly, Judges Daly, Bosworth, Barnard, and Hogan, Colonel James Fisk, Jr., in blue coat and brass buttons, the Hon. S. S. Cox, member of Congress from New York, Sheriff Brennan, Superintendent Kelso, Chauncey Depew, Mr. James H. Ingersoll, Coroner Schirmer, and Mr. Andrew J. Garvey, the Prince of Plasterers.

The presents were "a chief centre of attraction to the guests. They filled all four sides of a large room on the second floor, and "represented in cash seven hundred thousand dollars," according to Mr. James Gordon Bennett of the *Herald*. Mr. Bennett surmised that this was "a display of wedding presents unsurpassed by the collection of the celebrated Oviedo diamond wedding, or of any occasion of the kind, we dare say, since the marriage, two or three years ago, of a daughter of the Khedive of Egypt, and completely eclipsing the jewelry presents to the British Princess Louise, on the occasion of her union with the heir of the great Scottish Duke of Argyll." There were, for instance, 40 sets of sterling silver, one of which contained 240 separate pieces. James Fisk, Jr., sent a huge frosted silver iceberg, intended for ice cream. Arctic bears reposed on the icicle handles of the bowl and climbed up the spoons. Superintendent Kelso, of the Police, sent an exact duplicate of Jim Fisk's contribution. Aunt Millie gave a pair of monogrammed shoulder clasps. Thurlow Weed, the Republican boss of New York State, sent a silver sugar bowl, in the form of a beehive, with plate and spoon. Jay Gould gave a set of silver nut pickers with squirrel heads, and Mr. Lewis G. Kirk sent a set of silver pickle forks. Grandma and Grandpa gave "a richly bound Bible." "Peter B. Sweeny's card appeared on diamond bracelets of fabulous magnificence." One piece of jewellery, with diamonds as large as filberts, was known by the *Times* to have cost $45,000.

Mr. Eustace Roberts, who designed and cut the bride's trousseau, was given *crate blanche*, and merely told, according to the *Times*, that it should be "the richest ever produced, and fit for a Princess." One of the features of this magnificent outfit was "a black walking suit in heavy rich gros grain, in which thirty-five yards of silk were used. . . . Three hundred and eighty-two bows are used in the trimmings." "A purple silk reception dress containing thirty yards" cost "$900, and a silver gray reception dress containing thirty-two yards" cost $1,000.

The dinner was catered by Delmonico's, which had been occupied for two whole days preparing it. Grafulla himself played in the band, which furnished the music for the dancing. At eleven o'clock Mary Amelia and Arthur Ambrose Maginnis left for a short tour of Philadelphia, whence they returned to New York to sail on the *Batavia* for an extended trip in Europe.

James Gordon Bennett commented editorially apropos of the presents in the *Herald* two days after the wedding:

"Seven hundred thousand dollars! What a testimony of the loyalty, the royalty, and the abounding East Indian resources of Tammany Hall! Was there any Democracy to compare with thy Democracy, in glory, power, and equal rights, under the sun? Never! And it is just the beginning of the good time coming. Don't talk of Jeff Davis and his absurd Democracy; don't mention the Democracy of the Paris Commune, as representing true Democratic principles; but come to the fountainhead of Democracy, the old Wigwam, and you will get it there —if you get within the lucky circle of the 'magic' Ring. There you get into a Democratic placer which gives you, without the labor of digging, but with some deep diving, the pearls of Ceylon, the silver of Mexico, the gold of California, and the diamonds of Golconda, South America and Alaska. And they say that, by the 'rule of three,' it all comes out of the Tax Levy, and from the abounding blessings of municipal sovereignty and a municipal and a munificent emperor, who needs only a crown of brilliants and a throne of ivory, surmounted by a golden peacock as large as life, with an outspread tail blazing all over with diamonds, to rise to the Oriental Splendor of the Great Mogul."

Tweed held small sums of money in great contempt. Once a city creditor appealed to him to request Comptroller Connolly to pay his bill. He had asked for it again and again and was told that he could only get paid by remitting 20 per cent. of the

amount to the Comptroller's paymaster. Tweed hastily wrote
the following note to Comptroller Connolly:

DEAR DICK: For God's sake pay —— 's bill. He tells me your
people ask 20 per cent. The whole d——d thing isn't but
$1,100. If you don't pay it, I will. Thine.

WILLIAM M. TWEED.

The bill was paid.

Tweed gave large amounts to charities, and his Christmas
contribution of $50,000 in 1870 for poor relief in the Seventh
Ward gained him considerable publicity. It was said that, when
he was approached by Police Justice Shandley to put down his
name for a contribution, he had written $5,000. "Oh, Boss,
put another nought to it," Shandley said, half in jest. "Well,
well, here goes!" Tweed said, and wrote $50,000. Tweed also
had to hand out large amounts of money to his political supporters from his personal fortune. He had to buy innumerable
tickets for innumerable raffles, picnics, and shooting matches.
When he was asked on the witness stand how much he had
contributed in 1868 to the Democratic Party, he answered:
"I think it would frighten me if I told. I do not know. It was a
continued dribble—a hundred dollars, fifty dollars, five dollars,
two dollars, and one dollar. Perhaps I contributed entirely
about $10,000." Besides his own private charities and contri-
butions, the city treasury was made to contribute largely. In
the years 1869, 1870, and 1871 the Catholic Church in New
York City received from the city government $1,396,388.51
for its schools and charities. The Protestant Episcopal Church
received $56,956.74, the Hebrew $25,851.56, the Presbyterian
$13,960.52, the Baptist $5,325.63, the Methodist Episcopal
Church $7,270.95 and miscellaneous religious organizations re-
ceived $194,044.02 during the same period."[1]
The social life of the Ring was very costly. It organized and
controlled several clubs of great magnificence. The most elaborate of these was the Americus Club at Greenwich, Connecticut.
The great social event of the spring of 1871, in political circles,
next to Tweed's daughter's wedding, was the opening of the

---

[1] New York Council of Political Reform, Five Reports, p. 16.

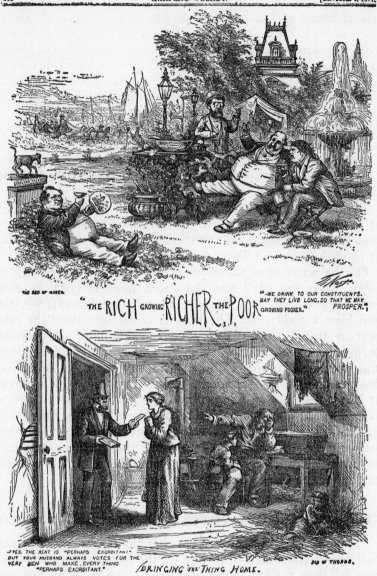

THE BED OF ROSES.

"THE RICH GROWING RICHER THE POOR GROWING POORER."

"WE DRINK TO OUR CONSTITUENTS.
MAY THEY LIVE LONG, SO THAT WE MAY
PROSPER."

"YES. THE RENT IS "PERHAPS EXORBITANT!"
BUT YOUR HUSBAND ALWAYS VOTES FOR THE
VERY MEN WHO MAKE EVERY THING
"PERHAPS EXORBITANT."

BRINGING THE THING HOME.

BED OF THORNS.

"THE TAMMANY LORDS AND THEIR CONSTITUENTS"

new clubhouse of the Americus Club, which overlooked Long Island Sound at Indian Harbour. On June 10, 1871, the politicians of New York gathered for the formal opening of the new $300,000 clubhouse. The reception room of the club was known as "Tweed's den." Inside the building were many luxurious parlours and a grand dining hall one hundred feet long. A piazza sixteen feet wide went around the entire building, and from there the view was said to be "romantic and enchanting." The carpet for the club rooms had been manufactured in England at a cost of $3,600. One of the members of the Americus Club proudly remarked that the famous imported carpet was "as thick as a beefsteak." The club owned three yachts, the largest of which was called the *William M. Tweed*.

Besides Tammany Hall and the Americus Club, the members of the Tweed Ring and their henchmen gathered at the Blossom Club, a political organization which occupied a building at Fifth Avenue and Twenty-third Street.

On the occasion of the celebration of the Fourth of July in 1870, Tammany Hall was decorated more elaborately than ever before. Andrew J. Garvey did not limit himself, for that had been a good year. The booklet commemorating the celebration stated that, "Every conceivable kind of patriotic decoration abounded." Sachem A. Oakey Hall had collected and presented to the Tammany Society examples of Indian dress and fighting equipment. Grafulla's Band, which played at Mary Amelia's wedding, played national airs for this occasion. Tweed made the only recorded speech of his career outside a legislative body. It was not stirring, and it was not well-rounded, but it seemed to serve the purpose for which he intended it. Keeping his hat on his head, which was the custom of the Grand Sachem, he said:

"FRIENDS AND FELLOW-CITIZENS, AND BROTHER DEMOCRATS:

"We are pleased to-day to see that the old interest of times past has been manifested by you for the words of wisdom which may fall from the lips of our brothers to-day, to be by you conveyed to your associates. We consider this bright auspicious day as forerunner for another when the great Democratic party, through which alone this great country can be properly reconstructed, shall again resume sway, and place us in the condition of constitutional prosperity we were in before the late civil war. (Applause.) I trust that the words that will be said here to-day by those who have prepared themselves for the occasion, will be duly pondered. We believe that the doctrines enunciated on this platform will be such as to warm the heart of every true friend of his country and every Democrat in the world. Brothers, as there will be much good talk by the warriors and braves, I will spare you the infliction of a speech from me, except these welcoming words to the Wigwam, and tell you how deeply we all feel the enthusiasm you have manifested by your attendance here to-day."

The Declaration of Independence was then read by Edmund Randolph Robinson, grand-nephew of Thomas Jefferson. "The Declaration," wrote the Tammany historian of the occasion, "was read with that fervor and appreciative emphasis which one would expect from a gentleman who had been lineally impressed with the historical incidents of the great document."

Tweed was now at the peak of his prominence, and men aimed to please him as they do an emperor whose power is absolute. With that trembling solicitude with which all men are treated whose will can be transmitted into action by the mere expression of it, his followers went out of their way to conciliate him, and spent time in thinking up new ways of winning favourable notice from their monarch. This was true of people in all classes of society. Millionaires found it useful to know the Boss of New York and to please him, and dock labourers were happy if they could gain his attention. It must be said for his personality that he was never arrogant, in spite of this provocation.

Frank Duffy, whose hat was slouched in the manner of Buffalo Bill, and whose moustache was waxed like that of Napoleon III, used to boast that, when Tweed was foreman of the "Big Six" Engine Company, he, Duffy, was a member thereof. He also claimed to be the creator of the Tiger symbol for Tammany Hall. But in spite of all these obvious accomplishments, Tweed did not take to Duffy, and he gave him no jobs. In order to win the attention of the great man, Duffy, who had noticed that the shop windows were displaying two engravings, entitled "Napoleon and His Generals," and "Grant and His Generals," conceived the idea of issuing a picture of "Tweed and His Generals," which would include portraits of the great man and all the leading public officials of New York City. Duffy thought that, besides pleasing Tweed, he would make some money out of the enterprise, for he received money from those who wished to be included, and he charged a special rate for those who wanted to cluster near the Boss. The picture appeared, but Duffy was disappointed in his effort to win Tweed's favour, because the Republican press ridiculed the picture so much that Tweed was annoyed rather than pleased, and, as Matthew P. Breen remarked, Duffy received "'cold shoulder' instead of 'taffy on toast.'"

Another effort to please the Boss had its origin in the campaign of the New York *Sun* for a statue to Tweed. The *Sun*, which, under the editorship of Charles A. Dana, enjoyed a hoax as much as it did news, was the first newspaper to take up the suggestion, which, it was said, originated as a joke among some merry members of the Blossom Club. It was also said that Tweed was consulted before the movement was started, and that he was persuaded to consent to it so that he might see who were his friends and who were not by the list of subscribers to the fund. The Tweed Testimonial Association was organized, and subscriptions were invited. It was hoped the amount necessary for a fine statue would be forthcoming by April 3d, the Boss's birthday. The *Sun* published this editorial on December 12, 1870:

"We propose that the statue shall be executed by Captain Albertus de Groot, who made the celebrated Vanderbilt bronzes, but we have not yet decided whether it shall represent the favorite son of New York afoot or ahorseback. In fact, we rather incline to have a nautical statue, exhibiting Boss Tweed as a bold mariner, amid the wild fury of a hurricane, splicing the main brace in the foretopgallant futtock shrouds of his steamyacht. But that is a matter for future consideration. The first thing is to get the money; and if those who claim to be Mr. Tweed's friends don't raise it, we shall begin to believe the rumor that the Hon. P. Brains Sweeny has turned against him, and has forbidden everyone to give anything toward the erection of the projected statue."

The *Herald* offered several designs by its own editor. On January 21, 1871, this editorial appeared:

"And so now the faithful followers of the 'Boss' are going to build him a monument. Committees, we understand, have been appointed in the several wards to raise the money, and, modest enough, fifty thousand, they say, is the figure. The site selected is the new Tweed plaza, at the junction of Broadway and Grand Street—a generous recognition of the claims of the east side of the town. And the design adopted for the monument, as we are kindly informed, is the happy conceit of a colossal hollow figure in brass of the 'Boss' as the big Indian, seated in an arm chair, holding in his right hand the scroll of our new city Charter, and in his left the pipe of peace.

"Exquisite design, this. Couldn't be better. Mark how harmoniously it blends the majesty of the Grand Sachem with his starting point to grandeur and glory,—that 'old arm chair,' bearing the inscription:—

> "'I love it, I love it, and who shall dare
> To chide me for loving this old arm chair.'

"This is the design selected. Among others submitted was one intended to represent the 'Boss' inspecting a group of fast horses in front of his splendid stable; but it was rejected as trenching upon the superior claims of Bonner's Dexter and Jo Elliott. Another plan, representing our hero in a standing position, holding up his new tax levy, was declined because it too nearly resembled the melancholy statue of 'Honest Old Abe' at Union Square. Lastly, a very elaborate design—intended to perpetuate in a railway train, under a full head of steam, that famous night trip of the Grand Sachem, from the squelching of O'Brien at Tammany Hall to the snuffing out of Genet at Albany on the Charter—was rejected, because the general idea, and more too, is embodied in the Vanderbilt bronze on the top of the railway depot in Hudson street. Is there anything in the world to compare with that Vanderbilt bronze? No. . . .

"But we have a much grander idea to propose, an idea which embraces all our City Fathers under the new dispensation. . . . Have all our city officials done in that style in brown stone, and have them arranged in the form of a grand circle or 'ring' around the sheep walk of the Central Park, with the 'Boss' in the centre, on a pedestal five hundred feet high, and in his unrivaled act of opening a bottle of champagne. . . .

"Let it not be a plan that it will take as long to complete as the Cathedral of Cologne or our new Court House, but something which can be carried out right off, and which our reigning city authorities can see for themselves in its perfection before it is too late for them. Life is short and power is fleeting, and we have no time to lose in monuments intended to curry favour with living men or reigning potentates."

It was said that the rank and file of the Democracy were more enthusiastic about a statue to Boss Tweed than the leaders and office-holders. Subscriptions were taken, and $7,973 was raised in a few days. All the publicity, however, was not favourable; the following letter appeared in the *Sun:*

SIR:

Inclosed you will find nine cents, my contribution towards the erection of a statue to Hon. W. M. Tweed.

I send this for the purpose of showing my appreciation of the man who, for the last ten years, has defrauded the public, more especially the poor man, out of millions of dollars—so that his image may always remain to the public gaze for generations to come. I want to show the man who has increased our taxation and deprived the poor man of his hard earnings. Then their children may point their fingers and say: "It was he who drove my father to destruction by the enormous rents we had to pay."

THOMAS McCUE,
(No. 82 Carmine St.)

Others sent in suggestions for designs. One of these represented Tweed in a Roman toga, but he objected to that style of coat, as he called it, remarking that it made him look too much as if he were going to take a bath. Finally, Tweed saw that the statue publicity was making him ridiculous and much too notorious. He sent the following letter to Police Justice Shandley, who was head of the Tweed Testimonial Association:

Senate Chamber
Albany, N. Y., March 13, 1871.

To the Hon. EDWARD J. SHANDLEY.

MY DEAR SIR:

I learn that a movement to erect a statue to me in the City of New York is being seriously pushed by a committee of citizens of which you are Chairman. While I am gratified by the friendly feelings which have prompted you and the gentlemen who are associated with you in this demonstration to do me honor, I most emphatically and decidedly object to it. I had no idea until yesterday, when my attention was called to public circulars soliciting contributions to that object, that it was gravely entertained. I was aware that a newspaper of our city had brought forward the proposition, but I considered it one of the jocose sensations for which that journal is so famous. Since I left the city to engage in legislation the proposition appears to have been taken up by my friends, no doubt in resentment at the supposed unfriendly motive of the original proposition, and the manner in which it had been urged.

Statues are not erected to living men, but to those who have ended their careers, and where no interest exists to question the partial tributes of friends. There are exceptional instances in which important deeds have been thus commemorated, or the vanity of the individual flattered. I claim to be a live man, and hope (Divine Providence permitting) to survive in all my vigor, politically and physically, some years to come.

The only effect of the proposed statue is to present me to the public as assenting to the parade of a public and permanent testimonial to vanity and self-glorification, which do not exist. You will thus perceive that the movement, which originated in a joke, but which you have made serious, is doing me an injustice and an injury; and I beg of you to see to it that it is at once stopped.

I hardly know which is the more absurd, the original proposition or the grave comments of others, based upon the idea that

I have given the movement countenance. I have been about as much abused as any man in public life; but I have never yet been charged with being deficient in common sense.

Yours very truly,

Wm. M. Tweed.

The *Sun* headed this letter: "*A Great Man's Modesty. The Hon. William M. Tweed Declines the Sun's Statue. Characteristic Letter from the Great New York Philanthropist—He Thinks*

THE REHEARSAL

Shandley (*as Puck*). "Allow me to immortalize you, Boss!"
Tweed (*realizing his part*). "I most emphatically and decidedly object to it. I am not deficient in common-sense."

That Virtue Should Be Its Own Reward—The Most Remarkable Letter Ever Written by the Noble Benefactor of the People." The *Sun* reminded Tweed in an editorial that the Duke of Wellington had seen dozens of statues erected in his honour before he died, that Commodore Vanderbilt had just had one, and "that Washington allowed a statue of himself to be sculptured by Houdin for the state of Virginia, and even stood naked before the sculptor while he was modelled."

The money subscribed for the Tweed Statue was returned, but, it was said, the list of subscribers was turned over to

Tweed, who knew from it who were generous in their affection and who were not, for the Committee furnished Tweed with the reasons offered by those who refused to subscribe. "As one of them afterwards expressed himself," wrote Matthew P. Breen, "'It would have cost so damn little to have put one's name down for a thousand dollars.'"

The Ring, now all-powerful in the City and the State, entertained national aspirations. The plan was, according to some political observers, to make Governor John T. Hoffman President of the United States in 1872, to make A. Oakey Hall Governor of New York, Tweed United States Senator from New York, and to let Connolly continue to rule the New York treasury as Comptroller. Sweeny, it was said, had no further aspirations than to remain the power behind the throne, but one newspaper credited him with ambition to represent New York in the United States Senate, where he would not have to talk much but could manipulate national affairs for personal profit. But Tweed was also said to have told his friends that he was working too hard, that he was rich and needed a change. In the event of Governor Hoffman's election as President, it was said that he wished to represent the United States of America as ambassador to the Court of St. James's.

In the election of 1870, the Ring had been eminently successful, and Tammany continued in complete power in New York. The *Standard* gave this burlesque description of the rulers of New York receiving the returns at the Metropolitan Hotel:

"All day yesterday any effort to elicit from Mayor Hall an estimate of his expected majority failed. Although wearied mentally and physically with the campaign, he betrayed no sign of anxiety. In the evening, at his rooms in the Metropolitan Hotel, he patiently and carefully received the returns, jotted them in order on his memorandum, chatted about yachting and journalism, and ate Malaga grapes.

"Mr. Sweeny sat in one corner, apparently asleep. When the returns came in he never awoke, but seemed to be dreaming of the parks beneath the collar of his coat.

"Mr. Tweed offered to bet him a thousand dollars that Hall would get 35,000 majority, but the great politician was immovable. At last Mr. Tweed was compelled to offer a game of

crack-loo to Governor Hoffman, who was standing upright by
the mantel in fear of bagging the knees of his doeskin panta-
loons. He answered the Commissioner by arranging the plaits
of his shirt front with dignified care. In and around the political
headquarters bets were freely offered on Mayor Hall receiving
30,000 majority, with few takers. The Mayor and his friends
seemed to think that Ledwith would poll a much larger vote
than was popularly expected. Said Tweed, 'If Oakey could
have made six such speeches as the Brennan meeting oration,
he would have carried every ward in the city. Ledwith will get
50,000 votes.' Then Sweeny nodded in his sleep, and Tweed
quietly dropped a grape-skin on Hoffman's boot. The great
statesman used his smelling bottle and retreated to the window.

"At eight o'clock Tom Fields dropped in and offered to take
the whole party on a drunk, up to Harlem Bridge. Nobody
would go. At ten o'clock the result was certain. Sweeny suddenly woke, walked to the door and disappeared. Hall took
another grape and vanished, rewarding the lackeys on the
landing with handfuls of posters. Tweed offered to play Hoffman a game of sugar-loo for ten dollars; but the great statesman
stroked his chin with his gloved fingers, and uttering the mysterious axiom, 'early to wealth and healthy to wise, will make a
bed rise wealthy and early,' he slowly meandered, like an un-
lighted wax candle, down the halls. As the door closed behind
him, Connolly and Tweed were beginning a game of leap-frog,
and Tweed was 'downer.'"

Tweed and his associates felt solid and comfortable. They
had worked hard for a few years and had managed to control
the City absolutely and the State as much as they needed.
They were rich. Tweed and his friends looked forward to a quiet
summer on the yachts owned and operated by the Americus
Club. But just as the hot weather came on, the New York
Times began the famous disclosures which heralded the beginning of the end.

VI

For more than a year the New York *Times* and some of the
other newspapers of New York had been calling the members
of the Tweed Ring thieves and marauders. Horace Greeley,

"ON TO WASHINGTON!"

in the *Tribune*, as early as 1870, wrote that the Ring "was the most corrupt gang of political adventurers that ever ruled and robbed a helpless city." In 1866 the Rev. Henry Ward Beecher had said in his pulpit that perhaps the government of the City of New York did more moral harm to the people of New York than all the churches together did good. The *Times* remarked, on October 3, 1870: "We think it is quite as true now as when old President Dwight said it, that although every Democrat is not a horse-thief, it is quite certain that every horse-thief is a Democrat."

The *Times* began to be somewhat discouraged at the obvious ineffectuality of its attacks.

"Can this island be the culminating point of the enterprise, the culture, the wealth and power of the continent," asked the editor of the *Times*, "yet its people be incapable to shake off the rule of the dozen sordid men of selfish hearts and narrow brains who have plundered us of millions yearly, obstructed our material growth, made our markets, our wharves and piers and streets, mere monuments of their rapacity, our elections a farce, and now have put up Judges in our very Court-house to sell injustice for a price?"

But in spite of all that the *Times* and *Harper's Weekly*, with the aid of the great talent of Thomas Nast, its caricaturist, could do, the Ring grew more powerful and more corrupt daily, and the people did not seem concerned.

One reason for the public indifference was that generalities were unimpressive, and neither the *Times* nor *Harper's Weekly* had definite figures and actual facts. To call Tweed a thief was futile until they could prove how much he had stolen in dollars and cents, and while everybody knew that it was true, nobody seemed to be able to do anything about it, because, for one thing, almost everybody wished to share in the plunder rather than to limit the opportunities of the thieves.

Another reason for public indifference was that the Ring kept up a careful counter attack in the newspapers which it owned or which it bought. Six or eight men on almost every newspaper in New York were put upon the City's pay roll at salaries of from $2,000 to $2,500 a year. They were engaged in no municipal business, but their duty consisted in writing blurbs in favour of Tweed and his associates as part of their newspaper work, for which they also received pay. Another effective method of controlling the press and public opinion was by means of corporation advertising. The Ring gave legal and municipal advertising to twenty-six daily and fifty-four weekly newspapers at exorbitant rates. Writers were also hired to send letters to newspapers in other cities praising the members of the Ring individually, Tammany Hall as an organization, and the administration of the City generally. These were copied by the New York papers after they appeared elsewhere, and they created the impression that the entire nation admired the city government. The *World*, whose editor, Manton Marble, later sold himself and his newspaper to the Tweed Ring, said of its contemporary the *Herald* on March 26, 1870:

"The *Herald* is measly and mottled with the frantic froth which the eight stipendiaries of the Ring employed upon it snort out in their efforts to save their places. . . . Who cares for the marriage certificate when he has seen them leap the broomstick and seen the features of their issue?

"'She was a harlot, and he was a thief,
But they loved each other beyond belief.'"

The Ring newspapers attacked the *Times* for attacking the Ring, and it was gravely pointed out that the editor of the *Times*, Louis Jennings, was not only an Englishman, but also the husband of an actress.

Just before the election of 1870 the members of the Tweed Ring thought that the efforts of the *Times* and *Harper's Weekly* might affect their success somewhat. Therefore Tweed obtained from the six wealthiest and most respectable members of the community, John Jacob Astor, Moses Taylor, Marshall O. Roberts, George K. Sistare, E. D. Brown, and Edward Schell, a statement that they had personally examined the books of the City, and that the finances were in excellent condition. The statement said that at the current rate of progress the entire city debt would be wiped out in twelve years—but the distinguished members of the "whitewashing" committee did not indicate whether or not this consummation was to be accomplished by bankruptcy. It was charged that in return for this splendid coöperation taxes were not collected from certain wealthy members of the community for 1868, 1869, and 1870, but it has also been alleged since that the members of the committee were threatened that, if they did not make this favourable report, their taxes would be increased enormously.

On October 27, 1870, a large meeting was held at Tammany Hall. The streets were jammed for blocks with people anxious to demonstrate their faith in the virtues of Tweed, Sweeny, Connolly, and Hall, who were being attacked continuously by Nast and the *Times*. On the platform sat Horatio Seymour, former Governor of New York, and Democratic candidate for President of the United States in opposition to General Grant, Governor John T. Hoffman, William M. Tweed, Samuel J. Tilden, and other politicians who went by the name of statesmen. August Belmont was the chairman of the meeting, and after he had called upon several of the trained orators for speeches, he called upon James Fisk, Jr., who sat beside Tweed. Fisk told the enthusiastic audience: "I never yet voted the Democratic ticket, but now I will vote for it on account of my friend Tweed; yes, vote for it, if I can, three times a day, and I will bring with me the 25,000 men under me!" There was boisterous applause, and Jim Fisk was generally considered to be the hit of the evening.

But envy was a more potent source of trouble than honesty, and rancour was more dangerous than principle. When Tweed and his associates made an enemy of Jimmy O'Brien, the Sheriff of New York, they made the mistake of their political and personal lives. The Sheriff's office was one of the most lucrative in the City for its occupant, because the Sheriff was entitled to the fees he collected instead of a salary. O'Brien had just completed in the spring of 1871 a prosperous term as Sheriff, but O'Brien was very much interested in money, and he put in a bill for "extras" amounting to a quarter of a million dollars. The omnipotent Board of Audit met to consider this claim and also a claim by the stationers to the City, Edward Jones & Company, for about one million dollars. The meeting was not harmonious. A letter was read from ex-Sheriff O'Brien in which he threatened that, unless his bill was sanctioned, he would publish the exorbitant bills which had already been approved by the Comptroller and paid. Some members of the Board of Audit wished to give O'Brien what he wanted, but one member of the Board maintained that it was illegal to pay out money on any claims that were alleged to be for work performed before the Board was constituted by the new charter, and he refused to allow the claim. This member, it was said, was Sweeny. It was just after that stormy meeting of the Board that the New York *Times* began to publish the exact figures from the Comptroller's books which showed in startling and vivid manner how much had been stolen from the people by their representatives.

These figures would not have come into the possession of Jimmy O'Brien at this time, and through him would not have been available for the *Times*, if James Watson, City Auditor, had not been so fond of horseflesh. While driving one of his fast trotters in the Central Park behind a sleigh during the winter of 1870–1871, Watson was killed. The Comptroller's office then needed another man, and a friend of O'Brien's named Copeland was appointed to work on the books in the Auditor's office. Copeland noticed some accounts that looked suspicious, and well he might become suspicious, for bills to the amount of hundreds of thousands of dollars for shades and millions of dollars for plaster would raise the eyebrows of an Arcadian. Copeland copied out choice samples of suspicious accounts and showed them to his friend O'Brien, who instructed him to continue quietly copying out all the figures he could find.

Meanwhile, O'Brien, with the coöperation of State Senators Norton, Genet and Creamer, and financed by Edward Jones & Company, who felt that Tweed and his associates could have inserted their fraudulent claims in the City's tax levy if they had wanted to, organized the Young Democracy in order to combat the Ring and to gain power for themselves. We have already seen how Tweed defeated their aims by the liberal use of money in Albany. At that time O'Brien did not have possession of the damaging figures, but as soon as he got them, and his threat to publish them was ignored by the Ring, he took them to the New York *Times*, where they were joyfully greeted as manna from heaven, for the *Times* had called the Ring thieves over and over again and was wondering what next to say.

The New York *Times* was owned at this time by George O. Jones, and his editor was Louis Jennings, a person who knew how to use epithets and invective. But neither epithets nor invective were necessary now. The *Times* analyzed the figures carefully and began to publish them in July, 1871. All summer long the *Times* kept up the publication of the damaging accounts and sent reporters everywhere to gather more evidence of the colossal frauds, while Thomas Nast in *Harper's Weekly* kept up a barrage of the most devastating caricatures that have ever appeared in an American publication.

The members of the Tweed Ring were now worried. Before the *Times* began to publish its figures, Tweed and his associates discovered that the paper had possession of them. Every man Tweed had ever seen or heard of had his price. One afternoon in the early summer of 1871, an eminent lawyer, who was friendly with George Jones, called at the *Times* office. He asked Jones to come to his office for a business consultation, and when Jones arrived he found that only one man was in the office— "Slippery Dick" Connolly. Connolly came to the point quickly and offered Jones $5,000,000 if he would not publish his figures. "I don't think," Jones was said to have remarked, "that the devil will ever bid higher for me than that." Connolly took the remark as encouraging and pictured to Jones what he could do with $5,000,000. "Why," he said, "you could go to Europe and live like a prince." Jones refused to live like a prince, and Connolly went away more worried than ever to tell his cronies the incredible, sad news that there was at least one man in New York who had no royal aspirations.

Tweed had never paid much attention to what the newspapers said about him, except his own newspapers. But there was one thing that worried Tweed for months, and that was Thomas Nast's art. He was keen enough to realize that Nast was more vivid than figures, and he once remarked that he did not care what all the papers in the world said of him, but he did wish that picture man would let up on him. A friend tried to comfort him with the assurance that the pictures were such

broad caricatures that people would never believe them. But
Tweed answered sadly that if the people got used to seeing him
in stripes, they would soon put him in them.

A well-known banker was sent to see Thomas Nast. The
banker remarked that he admired Nast's art tremendously,
and that he had certain friends who also admired it; that these
friends were so much interested in Nast that they were willing

THE "BRAINS"

THAT ACHIEVED THE TAMMANY VICTORY AT THE ROCHESTER
DEMOCRATIC CONVENTION.

to put up $100,000 for Nast's expenses while he was developing
his genius in Europe.

"Do you think I could get $200,000?" Nast asked inno-
cently.

"I believe," said the banker, "from what I have heard in the
bank that you might get it."

Nast thought a few moments. "Don't you think," he asked.
"I could get $500,000 to make that trip?"

"You can," the banker answered enthusiastically. "You can
get $500,000 to drop this Ring business and get out of the
country."

"Well, I don't think I'll do it," Nast answered. "I made up my mind not long ago to put some of those fellows behind the bars, and I am going to put them there."

"Only be careful, Mr. Nast," remarked the banker, "that you don't put yourself in a coffin first," and he left the room.[1]

On September 8, 1871, Tweed told a reporter for the *Sun:*

"The *Times* has been saying all the time I have no brains. Well, I'll show Jones that I have brains. You know, if a man is with others he must do as they do. If I had been alone, he would have a good time of it. But, you know, if a man is with others he must take care not to do a rash act. It would hurt them all, you know. . . . I tell you, sir, if this man Jones had said the things he has said about me, twenty-five years ago, he wouldn't be alive now. But, you see, when a man has a wife and children, he can't do such a thing (clenching his fists). I would have killed him."

The *Times* said in the course of its attacks:

"If Mayor Hall and Controller Connolly object to being branded as thieves and swindlers, as we once more brand them now, they can sue us for libel, and we will prove our charges in a Court of law. What is more, we will prove our charge by means of Controller Connolly's *own books*. It will not do for Hall to try and sneak out by saying that he is 'used to newspaper attack.' We do not attack him now on political grounds, or in wild language—but we call him a thief because we can prove him to be one."

Mayor Hall tried at first to parry the attacks by the public use of his curious sense of humour. When reporters came to him, he refused to comment on the facts and figures, and in the paper which he edited, the *Leader*, he merely remarked at the height of the attack: "Counts at Newport are at a discount"; "Shocking levity—the light-ship off Savannah has gone astray"; and, "These warm, yet occasionally breezy days, with charmingly cool mornings and evenings, are an indication that we are likely to have what befell Adam—an early Fall."

---

[1] *Thomas Nast*, by Albert Bigelow Paine, p. 182.

The Mayor finally consented to mention finances to a *Herald* reporter. He said that he had been intending to issue reports concerning the state of the City's finances for some time, but that the reports were so voluminous that they required care and time to prepare.

"These statistical tables," he said, "were behind, but in progress, when the Corinthian type of the *Times* fired its volley

"GROSS IRREGULARITY NOT 'FRAUDULENT'"

Boss SWEED. "To make this *look straight* is the hardest job I ever had. What made WATSON go sleigh-riding?"

of secret account bullets. Corinthian type and startling headlines are tremendous influencers of public opinion. If any paper should print in gigantic type, 'The cholera has come,' I believe half its readers would be in collapse before tea time, when if the announcement was in brevier no effect could be found."

The Mayor forgot, however, that the public would have quickly recovered from collapse when it was discovered that the cholera was not with them, but he made no attempt to convince the public that they were not assailed by unprecedented corruption. He told the *Herald* reporter that his reports on finance would be published "next week." "Why not before?" asked the reporter. "*Festina lente*," answered the Mayor with a smile.

The Tweed group were evidently of the opinion that everything would blow over, as the Mayor himself expressed it. When Tweed was asked concerning the *Times* revelations, he boldly asked, "What are you going to do about it?" This was a mistake; such defiance bred resentment against him, for not even the most acquiescent public opinion liked to think of itself as impotent.

Meanwhile, the members of the Ring tried to stop the revelations of the *Times* and *Harper's Weekly* by direct attacks on their business. All publications of Harper & Brothers were barred from the public schools. On August 31, 1871, the *Times* published the following comment:

"By the by, Mayor Hall has, we are informed, privately caused a recommendation to be isued through his favorite newspaper to the effect that all persons employed in the City or County offices should refrain from eating or drinking in the restaurant under the Times Building. Is not this a revenge worthy of the excellent Mr. Hall? The City clerks now are not to be allowed to eat their dinners where they like. Decidedly the City authorities are carrying on a defensive warfare in a dignified manner. *Quos Deus vult perdere*, etc., as the accomplished and learned Mayor would say."

At the height of the excitement Oakey Hall and his friends made a great blunder. They dug up the title of the building in which the *Times* was located, formerly the site of the Brick Church, and in the name of the City started suit for the premises, because the City had formerly owned the land, and the attempt was made to show that the title of the *Times* was defective. This was practically a confession of guilt in the form of determination on the part of the criminals to punish their accusers. It aroused the newspapers throughout the country; they had been jealous of the *Times* before, but now they cried free speech and defended their colleague. The proceedings were silly, for the *Times* title was perfect, and the exposures had already gone too far to enable the Ring to use its corrupt judges to sustain its absurd contentions. Tweed was losing his temper and with that he lost his judgment. The Ring also attempted to show by means of their own newspapers that the reasons for the attacks of the *Times* and the Harpers were that the *Times* had not been allowed a claim for $13,764.36 against the city government, and that the Harpers' textbooks were not purchased by the City. But, as we have just seen, the *Times* could have had five millions of dollars instead of $13,764.36, if its main interest had been money, and the Harpers' books were not barred from the schools until after Nast's pictures had appeared for some time.

The Mayor wrote two editorials in his paper, the *Leader*. One was called "The *Times* out of Joint," and the other "A Penny or a Paper." He wrote in his characteristic manner in the latter editorial:

"There is a point on the railway from New York to Philadelphia where the cars stop for a time beside an enclosure railed off from the road by a high white picket fence. If you dare to look out of the window towards this fence, you will find yourself the cynosure of a small mob of boys impaled behind it, whose shrill voices will forthwith send up a flattering chorus of 'Please, Mr. Gentleman, give us a penny or a paper—please, Mr. Gentleman, give us a penny or a paper.' If, trained in political economy, and ever considering the greatest good of the greatest number, you turn a deaf ear to these solicitations, as the cars move away the flattering cries will suddenly acidulate into a consentaneous yell of 'Ah! get along, you d——d old fool! ah! get along, you d——d old fool!'

"As it is with the naughty little Jersey boys, so it is with the gray-bearded Harpers of Franklin Street. So long as the city authorities could be enticed into giving them 'a penny or a paper,' into sending them advertisements, or buying from them tons of school-books, irrespective of age or sex, their most sweet voices would incessantly salute 'Mr. Government.' Give them their penny or their paper, and you should see Mr. Tweed, who grovels to-day in the dust of a grub, soar in some Nasty heaven of invention, an angel winged with gold. P. B. Sweeny then would become with them *Pontifex Benedictus*, building a golden bridge to carry them over from the deserts of Radicalism into the Goshen of Democracy, flowing with milk and honey, where bankers do not check nor butter merchants beslobber the progress towards perfection. Even the Mayor would be hailed by them *Augustus Optimus;* for they are very classical, these Harpers, and have made a very good thing out of Anthon [Professor Charles Anthon] and the heathen gods, a much better thing probably than either Anthon or the heathen gods, or the City Government, or the Radicals, or the Southern slave-drivers, ever have made or ever will make out of them."[1]

When a reporter asked Mayor Hall whether a report in a newspaper that he was going to resign was true, this scene took place: "Sonny," said the Mayor, taking the representative of the Press by the hand in the most fatherly manner, and leading him to a corner of the office, "do you see that?" pointing to a certificate of the Mayor's election. "Well, when I am going to resign, that will be taken down and a beautiful picture of 'Resignation,' which I saw this morning in Nassau Street, will appear in its place." The Mayor also said that he had long ceased to read newspaper comments upon himself. He followed, he said, the rule of the late Abraham Lincoln, and always turned to another part of the paper when he saw his own name mentioned. Whether or not this was true of Lincoln, it was certainly not true of A. Oakey Hall, for he collected every newspaper clipping he could find about himself, and the fourteen large ledger volumes in which they repose were donated by his daughter to the New York Public Library and now form part of the collections of that institution.

While the exposures of the Ring frauds were being published, some of the newspapers published an account of how the Mayor had saved a small child from drowning when she fell overboard from a yacht. The Mayor, hearing the mother's screams, was said to have hurled himself into the turbulent waters and fished out the child. He sent this note of denial to the newspapers:

"The newspapers have put me in a good deal of *hot water* lately, but I must disclaim the *cold water* heroism they have so generously given me credit for. I think the story of my romantic bravery is simply a clever hoax of that king of prac-

[1]New York *Leader*, July 22, 1871.

tical jokers, Alderman Jerome. I am an expert swimmer, and
have often jumped off docks and other places, and picked out
drowning people, but I do not desire credit for an act not performed. The whole story is founded upon the simple incident of
two little children floundering in a brook. They were in no
danger, and were brought ashore without any display of heroism. If a bad pun will *pun*-ish the not *pun*-y act of the Alderman
in relating his yarn, I will characterize it a (Je)rome-antic
story."

When the *Times* began its publication of the figures that told
the story of the Tweed Ring's frauds, many people were out of
town for the summer. The weather was hot, and public opinion
was lethargic. But the *Times* carefully nursed its campaign, and
in the fall, when people returned to the City, the best ammuni-
tion was used. Citizens were annoyed at first, and then, when
Tweed put his back against the wall, feeling safe in his omnipotence, and asked, "What are you going to do about it?" indignation sought action. "Th' public," remarked Old Mike,
one of the characters in Alfred Henry Lewis's *The Boss*, "is a
sheep, while ye do no more than just rob it. But if ye insult it,
it's a wolf."

A public mass meeting was called for Monday, September
4, 1871, at Cooper Union, and most of the leading merchants
and business men of the City attended, for they suddenly
awoke to the fact that it was they who were being robbed.
Former Mayor William F. Havemeyer, the sugar merchant, was
the chairman. "His manner," wrote Matthew P. Breen, "was
what might be expected of a bank president, who had to
make to the directors the painful announcement that the bank
had been robbed." Judge James Emmott carefully analyzed the
figures for the crowd. "'Gentlemen,' said Judge Emmott,
'there is no denial of these fraudulent payments, and there is
no fabrication of their amount. Now, what are you going to do
with these men?' (A voice, 'Hang them!' This answer brought
immense applause from all parts of the house.) 'I tell you,
gentlemen,' continued the Judge, 'that the world—the world is
waiting to see if the men of New York believe in honesty or wor-
ship fraud.' (Great applause.) 'We must repeal this charter;
we must punish the guilty, and recover the money to the City.

If the citizens of this great metropolis work in earnest, they cannot be resisted. There is no power like the power of a people armed, aroused, and enkindled with the enthusiasm of a righteous wrath!"

How the people began to turn against Tweed is illustrated by the reaction to a part of Judge Emmott's speech: "'Who, gentlemen,' asked the Judge, 'are these men who appear in these accounts by these singular and fictitious names? Who is Donnaruma? Who is Mr. Ingersoll's partner?' (Voices, 'Tweed.') 'Who shares with Keyser?' (Voices, 'Tweed, Tweed.') 'Who takes half of Garvey's plunder?' (Voices, 'Tweed, Tweed.') ... 'Now, gentlemen, there is no justification for these payments, and no denial of their amount!' (Voice, 'Send them to Sing Sing.')"

When Joseph H. Choate mentioned the name of William M. Tweed, there was an outburst of epithets, and cries of "Pitch into the Boss; give it to him; he deserves it." Tweed was a large man and well known to the people; he himself testified: "Nine men out of ten either know me or I know them; women and children you may include." It was his one-syllable name attached to his bulky personality that rapidly became the symbol of corruption which the imagination of the mob required.

Thousands of people tried to get into the hall of Cooper Institute, and when all could by no means be accommodated, another meeting was organized outside the building in Astor Place. A platform was improvised out of two large hogsheads, upon one of which stood the impromptu chairman, Mr. C. Scharzwaelder. Several thousand persons gathered around. M. M. Vail, a lawyer, was the first speaker. He said that his thoughts could not be expressed better than by the words of the poet:

"'Ill fares the land to lasting ills a prey,
Whose wealth accumulates and men decay;
Princes and lords may flourish or may fade,
A breath can make them, as a breath has made.
But a bold peasantry, their nation's pride,
When once destroyed can never be supplied.'"

W. T. Jennings remarked that it was essential to probe the cancer that was eating into the very heart of the City and de-

HARPER'S WEEKLY.

A JOURNAL OF CIVILIZATION

VOL. XV.—No. 773.]   NEW YORK, SATURDAY, OCTOBER 21, 1871.   [WITH A SUPPLEMENT.
PRICE TEN CENTS.

Entered according to Act of Congress, in the Year 1871, by Harper & Brothers, in the Office of the Librarian of Congress, at Washington.

THE ONLY THING THEY RESPECT OR FEAR

"We presume it is strictly correct to say that the one consequence of thieving which——
would now dread is a violent death. Public scorn, or even the penitentiary, has little terrors
for them."

"We do not know how the affair may end, but we do know that if —— close their careres
in peace, and ease, and affluence, it will be a terrible blow to political and private morality."
—*The Nation.*

stroying the body politic. But there were some Tammany adherents present. When one of the speakers remarked with great passion, "Those men have plundered us—those men have built splendid city and country residences at our expense!" someone in the crowd shouted, "Three cheers for *those men!*" He was hooted down. There were suggestions at the meetings inside and outside the Hall of lynching for the culprits, but the men on the platform who believed in law and order hastily deprecated any such intention. Some citizens suggested, however, the formation of a vigilance committee, a method so effective with criminals in California just after the gold rush, and the immediate hanging to conspicuous lamp-posts of Tweed, Connolly, Sweeny, and Hall. It was argued by these men that nothing else would be effective, for the Tweed Ring controlled the courts. The *Nation,* which was then a singularly sober weekly publication, took up this plan. An editorial in that paper for September 2, 1871, a few days before the mass meeting, read as follows:

"What we say is that, in our opinion, Hall, Connolly, Tweed, Barnard, and all the class to which they belong, and of which Louis Napoleon was the most conspicuous member, fear no penalty for their misdeeds except a violent death. They are indifferent to public opinion and have matters so arranged that the prison pen has no terrors for them, and a natural death they calculate on. But the prospect of a violent death, which would suddenly stop their champagne, knock the satin sofas from under them, shut out the velvet carpets from their view, cause their fast horses to vanish into thin air, and launch them into the cold unknown, would terrify them exceedingly; and such a death, we repeat, a large and growing body of respectable citizens think they ought to die—first and foremost in order to stop their thieving and rid the community of them, and secondly, to prevent an unwholesome influence on public and private morals of the spectacle of the peaceful close of their career in the enjoyment of their stealings. . . .

"An appeal to force, in New York, would mean civil war; and those who talk of appealing to force must make up their minds to civil war, and must be prepared for some fighting. Should they succeed in securing the persons of the malefactors,

"WHO IS INGERSOLL'S CO?" N.Y. TRIBUNE.   MR. INGERSOLL. "ALLOW ME TO INTRODUCE YOU TO MY CO?"

TWO GREAT QUESTIONS.

"WHO STOLE THE PEOPLE'S MONEY?"—DO TELL. N.Y. TIMES.   'TWAS HIM.

and in bringing them to punishment, their act will, however, be no more lynching than the execution of Robespierre and Rigault was lynching. It might be called high-handed, or cruel, or remorseless, or various other things, but it would have in it a solemnity which in Lynch law is wanting."

However, the advocates of law and order prevailed, and a Committee of Seventy was organized, with such men as Samuel J. Tilden and Joseph H. Choate as members. The members of the Ring were now thoroughly frightened. They had held many conferences, which usually ended up in their abusing each other. They were all seeking personal safety, and each demanded that the other become a "vicarious sacrifice"; but there were no volunteers for the job. Sweeny and Hall suggested that Comptroller Connolly be indicted because he was responsible for the accounts, and that Tweed resign his various positions and go to Europe. Hall tried desperately to get Comptroller Connolly to resign, but Connolly refused. The *Herald*, which was Mayor Hall's friend, demanded daily the resignation of the Comptroller. Connolly was terrified, and he looked around for means of protecting himself. On September 6, 1871, two days after the mass meeting at Cooper Institute, Connolly's wife transferred half a million dollars' worth of registered United States bonds to her son-in-law, Joel Fithian. She herself, it was said, retained three and a half millions of dollars' worth of the same securities in her own name.

Meanwhile, John Foley applied to Judge Barnard for an injunction prohibiting the payment of any money from the city treasury. This application was made on September 6th, the same day that Mrs. Connolly transferred some of her bonds. The Judge, however, did not appear in court, for he was at home ill with the gout. The *Tribune* reported that the Judge, though his foot was so swollen he could not walk, received many visitors during the day, and that paper remarked, "It was generally thought that the Ring was sicker than the Judge." Judge Barnard's decision was awaited with tense expectation. The next day, to the surprise of many, he granted the Foley injunction. The instinct for self-preservation was highly developed in Judge Barnard's character, and when people began to talk of hanging civic thieves to municipal lamp-posts, he controlled his sense of humour. The *Tribune* remarked apropos of the granting of the injunction: "It has been clear for some days that Tammany is more dangerous as a friend than as an enemy, and the cry of its old supporters is getting to be, 'Stand from under.'" Oakey Hall, when he was asked to comment on the granting of this injunction which prevented the Comptroller from functioning, remarked to the *Sun* reporter:

"Foley is a crazy fellow who, I have been told, claims to be a lineal descendant of the daring youth who fired the Ephesian dome. In its practical effect, the granting of the injunction is one of Judge Barnard's stereotyped jokes. . . . Foley thought that he had planted the nettle danger in the Court House; but from what I know of farming I think we shall pluck the flower safely from it."

Hall then went on to say that it was all a plot on the part of General Grant and the Republicans to gain control of the city administration for purposes of corruption. Meanwhile, Hall and Sweeny continued their efforts to sacrifice Comptroller Connolly.

While the members of the Ring were thus sparring with each other and endeavouring to sacrifice each other, New York was startled by exciting news. On Sunday night, September 11th, someone broke into the Comptroller's office and stole the vouchers for the year 1870 which contained the evidence of Ring frauds. The glass door had been cut with a diamond while the watchman was out getting his supper, and thirteen bundles of vouchers were removed from the office. Who was the instigator of this theft has remained a mystery, but it looked very much at the time as if Mayor Hall wished by this means to force Comptroller Connolly to resign, for on Monday afternoon he wrote the following letter to Connolly:

Mayor's Office,
Monday, P.M., September 11, 1871.

MY DEAR SIR:
I have just been informed by the Superintendent of Police that last night the offices of the Finance Department were secretly invaded, and that, as a consequence thereof, valuable

vouchers, evidences of payment and cancelled warrants (together representing a large amount of discharged city liabilities), are alleged by some of your subordinates to have then disappeared.

The Superintendent and the Mayor immediately had full conversation regarding the means of investigating the untoward circumstances of the alleged burglary; and so as to punish the guilty, procure restitution of such papers as may have been taken, and protect the interests of the city.

Our constituents will have a right to hold you responsible, and in a measure withhold from the Finance Department desirable public confidence. It is impossible not to perceive that the city credit will suffer, and in a very critical period of municipal government.

With great personal reluctance I officially reach the conclusion that the exigency requires your retirement from the head of the Finance Department, in order that I may place there another gentleman who will be enabled thoroughly to investigate its affairs, and restore public confidence.

I cannot suspend any head of department, not even pending an investigation. I can only prefer charges to the Common Pleas, who alone can remove, after a considerable time for trial.

I am compelled to throw myself, therefore, as Mayor, in this unexpected and sudden emergency, upon your magnanimity, and ask, under the circumstances, for your resignation.

Yours very truly,

A. OAKEY HALL, *Mayor.*

The HON. R. B. CONNOLLY, *Comptroller.*

Connolly answered:

Comptroller's Office,
New York, September, 12, 1871.

HON. A. OAKEY HALL, *Mayor.*

MY DEAR SIR:

Your letter of September 11, asking my resignation as Comptroller, was presented to me last night at 11 o'clock, at an interview sought by yourself.

Similar verbal requests, from yourself and others, have been, within the last few weeks, received and delivered. The official source and subject matter of your note, as then read to me, and as published by you in this morning's press, demanded and has received my earnest consideration. A criminal abstraction of papers from the Finance Department seems the reason for your letter, so far as any is therein suggested.

In common with other city officers, I now stand before the public and "our constituency" charged with malfeasance in the administration of high trusts so long confided to my care. The legal proceedings wherein such charges are made, and to be substantiated, if at all, is now on hearing before a fearless and just tribunal. My answer thereto, is before the public and my complete defence ready to be presented both to that high court, "our constituents," and to the citizens of New York at large. My counsel has urged, by my wish, a speedy trial and rigid investigation. I am fearless of the result, and anxious for the procedure. During the many years of my administration of this office I have not seen, and fail now to see, any diminution of public confidence, and such fact would have been readily marked, nothing being more sensitive to general opinion than financial administration. I beg leave to differ from your Honor in thinking the robbery of my office creates any "unexpected or sudden emergency." I am not apprehensive that either yourself or this community will suspect that I am an accomplice in that depredation. I am happy to assure you that it has effected no serious mischief, the archives of the department containing ample abstracts of all the stolen papers. Whoever planned or executed the crime has reaped no benefit and inflicted no injury upon public interests.

Would not my resignation at this particular time give the advocates of the partisan attacks upon the city government just cause to believe me to plead guilty not only to participation (at least passive) in the burglary, but as well to all the charges now made in the legal proceedings? So it seems to me. My official acts have been supervised and approved by your superior vigilance. So far as my administration is questioned, equal responsibility attaches to yourself.

In your answer and affidavit, read in the pending litigation, you have adopted and vindicated those acts. You could not justify yourself without so doing. Consequently I do not perceive why my resignation should be asked, or how if tendered, it would have any just influence in appeasing popular clamor. Confident, therefore, in the steadfast good opinion of friends, in the ultimate judgment to be rendered by the courts, I cannot, consistently with self-respect, accord to your desire. I am unable to submit myself a vicarious sacrifice to satisfy the hungry appetite of adversaries for a victim, or at this juncture and under these circumstances betray weakness of position or fear of rigid investigation by tendering my resignation.

'I cannot now anticipate the effect upon this determination future events may produce. When my past administration shall be vindicated, and pending accusation shall be repelled, I shall not fail to act as may seem to be demanded by the changed circumstances which may then exist.

Very respectfully, your ob'dt servant,
RICHARD B. CONNOLLY, Comptroller.

These letters, of course, were merely for newspaper publication and public consumption. Connolly, terrified at the prospect of being thrown to the lions, had consulted with the Committee of Seventy, and his action was based upon the advice of Samuel J. Tilden. Connolly had visited Tilden, revealed all he knew of the Ring frauds, and placed himself at the mercy of the reformers, offering to do anything to save his own neck. He was urged by Tilden and Charles O'Conor, the most eminent lawyers of the period, to hold on to his office until they told him what to do, for the reformers were afraid that, if Connolly resigned, Hall would appoint as Comptroller some friend who would cover up the frauds rather than uncover them. Finally, Tilden told Connolly to appoint Andrew H. Green Deputy Comptroller with the full powers of Comptroller. The Comptroller had this right, which had been slipped into the city charter when Connolly contemplated taking a trip to Europe during his term of office. Mayor Hall refused to recognize this appointment at first, and he appointed General George B. McClellan Comptroller. There was more talk of a vigilance committee if Mr. Green was interfered with in the administration of the Comptroller's office, and armed men were stationed in that office to guard the records.

Wild rumours now flew about the City. One of them was that Mayor A. Oakey Hall was mad and had to be held down by

VOL. XV.—No. 770.]   NEW YORK, SATURDAY, SEPTEMBER 30, 1871.   [WITH A SUPPLEMENT. PRICE TEN CENTS.

Entered according to Act of Congress, in the Year 1871, by Harper & Brothers, in the Office of the Librarian of Congress, at Washington.

"WE KNOW NOTHING ABOUT THE STOLEN VOUCHERS." "TOO THIN!" "WE ARE INNOCENT."

four men who took him home every day in his carriage. It was
difficult to find Hall, Sweeny, or Tweed during this period, for
they ran from newspaper reporters as from a plague. After
Hall's attempt to enforce the appointment of General McClellan as Comptroller had failed, he finally consented to talk with
reporters. He called them into his office in the City Hall, and
announcing his submission to the appointment of Andrew H.
Green, he said: "Gentlemen, some of you yesterday said that
I had received a severe check, and, *in testimonium veritatis*, I
have, as you see, put on a check suit."

The Committee of Seventy, under the leadership of Samuel
J. Tilden, was now beginning to gain control of the City. Samuel
J. Tilden had become one of the leading Democratic politicians
of the nation. In his boyhood he had heard political discussions
from prominent, crafty managers in his father's house, and by
the time he was fifteen he knew more inside politics than most
of his contemporaries. He studied law, and by his painstaking
abilities rose to the first rank in that profession. Realizing that
power required money, he became one of the first corporation
lawyers of any prominence in this country, and he accumulated
a large fortune as legal representative of leading railroads.
When Tweed and his associates began to steal, Tilden was a
member of Tammany Hall in good standing, and, though he
must have known of some of their deals, for it was his business to know everything in politics, he did not oppose them.
As he, perhaps, would have put it, the time was not ripe. Tilden
was cold, calculating, and inordinately ambitious. He was
frugal, cautious, and careful to control any hampering emotions.
Harry Thurston Peck wrote of him that, "He treated his
friends as though at some time they might become his enemies."

Tilden and August Belmont were interested in municipal
honesty because it was good business, but they were also
interested in the Democratic Party, because their personal
ambitions were involved in its success. Tilden wished to take
the lead in the reform movement, for he saw that such action
would be of political advantage to him, and the part which
he played in the Tweed Ring prosecutions did make him
Governor of New York in 1874 and was an indirect cause of
his Presidential nomination two years later. He was never
zealous for a justice stern enough to injure the interests of the

HARPER'S WEEKLY.

JOURNAL OF CIVILIZATION

VOL. XV.—No. 778.]   NEW YORK, SATURDAY, NOVEMBER 25, 1871.   [WITH A SUPPLEMENT. PRICE TEN CENTS.

Entered according to Act of Congress, in the Year 1871, by Harper & Brothers, in the Office of the Librarian of Congress, at Washington.

"WHAT ARE YOU LAUGHING AT? TO THE VICTOR BELONG THE SPOILS."

Democratic Party. An entirely different personality was Charles O'Conor, counsel to the Committee of Seventy, to whom was intrusted the prosecution of the Tweed Ring frauds. Mr. O'Conor was an honest man, for he had no political aspirations. O'Conor once wrote to Tilden:

"Your speeches make the welkin ring. Why did you not touch them up at Rochester? Is there a strong peculation clique there? 'Begad, I begin soospec', as the Frenchman said when he caught a man in bed with his wife."[1]

Politically, the first thing for the reformers to do was to win the election of 1871, which took place in November. The advance work had been done by the *Times* and *Harper's Weekly*, and the publicity of the startling exposures was a great weapon. But Tweed and his associates did not intend to give up easily, and they still enjoyed a powerful popularity among members of the community who regarded them as personal benefactors rather than as public marauders. In spite of all the revelations, Tweed was unanimously reëlected as chairman of the General Committee of Tammany Hall. At the State Convention of the Democratic Party, which was held in Rochester, Tweed was in control. Gangs of New York thugs were imported to Rochester free of charge over the Erie Railway in order to second more effectively the nominations which Tweed wished to be made. There were anti-Tammany delegates present, but Tweed and his followers threatened to use their thugs if these men were seated instead of the regular Tammany delegates. Bribery was also used, and all of Tweed's men were nominated for the Legislature. Tweed thought that if, by the election of his candidates, he could control the next Legislature, all would still be safe.

The reformers realized that they must put up a powerful ticket in opposition to the Tammany nominees. They nominated a German, General Sigel, for Register, to conciliate the German vote, and two Irishmen, O'Brien and O'Donovan Rossa, to cater to the Irish vote. Tilden himself ran for the Legislature. Tweed was also a candidate for reëlection to the State Senate.

The election was one of the most exciting ever held in the City of New York. In spite of the fact that the Chicago fire

[1] *Letters of Samuel J. Tilden*, Vol. I, p. 385.

DOWN WITH THE RING! THE BATTLE CRY OF FREEDOM

THE POLLS

"THE REASONS WHICH HAVE PROMPTED THIS ACTION — THESE REASONS ARE OF AN OVERWHELMING CHARACTER."

"THE REASONS WHICH HAVE PROMPTED THIS ACTION — THESE REASONS ARE OF AN OVERWHELMING CHARACTER."

"THE FACT SHALL NOT BE MADE KNOWN UNTIL AFTER THE ELECTION."

I HEREBY TENDER MY RESIGNATION."

TAMMANY RING LOST

"I SEVER MY CONNECTION"

THE POLITICAL SUICIDE OF PETER "BRAINS" $WEENY.

THE TAMMANY BRAINS

HILTON

WHAT WILL THE JUDGE DO WITHOUT HIS "BRAINS"

BRAINS

$

"THE TIMES HAVE BEEN THAT WHEN THE BRAINS WERE OUT, THE MAN WOULD DIE AND THERE AN END." SHAKESPEARE

THE "HEAD" AND "BRAIN" GONE, THE BODY GOES TO

SING-SING OR ALBANY THE STATE'S PRISON.   or   SENATE

Th. Nast.

and the arrival of the Grand Duke Alexis competed for attention with the political contest, the public remained somewhat interested in its business. Clergymen preached to their congregations the necessity of doing their duty by defeating the thieves at the polls. The students of New York University, who had listened with interest to the wit of A. Oakey Hall, now tore his portrait from the walls of the lecture room. Even A. T.

TOUCHSTONE

Tammany (O. K.) Hall Jester (*Reads*). "'Where Ignorance is Bliss, 'tis Folly to be Wise.' *I am in Blissful Ignorance of Every Thing that has happened since I have been Mayor of New York.*"

Stewart closed his large store on election day so that his clerks might vote. Four regiments of militia supplemented the police, and the soldiers were placed in large express wagons ready for rapid dispatch to any places where disorder might break out. Some efforts were made to throw out reform votes and to use repeaters, but the reform ticket won by an overwhelming majority. Tweed, however, was reëlected by a large majority to the State Senate, for the people of his district still clung to him loyally, because he had always distributed plenty of money about the ward, and they were not concerned with where he got it.

VII

After the election had been won by the reformers, efforts were made to prosecute Tweed. Soon after the election Sweeny announced that he accepted the will of the people, and that he was withdrawing from public life. Pretending to ill-health, he left hurriedly for Canada. The lesser members of the Ring, the contractors and the manufacturers, were frightened. Andrew J. Garvey, the Prince of Plasterers, hinted that Tweed and Woodward were responsible for his exorbitant bills, and that he himself was innocent. A man named J. Hennessy Cooke called upon the plasterer and assured him that if he did or said anything to injure "the old man," as Tweed was called affectionately by some of his followers, he would be murdered. "The job has been put up," Mr. J. Hennessy Cooke added encouragingly, "and I am to do it. There won't be any pistols or noise, but you will be got out of the way so that nobody won't know." Garvey left for Europe. Woodward went to Montreal.[1]

Mayor Hall clung to his office, in spite of demands that he resign, and he insisted that he had been innocent of the fraudulent ways of his best friends. Connolly was in the hands of the reformers.

Tweed stood alone. He was indicted by the Grand Jury on 120 counts, among which there were four for felony, three for forgery, two for grand larceny, two for misdemeanour, one for false pretences, and one for conspiracy. He was arrested on December 16, 1872, by his friend, Sheriff Matthew T. Brennan, who went to Tweed's office in the evening, touched him on the shoulder, and said, laughing, "You're the man I'm after, I guess." The Sheriff and his prisoner spent the night at the Metropolitan Hotel, which Tweed owned, and in the morning he applied for bail before Judge Gunning Bedford, whom he had made a judge. In the courtroom Tweed was greeted with both cheers and hisses. Judge Bedford refused bail and committed Tweed to the Tombs on the misdemeanour charge. Tweed resented the action of Bedford, and he was said to have remarked: "Why, if I couldn't spit twenty Bedfords an hour, and have each a giant alongside of Gunnie, I ought to be hung." But Tweed and his counsel did not go to the Tombs.

[1] *North American Review*, Vol. CXXIII, pp. 373–391.

"THE ARREST OF 'BOSS' TWEED—ANOTHER GOOD JOKE"

THE SHADOW OF JUSTICE. "I'LL MAKE SOME OF YOU CRY YET."

"Sheriff BRENNAN merely nodded to Mr. TWEED, bade him 'Good-day,' and laying his
hand tenderly on his shoulder, said, laughingly, 'You're my man!' It seemed like a deliciously
cool joke, and, judging from the faces, it was."—*New York Tribune.*

They sought out Judge Barnard, who was holding court in the new County Court House, which Tweed had helped to build. Barnard was asked to review the decision of the lower court immediately. The crowd followed into the Supreme Court chamber. Tweed sat in front of a life-sized painting of himself, which hung in back of the Judge's chair. Charles O'Conor protested against the granting of bail, ending his argument with the following quotation:

> "Plate sin with gold,
> And the strong lance of justice hurtless breaks;
> Arm it in rags, a pygmy's straw does pierce it."

Barnard listened, quite bored, to O'Conor's speech, and then he reversed the decision of Judge Bedford and granted Tweed bail at $5,000, which was paid at once. Tweed resigned as Commissioner of Public Works, as a director of the Erie Railroad, and as Grand Sachem of the Tammany Society. His only remaining position was that of State Senator, to which he had been recently reëlected.

Tweed's trial was postponed several times on the grounds that his counsel needed more time for preparation. Every possible excuse for delay was invented, for it was the object of the defendant and his attorneys to put off the trial until the public should have forgotten its resentment. Those who were fighting Tweed were willing to submit to some delay, because as yet there were too many Ring judges on the bench, and the District Attorney was Tweed's friend. The reformers were hoping that at the election of 1872 the people would elect an anti-Tweed judiciary. After the election the trial was pushed forward, and on January 7, 1873, the case finally came up before Judge Noah Davis in the Court of Oyer and Terminer. He refused the application of Tweed's counsel for an adjournment. The attorney said that he had been preparing his case for months, and that he was not "yet through with the beginning of the beginning." Judge Davis replied that "considering the brevity of human life, this rate of preparation would postpone the trial to the next generation."

Tweed had employed seven of the leading lawyers of the day, including David Dudley Field, John Graham, William O.

"CAN THE LAW REACH HIM?—THE DWARF AND THE GIANT THIEF"

Bartlett, Willard Bartlett, John E. Burrill, William Fullerton, and Elihu Root, who was then a young man, coming into prominence in his profession. The first trial lasted a long time, and much damaging testimony was introduced. Lyman Tremain, one of the special counsel employed to prosecute Tweed, assured the gentlemen of the jury that:

"Only fifteen short months have elapsed since the people of this city and State were aroused by intelligence that came flashing upon them like a clap of thunder in a clear sky, which alarmed them like the alarm-bell of fire at midnight. Men awoke from their fancied security in peace, and discovered that in the very heart of the commercial emporium of the western world a series of systematic crimes had been perpetrated, which, in enormity and the colossal character of the offences, the manner in which they were perpetrated, and the agents by which they were committed, as well as the secrecy and the success with which they were perpetrated, far transcended in interest and wickedness anything recorded in the history of crime in the civilized world from the morning when creation dawned upon the world."

There was, he said, no precedent in English or American law for such colossal crimes by public servants as had been committed by the members of the Tweed Ring, for our ancestors never dreamed that public servants would thus violate their trust, and therefore there was no criminal law on the subject.

"We have no law," he said, "adapted to the punishment of the priest at the altar who poisons the devout communicants who come to receive the symbols of a Saviour's love, or the judge who takes advantage of his position to bribe with golden arguments the jury who receive instruction from his lips. . . . The clerk who embezzles $25 goes to State prison. The man who by his neglect robs the treasury of $6,000,000, over $900,000 of which are traced to his pocket, can only be punished for a simple misdemeanor."

But Mr. Tremain offered this consolation: "Verdict, or no verdict, you cannot whitewash the defendant so that men would boast of being his personal friend."

The leading witness at Tweed's first trial was Andrew J. Garvey, who had returned from Europe. Mrs. Garvey had arrived in New York before her husband, and she announced to the prosecuting attorneys that Garvey had instructed her to say that he would disclose all he knew on condition that he receive immunity from prosecution. Mrs. Garvey intimated that her husband's revelations would implicate A. Oakey Hall and

"THE SUDDEN APPEARANCE OF THE DEMON GARVEY."

Sweeny as well as Tweed. When a reporter for the *Herald* showed this statement to the Mayor, he said:

"My fair haired young friend, I can tell you and I can tell anybody—tell the entire world—that there does not live a man, nor has any man died, who can or ever could make any revelation which would implicate me in any dishonorable professional or official act, nor impugn my professional or official integrity. . . . I can't say whether Mrs. Garvey has made any such statement or not; and as to those statements of my being implicated I am certain no man can make any, much less substantiate them."

Then he added with a genial smile:

> "If any such Zaccheus there be,
> Up a tree, let him come down and see."

Garvey testified that he had supplied Tweed with some of the money used to bribe legislators to pass the new charter—a fact which Tweed did not admit until some years later. He also testified that when an investigation of the Tweed Ring was threatened by the Senate, Tweed had told him that it was necessary to buy the Committee, and that Garvey and the other contractors would have to contribute. Garvey was very nervous on the stand, and he found it difficult to look at Tweed, who kept glaring at him. John Graham, one of Tweed's lawyers, shouted rhetorically at the jury: "Watch that man's face as he looks at Mr. Tweed," whereupon Judge Noah Davis asked: "Do you want me to appoint somebody to watch his face?" During the recess, Tweed approached Garvey and said something to him in his ear. When Garvey was asked what Tweed had said, he answered: "His language was blasphemous."

At the first trial the jury disagreed, and it was charged that Tweed had used money to bring about this disagreement. A new trial was ordered for the following term of the court, and Tweed was tried again ten months later. When the second trial began, Tweed's lawyers handed Judge Noah Davis a document in which they all concurred in protesting against the same judge presiding at the trial, on the grounds of bias and prejudice, inasmuch as he had decided points of law against the defendant at the first trial. The Judge was outraged at the suggestion that he could not be impartial, and he considered the document such an extraordinary breach of legal etiquette that he called a recess of the court in order to consult his fellow judges as to his action on the document. He then ordered the case to go on and announced that he would take action later on the document of Tweed's lawyers.

Great precaution was taken this time that jurors who were favourable to Tweed should not be smuggled on to the jury, and the prosecution used detectives to gather information concerning prospective jurors and their attitude toward Tweed in the past. Tweed's agents, it was said, hired detectives to watch the detectives. Finally, a jury was completed, and the same testimony heard, except that the prosecution, much to the dismay of Tweed's lawyers, did not call Garvey this time, for Garvey's general character was such that the lawyers for Tweed intended to cross-examine him thoroughly. Tweed also did not testify. The trial was brief, and on the morning when the jury was expected to render its verdict the courtroom was packed. Hundreds of people waited outside to hear the result. The jury returned a verdict of guilty.

A few days later Tweed was brought by the Sheriff into court to hear his sentence. It was generally thought that the maximum punishment for Tweed would be a fine of $250 and one year in prison, but Lyman Tremain pointed out to the Court that Tweed was subject to that penalty for each offence, and he had been found guilty of 102 offences. This would have subjected him to imprisonment for 102 years and a fine of $25,500. John Graham, Tweed's most passionate counsel, invoked the Universal Prayer and other pleas for the quality of mercy, and finally broke into sobs at the picture of misery he had himself painted. But the Judge remained unmoved. He called Tweed to stand and listen to his sentence, and he told him:

"Holding high public office, honored and respected by large classes of the community in which you lived, and, I have no doubt, beloved by your associates, you, with all these trusts devolved upon you, with all the opportunity you had, by the faithful discharge of your duty, to win the honor and respect of the whole community, you saw fit to pervert the powers with which you were clothed in a manner more infamous, more outrageous, than any instance of like character which the history of the civilized world contains."

The Judge then sentenced Tweed to spend twelve years in prison and to pay a fine of $12,500.

Tweed was taken to the Tombs prison, but people in the City could not yet believe that such a rich man would go to jail. "The baser newspapers," wrote George William Curtis, "evidently regarded him as the French nobleman regarded himself

who was firmly convinced that the Almighty would think
twice before condemning such a gentleman as he." Improvements were made in his cell—or room, as it proved to be—the
floor was carpeted with a pleasing dark green material, and
some cracked window panes were replaced with new glass;
there was a leather lounge in one corner, five chairs for visitors,
and a comfortable rocker. When Tweed registered at the jail,
the warden asked him his occupation. "Statesman," he

"STONE WALLS DO NOT A PRISON MAKE."—*Old Song.*
NO PRISON IS BIG ENOUGH TO HOLD THE BOSS." IN ON ONE SIDE, AND OUT AT
THE OTHER.

answered, and when he was asked his religion, he said, "I have
none."

Tweed served twelve months in the Tombs and on Blackwell's Island and paid a fine of $250. His lawyers contended
that this was the only legal penalty, but he was still held in
Ludlow Street Jail awaiting the final decision of the Court of
Appeals.

Tweed's seven lawyers were summoned to appear before
Judge Davis to answer for their unprecedented document.
Judge Davis declared his opinion that the paper they had pre-
sented to him was intended to intimidate him in the discharge

of his duty, to prejudice before the people his conduct of the case, and to question his fair-mindedness. The Judge then said:

"I fine William Fullerton, John Graham, William O. Bartlett, $250 each, and order that they stand committed until the fine is paid. Mr. Burrill's position has already been explained, and Mr. Field is three thousand miles away from the jurisdiction of the Court. In respect to the younger members of the Bar, who have signed the paper—Elihu Root, Willard Bartlett, and William Eggleston—I have this to say: I know how young lawyers are apt to follow their seniors. Mr. Eggleston did not take active part in the trial, and I do not speak of him. The other two younger lawyers displayed great ability during the trial. I shall impose no penalty, except what they may find in these few words of advice: I ask you, young gentlemen, to remember that good faith to a client never can justify or require bad faith to your own consciences, and that however good a thing it may be to be known as successful and great lawyers, it is even a better thing to be known as honest men."

It was rumoured at the time that the younger members of Tweed's counsel had suggested the irregular proceedings and had written the document.

The attitude of Tweed's distinguished lawyers in their effort to save their client was described in a letter which Charles O'Conor, who had charge of the Tweed prosecutions, wrote to Governor Samuel J. Tilden in 1876:

My object in addressing you is to submit certain suggestions for consideration.

When the present leading counsel for Tweed fell into a line of practice which, steadily pursued for years as it has been, might well have led to his being dubbed Attorney-General for Rascals, it was my lot to be much in professional antagonism to him. I found him to be neither wise, learned, nor, properly speaking, able, but essentially a trickster. He seems capable of being very troublesome, and to a *negligent* or unskilful adversary he may be regarded as dangerous.

In dealing with his class, one will generally find a central device around which all their series of tricks revolve, and from which all their force and effectiveness are drawn. This man's course and career furnish an admirable illustration of this fact.

Our multitude of judges, with equal powers, were perceived by him to furnish a hopeful quarry. One wicked, weak, or manageable could be found somewhere. The next item in his scheme for making judicial proceedings do the work which a bolder thief might seek to accomplish by piracy, highway robbery, or counterfeiting was to engage himself in quarrels where an unlimited number of separate suits by separate plaintiffs might be brought before different judges—all aimed at the same substantial object. This enabled him to make almost at random all sorts of harassing movements against the same parties. . . .[1]

Mr. O'Conor then went on to suggest the repeal of certain statutes which enabled attorneys to use obstructive tactics in the name of taxpayers. Tweed had plenty of money, and he was paying it out liberally in the effort to save himself. O'Conor wrote to Governor Tilden on April 28, 1876:

If *their* judges have resolution equal to their wishes they can defeat us, in despite of any legislation. But it is to be hoped that *fear*, like the cackling of the Roman geese, may save the State.

It is said that one of our N. Y. judges has pledged himself to save Sweeny. Very likely. And, I guess, whenever he has a chance, the Mayor will appoint as a corporation counsel a known friend of that absent functionary.

My precise motive in writing at this time is to warn you of the necessity of watching closely all amendments of the Code of Procedure, and any statutes concerning practice. There is great likelihood of an attempt to smuggle some baffler of that sort through the Legislature.

Yrs., etc.,
CH. O'CONOR.[2]

While his lawyers were trying every expedient to relieve him from the penalty of his offences, Tweed was waiting in Ludlow

[1] *Letters of Samuel J. Tilden*, Vol. II, pp. 395–398.
[2] *Ibid.*, Vol. I, p. 379.

Street Jail. A civil suit for $6,000,000 had been started against him, and the prospect was dark. He was treated with consideration by his jailers, who had been his political henchmen; frequently he was permitted to drive out in a carriage in the custody of deputy sheriffs, and to dine with his family. On the morning of December 5, 1875, the town was startled to read in the newspapers that Tweed had escaped from his custodians.

Tweed left Ludlow Street Jail with his son William, Warden Dunham, and Keeper Hogan, at about ten o'clock in the morning of December 4th, and entered a carriage. After a drive to Harlem Bridge in order that Tweed might get the fresh air, they stopped at Tweed's house at Fifty-ninth Street and Madison Avenue. It was then about half-past four in the afternoon. After they had been sitting in the parlour for a time with Tweed's son-in-law, Mr. Douglas, Tweed arose and said he would like to go upstairs to see his wife. The warden remarked after about five minutes that it was time to be going back to jail, and he asked Tweed's son to go upstairs and call his father. William Tweed returned and announced that his father had not gone upstairs. Keeper Hogan was instructed to search the upper part of the house, while Warden Dunham went into the basement and cellar and looked around outside. Tweed had left his overcoat on the rack in the hall, but he had taken his hat. Keeper Hogan told a *Times* reporter later that Tweed's son pulled at his own hair excitedly and said that his father had ruined the family. Mrs. Tweed also seemed excited. "The son-in-law," remarked Hogan, "acted like an insane man." Dunham and Hogan went to the nearest police precinct, and an alarm was sent out immediately to all stations announcing Tweed's escape. They also telegraphed to the chiefs of police of Boston, Philadelphia, Brooklyn, and New Jersey. Police Inspector Thorne searched Tweed's house again, and he noted that, when they returned for the second search, all the gas lights in the house were lighted, as if inviting inspection.[1] A reward of $10,000 was offered for Tweed's capture.

Sheriff Conner, who was responsible for Tweed as a prisoner, told reporters that he had always been opposed to the privileges which had been permitted by Warden Dunham, and he said

---

[1] Account of Tweed's escape, from New York *Times*, December 5, 1875.

that, in view of the laxity with which the prisoner was treated, it was a wonder that he had not escaped sooner. Charles O'Conor had written to Governor Tilden almost a year before:

MY DEAR SIR:

Perhaps I am too suspicious or too prone to evil constructions, but I cannot resist the belief that there is a complete conspiracy. And for aught I see, it may succeed. . . .

All the scamps have fled except Tweed. Field is hurrying up Tweed's criminal case, and the moment he gets a reversal, which is pretty sure, Tweed will fly. No civil process of arrest being out against him, this is easy.

What are we to do?

Yrs., &c.,
CH. O'CONOR.

The Court of Appeals had decided that Tweed could only be sentenced to one year and a fine of $250, and O'Conor's suspicions were well founded, for Tweed escaped soon after this decision, and while the civil suit for $6,000,000 was still pending.

A graphic account of Tweed's escape and subsequent adventures was published in *Harper's Weekly* for April 14, 1877. The author, Cornelius O'Brien Bryant, was a press agent of the period, who claimed that he got his information from Tweed himself. One of Tweed's lawyers, John D. Townsend, remarked in the course of the Board of Aldermen's investigation: "I will simply say for him, however, that the report of his escape published in *Harper's Weekly* was perfectly correct; and any one who wanted to read the romance of Mr. Tweed's life could get it there."[1]

Allowing for certain picturesque and lyric touches, Cornelius O'Brien Bryant's narrative was an accurate picture of this phase of Tweed's life. According to this story, and from other sources as well, we know that Tweed's closest friend among the prisoners in Ludlow Street Jail was Charley Lawrence, silk smuggler. The *Times* remarked the day after Tweed's escape:

"It is a somewhat significant fact that the room next to Tweed's apartment is at present occupied by the smuggler

[1]Tweed Ring Investigation, p. 375.

Lawrence, an intimate friend of Tweed. The two rooms opened into each other, and the bosom friends were always in constant companionship. Last night up to a late hour Lawrence was entertaining several lady friends in his room."

It was also said that Lawrence had been secretary and chief steward of the Americus Club. Lawrence's case required a complete knowledge of the extradition laws and treaties, and Tweed gained information from him.

Another fellow prisoner was a man known as Bliss who had been the leader in the robbery of the Northampton Bank, and he had offered for a consideration to remove the iron gratings in front of Tweed's window whenever convenient, so that both of them could escape. But Tweed refused the offer, for he felt that it would be impossible for him to hide successfully since, according to his own statement, he was known to nine out of every ten men, women, and children in New York. Bliss guaranteed to arrange for Tweed's seclusion but he insisted that no one must know of their plans, not even members of Tweed's family.

"Tweed understood," wrote Bryant, "that he was to be taken in charge by a well-organized body of men, distributed throughout the country, having every facility, their connections and method being thoroughly tested and well established. He was furnished with a short key for telegraphic communication, and one for postal facility. The latter included a system of inclosures through five different envelopes, with addresses at removed points."

The agreement guaranteed his safe landing in Spain. Tweed was given the name of John Secor, by which he was to be known to his confederates and to strangers. According to Bryant, the day of Tweed's final escape was to be indicated by a secret mark on the stoop of his house, which he could see as he went up the steps. How he escaped from his house we already know.

When Tweed found himself on the street, according to Bryant, he waited a moment until a tradesman's wagon arrived, and he saw a man's arm reach out from the cover; another man was passing the stoop, and he said to Tweed, "All right, get in the

WILLIAM M. TWEED
A photograph taken just after his arrest.

wagon." When Tweed got in, the wagon drove quickly around to Madison Avenue. It was delayed there several minutes because a trolley car had gone off the track. When the wagon was able to start again, it drove by a zigzag route to the Hudson River. The wagon stopped at a pier, and the driver said to Tweed, "Get on the river side." A truck covered him from observation as he got out of the wagon. A man standing near the truck told Tweed to get into a rowboat, and he was rowed quickly to the Jersey shore, where he was driven in a wagon that was waiting for him to the lonely wooded region in back of the Palisades. He was taken to an old farmhouse, where he was greeted by another of his new companions. The second floor of the house, because it was less likely to be observed, was chosen for his residence.

For three months Tweed lived in this house across the river from New York, where men were hunting for clues to his whereabouts. His first duty was to transform himself into Mr. John Secor, an invalid gentleman who needed rest, fresh air, and relief from business pressure. His beard and whiskers were shaved off, his hair clipped, and he wore a wig and a pair of gold-rimmed spectacles.

The newspapers published various rumours concerning Tweed's whereabouts. It was said that he had been carried off in the cage wagon of a travelling menagerie and was already three hundred miles away. The New York *Times* said that he was in Havana, and the *Sentinel*, of Augusta, Georgia, that he was in Savannah. The *Times* also reported that he was in the wilds of North Carolina, where a bodyguard of fierce men, armed with swords and pistols, protected him. He was also said to have been seen in Canada, wearing coarse clothes, green goggles, and a gray wig.

Tweed, meanwhile, was reading the newspapers carefully to learn the public reception of his escape. He was also intensely interested in the outcome of the civil suit against him for $6,000,000 which was rushed to trial. This trial had been delayed because Charles O'Conor was ill. O'Conor appeared finally in court, when Tweed's lawyers had expected that he was too ill to leave his bed, and his dramatic entrance and stirring speech to the jury caused them to bring in a verdict of guilty against Tweed. It was for this event that Tweed was waiting. If he had won his case, he could return to New York and be free from imprisonment, for he had already served his full term for misdemeanour. Now, however, he could be imprisoned again as a result of this verdict, and he decided to leave New Jersey, which was far too near New York.

Tweed left the farmhouse for a shad fisherman's hut on Staten Island off the Narrows of New York Harbour, where he awaited the preparation of a small schooner which had been hired for his escape. It was said that the ship went to Florida, where he parted from his New York guides and lived in the Everglades. He went in a fishing smack to Cuba, with his Florida guide, a man named Hunt, with the intention of sailing from there for Spain. They were landed on the coast near the harbour of Santiago, and then they arranged to be taken to the city in a fishing boat. The Spanish officials demanded their passports, which lacked a Spanish visa, and the two men were arrested and placed aboard the Spanish warship *Cherucca*. Cuba was then clamouring for independence; at a mass meeting held in New York a few months before, Mayor A. Oakey Hall had expressed the sympathy of the people of the City with the movement. Everybody who arrived on the island was suspected by the Spanish authorities, as a possible revolutionist, and two men dumped ashore from nowhere in a fishing boat were naturally objects of suspicion. The American consul, who did not recognize Tweed, obtained their release on parole, and Tweed made no attempt to hide from the local Spanish and foreign society while awaiting the final decision of his status by the Spanish authorities. He spent the long days of official delay learning Spanish. Finally, he was permitted to take passage on the bark *Carmen*, bound for Barcelona and Vigo.

During the voyage Tweed was so seasick that his weight was reduced from 280 pounds to 160, and the Spanish cuisine, with its inevitable oil and garlic, did not add to his comfort on the sea. After a voyage of forty-two days the *Carmen* arrived at Vigo on September 6th, and Tweed was arrested immediately, for, while he was on the ocean, his identity had been discovered in Cuba, and Hamilton Fish, Secretary of State for the United States, had requested that he be imprisoned upon his arrival in Spain.

The Spanish authorities had sent to London for a picture of

VOL. XX.—No. 1018.]　　　NEW YORK, SATURDAY, JULY 1, 1876.　　　[WITH A SUPPLEMENT. PRICE TEN CENTS.

Entered according to Act of Congress, in the Year 1876, by Harper & Brothers, in the Office of the Librarian of Congress, at Washington.

POLITICAL "CAPITAL"

The "people are in a very puzzled and despondent state of mind about the political situation, and have got beyond the point at which they look for the appearance of the ideal statesman uniting the purest motives with the highest ability. They can get the pure motives, and they can get the high ability; but somehow, owing to no matter what circumstances, to get a man who unites both into a leading place in the government is a work of such difficulty that most people have given it up as (for the present at least) a bad job, and are willing to content themselves with any man who, for whatever motive, will do good work. It so happens, too, that the work to be done at this moment is not work which calls either for the highest order of genius or the highest aspirations. A man may do it very well without being a Moses or a Washington—without, in short, being either a prophet or a hero. He has neither to lead a race out of captivity nor call a nation into existence. The task before the American politician of to-day is the simple and somewhat homely one of preventing public officers from stealing and dividing the public money, and of preventing the government from cheating its creditors; and when a man offers himself for this work, there is no general disposition to ask whether he is a statesman of the first rank, or whether his political judgment has always been sure or his voice been always heard on the right side. In fact, they go so far as to say that to make capital in this way is a good thing to do, and they wish all politicians to engage in it. They are ready to forbear all curious inquiries into the motives or antecedents of men who will undertake to put an end to cheating and stealing. In fact, the voters of the country are sticking notices up offering the highest offices in their gift, and "no questions asked," to any body who will bring in a few plunderers of the state. Mr. Tilden has achieved his present success simply owing to his having, before any body else of his class, understood the exact nature of the situation. He perceived sooner than his competitors that the time had come to stop preaching, and to begin making arrests and drawing up indictments. He now finds, and his competitors find, that his acuteness has rendered him the highest service, and his enemies actually play into his hands."—*The Nation*, October 7, 1875.

TWEED-LE-DEE AND TILDEN-DUM.

Reform Tweed. "If all the people want is to have somebody arrested, I'll have you plunderers convicted. You will be allowed to escape; nobody will be hurt; and then Tilden will go to the White House, and I to Albany as Governor."

THE CARTOON BY THOMAS NAST USED BY THE SPANISH
AUTHORITIES TO IDENTIFY TWEED

Tweed and had received one of Nast's caricatures, in which a symbolic baby was suffering at the hands of the politician. This gave the Spanish populace the impression that Tweed was a famous American kidnapper, and the people of Vigo who loved their babies were enraged. It was reported by cable from Madrid that an American, "Twid Autelme,"the Spanish interpretation of William Tweed, who had kidnapped several wealthy American children, had been captured in Spain, and another dispatch announced that one "Twid," "presumed author," who had embezzled $6,000,000, had been caught and turned over to the American authorities.

The United States cruiser *Franklin*, which was in the Mediterranean, was instructed to bring Tweed back to New York. He was taken to the wharf from the fortress of Vigo by a military guard of thirty soldiers at ten o'clock at night, in order to prevent any violent expression of sentimental indignation upon the part of the Spanish populace against the great American kidnapper.

Instructions to the commander of the *Franklin* were that Tweed was to be treated with courtesy and consideration for his comfort, but that he was to be guarded carefully to prevent his escape or his suicide. He was assigned to a suite on the gun deck which had formerly been occupied by Admiral Worden. The portholes were fastened securely and caulked tightly so that no one could pass any weapon to Tweed. A sentry guarded the rooms night and day, and two officers were detailed to watch Tweed all the time that the cruiser was in port.

When Tweed arrived on board the *Franklin*, his personal appearance contrasted oddly with the luxury of his accommodations. His linen shirt was soiled and lacked a collar; a black alpaca coat no longer fitted him and sagged in various places, and he wore a dirty brown vest and a pair of frayed checked trousers. His baggage had been sealed and was kept with the seals unbroken until the ship reached New York. Every half hour an orderly visited the cabin in which Tweed's papers and baggage were kept and reported that the seals were still intact. When he arrived in his cabin, Tweed said to the Captain, after looking himself over, "You see I've been trying to brush myself up a little out of respect to the people that I am going to see." He also expressed himself as happy to return to New York.

Tweed spent most of his time reading whatever newspapers and books were on the ship, and in the evening officers dropped into his cabin to smoke and to play whist and euchre. He also entertained them with stories; as one of the officers put it naïvely, "he seemed to be thoroughly posted in New York politics." He told, according to this officer, "funny stories about how elections had been carried in this City."[1]

When the *Franklin* arrived in New York Harbour, Tweed was taken off in a tug and landed at Pier 46, where a large crowd gathered to see him. As Tweed walked slowly and carefully down the plank to the pier, people shouted, "There he is"; "The Boss, here he is"; and they began to cheer. Tweed was nervous, and in trying to control his steps on the steep incline of the plank from which he was descending as the cheers of the crowd broke out, he gathered momentum and found himself running down the plank in a most undignified manner; missing the boards over which he was to walk he plunged into a heap of coal. An Irishman who was standing near grasped his hand to help him and shouted, "Hurrah for the old Boss!" The crowd repeated the cheer. The carriage that was waiting was surrounded with men and boys who tried to get a glimpse of "the old man." Tweed was driven hurriedly to the Ludlow Street Jail, followed by carriages filled with officials and reporters. People along Broadway and the Bowery hurried from shops and houses to watch the speeding cavalcade.[2]

Tweed's sons, William M. Tweed, Jr., and Richard Tweed, and his secretary, S. Foster Dewey, visited him in jail, and remained with him until a quarter before midnight, telling him of the fate of old acquaintances and the state of his affairs. When he was asked what he had expected to accomplish by his flight, Tweed said that he had been advised several times to escape, and that some friends had urged him to go to Turkey or to Egypt, where the telegraph could not so easily locate him. He had rejected that plan, because those countries were too far away, and he had chosen Spain because he was told that there was no extradition treaty between that country and the United States, and therefore it was to be hoped that

[1] New York *Times*, November 25, 1876.
[2] The *Sun*, November 24, 1876.

the Spanish authorities would not surrender him. He also said that he had chosen Spain because it was "much easier to get to, and is somewhere when you get there. Then I thought of my old friend Connolly, who is in Spain, and what a good time we could have together there." He also would have been near his old friend Sweeny, who was in Paris. Tweed had planned to set his sons up in business in Liverpool and in Paris. He himself had intended to give his attention to railroad construction in Spain.[1]

Tweed later testified that his expenses in connection with his escape were $60,000.

As Tweed sat at the window of his room in the Ludlow Street Jail, which, as a member of the Board of Supervisors, he had helped to build, he would call out the names of one out of every four persons who passed by during the day, and he could give details of their business, residence, relations, and events in their lives to the few intimates who dared to visit him.

Efforts were made to obtain Tweed's release, and only after every other effort had failed did he offer to testify against himself and his associates. He wrote to Charles O'Conor on December 6, 1876:

"I regret to say that my means have become utterly inadequate. I would not make this offer, if I had not some assurance, through unpublished statements, that the vindication of principle, and the prospect of purifying the public service are objects you have in view, as being more desirable than the receiving of money. I am an old man, greatly broken down in health, cast down in spirit, and can no longer bear my burden. To mitigate the prospect of a hopeless imprisonment, which must speedily terminate my life, I should, it seems to me, make any sacrifice or effort. Viewing the fact of my return to the wards of this prison, realizing the events in the city and in the state, which I am brought here to confront, it will not, I hope, seem to be an insincerity in me to say, I am indeed overwhelmed; that, all further resistance being hopeless, I have none now to make, and only seek the shortest and most efficient manner in which I can yield an unqualified surrender."

---

[1] The *Sun*, November 24, 1876.

O'Conor was in favour of releasing Tweed on condition that he would confess all he knew about everybody's connection with the frauds, but that was just what most of the politicians who held high positions in the affairs of the City and the State did not wish to happen, and nothing came of the negotiations. A petition was circulated by Tweed's friend and associate Hugh J. Hastings, editor of the *Commercial Advertiser*, urging Tweed's release.

Tweed testified in several minor suits brought by the City. Then John Kelly, who had taken over the affairs of Tammany Hall and was now the Boss of New York, arranged with Tweed that if he would testify before a committee of the Board of Aldermen to the truth, the whole truth, and nothing but the truth, he would be released from prison, and that he would receive immunity from any further prosecution. Tweed testified fully, as we have seen from the testimony quoted throughout this story of his career, but the Attorney General of the State and the Governor, Lucius Robinson, refused to carry out the bargain. This placed John Kelly in the position of having fooled a broken old man, and the new Boss of Tammany Hall was furious. His political hostility to Governor Lucius Robinson and Charles S. Fairchild, the Attorney General, continued for the rest of Kelly's reign.

The investigation by the Board of Aldermen Committee took place, however, and it shed much light on the methods and manners of the Tweed Ring and its members. As the counsel for the Committee remarked, "We are not sitting here as a Court, but as an inquest." On the witness stand, Tweed maintained that he was a poor man. "I think I can fairly say," he testified, "and am willing to the best of my knowledge and belief to testify, that in the year 1871, the costs of the real estate I owned, together with my personal estate, was about two millions and a half of dollars, at no time in my life, was I worth more than that amount to three million dollars." "I now affirm," he added, "and am willing to submit to the closest investigation in regard to it, that I am not to-day the owner of any money or property of any kind whatever, from which five thousand dollars could be realized."[1]

---

[1] Tweed Ring Investigation, pp. 306–307.

How some of this money went was indicated by this item in his testimony:

"Paid after November, 1871, and during years 1872, 1873, 1874 and 1875 for Legal Printing, Expenses in the various Trials, Detectives, Stenographers, and Travelling Expenses, and in Counsel Fees to the following gentlemen: David Dudley Field, William Fullerton, A. J. Vanderpoel, Augustus L. Brown, John E. Burrell, W. O. Bartlett, Willard Bartlett, William Edelstein, George F. Comstock, John Ganson, Elihu Root, E.R. Bacon, John Reynolds, Field & Deyo, E. W. Stoughton, John Graham and others through the State . . . 400,000."[1]

Tweed also said that he was testifying to the best of his ability concerning the City's affairs during his régime. "I will do the best I can," he said, "but men who could inform me and come in to see me are afraid. When they come in they tremble all over until they get out. They think they are going to get hurt. They think it is the next thing to being indicted to come where I am."[2] The note of sadness and bitterness in this statement is obvious, and Tweed was hurt more than anything, perhaps, by the treatment he received from the men who had courted him and whom he had created when he was in power. He was particularly enraged at statements made concerning him by the pugilist-politician, John Morrissey, who was at that time, 1877, a candidate for Congress. A reporter for the *Sun* interviewed Morrissey and asked what he thought of the investigation of the Ring frauds by the Committee of the Board of Aldermen.

"I did not intend to say anything about it," Morrissey answered, "but as my name has been mentioned by Tweed and by the Tammany General Committee's organ, I will answer your question. I think that such an exhibition as has been made in the Common Council's chamber, in connection with this investigation, would not be tolerated for one moment in any other country in the world. Just look at it. Here is this man Tweed, acknowledging under oath that every man who did legitimate work for the city, from 1861 to 1870, was compelled

---

[1]Tweed Ring Investigation, p. 311.

[2]*Ibid.*, pp. 210–211.

to pay fifteen per cent. of the amount of his bills to have them passed by the Board of Supervisors, of which he was the head; that he made seven-eighths of these men thieves by making them raise their bills fifteen per cent., so that they could pay him and his band the percentage which he demanded. I notice that in his testimony he uses the word 'tradesmen.' I think that the public would rather have their names. I know of one or two of them who have plenty of money. I now have in my mind one, who came from Albany, and was the clown for the Ring for a number of years. Tweed also acknowledges that he is the most notorious thief that the world has ever seen, and that no man ever did more to make public officers thieves. Why, the community knows but little of this man's transactions. For years he had two mistresses, one of whom lived within a stone's throw of his house in Fifth Avenue, and in the summer as near his residence in Greenwich. Rumor says that he gave those two women $1,800,000 of the public money which he stole from the city treasury. I understand that Wheeler H. Peckham has traced to one of them more than $1,000,000 of the public money. Tweed gallanted her from Maine to California, and through Fifth avenue and other streets in this city, in defiance of public decency. I hope that he will tell the public through this committee whether or not this is so."[1]

One morning, when the session of the Board of Aldermen Committee opened, Tweed pulled a paper from his pocket and began to read the following statement:

"From the testimony I have given before this committee, I think no one will believe that I favor myself as a good, honest man. I have now been doing what most of the papers and what all have advised me to do—tell the whole history of the ring. I believe I am doing right, and am willing to submit myself to the just criticism of any and all honest men. It is hardly fair to me, however, that the public should be called upon to judge of me out of the mouths of people worse than myself. Not only my public, but my social relations have been made an object of criticism by the Hon. John Morrissey. I have known him for about twenty-four years, and of him much longer. When I am

[1] The Sun, September 17, 1877.

made a subject of criticism by him, it is but fair the public should know who he is. At a Court of Oyer and Terminer in the City of Troy, in the December term of 1848, this man was indicted for assault with intent to kill. In the April term of 1849, he was indicted for burglary; and at the same term indicted for an assault and battery; and at the same term convicted and sentenced to jail for sixty days, having been tried on the two indictments for assault and battery and burglary. At the June term, 1849, he was indicted for burglary. In the City of Albany, on the 15th of July, 1861, he was convicted of breach of the peace, adjudged to be fined $50 and sentenced for a term of three months in the Albany Penitentiary at hard labor in case of non-payment. He spent nine months in the Albany Penitentiary in serving out his terms. In 1857 he was indicted in this county for an assault with a dangerous weapon upon Thomas H. Bulmer with intent to kill him. In the same year and on the same day he was indicted for a felonious assault upon William P. Conway with intent to kill him; on the same day he was indicted for a felonious assault upon John F. H. Dagget with intent to kill him. These last three indictments were found while A. Oakey Hall was District Attorney for this county. During the whole of that time, and up to that time to within a very few years past, he has been a professional prize-fighter and public gambler—a proprietor and owner of the worst places in the City of New York, the resort of thieves and persons of the lowest character. Perhaps one of the worst faults which can fairly be attributed to me, is having been the means of keeping his gambling houses protected from the police. As an organizer of repeaters he had no superior, and at the time when the ring was in power, such capacity was always fully recognized. It is hardly fair that respectable papers should copy his criticisms upon me as an inducement to public belief and faith."

When Tweed had finished reading this statement, there was a silence for several moments. Then Mr. Cole said:

"I am very sorry that you have felt called upon to read that before this committee in public. We are not authorized to let a matter of that kind emanate from this body, and I, for one, should be strenuously opposed to it. I have nothing to say for

Mr. Morrissey, but I feel that to use this committee in this way is wrong. I don't think we shall sit here and allow it."

"Must I sit here," Tweed answered angrily, "and be abused by every thief that stands on the corner without an opportunity of defending myself? I am tied hand and foot, am in jail, confined, with no means of sending out communications to anybody. This man, Morrissey, has said that he has given me one dose and will give me another, and I will give him another after he has given me that. He sends this paper here to hurt me all he can. I intend to fight back at everybody that fights me."[1]

After he had given his testimony, Tweed returned to Ludlow Street Jail and waited to be released, but no release was forthcoming. On the 26th of March, 1878, he was summoned to testify in the suit of Charles G. Waterbury against the City. When his name was called, he took the witness stand and read a paper, saying that the City had not kept its promise to give him liberty after he had testified before, and that, by advice of counsel, he declined to testify until the promise was fulfilled. He could not be put in jail for contempt of court, for he was already in jail, and it was therefore impossible to compel him to testify. He was taken back to Ludlow Street. While coming from the courtroom, Tweed caught a cold, which developed into pneumonia. Tweed's wife and his sons William and Richard were in Europe. His daughter, Mary Amelia, was living with her husband, Mr. Maginnis, in New Orleans. His daughter, Mrs. Douglas, was the only relative in the jail with him.

In the morning of April 12, 1878, Tweed began to die. His daughter had gone out to get him some delicacies. Luke Grant, a Negro attendant, was at his bedside, and Mary Fitzsimmons, the daughter of the matron of the jail, also attended him. Tweed's heart had been weak for some time, and he had given up hope of recovery. S. Foster Dewey, his secretary, said that Tweed told him "as many as five hundred times since his return from Spain that he wanted to die." In the course of the morning, he drank a little flaxseed tea and barley water. He called Mary Fitzsimmons, who had prepared these for him, to his bed and said: "Mary, I have tried to do good by everyone; if I have not,

[1]Tweed's statement concerning Morrissey was expunged from the records of the Committee. It is copied here from the New York *Tribune* of September 19, 1877.

it is not my fault. I am ready to die, and I know God will receive me." At about ten minutes to twelve in the morning, he called his lawyer, Edelstein, to give him a drink and said in a loud voice: "William, I guess Tilden and Fairchild have killed me at last. I hope they will be satisfied now." As the Essex Market Clock struck noon, Tweed died.

The newspapers reported various last words, including some concerning the angels. S. Foster Dewey, who was at the bedside, denied this with the comment: "He never thought of angels in his life." Mr. Dewey said that Tweed's last words were: "I have tried to right some great wrongs. I have been forbearing with those who did not deserve it. I forgive all those who have ever done evil to me, and I want all those whom I have harmed to forgive me."

Shortly before his death Tweed remarked to S. Foster Dewey: "This is a moral for the world. They will be preaching sermons about me, saying, 'Look at the record of this evildoer!'" He was right. Dozens of inane sermons were preached about the moral of his rise and fall. The Rev. Dr. T. De Witt Talmage, the most eminent clergyman of the period, drew a large crowd the Sunday after Tweed's death. He took as his text the sentences from Samuel II, xviii, 29: "And the King said, Is the young Absalom safe?" Then, according to the *World*, "he opened his ample mouth and spoke as follows":

"To prove that this life is an awful peril, I point to the wreck of Friday at Ludlow Street Jail, showing on what a desperate coast a strong craft may crash and part. . . . Ah, my friends, let us remember that this man made full expiation to society for his crimes against it. Remember that by pangs of body that no doctor could arrest, and that by horrors of soul that no imagination can describe, he fully paid the price of his iniquity. Let others do what they may, I will never throw one nettle or one thistle on that man's grave.

"I couldn't allow the event of last week to go by without deriving from it the fact that a man has an awful peril without the religion of Jesus Christ and that the way of the transgressor is hard. No stronger heart ever started out in this world than Tweed. . . . Alas! Alas! young men, look at the contrast—in an elegant compartment of a Wagner palace car, surrounded by

DEATH OF WILLIAM MARCY TWEED IN LUDLOW STREET JAIL, FRIDAY, APRIL 12th

A CONTEMPORARY ARTIST'S CONCEPTION OF TWEED'S DEATH

wine, cards and obsequious attendants, going to his Senatorial place at Albany; then look again at the plain box in an undertaker's cart at 3 o'clock last Friday at the door of a prison. Behold the contrast!—the pictured and bouqueted apartments at the Delavan, liveried servants admitting millionaires and Senators, who were flattered to take his hand; then see an almost friendless prisoner on a plain cot throwing out his dying hand to clutch that of Luke, his black attendant. Behold a wedding party at the mansion, the air bewitched with crowns and stars and harps of tube-roses and japonica. Forty sets of silver; fifteen sets of diamonds—one that cost $45,000; a wedding dress that cost $4,000, with trimming that cost another thousand; two baskets of silver-ware representing ice bergs to contain the ices, and polar bears of frosted silver lying down on the handles of the baskets. Then behold the low-studded room, looking out upon a mean little dingy court where, a prisoner, exhausted, forsaken, miserable, betrayed, sick, William M. Tweed lies a-dying. From how high up to how low down!

"Never was such an illustration of the truth that dishonesty will not pay."

Then the Rev. Dr. T. De Witt Talmage went on to tell his audience that love of home was the only safeguard against disaster.

"What," he asked, "are the frescoes on city walls compared to the little trinkets that adorned the little farm-houses you were born in? The porter in fine livery swings open the carven door of a metropolitan mansion; is it as much to you as the little gate, you on one side and on the other your sister, who went fifteen years since into glory singing the songs of childhood?"

"One other story Mr. Talmage told," reported the *World*, "in drawing lessons from the life of Tweed, which was that of a young man who went to the Park Theatre and lost his soul. There were two young men who set out to go to the theatre, but one fortunately turned back, his conscience getting the better of him on the way. The play set forth that there was hypocrisy in the Christian religion and had been condemned by even the secular press. The young man who went was drawn afterwards into successive vices, and at last 'died an awful death without one star of mercy shining on him.' The young man who turned back from the theatre was Mr. Talmage. In conclusion the preacher exhorted his hearers to 'Go somewhere. Start this morning for heaven.'"

Other men were learning lessons from Tweed's rise and fall, slightly different from those offered by the Rev. Dr. T. De Witt Talmage and his colleagues. Chris Magee, Republican Boss of Pittsburgh, made a special trip to New York and remained there several months studying the reasons for Tweed's downfall. When he returned to Pittsburgh, he told his associates that he now had a system which could not be beaten or broken, and it never was. John Kelly and Richard Croker were also studying Tweed's mistakes. And all of these men died in their own beds.

The New York *Nation* pointed the most sensible moral to adorn the tale of Tweed. The *Nation* considered the flood of funeral discourses a waste of eloquence and fervour.

"There is no city in the civilized world," wrote the editor, "that does not contain plenty of men capable of doing all that Tweed did and more, if they get a chance. London, Paris, Vienna, Berlin, Boston, and Philadelphia, all have them in abundance; men, we venture to say, with full as much ability and audacity, with as huge a greed for money, and as capacious stomachs. In every one of these cities there are scores of 'mute inglorious' Tweeds, waiting for an opportunity to play his part. If we never hear of them the reason will be, not that *he* was a man of matchless powers of mischief, but that the community they live in will not give them a chance of imitating him. He was undoubtedly an eminent man in his field, but he was not an eminently bad man. With similar culture and manure dozens like him could be raised in a year in any great capital, and by going to any State prison much more valuable illustrations of the consequences of knavery might be produced for the use of the Sunday-school teacher.

"To say that he was produced by certain social conditions is, however, not strictly accurate. He was produced by certain political conditions which grew into existence almost without the knowledge of the American public, and to which their eyes were only fairly opened by his rise and fall. American political theories and traditions had made absolutely no provision and provided no place for the community which raised him. According to these theories and traditions, when a number of capitalists, owning or controlling vast amounts of property, collect for the transaction of business at the mouth of a great river and draw around them hundreds of thousands of poor, ignorant, or shiftless persons to work for them in their warehouses and factories and docks, these hundreds of thousands become animated by an eager desire for efficient, orderly, and economical municipal government, and united with the property-owners for its creation and maintenance; they become, in short, the personage known in American jurisprudence as 'the people,' inheriting the supposed attributes of the sovereign of the Old World—that is, a perspicacious, vigilant, upright master, keeping a watchful eye over the public interests and careful in the selection of public servants. In fact, however, the growth of American cities has followed no such lines. The population by which they have been rapidly built up during the past twenty-five years has had many of the characteristics of a plebs, and rapidly began to ask for leaders which should put it in the way of living off the rich without violating the law. Tweed succeeded because he was the first to discover the way of doing it. Having once secured, through the ignorant, greedy vote, the control of the local taxation, he introduced Americans to another startling novelty—the wholesale corruptibility of legislatures composed of country farmers and lawyers of small means, by the use of sums which far exceeded with most of them the possible savings of a frugal and successful life. With the instruments in his hands, his work, as we all know, was perfectly easy. He met with no check from the very first, until the exposure came. And let us remember that he fell without loss of reputation among the bulk of his supporters. The bulk of the poorer voters of this city to-day revere his memory, and look on him as the victim of rich men's malice; as, in short, a friend of the needy who applied the public funds, with as little waste as was possible under the circumstances, to the purposes to which they ought to be applied—and that is to the making of work for the working man. The odium heaped on him in the pulpits last Sunday does not exist in the lower stratum of New York society. . . .

"A villain of more brains would have had a modest dwelling and would have guzzled in secret. He found, however, the seizure of the government and the malversation of its funds so easy at the outset that he was thrown off his guard. His successors here and elsewhere will not imitate him in this, but that he will have successors there is no doubt. The resolute refusal of the community which he spoiled and corrupted to make any essential change in the system by which he rose, or even to acknowledge the desirableness of a change, is a kind of standing invitation to all the demagogues of the world to come here and try their hands on us again, and the taxing system of nearly every city in the Union offers them a ready instrument for the attempt."[1]

The editor of the *Nation* spoke well. Tweed, in spite of the clergymen and moralists, was not a bad man in the popular sense in which that term would be used; he was merely a business man. In the words of George Washington Plunkitt, "He Seen His Opportunities, and He Took Them." Had he not been detected, he probably would have lived to a genial old age, to found hospitals and asylums for those of his period whose self-respect prevented them from raking in other people's hay while the sun shone. And we shall see presently that Tweed did have his successors, who applied the same system with certain safeguards.

Mr. Richard Tweed, the brother of the deceased, arrived at Ludlow Street Jail just too late to see his brother alive. He said to the matron, when he was leaving: "Well, Madam, we are all relieved of a great deal of trouble and anxiety. I am glad the end has come. We can never forget the loss we have sustained."

Tweed's body was followed to Greenwood Cemetery by a delegation of Freemasons, a few personal friends, and a sprinkling of the more courageous and less important politicians who had known him and worked with him. A large number of people gathered in front of the house of Tweed's son-in-law at 63 East Seventy-seventh Street, to get a last look at the man who had received so much publicity. They were mainly workingmen and their wives. As many as could be admitted were allowed to pass by the coffin. The rest stood on the steps of houses near by and

---

[1] The *Nation*, April 18, 1878.

waited for the funeral procession to pass. The pallbearers were ex-aldermen and ex-commissioners. The Rev. Dr. Joseph H. Price, who had married Tweed and had officiated at the magnificent wedding of Mary Amelia, read the Episcopal funeral services. Dr. Price said that, in accordance with the request of those in charge of the arrangements, he would deliver no funeral address, but he could not resist the remark that, "For the one who had gone, he trusted that He who looked in pity on Lazarus would not fail to have mercy on him."

VIII

When he was summing up before the jury in one of Tweed's last trials, David Dudley Field, Tweed's lawyer, said:

"Now on this point I propose to make an illustration, taking the case at the standpoint of the prosecution.

"A merchant finds that his clerks have robbed him of $6,000,000. Each has taken his share. He seizes one by the throat and says to the rest, '*Run* with your spoils; I have got this man. You are equally in my power, but you may go and keep what you have got. This man, it is true, has got but $1,000,000, or thereabouts, but I shall keep him and hold him for *the whole*. Bless you, my boys. Go and enjoy yourselves, and spend my stolen money as you please. He is rich. He is a man of political influence. I want to break him down. I shall keep him in Blackwell's Island, or in Ludlow Street Jail, or wherever I can hold him, till I squeeze the life out of him. I do not care so much for the *money*. It is the *man* I am after.'

"Is it fair that the merchant should collect from the man the entire amount of all that was taken, not what he took alone, but what the others were permitted, nay, *invited* to take off with them?"

This statement represented accurately the prosecutors' attitude toward Tweed, even though David Dudley Field was illogical, for whatever Tweed possessed did not approximate the amount he had stolen. Tweed's associates were more interested in their money than he was in his, and they took cunning precautions. They deposited the spoils in the names of their brothers and their wives and their close friends. They ran to Canada and they

ran to Europe. The City seemed to despair of getting back
what was due it, for to get back all was impossible. And the
public imagination was satisfied with the sacrifice of Tweed
as a glowing example of justice vindicated and morality
pleased.

An example of the way the City settled with some of the other
thieves was given in the testimony of Henry M. Taintor, the
expert accountant, before the committee of the Board of Aldermen:

"Q. The People against Woodward—is that suit pending?

"A. That suit was compromised and settled. . . . I had
evidence inculpating him in obtaining $8,000,000 to $10,000,000
additional.

"Q. What was that suit brought for?

"A. For the whole $6,000,000.

"Q. How much was it settled for?

"A. $155,000; I get my information from the newspapers.

"Q. Do you know how much of that was actually paid into
the treasury?

"A. I think $100,000.

"Q. Where is the other $55,000?

"A. That I do not know. . . . I merely suppose that it was
agreed upon on the ground of his inability to pay more."[1]

E. A. Woodward testified himself concerning his settlement
with the City, and he was insolently defiant:

"I am willing to swear that if I had to do the thing over
again, I would not have made any settlement at all," Woodward
testified.

"Q. What would you have done?

"A. I think I should have stayed away.

"Q. You settled then under a misapprehension. Do you think
you did yourself an injustice in making the settlement? Do you
think the city profited by the settlement—got more than its
just due?

"A. No; I mean that if I had known beforehand how little
I would have left after settling, I wouldn't have settled at all,

---

[1] Tweed Ring Investigation, p. 420.

but would have stayed away altogether, and never have come
back.

"Q. Why, what you have left gives you a good living, doesn't
it?

"A. Not much.

"Q. What are you doing now?

"A. Oh, I'm farming, tinkering around, speculating a little.
But it's my own business what I'm doing now, not yours.

"Q. I only wish to ascertain if you really had not enough left
to enable you to live like a prince.

"A. I've seen a good many princes abroad that didn't live
very well."[1]

Alderman Cowing asked Woodward, who, it will be recalled,
was the assistant paymaster of the Ring, a few questions to
which he received the following frank and brusque replies:

"Q. Now, how much more could you restore if compelled by
a moral conviction of the necessity of dealing with the city with
perfect honesty?

"A. I couldn't restore another dollar. The $150,000 was all I
could restore, and I don't think you have any right to ask me
those questions.

"Q. I wish to see if you are reformed?

"A. I am not a reformer.

"Q. And you would still do the same thing over again if you
had a chance?

"A. I don't think there's one in this room who wouldn't do it
if they had a chance.

"Q. That is not complimentary to the people in this room.
Do you include yourself?

"A. Oh, yes, of course I do.

"Q. Then the city's compromising with you has not made
any better man and citizen of you?

"A. I am not a citizen of New York, and have got nothing to
do with it. [Woodward was then a resident of Connecticut.]

"Q. I am trying to get at your idea of what might honestly
be expected of you.

"A. You have no right to ask me those questions, Alderman:

---

[1] Tweed Ring Investigation, pp. 717-718.

but if you ask my opinion of politicians, I can only say I never met an honest one, and I don't believe there's an honest politician in the world. . . .

"Q. You don't estimate the honesty of your fellow-men very highly?

"A. I never saw an honest politician in my life.

"Q. Never did?

"A. Never, sir; my experience is about as good as anybody's in this room.

"Q. Have you met all politicians?

"A. I have met all stripes of them.

"Q. And never found an honest one?

"A. Never.

"Q. What do you predicate that on?

"A. On my intimacy with them. . . . I may have been more unfortunate than others, but I don't think so."[1]

Woodward also made the statement: "I believe that this city is now, and always will be, swindled."

At first the prosecution of the Ring culprits was conducted on the principle that punishment of all the offenders was of prime importance and the recovery of the plunder secondary to that. While the case was being handled by Charles O'Conor, whose theory was that the punishment was more important than the money, the associates of Tweed managed to hide their property from the law, and to leave the country themselves. After O'Conor retired from the prosecution, the efforts of the City's representatives were turned to the recovery of the stolen money, and compromises were entered into with Sweeny, Woodward, Connolly, Garvey, and others, who were guaranteed immunity from personal prosecution for their thefts on condition that they returned a portion of them. Most of their property being by this time beyond the reach of the law, the City had to be content with whatever they offered to pay. Sweeny, from the safety of his Paris residence, offered to pay the City $150,000 in cash and $250,000 in notes if he was allowed to retain his freedom. This offer was accepted, and he was permitted to return to New York. When a reporter for the *World* interviewed Peter B.

---

[1]Tweed Ring Investigation, pp. 710–712.

"NEXT!"

Sweeny in 1889, he was living in the home of his brother-in-law, State Senator John J. Bradley, where, in the "sumptuously furnished parlours," a statue in black marble portrayed Othello clutching Desdemona's handkerchief. Mr. Sweeny insisted then that he had had nothing to do with the Ring frauds and that he had not profited by them personally.

Comptroller Connolly went to Europe in 1872. He spent most of his time at first in Egypt; an American tourist reported rather melodramatically that he saw Connolly sitting upon the piazza of his hotel, "shunned by everybody, with trembling hands and vacant eyes."

The Committee of the Board of Aldermen which investigated the Ring frauds found it outrageous that some of the leaders of the Ring had been permitted to go free. The majority report contained this statement:

"In the opinion of your Committee the prosecuting officers have made a very serious mistake in granting immunity from punishment to a single one of these criminals, either for a moneyed consideration or on any other pretext. The precedent is a bad one. It is saying to all officials, steal all you can, and if you will return a portion, you may keep the balance and be admitted back to live in peace and quietness in that society whose rights you have outraged, and may enjoy the balance of the plunder and go unpunished. It is respectfully submitted that the manner in which most of these Ring thieves have been treated has done almost as much to demoralize society as have the crimes they committed."[1]

In 1877 the City had recovered only a total of $876,241.84.

The only other member of the Tweed Ring besides Tweed who was brought to trial was Mayor A. Oakey Hall. Hall insisted that he had had nothing whatever to do with the Tweed Ring frauds, that he had audited the bills presented to him as part of the routine business of his office, and that it could not be expected that he should have investigated every bill that he was asked to audit. He also maintained that he had not received a cent of the spoils himself, in spite of Tweed's testimony to the contrary and the

---

[1] Tweed Ring Investigation, pp. 33–36.

general opinion of mankind. Mayor Hall wrote a letter to Tilden which reflects his personality vividly, if not admirably:

13 West 42d St., Sunday, A. M. (1872).

MY DEAR SIR:

It was remarked in my hearing last evening, after you so gratified the club and its guests, "Mr. Tilden looks as if he not only had a great head, but also a large heart." I propose to address the latter, if you will graciously pardon the intrusion.

I learn that Mr. Peckham intends procuring from the Oyer and Terminer G. J. a duplicate charge agst. me for official neglect. It is in your *power* to advise against and prevent this. I think, sir, I can satisfy you that such advice will be in harmony with that unflinching standard of justice by which you measure all men and all things.

"I have filed an unqualified stipulation that pending charges be removed to the O. and T. The removal order has been entered. . . . There is, therefore, no legal necessity for a duplicate. To press one now is only to wound the feelings of my very interesting family by arousing fresh (and doubtless, at this partisan pitch, cruel) newspaper criticism, and without accomplishing any better oblation to justice (either to me or the people, as the case may prove) than could be attained with existing pleading. And especially when some weeks ago I wrote to Atty.-Genl. Barlow I should always be ready for his convenience.

"I think, sir, that ever since, in Sept., 1871, I became convinced of the monstrous frauds (committed by men whose offences are condoned, or whose battles are carried on over my shoulders, because I neither skulk nor avoid fight) I have done much to atone for any imputed neglect in my acts as an auditor during the month of terrible mental trial to me which followed the inauguration of the new charter (May to June, 1870), as well as to entitle me to consideration upon a mere question of discretion like this I now ask you to prefer to Mr. Peckham. I say discretion, because, were it a question in his mind of imperative right towards his affirmative action, I could not insult you, nor him, nor myself by the request to forego it. I shall always be willing to meet the *necessary* exactions of the law without asking favor. It is only against unnecessary applications I respectfully protest. Surely my unassailed administration as Dist. Atty. during *12* years; my bearing and course as Mayor in all save these unfortunate audits or non-audits (as you please to phrase it); the character of my appointments since Nov., 1871; my uniform support of Mr. Green in his trying position; and my surrender of much personal pride to aid even personal enemies in accomplishing public good, ought to entitle me to ask from Mr. Peckham to be spared all unnecessary stigmas.

Pray pardon *me* for thus annoying you who, at this crisis, must be almost overwhelmed with duties. But when I heard the remark with which I began this note, the suggestion came to me with almost the intuition of a woman, and as if the whisper of a daughter—"appeal to his heart."

This does not require reply, nor is one expected.

With great respect and regard,

Your obt. sert.,

A. OAKEY HALL.

HON. S. J. TILDEN.[1]

A. Oakey Hall arrived at the courtroom for his first trial on horseback. He was dressed carefully and fashionably. He was permitted to retire without bail, and this decision of the Judge was greeted with cheers by some and with hisses and shouts by others. The Mayor then mounted his horse, after shaking hands with friends, and rode to City Hall. At the first trial, Hall was his own attorney, and he challenged two jurors on the grounds that they were older than he was. The trial proceeded, but in the middle of it one of the jurymen died, and it had to be discontinued. He was tried again on December 22, 1872. He conducted his own defense, saying that he had not had an opportunity to consult his counsel since the previous Saturday, because: "I could not consult with them on Sunday. I could not fly in the face of that Providence that has so kindly taken care of me unto this moment, and on whom I rely to vindicate my innocence."

In spite of Garvey's sudden and dramatic appearance in court to testify against him, it was impossible to connect

---

[1] *Letters of Samuel J. Tilden*, Vol. I, pp. 295–296.

Mayor Hall definitely with the corruption. The jury retired on Christmas Eve, and Hall chatted with his friends. He told them how he had once sat up on Christmas Eve when he was District Attorney to await the verdict in a murder case, and he recalled to them that he had written an imitation of Charles Dickens called *The Christmas Juryman*. The jury returned at ten o'clock at night with a verdict of not guilty. Oakey Hall bowed his head

"OUR MARE STILL LIVES."

on the table in front of him, ostensibly overcome with emotion. Then he recovered himself and received the congratulations of his friends. As he left the courtroom, there were shouts of "Merry Christmas!" At the Mayor's trial there was present in the courtroom what one newspaper described as, "a horrid woman with her hair cut like a man's."

Although some newspapers demanded that he resign his position as Mayor of New York, Oakey Hall served out his full term and refused to abandon the office until January 1, 1873, when the new Mayor, William F. Havemeyer, was inaugurated. He also did not abandon his practice of punning. Soon after his term as Mayor had expired, Oakey Hall fell on the ice and broke his leg. While he was at home in bed, he wrote to a friend:

13 West Forty-second Street
Sunday, January 26.

I thank you for your words of sympathy. Sympathy knits friendship—why not bones? What says the good book about marriage? Bone of my bone and one flesh. Some men talk of bringing life to a head. Now mine converges round a leg. It is the pole-star of my sick man's egotism.

If my mind turns to law, I think first of *lex talionis;* no reference here to Taglioni the dancer. If to practice, I ask how many clients I shall save from limbo? If to poetry, I think of Gray's Elegy, or Hood's Miss Kilmansegg and Her Precious *Leg.* If to the theatre, I wonder if Daly is going to do the *leg*itimate. If to traveling, I think of Cork or *Leg*horn. If to music, Billy Chapman's old ballad runs through my head, respecting Mynheer of Rotterdam,

> "Who, when he'd stuffed him as full as an egg,
> Found a poor relation come to beg,
> And in kicking him out he broke his leg.
> With a chorus of My-di-to."

If I think of politics, I wonder if I shall be qualified for the position of secretary of *leg*ation or *leg*ate to the Pope, and if my thoughts turn to gastronomy, I say: "*Donnez moi des* leg*umes.*"

I am inundated with ball tickets from all parts of the country, two or three being appropriately in aid of hospitals. Circulars also begin to arrive about cork legs, reclining and wheel chairs, bed-rests, crutches, etc. Although I fortunately had a policy in an accident company, prospect uses from other companies are sent, as possible reminders of the future, and one kind friend has sent me a vase of Fall leaves.

In every way I realize that I am like poor France—disordered—and especially in the Bonepartes.

I shall be a *Home* Journal for at least a fortnight more. Luckily I am no longer a public man, or my leg would be in everybody's mouth.[1]

---

[1] *Hall Scrap Books,* New York Public Library Collections, Vol. IX, p. 7.

Two years after he left the office of Mayor, A. Oakey Hall appeared on the stage of the Park Theatre in New York, in a play which he had himself written, called *The Crucible*. The first-night audience consisted of politicians, Congressmen, and legislators, as well as literary men and women, lawyers, and the omnipresent Henry Bergh, of the Society for the Prevention of Cruelty to Animals. The ex-Mayor was received with great

"ANOTHER FALL, MY COUNTRYMEN! NEXT!"

applause. The plot of the play concerned the false accusation of the hero, acted by A. Oakey Hall, of robbing his employer's safe, and his subsequent vindication in court. The dialogue was sprinkled with puns. The play had twenty-two performances and was taken off. Then Oakey Hall went back to the practice of law. He was also at one time city editor of the *World*. He gave up this position and went to London, where he was admitted to the bar, and he practised law there for some time. He also took charge of the New York *Herald* bureau in London at the request of his friend James Gordon Bennett, the younger. In 1889, Oakey Hall sued James Bryce for libel, because a chapter on the Tweed Ring in the first edition of *The American Common-*

wealth referred to him as one of the culprits. Hall demanded £10,000 damages. The action dragged along for nine years, and Hall did not prosecute it to its end; he never paid the costs which were charged against him.

Of the Tweed Ring judges, Judge Cardozo resigned, and Judge Barnard was impeached and removed after a long trial. While charges were being heard against him in New York, Judge Barnard still held court, and one day he interrupted an attorney in his argument before him with the remark: "Beg pardon; don't wish to interrupt you; but I desire to say that if there is any member of the Bar Association here, he can have an additional specification in the charges against me, for I am going to scratch my head." Whereupon His Honour proceeded to scratch himself.

CHAPTER V

"HONEST JOHN" KELLY

I

AFTER the defeat of the Tweed Ring at the polls in the election of 1871, Tammany Hall was in bad repute, and its members no longer enjoyed the lucrative jobs which they had been accustomed for so many years to regard as their right. Reformers held the power in the City's government, and therefore the only way for Tammany to regain prestige with the public after the startling disclosures which had sent some of its members to jail and others to Europe, was to reform itself. John Kelly, who had been a prominent Democrat in local politics for some years, was the man who undertook the job of making Tammany Hall spotless. It was an ambitious undertaking. Dr. Talcott Williams remarked concerning John Kelly's achievements in Tammany Hall: "He found it a horde. He left it a political army." Hugh J. Hastings, Tweed's friend, wrote the following figurative description of John Kelly's problem:

"Beasts of burden may easily be managed by a new master. But will the wild ass submit to the bonds? Will the unicorn serve and abide his crib? Will the leviathan hold out his nostrils to the hook? The mythological conqueror of the East, whose enchantments reduced wild beasts to the tameness of domestic cattle, and who harnessed lions and tigers to the chariot, is but an imperfect type of the man who can control the wild, whiskey-drinking and fierce spirits that make up the worst elements of this great city. It requires a great man to stand between the City Treasury and this most dangerous mass. It demands courage, activity, energy, wisdom, or vices so splendid and alluring as to resemble virtues. Again we say, dethrone Kelly, and where is the man to succeed him?"

During the excitement of the Tweed Ring exposures John Kelly was in Europe, familiarizing himself with the topography of the Holy Land. He had recently retired from the office of Sheriff of New York County, one of the most lucrative in the City's gift, and he could therefore well afford to devote his time to his religious interests. One of his biographers assures us that "his letters at this period dwell much upon the Mount of Olives, the Way of the Cross and the Holy Sepulchre." While he was abroad, rumours reached New York that John Kelly had retired from the world to spend the rest of his days in the calm of a monastic retreat. But it was not long after this rumour that John Kelly himself returned to New York to spend the rest of his days in Tammany Hall. He brought with him four great oil paintings representing the Baptism of the Lord, the Marriage at Cana, the Return of the Prodigal Son, and St. Patrick Preaching at Tara, which he had commissioned an Italian artist to execute for him, and he presented these to St. Patrick's Cathedral in New York. After the solicitations of "hundreds of leading men," as he himself put it, John Kelly consented to lead the New York Democracy against the hordes of deposed Tweed men and the degenerate Grant Republicans.

John Kelly was born in Hester Street, New York, in 1822. His mother was said to have assured a neighbour that her son "thinks a great deal more than he talks, but be sure he is not dumb," and it was John Kelly who began the silent man régime of Tammany Hall which was carried on after him by two other models of taciturnity, Richard Croker and Charles F. Murphy. Kelly came from a poor Irish family, and he started his career as office boy to James Gordon Bennett, editor and owner of the *Herald*. He left that position to become a grate setter and soapstone cutter. Bennett advised him to remain in the newspaper business, but apparently he offered no money as an inducement, for Kelly found grate setting and stone cutting more attractive, and he was soon operating a workshop of his own.

Kelly was handy with his fists, and he found that they were useful in his neighbourhood. He was a member of the Volunteer Fire Department at the same time as Tweed was, and he took part in the battles of the rival engine companies. Kelly's friend and biographer, McLaughlin, wrote that in his youth John Kelly "would not loiter with the crowd at street corners of evenings, nor haunt the purlieus of the city where youth loses its innocence, and flaunting vice slopes the way to ruin." In spite of this, wrote McLaughlin, he was "a favorite among his companions, and they all soon came to look upon him as a sort of leader." At night Kelly frequented the Ivy Green, a saloon in Elm Street, where he met the leading politicians of the day, and those who were soon destined to rise to notoriety. It was here that Kelly used to talk with Peter B. Sweeny, John Clancy, who became Tweed's secretary, and David C. Broderick. He sometimes visited the Comet, in Mott Street, where Tom Hyer, "Yankee" Sullivan, John Morrissey, and other prize fighters gathered. Kelly was also the organizer of an amateur dramatic association, and he played the parts of Macbeth, Hamlet, "Toodles," and Othello.

Early in his life Kelly took part in the violent politics of his ward, and he was at that time always on the Democratic side against the anti-Irish Know Nothing Party. In 1853 he was elected Alderman, and two years later he defeated Mike Walsh for a seat in Congress by eighteen votes. Kelly served two terms in Congress, where he championed the rights of foreigners, Catholics, and Democrats. Kelly had been made a member of the Tammany Hall General Committee, and he took part in the campaigns of the organization. After serving in Congress, Kelly won for himself the nomination to the valuable office of Sheriff of New York, which entitled the occupant to no salary but all the fees of the office. He was elected Sheriff in 1858. The *Times* accused Kelly of taking more than thirty thousand dollars which he was not entitled to for the care of prisoners and of charging the City 133 per cent. more than the legal rate for conveying prisoners to and from Blackwell's Island. Kelly served three terms as Sheriff of New York and grew rich. He also gained the prefix to his name of "Honest John." Mayor William F. Havemeyer, who succeeded A. Oakey Hall, wrote to Kelly concerning his administration of the Sheriff's office:

"Fraud permeates every part of your bills to such an extent that one honest spot would be a sort of relief. In such a matter as conveying convicts to prison, it does seem that you might be satisfied to be honest. . . . I think that you were worse than Tweed, except that he was a larger operator. The public knew

Accept for yourself my esteem and obligation yours truly

John Kelly

"HONEST JOHN" KELLY

that Tweed was a bold, reckless man, making no pretensions to purity. You, on the contrary, were always avowing your honesty, and wrapped yourself in the mantle of piety. Men who go about with the prefix of 'honest' to their names are often rogues."[1]

Kelly was opposed to Tweed and his associates because he was not one of them, but his opposition did not take an active form until 1868, when he considered running as an opposition candidate for Mayor against Tammany's man, A. Oakey Hall. Kelly withdrew from the contest just before the election on account of his health and went to Europe, but Mayor Hall remarked flippantly, "I am the medical adviser who drove Kelly to Europe."

One of Kelly's first moves in the renovation of Tammany Hall was the selection of prominent persons as sachems of the Society, so that the discredit of the Tweed régime might be overcome. The venerable Augustus Schell was persuaded to become the successor of William M. Tweed as Grand Sachem. This appointment was a wise one, for the public knew that Mr. Schell was too old to be very actively dishonest whatever his worst inclinations might be. Tilden, Horatio Seymour, Sandford E. Church, August Belmont, Abram S. Hewitt, and other reputable men became associated with the Tammany Hall organization, and the new régime was hailed as a congregation of the City's honest men.

Soon after the excitement of the Tweed Ring exposures had died down, New York enjoyed another, but milder, political sensation, which was manipulated by John Kelly. Two police commissioners of Mayor Havemeyer's reform administration were charged with a misdemeanour when they removed an election inspector, John Charles Sheridan. A. Oakey Hall was the counsel for Charlick and Gardner, the Police Commissioners, and he fought the new Tammany's attempt to discredit them. When he entered the crowded courtroom, ex-Mayor Hall remarked: "Once more into the breach, dear friends, once more." In June, 1874, the police commissioners were convicted, because they removed Tammany Hall election inspectors, and

[1]New York *Herald*, June 2, 1886.

appointed in their place men who suited their own interests. They were fined $250.

The conviction of these police commissioners was only a device on the part of the new Tammany Boss to discredit the reformers, so that he might make his power supreme in the City. They were guilty of the offence charged against them, from the evidence presented, but they were especially guilty of not being regular members of Tammany Hall. If there is anything a machine politician hates it is reform; Roscoe Conkling, who was a New York State machine politician of the regular stamp, once remarked in the Senate of the United States that when Dr. Johnson defined patriotism as the last refuge of a scoundrel, he had ignored the vast possibilities of the word reform. After the Tweed Ring reformers had gained power, and after John Kelly had rehabilitated Tammany Hall, it was necessary to discredit the independent office holders, who, however inefficient they sometimes were, could never be so efficiently dishonest as those who worked with the powerful machine as an engine.

Mayor Havemeyer, whose large sugar business made it possible for him to remain personally incorruptible, wrote a long open letter to Governor Dix on August 6, 1874, in which he indicated the reasons for the opposition of the Tammany and other machine politicians to his administration.

"All the corrupt elements have, as if by instinct, struck hands together to render every man who makes an honest endeavor for good government odious. And the elements thus arrayed are formidable. They embrace the machine politicians of both political parties; the numerous adherents of the late corrupt ring against whom prosecutions are pending, and to be brought, to compel the restitution of millions of moneys plundered from the Treasury; the still more numerous class holding fraudulent claims against the city to the amount of millions more; the army of contractors, who look for subsistence to the prosecution of extended public works and the consequent increase of the public debt; and with these the numerous horde of lobbyists and adventurers accustomed to be fed, directly or indirectly, out of the public crib. All these play the same game, which is to foster a laxity and indifference in the public mind leading to the notion that all who labor for reform in public administration have merely personal interests in view; that there is no substantial difference between the officials of the Tweed *régime* and those who have succeeded them; that the Committee of Seventy was itself but a ring of place seekers, and, in short, that one man is as good as another. . . . In this way they seek to discourage all resolute effort to correct the tendencies to demoralization and corruption, to the end that in the indifference of the general mass of citizens the compact and trained bands organized and led by corrupt chiefs may make an easy capture of the places of power. It is from a union of these forces, always ready to combine, however widely divided in their political professions, that this city has before been brought almost to the verge of bankruptcy, and may, at no distant period, be brought still nearer to it. It is one of their favorite arts, which they practice with occasional success, to allure to their side, by specious pretenses, men of irreproachable characters and purposes, who allow themselves, by the failure to exercise sufficient caution, to be misled."

It was inevitable that a man like Havemeyer, who had been Mayor of New York in 1845, in 1848, and now had been recruited at an advanced age into the services of reform, and a man like Kelly should clash. Havemeyer considered the government of the City of New York a business which should be run efficiently for the purposes of the corporation, just as the sugar business was run for its corporation, and to Kelly the government of the City of New York was a business which should be run efficiently for the purposes of the men who held subordinate positions under it; the one believed in corporate finance for the good of the corporation, and the other believed in prosperity for the greatest possible number of officeholders. If Mayor Havemeyer succeeded, John Kelly and Tammany Hall lost money and prestige, and if Kelly succeeded, the City and its citizens, in the opinion of Mayor Havemeyer, lost money and character. Kelly therefore was compelled to attack Havemeyer at every possible point of attack, and Havemeyer retaliated by calling Kelly corrupt in public. In order to justify his prefix of "Honest John," Kelly found it necessary to sue Mayor Havemeyer for libel, and he did so. The day that the trial was to begin, the Mayor, who was then almost eighty years old, dropped dead of apoplexy in the Mayor's office, and John Kelly succeeded in electing his henchmen to the Mayor's office for the next two succeeding terms.

There was one other reformer whom it was necessary for John Kelly to defeat, if he was to succeed in his efforts to consolidate Tammany Hall, and that was Samuel J. Tilden, who was Governor of New York. Tilden had always played with Tammany Hall and its bosses so long as it was to his personal advantage to do so and so long as doing so did not necessitate a dangerous expansion of the principle that honesty was the best policy.

Kelly's aim, from the beginning of his rule in Tammany Hall, was to make his power absolute, and it was he who established the system of one-man power which prevailed for the next fifty years, with very short intervals. Kelly believed in obedience, and once he had made up his mind to a policy or an appointment, he refused to listen to arguments or to threats: he was sometimes called by the less imaginative newspaper writers, "the Bismarck of New York." If a man opposed his rule, John Kelly never forgave him. He was just under six feet in height and weighed two hundred and thirty pounds. His jaw was heavy and firm, and his whole manner denoted stubborn power. He bore a strong physical resemblance to his protégé and successor, Richard Croker, who carried Kelly's methods and manners to their logical extreme.

Kelly's manners in the state conventions in which he took part were arbitrary, and he attempted to seat the Tammany Hall delegates in defiance of all opposition. In this attempt he was at first eminently successful, for he was then working along with Governor Tilden, who had his own private political machine, kept running by his personal friends and his personal fortune. But it was inevitable that a man like Tilden and a man like Kelly should quarrel, for each desired power at the expense of the other. Kelly gave Tilden passive support when he was nominated for President of the United States in 1876, and it was said that he was not unhappy when Tilden was denied the place after a close fight.

Kelly denied a renomination to Tilden's friend, Governor Lucius Robinson, who had refused to give Tweed his freedom when the latter agreed to testify, for Kelly's power to accomplish his ends had thus been denied, and his word had been broken. He wished revenge, and when the state convention nominated Robinson, Kelly withdrew the Tammany delegation and had himself nominated for Governor, though he knew that he could not be elected. His object was not to be Governor, but to see to it that Lucius Robinson was not Governor, for he never forgave a man who did not obey him. The Republican candidate, Alonzo B. Cornell, was elected, and this was one of the first instances of Tammany Hall's method, which was sometimes practised later, of "knifing" its own party's candidate because the Boss of the Hall had a grievance against him.

As part of the machinery for the development of his personal power, John Kelly controlled two New York City newspapers, the *Star* and the *Evening Express*. Kelly kept alive the influence of the *Star*, of which he held the stock, by ordering the Board of Excise Commissioners not to grant a license to any saloon keeper who could not show paid-up subscription receipts for two subscriptions to the *Star*. In this way, Kelly's newspaper gained about six thousand subscriptions, and his political propaganda circulated in the places where men congregated. The scheme was also effective in keeping opposition newspapers out of the saloons, for a saloon keeper who was compelled to pay for two subscriptions to one newspaper was not likely to be extravagant enough to supply his patrons with any other journal of opinion.

Kelly also used the services of competent "spouters." One of these was General Francis B. Spinola, who in one of his impassioned orations said:

"The Saviour of mankind could not protect himself from a Judas. But we can look out hereafter for the Judases of Tammany. . . . We may not have an office under the City government, but they cannot destroy Tammany Hall. It had its birth with the Republic, and it will never die until it is laid side by side in the same coffin with the Republic."

In spite of all his efforts, John Kelly's battle for absolute power was fought with difficulty. Leading Democrats who were opposed to his autocratic rule seceded from Tammany Hall and formed opposition organizations. George Washington Plunkitt once said of these attempts to set up rivals to Tammany:

"You might think that it would cost a lot of money to get up one of these organizations and keep it goin' for even one campaign, but, Lord bless you! it costs next to nothin'. Jimmy O'Brien brought the manufacture of 'Democracies' down to an exact science, and reduced the cost of production so as to bring it within the reach of all. Any man with $50 can now have a 'Democracy' of his own.

"I've looked into the industry, and can give rock-bottom figures. Here's the items of cost of a new 'Democracy':

```
"A dinner to twelve bone-hunters . . . . . .  $12.00
 A speech on Jeffersonian Democracy  . . . .   00.00
 A proclamation of principles (typewriting) . . .    2.00
 Rent of a small room one month for headquarters .   12.00
 Stationary . . . . . . . . . . . . .    2.00
 Twelve second-hand chairs. . . . . . . .    6.00
 One second-hand table . . . . . . . . .    2.00
 Twenty-nine cuspidors . . . . . . . . .    9.00
 Sign-painting  . . . . . . . . . . . .    5.00
```

"If you land even one small job, you get a big return on your investment. You don't have to pay for advertisin' in the papers. The New York papers tumble over one another to give columns to any new organization that comes out against Tammany. In describin' the formation of a 'Democracy' on the $50 basis, accordin' to the items I give, the papers would say somethin' like this: 'The organization of the Delicatessen Democracy last night threatens the existence of Tammany Hall. It is a grand move for a new and pure Democracy in this city. Well may the Tammany leaders be alarmed. Panic has already broke loose in Fourteenth Street. The vast crowd that gathered at the launching of the new organization, the stirrin' speeches and the proclamation of principles mean that, at last, there is an uprisin' that will end Tammany's career of corruption. The Delicatessen Democracy will open in a few days spacious headquarters where all true Democrats may gather and prepare for the fight.'"

The opposition to Tammany Hall in the Democratic Party in New York formed what they called the Irving Hall Democracy after the name of their meeting place. Mayor Edward Cooper was the leader of this faction, and they fought Tammany bitterly, until it was decided by both sides that it would be more profitable personally and generally to combine together for the purpose of winning elections rather than to fight for the purpose of defeating each other. Tammany Hall's leaders and Irving Hall's leaders met one evening just before the election of 1880 on neutral territory, the Westminster Hotel, which was near both halls. The main duty of the reconciliation committee was to settle the number of congressional and assembly districts that should be the property of each faction, and never before had the attitude of Tammany and its associates been expressed so frankly. Hitherto there had been a surface assumption that the voters had something to say in the selection of their candidates for offices, but long years of disregarding the voters' wishes had developed brazen carelessness in the manners of politicians. Kelly for Tammany Hall, and Hubert O. Thompson for Irving Hall, stood opposite each other, and the numbers of districts were placed in a hat between them. They drew for the right to control Democratic nominations in the respective districts, but the system did not prove favourable enough to Tammany Hall, for Kelly had bad luck and kept drawing districts which were strong in Republican voters. Then a compromise conference was held, and the districts were distributed more equitably. Whenever it was impossible to agree on particular districts, someone got out his hat, and the lottery system was resorted to. This went on for weeks, and finally agreements were reached. The other problem to solve was the selection of a candidate for Mayor, and both factions finally agreed on William R. Grace. So much time had been spent in agreeing on candidates that only two weeks were left for the election campaign, and the Democratic majorities were small that year, although Mayor Grace was elected.

After this unsuccessful election, the opposition to John Kelly grew, and an attempt was made to oust him from the leadership of Tammany Hall. Kelly fought this movement strenuously. The election of sachems and other officers of the Tammany

Society took place in Tammany Hall in 1881. The reformers, who were members of another organization known as the New York County Democracy, had their ticket, and Kelly had his, including his own name for sachem. More than eight hundred members of Tammany attended the election, which was four times the number usually present at the elections of the Society. At the left of the Grand Sachem sat the treasurer of the Tammany Society with his cash box, and at his left sat the secretary with his membership book. As each member came up to the table, he was required to pay his poll tax of one dollar. Then he received a receipt which entitled him to vote. The supporters of "Honest John" Kelly for leader had been provided with receipts beforehand, and the first part of the long line, which stretched down the stairway and into the street, consisted almost entirely of the supporters of Kelly, who received their authorizations to vote without delay. The opposition was kept further back in the line, and the Secretary found it more difficult to find their names in his book than he did those of Mr. Kelly's friends. Some of the opposition were thus prevented from voting until after it was too late. In the line ex-Senator Ecclesine and Mr. Edward T. Fitzpatrick bumped each other accidentally. Senator Ecclesine pushed Mr. Fitzpatrick, who was an ardent supporter of John Kelly, and there were words, whereupon the Senator hit Mr. Fitzpatrick over the head with his cane, indenting the latter's bowler hat. It was announced late that night that John Kelly had won the election.[1]

Perhaps John Kelly's most troublesome political and personal opponent was John Morrissey, whose previous part in New York politics has already been noticed. Morrissey had opposed Tweed, and he acted with Kelly and Tilden in the campaign against the Ring. His personal following was large, and his tendency was toward eccentricity rather than obedience, for his personal experience as prize fighter and gambler had taught him independence. Kelly soon found that John Morrissey was an obstacle in the way of his autocratic domination of New York politics, for Morrissey was a disturbing influence in Tammany Hall gatherings, and his wishes often were opposed to those of Kelly. It was not possible for both men to remain in Tammany

---

[1] *Thirty Years of New York Politics*, by Matthew P. Breen, pp. 52 ff.

HARPER'S WEEKLY.
A JOURNAL OF CIVILIZATION

Vol. XVII.—No. 879.]   NEW YORK, SATURDAY, NOVEMBER 1, 1873.   [WITH A SUPPLEMENT.
PRICE TEN CENTS.

Entered according to Act of Congress, in the Year 1873, by Harper & Brothers, in the Office of the Librarian of Congress, at Washington.

"TAMMANY HALL WILL WHIP CREATION THIS FALL."

HERCULES MORRISSEY. "Stand aside, Boys. I'll show you what Muscle can do."

Hall, if Kelly was to be the monarch. Charges were made that Morrissey and his friends were not responsive to the demands of the Democratic Party, and they were expelled from Tammany Hall. This took place just before the fall of 1875, when there was an election for State Senator in the Fourth Ward, a Tammany stronghold which had sent Tweed to the Senate. Morrissey decided to be a candidate from that ward. The district had always been worth a majority of 11,000 votes to Tammany Hall, and Morrissey succeeded in defeating the Tammany candidate, John Fox, by 3,377 votes.

Morrissey voted in the Senate for every anti-Tammany measure, and he introduced some of them himself. Tammany Hall leaders, and Kelly particularly, were very angry. It was said against him that only the district which had elected Tweed would be guilty of sending a vicious thug, a rowdy prize fighter and a notorious gambler to the State Senate. This annoyed Morrissey, and in 1877 he decided to be the candidate for the Senate of the Seventh District, the most reputable in the City, where his Tammany opponent was the venerable Augustus Schell, the director of the Vanderbilt railroads and the Grand Sachem of Tammany Hall. The Republicans endorsed Morrissey, and he gained the support of all the anti-Tammany elements. In the course of the campaign, Tammany orators denounced Morrissey as a gambler, a prize fighter, a ballot-box stuffer, and a burglar. It was also said that when he was a member of Congress, he had a percentage in the leading faro game in Washington. John D. Townsend, the lawyer who made these charges, ended his speech with this peroration: "I know of nothing since the time when Fisk used to parade his mistress at watering-places and through the public streets, when Judges sat in his box at the theatre and at the table of his mistress, that could do more to destroy virtue in the minds of the young, than the election of John Morrissey from one of the most respectable, literary and high-toned districts of the City." But this most reputable, literary and high-toned district elected John Morrissey by a majority of 3,874, and his triumph over his enemy John Kelly was complete, for he had defeated him once in the poorest district in New York and again in the most fashionable.

Early in John Kelly's administration of Tammany Hall, the organization had split into two factions, popularly known as the

"Swallow-tails," consisting of the rich men of Tilden's group who had been brought in by Kelly for his show window, and the "Short-Hairs," who were the workingmen and pugilists led by Morrissey. In 1874, Tammany elected a reputable business man, William H. Wickham, Mayor of New York. He introduced more businesslike methods in the City Hall, and among his innovations was an attendant at the door of the Mayor's

DEMOCRATIC COMPANIONS (?) IN ARMS.

"Short-Hair" to "Swallow-Tail," "Oh, yes, it's all very well now, after I have done all the dirty work for our—I mean *your*—election, and now you will not let me share the plunder."

office, whose duty it was to receive the cards of visitors. One day, about a month after Wickham had taken office, John Morrissey, being in the neighbourhood, called at the City Hall to see his friend, whom he had been instrumental in placing there. He started for the Mayor's inner office, as he had been accustomed to do when friends of his were mayors of New York, and the attendant grabbed his arm and asked for his card. Morrissey was amazed, and he was also mortified, for several of his friends were waiting in the anteroom. "By whose orders are you acting?" Morrissey asked. "By order of His Honour Mayor Wickham," answered the attendant. "Is that so?" said

Morrissey. "Well, give my compliments to His Honour Mayor Wickham and ask him to tell 'Billy' Wickham that when John Morrissey has time to put on French airs, he may call again. Good-day, sir!" A few days later, a friend met John Morrissey in City Hall Park. He was dressed in a swallow-tail coat, patent-leather boots, white kid gloves, and he carried a light coat over his arm. In his other hand was a thick book. His friend, John B. Haskin, said: "Hello, John, what's up now? Going to a wedding?" "No," answered Morrissey, "not so bad as that. I've just bought a French dictionary to help me to talk to our dandy Mayor. I'm going in full dress to make a call, for that is now the style at the Hotel Wickham," pointing to the City Hall. "No Irish need apply now," Morrissey added. He paid his call, and the Mayor received him with a laugh and apologized for the mistake of his attendant, who did not know that there were exceptions to all rules, and that the Hon. John Morrissey was one of them.[1]

Morrissey had married a very beautiful woman. Joseph Smith, the usher of the United States Hotel at Saratoga, where Morrissey owned a large interest in the race course and where he operated the leading gambling establishment, wrote in his naïve book of reminiscences that when he was engaged at the Saratoga railway station in the transportation of guests to the hotel, the first request made by all arriving guests was, "that I should point out to them William H. Vanderbilt and Mrs. John Morrissey."

Morrissey had made a great deal of money in gambling and in Wall Street, and he wished to buy a house in the aristocratic section of his native city, Troy, New York. When the neighbours learned that a prize fighter and a gambler was about to be a neighbour, they organized and bought the house Morrissey was interested in. Morrissey was angry, and he purchased a lot in the rear of the fashionable district and set up on it a soap factory, which in the course of turning out its product emitted the vilest smell obtainable by chemical processes. The neighbours were compelled to buy Morrissey's property for a very high price.

John Morrissey did not enjoy his triumph over

---

[1]Breen, pp. 532-533.

John Kelly for long. During his election campaign, he had contracted pneumonia, but he kept on making speeches. After the election, his health grew worse, and he died on May 1, 1878, at Saratoga, before he was able to take his seat in the Senate again. Eulogies were delivered in which the favourite themes were his honesty and the triumph of his struggles against formidable obstacles. Senator Thomas C. E. Ecclesine, the same who had crashed in Mr. Fitzpatrick's bowler hat, said:

"He is dead. It is the common heritage of the sons of men. He has gone to that land of shadows, toward which we are hastening; but he has gone, buoyed up and soothed by the hopes of a blessed immortality, hopes that lift the dark pall from the portals of the tomb, rob the grave of its victory, and death of its sting. And while, in the language of the old Latin poet we may say 'sit terra tivi levis,' 'May the earth lie light on his body,' we may also add the words of that Church in whose faith he died, 'May Heaven have mercy on his soul.'"

II

In spite of the defeats he suffered when he endeavoured to dominate national politics and the politics of the State of New York, John Kelly managed to retain his control of Tammany Hall and the city government during most of his reign from 1872 until 1886. Kelly had realized even during the Tweed era that Tweed's ribald corruption was not the way of permanent power, and it was among Kelly's ambitions to die in his own bed and to make the years before the inevitable end as comfortable as possible.

Kelly's golden calf was the organization, and he believed that the greatest amount of money and power could be obtained with the utmost safety if individuals relied on the organization of Tammany Hall and did nothing to interfere with its perfect progress.

John Kelly originated the system of assessing candidates large sums of money for their nominations to office. He saw that for candidates to spend money in individual campaigns was both wasteful to themselves and of no permanent value to Tammany Hall, and he persuaded his candidates to pay into the organization a fixed sum of money so that a general campaign might be waged, and he also compelled small office holders to contribute a percentage of their salaries to the organization at election time. This had been done before, as we have seen, but never in such an organized and thorough way as during the Kelly régime.

After Tammany Hall had won an election, it was then the custom for the leader to submit a list of names to the Mayor for all the vacancies in the city government, and the Mayor, if he wished to retain the respect and the support of Tammany Hall, was compelled to appoint those men to the offices designated. Each district leader was provided with places for himself and his constituents, and the system developed into an orderly and permanent machine for the exploitation of the City's offices rather than a diffuse and inefficient scramble for places.

Tammany Hall under John Kelly perfected an organization that was, as Richard Croker described it, "admirable in theory, and works excellently well in practice." The voters in every Assembly District in the City who wished to be known as Democrats were, if they enrolled with the Democratic Party, entitled to vote for delegates to the Tammany Hall General Committee, which consisted of more than four thousand members. Every Assembly District also had its district, or ward, committee, which took charge of affairs in the particular district, and each district had its district leader and its election district captains. A Committee on Organization of Tammany Hall consisted of members from each Assembly district and also the officers of the Tammany Hall General Committee. This Committee on Organization took charge of primary elections and regular elections in all their details, for, as we have seen, the state intrusted the details of elections to the political parties, and Tammany Hall in New York was the official representative of the Democratic Party. There was also an executive committee, consisting of the district leaders of each district in the City, and this committee decided problems of policy and the issues which should and should not be discussed in campaigns, as well as who was and who was not to get a job after a victory.

In short, the system consisted of a boss, who was chairman of the Finance Committee, and a member of the other important committees, and a subordinate boss in every district in the

City, who was supreme in his neighbourhood, but who did the bidding of the Boss of Tammany Hall. Each district leader had a clubhouse in his district, and the general meeting place was Tammany Hall. Tammany controlled the delegates to state conventions, who nominated the candidates for Governor and other offices, by seeing to it that only men who could be trusted to obey were selected as the regular delegates of the party in each district. If there was opposition in any ward to the selections of the Boss of Tammany Hall and his subordinate district bosses, the opposition meetings were broken up by gangs, and the primary election was insured for victory by stuffing the ballot boxes with extra ballots or by preventing the opposition from entering the polling places until it was too late to vote. In these endeavours, fists, vegetables, and decayed eggs were used. The police, owing their positions to Tammany Hall, refused to interfere. The object was, however, to win a primary election without unnecessary bloodshed. "Blood's news," remarked Big John Kennedy; "it gets into the papers."

The Monday before election day was known in the period of "Honest John" Kelly and Richard Croker as "Dough Day," for it was then that Tammany distributed the money that was to be spent in the election campaign of the next day. Each district leader received as much as he thought he would need for his district, to pay the men who would help get the voters to the polls, for the hire of carriages to take the lame, the sick, and the blind to vote, for the purchase of fireworks and the hire of orators. William M. Ivins estimated that in the 1880's it cost the candidates $211,200 for the legitimate expenses of election in the City, and he also estimated that in an average year during this period the legitimate expenses of both parties totalled $407,500 in addition to the City's appropriation of $290,000 for the expenses of the election, making a total of approximately $700,000. A Presidential election cost more.

The difference between the $211,000 which was paid in assessments by the candidates themselves and the $407,500 which was required by the parties was paid by levies on contractors, corporations, rich men, and people who wished to break the law with impunity in one way or another. In each district of the City saloon keepers, owners of houses of prostitution, grocers who wanted to obstruct the sidewalks, builders who wished to violate the building regulations of the City, paid tribute at election time to the district leaders, who turned the money over to the general campaign fund of Tammany Hall. The organization collected not only from those who wished to violate laws, but also from those who wished to live peacefully without having the windows of their shops smashed by the district leader's gang, or without being unnecessarily molested by the police.

The efficiency which the Tammany Hall organization attained under John Kelly and has maintained ever since was due to the fact that the organization consisted of groups of men who were working at the business of politics every day in the year. The Boss, when he was not taking his vacations during the months when there were no pressing problems, could be found in his office in Fourteenth Street every day, where the district leaders could consult with him on the affairs of their neighbourhood. These district leaders, on the other hand, never took vacations. Everybody in the district knew the leader, for it was his business to know everybody. His duties consisted of getting jobs for the people in his neighbourhood, paying their rent when they could not afford to do it themselves, getting them out of trouble when they were arrested, and keeping them amused with outings in summer and dances in winter. The duties of a district leader of Tammany Hall were vividly portrayed in the following record of a day's work which was furnished by George Washington Plunkitt:

"2 A. M.: Aroused from sleep by the ringing of his door bell; went to the door and found a bartender, who asked him to go to the police station and bail out a saloon-keeper who had been arrested for violating the excise law. Furnished bail and returned to bed at three o'clock.

"6 A. M.: Awakened by fire engines passing his house. Hastened to the scene of the fire, according to the custom of Tammany district leaders, to give assistance to the fire sufferers, if needed. Met several of his election district captains who are always under orders to look out for fires, which are considered great vote-getters. Found several tenants who had been burned out, took them to a hotel, supplied them with clothes, fed them, and arranged temporary quarters for them until they could rent and furnish new apartments.

"8:30 A. M.:Went to the police court to look after his constituents. Found six 'drunks.' Secured the discharge of four by a timely word with the judge, and paid the fines of two.

"9 A. M.:Appeared in the Municipal District Court. Directed one of his district captains to act as counsel for a widow against whom dispossess proceedings had been instituted and obtained an extension of time. Paid the rent of a poor family about to be dispossessed and gave them a dollar for food.

"11 A. M.: At home again. Found four men waiting for him. One had been discharged by the Metropolitan Railway Company for neglect of duty, and wanted the district leader to fix things. Another wanted a job on the road. The third sought a place on the Subway and the fourth, a plumber, was looking for work with the Consolidated Gas Company. The district leader spent nearly three hours fixing things for the four men, and succeeded in each case.

"3 P. M.: Attended the funeral of an Italian as far as the ferry. Hurried back to make his appearance at the funeral of a Hebrew constituent. Went conspicuously to the front both in the Catholic church and the synagogue, and later attended the Hebrew confirmation ceremonies in the synagogue.

"7 P. M.: Went to district headquarters and presided over a meeting of election district captains. Each captain submitted a list of all the voters in his district, reported on their attitude toward Tammany, suggested who might be won over and how they could be won, told who were in need, and who were in trouble of any kind and the best way to reach them. District leader took notes and gave orders.

"8 P. M.: Went to a church fair. Took chances on everything, bought ice-cream for the young girls and the children. Kissed the little ones, flattered their mothers and took their fathers out for something down at the corner.

"9 P. M.: At the club house again. Spent $10 on tickets for a church excursion and promised a subscription for a new church-bell. Bought tickets for a base-ball game to be played by two nines from his district. Listened to the complaints of a dozen pushcart peddlers who said they were persecuted by the police and assured them he would go to Police Headquarters in the morning and see about it.

"10:30 P. M.: Attended a Hebrew wedding reception and

dance. Had previously sent a handsome wedding present to the bride.

"12 P. M.: In bed."[1]

There was only one return expected of the beneficiaries of the district leader's benevolence, and that was that those who were helped or pleased should vote for the Tammany Hall candidates on election day, a simple and modest request, for most of the people did not care for whom they voted.

Plunkitt said that when he heard of a young man in his neighbourhood who was proud of his voice, he gave him a chance to sing at the district glee club, and when election time came he voted for Plunkitt's choice. Those who liked rowing, prize fighting, or waltzing were also given opportunities to display their talents. "I rope them all in," remarked Plunkitt, "by givin' them opportunities to show themselves off. I don't trouble them with political aguments."

Plunkitt had a vast contempt for campaign literature:

"No, I don't send them campaign literature," he said. "That's rot. People can get all the political stuff they want to read—and a good deal more, too—in the papers. Who reads speeches, nowadays, anyhow? It's bad enough to listen to them. You ain't goin' to gain any votes by stuffin' the letter boxes with campaign documents. Like as not you'll lose votes, for there's nothin' a man hates more than to hear the letter-carrier ring his bell and go to the letter-box expectin' to find a letter he was lookin' for, and find only a lot of printed politics. I met a man this very mornin' who told me that he voted the Democratic State ticket last year because the Republicans kept crammin' his letter-box with campaign documents."

District leaders never wrapped a sandwich in wax paper printed with "Vote for Mulligan" before they gave it out.

"If a family is burned out," said Plunkitt, "I don't ask whether they are Republicans or Democrats, and I don't refer them to the Charity Organization Society, which would investigate their case in a month or two and decide they were worthy of help about the time they are dead from starvation.

[1] *Plunkitt of Tammany Hall*, pp. 167–183.

I just get quarters for them, buy clothes for them if their clothes were burned up, and fix them up till they get things runnin' again. It's philanthropy, but it's politics, too—mighty good politics. Who can tell how many votes one of these fires bring me? The poor are the most grateful people in the world, and, let me tell you, they have more friends in their neighbourhood than the rich have in theirs."

Life in New York City was a close struggle for very many people in certain sections of the town. Therefore, any favours meant much in immediate advantage and were always thankfully received. The character of this struggle was illustrated by the following comment in the report of the Metropolitan Board of Health for 1880: "As the matter now stands, in some portions of the Sixth, Eleventh, Fourteenth, Seventeenth, Eighteenth and Twentieth Wards, the living have very little more ground space than is appropriated to the dead—a distribution which is not less fatal than it is impartial." Whatever the Tammany district leader contributed might mean more than can be imagined. That it was not philanthropy but politics was admitted by Plunkitt, but it is illustrated in a more sinister way by the fact that the Tammany system contributed so largely to the conditions which it could only hope to ameliorate in a small way. Professor Merriam in his book on the American party system pointed out that the Boss "gives $100 to charity but accepts $1,000 for voting against an ordinance for better housing. He pays the funeral expenses of the man who dies because the boss killed the law to safeguard the machinery on which he worked. He helps the widow, whose suit for damages was blocked under a system he was paid to perpetuate. As the government broadens the range of its generally recognized social duties, the occupation of the spoilsman is taken away and the interest of the citizen in his own government is stimulated."

Tammany Hall, under the system which was inaugurated by "Honest John" Kelly, did not have to steal openly. It had created a vast design to which every phase of New York life contributed its pleasantly profitable section. "The politician who steals," remarked Plunkitt at a time when this design had reached its completion, "is worse than a thief. He is a fool. With the grand opportunities all around for the man with a

political pull, there's no excuse for stealin' a cent." "It makes
me tired," he also remarked, "to hear of old codgers back in the
thirties or forties boastin' that they retired from politics without
a dollar except what they earned in their profession or business.
If they lived to-day, with all the existin' opportunities, they
would be just the same as twentieth century politicians. There
ain't any more honest people in the world just now than the
convicts in Sing Sing. Not one of them steals anything. Why?
Because they can't. See the application?"

After a Tammany district leader under the business system
of political manipulation had aided his constituents and had
thus won their votes, he was in a position to aid himself. The
expenses of philanthropy were large, and it was necessary to
get the money by office-holding or by contracting work for
the City. George Washington Plunkitt boasted that he held
a record—he filled four public offices in one year and drew
salaries from three of them at the same time. He spoke to
his friend Riordan one day on his rise in politics and gave
this picture of the process as it was practised in the 'eighties
under "Honest John" Kelly:

"After goin' through the apprenticeship of the business
while I was a boy workin' around the district headquarters and
hustlin' about the polls on election day, I set out when I cast
my first vote to win fame and money in New York City politics.
Did I offer my services to the district leader as a stump-
speaker? Not much. The woods are always full of speakers. Did
I get up a book on municipal government and show it to the
leader? I wasn't such a fool. What I did was to get some marketable goods before goin' to the leaders. What do I mean by
marketable goods? Let me tell you: I had a cousin, a young man
who didn't take any particular interest in politics. I went to
him and said: 'Tommy, I'm goin' to be a politician, and I want
to get a followin'; can I count on you?' He said: 'Sure, George.'
That's how I started in business. I got a marketable commodity
—one vote. Then I went to the district leader and told him I
could command two votes on election day, Tommy's and my
own. He smiled on me and told me to go ahead. If I had offered
him a speech or a bookful of learnin', he would have said, 'Oh,
forget it!'

"That was beginnin' business in a small way, wasn't it? But that is the only way to become a real lastin' statesman. I soon branched out. Two young men in the flat next to mine were school friends. I went to them, just as I went to Tommy, and they agreed to stand by me. Then I had a followin' of three voters and I began to get a bit chesty. Whenever I dropped into district headquarters, everybody shook hands with me, and the leader one day honored me by lightin' a match for my cigar. And so it went on like a snowball rollin' down a hill. I worked the flat-house that I lived in from the basement to the top floor, and I got about a dozen young men to follow me. Then I tackled the next house and so on down the block and around the corner. Before long I had sixty men back of me, and formed the George Washington Plunkitt Association.

"What did the district leader say then when I called at headquarters? I didn't have to call at headquarters. He came after me and said: 'George, what do you want? If you don't see what you want, ask for it. Wouldn't you like to have a job or two in the departments for your friends?' I said: 'I'll think it over; I haven't yet decided what the George Washington Plunkitt Association will do in the next campaign.' You ought to have seen how I was courted and petted then by the leaders of the rival organizations. I had marketable goods and there was bids for them from all sides, and I was a risin' man in politics. As time went on, and my association grew, I thought I would like to go to the Assembly. I just had to hint at what I wanted, and three different organizations offered me the nomination. Afterwards, I went to the Board of Aldermen, then to the State Senate, then became leader of the district, and so on up and up till I became a statesman."[1]

The district leader always endeavoured to quarter his election district captains on the City by getting them sinecures in the city government. There was an unwritten, unmentioned agreement between the Democrats and the Republicans to take care of each other's election district captains with jobs even when one party was not in power. The great foe of this system, which John Kelly was perfecting patiently, was civil service reform, which began to become popular in the period of his reign. George

[1]*Plunkitt of Tammany Hall*, pp. 14–17.

Washington Plunkitt grew indignant whenever the words civil service examination were mentioned in his hearing, and he once said:

"It would be all a mess if every man who wanted a job would have to run up against a civil service examination. For instance, if a man wanted a job as a motorman on a surface car, it's ten to one that they would ask him: 'Who wrote the Latin grammar, and, if so, why did he write it? How many years were you at college? Is there any part of the Greek language you don't know? State all you don't know, and why you don't know it. Give a list of all the sciences with full particulars about each one and how it came to be discovered. Write out word for word the last ten decisions of the United States Supreme Court and show if they conflict with the last ten decisions of the police courts of New York City.'

"Before the would-be motorman left the civil service room, the chances are he would be a raving lunatic. Anyhow I wouldn't like to ride on his car."[1]

Plunkitt also remarked: "I know more than one young man in past years who worked for the ticket and was just over-flowin' with patriotism, but when he was knocked out by the civil service humbug he got to hate his country and became an Anarchist."

But Plunkitt was optimistic: "I see a vision," he said. "I see the civil service monster lyin' flat on the ground. I see the Democratic party standin' over it with a foot on its neck and wearin' the crown of victory. I see Thomas Jefferson lookin' out from a cloud and sayin': 'Give him another sockdolager; finish him.' And I see millions of men wavin' their hats and singin' 'Glory Hallelujah!'"

III

John Kelly succeeded in keeping his administration of Tammany Hall free from scandal and in accumulating a personal fortune of half a million dollars. The only scandal during his régime was the bribery of the Board of Aldermen by Jacob

---

[1] *Plunkitt of Tammany Hall*, pp. 102–103.

Sharp to pass a franchise giving him for nothing the right to run a street railway along Broadway. As a result of this deal, most of the Board of Aldermen went to jail or to Canada, but Tammany Hall was not directly involved, and there is no indirect evidence of the participation of Kelly or any of his henchmen. In fact, Hugh J. Grant, who was Kelly's friend and Croker's friend, was the only Alderman who voted against the free granting of the franchise for which another company had offered $1,000,000. Kelly's rule, therefore, may be considered successful to Tammany Hall and to himself.

It was when Kelly attempted to step outside of New York City that he almost invariably failed. We have seen how Samuel J. Tilden opposed him in the State, and Kelly's next opponent was Grover Cleveland. Cleveland had committed, while he was Governor of New York, that sin which was the worst in the eyes of a Tammany Hall leader, independence of party dictation. And Cleveland carried stolid incorruptibility to what John Kelly regarded as a vice. Cleveland had also written John Kelly a letter in which he asked that the Boss of Tammany Hall should please see to it that Thomas F. Grady, the silver-tongued orator of Tammany at the moment, did not receive a seat in the New York Legislature again because of his obstructive tactics directed against Governor Cleveland's measures and purposes. Grady did not receive another nomination, but Kelly used the letter against Cleveland when the latter was a candidate for the nomination for President of the United States, and Thomas F. Grady delivered a long speech against Cleveland on the floor of the national convention. It was in answer to this speech that General Bragg of Wisconsin arose and made the statement which became a slogan: "We love him most for the enemies he has made." Cleveland's supporters maintained that he was independent and honest, and that those were two traits which Tammany Hall had never been able to make much use of in its business.

Kelly had predicted the defeat of Grover Cleveland for President, and he had put all his efforts into electing Hugh J. Grant Mayor of New York against William R. Grace, whom Kelly hated for ingratitude, or as Grace would have preferred to call it, independence. Cleveland was elected, and so was Grace. Kelly was crushed. He became ill and could get no sleep except by the use of opiates. In 1885 he practically retired from active management of the affairs of Tammany Hall, which had fallen from his hands into those of his protégé, Richard Croker. Kelly sat in a chair in his house in West Sixty-ninth Street, where Croker went to see him every afternoon. He consulted with the broken boss and carried out his orders.

But there were those who said that Richard Croker consulted with his sick friend and then did as he pleased, and this is not unlikely, considering Croker's traits. "Brutus killed Cæsar with a dagger," wrote John D. Townsend, Tweed's last lawyer, who hated Croker, "but Croker broke the heart of John Kelly by the ingratitude he manifested." Croker, according to Townsend, manipulated the delegates to insure the nomination of his friend Hugh J. Grant for Mayor, against John Kelly's advice and better judgment, for Kelly believed Grant too weak to win against his enemy, William R. Grace, which proved to be the fact. The one thing John Kelly preferred above all was revenge against a man who had disobeyed him, and he wished that revenge against Grace, who had refused Kelly as much patronage as he considered Tammany Hall must have. But Croker wished Hugh Grant to be nominated, for he knew how to manage Hugh Grant, as we shall see, and he only informed his sick friend about what he was doing after he had made sure of the nomination and it was too late to change it.

"Honest John" Kelly died on June 1, 1886. Simple services were held for him in St. Patrick's Cathedral, which was crowded for the occasion with city officials and workingmen.

CHAPTER VI

CROKER

I

JOHN KELLY had changed Tammany Hall from a disorganized and sociable political society for the development of the financial interests of its members into an efficient association for complete political exploitation. Before he died, he had impressed upon his followers the great importance of organization, obedience, and coöperation. Richard Croker, who had been Kelly's protégé for years, inherited his mantle. When Kelly died, nothing was said about a successor, for during the last years of his master's life Richard Croker had become the leader unobtrusively but unquestionably. No one knew quite how it had come about, but no one thought of opposing the succession. The leadership of Tammany Hall was, as one of its leaders once pointed out, a growth and not an appointment.

Richard Croker was born in County Cork, Ireland, November 24, 1843. His father's name was Eyre Coote Croker, and the Crokers were credited with descent from an old Irish family whose members were officers in Oliver Cromwell's army. These early Crokers were said to be extremely fond of fighting, dice, cards, and horses. Eyre Coote Croker found living difficult in Ireland for himself, his wife, and his seven children, and he emigrated to New York when Richard was three years old. Eyre Coote Croker had to do with horses in Ireland as a blacksmith and a veterinary, and in New York he practised the science of the veterinary.

Richard Croker went to school for a few years in East Twenty-seventh Street, and then he took a job in a machine shop operated by the Harlem Railroad, where he helped to build locomotives. Living and working in the district near Third Avenue and Twenty-third Street, where gangs were rampant and powerful, Richard Croker soon developed skill as a

fighter, and he became the leader of the notorious Fourth
Avenue Tunnel Gang. It was said that on one occasion he had a
fight with Patrick Kelly in a liquor saloon at Thirty-fifth
Street in the course of which Kelly lost an ear, but the battle
which made Croker famous in his neighbourhood was that with
Dick Lynch, a professional pugilist. It took place one Sunday
morning in Jones's Wood; all of Lynch's teeth were knocked
out, and he received other serious injuries. After this fight Dick
Croker was taken up by Jimmy O'Brien, the man who delivered
the proofs of the Tweed Ring frauds to the New York *Times*.

Otto Kempner, who was a vehement opponent of Richard
Croker after Croker became Boss of New York, wrote this
description of one of the Boss's early battles for prestige: "A
great number of the local sports still recall the fierce 'shindy'
in Jim Cusick's rat-and-dog pit on the west side. Cusick was
known as the 'Man Eater,' and had the reputation of being able
to kill more rats with his mouth in an hour than any dog could
in a day. On one occasion Croker's dog was matched to fight
Cusick's dog. The pit was packed with the backers of both kinds
of dogs—the two-legged as well as the four-legged ones. When
Croker's was getting to be the under dog, the excitement became intense. The men went to the aid of their quadrupeds with
fists. A general battle followed. For three quarters of an hour,
both species of brutes bit, gouged, and punched each other
promiscuously. When the smoke of the scuffle cleared away,
the bloody pit was seen to be strewn with parts of human ears
and pieces of human fingers." One "Ed" Quigley was the only
man credited with the ability to beat Richard Croker in a
fight, and he was found one day in the Tunnel with both legs
cut off by a train.

Croker, like Tweed and so many other rising politicians, had
been a member of the Volunteer Fire Department. Croker's
friends and associates when he was young were John Scannell
and his brother Florence, Thomas F. Gilroy, whom Croker
later made Mayor of New York, and other fighting men of the
district who became prominent in the government of the City
of New York when their friend rose to power. One of Croker's
rivals in his youth was Owney Geoghegan, leader of the Gas
House Gang. He and Dick Croker were scheduled to fight,
but perhaps it was better for the future of Croker, if not for the

future of New York, that the fight never took place, for during
one of his fights Owney Geoghegan was found to have horse-
shoes in his gloves. On another occasion, when he was fighting
with Con Orem, he suddenly shouted, "He's got a set of brass
knuckles in his hand," and when Orem opened both his hands
to show that it was not true, Owney Geoghegan rushed in and
knocked him senseless before he could guard against the attack.
Owney Geoghegan owned a "sporting house" at First Avenue
and Twenty-first Street, which was the headquarters of the
Gas House Gang, and Geoghegan was also a member of Tammany Hall and an active worker for its interests on every election day.

Croker, too, worked for Tammany Hall on election day. "In
the year 1864," Richard Croker once wrote, "at the age of
twenty-one, I cast my first ballot. I felt then that the Democratic Party was the young man's party; that the young blood
of the nation must naturally be drawn toward Democracy,
which made a ready place for the newcomers, and welcomed
them to a share in the management of the affairs, even into the
councils, of the nation." In fact, Croker felt so strongly that
the Democratic Party was the young man's party that, in
1865, at the age of twenty-two, he did even better: he voted no
less than seventeen times for William H. Lyman, the Democratic candidate for Constable in Greenpoint.[1]

Alfred Henry Lewis wrote two books dealing with the life
and times of Richard Croker. One of them, a work of fiction
called *The Boss*, approximated the truth, and the other, an
idealization called *Richard Croker*, compared the Boss of New
York with Cromwell, Napoleon, and allied artists. Describing
Richard Croker's early life, Lewis wrote in the latter work:
"There was no youth more moral in the city. He drank no
liquors, he visited no saloons, he did not set foot in a brothel,
and his language was without taint of profanity or violence.
These were characteristics of his young manhood; they have

[1]Ex-Sheriff James O'Brien, at a political meeting in 1901, charged Richard Croker
with voting fourteen times for Lyman and remarked, "Now, Mr. Lyman himself
will tell you if I am telling the truth." "He speaks in part the truth," said Mr. Lyman,
"when he charges that Richard Croker voted for me fourteen times in one day. The
only mistake he made was in the number. Richard Croker voted for me seventeen
times in one day, and he was at the head of a gang of repeaters that day." Richard
Croker never denied this statement. New York *Times*, February 9, 1901.

found emphasis with every day he has lived. Richard Croker has been, and is, in the matter of personal morals, a lesson." What Richard Croker thought of this lyric biography, which was published when Croker was at the height of his power, was indicated by a news item published in the New York *Times* for October 26, 1901:

"Tammany men are discussing with interest Richard Croker's view of the book about himself written by Alfred Henry Lewis. They have learned that the Tammany chieftain, upon reading the work while aboard the steamship bound for home, became so angry that he threw it over the rail.

"Until this incident became generally known Croker's lieutenants read with pride the book in which the Tammany Boss is compared with Julius Cæsar, Napoleon, George Washington, and other great figures of history.

"Mr. Croker had no opportunity to read his official biography until he got aboard ship. Before he had gone half way through the work he rose from his chair, stepped to the rail and flung the book out in the waves."[1]

Young Richard Croker's usefulness was not only recognized by Sheriff O'Brien, but also by "Slippery Dick" Connolly, the Tweed Ring Comptroller, and Croker's name was placed on the city pay rolls as an attendant in the Court presided over by the notorious Judge Barnard, at a salary of $1,200 a year. At this same period Richard Croker was said to have operated a saloon on Second Avenue, but he denied before an investigating committee of the Legislature that he ever in his life owned a liquor store or had the slightest interest in one. Croker also worked as an engineer on one of the City's steamers, and while he was an engineer he was elected Alderman. This was the year 1868, when Tweed and his associates were climbing to unlimited power. Croker was elected to fill the vacancy caused by the elevation of his friend Jimmy O'Brien to the office of Sheriff of New York. It was at this time that O'Brien was beginning to fight Tweed and his associates, and Croker, who had been an enrolled member of Tammany Hall for some years and whose

---

[1] New York *Times*. October 26, 1901.

father was also a member, joined O'Brien's faction. Croker was reëlected to the Board of Aldermen in 1869, and he was one of the eight Aldermen who signed an agreement not to vote for any appointment or measure until they had consulted with Tweed's opponents, the Young Democracy leaders, Genet, Norton, and Creamer. Croker was then put out of office by the provision of the Tweed charter which called for a new Board of Aldermen. But the dissenters, as we have seen, were not long in making friends with Tweed, and they were taken care of by him. Croker was given a position in the Comptroller's office under "Slippery Dick" Connolly, and he was a subordinate in that office when the Tweed Ring exposures began. When the reform Comptroller, Andrew H. Green, took office, Croker was removed.

Meanwhile, Croker had thrown his local influence among his friends on Second Avenue and Third Avenue to "Honest John" Kelly, and when Kelly became Boss of Tammany Hall, Richard Croker was made a city marshal by Mayor Havemeyer. In 1873 John Kelly nominated and elected Richard Croker Coroner of New York, an office which was then worth about $15,000 a year in fees.

Croker's main usefulness to his political leaders at this time was as a fighter. It was Croker's gang who in 1868 assaulted Christopher Pullman, a Republican politician, on the corner of Thirty-second Street and Second Avenue. Pullman was knocked unconscious by the Croker boys, and he received injuries from which he never recovered. This significant item appeared in the New York *Times* of September 8, 1871:

"On last Tuesday evening, Sept. 5, about 8:45 P. M., ex-Alderman Richard Croker, of the Twenty-first Ward, who is the leader of the St. Patrick's Alliance (Dick Connolly's secret organization in that ward), with the assistance of another individual, who can be identified by parties who were present, assaulted a man named James Moore with a slung-shot, knocking him down and kicking him, at the corner of Twenty-first Street and Third Avenue. The ex-Alderman is now holding a sinecure position under Dick Connolly, and is occasionally appointed as a commissioner on street openings. He is also the individual who put in a bid for Washington Market (it is supposed) as a blind for 'Slippery Dick.'"

Just after he was elected Coroner an incident occurred which almost closed the promising political career of the Second Avenue Slugger who was destined to rule New York for so many years. Croker had quarrelled with his friend Jimmy O'Brien and had become a follower of John Kelly instead. In the campaign of 1874 Kelly was supporting Abram S. Hewitt against Jimmy O'Brien for Congress. At a quarter past seven on the morning of election day, 1874, John McKenna, thirty years old, one of O'Brien's supporters, was shot to death on the corner of Thirty-fourth Street and Second Avenue. Richard Croker was accused of the murder and arrested for it.

The antagonism between the faction of James O'Brien and the district faction of Tammany Hall led by Richard Croker was bitter. O'Brien was fighting particularly hard in this election, for if he lost this time, it was rather certain that he would never again take a leading part in the politics of the Twenty-first Ward and of the City. O'Brien's followers, led by his brothers Larry and Steve, travelled around the ward early in the day, upsetting polling places and ticket boxes and beating citizens who wished to vote against them. Owney Geoghegan was using his fists vigorously in the interests of Jimmy O'Brien.

Croker and his friends George Hickey and John Sheridan met Jimmy O'Brien and Billy Borst at the corner of Thirty-fourth Street and Second Avenue. Borst belonged in a West Side district, and Croker asked him what he and his friends were doing in the Twenty-first Ward. At this moment Jimmy O'Brien came up to the group and asked, "Billy, what is that damned loafer saying to you?" "I am no damned loafer," Croker answered. "You are a damned loafer, and a God damned loafer, and a repeater," O'Brien said. The crowd began to grow larger. "You are a damned thief," Croker said to O'Brien. And O'Brien was credited by eyewitnesses with the following remark: "You damned cur, I picked you out of the gutter, and now you're supporting a rich man like Hewitt against me for Congress." When Croker repeated that O'Brien was a damned thief, the ex-Sheriff hit the future Boss on the back of the head, and Croker followed with a blow which cut O'Brien's mouth. The other men joined in the fight. Then suddenly shots were fired, and when the police finally thought it time to interfere, it was found that John McKenna, a car-driver, had been shot in the head. He was taken to Bellevue Hospital, where he died a few hours later.

Police Sergeant Frank B. Randal testified later that he spoke to John McKenna in a drug store directly after the shooting. He knew McKenna and asked him who shot him:

"He said, 'Dick Croker'; I said to him 'John, it is my place to know how this occurred, I wish you would tell me how it happened'; he said, 'For God's sake give me a drink of water'; somebody proposed to give him some brandy; I then asked him again if he could tell me how it occurred; he said he would; that he saw the Senator [O'Brien] and Mr. Croker strike each other, and he ran across, and he said George Hickey said, 'Let's give it to the sons of bitches' and as he said so he struck him, then Coroner Croker shot them, and he said, 'When I fell George Hickey fired two shots at me.'"

Coroner Croker was arrested soon after the death of McKenna. He made a statement in which he denied any part in the shooting and added: "I never carried a pistol in my life, and never will as long as I can use my hands." John Kelly and Abram S. Hewitt both appeared in the Coroner's court, and Croker was released on $2,500 bail, which was furnished immediately, but later he was placed in the Tombs, awaiting his trial. Kelly realized that Croker was in great danger, and he hired the best lawyers for his protégé, among them Henry L. Clinton, who had helped to prosecute Tweed.

While Croker was in the Tombs his companions were John Scannell, who had shot and killed the man who murdered his brother Florence Scannell, and Edward S. Stokes, who had shot and killed James Fisk, Jr. The three got to be close friends. Scannell was sent to an insane asylum for one year, and when he came out he resumed work for Tammany Hall and during Croker's régime became one of the Boss's confidential henchmen. Stokes served seven years in Sing Sing Prison and was then pardoned. He became the proprietor of the Hoffman House, and his prison friend Richard Croker aided him by making that establishment the headquarters of Tammany Hall politicians during election campaigns. It was said that in one night at election time the receipts of the Hoffman House bar were more than $2,200.

The jury in the trial of Richard Croker consisted of six Democrats and six Republicans. The evidence was conflicting and thin. Eyewitnesses testified that they saw Croker fire the shot, and others testified that Croker did not have a gun and never carried a gun. The jury remained out for seventeen hours and then returned to make the announcement that they stood equally divided, six for conviction and six for acquittal, and that they could not agree. Croker was released, and he was never tried again. It was generally believed in later years that he did not fire the shot that killed McKenna, but that it was fired by his friend George Hickey. General Wingate, who was of Croker's counsel, said at the time of the death of Croker that the man who fired the shot was standing next to Croker during the trial and intended if the verdict was one of guilty to declare himself the murderer. Croker, according to his lawyer, refused to permit proof to be submitted that his friend had fired the shot.

Judge George C. Barrett, who presided at Croker's trial, was a candidate for renomination some years later, when Croker controlled New York, and the Boss gave the Judge the renomination. Judge Barrett stated at this time that from what he had learned since the trial he was convinced that Richard Croker had not fired the shot that killed McKenna.

The notoriety resulting from this murder trial made it impossible for Croker to hold public office for a few years, but it did not hinder his advancement in Tammany Hall. In fact, it contributed to his eminence there, for he was generally regarded by his friends and fellow members as a martyr to the sacred cause of organization; even if he had fired the shot that killed McKenna, Tammany politicians would have extolled him as a man of the proper collegiate spirit, who would even commit murder for good old Tammany Hall. Mayor Edson refused to appoint Croker to be a police judge until it was established that the public would not be indignant at the appointment to civic office of a man who had been charged with murder, and therefore it was arranged that Richard Croker should be a Tammany Hall candidate for alderman in order to test the popular opinion of his character. In 1883 John Kelly nominated

Richard Croker for alderman, and he was elected, but he never took his seat, for, seven days after the election, Mayor Edson appointed Croker a Fire Commissioner of New York.[1]

While recovering from his disgrace, Richard Croker had not been idle. He had worked hard in the Eighteenth District and had converted it into one of the strongest Tammany districts in the City. His success placed him in the position of natural successor to John Kelly as leader of Tammany Hall. When Kelly became ill, it was customary for Tammany district leaders to consult Croker on appointments, nominations, and the other important affairs of their particular districts. After Kelly's funeral in 1885 Richard Croker sat at the Boss's desk in Tammany Hall, concerning which one of Croker's opponents once said that all during his reign it showed no ink stains.

II

In his first important campaign Richard Croker insisted on the nomination of Abram S. Hewitt for Mayor. Hewitt was a son-in-law of Peter Cooper and a member of the firm of Cooper, Hewitt & Co. He was a millionaire who desired also to be a statesman, but he always refused to sacrifice either his principles or his feelings to his ambition. Most of the Tammany leaders would have preferred a regular organization man, but Richard Croker insisted on Hewitt, because he knew that Tammany Hall needed Hewitt's reputation, and because Hewitt had helped Croker at the time of his murder trial with advice, influence, and money. Hewitt visited Croker soon after the murder, with which he was slightly involved, because the origin of the quarrel was the election to Congress of Hewitt against O'Brien. He was convinced that Croker was innocent. "I was told then and there who fired the shot," Hewitt said. "It was a man named Hickey. . . . Knowing that he was innocent, I became personally interested in his acquittal. . . . I spent over $4,000 in helping Croker out of his difficulty."

The campaign was a close one, for the opposing candidates were Henry George, whose Single Tax doctrines were beginning

---

[1] *Testimony Taken Before the Senate Committee on Cities Pursuant to Resolution Adopted January 20, 1890*, Vol. II, pp. 1706–1721. Hereafter this investigation will be referred to in footnotes as the Fassett Investigation.

to gain great popular support, and Theodore Roosevelt, whose independence was winning notoriety. Hewitt was elected by a close margin. He reappointed Richard Croker Fire Commissioner.

But Tammany and Croker did not find Hewitt congenial or tractable. He was irritable and refused to be bossed. When a committee of the Irish societies called on the Mayor in March, 1888, and asked him to review the St. Patrick's Day parade that year, the following scene took place:

"Mr. Carey introduced each committeeman by name, saying: 'They are all good Democrats, Mr. Mayor. . . .'

"In a husky staccato tone that has rattled many a delegation before, the Mayor broke in and said:

"'Let us understand each other. I am Mayor of the city and you want me to leave my official duties to review your parade. . . . You started off by a reference to the Irish Democratic vote. Let us understand each other thoroughly. I may be a candidate for Mayor or for Governor, or for President' (here the Mayor turned a humorous glance on the bystanders), 'and I may want all the Democratic votes I can get. We all know that the Irish vote is strong enough to elect any candidate in this city for which it is cast. But for the purpose of getting that vote I shall not consent to review any parade, be it Irish or Dutch or Scotch or German or English. I tell you now that I shall review no parades except those which I am officially required as Mayor to review.'

"This unexpected flat refusal took the committee's breath away for a moment. Then Mr. Carey said that every Mayor for thirty-seven years had reviewed the procession on St. Patrick's Day, and none of them thought it was lowering his dignity to do so.

"'We do not ask this as Irishmen, but as Irish Americans,' he said. 'Previous Mayors thought themselves honored in being asked to review the parade of Irish societies. Even you yourself last year asked to be excused not because you objected to doing so, but on account of your rheumatism. We believed that St. Patrick had taken the rheumatism all out of you, and it would give you pleasure to review us. We believed that in honoring us with your presence, you also were honoring yourself.'

"But by this time the Mayor was ushering the committee toward the door.

"'Gentlemen, you have my answer,' he said, 'I shall not review your parade on St. Patrick's Day.'"[1]

Tammany Hall could not use a man of such a character, and Richard Croker's gratitude had limits. Besides, Croker no longer needed Hewitt, for his temper and irritability had made him unpopular, and the position that he occupied because of his immense wealth and the place he held in New York society was not an advantage in the estimation of the large body of voters, who never enjoyed being ruled by a man who did not have homely or genial manners, no matter how honest or how efficient he might be. Croker did not give the renomination to Abram S. Hewitt, but he nominated instead his old friend Hugh J. Grant, who was elected by a large majority over Joel B. Erhardt, the Republican, and Abram S. Hewitt, who was the candidate of the County Democracy, a faction opposed to Tammany Hall.

Hugh J. Grant was the first regular Tammany Hall man to be elected Mayor since the days of Tweed, and Croker now had his hands on all the offices and all the contracts in the City's gift. Mayor Grant immediately appointed Richard Croker City Chamberlain at a salary of $25,000 a year. This was the office which Peter B. Sweeny had held under the Tweed Ring. Croker held this office until the beginning of 1890, when, because of his ill health, he resigned and went to Europe.

In the same year the Republicans began an investigation into the affairs of the government of the City of New York, known as the Fassett Investigation, which revealed much concerning the relations of Hugh J. Grant and Richard Croker, and the relations of the government of the City of New York and Richard Croker. One of the star witnesses before this committee was Patrick H. McCann, Mrs. Richard Croker's brother-in-law. McCann claimed that Richard Croker held the lease to a restaurant in Central Park, called the Mount St. Vincent. This house had been built by the State after John Kelly had forced through the Legislature a bill providing for its establishment. Kelly did this for his friend Croker, according to

[1]The *Sun*, March 7, 1888.

McCann. Croker tried to run the business with Cornelius S. Conklin, but they lost money, and then Croker persuaded his wife's brother-in-law, McCann, to take over Mount St. Vincent and assume the obligations which he had contracted. Croker and Hugh Grant patronized the restaurant, and other Tammany Hall politicians made it the place for their parties, but McCann said that they never paid the checks. Then Hugh Grant told Croker that his brother-in-law was giving notes and indorsements freely, and that if he did not stop his credit would be ruined. Croker mentioned the matter to his wife, and Mrs. Croker told her sister, Mrs. McCann. McCann became angry and told Grant next time he came to Mount St. Vincent that he did not want him to come there any more, and that he did not want "anything to do with a man who would try to make trouble in a man's family." Grant told Croker what McCann had said, and Croker was very angry. He issued orders to Tammany Hall men not to patronize the Mount St. Vincent house any more, and he threatened to "freeze" McCann out. Croker believed that when the patronage of Tammany men was withdrawn, McCann would not be able to make the restaurant pay, but McCann did make money, and he made more money than ever before, because the Tammany Hall politicians had never considered it necessary to pay for their food and drink, while his other customers did. Croker and Grant then did everything they could to ruin the reputation of the restaurant, and Grant told Croker, according to McCann, "that nobody went there but Jews and loose women." When these tactics failed, Croker told the Park Commissioners not to renew McCann's lease, and the lease was given instead to one Gabe Case.

When Patrick McCann was called as a witness before the Fassett Committee, he was angry with Richard Croker, and especially with Hugh Grant, who was now Mayor of New York. He was ready to tell almost all he knew, and to the consternation of Tammany Hall politicians he did so. The only questions that McCann refused to answer were what he called private family matters. It was a well-known fact that Richard Croker and his wife were not friendly. She was of a respectable family and resented the slurs that the newspapers cast on her husband's reputation when he began to come into power, and he had his reasons for disliking her which have never become public.

The fact is, however, that during the last years of her life and of his they lived apart. McCann told the Fassett Committee: "This is no place to wash family linen, and I do not propose to come here and wash family linen; it is exceedingly painful to me to have to come here and interfere with innocent children and women." "I should suppose it to be," said Bourke Cockran, who was the lawyer representing the interests of Tammany Hall. "Women," answered McCann, "that those people are not fit to black the boots of."

But concerning the relations of Richard Croker and Hugh J. Grant, whom he hated, McCann was voluble and willing to testify. In the fall of 1884 Croker was anxious to obtain the appointment of Hugh J. Grant as Commissioner of Public Works of New York. McCann testified:

"Q. Did you ever hear that Mr. Grant or Mr. Croker believed they could get Mr. Grant appointed commissioner of public works in case they could guarantee a confirmation by the board of aldermen?

"A. Yes, sir; I heard so. . . . Oh, I heard it at the Hoffman House from dozens of men, at the time it was in existence, that he was a candidate; general talk among the people. . . .

"Q. Did Mr. Croker ever go to your store, having with him a sum of money, and telling you that that was the amount of money that had been raised for the purpose of securing sufficient votes in the board of aldermen to confirm Mr. Grant; that you will know of your own knowledge?

"The Witness—Must I answer it?

"Senator Fassett—Yes.

"The Witness—Yes.

"Q. You say yes; did you see the money?

"A. Yes. . . .

"Q. Did Mr. Croker tell you how much it was?

"A. Yes.

"Q. How much was it?

"A. About $180,000.

"Q. What form was it in?

"A. Bills.

"Q. You saw it in bills?

"A. He had it in a satchel.

"Q. How did Mr. Croker come to tell you about that at that time?

"A. He came to me to know if I knew some people in the neighborhood that he would like to meet. . . .

"Q. As relating in any way to this business?

"A. Yes.

"Q. Did Mr. Croker tell you who had raised this money, and from whom it had been raised?

"A. He mentioned the name of Maloney and somebody else.

"Q. Billy Maloney, so known?

"A. Yes, sir. . . .

"Q. Did he say it was raised by way of subscriptions in Tammany Hall?

"A. No; he said it was raised by the organization. . . .

"Q. By the 'organization,' meaning Tammany Hall?

"A. I suppose so; he did not mention Tammany Hall. . . . That was my inference at the time.

"Q. Did he tell you that Mayor Grant had contributed any part of that money?

"A. Yes.

"Q. How much did he tell you Mr. Grant had contributed towards this money for use in the board of aldermen, to secure confirmation?

"A. Eighty thousand dollars. . . ."[1]

McCann was cross-examined by Bourke Cockran for Tammany Hall and testified:

"Q. Were you surprised when Mr. Croker came to you with $180,000?

"A. No; not much. . . .

"Q. And was that a startling thing to see a man with $180,000 in greenbacks in your store?

"A. Not in those times; it was very plenty around.

"Q. Had you ever seen another citizen in this city armed with a bag with $180,000, or any other similar amount in it?

"A. Not on that mission.

"Q. Did you ever see anybody with a bag, or any other person

---

[1] Fassett Investigation, Vol. I, pp. 655–658.

walking around the town with $180,000, or any other similar amount in a bag?

"A. Not that I know of; no.

"Q. And yet you say it was not an unusual thing?

"A. With those people at that time; no.

"Q. With which people?

"A. With the people connected with the board of aldermen.

"Q. Do you know that, or had you heard of it?

"A. Only heard it. . . .

"Q. Now, he came into the store with this bag with $180,000 in it, and what did he say, Mr. McCann?

"A. He says, 'Mac, I hear you talk a good deal of that man Adams; do you think you could trust him?' I said, 'I had trusted him with everything I had had in the world and would trust him if I had millions.' 'Well,' he says, 'I would like to meet him.' . . .

"Q. Did you know at the time Adams was sent for by Mr. Croker, that his purpose was to make him the stakeholder of this $180,000?

"A. From the question Mr. Croker asked me, if he could trust him, I supposed there was something in the matter. . . .

"Q. Then you knew the object of this interview was to enlist Mr. Adams in the business or job of holding this money as the stakeholder for these aldermen?

"A. Yes. . . .

"Q. Did Adams say anything to you when he came back?

"A. After the confirmation was made, he did; yes. . . . Well, he said, 'Mac, I am sorry I didn't get that money, or if I had got it, I would keep half and give you half, and let them go to hell.' . . .

"Q. What did you say to that lofty sentiment?

"A. I don't know what I said, just now.

"Q. Did you greet the suggestion with the same approving smile that you did just now?

"A. I don't think I did; no. . . ."[1]

The $180,000 in bills in Croker's satchel was to be used, McCann testified, to bribe two aldermen to vote for Grant's confirmation as Commissioner of Public Works. After further

[1] Fassett Investigation, Vol. I, pp. 683–690.

questioning, McCann told why Croker and Hugh J. Grant were so much interested in getting Grant appointed a Commissioner of Public Works, and why they were willing to pay such a large amount of money to bribe two aldermen to confirm the appointment.

"Well, he [Croker] told me," McCann testified, "there was a manufacturer of cement on the Hudson River near Newburgh, I think, or some place about the Catskills, that was making a cement just as good as the cement that was used, and that if Grant was appointed Commissioner of Public Works that they would adopt his cement, and that he was to receive ten cents a barrel for every barrel that would be used in the department." "Mr. Croker was to receive ten cents a barrel?" asked Senator Fassett. "Yes, sir," answered McCann.[1]

McCann also testified that Mrs. Croker told him that her husband had brought the $180,000 home, "and he left it in the bureau and told her there was a great deal of money there and to be careful of it; it unnerved her so that she sat before it for fear the bureau would run away." Grant was not appointed a Commissioner of Public Works by Mayor Edson, and the money was then returned, McCann said he was told, to those who had contributed it.

When Hugh J. Grant was made Sheriff of New York, Croker benefited financially by the appointment. The testimony which Patrick McCann gave on this point was revealing of the methods sometimes used by Tammany Hall leaders in the transfer of money, and the testimony of Mayor Grant himself furnished amusing details. Grant did not give Croker money, but he gave Croker's baby daughter, Flossie, envelopes containing, he admitted, $10,000 in bills, but others stated they contained $25,000 in bills. When McCann was asked concerning these transactions, and it was decided that the question was proper, he broke down: "Then I refuse to answer. I will not," he said. "I will not interfere in family matters. Do with me what you like." Then the following questions were asked and answered:

"Q. Mr. McCann, have you ever heard that Mr. Grant gave the sum of $5,000 for instance to any member of Mr. Croker's

[1] Fassett Investigation, Vol. I, pp. 695 ff.

family; I do not ask you now who told you, I ask you if you ever heard it?

"A. Yes.

"Q. Have you ever heard that Mr. Grant gave $5,000 to any member of Mr. Croker's family on more than one occasion?

"A. Yes.

"Q. Have you ever heard that Mr. Grant gave $25,000 in that way to a member of Mr. Croker's family?

"A. Yes.

"Q. While he was sheriff?

"A. Yes. . . .

"Q. Has Mr. Croker a child named Flossie?

"A. Yes. . . .

"Q. What is her age?

"A. About six years old.

"Q. Have you ever heard that Mr. Grant on five several occasions gave an envelope addressed to Miss Flossie, which envelope on each occasion contained $5,000?

"A. I heard so; yes.

"Mr. Ivins—Now it is for the committee to say in view of the foundation that I have laid as to whether this witness should be compelled to tell who told him so.

"The Witness—Don't, don't, gentlemen, please don't ask me that.

"Senator Fassett—Mr. McCann, it seems as if it was due to Mr. Grant and to the public, and to yourself and to the committee that you locate the source of your information. The committee do not want to force you to do anything that is personally painful, and yet it is a very serious matter.

"Q. Mr. McCann, was it a man who told you?

"A. No, sir.

"Q. Was it a woman?

"A. Yes.

"Q. Was it your wife; if so, we cannot ask you to disclose just what she said?

"A. She was one of the parties; yes.

"Q. Who was the other?

"A. Her sister.

"Q. Her sister, Mrs. Croker?

"A. Yes.

"Q. Then we understand that Mrs. Croker told you that during Mr. Grant's term as sheriff he gave $25,000 to Flossie?

"A. Yes.

"Q. It was handed to her father?

"A. No, I believe not; given to the child.

"Q. Did you ever hear what was done with that money?

"A. Paid for the house they live in. . . . Mt. Morris avenue. . . ."[1]

Hugh J. Grant was Croker's protégé, just as Croker had been "Honest John" Kelly's protégé. He was grateful to Croker for favours and advice. At the time when the aldermen were being bribed by Jacob Sharp for the Broadway street railway franchise, Hugh Grant was the only Tammany alderman who was not involved. On the advice of Richard Croker he had refused to have anything to do with the deal. Croker was too canny to subject himself or his protégés to the chances that Tweed and his associates took so incautiously.

When Hugh J. Grant, then Mayor of New York by the grace of Richard Croker, was examined by Joseph H. Choate, who in conjunction with Bourke Cockran represented Grant and the other Tammany Hall leaders before the Fassett Committee, he testified that Flossie Croker was his godchild, that when he undertook the responsibilities of godfather he meant to provide for the child, and that he gave the child $10,000 and intended to provide for her in his will, because he had no near relatives of his own. Mayor Grant was cross-examined as follows by Albert B. Boardman, one of the attorneys for the Committee:

"Q. How many other godchildren have you got besides Flossie?

"A. None, and I have always refused to have any owing to the fact that I believed it was a great responsibility, and I do not think there is much probability of my being godfather for any more. . . .

"Q. What was the date when you made the first present to Miss Florence?

"A. I cannot recall the date, sir.

[1]Fassett Investigation, Vol. I, pp. 661–665.

"Q. Was it after you became sheriff?

"A. I rather think it was.

"Q. How long afterwards do you think?

"A. Well, I could not say; let me see; I rather think it was some time about the anniversary of its birthday.

"Q. How old was the child?

"A. I think the child then was two years old.

"Q. Had you given the child any substantial presents in money up to that time?

"A. No, sir; my presents up to that time had been in the nature of some silver, I think; I gave the child some silver.

"Q. Well, the ordinary presents that men give to their god-children?

"A. It depends upon what the ordinary is; I had great affection for this child, and I think I made it a little better than the ordinary.

"Q. Did you give it any money prior to the time you became sheriff?

"A. I think I did; I think on the child's first birthday I gave it a gold piece. . . .

"Q. Passing that by, you gave it no money until you became sheriff?

"A. No, sir.

"Q. And then you gave it $5,000?

"A. Yes, sir. . . .

"Q. That is, when the child was a year old you intended to make it a present?

"A. Yes, sir; but at that time Tammany Hall found itself without a candidate for sheriff, and I was obliged to accept the nomination with very little preparation—that is, I was not obliged, but I did accept the nomination with very little preparation.

"Q. And it took all the loose money you had?

"A. I did not feel so much at that time like making the present then, and I think I made it subsequently; whether I made it at the next birthday, or before that, I would not like to swear to now. . . .

"Q. The child was in the custody of a nurse, was she?

"A. No; I rather think the child was just able to toddle over to me. . . .

"Q. Did you hand the envelope to the little child?

"A. Yes, sir.

"Q. And what did the little child do with the envelope?

"A. The child rather held the envelope.

"Q. And finally somebody took it away?

"A. Yes; I think the mother took it. . . .

"Q. That was in bills, too, was it?

"A. Yes, sir.

"Q. Why did you take that mode of transferring money to this child, giving the child bank bills; why didn't you create a trust for the child and put the money in a trust company?

"A. Because I did not think I was exactly in that position; my idea was that if anything should occur to me this child should be provided for.

"Q. You do not usually pay sums of money of that sort in bank bills, do you?

"A. I think that was the proper way to do it. . . . I don't know how I could have given that child a check drawn to the child's order so that the child could indorse it. . . .

"Q. You think it is quite customary for godfathers to go through that little performance about once a year?

"A. No, sir; but I think if you will look over the obligation that one accepts when they become a godfather—of course, I must say that I feel very delicate about discussing such a subject here because it is a matter that I always considered sacred until this committee saw fit to go into it."[1]

Mayor Grant's sacred obligation, however, did not continue after he ceased to be Sheriff of New York County. "You have made no such presents since you left the sheriff's office?" asked Mr. Boardman. "No, sir," answered the Mayor; "I thought that was quite ample."[2]

The scene in the Croker parlour would have made a charming charade on the word Graft: The baby toddled up to Sheriff Grant, took her $5,000 in United States bills with a "Goo, goo," and toddled over to her mother with the bulky envelope, while the leader of Tammany Hall and the Sheriff of

[1]Fassett Investigation, Vol. I, pp. 745-750.

[2]Ibid., p. 757.

New York looked down benevolently on the blissful domestic scene.

The money, Richard Croker testified, when he returned from Europe, was handed by the child to her mother, who put it in a safe. More than a year later, the domestic scene was repeated, and then Croker added $6,500 to the $10,000 which Sheriff Grant had given his daughter and bought a piece of real estate. No memorandum, however, was ever made to the effect that this particular piece of property belonged to Miss Flossie Croker, and it could never have been distinguished by a surrogate from the other property held in the name of Richard Croker, had he died at that moment. When Croker was asked why he did not put the money in a bank account so that it might earn interest while he was waiting to invest it in a piece of property, he answered that he did not trust banks. "I have always had very peculiar notions about putting money in banks," Croker said, "and I have always kept money around the house; we never kept a bank account, and this money was turned right over to her."[1]

Hugh J. Grant's administration of the Sheriff's office was the subject of investigation by a grand jury, which reported that it had been "tainted and corrupt," had been characterized "by an utter subversion of the public interests to personal gain, and the employment of men of ignorance and cupidity to discharge its ordinary duties," and that the management of the office had been "mercenary, slovenly, and wholly indecent."

Grant was the son of a liquor dealer who died when the Mayor was a young man and left him large liquor properties. He was brought up by his guardian, a pawnbroker, named McAleenan, who started him in politics in 1883 as an alderman. His reputation for honesty, gained by not accepting the bribe for the Broadway street railway, led Tammany Hall to run him for Mayor against William R. Grace in 1884, but he was defeated. He had borrowed large sums of money from McAleenan to pay for his mayoralty campaign, and his fortunes were low. In consideration of this, Croker and Kelly gave him the lucrative office of Sheriff, and he made the most of it, and somewhat more than was legal.

---

[1] Fassett Investigation, Vol. II, p. 1733.

Grant and Tammany Hall shared in the patronage of the Sheriff's office, not only directly in the fees which the Sheriff was entitled to for his services, but also they appointed the official auctioneers who worked for the Sheriff, and whose business was sometimes very valuable. John F. B. Smyth, a neighbour of Hugh J. Grant's, who was active in Grant's first unsuccessful campaign for the mayoralty, and who helped him in his campaign to win election as Sheriff, testified before the Fassett Committee that Grant rewarded him by making him Sheriff's auctioneer. Grant told him, however, that the business was so large that he would have to give him a partner. "And you took a partner at his suggestion?" Mr. Smyth was asked. "Hoping I would make a barrel of money; yes, sir," he answered. His partner was an alderman named Kirk, who was a district leader of Tammany Hall. "What reason did Mr. Grant give you for imposing this man upon you as a partner?" Mr. Smyth was asked. "That it was the most valuable gift he had at his disposal," he answered, "and the organization insisted upon one-half of it going to somebody else." "By the organization, what did you understand him to mean?" "Why, at Tammany Hall," Smyth answered.[1]

During Hugh J. Grant's administration as Mayor and Croker's administration of Tammany Hall, the City was regarded as a vast source of financial profit which, if handled carefully, would yield large returns at little risk. Tammany Hall was in complete control of the City, and it was considered fitting and proper that subordinates as well as principals should all make as much money as possible. One source of profit was the administration of the Ludlow Street Jail, where civil prisoners were kept. These frequently included rich business men who had got into difficulties, either domestic or financial, and they paid heavily for extra jail privileges.

Nelson Hersh, a New York *Herald* reporter, testified:

"Q. During the time that you were confined in Ludlow street jail, or supposed to have been confined there, did you go out of the jail?

"A. I did. . . . Once. . . . With Mr. Keating, the warden. . . .

[1] Fassett Investigation, Vol. I, pp. 283-284.

"Q. Tell the committee how you came to go out of the jail and what occurred between Mr. Keating and yourself, from the time that you asked to go out of the jail until the time that you came back?

"A. I spoke to him on the afternoon of Sunday, the twenty-third, I believe; asked him if I could get out and go uptown in the evening and afternoon; he told me that it would be pretty expensive; I asked him how expensive, and he said about twenty dollars; I told him that I had spoken to one of the keepers before, on Saturday, who said it would only cost about fifteen dollars; Mr. Keating explained that as I wanted to be out a longer time than I had spoken to the other man about, it would cost me about five dollars more; I then told him that I was willing to pay that; but I would not stand on the question of a five-dollar note; he asked me if I could go out in the afternoon instead of the evening, as I had originally proposed; I said yes, that would suit me quite as well; and suggested that we go over to the barber shop near by first as I wanted to get shaved; we went over there. I was shaved and as we came out of the barber shop paid Mr. Keating the twenty dollars and we started up town; I will tell as much more as you like, Mr. Ivins.

"Q. How long were you out?

"A. It was about 3 o'clock when we left the jail, and back about half-past six. . . .

"Q. After you were under arrest you went to the tneater?

"A. Yes, sir; on Friday evening the twenty-first of February. . . .

"Q. What did you pay for the privilege of going to the theater?

"A. Forty dollars I paid to Mr. McGonnegal who arrested me, for the privilege of staying out that evening and going where I chose.

"Q. Did he go with you?

"A. Yes, sir. . . .

"Q. Did you pay the expenses at the theater?

"A. Yes, sir.

"Q. Did you and he dine together?

"A. We ate together and drank together a number of times.

"Q. Was that in addition to the forty dollars?

"A. Oh, yes; entirely in addition to the forty dollars.

"Q. Who paid for it?

"A. I believe Mr. McGonnegal bought one drink or one or two drinks during the afternoon and evening; I paid for all the rest. . . .

"Q. Mr. Hersh, on what process were you arrested?

"A. Civil process; for obtaining money under fraud. . . .

"Q. I would like to ask you one more question; did you pay anything to anyone for accommodations inside of Ludlow street jail?

"A. I paid fifteen dollars for board the night I went in, supposed to be a week's board. . . . I paid that to the night keeper. . . .

"Q. What accommodations did you get for that; accommodations differing in character from those of the other prisoners?

"A. Not having seen the accommodations of the other prisoners I can't say; but I understood this was to be board at the warden's table and some particular arrangements about the bed and the room where I slept myself; had sheets and one thing and another. . . .

"Q. Were there any prisoners in the jail who did not eat at the warden's table?

"A. I think there were; I saw a number of prisoners in the jail whom I never saw at the warden's table."[1]

Charles G. Francklyn, a wealthy business man who spent a week in Ludlow Street Jail, testified that he paid $100 a day for the privilege of going to his lawyers' offices in the company of two deputy sheriffs and dining later with his family. Henry S. Ives, who failed in business for $20,000,000 and who was imprisoned in Ludlow Street Jail from January 29, 1889, to March 17, 1890, with his partner George H. Stayner, testified that he paid about $1,000 for the privilege of staying in a hotel for two days, from Saturday to Monday night, instead of going to jail immediately after his arrest. Then he went to the jail, and he paid heavily for the special privileges of living downstairs and eating at the warden's table. "Can you tell, Mr. Ives," he was asked by the examining attorney, Mr. Ivins, "approximately how much money you paid—Mr. Stayner and you together, I mean—how much you paid to the warden

[1] Fassett Investigation, Vol. I, pp. 190–192.

while you were there?" "Yes, sir," Ives answered; "about $10,000." For this money Ives had a different bill of fare and dined later than the regular prisoners, was permitted to have three stenographers in his suite of rooms and a servant. There was also a bar in one of the cells for the accommodation of the warden's special paying guests.[1] Stephen Keating, Warden James P. Keating's son, a student at Columbia College, was on the salary list of the jail as a cleaner and received sixty dollars a month. The prisoners did not see him cleaning, and when Ives was asked if he knew of any reason why Stephen Keating should be on the salary list for sixty dollars a month, he answered, "Sixty dollars a month."

While these revelations were being presented to the public of the private and public affairs of Richard Croker, Croker's young son wrote the following letter to Leicester Holme, Mayor Grant's private secretary:

Hotel Victoria, Wiesbaden, March 17, 1890.

MY DEAR MR. HOLME:

I hope this letter will find you and Mr. Grant in good health. The doctors have blistered papa's side, which makes it very sore, but he is getting along very nicely now. He drinks the waters, takes the baths, and walks for eight miles every day, and is now commencing to feel very different. He said he slept better the other night than he has for six months, so the doctors say that is a good sign.

I wish mamma and all the family were here, as I know it would make papa feel much better. You might be able to come over with her, as I am sure it would do you much good. We expect to leave here in the latter part of May for Switzerland. If you come we will have a fine time riding the donkeys and horses over the beautiful mountains in Switzerland. Be sure and come, for we will have a daisy time. I hope Mr. Grant is well. Papa is gone to take his daily walk, so I take this opportunity to give the particulars of how we are getting on.

Just before papa went out he told me to remember him to you and Mr. Grant. We hope you will continue to write. Richy, Bertie, and I send you our love. I remain yours most truly,

FRANK H. CROKER.

---

[1] Fassett Investigation, Vol. I, pp. 242-249.

But ex-Justice Leicester Holme was having a daisy time helping to ride the donkeys in New York, and he could not leave the fertile fields of the City for the beautiful mountains in Switzerland. Croker himself returned to New York before the Fassett Committee had finished its investigations, and he testified before it, giving much information, which has been used above, concerning his early career and his present status.

In spite of revelations of dishonesty in almost every department of the City's government, Croker succeeded in renominating his friend Hugh Grant for Mayor, and he was reëlected in 1890 by a large majority.

After Mayor Grant was reëlected, Croker dictated most of his appointments to office. Croker demanded that his personal friends be placed in the offices of the heads of city departments, and Grant was acquiescent in most cases. It was said that there was one appointment, however, that Grant baulked at, and that was said to be the cause of the break between him and Croker. Croker wanted his prison mate, John J. Scannell, appointed Fire Commissioner, and Mayor Grant was afraid of what the newspapers would say if he appointed to high office a man who had been found guilty of emptying four chambers of his revolver into another man and thereby killing him. With tears in his eyes, the Mayor refused, and when Mayor Grant's term expired, he never held public office again.[1]

III

In less than five years Richard Croker rose from an inconspicuous but energetic political follower to the most powerful leader New York politics had ever known, and his personal fortunes increased accordingly. Tammany Hall was the fulcrum he used to raise himself, and he took thousands of people along with him to realms of money glory to which they had not even dared to aspire. In 1888 Mayor Grant swore that his friend Richard Croker was in 1886 "very poor indeed." But by the end of 1893 Croker had invested $250,000 in a stock farm of race horses, $103,000 in race horses, and $80,000 in a Fifth Avenue mansion; he had also paid salaries of $12,000 a year to one of his jockeys and $5,000 to the manager of his stock farm. When he

[1]*Thirty Years of New York Politics*, by Matthew P. Breen, pp. 770–771.

took a trip to the Pacific Coast in 1894, Richard Croker travelled in a private car which cost him $50 a day. In the words of the popular song, "How He Did It His Books Don't Show," but we are fortunate in the possession of masses of testimony sworn to before legislative investigating committees which reveal the manifold sources of profit for an all-powerful boss of Tammany Hall and his subordinates.

The investigations known as the Lexow Investigation, which took place in 1894, and the Mazet Investigation, which took place in 1899, were the most valuable contributions to the political history of New York City that were ever made by a legislative body. Inspired by the partisan enmity of Thomas C. Platt, the Republican Boss of New York State, and by the moral prejudices of Dr. Charles H. Parkhurst, one of the City's leading clergymen, these investigations succeeded by means of their more than thirty thousand pages of fascinating testimony in bringing into high relief the entire system of Tammany Hall in most of its ramifications. "Things hinted at, suggested, the subject of rumour, have now been fixed beyond the possibility of denial, in permanent form," said the report of the later committee, of which Robert Mazet was chairman.[1]

During the period of the 1890's, when Richard Croker and Tammany Hall were demoralizing the City of New York more systematically and more efficiently than it had ever been done before or has ever been done since, another and wider demoralizing force was at work even more efficiently, if not so systematically, in the form of that listless but energetic, polite but firm, cautious but essentially dishonest Republican politician, Thomas C. Platt, who, more than any one man in the history of America, was responsible for the corrupt alliance between millionaires and their corporations and those whose business was supposed to be the government of the state. Thomas C. Platt and Richard Croker, like Chinese bandits, worked together frequently in spite of the fact that they were the leaders of opposite parties, but, since their interests were both essentially predatory, they sometimes found themselves in conflict.

---

[1] *Report of the Special Committee of the Assembly Appointed to Investigate the Public Offices and Departments of the City of New York and of the Counties Therein Included.* Albany, 1900, 5 volumes, Vol. I, p. 35. Hereafter this report and testimony will be referred to in footnotes as the Mazet Investigation.

One of these conflicts occurred when Platt wanted some appointments from Mayor Hugh J. Grant. They had been promised to him by Tammany Hall, but the promise was not kept, for the Boss considered that he was at the moment powerful enough to ignore it. Platt was angry, and he wished to show his own power of interference, at least, and so he commanded the New York State Legislature to hold the investigation of which Senator J. Sloat Fassett was the chairman. We have already quoted from the testimony of this investigation concerning the relations of Richard Croker and Sheriff Grant. These revelations had served Platt as revenge and as a warning that promises to him must be regarded with rather more sanctity than Croker and his henchmen had exhibited, and they had also furnished Platt with detailed information concerning the tactics of his opponents.

In 1894 Platt consented to the Lexow Investigation, because Dr. Parkhurst, as we shall see later, had been making a powerful nuisance of himself to politicians by his personal revelations from the pulpit of New York's vice as stimulated and protected by Tammany Hall. Anything that hurt his opponents and did him no harm was welcome to Platt, but he was not especially interested in this remarkable investigation, for he was then in political power, and he had made his deals with Croker. Also, Platt was not particularly interested in the revelation of sin, for he had his private experiences with it, and the revelation of some of them by his political opponents, who had climbed up to a window in the Delavan House in Albany to make their investigations, had caused him some embarrassment. Platt was, however, a regular attendant of Dr. Parkhurst's Madison Square Church, and he approved heartily of the vigorous sermons of that enterprising clergymen, until one Sunday morning when Dr. Parkhurst announced from the pulpit that one Thomas C. Platt was worse than five Richard Crokers. Platt changed his church affiliations the following Sunday. Theodore Roosevelt, who worked with Platt, and whose work as Governor of New York was frequently hindered by the man who was known to his friends as the "Easy Boss," once remarked that he never could find that Platt had "any tastes at all except politics, and on rare occasions for a very dry theology wholly divorced from any moral implications."

In 1899 Platt instigated and supported the Mazet Investigation, for at that time he wished to break Tammany Hall's power in New York County and to strengthen thereby the hands of his lieutenant, Lemuel Ely Quigg, the Republican leader of New York County. The Mazet Committee brought forth five volumes of testimony of great value as sources of historical information concerning the fortunes of Tammany Hall and of Richard Croker, politically and personally.

Croker was very angry with the investigating committees and with their counsel. In a statement he made to newspaper reporters at the time of the election following the Mazet Investigation he said: "I don't believe the citizens of New York are going to allow a combination of Republican wolves and disappointed office-seekers to break into the fold in order to eat up the lambs." It was the first time the Tiger had been referred to as a lamb. While the Lexow Investigating Committee, whose counsel was John W. Goff, was holding the sessions that thrilled and startled New York by their daily revelations of unheard-of vice and unprecedented crime, Croker was in Europe racing his horses on English tracks. He returned too late to testify. "The Satirist" in *Town Topics* imagined the following scene descriptive of the situation:

The Return of the Wanderer

MR. CROKER IS AGAIN IN THE HANDS OF HIS FRIENDS

Scene—The deck of the *Majestic* as the steamer is making her landing. A man with a shoe-brush beard and a pale, frightened eye is dodging about excitedly. On the pier are Patsy Squilligan, Mick Dooley, Jimmie O'Stufferty, Barney Dunphy, Eddie McGint, Buttsy Clancy, and Fink Burke, members of the Tammany committee that have been deputed to meet the Boss.

Fink Burke (*shouting*)—Hi dere! Dickey, me bye. How's yure malary?

Mr. Croker puts his head over the rail for an instant and then disappears.

Mick Dooley—Misther Crokey! Have you still the loombaygaw in yure trawt?

Mr. Croker puts his head above the rail.

Mr. Croker (*calling feebly*)—Has the Lexow Committee adjourned?

The terriers do not hear him.

Eddie McGint—Yu're lookin' like a t'ree-year-ole, Richard. For hivun's sake, dawnt keep us in suspinse. How's yure liver?

Mr. Croker (*again calling with all his vocal force*)—Has the Lexow gang adjourned?

The terriers still cannot hear him.

Buttsy Clancy—Dthere's a basket av cawld bottils, me bye, waitin' for you at dther Hall. But aise our flutterin' harruts. How's yure chilblains an' dyspepsy?

Mr. Croker groans and halloos through his hands.

Mr. Croker (*with a despairing wheeze*)—Have the Lexow goats stopped their questions?

The terriers are still deaf.

Patsy Squilligan—Long life to ye, Dickey. If ye love us sind wurrud over the intervaynin' wathers if yure browncutus have lift you.

The steamer by this time is quite near the dock. Mr. Croker again raises his head and screeches at the group on the pier.

Mr. Croker—Is Goff still at it?

The terriers hear the name of Goff.

Fink Burke—Be he ashkin' about Goff?

Jimmie O'Stufferty—He be.

The terriers jump into the air.

The Terriers (*howling in chorus*)—Goff has flew the coop.

Mr. Croker rises like a Phœnix bird to his full height, lights his cigar and calls out in a voice as robust as Edouard de Reszke's:

Mr. Croker—Hellow, Patsey! Hellow, Fink! Ah, there Mickey! Boys, I'm feelin' like a bird. I left me malaria in a London safe deposit.

When the steamer is made fast Mr. Croker walks jauntily ashore.

Mr. Croker (*to Mick Dooley*)—Say, Mickey, I'm awful glad to get home, but I'm sorry Goff didn't wait for me. I hurried back to give my testimony, and now you see I'm just too late.

And Mr. Croker is driven in the direction of the cold bottles.[1]

---

[1] *Town Topics*, July 5, 1894, p. 16.

In order to give a coherent picture of Tammany Hall under Richard Croker, the material revealed by the legislative inquiries will be used first to demonstrate Croker's personal sources of wealth and power, and then we shall see how the money and the prestige were garnered from the life of New York City. The Mazet Committee Report said: "We see the central power, not the man who sits in the Mayor's chair, but the man who stands behind it." The Committee also saw this picture:

"We see the same arbitrary power dictating appointments, directing officials, controlling boards, lecturing members of the Legislature and the Municipal Assembly. We see incompetence and arrogance in high place. We see an enormous and ever increasing crowd of office-holders with ever increasing salaries. We see the powers of government prostituted to protect criminals, to demoralize the police, to debauch the public conscience and to turn governmental functions into channels for private gain. The proof is conclusive, not that the public treasury has been directly robbed, but that great opportunities have been given by manipulations of public offices to enable favoured individuals to work for their own personal benefit. The enormous increase in the budget of the City of New York, the inefficiency and wastefulness in the public service, the demoralization of many of the departments are due absolutely to this abdication of power by the officers of the people to an organization, the ruler of which, an autocrat, has testified that he was working for his own pocket all the time."[1]

Croker had escaped the withering and efficient cross-examination of John W. Goff, the counsel to the Lexow Committee, but he was subjected to a complete examination by Frank Moss, the counsel to the Mazet Committee. He was angry and at times ferocious in his answers to questions concerning his personal sources of profit and those of the members of his family. The spectators who crowded the sessions of the committee saw a harassed animal with the powers of speech expressing his opinion of his enemies. The squat, heavy-set little man with the powerful jaw and scrubby beard, whose eyes were fright-

[1]Mazet Investigation, Vol. I, p. 6.

ened and fierce, defied the Committee, the counsel, and the world.

"You are the leader of the political organization generally known as Tammany Hall, are you not?" asked Frank Moss.

"I don't know about that," Croker answered.

"But you are simply the leader of the Tammany Democracy, are you?"

"Yes, sir, you say so and it must be so."

"You admit it?"

"Yes. I don't deny that."

"There is a difference between the Tammany Society——"

"(Interrupting) It is not necessary to bring all that up, I should not imagine, because everybody knows they are. There is no use playing to the galleries."

"Mr. Moss: We are making the record."

"The Witness: Give good straight talk and let us get through. There is no use making speeches. They all know everything you have said here. I am the leader of the party and I acknowledge it, and all these people are my friends and I am going to stick to them all the time. I don't shy away from them. (Applause from the audience.)"

"Mr. Moss: That is right. I hope the chairman will allow that once in a while."

"The Witness: No, we don't want it. Just give me good straight talk and let us settle it. That is all unnecessary. All those gentlemen know that I am considered the leader, and all those gentlemen are my friends, and yet you have taken a half hour up for nothing. Now, what is the use?"[1]

Moss then asked Croker concerning his official position in the city or national or state government and obtained the admission that he had none. "And your relation to these public affairs," asked Mr. Moss, "is the political position which you have in Tammany Hall?" "That is all," answered Croker. "But that does give you a practical relation to these matters, does it not?" Mr. Moss asked. "Well, no," Croker said, "No; the same as any other citizen who is recognized and who is liked and respected. That is all." "Do you know of another

[1] Mazet Investigation, Vol. I, pp. 323–327.

citizen who has to-day his wishes respected as you have?" "Some has," Croker answered, "in this city; yes, sir. . . . Not at this present time, probably. Not so much as me. There are others have their influences, but probably not to such an extent as me." "So that at the present time your influence, politically, is larger than the influence of any other man that you know of?" "I don't know about that." "You may be a little modest about it, but if I say so, you will not contradict me, will you?" "You can say so. No; I won't contradict you."[1]

After he had obtained so much, Frank Moss went into the personal financial profit from his position of Croker and his sons, and that phase of the examination threw Croker into a rage. This quiet series of significant questions and answers was the prelude.

"Let us see if my deductions are correct," Mr. Moss demanded. "The judges elected by Tammany Hall appoint referees, who, in line with their party obligation, appoint auctioneers. . . . And it is the duty of those auctioneers——"

"That referee," broke in Mr. Croker, "is appointed by the judge, and he appoints whatever auctioneer he pleases."

"But if that referee is a good Tammany man," Moss asked, "he should appoint an auctioneer who is in line with the party, should he not, as part of the patronage?"

"It all depends," answered Croker, "on the kind of a Tammany man he is."

"If he appoints your firm [Croker was a partner with Peter F. Meyer in a firm of auctioneers] he does a good party act, does he not?"

"Yes, sir."

"Why? If he appoints your firm he does a good party act, you say. Now, I ask you why does he do a good party act when he appoints your firm?"

"Well, all things being equal, he has a right to do it. He is a Democrat himself and he ought to appoint Democrats."

"And he ought to do that thing which puts into your pocket money, because you are a Democrat, too?"

"Yes, sir."

[1]Mazet Investigation, pp. 336–337.

"So we have it, then, that you, participating in the selection of judges before election, participate in the emolument that comes away down at the end of their judicial proceeding, namely, in judicial sales?"

"Yes, sir."

"And it goes into your pocket?"

"I get—that is, a part of my profit."

"And the nomination of a judge on the Tammany Hall ticket in this city is almost equivalent to an election, on the history of the parties, is it not?"

"Yes, sir."

"So that, if you have a controlling voice in the affairs of your party, and secure the nomination of true men, you may be sure that at least in the real estate exchange and in the firm of Meyer & Croker you will, as a true Democrat, get some of that patronage?"

"We at least expect he will be friendly to us."

"And you get some of the patronage?"

"We hope so."

"Then you are working for your own pocket, are you not?" demanded Mr. Moss.

"All the time; the same as you," snapped Croker.

This last question and answer startled New York when it was printed in the newspapers that day, and for many years it was used against Croker to great effect in political campaigns. Although everyone knew it was the fact, no one had ever admitted before on the witness stand or anywhere in public that a Tammany Hall boss was working for his pocket and not for undying patriotism and the love of his fellow creatures.

Then Mr. Moss asked:

"It is not then, a matter of wide statesmanship or patriotism altogether, but it is a wide statesmanship, patriotism and personal gain mixed up, is it not?"

"It is 'to the party belongs the spoils,'" said Croker. "I tell you that now right out, so that you can make it all right here. We win and we expect everyone to stand by us."

"To the party belongs the spoils and to the boss belongs the lion's share of the plunder?" asked Moss.

"Not plunder; no," said Croker. "You may call it plunder—if you call it plunder because the men are loyal to us; but you will send your bill in to the Legislature for the work you have done by and by, and you may as well call it plunder." (Cries from the audience of "Good boy." The Chairman threatened to clear the room if there were any more demonstrations from the audience.)

"You believe that I am working for money here?"

"Yes, sir."

"You believe and say that you are working for your share of the money, as the boss of Tammany Hall?"

"No; I am not. There is no 'boss' at all."

"As a member of Tammany Hall you are working for your share of the money, as well as the glory?"

"I want to get a living; yes, sir. . . ."

"And you do not see any reason why you should not have a real estate business, or any other business, to which the referees' fees or the auctioneers' fees and such things as that should come, do you?"

"I don't know about other business, but I know that the business I am in, it comes all right; legitimate. . . ."

"And you are willing to do a similar thing wherever it can be done?"

"It all depends what sort of business it is."

"If it is an honorable business you are always willing to do it?"

"I am not prepared to go into any other business at present. I have all I can do now."

"You think that Tammany men should stand together even in matters of business, do you not?"

"I do; yes, sir."

"You believe that they should stand together not only as to politics, but when they can help each other they should stand together in business matters, do you not?"

"No; I do not; not the way you are trying to say."

"How do you believe that?"

"I don't believe the way you are trying to put it at all. You are trying to bring about a state of things that there is a conspiracy to plunder the people. I don't believe in that at all. If you are trying to lead me to that, you can't do it."

"No; you are mistaken. My questions are meant to be perfectly straight, and meant to be somewhat in the language of the discipline of one of the churches that I remember having read—'Brothers should deal with brothers in matters of business, preferring each other.' That is a free rendering of something I have read in the discipline of one of the churches, as a rule of the church. Is it not so in matters of Tammany Hall; all things being equal, members of the organization should support each other in business matters?"

"I don't know what you mean by that. I can't understand what kind of business you mean. . . ."

"You see the trouble is," said Mr. Moss, "you are looking beyond my question and fearing something."

"No; I am not fearing anything," Croker answered sharply. "I don't fear you at all. Don't you be alarmed about that."[1]

Then Frank Moss began to ask specific questions concerning Croker's holdings in various companies and inquired how he got his stock. The result was a sharp and lively duel:

"You are a member of the Air and Power Company?" asked Moss.

"Yes, sir."

"What is the capital stock of that company?"

"Ten million dollars."

"How much of that stock do you hold?"

"Well, it has not been settled up yet. It ain't out on the market at all. It is in the treasury yet. . . ."

"You are to have some of it, are you not?"

"That I can't tell you."

"You are taking a lively interest in the Air and Power Company, are you not?"

"Yes, sir."

"You expect to have your hand in it, do you not?"

"Expect that is going to be a good thing."

"And this air and power will be supplied to anybody who wants to use the air and power all over this city?"

"Yes, sir."

"Including the public buildings?"

---

[1] Mazet Investigation, Vol. I, pp. 352–357.

"If they think it is a good thing. There is no chance to use them in public buildings, that I know of."

"Can you not devise some way to make them useful in public buildings?"

"We haven't got to that yet."

"Is it possible?"

"I don't know. I am not one of the inventors, you know. . . ."

"Who first proposed to you to go into that company?"

"Mr. Hoadley himself spoke to me about it. Mr. Knight, the engineer. Mr. Hoadley, I think was the first."

"Did he propose that you should put money into it?"

"I decline to answer that question. I told you before that I won't answer any questions concerning my private affairs."

"You have answered about the Consolidated Ice Company."

"I told you that just because you were so anxious."

"I am anxious about this."

"You won't know anything about this."

"Why not?"

"Because that is my own affair personally. It does not concern New York; no city department or anything else. It is not a thing to go to the people in general. The city has nothing to do with it at all."

"I will tell you frankly how it does concern the people of New York," explained Mr. Moss, "and I want you to understand what is in my mind while I am asking you these questions. There was a time when it is on record that you were a poor man, and you will not deny that there was a time when you were a poor man."

"I was a poor man when I was a boy, yes; and I don't know how poor you are now. You have been in the Police Department and you ought to know how it is."

"I am here conducting this investigation, and I am right before you and you own the Police Department now. I am not going to Europe this summer."

"You are conducting this investigation by a minority vote of the people of this city, and I am sitting here representing my friends with a big majority vote. You have been put out of the Police Department by the people. The people put you out of the Police Department, and the Police Department has thrived and has benefited since you left it."

This was an extremely important confession, for Croker in his anger had unconsciously admitted that the Police Department was the great source of personal profit for those concerned with it, and Moss had got on the record without denial that Croker through Tammany Hall owned the Police Department. As we shall see presently the control of the police at this period by Tammany Hall was one of its most valuable weapons, and the ramifications of that control extended throughout the life of the City. The recriminations were stopped by the chairman, and Moss continued:

"I was about to tell you what lines of thought were in my mind upon which these financial questions were being shaped, and I had said that there was a time which you remember and which the people remember, and which I think appears in testimony in a former investigation, when you were, comparatively speaking, a poor man. Since that time it does not appear that you held any official position, that you have been in receipt of any salary, that you have been in control of a political organization, which has many times dominated the city and over which you have had a large control, as you have to-day. It is now very apparent that you are a wealthy man, because you are able to indulge in those things in public which nobody but wealthy men can indulge in."

"What are those things I indulge in?" asked Croker.

"Wait a moment. And the people are interested in knowing how you got that money, and I propose, in as gentlemanly a way as possible, but in as firm a way as I may have to, to ask you those questions——"

"Yes, sir."

"Where you got it."

"Yes, sir. You have been reading the *World.* You are just catering for that paper now. Now, let me tell you something. You are asking me now. I will ask you back——"

"Will you stop the witness?" Moss asked the chairman. . . .

"We will show you the books," Croker said. "There is Peter Meyer's there, and I want to say to you now that my half in that business has amounted to anywhere from $25,000 to $30,000 for the last seven years, right along."

"That is simply the real estate business?"

"Real estate, and I have got more money now than I had when I was in a public office. I had none or very little when I was there. It is since I got out of that. My speculations in Wall Street, or any other place I am not going to tell you now. If you can show me where I have taken a dollar from this city you can cut that right arm off—or encouraged it, either."

"We have this, then: That you have prospered more since you left public office?"

"I think I have."

"And that was quite some years ago?"

"Yes, sir."

"Do you mean to say that all of your business transactions, all of your business income, is shown upon these books that you have referred to?"

"The income, yes, sir; outside of any speculations that I might make with my friends. No, Mr. Moss, you are a pretty smart man——"

"I do not know whether I am or not, when you are here——"

"And I want to say this. I have got nothing to hide at all, and if anyone tells me of a nice stock to buy, and I can make a little turn on it, I am going to do it, and I have done so. There is nothing to hide at all, and you will do it yourself, if you get a chance. . . . So any questions you ask me about my personal business, I decline to answer."

Both men were talking at once by this time, and Mr. Moss was saying while Mr. Croker made the last statement, "You have more at stake than I have in the matter. It is well for you to consider that."

"Not a bit," said Croker.

"A man who is so public a character, and who has such a tremendous power in this city—his affairs should be as transparent as glass," suggested Moss.

"I don't know that he should" . . .

"Did you ever have any stock of the so-called Huckleberry Railroad, more properly known as the Union Railroad?"

"I decline to answer any more of those questions."

"You will not answer any more of those questions?"

"No, no more questions."

"Why?"

"I told you why a little while ago."

"Who gave you the stock of that road?"

"I told you I would not answer you. . . ."

"How much did you pay for it?"

"I told you I wouldn't go into my personal matters. . . ."

"Would the answers to these questions tend to degrade you?"

"I don't know."

"Would they tend to convict you of a crime?"

"I don't know."

"Is it because you have doubts on those subjects that you do not answer the question?"

"No; not the slightest."

"But you are not certain?"

"I am certain I do not want to answer you those questions."[1]

The next day, when the sessions of the Committee began, Frank Moss took up the question of cutting off Croker's right arm:

"Mr. Croker," he said, "you said yesterday that if it should be proven that you had ever received any dishonest or dishonorable money in the affairs of the city you would allow your right arm to be cut off?"

"Yes, sir," Croker answered.

"Well, don't you think it was a peculiar proposition to be made in this enlightened and civilized community?"

"No, I do not."

"You didn't expect hardly that any tribunal would sentence you to have your arm cut off, or that any official authority would allow you to part with your good right arm, did you?"

"No; if they are willing to do it, they could do it."

"But you didn't hardly believe there was anyone to carry that out, did you?"

"No."

"Are you willing to make the proposition that if dishonorable

---

[1]Mazet Investigation, Vol. I, pp. 422–435.

money or dishonorable transactions are laid at your door you will part with your fortune and part with your liberty?"

"Yes."

"That is more to the point and more to the purpose? You are willing to say that, are you?"

"Yes, sir."

"I was led to put that question, Mr. Croker, because of your suggestion early in the examination yesterday that there wouldn't be any playing to the galleries, and it appeared to me that your answer was subject to that criticism, but now we have it down on a business basis and in a position where it really amounts to something and that you and I recognize?"

"Yes, sir."[1]

Then Frank Moss attempted to show that Croker or his sons, because of his position as the leader of Tammany Hall, had been given an interest in various companies which did work that the City might use, and that he had not paid any money for his interest in those companies. Croker refused to admit or to deny the charge on the ground that it was his private business, and he would not answer questions concerning his private business.

One of these enterprises was the Auto-Truck Company. "Were you given $140,000 of that company's stock?" Moss asked. "I decline to answer," said Croker. "Without the payment of a dollar?" continued Moss. "I decline to answer," said Croker. Moss read into the record the following from the New York *Tribune* of January 16, 1899:

"When Mr. Croker was seen at the Democratic club last night he said that he was interested in the New York Auto-Truck Company, and that the company was going to do a general trucking business in the cities of New York and Jersey City, and suburbs adjacent. Mr. Croker said also that in his opinion the horse, as a pet, for pleasure driving, speeding purposes and as a 'play toy' in general would, for all time, hold a place in the affections of mankind, but for business purposes, the carriage of freight, passengers and drayage along the wharves and piers and in the streets of the larger cities and

---

[1]Mazet Investigation, Vol. I, pp. 447-448.

towns, he must recede before the progress of civilization and the requirements of the present inventive age."

In connection with the influence which he exerted in behalf of the New York Auto-Truck Company, Croker visited George Gould, President of the Manhattan Elevated Railroad Company. He demanded of Gould the privilege of attaching compressed-air pipes to the elevated railroad structures on all the streets covered by their lines, for the use of the New York Auto-Truck Company. Gould answered courteously that if Croker would have his plans submitted, he would consult the chief engineer of the elevated railroad in order to find out if the structures would carry the load. He also wished to find out from his lawyers whether the Manhattan Company had authority to permit the attachment of the pipes. Whereupon Mr. Croker answered: "Oh, hell! I want the pipes put on, and I don't want any circumlocution." "Don't you think it would be better to give me an opportunity to consult my officials?" asked Gould. "No," Croker said, "we want the pipes put on, and we don't want any fuss about it." "Under the circumstances, Mr. Croker," Gould was quoted as answering, "I will settle the question now, without referring it to my officials. I will say to you now that we will not permit you to attach your pipes to the elevated structures."[1]

The city officials began to attack the Manhattan Elevated Railroad Company immediately. The Board of Aldermen passed some laws that required the company to spend millions of dollars in improvements. One of these insisted that the company must place large drip pans under its structures at every street crossing, and another compelled it to run trains every five minutes during the entire twenty-four hours of the day and night, and provided for a fine of $100 for each violation. Another ordinance required the company to enclose all its stations with glass, and it was forbidden to sell newspapers, magazines, chewing gum and candies or other goods on the stations. The storage of cars on a third track at the end of the line was also prohibited, and the Park Department ordered

[1]*Some Things Richard Croker Has Said and Done*, a pamphlet published by the City Club of New York, July, 1901, pp. 29–30.

the company to remove its tracks from Battery Park immediately, a demand which the City was entitled to make under the original franchise.[1]

It was charged that Croker and his friends even profited personally by the discomfort they visited on the Elevated Railroad Company, for they sold short the stock of the Manhattan just before the Board of Aldermen began to attack the company. When he was asked concerning this transaction in Manhattan stock, he declined to answer on the grounds that it was private business. "Working for your pocket all the time?" asked Moss. "Yes, sir; as you are working for criminals in New York," Croker answered angrily. "Just as I am after criminals?" asked Moss. "Yes," said Croker, missing the implication. "I take your language," said Moss. To which Croker answered sententiously: "Every man in New York is working for his pocket."[2]

"Ground is not wanting," wrote the author of the City Club's pamphlet, *Some Things Richard Croker Has Said and Done*, "for the belief that the power of Mr. Croker is sustained, directly and indirectly, by 'respectable and prominent citizens' who believe that it is better to uphold the bosses than to 'imperil the interests, perhaps those of widows and orphans, committed to their charge.' In other words, the theory is that a citizen is justified, when acting as a director, or as the manager, of a company in 'doing business' with a political machine, however corrupt and however dangerous to the state."

Whether or not it was out of due respect for the interests of their widows and orphans,[3] the Manhattan Elevated Railroad Company soon "did business" with the city officials, for the laws passed against it were never executed.

Another source of Croker's personal fortune was the United States Fidelity & Casualty Company, of which his closest friend and business associate, Andrew Freedman, was the vice president. This company bonded the employees of the City whose positions required bonding, and Croker's influence ob-

---

[1] *History of Public Franchises in New York City*, by Gustavus Myers, pp. 171–172.

[2] Mazet Investigation, Vol. III, p. 2963; Vol. I, pp. 455 ff.

[3] Professor Charles A. Beard once said in the course of his remarkable lectures on politics at Columbia University that someone should write the natural history of widows and orphans: they have been used so frequently in the history of American corporate finance to represent the virtuous responsibilities of business organizations.

tained the business for the company. When Freedman was asked by Frank Moss whether he divided his commissions with Croker, he admitted that Croker received a proportion of them, but when Moss asked what that proportion was, he answered that it was none of his business. Freedman refused to say how much money he had given Croker, but admitted that he gave the money in bills and that no records were kept of the transactions. He was asked whether he carried money on his person and handed it to Mr. Croker when he felt like it. "That I wouldn't care to tell you because I don't want to let you know how much money I carry on my person," he answered.

Croker also owned the Park Row Building, and the offices of some of the City's departments were moved into that building at higher rents than they were offered elsewhere because the Boss of Tammany Hall was the landlord.

Some of the business which Croker did, it was alleged, he did through his sons. When he was asked whether he gave his son money to buy stock in the Roebling Construction Company, which built the Brooklyn Bridge, or whether his son got stock in that company for nothing, Croker refused to answer. The Roebling Company was interested in selling a system of fireproofing to the City for its public buildings. The Mazet Investigation brought out that until Frank H. Croker, who was just twenty-one years old, became a partner in the Roebling Company, a terra-cotta fireproofing system was used in city buildings. Croker gave his son $17,000 in cash to pay for stock in the company. Frank Croker was made secretary of the company, and after this transaction blue prints of the construction of two public-school buildings in New York were specifically marked by the Building Department "Roebling system." Previous to this the Building Department had refused to use the Roebling system of fireproofing by wire and concrete.[1]

Croker was also charged with taking money from the New York Telephone Company for a city contract. Henry M. McDonald testified that he was acquainted with the affairs of the Flushing Gas Company, and that that company tried to get a contract from the City for additional street lamps in Flushing, but it was unsuccessful. Finally, it was arranged between Croker and a member of the company, according to McDonald,

[1] Mazet Investigation, Vol. I, p. 241.

that the stockholders of the company should turn over 20 per cent. of their stock to Andrew Freedman. Freedman was also elected a member of the Board of Directors of the Flushing Gas Company, and the arrangement was that the company should then receive a contract for at least five hundred additional street lamps and possibly one thousand. Freedman denied that the Flushing Gas Company received any additional lights after he became a member of the Board of Directors.[1]

There were many other deals in which the Mazet Committee attempted to show Croker's participation, but it was frequently unsuccessful because of the refusal of witnesses to answer questions. Croker had established the precedent for his friends and associates by defining all business he was engaged in as personal and private, and he refused to admit that he had any official influence in the affairs of the City. Frank Moss explained that Croker was not in the same position as every other citizen, but Croker refused to recognize the distinction or to answer questions. Mrs. Euphemia Vale Blake remarked that the Committee had met "a foeman worthy of their steel," and she chronicled with satisfaction that after the hearings were finished, Richard Croker left for his usual trip to Europe "amid the vivas of the multitude that blocked the streets and steamer wharf." The New York *World* published verse called "Myself and Me," in which another point of view was expressed:

> "Those Mazet people make me smile,
> Inquiring how we made our pile
> And why we own Manhattan Isle—
> Myself—and Me.
>
> * * *
>
> "They'd pry into our bonding scheme,
> And find out how we skim the cream
> Of all the business—that's no dream—
> Myself—and Platt.
>
> "They've had us on the witness rack;
> Now we'll seek pleasure at the track,
> And if we lose, why, we'll come back—
> Myself—and Me."

[1] Mazet Investigation, Vol. I, pp. 596-597, 604.

IV

More important than Croker's personal profit from his position as the Boss of Tammany Hall was the profit of the thousands of supporters of the organization on the police force and in the other departments of the City's government. The ramifications of the system which Tammany Hall organized and executed extended to the social agencies of the City's life, such as the saloon and the brothel.

On Sunday morning, February 14, 1892, in the Madison Square Church, Dr. Charles H. Parkhurst delivered a sermon that startled New York. Dr. Parkhurst took as his text, "Ye are the salt of the earth," and he pointed the moral that the salt had lost its savour to a considerable degree.

"There is not a form under which the devil disguises himself," said the Rev. Dr. Parkhurst, "that so perplexes us in our efforts, or so bewilders us in the devising of our schemes as the polluted harpies that, under the pretence of governing this city, are feeding day and night on its quivering vitals. They are a lying, perjured, rum-soaked, and libidinous lot."

The Doctor deplored the sad fact that while he in his small way and the Church in its large way were making efforts toward morality and virtue, Tammany Hall and its mayors were far more efficient in their stimulation and patronage of vice.

"But after all that has been said," Dr. Parkhurst remarked sadly, "the great fact remains untouched and uninvalidated, that every effort that is made to improve character in this city, every effort to make men respectable, honest, temperate and sexually clean is a direct blow between the eyes of the Mayor and his whole gang of drunken and lecherous subordinates in this sense, that while we fight iniquity they shield and patronize it; while we try to convert criminals they manufacture them; and they have a hundred dollars invested in manufacturing machinery to our one invested in converting machinery."

One can imagine Thomas Platt, rather shrivelled and somewhat dry, sitting up in his pew at Dr. Parkhurst's church and exulting at the statements which the servant of the Lord was making in favour of the Republican Party. Dr. Parkhurst's intentions were of the best, but Mr. Platt could calculate as he carefully held his silk hat between his knees the number of votes that sermon would produce.

The sermon provoked great attention. The newspapers took up Dr. Parkhurst's words, and they visited them upon the city officials. Tammany leaders and city officials made a great blunder. They denied the allegations and defied Dr. Parkhurst, calling him names, instead of maintaining an aloof silence. The Mayor, Hugh J. Grant, issued a statement in which he challenged Dr. Parkhurst to prove his general statements with specific evidence, and the *Tammany Times*, the house organ of Tammany Hall, said editorially:

"A 'loose idea' in a man's head is a serious thing. Every once in a while an idea probably forms in Doctor Parkhurst's head, and then it gets loose and rattles around at such a great rate that it drives the poor man crazy. It keeps rattling around until the next idea forms and drops off, and that is the reason he seems to be crazy all the while."

The Doctor, however, accepted the challenge. He was at the moment an active member of an organization known as the Society for the Prevention of Crime. It was one of those associations of earnest and pious gentlemen of means who viewed with alarm the growing sins of their neighbours, and in the endeavour to correct those sins it was the greatest rival of Anthony Comstock and Henry Bergh. A personality equivalent to either of those in energy and picturesque intrepidity had not, however, been connected with the Society until Dr. Parkhurst accepted a share in its responsibilities. The Doctor, using the agents of the Society and its funds, proceeded quietly to collect the material proof of his general assertions. He hired a detective, Charles W. Gardner, who, fortunately, wrote an interesting account of his vice tour with the minister, and it is from Gardner's book, *The Doctor and the Devil, or Midnight Adventures of Dr. Parkhurst*, that we learn much of this historic journey into the inferno.

Gardner promised to show the Doctor the town for six dollars a day and expenses. When they had settled terms, the detective looked the minister over critically and suggested the necessity for a disguise. The Doctor agreed, but said that he would like to keep his whiskers, if possible, because they protected his throat, but, if necessary, he would make even that sacrifice in the cause of reform.

"If due caution is taken," Gardner wrote that he replied, "I don't think it will be necessary to harvest your lilacs at present." "Dr. Parkhurst laughed," wrote Gardner. "He is a very jovial man, and appreciates a joke. I must say that as a companion no 'rounder' is better company than the celebrated apostle of reform." Gardner called on the appointed evening for Dr. Parkhurst and his young society friend, Mr. John L. Erving, who was to accompany them on the tour. The two men had attempted to disguise themselves, but the Doctor looked too much like a preacher to suit the detective, and Erving "looked like a costume plate of a dead year, just a bit run to seed." Gardner took the two men to his room in Eighteenth Street and dressed them up for their parts. This is what he did to the Rev. Dr. Parkhurst:

"First I gave him a pair of checked black and white trousers. They were seedy, to be sure, but loud enough in pattern to make a noise in the next block. Dr. Parkhurst is about twelve inches shorter than I am, and when he got himself into the trousers their waist band was about on a level with his shoulder blades. To get into his hip-pocket the Doctor would have had to run his hand down the neck of his shirt.

"Then I gave the clergyman a shirt which had been worn before, and was not particularly clean. Next I gave him a double-breasted reefer jacket, sadly the worse for wear, and then I looked at him. Somehow or other, he hadn't shaken off the clergyman air. I thought I could make him look a little more worldly by adding a necktie to his apparel. So I ripped out a sleeve of an old red-flannel shirt that I had in my room, and tied it around the clergyman's neck. Still he looked of the celestial rather than of the half world, and I was puzzled to find what was the matter. I got a brown, dirty old slouch hat out, and put it on the Doctor's head. It made him look a good deal more like a battered sailor, but still there was that pulpit air about my client. It came to me like a flash, finally, what I wanted to fully complete the metamorphosis.

"'Dr. Parkhurst,' I ventured, 'I think that hair of yours queers you. Let me fix it for you.'

"So I procured a bar of common laundry soap and rubbed it on the doctor's luxuriant hair, which curled enticingly down his neck. I never believed much up to then in the theory that dress has much to do with the making of the man, for the liberal application of soap absolutely changed the doctor's appearance in a trice. If ever man looked the 'tough' that man was the Rev. Dr. Charles H. Parkhurst when I had soaped his hair from its natural curl to a sober straightness.

"'Why, if I was a "cop,"' I said, as I critically examined my work, 'I would run you in on suspicion.'

"'Good,' replied the Doctor, 'I would like to have that happen, if I was sure that I wouldn't be recognized in a police court the next day.'"

Then Gardner turned his attention to Mr. Erving. "His feet were as small and delicate as a woman's," he wrote, "so I made him put on a pair of rubber boots." He made other changes in trousers and suit, and, "Then I insisted on his mussing up his blond hair, because if he was found to be parting his hair in the middle where we were going, I knew there would be trouble." Gardner also wound a red necktie around Erving's neck.

The first place the extraordinary trio visited was Tom Summers's saloon in Cherry Street. "Tom Summers," Gardner wrote, "is not half as bad as his customers and the embalming fluid he sells as whisky." Summers also dealt in the pawn tickets of thieves, and Gardner introduced Dr. Parkhurst "as an uncle of mine, who wanted to buy a watch." They had a drink first, and the Doctor swallowed a large dose of Cherry Hill whisky. "He acted," remarked Gardner, "as if he had swallowed a whole political parade—torchlights and all." The Doctor watched intently the flow through the swing doors of boys and girls about ten years old who had come to buy pints of whisky for ten cents to take home to their fathers and mothers. "A civilization is being cradled here," the Doctor preached to Gardner when they got on the street again. "Good God! what will the man be whose babyhood was lived out in this reeking, pestilent hole? I admit that this is bad enough, but I want to see worse." Gardner was willing, and they stopped in front of 342 Water Street, where women stood in the doorway "soliciting people to enter the resort with the same air that a Grand Central Station hackman asks you to 'have a cab.'" "And as we were passing, two of the women caught the Doctor by the arm, and before he knew what had happened, whirled him into the place and sat him down in a chair. A big, fat, greasy, and not very pretty woman, meanwhile had done the same for Erving. I, too, had been 'steered' into the place by a black-haired woman, old enough to have been the mother of Columbus; so there we were, a happy little family party." "The Doctor chatted with the women a few moments, and had no trouble, apparently, in withstanding their blandishments."

The next place visited was a five-cent lodging house in Park Row, where the reek of the perspiration from the naked men who were lined up on cots disgusted the visitors, and the Doctor remarked on the street: "Yet from just such sad places at election time comes a host of men to cast their ballots. I feel like revolting against my generation, when I think that from just such lodging houses are built up political careers."

The party went that night and on succeeding nights to houses of prostitution, to cabarets where prostitutes performed, to Chinese opium houses, and to "Tight Houses," so called because all the women wore tights. But the climax was reached when Gardner led his clients to the Golden Rule Pleasure Club, a four-story brick house in West Third Street. A woman known as "Scotch Ann," the proprietress, greeted them with a pleasant "Good-evening." "The basement," wrote Gardner, "was fitted up into little rooms, by means of cheap partitions, which ran to the top of the ceiling from the floor. Each room contained a table and a couple of chairs, for the use of customers of the vile den. In each room sat a youth, whose face was painted, eyebrows blackened, and whose airs were those of a young girl. Each person talked in a high falsetto voice, and called the others by women's names." Dr. Parkhurst was puzzled. He turned to Gardner and whispered a question. "I explained. The Doctor instantly turned on his heel and fled from the house at top speed. 'Why, I wouldn't stay in that

From *"The Doctor and the Devil" by Charles W. Gardner*
"THE DOCTOR AND HIS COMPANION IN DISGUISE"

house,' he gasped, 'for all the money in the world.'" It was the only abode of sin in which the Doctor found it impossible to remain even for a few minutes.

Gardner wrote that this tour was not a pleasure trip to him, though he had been presented to the public as a man who enjoyed taking a clergyman "slumming." "In the first place," he wrote, "not only did I have to keep the Doctor from trouble, but he was a very hard man to satisfy. 'Show me something worse,' was his constant cry. He really went at his slumming work as if his heart was in his tour."

Gardner arranged for the edification of Dr. Parkhurst a "dance of nature" at the abode of Hattie Adams. He ordered five girls "at a cost of $15, or $3 for each gymnast dancer. Each girl was dressed in the usual garb or a Mother Hubbard gown, so fashionable in the circles we were in. The story of the disrobing has been told in court and need not be reproduced here. I meanwhile blindfolded 'the Professor,' as the broken-down musician who sat in the parlor to furnish music was called, as the girls refused to dance before him. Then the five women, to a lively jig played by the 'Professor,' danced the 'can-can.' . . . As I could not dance, and the Doctor, of course, would not if he could, Erving was forced to do the dancing for the visitors. . . . Then came the celebrated 'leapfrog' episode, in which I was the frog and the others jumped over me. The Doctor sat in the corner with an unmoved face through it all, watching us and slowly sipping at a glass of beer. Hattie Adams was quite anxious to find out who Dr. Parkhurst was. I told her that he was 'from the West,' and was 'a gay boy.' Then Hattie tried to pull Dr. Parkhurst's whiskers, but the Doctor straightened out with such an air of dignity that she did not attempt any further familiarities."

"The celebrated leapfrog episode" became celebrated because city officials gave it out to the newspapers that the Rev. Dr. Parkhurst had enjoyed himself playing leapfrog with naked prostitutes while pretending to investigate vice conditions in New York.

Dr. Parkhurst, having gathered a mass of evidence of the existence of vice, proceeded through the agency of the Society for the Prevention of Crime to demand that the District Attorney and the courts close the places which he had visited.

First, however, he delivered another sermon in which he told his fascinated audience of his trip through the underworld of New York and arraigned Tammany Hall as the protector and the instigator of these conditions for the sake of the money the police and the police justices, who were members of the Hall, received for themselves and their district leaders from those who sold vice. As the police justices were most of them Tammany Hall men, Dr. Parkhurst found it impossible to get warrants for the arrests he wished to make. Agents of Dr. Parkhurst were mobbed by a crowd of about five hundred people when they came out of the Essex Market Court after having given evidence against disorderly house keepers in the neighbourhood. Policemen refused to interfere, but the men escaped serious injury by jumping on a passing street car.

Inside the Essex Market Court, just before the mob chased the detectives of Dr. Parkhurst's Society, Frank Moss, counsel for the Society, had been prosecuting cases against disorderly house keepers. Information had come to him that a man in the courtroom had warned a defendant so that she was able to evade arrest. Moss pointed out the man to Judge Voorhis, and the Judge directed the court officers to bring him to the bench. They went toward him, but when they saw him, they turned pale and refused to go further. Moss said to the head officer, "Why don't you bring that man here? If you don't bring him I will bring him myself." Still the officer did not move, and Moss, taking the man by the arm, ordered him to come to the bench, and he gave him a push. The Judge said: "You are accused of having warned a defendant in this case that the officers were after her. What do you say to that?" The man would not answer. "What is your name?" "Max Hockstim," the man said, and there was a stir in the courtroom. It was clear now to everybody why the officers had not moved. Max Hockstim was a leading saloon keeper on the East Side, and with "Silver Dollar" Smith and Martin Engel he controlled the Eighth Assembly District in the interests of Tammany Hall and Richard Croker. He was an election district captain of Tammany Hall, and there was a Max Hockstim Association which worked for Croker on election day. Hockstim controlled a gang of thugs who assaulted anyone who opposed them or their leader. The Judge, who was not a member of Tammany Hall, gave Hockstim a lecture and ordered him to keep away from the courtroom. Hockstim went to the attorney for the defendants and asked him if he thought it would cost him more than one hundred dollars to demolish Frank Moss's face. Then he went outside, and when the Court adjourned, the agents of Parkhurst's Society were chased by the mob of five hundred people.[1]

Dr. Parkhurst's persistence had awakened New York to some of the realities of its existence. The Republican Party in the State of New York saw a great opportunity to profit by the sins of its Democratic brethren. Therefore, the Legislature appointed the Lexow Committee to investigate the Police Department and its relation to the politics and degradation of New York City. This investigation, with which Dr. Parkhurst found it impossible to coöperate fully, because he felt that it would not go far enough, since its objects were political rather than thorough, through the able inquisition conducted by its counsel, John W. Goff, brought to light more concerning the life of the City of New York than any other agency that has ever operated in the City. The five volumes of its report, containing almost six thousand pages of testimony, are startling and vivid in their human interest even to-day, more than thirty years after the events which they describe.

In these pages is revealed the secret of Tammany's clutch on the City during the reign of Croker, and that secret was the absolute control of the police force, for without that control Tammany Hall and Croker could do nothing. They could not make certain of elections by fraudulent means if policemen were honest in their efforts to arrest lawbreakers, and they could not collect vast sums of money for their personal comfort and for the insurance of the eternity of their power, if policemen arrested the prostitutes, the saloon keepers, the pimps, the race-track gamblers, the thieves, and the business men who paid for the privileges of violating the law.

Just how Tammany Hall under Croker controlled the police force is evident. The first step was to control the appointment, transfer, and promotion of members of the police force. James J. Martin, Tammany Police Commissioner in 1894, admitted to the Lexow Committee that of all the appointments, transfers,

---

[1] *The American Metropolis*, by Frank Moss, Vol. III, pp. 237-239.

and promotions he made to the police force, from 85 to 90 per cent. were recommended by district leaders of Tammany Hall for the district in which the applicant or the policeman resided. He was then asked if the men who received appointment and promotion on the recommendation of Tammany Hall leaders did not feel grateful and under obligation to Tammany Hall and its leaders. He answered that it would be natural to expect that. "So far as your recollection goes," Commissioner Martin was asked, "with the exception of two instances, so long as you have been Police Commissioner, you have not recommended for appointment, promotion, or transfer, a single man, except one who was backed by political influence?" "I do not recollect of any others," he answered, "I think there are others of them."[1]

General Theodore A. Bingham, who was Police Commissioner of New York, but not a Tammany man, wrote that it was natural for policemen to ignore the Mayor and the Police Commissioner in their desire to please, because those officials only held office for short terms, while the policeman himself held office for life. The only man as permanent as the policeman was the Tammany Hall leader, and it was therefore necessary to cater to him and to take his orders rather than those of the head of the department.

"I had scarcely moved into the office on Mulberry Street," wrote General Bingham, "when political leaders began to call upon me, for the most part to secure a continual shifting of the police for plausible but mysterious ends of their own. . . . I found immediately that among the officers of the force there were very few I could trust to carry out my orders in good faith. . . . I could not at that time even choose the leading officers of the department whom I wanted to carry out my orders."[2]

Frank Moss was once talking with a veteran police captain:

[1] *Report and Proceedings of the Senate Committee Appointed to Investigate the Police Department of the City of New York*, 1895, 5 volumes, Vol. I, pp. 446–448. Hereafter this report will be referred to as Lexow Investigation.

[2] *McClure's Magazine*, Vol. XXXIV, p. 62, article by General Bingham, "The Organized Criminals of New York." General Bingham was writing of conditions under Murphy and not Croker, but the same condition existed to a greater extent in Croker's period.

"I said to him: 'Captain, Commissioners may come and Commissioners may go, but the Old Guard seems to hang on. You are always here. Will you tell me what kind of a Commissioner you men prefer?' He said: 'We like a nice honest gentleman who does not know that he is alive.' I said, 'Explain that.' He answered, 'He makes a good front to the public and prevents public suspicion, while the insiders do the business behind his back.' I said, 'But why do you men take this dirty money?' He said, 'Wouldn't we be fools if we didn't?' 'What do you mean by that?' I asked him. He said, 'Everybody in New York works his job, even the ministers.' 'Do you believe that?' He answered, 'I know it.' 'But,' I said, 'this money is so dirty.' He answered, 'We fumigate it. It is clean after we get it.'"[1]

Judge Roesch was a Tammany Hall district leader on the East Side of New York, and he testified before the Lexow Committee that he asked the Police Commissioner to transfer police sergeants from one post to another because men in the organization of Tammany Hall wanted their places. John W. Goff asked if that was a good enough reason. "I will tell you," Roesch answered; "when a man comes to me and wants to get an appointment or transfer, or anything like that, I never stop to consider who is in the place he wants to go to, but my object is to get him there; necessarily, somebody has got to get out of the way, and here it happened to be Sergeant Schryer." "I believe," Judge Roesch admitted later, "if this political influence, if you will call it that way, were entirely removed, absolutely, if it could be, from the Police Department, necessarily the force would be better, all the way through."

A man who was not a member of Tammany Hall and who still desired to remain a policeman had a more difficult life than a man who joined the organization. James Curry, a retired patrolman, testified before the Lexow Committee:

"Q. You were doing special duty in Jefferson Market court?
"A. I was doing duty there; was detailed there to inside work that I could do for years if I had been left alone, but I couldn't go out and do six hours' patrolling; I had rheumatism and sciatica.

---

[1] *Literary Digest*, August 10, 1912, Vol. XLV, p. 207.

"Q. Your experience made you useful in the Jefferson Market squad?

"A. Yes, sir.

"Q. That is a place at a premium?

"A. There is no premium now; if you were a Republican you couldn't stay there.

"Q. You had the misfortune to be a Republican?

"A. All my life.

"Q. And you are not willing to give it up?

"A. Never will.

"Q. Even to have a soft position in Jefferson Market?

"A. No.

"Q. You are a partisan?

"A. Yes, sir; always was; I know it done me harm and a great deal of it; I have been searching ever since to try and get a light job for a man that has been on duty all his life from 13 until I became 60, he wants something to keep his old brain in motion, but I couldn't get it.

"Q. And from the fact that you were a Republican; that was against your interest there?

"A. Very much. . . .

"Q. You know a thing or two about politics in this city?

"A. I might think I did and not know it after all. . . .

"Q. What led you to think that your Republicanism interfered with your getting that position in Jefferson Market?

"A. Well, I know Mr. Martin went for me.

"Q. How did he go for you?

"A. Because they sent me word that if I didn't get in there I had better go out. . . . I got word through the leader of the district. . . . I got it from a fellow by the name of Callahan and another by the name of Duress. . . .

"Q. You understood them to be Tammany leaders in the district?

"A. Yes, sir.

"Q. What did they say to you?

"A. Asked if I wouldn't join Tammany Hall and I would be taken care of, and I said no.

"Q. After you refused to join Tammany Hall, what happened to you?

"A. I was sent on post.

"Q. But you made your application to be sent back to Jefferson Market?

"A. I got friends to go and see McClave, and I found it was of no use."[1]

Police Captain Max F. Schmittberger testified that the politician of Tammany Hall usually exercised his influence in favour of his friends on the force through the police sergeant, and that the sergeant had to obey his orders if he wanted promotion or wished even tranquillity.

In addition to obeying the orders of Tammany leaders, policemen and police officers were compelled to pay money to individual Tammany Hall politicians for their jobs and for promotions, and they were also expected to contribute to the Tammany Hall campaign fund. Captain Schmittberger also testified that it was considered wise for police officers to belong to the Pequod Club, a Tammany district club presided over by John C. Sheehan, who was a close friend of Richard Croker's and a police commissioner of New York during part of Croker's reign. They were also expected to sell tickets to the outings and dances of the Tammany clubs to saloon keepers, who realized that if they did not buy tickets at five dollars each, the excise laws would be enforced more rigidly than was convenient for their business.

The regular price required from a man who desired a job as an ordinary patrolman during Croker's reign in Tammany Hall was $300. Then the price for promotion went up and up until it reached as high as $15,000 for the position of police captain in a profitable district, that is, in a district where the graft from prostitutes, saloon keepers, gamblers, and merchants was rich. Captain Schmittberger gave the following instance in his experience of payments for promotion:

"Captain Martens was a patrolman in my precinct when I was a sergeant; he asked me to help him to be made a roundsman; he said he had been trying for some time and wanted to be made a roundsman; I told him he couldn't get it unless he paid for it; he asked me how much it would be; I told him I thought I could make connections with Captain Williams,

---

[1] Lexow Investigation, Vol. V, pp. 4632 ff.

that he could do it for him. . . . I asked Captain Williams how much it would cost to make Martens roundsman; he said, $300; he said, 'You get the money and I will make him'; I got the $300 from Martens, handed it to Williams, and he was made a roundsman. . . . Martens became a candidate for sergeant; he came to me again and wanted to know how much it would cost. I told him I didn't know; I would find out; I saw again Captain Williams, asked him how much it would cost to make Martens sergeant; he said, $1,600; Martens brought me the $1,600 and I handed it to Williams; Martens was not made a sergeant for quite a while, and he commenced to run to my house and bother me about this money . . . and finally he began to press me so hard for the money that I couldn't hold him any longer; he wanted to know what he was to get for the money, I told this to Williams, and Williams put on his hat and coat and went down to headquarters and Martens was made a sergeant that day.[1]

"Do you know of any other cases than the two that you have testified to?"

"Well, I had a conversation with Martens about his captaincy when he was a candidate for captain; yes, he told me then it would cost him $14,000."[1]

Captain Alexander Williams, of the New York police force, to whom Captain Schmittberger referred in his testimony, was, next to Chief of Police William S. Devery, of whom we shall hear more, the most famous member of the force. He was known by some as "Clubber Williams" because of the inordinate use to which he put his club in dealing with citizens. In his insolent testimony before the Lexow Committee, he remarked proudly, "I am so well known here in New York that car horses nod to me mornings." It was Captain Williams, too, who gave the Tenderloin District its famous name. This district extended from Fourteenth Street to Forty-second Street and from Fourth Avenue to Seventh Avenue. When Captain Williams was transferred from a precinct far uptown to the precinct which took in this district, he remarked to his friends that he was leaving the rump to feed on the tenderloin. How rich and juicy the tenderloin was we shall soon see.

[1]Lexow Investigation, Vol. V, pp. 5378-5379.

One of the most interesting bits of testimony taken by the Lexow Committee concerning the method of gaining advancement on the police force was that of Captain Timothy J. Creeden, who reluctantly exposed the bribery connected with his own advancement:

"After the first question was asked you, Mr. Goff said, touching the payment of money for your appointment as police captain, you hesitated a long time before you answered; can you give us any explanation this morning why you hesitated so long?"

"Yes, I can," Captain Creeden answered. . . "I had no desire, and did not wish to implicate anybody else, especially people whom I supposed were my friends, and were present in court; I did not wish to be placed in the light of an informer; and that is the particular reason. . . ."

"In other words, you were determined to sacrifice yourself sooner than be called an informer—that is true?"

"That is true."

"That is your nature, captain?"

"Yes, sir."

"And a distinguishing feature of your race?"

"With my family particularly so."

"For what reasons particularly?"

"Being revolutionists."

"Revolutionists in Ireland?"

"Yes, sir."

"So that the word informer carries with it a terrible significance there?"

"It does, sir."

"More than it does even in our own country; hence you have hereditary dread of having that name applied to you?"

"Yes, sir."

"And it was that dread and terror that caused you to hesitate yesterday in giving your testimony?"

"Yes, sir."

"Well, captain, this investigation does not involve treason to our country nor treachery to one's friends surrounded and guarded as it is by the provisions of law applicable to it; and since we are not in Ireland, since you have not to deal with the informer in Ireland, and cannot be accused reasonably of being such here, I ask you, captain, after your night's consideration and after reflection as to how this committee has treated you and the opportunity it has given to you, if you wish to state anything different from what you stated yesterday?"

"Yes. I have reconsidered the whole matter, reflected over it after a consultation with my family."

"You have got a large family, I believe?"

"I have."

"How many children?"

"Eight."

"Well now, captain, tell us all about that transaction, and inasmuch as we are to hear it, the best way is the right way and the truthful way, and I have no doubt but what the great majority of people in this city, considering your record and your service to our country, will sympathize with the unfortunate position in which you have been placed—now, tell us the whole transaction."

"I was an applicant for the position of captain in the department that I was connected with so many years, from 1887, and went before the civil service board at the first examination they had here under that law, after which, having passed a creditable examination there, my name had been placed on the eligible list, but was never able to reach the place; I went through the same course a second time, with the same result; and friends of mine used to say to me, 'What are you going there for, you are only wasting your time; if you don't make up your mind to do one thing, why you are losing your time and you had better stay at home,' and that was the situation of things down to the time that this vacancy was that I now fill; I remember very well at the time in December, I think it was the 29th of December, 1891, it was said the appointments or promotions were to be made, and if I remember right now the names were spoken of who were going to receive the places; I didn't come in on it, notwithstanding that I was on the list; a friend of mine says to me, 'Why don't you bring some influence to bear on one of the commissioners, see him or have somebody see him.'"

"What commissioner?"

"One of the commissioners; the one who had this vacancy to fill, 'And you must do it or else let the thing go by default';

I was sitting at the desk in the station at the time, I was on desk duty, and I says to him, 'Who can I see?' 'Well,' he says, 'Mr. Reppenhagen is the representative of the New York Democracy in this district, and he represents Mr. Voorhis.'"

"That was Commissioner Voorhis?"

"Yes, sir; he says, 'I will go around and see him and see what he thinks of it.' I says, 'All right'; in the course of half an hour he returned saying, 'Mr. Reppenhagen will be here in a few minutes and wants to see you'; he came and we had some conversations. . . . It was in relation to the appointment; I cannot remember now the exact words."

"It was Reppenhagen who came?"

"Yes; he came to the station-house. . . . He says, 'I will go right over and see Commissioner Voorhis and see what can be done; I will be back here again'; he returned some time after; I don't know how long now; before I left the desk; and stated that Commissioner Voorhis would not make the appointment that day, and that he would see me again; the other appointments were made that day; he saw me subsequently and stated that the place could be had for $12,000; I told him that was considerable money, that I didn't have it; I didn't know how I could reach it."

"You were a poor man?"

"I was; but I said to him that I would see my friend and see what would be the result, and let him know; I called upon Mr. Barney O'Rourke, a friend of mine, and stated the circumstances to him; and he called the two friends together and talked the matter over; I, in the meantime, telling them that whatever they would agree upon I would stand by . . . and they agreed to make up a certain sum of money between them, and while they were working on it Mr. Reppenhagen came to see me again, saying there was another man at $12,000 up, and if I wanted the place, I must put up $3,000 more. . . ."

"Well, captain, he said that in addition to you being made a captain you were to be assigned to the command of the precinct you were then doing duty in as sergeant?"

"Yes, sir."

"That was the Eleventh precinct?"

"Yes, sir; that is right. . . . I said to him that I didn't know about that, that I would have to consult my friends again, and

I went and saw my friends and laid the new proposition before them and they decided, said that it was all right, and I said if you think so I am satisfied. . . ."

"In speaking of your friends, you refer to Mr. O'Rourke?"

"And the other gentlemen who were interested in the affair; I then, and because of their desire, went to a stationery store, bought a blank-book, small book with blank notes, and went to the office and signed, I think, about a dozen of these notes, and then handed the book to Mr. O'Rourke."

"The amounts were not filled in?"

"No, sir; he was to fill in according to what those people would do, his friends—my friends and his, that I didn't know anything about; the arrangement was to be carried out in that way. . . ."

"Now, was there not something said then, captain, about a life policy?"

"There was. . . . I brought it up myself. . . . I volunteered that myself, in case of anything occurring, life being uncertain, I wanted to protect my friends. . . ."

"What next took place?"

"The matter went along for a number of days; I heard no more about it until, one afternoon, John J. Martin came to the station-house looking for me and told me that Commissioner Voorhis wanted to see me; I went over to headquarters and saw Commissioner Voorhis, and he put some questions to me in relation to my time on the force, etc.; and he then said it was rumored—told me that he wanted to appoint me; that he had it in his mind he would appoint me to the position of captain, but that he wanted to speak to me, as he heard rumors that there were a number of people over in the Tenth ward who made up a sum of money, and wanted to know if I had any knowledge of it; I told him I had no knowledge of it at all; and with that I left and came back to the station-house, and about five minutes after arriving at the station I was telegraphed for to come back again to the office; when I got there I was appointed and assigned to the First precinct. . . ."

"By Chairman Lexow:

"I would like to ask the captain before he continues if he can give us the whole of the conversation he had with Commissioner Voorhis?"

"That was the substance."

"Give us as nearly as you can his words, and the words you said in answer?"

"He asked me if I had any knowledge of a rumor that there were a number of liquor dealers who had pooled, made a lot of money up in my interest, I thought at the time he wanted to see what I would say, and I naturally denied it. . . ."

"You assumed at the time that was a question put to you by the commissioner to provide a kind of retreat for himself; your opinion at the time was that the commissioner was simply providing for his own retreat in case of necessity?"

"That is the conclusion I came to. . . ."

"By Mr. Goff:

"Now, captain, you reached the point of your appointment and assignment to the First precinct; you felt disappointed at that, did you not, at the latter portion, being assigned to the First precinct?"

"I was somewhat disappointed; yes. . . . Well, the money was not paid right away."

"Why, captain?"

"Well, there was no particular reason it was not paid, and Reppenhagen came down to the station-house to see me about it, and I told him he had better go up and see Mr. O'Rourke; says I, 'They have got the matter in their hands; whatever they do is satisfactory to me'; and I believe that one of the reasons—I think there was a reason why the money was not paid at the time. . . . Mr. O'Rourke was not exactly satisfied because he claimed that they broke their contract in sending me to the First precinct instead of the Eleventh. . . . They withheld the money some few days . . . and meantime I saw Mr. O'Rourke and I told Mr. O'Rourke he might as well let the thing go; there was no fighting it; that I would have to stand the loss if there was any loss into it. . . . If there was any difference in the precinct, I would have to stand it, and I learned afterward that on an order the money was paid over to Mr. Snell; . . . I don't know that Mr. Reppenhagen got the money; that I don't know, except that I was told he received it."

"And, of course, you heard him testify last night that he did get the money?"

"Yes, sir. . . ."

"Now, captain, before you made application this time that you received the promotion, had you before that made application for promotion?"

"Yes, sir; three or four times."

"And you passed the civil service examination each time?"

"Yes, sir. . . . The first examination I received a percentage of 97.82. . . ."

"Now at either of the two previous examinations, the first and the second, were you approached by any persons and told that you would not get the promotion unless you paid for it?"

"I was."

"Was that the first examination or the second?"

"First."

"Was there a price named?"

"There was. . . . Six thousand dollars. . . . Eighty-seven, I believe that was the year; I am not positive."

"What was your answer to the proposition?"

"I refused. . . . I told them I did not think it was right; that I wouldn't go into it. . . ."

"Now I ask you, captain, if you did not understand at that time, at the time of your promotion, that the system in the department had become so universal in its application that no man could get promoted unless he paid for the promotion?"

"Well, that was the understanding."

"That was the understanding; and had it got to a point in the department, captain, and it was well understood by every man in the department, as far as common rumor and your understanding went, that any man that sought promotion, no matter what his merits may have been, had to pay for that promotion?"

"Yes, sir."

"And under those circumstances, you felt that you had to bow down to the system then in operation?"

"That was it."

"Then you knew the system was corrupt and bad; you had to bow down to it?"

"Yes, sir."

"The promotion that you felt should be yours upon the strength of your merits and service, you felt never could be yours, if you did not comply with the corrupt system then in existence?"

"That is so. . . ."

"Did Reppenhagen ever say anything to you about his giving that money, or any portion of it, to anyone?"

"He did not."

"But that he was to give it to the commissioner who was to appoint you was a fact impressed upon your mind by his conversation?"

"That is so."

"No question about that?"

"No, sir."[1]

The Lexow Committee assured Captain Creeden at the end of his testimony that because he had told the truth he would be protected in his position, but the Tammany Hall police commissioners, at the request of Superintendent of Police Byrnes, preferred charges against Captain Creeden at their next meeting, and they ordered him to be suspended from the police force. The Lexow Committee then called Commissioner Martin and Superintendent Byrnes to the stand, questioned the justice of their action, and the order suspending Captain Creeden was rescinded.

Officer Mooney, who was the go-between for Captain Creeden with the politician, Reppenhagen, whose influence was not with Tammany Hall but with a faction that had split from Tammany, the New York Democracy, testified to this colloquial interview with Mr. Reppenhagen:

"I went in where he was sleeping, in a front-room on a folding-bed, and I passed the time of the day with him; and he says, 'Sit down'; and I sat down on the edge of the bed; and I says, 'Repp, I came up here to see if you cannot do something for Tim.' . . . Sergeant Creeden; he said, 'What is the matter with Tim; is he in trouble?' I says, 'No; he is in no trouble, any more than he would like to see if he can be made captain'; 'Well,' he says, 'Mooney, why didn't you come up a week before; it is pretty late now; Wiegand is slated to be made by Commissioner Voorhis, and he is the only one I can possibly reach'; or something like that. . . . Yes, sir; I know he said it; and he says, 'I don't know—it is so late—that I can do anything, but I will get up and go to headquarters and see if I can reach Mr. Martin'; and he says, 'That Wiegand was slated to be made for $12,000'; and he says, 'The money was up'; he says, 'I don't know what he can do now'; 'Well,' I says, 'if you will make Creeden captain, I will raise the ante $3,000'; and he straightened up on his elbow in bed, and he says, 'God; that is pretty good'; and he says, 'Well, I will have to go and get shaved first'; and I says, 'All right'; he got up, and says he, 'Now, Martin has run for coroner and got defeated; and spent a good deal of money, and I have been to a good deal of expense'; and he says, 'There is $5,000 for me, and $5,000 for Martin, and $5,000 for Voorhis'; and he says, 'It will help us all out in our election expenses;' and he says, 'You meet me before noon, between 11 and 12 o'clock, and I will tell you'; and I says, 'All right'; I met him, and he says, 'Wiegand's appointment has been deferred.'"[1]

John W. Reppenhagen testified. At first he refused to answer questions, but when he was assured of protection as a state witness and threatened with prosecution for perjury, he admitted the transaction for Captain Creeden's promotion. Goff also brought out in the testimony of this witness the necessity for Captain Creeden's assignment to "a good, fat precinct."

"Don't you remember," asked Goff, "that there was a discussion between yourself and Snell at that time, in which it was said that Creeden having been sent to a precinct where no money could be made, that he could not expect to pay back the $15,000 unless he was sent to a good, fat precinct; don't you remember that?"

"Yes," answered Reppenhagen, "there was something said of that kind."

"And that if he had been assigned to the command of the Eleventh precinct where he was known, and where his friends were, that he would soon make money enough to pay that back; wasn't that so?"

"Yes, sir."

---

[1] Lexow Investigation, Vol. V, pp. 5254-5255.

"But the fact that he was sent down to the Old Slip station-house where there was very little money to be made, that his friends did not feel justified in giving up the money, because there was no chance of his getting that back; isn't that so?" "Yes, sir."[1]

General Theodore A. Bingham testified some years later that "there is a wonderful 'underground' telegraph in the Police Department," and that the news of promotions spread so fast that he found it necessary to write out papers concerning promotions in his own handwriting behind the closed doors of his office, to prevent policemen from being subjected to extortion by politicians who claimed that they had arranged the deals and deserved money.[2]

In addition to purchasing preferment for policemen, politicians of Tammany Hall helped policemen to get out of trouble if they incurred it. George A. Sipp, who ran the Baltic Hotel at One Hundred and Twenty-fourth Street and Lexington Avenue, where, he admitted, men and women were not asked for their marriage certificates, nor were they suspected if they did not carry baggage, had trouble because he was competing with a similar institution near by, in which politicians and policemen were personally and financially interested. He complained against a policeman who had been persecuting him and who had charged the city $54 for champagne supposed to have been purchased in line of duty in the pursuit of prostitutes at the Baltic Hotel. Mr. Sipp maintained that he had not sold a bottle of wine in six months. "I don't think," Sipp testified, "there is a Tammany Hall politician in New York that was not ringing my doorbell, and asking to let them go because he had a sick mother or wife and children, and I said, 'He did not think of mine when he was trying to put one over on me.'"[3]

If a policeman did not wish to play the game, he was not permitted to remain in the enjoyment of ordinary comfort,

[1]Lexow Investigation, Vol. V, p. 5023.

[2]*New York City Police Department. Stenographer's Minutes Special Committee of the Board of Aldermen of the City of New York Appointed to Investigate the City's Police Department. Pursuant to Resolution Dated August 5, 1912*, Vol. I, pp. 148–149. Known as the Curran Committee.

[3]Curran Investigation, Vol. III, pp. 2226–2227.

even if he did not desire promotion. We have already noted the
testimony of James Curry, who was removed from his post in
Jefferson Market Court because he was not a member of Tammany Hall. If a man proved recalcitrant, even if he was a member of Tammany Hall, he was shifted from precinct to precinct.
In order to make life more comfortable, policemen preferred to
house their families near their station houses. Those who wished
to be independent were permitted to get settled comfortably in
one place and then suddenly sent to the opposite end of the City.
This was kept up until they either asked to be retired or resigned. In Alfred Henry Lewis's novel *The Boss*, the politician
Big John Kennedy holds this conversation with the Chief of
Police of New York:

"'McCue!' returned the Chief of Police in tones of surprise.
'That man would never do! He's as honest as a clock!' 'Honest!'
exclaimed Big Kennedy, and his amazement was a picture.
'Well, what does he think he's doin' on th' force, then?' 'That's
too many for me,' replied the other. Then, apologetically:
'But you can see yourself that, when you rake together six
thousand men, no matter how you pick 'em out, some of 'em's
going to be honest.'"

v

The system of graft operated by the police of New York
during the reign of Richard Croker was one which worked
from the top down and then back to the top again. While
Tammany Hall officials saw to it that they got their share of the
spoils, which were estimated by Henry N. Taber, foreman of
the Grand Jury in 1894, as amounting to $7,000,000 a year,
the system was not so rigid that it did not allow for human
tendencies. It was not under the care of an efficiency manager,
for while Croker was a stern boss, he did not aim to gather in
every dollar he could without waste, but wisely acted upon the
principle that was expressed in one of the vaudeville *mots* of the
day, "Is everybody happy?"

Croker was now a wealthy man, as we have seen, and he did
not demand that policemen give him a percentage of their
graft, but the Tammany Hall finance committee, of which he
was the chairman, received heavy contributions every autumn

from the men who collected the graft and from the people who paid it, and the chairman of the finance committee of Tammany Hall has never kept books; it is one of the traditions of the organization.

By the standards of the men who engaged in the enterprise, it was altogether fitting and proper that Tammany Hall should share in the proceeds of graft, for Tammany Hall made the business possible. If Tammany Hall was out of power, police graft became dangerous, for there was no telling what the reformers might do, and Tammany Hall's safe and sane attitude had been enunciated by the proclamation of Croker, its Boss, that everybody in New York was working for his pocket all the time. A Tammany Hall administration meant for the grafters what a business administration at Washington meant for the corporations—"the right," as one of the statesmen of the period expressed it, "of a man to run his own business in his own way, with due respect, of course, to the Ten Commandments and the Penal Code." Tammany Hall went even further: it did not bother to place a strict construction on either the Penal Code or the Ten Commandments if the chances of getting caught were carefully observed, and a man who did not observe those chances carefully was considered a fool and not a criminal. The attitude was tersely expressed in the testimony of Edgar A. Whitney, who happened to be minding a gambling house for his friend Pease while Pease went to supper. Glennon, the policeman who collected graft for Chief of Police William S. Devery when Devery was a captain, entered and asked for Pease, and then left this message for him: "'Come to one side,' he said, 'the captain wants this game closed up until after election time; that if the Tammany Hall ticket is elected,' he says, 'we will protect you for anything from a poker game to a whorehouse.'"[1]

During the 1890's in New York City police bribery was so open and generally accepted that the particular motion of the hand behind the back and the palm turned up in the shape of a cup was used on the vaudeville stage then and later as the symbol denoting policeman. Like all good burlesque, it was based firmly on truth, for it was the traditional way in which

---

[1] Lexow Investigation, Vol. II, pp. 1602–1603.

large policemen really did take money from small Italian fruit vendors and portly German saloon keepers.

The Lexow Committee came to the conclusion in its report that there was in existence throughout the City "a system so well regulated and understood that upon the assignment of a new captain no conversation was necessary to instruct the precinct detectives or wardmen as to their line of conduct." Each police captain had his wardman, who had practically no other duties except to collect money from the proprietors of houses of prostitution, and from saloon keepers, criminals, business men, and other miscellaneous citizens in regular monthly amounts which had been agreed upon. Every month, soon after rent day, the wardman appeared in the house of prostitution and the saloon and got what he had bargained for, and the proprietors of these establishments were accustomed to regard the protection money as a part of the overhead of their business.

The wardman deducted 20 per cent. of what he collected for his services, and then he turned the rest over to the captain; the captain then visited the inspector of his division and paid over his percentage to him. The inspector, when called upon, contributed to the fortunes of the police commissioners and to the fortunes of the district leaders of Tammany Hall. General Bingham wrote that when he was Police Commissioner of New York: "it would have been an easy matter for me to have made $600,000 in bribe money, and $1,000,000 would not have been an excessive figure at all. . . . One day, shortly after my arrival at Police Headquarters, an acquaintance dropped into my office. 'Commissioner,' he said, 'there is a house at —— West Thirty-third Street, run very quietly. It will be worth $10,000 a month to *you*——,' but the sentence was never finished to my knowledge. As a matter of fact, the place had never been opened, and the man had been used as an agent to feel out the Department. A few months later, I was offered $5,000 in cash and $500 a month merely to be seen shaking hands with the proprietor of an upper Broadway café."[1]

General Bingham was a reformer. His refusal to take graft proved perplexing to the people who had become accustomed for so many years to pay it as part of their business expenses.

[1] "Policing Our Lawless Cities," by General Theodore A. Bingham, *Hampton's Magazine*, Vol. XXIII, September, 1909, p. 296.

He told of the proprietor of an East Side dance hall who suffered the following disturbing experience:

"Following a custom of years he had tendered his usual
quarterly 'assessment' to the patrolman of the precinct. Turned
down in that quarter, he had gone to the captain, then to the
inspector, both of whom, to his amazement, were square. He
had finally come to me in desperation, to learn who would take
his money in return for protection."

The Lexow Committee reported:

"The poor, ignorant foreigner residing on the great east side
of the city has been especially subjected to a brutal and infamous rule by the police, in conjunction with the administration of the local inferior criminal courts, so that it is beyond a
doubt that innocent people who have refused to yield to criminal extortion, have been clubbed and harassed and confined
in jail, and the extremes of oppression have been applied to
them in the separation of parent and child, the blasting of
reputation and consignment of innocent persons to a convict's
cell.
    "The coördination of all the departments of city govern-
ment, under the sway of the dominant Democratic faction in
that city, has produced a harmony of action operating so as to
render it impossible for oppressed citizens, particularly those
in the humbler walks of life, the poor and needy, to obtain
redress or relief from the oppression or the tyranny of the
police. Their path to justice was completely blocked. It is not
credible that the abuses shown to exist have been the creation
of but a short time. It is clear from the evidence that abuses
have existed for many years back; that they have been constantly increasing through the years, but that they did not
reach their full and perfect development until Tammany
Hall obtained absolute control of the city government, and
under that control the practices which have been shown con-
clusively before your committee, were brought into a well
regulated and comprehensive system, conducted apparently
upon business principles."[1]

_____
[1]Lexow Investigation, Vol. I, p. 27.

What some of these abuses and practices were that were enacted by the politicians of Tammany Hall and the police working hand in hand, we are in a position to see vividly from the mass of extraordinary testimony that was drawn from exceptional witnesses by the talents of John W. Goff and Frank Moss.

One of the most important sources of graft for police and politicians in New York came from the unhampered practice of female prostitution. The money from this source came from the individual street walkers, the houses of prostitution, the houses of assignation, flats and apartments used for sporadic prostitution, saloons with rooms to rent upstairs, restaurants where men and women made each other's acquaintance, and various miscellaneous agencies such as pimps and cadets. There were also side lines of graft which involved the sale of wines and beers to houses of prostitution, and the supply of cigars, cigarettes, food, clothing, jewellery, furniture, and medical attendance. These were usually considered valuable concessions to be enjoyed by a faithful Tammany man. The profits were large, and the purchases could be made compulsory by the threat of the law. There were also abortionists, midwives, and baby farmers, who worked with the police and the district leaders, or who paid them for protection from the laws. It was considered advisable, too, for the coroner to be friendly in case of the accident of death.

A perfect picture of this phase of New York life in the reign of Richard Croker was portrayed in the testimony before the Mazet Committee of Emma Hartig, a fifteen-year-old prostitute:

"I am not yet sixteen years old, and within the last four months I was in four or five different houses. . . . I wanted to go to work and earn some money, and I had no trade, and I thought perhaps I could be a waitress; and I took a newspaper called the German Herald and in that I saw advertisements for waitresses. And one such advertisement I found at No. 32 First street and I went there to be a waitress. I meant to go there and do a respectable business as a waitress, but when I got there I found myself in an improper place. I stayed there. They kept me quite nice there. I stayed because I would not return home. I did not like the place where I was, but I would not return home because the lady said to me if I stayed there and earned my living it would be quite right; I did not care what the people say; she takes the place of a mother to me. . . . I did not like to go back home because my father never treated me right. I had trouble at home. So this woman who kept 32 First street said she would be a mother to me, and I thought I would stay. I didn't know she wanted me to do anything wrong until I was there about two or three hours in the place. . . .

"From that place, 32 First street, I went to 212 Forsyth street. That was a bad house, too; 32 First street was a bad place. From Forsyth street I went uptown in Fourth avenue, No. 89. . . ."

"Now, tell me, Emma, were there any more very young girls at 89 Fourth avenue?"

"There is a girl there named Lillie, she is about thirteen or fourteen years old. . . . There were young girls in these other places too, about fifteen to sixteen. From Fourth avenue I went to Ella May, right next door. . . . I found out these different places through the girls in the places I was in. There were a good many girls in those places, and a great many young girls circulating through all those places on the East side. A few as young as I am. But a great many 16 and 17 years of age. There are a great many of those places where the young girls of the east side are taken in. I could not count them there is so many. I found out where McGurk's was. And I got going to McGurk's. Yes, three times. There are very rough people that go to McGurk's. Very rough men indeed—sailors, soldiers— longshoremen. And there are a good many young girls there. Most that go there have somebody to watch over them—a man. I do mean to say that girls like me, 15, 16, 17 years of age, are sitting around the tables drinking. I found it so. . . . Some of the girls live over McGurk's. They stay there altogether some times; they don't pay any; . . .

"There are a great many men living in that district who take money away from the girls when they earn it. Those men, first they commence to make out that they like the girls, and then after they say: 'Well, now, if you don't stick to me I'll tell the police,' and all that kind of stories, and they get kind of frightened, and then they commence to give their money to him, and sometimes if they don't give the money to him they get licked. I know such a man as that. He throwed a chair at me to make me give up my money. He hurted me. There are a great many cases of that kind. There were quite a number of such men hanging around McGurk's saloon and watching the girls and making them work for them. . . .

"The police never arrested me before I took the poison. I was one of the girls that got tired and took poison, at Mc-Gurk's and then of course I was arrested, and that resulted in my changing my life. It was a very good thing for me. I am living now outside of the city with decent people, and enjoying a comfortable, good life, and my friends are with me to-day. . . .

"I don't think the police were much good. Sometimes the police go in these houses and get treated to drinks and whiskey and they don't care much about it if a girl goes on the street. They do not. Sometimes they urge them to go with them themselves. They go into the houses and urge the girls. I have known that to happen myself. . . .

"Of course, the police are not particularly anxious to arrest girls that are good to them. A policeman once asked me for money. It was when I was in 89 Fourth avenue, and the lady sent me once out to go around the corner; it was night about ten o'clock; and I went around and there was a policeman, and I came there three or four nights after to go around the corner, and he was there, and I commenced to talk with him and invited him up, and he said to me: 'Do you know I can bring you up to jail, if you talk like that with me?' And then he commenced to ask me if I take some men in there I should give him every time a quarter. I said to him, indeed I won't do it; that men that take money from girls are pimps. That is what I call a policeman who takes money from girls. I do know whether the persons keeping those houses were paying any money to the police. I knew that was so. That was the general talk throughout with women of that kind, that they had to pay. That is well understood. Twenty-nine Eldridge street, Mrs. Fisher, she was the lady of the house, and she sent one day . . . with some man the money to the station-house, and it was sent back with a policeman—with somebody—I don't know exactly it was a policeman. . . . That is the amount of money that was sent was not enough, and it came back from the station house with the word that if we could not pay the fine for the month we would have to shut up the place, and we did shut it up. . . . A police officer in uniform came into that house regularly, one. He stayed there sometimes. He never paid. The proprietor of the house was glad to have policemen come, because if they come in it is easier for them to treat the policemen so they keep their mouth shut. I remember when I was at No. 32 First street, a police officer coming in at First street, not in 32, but by Mr. Jumbo on the corner. We used to call him Charlie; he used to come there once or twice a week, and sometimes oftener, and the madam would call me because I was the youngest girl in the house. I did not see that officer take any money from anybody—from any women. . . ."

"Do you not remember an officer taking money from one of the women who was a married woman?"

"That was not an officer; that was a detective. . . . He used to come in First street, No. 32 . . . and there was a married woman, she was there to wait on the table, and he used to come there, and he took her back once, and she gave him some money, and then she said she would leave the children for him. She would leave the children to go with the officer. All of this I experienced in five months. Pretty rapid life for a little girl. I am glad I am out of it."[1]

Graft was collected regularly from the street walkers themselves by policemen on the beat in the neighbourhoods where they worked and by the wardmen who represented the police captains. Lucy C. Harriott testified before the Lexow Committee that she paid one dollar a week for the policeman to the woman who ran the house where she lived and worked.

"In case of a new wardman coming there," asked Mr. Goff, "isn't he generally introduced by the madam to the girls?"

"As a general thing the wardman and detective come down Saturday night about 9 o'clock," answered Miss Harriott, "and they will go into the front room, and after the madam has seen him, if the girls are bold enough they will walk into the room, and laugh and 'kid' with him, and if you go in the room where they are you are spotted out, and she says, 'My girls, don't trouble them.'"

[1] Mazet Investigation, Vol. II, pp. 1996–2000.

"Have you ever heard the word 'cruisers' used?"

"Yes, sir."

"Is that the police name by which the madam introduces you to the wardman—as her 'cruisers'?"

"Yes, sir."

"Have you known of girls who refused to pay being arrested more frequently than those who did pay $1 a week?"

"Yes; I have."

"Can a cruiser, as she is called, cruise around the streets there at night unless she pays?"

"Not very well."

"She runs a risk of being arrested?"

"Yes, sir; at all times; whether you are doing any harm or not."

Policemen went so far as to threaten with arrest any women they saw alone on the streets at night unless they paid them money, and many of these were working women returning from their work. James J. O'Brien testified that he knew of such cases, "and one girl told me it was safer to turn up a dollar or so if she had it in her clothes, than go before a magistrate and be locked up." "Did you know the girl?" "I did." "Was she a decent girl?" "A respectable girl; hard worker; steady worker."[1]

Another girl told the Lexow Committee that she had been arrested 102 times and sentenced to Blackwell's Island each time. She never served her sentence more than once, and that was because she preferred to serve that time rather than pay politicians and lawyers to obtain a suspended sentence, for she had been arrested four times that week and had paid each time, "and the fifth one that came I thought I would go to the island," she said. "Can you tell us," Mr. Goff asked this girl, Hattie Ledyne, "how many times you have paid Lawyer Webb for getting you out?" "Somewhere about 34 or 40 times," Miss Ledyne answered.[2]

"You were liberated yesterday from the island?" Mr. Goff asked Miss Ledyne.

---

[1] Lexow Investigation, Vol. II, p. 2287. Lucy Harriott's testimony, Vol. IV, pp. 3614–3616, 3621.

[2] Lexow Investigation, Vol. IV, p. 3630.

"Yes, sir," she answered.

"And you have not served a month there?"

"No; three weeks sentence to-day."

"And you were sentenced to six months in the workhouse?"

"Yes, sir."

"Did you do anything to get out yourself?"

"No, sir; I only wrote to a friend of mine."

"And that friend of yours got you out, is that the idea?"

"Yes, sir."

"Do you know how much money that friend put up to get you out?"

"No, sir; I do not."

"Have you seen your friend since your discharge?"

"Yes, sir; I have seen him; and I did not ask him; but I suppose he will look for a house and lot; he is colored; he will look for a house and lot."

"He will expect a house and lot for getting you out?"

"Yes, sir. . . ."

"Have you had to pay your friends in every case where they have got you out?"

"Oh, yes, sir."

"Every time?"

"Sure; if I get $5 or five days, and haven't got it, I borrow $5, and I give him $10 for it."

"If you borrow $5 you give him $10 for it?"

"Certainly."

"Give us the name of your friend."

"Mike Stake."

"Where does Mike live?"

"He lives in Union Stock Yards Hotel, West Sixty-fourth street. . . . I know it is near Tenth Avenue."

"Did Mike ever get you out before?"

"Yes, sir; he got me out before."

"More than twice?"

"Yes, sir."[1]

The privilege of bailing out prostitutes was a valuable Tammany concession. Then the prostitute was permitted to walk the streets again to make money so that she might have some

[1]Lexow Investigation, Vol. IV, pp. 3637–3638.

when the policeman and the politician wished to arrest her again, for there was no advantage in killing the goose that laid the golden eggs when they could take the eggs as soon as they were laid.

William R. Nelson, the Tammany Hall district leader who controlled the bail monopoly in the Tenderloin district, found it lucrative. Nelson received five dollars from every prostitute he bailed out, and he was credited with bailing out from twenty to thirty prostitutes every night.[1]

Henry Hoffman, the proprietor of a house of prostitution on the East Side, testified before the Lexow Committee that the police sometimes arrested his girls while they were soliciting men from the stoop of his house, and that he went immediately to ex-Assemblyman Wissig, gave him five dollars for each girl, and they were bailed out so that they could go back to work the same night. The next day they were sentenced to two months or one month on Blackwell's Island; "and I paid $25 and they were discharged." Hoffman remarked: "I wouldn't have said all this, but, gentlemen, the dirty tricks they played me afterward forced me to do it."

We have seen how men turned against Tammany Hall and testified at the time of the election frauds during Tweed's régime because they had not been treated with consideration. The same was true in the 'nineties. The prostitutes and keepers of houses of prostitution were only willing to testify because Tammany politicians and policemen had been foolish enough to take their money and to treat them badly afterward. Their condition could not have been worse, and therefore they were unafraid of what the police might do.

"Silver Dollar" Smith, one of the leading Tammany men of the East Side, also did a flourishing business in bailing out prostitutes. "Silver Dollar" Smith got his name from the fact that his famous saloon across the street from the Essex Market Court had one thousand silver dollar pieces cemented in its floor, with a fifty-dollar gold piece in the centre. "Silver Dollar" Smith told James L. Ford that in the three days after he had completed this scheme of decoration he took in more than three times the amount of money in the floor from men who "wanted to see how this fool had wasted his money." Every silver dollar

---

[1] Mazet Investigation, Vol. II, pp. 1595–1602.

in the floor bore the date 1887. In back of the bar of his saloon
"Silver Dollar" placed a chandelier trimmed with 500 silver dollars and behind the bar there was a star and crescent a foot high
covered with silver pieces ranging in value from a dime to a
dollar. Smith also had a saloon on Thirty-first Street and Sixth
Avenue which was open all night in spite of the law providing
that saloons must close at 1 A.M. From 1892 until his death,
"Silver Dollar" Smith was a prominent member of Tammany
Hall. "Silver Dollar" Smith's real name has been variously
given as Charles Solomon, Charles Goldschmidt, and Charles
Finklestein, but the consensus of opinion was in favour of
Charles Solomon.

Henrietta Hensing, who kept a boarding house and saloon
on Fourth Avenue, was arrested together with the inmates of
her house because the police claimed that she rented rooms for
the purposes of prostitution. She and her girls remained in jail
overnight, and the next morning "Silver Dollar" Smith came
to visit them, "and he said he would bail out my husband and
myself if I would pay $100 for it; then he demanded $25 for
each woman; I paid $50 for three, and didn't have any more
money, and the others all paid $25 themselves; there were
married people visiting their friends in the house; they were all
arrested with the rest; they all paid "Silver Dollar" Smith $25
apiece; all the women were married and some of the gentlemen
were single; they paid $25 apiece to Mr. Smith."[1]

When "Silver Dollar" Smith's daughter was married in an
uptown hall, the ceremony was attended by a miscellaneous
gathering, "that ranged in social status," wrote James L. Ford,
who attended the wedding, "from Police Inspectors down to
the deaf and dumb bootblack of the Essex Market Court."
"The bride," Ford wrote, "was a girl of pleasing manners. She
told me that her father had a roof-garden on top of his house
built especially for her to play in and that she had been carefully kept off the streets from her earliest childhood."[2]

When "Silver Dollar" Smith died, his friend, the Rev. Gabriel Hirsch, who delivered the funeral sermon, said: "He never
broke his promise to a friend, and he had a warm and generous
heart."

[1]Lexow Investigation, Vol. II, pp. 1451–1452.
[2]Forty-Odd Years in the Literary Shop, by James L. Ford, pp. 170–172.

Hattie Ledyne, a prostitute, testified to relations with policemen that were genial but purely mercenary:

"Do you remember one time that you stole a diamond stud?" asked Goff.

"Yes, sir," Miss Ledyne answered.

"Do you know who it was you stole it from?"

"No, sir."

"He was one of the men you picked up on your cruise?"

"Yes, sir."

"And you slipped it out of his shirt?"

"Yes, sir; I would not like to know the man either. . . ."

"What did you do with the diamond?"

"I gave it to Captain McDonald."

"How did you come to give it to Captain McDonald?"

"We were fast friends."

"Did the captain ever say to you that if you picked up any little trifle like that to think of him?"

"Sure. . . ."

"Have any of the patrolmen or policemen abused you on the street?"

"No, sir."

"You were pretty sociable with them all?"

"Yes."

"Ever make any dates with them?"

"No, sir; because there is no money in it."

"No money with policemen?"

"No; I am looking for money, and so are they."[1]

Hattie Ledyne also testified that when she passed a policeman she frequently gave him a dollar to buy a cigar. "Sometimes," she said, "I would be half drunk, and I would have money, and I would give them a dollar, and tell them to go and buy a cigar." However, further questions brought out that if she forgot to give them their dollars she was quickly reminded that her rent was due.

The large sums of money, however, were collected from the proprietors of houses of prostitution and not from the prostitutes who worked for themselves. The girls had to pay what-

---

[1] Lexow Investigation, Vol. IV, pp. 3634–3636.

ever they could, but the houses of prostitution paid a fixed rate depending upon the locality, the number of beds, the number of girls, and the amount of their nightly proceeds. Some of these women and men paid money not only to the police but also to Tammany Hall district leaders. The testimony before the Lexow Committee of Mrs. Augusta Thurow illuminated this whole system.

Mrs. Thurow was a dressmaker who lived on Second Avenue. "What sort of house is that on Second Avenue?" asked Mr. Goff. "The first five years I kept it a straight house and the last four years it was a house of ill-repute. . . . I could not get tenants to occupy the rooms, and I took in women that said they lived with men that were their husbands. . . . I was then making dresses and sewing with five girls; and in the night they would bring men in; . . ." One of the policemen on the beat was the first to discover this tendency on the part of the sewing girls, for this branch of the police service was always vigilant and attentive to business. He told Mrs. Thurow what was going on in her house, and informed her that there would be trouble. "How can I stop it when I am asleep?" she asked. "I will send Bissart," he answered laconically. Wardman Bissart called, and he seemed to know all about what was going on in the house on Second Avenue. "Well, where this house stands you can never put a church, and you can go on in business, and I will see you in a month," he told Mrs. Thurow. Next time Bissart called, Mrs. Thurow gave him $10, and then he called every month and received sometimes $21, sometimes $12, and sometimes $15. When the rooms were empty and business was bad, he received no money. In two years, said Mrs. Thurow, he went away four times without any money. "At the time I paid him $20," Mrs. Thurow testified, "there were four girls in the house doing business at one time; he says, 'About $5 for every girl you have in the house is what we will charge.'" She paid "in bills, or in silver, or anything; if I gave him bills and silver both, I wrapped the bills around the silver, so there would be no click; he cautioned me that way. . . . He did not want the girls to hear the click; . . . and he said, 'Don't let them hear the click.'"

When a new police captain came into a precinct where houses of prostitution were flourishing, each keeper of every house had to pay what was known as the initiation fee for the new captain, and this usually was $500. Mrs. Thurow could not afford to pay this fee, and her house was raided by the police. But later Mrs. Thurow started in business again, and then she called at the station house and paid the captain himself $25. The wardman, Hoch, was not satisfied with Mrs. Thurow's stipend each month. When she protested that she did not make enough money to pay more, Hoch answered: "You have got the house, and why don't you make money? It is your own fault, and that house is situated in the right spot, and you can do all the business you want and we won't interfere with you, but you must do better than this."

Mrs. Thurow was worried, and she asked her husband to go to see Judge George F. Roesch, Tammany district leader of the Seventh Assembly District, for Mr. Thurow was a member of Roesch's Tammany Hall Club. Mrs. Thurow was then asked to visit Roesch at his law office. She explained her difficulties with the police, and he said: "I will fix that; . . . it will cost you $100 or $150." After paying Tammany leader Roesch $100, she was permitted to do business for a time, but the police bothered her again before long and arrested some of her girls for soliciting on the stoop. She paid more money to the police, and then she was permitted to do business again. One day Hoch called on her and said, according to her testimony: "Business are on the bumerina; Parkhurst is on the road, and you have got to lay low for thirty days. . . ."

In addition to paying the captain, his wardman, and the Tammany leader, Mrs. Thurow testified that she paid each policeman on the beat in the neighbourhood of her house two dollars every week, and whenever they were changed, which she said happened as often as seven and eight times in a week, she had to pay another two dollars. "Yes," Mrs. Thurow testified, "one told the other, I suppose; and they would stand in front of the stoop, and I would go downstairs, and they would say, 'You know what's the matter; I am as good as everybody else; I am flesh and blood, and want what the others get;' . . ."

When Mrs. Thurow told Wardman Hoch that she had paid money to the Tammany district leader Roesch, he was very angry, for there was constant competition between the politicians of Tammany Hall and their policemen for the spoils. "That is how it is with you," she said Hoch told her; "you people get us angry; you give the money to the politicians that belongs to the police. . . . Are the politicians doing for you, or are we doing for you?"[1]

The Tammany political clubs in the East Side districts of New York, where many of the houses of prostitution were located, collected money whenever they could get it from the owners of those establishments, and especially at election time. The testimony of Mrs. Rhoda Sanford illustrates the share of the political clubs in the spoils of prostitution:

"Chairman Lexow—Will you kiss the Bible?"

"The Witness—Suppose I don't believe in the Bible?"

"Senator Bradley—You don't believe in the Bible?"

"The Witness—No."

"Senator Bradley—Stand up then."

"The Witness—I don't believe in the Bible."

"Chairman Lexow—One moment; I will affirm you then. . . ."

"By Mr. Goff:

"How long did you reside in 24 Bayard Street?"

"Two years as a madam and one year as housekeeper. . . ."

"This house that you kept there was what we commonly call a house of prostitution?"

"Yes, disorderly house; the old-fashion name of house of prostitution. . . ."

"How did you come to give him $200?"

"I was told—some person called on me, and sent me a note and said I must pay some money, and I heard afterwards that it was a young political organization; I gave them money; . . . the gentleman that came said it was for a young political organization that had just been organized, do you see; and it was for that reason they came after the money. . . ."

"Did you ever buy any tickets for any excursions?"

"Yes; I often bought tickets for excursions."

"Five dollars a ticket?"

"Yes, sir. . . ."

"Do you know of others engaged in the same business living

---

[1] Lexow Investigation, testimony of Mrs. Thurow, Vol. I, pp. 1040-1115.

around in the same street near you there, paying similar sums to what you paid?"

"Well, I tell you, Senator, I don't know, because I always kept to myself; I never interfered with any of them, and never interfered with them, because they begrudge you your life; each side of you they think you are getting along better than themselves. . . . I don't know nothing of what my neighbors were doing . . . ; one time they came to me for $500 for another political organization; . . . and I know one day a gentleman called and said it was for a political organization, and I said do you want to get blood out of a stone, and I put them out."

"Didn't you know that other people engaged in the same business that you were engaged in were paying the same kind of contributions that you were?"

"No; because I don't know nothing about that; if I went to speak of it to any person, in regard to that, I would get a short answer, and anyone that spoke to me at the same time I would give a short answer . . . ; they would not speak of such a thing; any of the people in that business, they don't get very intimate among their neighbors in that business; outside it is all right; I don't know the next door neighbour. . . . Everyone keeps their own business secret and because, as in the dry goods business, everyone don't like to see their neighbor get along better than they do. . . ."

"Now, do you remember a fellow by the name of Charlie Keach?"

"No."

"Cock-eyed Louis?"

"Yes; those were the parties that came to me for the $500 for the political organization; I went to the door and put them out. . . ."[1]

Charles Priem, who kept a house of prostitution, testified that at election time workers for the local political clubs belonging to Tammany Hall visited him "and collected whatever they could." "Cock-eyed Louis," a worker in the Tammany Commanchee Club of the East Side district, was one of the leading collectors of the district. Mr. Priem also did not kiss the Bible, and when cross-examined by De Lancey Nicoll, Tammany's

[1] Lexow Investigation, Vol. I, pp. 983–1010.

representative before the Lexow Committee, who asked why he had not kissed the Book, he answered: "If it was a new one, I would not hesitate for a moment, but I suppose there are so many kisses on that it wasn't necessary." "You are so particular of whom you kiss or what you kiss?" asked Mr. Nicoll. "Yes, sir; in that line," answered Mr. Priem. Then Priem gave this account of how he came to go into the business of prostitution:

"I will tell you simply how I came about it; I was living, or I kept a room, in Third street, and the madam of this house kept the house in Bayard street; that was Mrs. Connelly, now Mrs. Granger; at that time I took a room there, and I got acquainted. I was a single man at the time, and I got acquainted with the servant of the house there, and as Mrs. Connelly was about selling her place, I made a proposition to my present wife, now living, that if she could arrange things, that I would marry her and we would take the place."

"That is, you proposed prostitution to your wife, that if she would marry you, you would open a house of prostitution?"

"That was the understanding. . . ."

"That was the marriage understanding?"

"Yes, sir; at that time. . . ."

"Who paid for the furniture in the house?"

"We bought the place through influence; my wife raised $1,000; she paid that $1,000 and the balance, amounting to four more thousand dollars, was made out in notes payable each month, a note of $300."

"From whom did she raise the $1,000?"

"From a well acquaintance of hers."[1]

Priem testified that whenever a new police captain was appointed to the precinct in which his house of prostitution was located, he had to pay an initiation fee of either $500 or $300, and that at Christmas time the wardman came around, and collected a Christmas present for the captain. "Now, Priem, Christmas is coming on, get ready," was the way it was put to him, he said. He understood from his friends in the business that all the keepers of houses of prostitution gave a Christmas

---

[1]Lexow Investigation, testimony of Charles Priem, Vol. I, pp. 953–982.

present of money to the police captain each time the anniversary of Christ's birth was celebrated.

The keepers of houses of prostitution had no love for Tammany Hall and the police, but they feared both institutions and cringed before their power. Miss Maud Harvey, who took in gentlemen and lady boarders by the night in a house in West Twenty-fourth Street, had a conversation with Edgar W. Whitney, who served a subpœna on her to appear before the Lexow Committee, which illustrated the attitude of many of these people to their extortionists. Miss Harvey was distressed when she saw the subpœna and asked, "Can they lock me up?" "Not unless you commit perjury," Whitney answered. "I must go and see somebody," she said. "Are you to go to see the police?" Whitney asked. "What, those God damned sons of bitches? No, the stinken bastards, I wouldn't go to them," answered Miss Harvey. Then she inquired if he thought the Lexow investigation would break up Tammany Hall. "I don't know whether they will or not," Whitney answered. "I hope to Christ they do break up Tammany Hall, and I can open my house again and make some money, which I have not done in the past," Miss Harvey said.[1]

Miss Mary Goode, a proprietress of a house of prostitution, told the Curran Committee: "Well, when a policeman don't take your money, when he is going to be your friend, always watch out." These women disliked the police and the politicians, because after working hard they found that they had no money left, for as soon as they had accumulated a surplus either the police or Tammany Hall workers took it away from them by threats of raids. Mrs. Matilda Hermann, known to the police in New York as "the French madame," and considered "a gold mine" for extortion, testified before the Lexow Committee that in the four or five years she was in that business, she had paid out more than $30,000, and that she then had no money of her own, although she had made a profit of $1,000 to $1,500 a month. "To-day," she said sadly, "I haven't got a dollar to my name."

In spite of the fact that she had paid more than $30,000 for protection, Mrs. Hermann suffered personal injury and in-

---

[1]Lexow Investigation, Vol. II, pp. 1594-1595.

dignity from individual police officers. She told the Lexow Committee the following amazing story:

"Once I was arrested, and a policeman did lick me," Mrs. Hermann testified. . . . "I never seen the policeman before; I only spoke with him, only my servant girl came to me and told me that the policeman wanted to arrest her; I told her you must do something to be arrested; she said madame, I am afraid to go in the street, for he will arrest me, and then—I have any kind of liquor in my house and beer—I had seen the policeman go in the saloon on the corner of Third Street and Sixth avenue, and I took a big pitcher and I never used to go for beer, and had plenty of beer—to speak to the policeman; the policeman was with five or six people drinking in a little place in the liquor-beer saloon, and I called him outside like this (indicating with her finger), and he told me what I want; then he came to me and got outside and came to me and said: 'What do you want?' I said, 'I watch you,' and he was awful mad, and he called me every kind of name; I said I do not want it. 'Here is a detective if you want to speak to him; you can speak to him.' I said 'no; I only want to speak to you'; and then he said: 'He is a detective, speak to him.' I asked him what is the matter with you, you don't understand me, and he commenced to be sassy, and called me evil names, and I was ashamed and I crossed over the street to go to my house, and the policeman followed me, and he took the pitcher out of my hands and threw the beer over me, and commenced to lick me, and called me a 'French bitch' and from that commenced to lick me."

"With his fists?"

"No; with his club . . . then I was awful ashamed, and lots of people outside, and he licked me, and I begged him to let me alone, and then he said, 'You will suffer for that; you doing something against my friends,' and he said 'here, here,' and he told me he would lick me more, and then he took me to the station-house, and I had a wrapper on, and I was all wet, and when I got to the station house, I felt my diamond earrings were out."

"Your diamond earrings were gone?"

"Yes, sir, then the matron was there, and I told my earrings is lost, and I said the policeman licked me awful bad, and she said, who do you want, and I send for somebody there, and I said——"

"The matron asked you how much you wanted to give, and she will send somebody there?"

"Yes, sir; then about 10 minutes after——"

"You said you would give her $15?"

"Yes, then 15 minutes afterwards she came back and told me the man did not find the earrings; if I wanted to pay a little more, she send two men for it, and sometime find it."

"Did you give her the $15 the first time?"

"No, I told her if she bring the earrings I have the money; about half an hour after this she brought me the earrings in a piece of paper, and I gave her $30; it was found in the place where the policeman licked me . . . I know it is two matrons, and it is the thinnest one of the two. . . ."

"You were put upstairs?"

"Yes, sir; and it is there I gave $30 . . . now I take a carriage and go home but I was ashamed to go in the street like I was, and was all wet; then I was out about 9 o'clock in the night, and after 9 o'clock I was lying in my bed, it was three or four days; I could not walk, he licked me; and I had a doctor; I was all the time sick, and I had a big operation, and you can think it had a good deal to do with it."

"And you have suffered ever since?"

"Yes, sir; I had my side here, was all black, and my side here and my stomach is sore, and then I saw my friend Mr. Helrung, and he said if I knew that was an old friend of yours, I would not have arrested her."

"That is, O'Hara said?"

"Yes, sir. . . ."

Soon afterward Mrs. Mathilda Hermann was arrested again and taken from her bed to the station-house.

"Well, the remembrance of that night, Mrs. Hermann, makes you sick, doesn't it?" asked Goff.

"Yes; they took me to the station-house . . . then I was put in $500 bail, and my case was tried long after; that was the 21st of January, and the 9th of February I had a big operation where

I had six doctors, and where I was in a very bad condition and those officers swore I was the madame; I called them in and there did sell me for a dollar, and I am 37 years old; and I never sell me for one dollar—not for a hundred dollars; and a bootblack swore I was upstairs for one dollar."

"And even the bootblack was brought in to swear against you?"

"Yes; everything was false, and everybody else knows I was innocent, and no one was in the house, and nothing was done."

"And even the bootblack, the boy, he swore that you sold yourself for a dollar, too?"

"For a dollar, yes, sir."

"To him?"

"Yes. . . ."

"Did he swear?"

"Yes, sir; he swore that he stayed with me for a dollar; never a man in New York or a Frenchman can say they stayed with me for a dollar; never yet I do it."[1]

Some women in this business, however, were more fortunate than Mrs. Hermann. They enjoyed unusual courtesies because of their intimate relations with city officials, judges, and prominent politicians. Police Captain Schmittberger gave the following testimony before the Lexow Committee:

"I will ask you, before it escapes my memory, to step back with me to the Twenty-second; while in the Twenty-second did you ever hear of Georgiana Hastings?"

"Yes, sir."

"Was she one of the women that paid?"

"No, sir."

"Why did she not pay?"

"Well, she was exempt for some reason or other."

"That is the point I want to get at, the exemption."

"I couldn't tell you myself."

"How is it that she was not assessed, and, if not paying an assessment, that she was not pulled?"

"Georgiana Hastings is a very peculiar character, and some of the gentlemen who visit her house probably would not like

---

[1]Lexow Investigation, Vol. IV, pp. 4172–4178.

to see their names in print, and I presume when I went to the precinct there, that that was the reason she was never interfered with; in fact, she keeps a very quiet house, and I was given the tip, so to say, if I didn't want to burn my fingers not to have anything to do with her, and I didn't; I never saw the woman, and I wouldn't know her now if she stood before me."

"From what source did you get the tip?"

"I couldn't remember now; I think I got it from Captain Devery, if I remember right. . . ."

"Is it not a fact that you were informed that certain public officials were in the habit of visiting Georgiana Hastings' house?"

"Yes, sir."

"And some officials that graced the bench?"

"Yes, sir."

"And some officials that held commissions in the city of New York?"

"Yes, sir."

"Mr. Goff—Now, Mr. Chairman, at this point I do not wish to bring in the names of men. We have been aware of the conduct of affairs in this Hastings house. Miss Hastings, or Madam Hastings, or whatever we will call her, is under indictment. It has been a very difficult matter for us to get her here, even under a bench warrant, and we have very positive information that one night when a bench warrant was sent there for execution, that there were two officials, one a judge of a court in this city—not of a civil court—in the house, and that that warrant was not executed. While we have been extremely careful not to mention men's names, and will be extremely careful, of course, sometimes it may force itself upon us as a duty, and if it does, we will have to do it, and only under those circumstances."[1]

Captain Schmittberger testified that when he went to take charge of the Twenty-second Precinct he received orders from Police Commissioner James J. Martin, who was also the Tammany leader of the Twenty-first Assembly District and a friend of Richard Croker, not to interfere with a row of houses of prostitution in the precinct.

---

[1] Lexow Investigation, Vol. V, pp. 5373-5374.

"Just give us his exact words," asked Mr. Goff.

"He said, 'You might leave them be there and not interfere with them until the school is built'; there was a school then in erection; 'after that is built you will have to drive them out of there'; I said, 'All right'; on another occasion he telephoned for me at half-past 11 o'clock at night to be in his office the first thing in the morning; I went down there; I had received a complaint about a disorderly house from some citizens, and I sent an officer to this house to make inquiries; that was the house 250 or 252 West Fifty-first street, Mrs. Sadie West; I sent Casey there to find out what kind of a house it was, and he rang the bell, and the woman was very reluctant to give him any information; and she asked him if he knew Commissioner Martin; he said, 'Yes'; this woman said, 'Commissioner Martin is a friend of mine, and don't do anything until you hear from him'; that same evening I received a message; that was in October some time—in September, I guess, last year. [1893]. . . I received a message to be at Commissioner Martin's office the next day, and he said, 'Did you send an officer around to such and such a house?' giving the mumber; I said, 'Yes, sir; the officer did it at my direction'; he said, 'Well, you send that man back there and make him apologize, say he made a mistake.' I said, 'Hold on, commissioner, this originates from a complaint of citizens.' 'Well, I don't care; I want you to do what you are told'; so I had to send that officer back and he had to apologize, beg the woman's pardon, that he was sent there to make an investigation; I desire to correct that number; it is 234 West Fifty-first street, instead of 252." . . .[1]

This house, Captain Schmittberger testified, was in the political district of which Commissioner Martin was the Tammany leader.

The police and the politicians of Tammany Hall not only made money by protecting houses of prostitution from interference by the law or protected them from such interference because of personal friendships, but they also owned financial interests in houses of prostitution, and sometimes they suggested to citizens who owned rooming houses that they turn them into houses of prostitution. Many of the Tammany Hall

[1] Lexow Investigation, Vol. V, pp. 5362–5365.

district leaders were accused of being partners in the business of wholesale prostitution in New York City, and the foundations of several large fortunes were said to have been made in that industry. Frank Moss asked Chief of Police William S. Devery: "What about the places of a disreputable and immoral character in which your friend Senator Sullivan [Big Tim Sullivan, Tammany leader] has an interest?" Devery was caught in the trap, for he answered without thinking: "Give them police attention, and if we get the evidence arrest them the same as we do the others." Moss followed up eagerly: "What place have you in mind when you say you send the police to the immoral and disreputable places that Senator Sullivan is in? What have you in mind?" Devery recovered himself: "I don't know of any that he has." "What did you think of when you answered that question?" asked Moss. "I said that if he had any disorderly places I would give them the same attention." "You do not know whether he has any or not?" asked Moss. "Oh, I know he ain't," said Devery.[1]

The complete facts concerning the financial investments of Tammany Hall leaders in the business of prostitution are not available, because the Tammany men always covered themselves carefully by using their friends' rather than their own names. We do know, however, by the testimony before the Mazet Committee of John C. Ellis, the proprietor of a cabaret known as the White Elephant, that the police encouraged, and even urged, men to engage in the business:

"I had a private house in Thirty-ninth street, a flat house," said Mr. Ellis. "I remember a police officer making a proposition to me about that house prior to Captain Price's time. I had an arrangement there with a party, during Captain Sheehan's time. It was Detective Becker. I think that would probably be 1897, I think in the fall. . . . Detective Becker[2] came to me and says: 'You have got the flat house 118 Thirty-ninth street?' I said: 'Yes, sir.' He says: 'I want to run that house.' He says: 'I don't want you to pay any attention to

<hr>

[1]Mazet Investigation, Vol. I, pp. 178–180.

[2]Whether this Detective Becker was the same individual who later as Police Lieutenant Becker was electrocuted for the murder of the gambler, Herman Rosenthal, I have been unable to ascertain.

it at all; I will take care of that house.' Well, I was surprised at the proposition. He says: 'I will attend to putting the tenants in that house and everything; I will pass on them; you need not go near the house.'"

"What was the character of that house when you were running it?"

"I have always had a good many nice people living in that house."

"Any disorderly or disreputable people in that house?"

"Not that I know of; I have always tried to keep clear of them as much as possible. . . . Becker said: 'I want to run that house.' He said: 'You will have to turn it over to me.' I says: 'I suppose I will have to do it, if you demand it then.' I says: 'What do you expect to get out of it?' He says: 'I want $75 a month out of you.' He says: 'I will take care of the house.' 'I never went near the house at all; my collector simply collected the rent; that went on for two months. I paid $70 each of those months. It was a very good investment for me. They paid more rent. I don't really know what caused that arrangement to be terminated. I only had my opinion about it. . . . I think Becker was going too fast. I think Captain Sheehan was perfectly honest; I don't think Captain Sheehan got a cent out of that money. . . . I think when Sheehan learned of it he stopped it. . . ."

"You paid money to Detective Becker; was anybody present?"

"No, sir."

"Where did you pay him the money?"

"Generally paid him along on Broadway in the neighborhood of Fortieth street. . . . Always cash."[1]

During the period of Croker's reign, the police not only shared in the proceeds of prostitution, but they shared in the proceeds of any robberies which prostitutes might commit at the expense of the men they solicited, and they refused to protect citizens who complained that they had been robbed. We have already seen from the testimony of Hattie Ledyne that Police Captain McDonald received a diamond stud she stole from one of her transient admirers and instructed her not to forget

---

[1] Mazet Investigation, Vol. II, pp. 1591–1595.

him whenever she picked up any little thing like that. Those
who were interested financially in New York's vice industry
urged the proprietors of cabarets to encourage robbery in their
establishments and endeavoured to share in the proceeds of
such robbery. Joel S. Harris, who was a special investigator
for the Mazet Committee, told the following story of his experiences in 1899:

"On the 6th day of July I was walking through Twenty-
sixth street, between Sixth and Seventh avenues. It was late
at night. As I was passing No. 116 West Twenty-sixth street,
on the stoop there were three or four, I think it was four,
colored girls; and one of them solicited me. In fact, all three
did, but one got up and grabbed hold of me while I was against
the rail and said, 'Come up stairs.' I said, 'No, I don't care
about going.' She says, 'Come on! come on!' and she put her
arms around me, and at the same time she went in my pocket
and took a dollar which I had there, with some other money,
make-believe money, counterfeit, stage money. . . . This girl
took the money out of my pocket, it was in my vest pocket,
and immediately ran up the stairs, saying before she did,
'Well, there is nothing in you. Good bye, Honey.' She ran up
the steps. So I felt and saw that I was robbed and I went to
look after an officer. I found an officer on the corner of Twenty-
fifth street and Sixth avenue. I said, 'Officer, I have got the
rinky-dink.' He knew what it meant all right. He said, 'Where?
Down at that wench house?' I said, 'I guess that is right.'
. . . I says, 'Will you come around?' and he says, 'I can't.'
He says, 'It is not on my beat,' or something like that. So I
says, 'I want an officer.' He says, 'You will have to find a man
around there.' He laughed. . . . I says, 'John, blow your
whistle,' and he did, and three or four policemen came running
up and asked what was the matter. I told them I had been
robbed. They said, 'Where?' I told him. He said, 'Come on.'
So we got to the house; the two officers came up with me and one
stayed down with Mr. Wood. I commenced knocking on the
doors and trying them, and the officer says, 'Here, don't do
that. You will have your brains blown out.' So I said, 'I will
take the chance.' He got up to the second floor front, and I
knocked on the door, and they looked in and said, 'Was that

the party?' The officers wouldn't do it. The officers were afraid. That is when they made that remark. I had to lead the way. I opened this door and I said, 'That is not the woman,' and closed it and went on up through the house; when a door was opened a big fellow came out, and he says, 'Are you the guy that lost something?' I said, 'I lost some money.' He said, 'Just wait a minute.' He said, 'Was it a dollar bill with a lot of stage money?' I said, 'That's me.' He said, 'Here I will get this for you.' He walked inside. The policeman was standing right there. He comes out with the money. When he goes in for the money the officer says to me, 'You are a cheap son-of-a-bitch making this holler all over a dollar. I wouldn't have budged.' He said, 'You are so light you would float, to make that holler over a dollar.' He showed the men that money. They were all kidding me, and calling me all kinds of names and everything else. Before he did come out they went to go downstairs. I said, 'Hold on here until I get this thing.' I had to call them half a dozen times. So they came back and all three roasted me. One of them handed out the money and showed it to the officers, and went to show by that how cheap I was. He said, 'I wouldn't have had it happen for ten dollars.' He said, 'Here, a nice-dressed fellow like you making all this fuss over a dollar.' He says, 'Here it is.' . . . They made no effort to arrest anybody, even when I said I would make a charge."[1]

Another witness of robberies on Twenty-sixth Street, Mrs. Mary Reardon, testified that when she asked an officer why he did not do something about the men who were being robbed every night, "he gave me a very insulting remark. I will not tell it; the remark was too indecent." Mrs. Reardon also testified: "I heard these women on the stoop say they paid Captain Price half what they made, they were talking among themselves; they wasn't talking to me."

It has perhaps been noticed in the testimony of the investigator for the Mazet Committee, that when he went to get his dollar and his stage money, a man came out and handed it to him. He never saw the woman who had robbed him. It will also be remembered that in her testimony Emma Hartig told

[1]Mazet Investigation, Vol. II, pp. 2351–2354.

how most of the girls she knew had men who ruled them under the guise of protecting them. An essential part of the design which included the prostitute-police-politician *motifs* was the pimp and his cousin the cadet.

The report of the Committee of Fourteen which organized to investigate vice conditions in New York City drew this distinction between the pimp and the cadet, and it noted that both were essential in the prostitution business of New York: "The cadet is the procurer of girls for houses of prostitution, and the pimp is the protector and sharer of their earnings, whom the girl usually falls in with after she has become a prostitute. A cadet introduces her to the game and then steps out of her life. The pimp takes care of her afterwards." The Committee of Fourteen Report contained the following account of the origin and progress of the typical cadet:

"Usually he is the boy who first became acquainted with immoral women as he played about the steps or in the street in front of his tenement home. As the acquaintance grew, the women engaged him to run errands, in return for which they gave him presents of candy, fruit or pennies. As the boy grew older he found that these women were sought by different men who gave him dimes and quarters to carry messages to them or take them to apartments where they lived.

"As time goes on, the boy becomes a member of one of the street gangs in his neighborhood. Often some of the more adventuresome girls of the same age in the district are taken into the secrets of the 'gang,' and enjoy the benefits of the petty thieving carried on. The boy and girl chums soon become very intimate, and the strange loyalty begins which afterward astounds judges when they seek to secure evidence against the boys appearing before them as 'cadets.' The boys in these street gangs who develop fearlessness and physical strength later attach themselves to political leaders, and become members of district clubs, associations and athletic clubs. It is not long before they become invaluable to the politicians in certain districts through their aid as repeaters and strong arm men at the polls on election day. In the meantime, they have acquired a taste for good clothes and idleness, and fail to choose a definite remunerative occupation."

The boy who usually attached one girl to himself, and because of her affection for him persuaded her to divide the proceeds of her prostitution, soon realized the prospects of profit in a larger business, and he made an endeavour to attach more women to himself. "The height of his ambition, to have a house, is now often gratified," reported the Committee of Fourteen, "and the combined earnings of a number of women make him a rich and dangerous member of the community. Instead of obtaining protection because of his activity in the district and at the polls, he pays cash for it. Attached to his house are young men who are being trained in the now highly specialized work of 'cadets.'"[1]

How the cadet usually gained the affection of his workers was indicated by the report of the Committee of Fifteen, the successor to the Committee of Fourteen:

"His occupation is professional seduction. By occasional visits he succeeds in securing the friendship of some attractive shop-girl. By apparently kind and generous treatment, and by giving the young girl glimpses of a standard of living which she had never dared hope to attain, this friendship rapidly ripens into infatuation. The Raines law hotel or the 'furnished-room house,' with its café on the ground floor, is soon visited for refreshments. After a drugged drink, the girl wakens and finds herself at the mercy of her supposed friend. Through fear and promises of marriage she casts her fortunes with her companion and goes to live with him. The companion disappears; and the shop-girl finds herself an inmate of a house of prostitution. She is forced to receive visitors of the house. For each visitor the girl receives a brass or pasteboard check from the cashier of the house entitling her to twenty-five cents. The 'cadet' returns to the house at frequent intervals, takes the checks from his victim, and cashes them at the cashier's desk.

"Within the last year [1901] six 'cadets' have been sent to State prison for abducting girls under the age of eighteen years. The facts were substantially similar in all the cases, and in

---

[1] *The Social Evil in New York City. A Study of Law Enforcement by the Research Committee of the Committee of Fourteen*, pp. 61-62.

the majority of them the victims were physical wrecks when rescued."[1]

The girl whose case was described as typical in the above report could not escape from the house where she was confined, because usually her clothes were taken from her. Meanwhile, her friend was dividing his time between making new female acquaintances and doing minor favours for Tammany politicians and the police, so that any appeals to the law against him might be eternally ineffective. Election Day was his busiest day, for then he rounded up all the assistants he could find and voted the straight Tammany ticket as often as possible without undue risk of jail. The risk was not high because he knew the men who made the judges.

The pimp usually did not work with a regular house of prostitution but controlled his own private flock of girls, who worked for him and turned over their earnings to him. Threats of arrest, and actual arrest, followed if the girl did not consent to give her friend her earnings. And sometimes, as Emma Hartig testified, force was used. Fictitious charges were brought in court against recalcitrant girls. Dr. Morris Behrman, an East Side physician, testified that in summer when the windows were open in Allen Street and Rivington Street, and when the people lived on the streets and the stoops of the tenements, he often saw the pimps fighting with their girls for the money they had just made.

"I heard them," he testified, "ask her for the money right on the street, and she will give up a half a dollar and he will say, 'There was more.' He will say, 'I saw two men go into the place—two or three men'; and she was trying to steal from him, or for herself a certain amount, and the first thing there would be a fight, and the poor woman gets the worst of it naturally; that is understood.

"It is pretty hard for us respectable people to sustain ourselves there," said Dr. Behrman, "it certainly is. . . . It seems complaints have no effect, or lately they have not had any.

---

[1]*The Social Evil with Special Reference to Conditions Existing in the City of New York. A Report Prepared (in 1902) Under the Direction of the Committee of Fifteen*, pp. 155–159.

... I presume it is because the district is managed from a political standpoint rather than from a civic standpoint. There is a boss in the district. That boss is recognized as potential in police matters. That is the way I understand it. That is the general feeling of the people in my district. Martin Engel is the boss of the East Side."[1]

General Bingham wrote concerning the relations of Tammany Hall and the pimps of the East Side:

"I do not and never have believed that Tammany, as much as I hate Tammany, officially recognizes these fellows. But if they pay their dues regularly and perform their part willingly at election time, Tammany does not ask questions, and when a faithful henchman runs afoul of the police, Tammany will 'take care' of him. Policemen know this. Some of them take bribe money to keep hands off, but even the honest men hesitate to arrest a man who is 'strong' with the organization. They know, too, that conviction is impossible without the woman's testimony, and in only one case out of a hundred will she testify against her master."[2]

Samuel H. London, a United States government expert on the White Slave traffic, testified before the Curran Committee, and made this significant statement:

"I say that in a great many instances which appeared in the reports handed to me, individuals of the Police Department, usually, I believe in most cases, the uniformed men, and in some instances others, would intervene between the pimp and a prostitute whenever she became obstreperous and refused to remain under his submission any longer, and in that way would help him get her back to him, or do some other things like that." When he was asked to estimate the number of such instances, he answered that there were a great many, and that he could not estimate them accurately. He finally estimated that there were more than a hundred such cases with which he had come in contact.[3]

---

[1]Mazet Investigation, Vol. II, pp. 2033–2040.

[2]*The Girl That Disappears*, by General Theodore A. Bingham, pp. 61–62.

[3]Curran Investigation, Vol. IV, pp. 3229–3230.

Mayor Robert A. Van Wyck, who was Croker's Mayor at the time of the Mazet Investigation, testified before that Committee concerning vice conditions in New York, and this was his reaction to them:

"And all the laws are better enforced now than they have been within your memory?" Moss asked.

"Yes, sir; I think there are a few harlots in town, and there is a lot of liquor sold, as there is all over the State, . . ." the Mayor answered.

"You have said there are a few harlots. Have you ever been solicited on the streets?"

"Oh, in days gone by, when I was a young fellow, yes, sir," the Mayor said.

"In your term of office?"

"No."

"Never have been? Do you know that we now have male harlots thronging the streets, who have their peculiar places of resort, which can be found as easily as any saloon can be? Do you know that?"

"No, I do not."

"But what do you think of the male department of that industry that has become so large in the city of New York in the last two years?"

"I know nothing about it. All I know about it is what occurred in London a few years ago. That is all I recollect about it." [The Mayor was referring to the trial of Oscar Wilde.]

"You never heard of it in the city of New York?"

"No, sir."

"How is that?"

"They didn't indulge in that when I was a boy," answered the Mayor.

"What do you mean by that?"

"It was not going on then."

"What has that got to do with the condition of New York now—your knowledge of the condition of New York now?"

"My knowledge of the condition is as I observe it, as I pass through."

"What has the condition when you were a boy got to do with

the condition now, while you are mayor of the City, for the last two years?"

"I think those boys do now what I did when I was a boy," answered the Mayor.

"You do?"

"Yes, sir, I don't think society is any worse than it was then."

"I did not think that you meant we should draw any inference from your probable course of life, and I am very sorry if you meant we should. I conceive this matter to be too serious a matter, and on too high a plane of public morals to deal with in any such way as that."

"Put a question. Ask a question and I will answer it."

"Mr. Moss—I am surprised that the mayor should discuss things in that way."

"The Witness—You are morbid about conditions of crime."

"Mr. Moss—It would be better for us if the mayor were a little more so."[1]

Chief of Police Devery was even more indifferent to complaints about vice. When he was a captain of police in 1893 Devery told the pastor of the Allen Street Memorial Church, the Rev. Mr. Hamilton, who came to the station house in complaint about prostitutes, that "Men that are looking for that sort of thing can find plenty of it." He also had a clergyman thrown out of the Eldridge Street station house who came to protest about prostitutes. But after he himself was solicited when he was walking in citizens' clothes on the East Side, he was very angry. Henry Hoffman, the proprietor of the house into which Devery was invited as he passed by, was called to the police station next morning. "I told him what my name was," testified Hoffman, and he says, 'You son-of-a-bitch, that is you, is it?' 'Well,' he says, 'if them women cows of yours call me up again, I will take you by the neck and throw you out of the house.'" A few days later, Captain Devery's wardman, Glennon, called on Hoffman and demanded $10 a month more because of the insult to Captain Devery. Hoffman also testified that he had paid Devery $500 when he opened his house.[2] It

[1]Mazet Investigation, Vol. I, pp. 940–941.
[2]Lexow Investigation, Vol. II, pp. 1538–1539.

was one thing for a police captain to receive $500 and $50 a month, but it was quite another for a respectable family man in citizens' clothes, who happened to be a captain of police during his working hours, to be annoyed by "women cows" when he was taking an unofficial walk through a New York street.

The conditions of prostitution revealed by Dr. Parkhurst, the Lexow Committee, and the Mazet Committee created a stir among certain classes of the community, and a committee was formed to investigate and to do something about prostitution in New York City. This committee soon found that one of the adjuncts to prostitution in New York was the Raines Law which had been passed by the New York State Legislature in 1896. Senator Raines, who was an ardent prohibitionist, was not so concerned with sexual relations, and though he did not foresee the effect of his law on prostitution, its effect was great. The Raines Law provided that only hotels could sell liquor on Sunday, and the Sunday saloon trade was extremely important to liquor dealers, for Sunday being a day of leisure, and an insufferably dull day because of that, men who worked all week had time and money to drink and to forget the surrounding lack of life. Every saloon that could manage it immediately became a hotel; something had to be done with the rooms that entitled the establishment to such official designation, and the most profitable thing to do with them was to rent them out to men and women who wished sexual intercourse, for people who wished comfort would not live above saloons.

An interesting scene took place in Albany in 1909. Senator Thomas F. Grady, Tammany's current silver-tongued orator, was somewhat notorious for his overindulgence in liquor. It was said in Albany that the only man who could handle him was Senator James J. Frawley, the Tammany leader, and that Senator Grady had even been known to threaten his friend Senator Frawley with a whisky bottle as a weapon in the President's room of the Senate, when Mr. Frawley was urging him strenuously to pull himself together. Senator Raines, who was then Republican leader of the Senate, took occasion during the session of 1909 to refer on the floor of the Senate by several innuendoes to the well-known failing of his Democratic colleague. Senator Grady, whose heavy features were not unimpressive in a scene, rose in his place and said to the Senate that he himself appreciated his failings, that he did his best to overcome them, but—and then turning to Senator Raines, and with his most effective oratorical gesture—he bellowed that no one had ever been able to accuse *him* of immorality with women. It was also well known to the members of the Senate and the population of Albany that Senator Raines had laid himself open to such accusations in a rather obvious manner. It is curious that the Senator who was responsible for the spread of prostitution by his law regulating liquor should have exemplified in his own personal prejudices the preference for women over whisky.

The laws that had been passed from time to time regulating the traffic in women and in liquor played into the hands of Tammany Hall and its leaders. New York has always contained a large pleasure-loving population, whose habits have been somewhat pagan. Any attempts to control too rigidly the desires of this population were of profit to Tammany men, who were the instruments for safe violation of the law. In return, they received a money consideration. In that way, the moralist was satisfied, for there was the law on the statute books; Tammany men were more than satisfied, for the profits in violating the law were large; and the people who wanted their vices were also satisfied, except that the cost of living that way increased. Tammany Hall helped people commit their sins, and there is no one more attractive than an efficient evil companion.

The Committee of Fifteen recognized this situation when it recommended a change in attitute toward prostitution, suggesting that a distinction should be drawn between a crime and a sin, and that prostitution should be taken from the first category and placed in the latter. "We hasten to add," the prominent members added, "that this proposition should by no means be understood as a plea in favor of laxer moral judgments. A sin is not less odious because it is not treated as a crime. . . . Nevertheless, some of the more grievous sins are not subjected to legal penalties, simply because it is recognized that such penalties cannot be enforced, and a law on the statute book that cannot be enforced is a whip in the hands of the blackmailer."[1]

---

[1] *The Social Evil*, Report of the Committee of Fifteen, p. 152.

Mayor William J. Gaynor, who said that he was a student of the problem of prostitution and had looked into the literature of the subject, "beginning with St. Augustine, and ending in our own times with Lecky in his *History of European Morals*," advised the Curran Committee not "to burn its fingers with this awful subject, mournful subject, one more to weep over than to try to make political capital of, without first having read the literature of it from St. Augustine down to yesterday and then they will know what the subject is, and they will know that if you—by the way we have now places to lock up about a thousand of these women, I think, but if we could take the whole 25,000 of them and lock them up, their places would be promptly taken by others, as everybody knows." "We have to deal with it," Mayor Gaynor added, "the best we can under the law and minimize it and put it into the hearts of people, of men, not to seduce women, and as to the merchants and store-keepers and manufacturers, to put it into their hearts to pay women wages that don't drive them on the town and into prostitution, and things like that we have got to do by slow degrees until the evil is done away with entirely. But for a man to pay a woman three dollars a week and then accuse me and say that there are too many prostitutes in the City of New York is infamous, and there are people here who are doing just that thing. (Loud applause by the spectators, and order rapped for by Chairman Curran.)"[1]

The Mayor also wrote in a letter that the tendency of prostitutes was to congregate in a few localities. "To prevent this tendency and scatter them all over the city," he thought, "would be the worst thing that could happen. By their example they would scandalize other women and girls all over the city and cause them to go astray." The moralists who were aroused by the revelations of conditions in New York endeavoured to scatter the prostitutes and succeeded in doing so; now there are practically no prostitutes on the streets of New York, but to what extent the "gold-digger" has become a type as common as the street-walker was, is a question open to research.

Another commentator viewed the situation sadly from an-

---

[1]Curran Investigation, Vol. I, pp. 40-42.

other point of view. John J. Hickey, Officer 787 retired, wrote
in his book, *Our Police Guardians*:

"Yes, my friends, they were the happy days in the old fourth
ward, A. D. before Dr. Parkhurst and his leap-frog tactics, when
the sailors of the seven seas would find their way to either
Water, Cherry, Roosevelt, or James street to greet the women
of their hearts' desire, spend their money with them, and when
all was gone reship and go get more.

"But since the Parkhurst crusade the poor sailor is as much
at sea in New York as he would be in the Indian Ocean, for he
knows not where to go to find his woman, but into some tenement or apartment house among decent people, yes, and into
some of our first-class hotels, and among the nobility of Riverside Drive. The poor unfortunate girls ran into every hole,
they have to live, and men and women must have their pleasures, hence this necessary evil existed in certain quarters of
this city, and in those quarters only the young man of that day,
after working hard all week, would visit Wooster or Greene
Streets or south Fifth Avenue on the west side, Forsyth or
Delancey on the east, and finish the job and go home happy for
another week, but now and since the Parkhurst crusade brought
about by investigation of the Mazet Committee, that wound up
like all other investigation committees, doing nothing but robbing the state treasury, and destroying the good name of little
old New York, more's the pity."

After the startling revelations of the Mazet Committee
Richard Croker realized that he must do something about vice,
and he therefore appointed his own vice exterminating Committee of Five. Croker called a meeting of the Tammany Hall
Executive Committee in November, 1900, and told the district
leaders that "he and Tammany Hall had not been and would
not be mixed up with any toleration of vice for profit." Coroner
Fitzpatrick, leader of the Fourth District, rose to explain the
difficulty of keeping vice out of the tenement house district.
Croker interrupted him and roughly denounced him as one
who tried to evade responsibility, warning him that once the
people understood what could be done on the East Side, they
would have no use for political leaders who could not be of

positive assistance to them. "Mr. Fitzpatrick," reported the *Sun*, "lost his temper when Mr. Croker said that even policemen had been solicited in the Coroner's district and retorted that more policemen had solicited women than had been solicited by women."[1]

After this singular repartee Mr. Isadore Straus told of conditions on the East Side, and Croker urged his district leaders to do everything in their power to aid Mr. Straus in his laudable effort to stamp out the evil of prostitution. "I am not talking for political effect," he concluded. "I am talking of what you should do as honest citizens." Then he himself thanked them for their "splendid work for Democracy in the city," bade them farewell, and sailed for his semi-annual horse-racing and pleasure trip to England.

Tammany Hall and the police also profited from the activities of various dives of a miscellaneous nature in the City. Some of these were known as Paresis Hall, Manila Hall, The Black Rabbit, and The Palm, where men of homosexual tendencies performed publicly for the benefit of any one who cared to admire them. Paresis Hall was on Fourth Avenue between Twelfth and Thirteenth streets.

Joel Harris, investigator for the Mazet Committee, testified:

"These men conduct themselves there—well, they act effeminately; most of them are painted and powdered; they are called Princess this and Lady So and So and the Duchess of Marlboro, and get up and sing as women, and dance; ape the female character; call each other sisters and take people out for immoral purposes. I have had these propositions made to me, and made repeatedly."

George P. Hammond, Jr., another investigator for the Committee, testified that in line of duty he had been in Paresis Hall a number of times:

"They have one woman who goes there they call a hermaphrodite. These male degenerates solicit men at the tables, and I believe they get a commission on all drinks that are purchased there; they get checks. . . . I have been received there with open

---

[1] The *Sun*, November 16, 1900.

arms. . . . One night we were there we saw Captain Chapman come in there and stand and look around about two or three minutes, and then speak to the proprietor four or five minutes, and then walk out."[1]

Two famous resorts protected by politicians and police were Billy McGlory's Armory Hall in Hester Street and Owney Geoghegan's place in the Bowery. Geoghegan boasted that Captain Foley's raid on his place cost the captain his position on the force; and after the raid Geoghegan held a mock wake over Foley in his establishment. McGlory and Geoghegan, who were intense rivals, were finally sent to prison and died soon after their release. "Geoghegan's funeral," wrote James L. Ford, "was an imposing event. Two wives attended, and the drivers of their respective hacks fought all the way to Calvary for the place of precedence directly behind the hearse, each widow hoping that in this fashion she could establish conjugal rights." Billy McGlory, after he came out of jail, conducted a livery stable, and he once remarked to a friend: "These horses can kick but thank God they can't go to the District Attorney."

Tammany Hall and the police protected the saloon keepers against arrest for violation of the excise laws, and the saloon keepers paid liberally for that protection. At one time during the Croker period an agreement was reached between the liquor dealers' association and Tammany Hall that the saloon keepers were no longer to pay cash for their protection to the police, but that instead they were to give the Tammany ticket complete support and to work in their saloons and outside for the election of the candidates of Tammany Hall.

How dependent upon the police and the politicians a man was who wished to operate a saloon in New York during the 1890's was illustrated vividly in the testimony before the Mazet Committee of Simon Buttner:

"I started a business on the Bowery between Houston and Bleecker streets in 1890," said Mr. Buttner, "I did not see any police captain at that time. I have seen politicians. I just came to the city of New York as a country jay, and I have seen a certain politician, and he told me I have got to see the police if I

---

[1] Mazet Investigation, Vol. II, pp. 1429, 1431–1432.

wanted to do business on the Bowery. I couldn't mention the name of the politician. I don't remember now. . . . I went to see Inspector Williams but I couldn't see him, only a man by the name of Price. That is the present captain, James K. Price. He was then a roundsman. I seen him and I told him what kind of business I have and where I am located, and he told me I can only do business with him, and I did it. He said to me I was to give him a hundred dollars a month, 'and anything that comes off.' I didn't know at that time what he meant by 'anything that comes off.' I didn't understand the slang at that time. But I gave him—I paid him regular $100."

"What about anything that comes off; what were you to do then?"

"I remember very well now what it means. If a trick is turned—what they call, in the slang—that he was to get half of it, or a third of it."

"That is, if somebody was robbed?"

"Yes, sir. . . ."

"Did any tricks come off?"

"Yes, sir, one. . . ."

"Will you just explain to the committee what the trick was? We want to know all about it."

"Yes, sir; that trick was: One day Price sent to me to meet him at the corner of Bleecker and the Bowery. He says, 'Buttner, how about that trick that came off last night?' I said, 'What is it?' 'Here is a man that lost $400 and a gold watch.' I said, 'I know nothing about it.' . . . He never spoke any more about it. There was complaint from the neighbors."

"What?"

"About the music being too loud. The houses in the rear, on Elizabeth street—they complained, and every time the complaint went to headquarters Price used to send for me or come around himself, and it cost me another $40 or another $50 or $25 to square it. Especially one certain man that has lived back there, by the name of Taylor, that owned that property. He was the most expensive what we called kicker in the neighborhood."

"He cost you something every time he kicked?"

"Every time he kicked, and he was a hard kicker and he couldn't be fixed. . . . I had nothing but a saloon and a little music in it."

"I suppose the people who patronized your place were not of the best character?"

"Well, it was not a Sunday school, that I dare say; but just as frequented as any other saloons. . . ."

Mr. Buttner prospered in his saloon with a little music in it, and he moved uptown into the Tenderloin district. Price, now a police captain, visited him again in his new establishment:

"When he came there the first night, he sent in for me, my bartender. I came out. He says: 'Hello, is that you here?' I says: 'Yes.' 'Since when are you here?' I told him since when, as we were old acquaintances, college chums. So he says: 'Well, what are you doing, what kind of business are you doing?' I says: 'I am doing a legitimate business.' He stood in the door and he looked inside, and he seen some French women in there. He says: 'Buttner, there are some French women in there. I want them out of there.' I says: 'Captain, that is hardly possible; they are very good customers; they are as good spenders as we have got. They do eat the best. I have got to look out for my expenses.' I was under rental of $8,000 a year. My expense was $800 to $900 a week in that place. Naturally I could not drive any trade away. I says: 'Captain, how can I do that?' He said: 'Well, we want to drive them into the houses. We don't want them around there.'"

"What houses?"

"That is the usual language that is used when they want them to go into the fast houses. I says: 'Captain, I always did as you tell me to do, didn't I?' He says: 'Yes, I know you did.' I says: 'Who will I have to do business with?' He says: 'I will let you know in a day or two.' He came along the following day, or the day after, and set the price. 'It will cost you $150 a month, and the same old thing, anything that comes off.' I says: 'Hold on, Captain, there is nothing comes off here. I don't let out a room. I am doing now a straightforward business.' He said: 'I don't care a God damn if you let out a hundred rooms a night. I want $150 a month.' Now, he is not a man that you can sit down and consult with him and speak gently with, because he is as liable to hit you as look at you, if you are always contradicting him. I know the best thing is to let him go. I says: 'Captain, who will I have to do business with?' He says: 'Bob Nelson.' I says: 'Who is Bob Nelson?' He told me who he was. I says: 'Oh, no, Captain, I ain't doing such things as that. . . . No, Captain, I am too old in the business to throw my liberty into the hands of Bob Nelson. If I can't do business with you, I don't do no business with no politician or no saloon keeper'; and he didn't like that at all; but he commenced to arrest."

"Arrest what?"

"To make excise arrests."

"Had you not had any excise arrests before that?"

"No, sir, not excise arrests. . . . I had never had arrests before until this last place in the Broadway Garden. I got them by the wholesale there. . . ."

"Well, you were not willing to go to see Bob Nelson?"

"Not to see him. So I thought the best was—I have got too much money invested; I must go and see him. I went there to see him at least a half a dozen times. He was always denied to me. Then I seen that the thing was too late, and I couldn't do no business with him. Then I was advised to go to see Al Adams."

"That is the policy king?" [Head of the syndicate of policy gambling shops.]

"That is the policy king. He is also brewer of the Karsh Brewery. He is the owner of this Karsh Brewery."

"What has that to do with it?"

"By taking beer from him you are all right. You will be protected. . . ."

"Did you get word from him?"

"He says: 'Buttner cannot be protected in this precinct.' My man asked him: 'What did he do?' He says: 'Well, he got in trouble over in Broadway there. He didn't do like the boys wanted him to do, and consequently they won't touch him.' . . . That was the message that came back."

"While you were having these excise arrests were there other places in the neighborhood that were open and doing business all night?"

"Yes, sir, and running in a fierce manner."

"What do you mean by a 'fierce manner'?"

"Well, it would be disgraceful to mention it here in the public. Like some of those places are running."

"Now?"

"Now, and had been at that time."

"You mean in an immoral manner?"

"In an immoral manner."

"And publicly so?"

"It was so, open doors day and night. . . . Free to enter for everybody and anybody."

"Did you have any other interviews with Captain Price after that, or with anyone connected with him?"

"Yes, sir, I had one interview with Captain Price. I went to see his brother, who was a perfect gentleman. It must have been some mistake between the two anyhow; and he made an appointment that I should meet his brother that same night. We met right in front of the Greeley statue. Sam Price, his brother, came and fetched me, and I went out to meet him out there, and I told him, 'Captain, how is that, that you and I can't get along?' 'Well,' he says, 'I will tell you Simon, I have got nothing against you personally; never did have anything'; but he says, 'You can't stay in this precinct. There is something else behind it. Now, the best thing you can do is to get out of the precinct.' 'Well,' I says: 'I have got too much money invested here. I have got at least eight to ten thousand dollars invested in the business. How can I get out?' He says: 'Try and sell out.' I says: 'Let me alone until I can sell out,' and I was willing to give up. So that was the understanding."

Apparently, Simon Buttner had offended Bob Nelson, the Tammany worker and King of the Tenderloin, by saying that he would not have dealings with him, and it was impossible for Buttner to keep a saloon in the Tenderloin after that. Whether or not Nelson wanted Buttner to give him an interest in his business, which was sometimes the proposition Tammany men made to dive keepers, the testimony did not bring out. The rulers of the district were determined to make trouble for Buttner and to drive him out of the Tenderloin, and an attempt was made to have a man robbed in Buttner's saloon. A waiter was hired to testify falsely that he was a witness to the robbery, and to implicate Buttner.

The difference between the protection and indulgence granted to a saloon keeper who stood in well with the authorities and the treatment of one who was out of favour was vividly illustrated by Buttner's testimony describing the scene when he was arrested for an excise law violation. The policemen who arrested him took him past the uptown saloon of the Tammany man, "Silver Dollar" Smith. Buttner described the scene of his arrest and his treatment in the station house:

"When we passed by when I went along with the officer, Silver Dollar Smith's place was open, and the noise loud enough to wake people fourteen blocks away. I says, 'Why don't you make an arrest there?' He says, 'I don't know, Captain Price told me to bring you, and that is all I know about it.' . . . They wouldn't accept no bail. Now, I think for my $1,600 I pay a year, I ought to have as much privilege as Silver Dollar Smith has, or any other of those dive keepers down in the Tenderloin, or any common prostitute that walks the street; she can be bailed out, and my work people that are working for a living to support their families—I think they ought to have as much rights; and they could never get bailed out; they were always held in. Of course, if I could get Bob Nelson, but Bob Nelson wouldn't bail me. That would be getting into their line. That wouldn't do."

"Does Bob Nelson bail most of the people up there?"

"All the women. Nobody else has a chance there. If he does, they will find fault with them immediately."

"It is well understood that they pay him for his kind acts?"

"The kind act is simply for—the way I understand, and on pretty good authority I am speaking, $5 for prostitutes, and $15 or $20 for larceny, and so forth."

"That is the current rate?"

"Yes, sir. As the *World* claims, it is better than a President's position; pays better, rather—not better, but it pays better. . . ."

Buttner described the following scene when he reached the station house:

"Was there anything special about Price's treatment of you?"

"Oh, he didn't handle me with kid gloves. He had none on."

"What did he do?"

"It was more what I done. If I had said a word, I would probably have been out of there as a cripple. . . . The first reception he gave me was, 'Buttner, I have got you.' 'For what?' 'I have got you'—grinding his teeth. . . . So, to shorten this, Captain Price tried in every way to corner me. I explained exactly how everything stood, how the circumstances were. But I might as well talk to a blind wall. He was going to railroad me. So he took me out to the desk, and said: 'Search this man.' They searched me, even my shoes and stockings and under my shirt I was searched. I says: 'Can I send out for counsel?' 'No.' 'Can I send out for a cigar?' 'No.'"

"With the lower jaw protruding in that way?"

"That always extends. Like a bull dog. He would not allow me counsel or a cup of coffee or anything there. 'If you bring an half a dozen justices here this time, you can't get bailed out.'"[1]

The proceeds from gambling in New York City were organized efficiently during the Croker period for the benefit of several leading men in Tammany Hall, and particularly for the benefit of "Big Tim" Sullivan. A syndicate was operated by Sullivan, who was then a State Senator and Tammany district leader of the Bowery district, Frank Farrell, the leading professional gambler of his day, and William S. Devery, Chief of Police of New York. Evidence of the existence of this syndicate was given to the Mazet Committee by Matthew McConnell, a retired policeman, who testified that he was instructed by Police Inspector Brooks to visit a pool room at 54 West Twenty-ninth Street where bets on horse races were placed. He was told to get evidence against the proprietor of this place, Frank Farrell. Then Senator Sullivan came down from Albany, called at Police Commissioner Sexton's office, and Patrolman McConnell was retired. Soon afterward Devery, "Big Tim" Sullivan's gambling-house partner, was made Chief of Police of New York.[1]

The New York *Times* reported in March, 1900, that there was in existence in New York City a secret gambling commis-

---

[1]Mazet Investigation, Vol. I, pp. 501–522.

[2]*Ibid.*, pp. 1006–1007.

sion consisting of "a commissioner, who is at the head of one of the city departments, two State Senators, and the dictator of the pool-room syndicate of this city, who was before the Mazet Committee, and who is allied to Tammany Hall." This commission, according to the *Times*, took in $3,095,000 a year in graft from gambling-house proprietors. Apparently, the Tammany leaders allowed the police to retain a large part of the graft from houses of prostitution and saloons, but this syndicate kept the gambling graft for its own. The *Times* gave the following itemized account of the annual proceeds:

"Pool rooms, 400, at $300 per month,
    $120,000 per year.................... $1,440,000
Crap games, 500, at $150 per month,
    $75,000 per year....................... 900,000
Gambling houses, 200, at $150 per month,
    $30,000 per year....................... 360,000
Gambling houses, large, 20 at $1,000 per month,
    $20,000 per year....................... 240,000
Envelope games, 50, at $50 per month,
    $2,500 per year....................... 30,000
Policy................................... 125,000
            "Total............ $3,095,000."[1]

No new gambling houses, crap games, policy shops, or pool rooms were permitted to open without the sanction of this un-official, but powerful, Tammany commission.

This was the period of the Spanish-American War, and the passwords used over the telephone in the racing pool rooms were taken from the slogans and battles of that war. When the man who answered the telephone in a racing pool room picked up the receiver, he was told to say "Havana," before he said anything else, and then to wait for the answer, "Remember the *Maine*," before mentioning his business. In case policemen who were not known were in the room at the time the telephone rang with the latest information from the race tracks, the man at the telephone was instructed to say "Siegel-Cooper," the name of the well-known department store, "and then put your 'phone away." "I will understand that that means danger and

[1] New York *Times*, March 9, 1900.

will call you up again in twenty minutes," James A. Mahoney, "the pool-room king," told his men. "If you don't answer, I will call you up again in twenty minutes, and will keep that up until I hear from you in response to my call."[1]

Richard Croker's own vice-investigating Committee of Five, with his friend Lewis Nixon as chairman, investigated and reported that conditions were not nearly so bad as they were painted, and that Tammany Hall was in no way connected with the criminality of the City. The committee men also found it impossible to discover any evidence of illegal gambling. The day after this report, William Travers Jerome, who was then a Police Court Justice, raided in person a pool room at 20 Dey Street. Usually, the gambling houses had been warned of raids as soon as the raiders applied for a warrant, but Jerome had put the warrant in his pocket after signing it and conducted the raid himself immediately, in company with Lewis Nixon and several others. He opened his court in the gambling house which he raided.

One man came to Jerome and said: "Mr. Jerome, I can't afford to be caught here; you must help me out." "You don't seem to understand that this is a courtroom," Jerome answered. "Hold up your hand and be sworn." When the man hesitated, he added: "You can take your choice, and take it quickly; go to jail for contempt of court, or hold up your hand." The man was sworn. "What is your name?" he was asked. "John Doe," he answered. "I shall be obliged to commit John Doe to the House of Detention in order to find him when I want him," Jerome said. "I do not know his residence." Then the man told who he was. His name was Maurice F. Holahan, and he was the President of the Board of Public Works of the City and a leading member of Tammany Hall. The next day Holahan explained to the newspapers that he was only in the gambling house looking for his wayward son. But the town laughed, and the son was indignant, and made a statement concerning his relations with his father:

"If my father had stopped with that original statement of his I would not have been heard from," Frank M. Holahan's statement read, "but he is piling it on pretty heavy. This, too,

[1]Mazet Investigation, Vol. II, pp. 1233-1234.

after he has been the cause of ruining my business, which netted the firm, which was run under my name in the Park Row Building, no less than $200,000 a year, and brought me personally no less than $50,000 a year. All, too, because I married the girl of my choice.

"The firm of which I speak was known after I left it as the Realty Protective Company. . . . We made a specialty of protecting property holders when condemnation proceedings had been brought by the city.

"In such cases as that my name—the name of my father, rather—helped us out wonderfully. I do not mean to imply that my father threw work into our hands because of his public position, but there is no doubt that his name and his advice did help us. Clients, for example, would not believe that my father would not help us in spite of our protests to the contrary.

"In order to compete with firms in our line we engaged solicitors. These solicitors never revealed the name of the firm until forced to. Then it usually occurred that the prospective client would ask:

"'What is the name of your firm?'

"My name was then mentioned, because the business was run under my name.

"'Is he any relation to President Holahan, of the Board of Public Improvements?' was generally the next question.

"It was then admitted that I was his son. That was enough.

"Our business was so prosperous that I at times refused to accept clients for no very good reason. We never took less than 10 per cent. for our work, and yet we did more business than any of our contemporaries who accepted 3 per cent. I was frequently pitted against my father, who represented the city, and who often won out. He made me mad at times, because he denied me fees that he could have thrown my way. My father goes to the extent of being Puritanical in his ideas about honesty. I do not go quite so far. I am content to be merely honest as honesty is understood between man and man nowadays. I think, for example, that when a man is in a position to throw business either into the hands of a friend or of a man whom he does not know he ought to give it to his friend."[1]

---

[1]*Ten Months of Tammany*, a pamphlet published by the City Club, pp. 62–63.

Besides the gambling-house business Tammany leaders managed the prize fighting in New York State during the period of Croker's reign. "Big Tim" Sullivan controlled a monopoly of prize fighting in Manhattan. Prize fighting was restricted by the Horton boxing law to athletic clubs, and immediately clubs were formed, but they had to get permission from the Police Department to operate, and no clubs were licensed which did not belong to "Big Tim" Sullivan. A profit of $50,000 during one year was said to come from the leading club of this kind. Fighters who refused to fight in Sullivan's clubs could not get permission to fight anywhere in New York State.[1]

Croker himself, as soon as he grew rich, became intensely interested in "the sport of kings." In 1892, he attempted to have a part of Central Park turned into a race course, but the publicity created by the passage of this bill for a semi-private track at the expense of the City was too harmful, and the bill was repealed. Croker owned an interest in several race tracks, and his horses ran at them. He was, therefore, anxious that people should go to the track and place their bets rather than do so through the pool rooms. All the pool rooms in New York were closed one day when Croker told Superintendent Byrnes of the Police that he wished them closed. Then Croker transferred his racing activities to England, and all the pool rooms in New York opened again.[2]

VI

Graft from prostitution, saloons, and gambling was not the only source of Tammany profit. The outstanding development of the Croker period in Tammany Hall was the beginning of an alliance between Tammany Hall and large corporate enterprise. Croker himself had started the relations between Tammany Hall and big business, but it was left for Murphy to carry that partnership to its perfection.

In the 1890's large corporations began the practice of contributing to the election funds of both parties, and Tammany Hall received its liberal allowance in New York City. Theodore Roosevelt testified in the libel suit which William Barnes, Jr.,

[1] *Harper's Weekly*, Vol. XLII, pp. 1045–1046, article entitled "'Wide Open' New York," by Franklin Matthews, 1898.

[2] *Harper's Weekly*, Vol. XLII, p. 1045; Mazet Investigation, Vol. I, pp. 299–300, 483.

brought against him that Barnes told him that Anthony Brady, the traction magnate, always contributed to the Democratic and the Republican campaign funds, "not as a matter of politics, but as a matter of business, because he could not have the great interests that he represented exposed to attacks by demagogues and scoundrels in the Legislature." "I believe," said Roosevelt, "that the expression he used was that it would be unjust to the widows and orphans who had invested in the concerns of which he was the head."[1]

Roosevelt testified that Mr. Platt also spoke to him of the responsibility to their widows and orphans of the millionaires who directed large enterprises. Neither the political bosses nor the corporation directors ever seemed to think of the millions of widows and orphans who were not in receipt of dividends from corporations. The latter were dependent upon the haphazard benevolence of philanthropic millionaires and Tammany Hall district leaders whose sense of righteousness was not always, perhaps, so reliable as the impersonal but protective action of the state might be, if uncorrupted by the combined efforts of bosses and corporations.

Tammany Hall was always anxious and willing to help a large corporation in return for money, and the Republicans were also just as willing wherever and whenever they were in power. The competition between the two parties sometimes put the corporation in a strategic position, and there were instances of men being placed in positions of political power by the corporations. Charles E. Hughes asked E. H. Harriman, during the insurance investigation of 1905: "Well, it has been openly charged that through your relations with Mr. Odell you have political influence; what would you say to that?" Harriman answered, "Well, I should think that Mr. Odell had political influence because of his relations to me."

Sometimes a corporation cheated Tammany Hall out of its spoils. In the campaign of 1893 the president of a corporation called a meeting of the directors to consider a contribution of $15,000 to the Tammany Hall campaign fund. The directors voted for the payment. It had been arranged that three checks should be drawn, one to the local boss, presumably Mr. Croker,

---

[1] *Barnes vs. Roosevelt*, Case on Appeal, Vol. I, pp. 216–217.

another to the state leader, and a third to the fund of the campaign committee. The checks were drawn on the Saturday before election and were to be called for on Monday, the day before election, but the cashier in charge of the safe where the checks were deposited was called away Monday, and when the checks were called for, they could not be taken out that day. The representative of Tammany was told to call on Wednesday. The election was held on Tuesday, and Tammany Hall lost control of the state legislature. When the checks were called for on Wednesday, the representative of the Boss was told that it had been decided not to give any money that year, inasmuch as the Democrats had nothing to deliver.[1]

Tammany politicians, and especially Croker, have always taken an intense interest in the transit facilities of the City of New York, and for some years they strenuously and effectively blocked the construction of a subway, because they felt that it would interfere with the business of the elevated railroad, in which they held stock. Whenever Croker was asked about the possibilities of a subway in New York City, he ridiculed the idea and called it a hole in the ground; it will be remembered that Tammany politicians in the first quarter of the Nineteenth Century called DeWitt Clinton's Erie Canal "a big ditch."

Tammany Hall and Croker were torn between two temptations. One was to continue to work for the street railway companies and the elevated railroad then existing, which paid them well and were certain of return; the other was to get the colossal contract for building the subway, which would amount to at least $50,000,000, and could be made to pay like a bank. Republican Boss Platt of New York State, and Governor Hill, its Democratic Boss, however, did not intend to give Tammany Hall such delightful pickings without a struggle, and, to guard against the possibility, they created the Rapid Transit Commission. The newspapers and the public were clamouring for a subway. London had had a successful one for many years, and it seemed absurd that New York should have nothing but overcrowded street cars and an overburdened

---

[1]The *Century Magazine*, Vol. XLVIII (n.s. Vol. XXVI), 1894, p. 670, article, "The Price of Peace," by Joseph B. Bucklin.

elevated railway. The act of the Legislature which created the Rapid Transit Commission gave the members of that body office for life, and it empowered them to name their own successors, for Platt and Hill were fearful that Tammany Hall might some day control the personnel of the board. The commission also had power to incur a huge debt on behalf of the City of New York, although it was a body appointed by the State. The members could spend the City's money without responsibility to any official of the City, and they could not be removed by either the Governor of the State or the Mayor of the City. They were not required to furnish the people with any account of their transactions or their acts.

Three years of deliberations passed, and then Tammany Hall and Croker were once more in full control of New York City. Mayor Van Wyck, Croker's servant, refused to attend the meetings of the Transit Commission, although he was by virtue of his office a member of that body. By obstructive tactics Tammany Hall managed to put off work on the subway, for the Tammany officials insisted that the authorized debt limit of the City was too low to include the appropriation for the subway. Then Tammany Hall, through Mayor Van Wyck, suggested that the work on the subway be let to a private company, and that the company should be given a perpetual franchise to operate the railway when it was built. The Metropolitan Street Railway Company was to be granted this right to build and operate the subway, and the Rapid Transit Commission approved a bill providing for this boon and had it introduced into the State Legislature. The Metropolitan Street Railway Company was not mentioned by name, but everybody knew who was to get the valuable franchise, out of which millions could be made. This arrangement was satisfactory to both Croker and Platt, for the traction magnates always took the precaution of contributing heavily to the Tammany Hall and the Republican campaign funds, and the two bosses were friendly to the Metropolitan Street Railway Company. Platt's lawyer, Boardman, in whose firm Platt's son was a partner, supported the bill, and the Tammany legislators at Albany had their orders to pass it. But some people became suspicious and mass meetings were held in New York, at which the deal was denounced; the labour unions particularly opposed it. Roosevelt was by this time Governor; he called the Rapid Transit Commission to his office; the explanations were embarrassing, and the bill was never passed.

Finally, as late as 1900, the Rapid Transit Commission began to ask for public bids for the construction of the subway. The street-car company expected that it would be the only bidder. But there was another, John B. McDonald, a contractor, a member of Tammany Hall and a friend of Richard Croker. McDonald had built the Jerome Park Reservoir. Croker and his friends saw the chance to get valuable sub-contracts for their contracting firms if McDonald got the contract to build the subway, and Tammany Hall also wished to enjoy the privilege of making from five to ten thousand Tammany voters labourers on the subway. McDonald was awarded the contract. But McDonald had no money, and he tried to negotiate with the street-car companies for financial backing; they would have nothing to do with him, for they thought that, if he failed to get the money to build the subway, the contract would go to them. McDonald, however, was a friend of Andrew Freedman, one of Croker's financial partners and closest friends, and a few days later it was announced that August Belmont was backing the construction of the subway with unlimited funds. Belmont was at that time, and had been for many years, the American representative of the Rothschilds. He had been kept out of several large deals by the traction magnates and their bankers. The subway was built, and it was said that after McDonald had done most of the hard work, he was forced out by Belmont and compelled to resign just before the subway was completed. At the dedication ceremonies of the new subway, McDonald was practically overlooked.[1]

One of the large business deals of the Croker period which involved leading members of Tammany Hall was the so-called Ice Trust manipulations. Charles W. Morse formed the American Ice Company, combining in it several other ice companies. The plans were to shut off competition by controlling the right to land ice at the City's docks, and in order to insure that this privilege should belong exclusively to it, the American Ice

---

[1]*McClure's Magazine*, Vol. XXIV, pp. 457–462, 1905. Article by Ray Stannard Baker.

Company gave stock to Mayor Robert A. Van Wyck, to his
brother, Judge Augustus Van Wyck, to Tammany Hall's Dock
Commissioner, Charles F. Murphy, later the leader of Tammany Hall, and to J. Sergeant Cram and J. B. Lounsbury, the
other Tammany Dock Commissioners. After it had obtained
control of the docks, the Ice Trust notified domestic customers
on May 1, 1890, that thereafter ice would cost sixty cents a
hundred pounds and that no five-cent pieces would be sold.
It looked as if that summer Tammany district leaders would
have to supply some portion of the ice which poor people would
not be able to buy for themselves owing to the new regulations
approved by the leaders of Tammany Hall.

The *World* investigated the situation, and, taking advantage of a provision of the new charter, which compelled
any city official to answer before a public examination, the
newspaper brought Mayor Van Wyck and the Dock Commissioners before the court of Judge William J. Gaynor. This provision of the New York charter had been passed in order that
New York City should never again have the difficulty in getting
information from city officials which was experienced at the
time of the Tweed frauds. Mayor Van Wyck admitted that he
had obtained 3,050 shares of preferred stock and 2,750 shares
of common stock of the American Ice Company, although the
city charter forbade such investment, even if he had paid for
his stock. His brother, it was discovered, also held stock in the
company, and John F. Carroll, one of Croker's leading associates, Croker himself and members of his family, Murphy,
J. Sergeant Cram, Hugh McLaughlin, the Boss of Brooklyn, and
others were found to possess stock of the American Ice Company. The *World* published in its issue of October 17, 1901, the
following tabulation from the stock books of the American Ice
Company:

	Par value.
Mayor Van Wyck—	
6,200 shares preferred	$620,000
6,100 shares common	610,000
Mayor Van Wyck's brother Augustus—	
2,025 shares preferred	202,500
2,850 shares common	285,000

Par value.

Mayor Van Wyck's Dock Commissioner, J. Sergeant
   Cram—100 shares preferred 10,000
   300 shares common 30,000
Mayor Van Wyck's Dock Commissioner, Charles F.
   Murphy—100 shares preferred 10,000
   300 shares common 30,000
Mayor Van Wyck's Dock Commissioner, Peter F.
   Meyer's confidential clerk, J. B. Lounsbury—
   1,000 shares preferred 100,000

The *World* commented:

"From the Mayor's admissions of dividends, it was found
that while his salary as Mayor was $41.09 a day, his dividends
from his Ice stock were $95 a day. The market value of all his
Ice stock was $678,000. The stock was going rapidly toward
par when the conspiracy was exposed and defeated. . . . Mayor
Van Wyck did not produce either checks or check stubs or
notes or any document whatsoever in support of his assertion
that he had paid for his stock and had not got it as a bonus for
his services."

Another leading business scandal during the Croker régime
was the Ramapo water deal. The Ramapo water company was
granted a two-hundred-million-dollar contract to supply the
City of New York with its water. The contract called for the
erection of reservoirs and a double steel pipe line eighty-one
miles long. William Dalton, who was Commissioner of Water
Supply under Mayor Van Wyck, was asked by Frank Moss
before the Mazet Committee: "If you have your pipe 300 feet
high in the air—think of that; as high as the steeples on St.
Patrick's Cathedral on Fifth Avenue, 300 feet high in the air;
two great steel pipes, eight feet three inches in diameter—what
is going to hold them up there?" "I don't know where they are
going to put those pipes," the Commissioner of Water Supply
answered. Moss then denounced the plan as a stock-selling
scheme to defraud the public, and he compared it with the
Great South Sea Bubble. There was, he said, no obligation to
carry out the contract, but only a great desire to sell the securities of the new company to the public. Investigation of the

colossal water contract resulted in its being rescinded, and the City operated its own water supply enterprises. When Mayor Van Wyck, upon his return from a vacation, was questioned by newspaper reporters concerning the Ramapo water contract, he replied, "The mosquitoes have been very numerous on Long Island this summer." "But about the Ramapo," the reporter insisted. "The mosquitoes were also of unusual size," said the Mayor.

The Mazet Committee testimony also brought out how Croker and Tammany Hall wrecked the Third Avenue Railroad Company, sending its shares from $242 to $50, and finally causing the company to go into the hands of a receiver in bankruptcy. One of the main causes of the bankruptcy was a contract for changing the motive power of the cars to electric power. The contract was made with Naughton & Company, a firm with which Daniel F. MacMahon, head of the executive committee of Tammany Hall, was associated. The previous contractor employed by the Third Avenue Railroad Company had offered to do the work for $7\frac{1}{2}$ per cent. of the labour pay roll and no commission on material, but he was removed from the job because he supported Judge Daly, who was refused a renomination by Croker. The work was then given to Naughton & Company, who demanded 15 per cent. on the labour pay roll and 10 per cent. commission on the cost of material. The men working on the job were members of Tammany districts, and they loafed. Photographs showing them in the evident process of loafing were produced before the committee. The job went on as slowly and as expensively as possible, and all the materials were furnished by Tammany firms, for no other contractors could get permission to open the streets.

It was not only in big business, however, that Tammany Hall found sources of profit. Nothing was too small to pay tribute. The Lexow Committee reported:

"It has been abundantly proven that bootblacks, pushcart and fruit vendors, as well as keepers of soda water stands, corner grocerymen, sailmakers with flag-poles extending a few feet beyond the place which they occupy, box-makers, provision dealers, wholesale drygoods merchants and builders, who are compelled at times to use the sidewalk and street, steamboat and steamship companies, who require police service on their docks, those who give public exhibitions, and in fact all persons, and all classes of persons whose business is subject to the observation of the police, or who may be reported as violating ordinances, or who may require the aid of the police, all have to contribute in substantial sums to the vast amounts which flow into the station houses, and which, after leaving something of the nature of a deposit, then flow on higher."[1]

Even the pushcart peddlers who sold their goods on the streets of New York were subject to tribute to Tammany Hall and the police. In a speech which he delivered during his campaign for District Attorney of New York in 1901, William Travers Jerome said concerning the pushcart peddlers:

"Have they not a right to sell without buying tickets to Tim Sullivan's chowder parties? . . . I have been told that all of a sudden, as this election was approaching, the police force descended upon the peddlers of the East Side. They had been getting on very nicely through the summer, with only an occasional shake-down from the plain-clothes man—well, of course, they had to pay that. Those who had most money had to take occasionally some tickets for a chowder party; well, they had to pay that. But I am told that as election time drew near, there was a great activity of the police force among the pushcart men, so that at last the association of the pushcart men betook themselves in all humility to Martin Engel and asked what they had got to do. And Martin Engel answered, 'You have got to support Tammany Hall.' Well, it was support Tammany Hall or get arrested. It was support Tammany Hall or be put out of business. Thereupon the Association answered, 'Yes, great one, we will support Tammany Hall.' But once inside the little box on Election Day, I find it difficult to believe the pushcart men will still be supporting Tammany Hall. Men will do much for friendship, that is human nature; when a man is kind to me, I for my part desire to help him all I can. And Mr. Shepard only the other day told Tammany Hall that somehow it had entwined itself in the hearts of the people. And up-town men say to me: 'Hang it, Jerome, those fellows somehow get

[1] Lexow Investigation, Vol. I, pp. 42–43.

down to the hearts of the people. You know they give them outings.' Mr. Hockstim, Mr. Katz, Mr. Engel, and the rest, they seem to think, have entwined themselves about your hearts. Heaven help you then, I think you must have let your hearts slip down into your pockets. It would be hard enough to know where else they can be found entwined."[1]

Jerome was right; Tammany Hall did entwine itself around the pockets of its constituents, but that was where their hearts were undoubtedly to be found, for most of them could not afford, or did not wish, to keep them anywhere else.

The people who towed garbage and the people who towed manure for the Street Cleaning Department all paid Tammany Hall for the privilege. Michael Moran, who was a garbage contractor for the Street Cleaning Department, sent Richard Croker a check for $50 on June 16, 1891, to help pay for the coming Fourth of July celebration at Tammany Hall. Upon being questioned further by Mr. Goff, he admitted that he didn't "give money away very easy," and that he wished Tammany a happy Fourth of July because he expected thereby to cart more garbage for the City.

Stables in New York had been in the habit of selling their manure. Tammany Hall under Croker passed a law providing that they must not sell it any longer, but that they must thereafter pay to have it carted away by certain licensed carters. "Tammany went so far, in one case, as to send in a bill for removing manure from a stable which had been closed during the whole period covered by the bill. The owner protested against being forced to pay for the fictitious carting of imaginary manure; but Tammany replied that if he did not use the stable it was his own fault. Tammany's licensee was ready at all times to do his duty."[2]

A contractor who did paving and gravelling in Central Park, James H. Perkins, testified before the Lexow Committee: "I never saw the inspector in our work but crowded on to me for money and he got it, except one, and he was a crazy man· his name was Smith and he died shortly afterward."[3]

---

[1] *A Fight for the City*, by A. Hodder, pp. 137-142.
[2] *Atlantic Monthly*, Vol. LXXIII, 1894, p. 251.
[3] Lexow Investigation, Vol. III, p. 2662.

"AN ENGLISH COUNTRY SEAT AND RACING STABLE COST A LOT OF MONEY—AND HE
KNOWS HOW TO GET IT"

Puck Oct. 23/01.

There was no form of business in which Tammany Hall did not share to the utmost of its opportunities during Croker's firm administration, and this applied even to the business of death. The traffic in the corpses of poor people by the men who had influence at the City's morgue was extensive. Wyndon Lynn, an undertaker's assistant, gave the following testimony before the Mazet Committee:

"I am engaged in the undertaking business. I was formerly employed by James P. Marren, an undertaker on First avenue between One Hundred and Nineteenth and One Hundred and Twentieth streets. Mr. Marren has had a monopoly of the caring for dead bodies at the Harlem Hospital. I have been with him a year and a half. Mr. Marren would get the first information and get hold of the body of any person brought dead to the hospital, or dying at the hospital, at the expense of any other undertakers. I know that Mr. Marren is a politician. A Democrat politician. He belongs to that assembly district. I mean the Tammany organization of that district. He does not hold any position under it. He claims he is associated with some of the prominent members of the Tammany organization in the city. . . .

"'When death occurs at the Harlem Hospital it is their duty to notify Bellevue Hospital by telephone. Then the authorities at Bellevue are supposed to notify the family so as to give the family an opportunity to employ its own undertaker, and to take charge of the body of the relative who is dead. He had an arrangement by which he was notified of the death before notice was sent to Bellevue in the regular way. His messenger or the clerks in the hospital would come to him in person. One clerk there was Edward Freeborn, another Edward Fitzgerald. . . .'"

"Did you have, or did Mr. Marren have any financial relations with Mr. Freeborn about these matters?"

"Yes; he paid Freeborn three dollars for every case he took. He paid Fitzgerald the same price. I know that money was paid because I have paid it myself. That has continued ever since I was with him; a year and a half. I have made in all twenty-three payments. Each time there was a dead body that I know anything about I paid, if took from there. I did pay that by direction of Mr. Marren. . . . I had to do it, or they wouldn't send the work, and they always came after the money the day after I took the case. . . . I know Mr. Marren has no relations with the Tammany leader of the district, Mr. Nagle. His relations, as stated by me, were with Mr. Carroll and Mr. Shultz. I know he claims he is acquainted with Mr. Croker."

"What does he claim he has done as showing his relationship with Mr. Croker?"

"Nothing; only I have heard him talk that he was personally acquainted with Mr. Croker."

"Hasn't he made some little unimportant but interesting presents to Mr. Croker and Mr. Carroll and Mr. Nagle?"

"He presented them with blackthorn sticks last summer, when he returned from Europe."

"A small matter, but showing an intimacy?"

"Yes, sir. . . ."

"Have you ever heard Mr. Marren say anything with reference to his being able to keep this, how long he could keep this monopoly?"

"As long as Croker and Carroll were in power."

"He said that, did he?"

"Yes."

"As long as Croker and Carroll were in power he would keep that?"

"Yes, sir. I know the other undertakers in Harlem have been considerably stirred up about this monopoly; I know it has been talked about in that business in Harlem. It is a matter of common knowledge and common rumor in Harlem and in all New York."

"Can you tell me something about coffins; coffins made and supplied by the city and obtained by Mr. Marren?"

"He used a great many of them. They are common city coffins. There is generally a dozen or fifteen stored at the Harlem morgue. These are coffins made by the city and paid for by the city. Mr. Marren gets them from the morgue people. He pays 50 cents and $1 apiece for those city coffins to the morgue people. I know that to be a fact, I have paid it. In the last ten weeks I have taken about eight coffins from there."

"Now, Mr. Witness, can you tell me anything about what are called 'still-born coffins'?"

"A still-born coffin is the smallest coffin that is made. If an undertaker sends a body to the Harlem morgue with a still-born in it, it is taken out of the coffin and the coffins are returned to Mr. Marren, and he allows them 25 cents apiece for them. So he gets everything in the way of dead bodies and coffins and still-born coffins. . . . I also stated that this monopoly existed at the time I went into Marren's employ; he claims it has been going on for ten years."[1]

Another employee of Mr. Marren's, Arthur L. Steckel, testi-fied that the undertaker made in the following manner some of the profits which enabled him to present blackthorn sticks to his political friends and to contribute to their campaign funds:

"I was employed by Mr. Marren. . . . He spoke to me about the practice of getting the bodies from the Harlem Hospital. He told me that he was the body snatcher of the Harlem Hospital, and that he got all the bodies from there, and that we were to use all power and means to take a body wherever we could do so; if a man dropped dead in the street, or anything, we were to get it, and he had got influence and good backing and he could protect us in anything that we did. . . . The day I went to work for Mr. Marren there was a body in the wagon that came from the hospital in a city coffin. I took that body to One Hundred and Eighth street and Lexington avenue, and the city coffin then was taken back and was removed to Daley's stable, One Hundred and Twenty-ninth street and Lexington avenue. We also brought another city coffin that a man by the name of Marty was buried in which the Charity Society, at One Hun-dred and Twenty-second street and Third avenue, paid Marren thirty or thirty-five dollars for the job. He was supposed to have a decent respectable coffin, but he got a city coffin covered with 69 cents worth of black cloth."[2]

Dr. O'Sullivan, Tammany's counsel before the Mazet Com-mittee, asked the witness if he knew what a body snatcher was. "The term amongst undertakers," said Mr. Steckel, "a body snatcher is if somebody dies to try and get the job."

---

[1]Mazet Investigation, Vol. II, pp. 1238–1246.
[2]Ibid., pp. 1246–1249.

VII

In order to control the vast revenues of the town, Tammany Hall under Croker had to control elections as completely as Tweed did when he ruled. As we have seen, Croker began his career as a personal controller of elections by means of extensive repeating and active use of his fists. As he grew in power, he no longer needed his own fists, and he only voted once himself, but the organization engaged others' fists and other names by the wholesale. Thomas C. Platt wrote in his autobiography:

"Tammany dominated the election boards by three to one, and Republican inspectors were helpless. Whole Assembly districts were declared by the Tammany boards to have gone Democratic by from eight to ten thousand, a meager few hundred votes being accorded to Republicans. Conservative estimates placed the total fraudulent vote in New York County alone, in the campaigns of 1891 and 1892, at from thirty to fifty thousand."

In its fraudulent activities at the polls Tammany Hall made use of the police and of criminals; both of these classes under Croker worked with each other and with Tammany Hall. It was one of the duties of the police to make up the poll lists of voters; policemen were also posted at the polls to see that no frauds were committed. Naturally, they worked for their masters in Tammany Hall rather than for their employers, the City, and they insured the facility of repeating by their negligence in the inspection of voters' residences and by their refusal to arrest repeaters at the polls.

John E. Leonard, a policeman on duty at the polls, who tried to prevent a Tammany Hall worker from electioneering where he had no business to electioneer, testified before the Lexow Committee that the president of the Lenox Hill Tammany Hall Club went immediately to the station house, and Leonard was ordered to go up to Seventy-sixth Street and Third Avenue to watch an empty lot instead of a polling place.[1]

Canute A. Dias, an inspector of elections in a district on the

----

[1] Lexow Investigation, Vol. I, pp. 950–953.

Bowery, testified before the Lexow Committee of his experience during the election of 1893:

"How many men were there who came and found that somebody else had voted on their names?"

"Thirty—30, at least, from the record I have. . . ."

"How many of these did you know personally?"

"I did not know them personally; I knew them only by sight, I remembered them from registration days. . . . In the case of Barnes, an old gentleman of 84 years of age; when he registered he said he was born in Marblehead, Mass.; the old gentleman had long flowing locks, and there was a lull during the time of registration when he came in that afternoon, and he conversed with the inspectors, and to show how active he was for an old gentleman he got up and danced and whistled Yankee Doodle; we could not help but remember it, and on the day of election a young man of about 22 or 23 years of age came in, and offered to vote on his name; I protested, and the chairman said, I was there through courtesy; that I had got along through registration very well, and that now he hoped that I did not wish to create any trouble or else I would be suppressed."

"Where was the policeman?"

"He was there all the time. . . ."

"How long was it after that before the old man came in?"

"It might have been two or three hours perhaps, and he thought it very strange that he should be disfranchised when he was told that he had voted."

"Who told him that he had voted?"

"The chairman; the chairman said, 'Your name has already been voted upon,' and the old man said, 'That is strange; I have not been here,' and the chairman said he could not help that."

"Did the old gentleman still have his flowing locks?"

"Yes, sir; he had."

"And he presented the same general appearance when he came to vote that he did on registration day?"

"Yes, sir."

"There was no possibility of mistaking him, was there?"

"No, sir; the chairman said, 'Your name has been already voted on,' and he said, 'I have not been here at all before,' and the chairman said, 'I can't help that; your name is voted on'; and the old gentleman said, 'I have voted for sixty years, and I think this is strange, that I should now be disfranchised,' and he said, 'Well, we can't vote but one name,' and the old man said to the chairman, 'Don't you remember me?' and the chairman said, 'Yes,' and the other Democratic inspector also recognized him, and so did I, and even then, the man was not allowed to vote after the entire board had said that he was the right party, and that they recognized him and then he went down to Judge Andrews and mandamused the board, and came back to vote; he was one of the seven."[1]

A Republican election inspector who tried to do his duty received rough treatment. Daily Williams testified before the Lexow Committee that when the people in the polling place where he was officially accredited to act as a watcher learned that he was the Republican watcher "they crowded around me, knocked my hat over my eyes, knocked it off two or three times, and threw every possible obstacle in my way.... The two police officers sat there, or one of them, certainly, and I remonstrated with them officers and asked him if he could not afford me the protection a watcher was entitled to; he said: 'I don't see anybody bothering you'; I said, 'It seems to me I feel a good deal of it; those people are knocking me around and knocking my hat off,' and finally I managed to live through it all, got disgusted and went out without any serious injury coming to myself."[2]
Police Captain Devery in the course of his instructions to his policemen one election day warned them that, "there is a lot of silk stocking people coming down from up town to bulldoze you people, and if they open their mouths stand them on their heads."
The Tammany Hall workers collected recently arrived Irish immigrants in the saloons of the East Side and voted them on Hebrew names. Frequently, according to Jacob Subin, a Republican watcher, they had difficulty pronouncing the names they were supposed to bear. They were somewhat like the repeater mentioned by George Washington Plunkitt, who, when he was asked his name at one polling place, answered, "William Croswell Doane." "Come off," said the poll clerk. "You ain't

[1]Lexow Investigation, Vol. I, pp. 277-278.
[2]*Ibid.*, pp. 87-88.

Bishop Doane." "The hell I ain't, you —— ——," answered
the ardent voter. When Subin challenged some of these incon-
gruous combinations, he was told that unless he stopped
"monkeying with the regular way of doing business" he
"would be thrown through the window." The watcher of the
Socialist Party, who did try to interfere with the regular way
of doing business, had his face punched and was thrown out of
the polling place. When he asked the policeman stationed there
to give him protection, "the officer stretched himself a little
and he said, 'Well, I guess I am pretty busy just now; I will see
you after 4 o'clock; I will have more time to spend'; and finally
but for the Tammany captain, if he had not interfered, they
would have handled him very roughly; but they made the
proposition to the captain of the Socialistic Labor party to go
right away, and in that case they would let him off, and so he
did go off very quickly."[1]

Frank Nichols, who was hit by a man with brass knuckles
on election day, 1893, because he wanted to vote, was asked by
Mr. Goff: "Did the police do anything at all?" "No, sir," he
answered, "he would not arrest a cat that day as long as it
belonged to Tammany Hall."

The Tammany district leaders, emboldened by their ability
to do what they pleased on election day without interference
from the police, told their subordinates that they wanted a
large majority at the election, that the inspectors were with
Tammany, and that the police were friendly. "You have the
police with you," John J. Ryan, the Tammany district leader
of the Twenty-fifth Assembly District, said in a little speech
to his captains, "and if you have not got enough, let us know,
and we will give you more; we will have a whole platoon sent
down, if necessary; those that are with us will receive our protection; those who are against us will receive nothing; and
should a Republican vote be challenged, why they have no
protection." He remarked in another election announcement:
"Now, I want you district captains to hand the secretary
the names of those police officers whom you think are friendly
toward our organization, and let him have them and I will see
that you have them at the polling place."[2]

---

[1]Lexow Investigation, Vol. I, pp. 303-304.

[2]Ibid., Vol. II, pp. 1368-1369.

Croker himself made an extraordinary pronouncement just before the Presidential election of 1900: "My advice to Democratic voters the country over," he told newspaper reporters, "is to congregate about the polling places on the evening of election day, count noses, and then, if the election returns for Bryan don't tally with their count, to go into the polling places and throw those fellows in charge of the returns into the street."

But the leading advocate of violence at elections and organizer of repeating operations in the interests of Tammany Hall was Timothy D. Sullivan, otherwise known throughout the city as "Big Tim" and "The Big Feller." Tim Sullivan was born in the old Sixth Ward in New York in 1863. When he was eight years old, he left school and sold newspapers. He sold newspapers during the Tweed Ring exposures and did a big business because of the public interest aroused at the time. He was known to the boys he worked with as "Dry Dollar," because of the historic occasion when he was found drying off a revenue stamp from a brewery keg under the impression that it was a dollar. "Big Tim" Sullivan's personal popularity was dated by one newspaper historian from the day when Sullivan saw a prize fighter beating a woman and after a hard battle beat the prize fighter. Sullivan started by running errands for politicians, and then he voted extensively. When he was twenty-three years old, he was elected to the Assembly on an anti-Tammany ticket from the district in which the Whyo Gang of thugs was dominant.

In Albany Sullivan met Tom Foley, an ardent Tammany leader under Croker. Foley suggested that Sullivan come over to Tammany, and pointed out the advantages to be gained; Sullivan realized them and turned his influence in the Bowery to Tammany Hall. His personal prestige on the Bowery was very great, and in the election of 1892 he reported to Richard Croker that the vote in his election district was 388 for Cleveland and 4 for Harrison. "Harrison got one more vote than I expected," Sullivan said, "but I'll find that fellow."

Sullivan had bought a saloon on the Bowery, and his headquarters were located there. His assistants in election work were his cousins "Little Tim" Sullivan and Florence Sullivan and "Soda Water" Riley, known as Sullivan's valet, because of his intense interest in the wishes of his leader. Even when he

was a State Senator, as he soon was, Sullivan attended personally to the business of repeating in his district. Harry Cunningham, a watcher at the polling place in Prince Street during the
election of 1893, testified before the Lexow Committee that
Senator Sullivan and Florrie Sullivan came into the polling
place after Cunningham had ordered a man arrested for illegal
voting. "Big Tim" took Cunningham by the collar of the coat,
pulled him outside into the street, and said, "If I wasn't running for Senator I would do so and so, . . . and Florrie Sullivan
and several others got at me and gave me a severe beating."[1]
It was said of "Big Tim" Sullivan that he once took the precaution to have the ballots in his district perfumed, so that he
could tell whether or not his followers were voting as they were
paid to vote. One trained observer of a band of repeaters remarked, "Dry Dollar would be sore if he saw that bunch.
They're all smooth-faced." "Well, can't a smooth-faced guy
vote as well as one with lilacs?" asked a friend. "Vote just as
well, onc't," said the expert, "but one vote lets him out, if the
inspectors are inclined to make trouble. Dry Dollar said once
that when you were getting repeaters in the district always get
guys with whiskers. When you've voted 'em with their whiskers
on you take 'em to a barber and scrape off the chin-fringe. Then
you vote 'em again with side lilacs and a moustache. Then to
a barber again, off comes the sides and you vote 'em a third
time with the moustache. If that ain't enough and the box can
stand a few more ballots clean off the moustache and vote 'em
plain face. That makes every one of 'em good for four votes."[2]
    The leading repeaters, however, whom "Big Tim" Sullivan
and his associates used at the polling places in New York were
not men with whiskers, but men with guns, whose activities the
rest of the year as gangsters were not interfered with by the
police and the courts if they devoted themselves earnestly to the
business of voting or intimidating hostile voters on elections.
"Monk" Eastman, the first general leader of East Side
gangs, was a friend of "Big Tim" Sullivan, and Eastman's
gang turned out from ten to fifteen repeaters on each election
day. "Monk" Eastman began his career as bouncer in "Silver
Dollar" Smith's saloon. Once when Eastman was arrested for

[1] Lexow Investigation, Vol. I, pp. 192–193.
[2] *Harper's Weekly*, October 18, 1913, p. 15.

assaulting the coachman of David Lamar, who had had a difference with his employer, he said to the policeman who was taking him away: "You're arresting me, huh? Say, you want to look where you're goin'. I cut some ice in this town. I made half the big politicians of New York." Senator Grady, Tammany's silver-tongued orator, defended "Monk" Eastman on this occasion, and he was acquitted. "Monk" Eastman, it was said, could be counted upon for between four and five hundred repeaters. His successor, "Kid" Twist, was said to be worth double that number. Paul Kelly, whose real name was Antonio Vaccarelli, was said to be good for one thousand repeaters from the ranks of his followers. At one Tammany Hall primary election in which Kelly's gang took part, his repeaters were furnished with food, cigars, whisky, and benches to sit on while they waited to vote repeatedly. It was in Kelly's saloon in Great Jones Street that several men were shot to death in the attempt of rivals to kill Kelly. A patrolman passing the saloon early one morning on his rounds heard no noise, which was unusual. He walked in. The legs of a dead man were sticking out of a closet; a clock was ticking loudly; and a large portrait of "Big Tim" Sullivan was hanging on the wall.

VIII

We have already noted that, after he had elected his friend Hugh J. Grant Mayor of New York, Richard Croker was supreme in Tammany Hall, and Tammany Hall was firmly established in power. Croker was then a factor to be considered in both the affairs of New York State and of the nation, for his absolute control of New York City, which he maintained with the aid of corrupt election tactics executed by his district leaders, meant that he could turn the vote of that section of the nation over to any candidate he chose. One of Croker's favourite cartoons about himself was that in which the draughtsman pictured him walking arm in arm down a gangplank with Thomas B. Reed, then Speaker of the House of Representatives, and the caption underneath read, "Who's Your Fat Friend?"

In 1892 Croker opposed the nominations by the Democratic Party of Grover Cleveland for President of the United States

and of David B. Hill for Governor of New York. Croker disliked
Cleveland because Cleveland refused to play the Tammany
game, and he hated Hill because Hill knew too well how to play
that game. In spite of Croker and Tammany Hall, however,
both Cleveland and Hill were nominated and elected. Croker
was a factor in State and in national politics, but he was not
practically the only factor, as he was in municipal politics, and
whenever Tammany Hall left its own realm, the City of New
York, and attempted to control the State or the nation, it usually lost, for its power was dependent upon careful and complete
control of a constricted area, where it had enough henchmen to
take care of each district thoroughly and to provide sufficient
repeaters at each election, if the popular sentiment was not in
favour of Tammany Hall's candidates. But to do that same
work throughout the State would have required an army
difficult to assemble and almost impossible to control. Besides,
Tammany Hall's reputation among the country gentlemen
and farmers of the upper portion of New York State, and among
the politicians and business men of the rest of the nation, was
not good. They both distrusted and feared the organization
whose methods were so well known and yet so successful. And
Tammany Hall's leaders usually found national issues, and even
state problems, too much for them. Croker's few public pro-
nouncements on national questions were direct but naïve in the
extreme. When the entire nation was agitated over the free-
silver controversy, Croker remarked one day in the Hoffman
House: "What's the use of discussing what's the best kind of
money? I'm in favour of all kinds of money—the more the
better." "See," said George Washington Plunkitt, "how a real
Tammany statesman can settle in twenty-five words a problem
that monopolized two campaigns!" "What do you mean by
Anti-Imperialism, Mr. Croker?" he was asked at the time when
he was strenuously opposing the imperialism of his Republican
opponents. "My idea of Anti-Imperialism," said Mr. Croker
promptly, "is opposition to the fashion of shooting everybody
who doesn't speak English." This was a good definition, but
natural from the leader of Tammany Hall, for, as the editor of
Harper's Weekly pointed out: "If every man who cannot speak
English were to be shot to-night it is doubtful if there would be
ten members of Tammany Hall left alive to-morrow."

In 1894 Croker was still in power, with his friend Thomas F. Gilroy as Mayor of New York, but in that year the Parkhurst revelations and the Lexow Investigation made Tammany Hall's corruption too obvious. When Croker returned from Europe in May, 1894, he announced his retirement from politics and his resignation as the leader of Tammany Hall. He told the executive committee of Tammany Hall that his health would no longer permit him to lead the organization, and that the responsibilities of the job were more than he could then carry. To reporters Croker said that he wanted time to attend to his health, time to attend to his real-estate business, and time to attend to his horses, of whom he had grown passionately fond. There were those, however, who maintained that Croker realized that the investigations of the Lexow Committee would cause Tammany Hall to lose the coming election no matter what efforts were made, and that Croker did not wish to be at the head of the organization when the inevitable crash came. The people of New York City were emotionally aroused by the tales of prostitutes, saloon keepers, and gamblers, and public-spirited excitement was at a point which had not been equalled since the days of the overthrow of Tweed. Committees were formed and vast preparations were made by zealous men to fight against Tammany Hall in the 1894 campaign for Mayor.

As the resentment against Tammany Hall, the revealed exploiter of prostitutes and the exposed blackmailer of business men, grew greater and greater, independent reform agencies came into being. There were Good Government Clubs, the State Democracy, the O'Brien Democracy, the Citizens' Union, the Independent Democracy, the Citizens' Association, and the City Club, among others. An attempt was being made during the summer of 1894 to fuse these diverse elements into one powerful opposition organization, but that was difficult to accomplish, for each element was jealous of the other and hesitated before making the necessary combination.

A large mass meeting was held at Cooper Union, and, in an attempt to reënact the drama of the Tweed Ring exposures, a Committee of Seventy was formed. A powerful candidate for Mayor had to be chosen, and John W. Goff, who had so ably conducted the examination of witnesses for the Lexow Committee, was considered for the position, but William L. Strong, a bank president of good reputation, was chosen as more likely to appeal to the solid portions of the community.

Thomas C. Platt, the Republican State Boss, was urged to join in the fusion movement, but he was cannily wary of it, for he distrusted the disorganizing results of which earnest reform was capable, and his life interest was not good government, but rather the construction of an impregnable Republican fortress in the City and State of New York, which would govern those communities with due regard for the dividends of widows and orphans, within the limitations imposed only by a loose construction of the penal code and the Ten Commandments. "Strong," Platt wrote in his autobiography, "was another of the fellows who wore a little bunch of whiskers under his chin." Platt disliked this symbol of uncompromising righteousness so much that he confessed: "One effect of my experience with him was to call for a barber and have my beard trimmed close, and studiously avoid permitting the growth of any tuft on my neck." Horace Greeley and Reuben E. Fenton, who were also distasteful to Platt, because they would not believe in their party right or wrong, but preferred to stand for what they considered to be right, also wore little bunches of whiskers under their chins, according to Platt. Thomas Platt was later to come into intimate contact with a more troublesome reformer than all, Theodore Roosevelt, who had only a moustache and rather prominent teeth. Roosevelt was a great trial to Platt, but it is nowhere recorded that the "Easy Boss" of the "Amen Corner" had his teeth extracted.

Croker took no part in this hectic campaign, and Tammany Hall was defeated completely. William L. Strong proved to be an efficient mayor who appointed honest and capable men to the leading offices in his administration. Platt, who was interested in building up a strong Republican organization in the City of New York that would be in a position to combat the extraordinary influence and power of Tammany Hall, was chagrined at Strong's appointments of men who disregarded the needs of the Party and considered only the needs of the City. "Colonel Waring," Platt wrote sadly in his autobiography, "was put in charge of the Street Cleaning Department, and no organization leader could get a place from him during his entire administration." This department had always been used by

Tammany to give jobs to thousands of men who were thereby worth thousands of votes at the next elections. It did not matter to Platt that Waring was the first man in charge of cleaning New York's streets who actually kept them clean and who did not steal or permit his friends to steal large sums of money for inefficient service. And Platt, from his point of view, was perfectly right. But his point of view was questionable. Reformers have never been able to understand the advantage of substituting one efficient machine for another, and they too were right, for machines have had a tendency to become astoundingly corrupt and ruthless in their use of the power which they so carefully developed. Whether it is better for the government of the City of New York to sway from Tammany to Republican, or by opposing Tammany alone, end some evils temporarily, it is difficult to decide.

"These reform movements," an East Side gangster once remarked, "are like queen hornets. They sting you once, and then they die." Tammany Hall has only one fundamental purpose: the greatest good of the largest possible number of its members; and this greatest good has always involved plenty of money for the members. Its opponents, on the contrary, have been groups of people with varied purposes. The clergymen and social workers who made up the ranks of reform were interested in the eradication of vice or the improvement of living conditions in a vague, general way. These were the people with high purpose. The business men, who made up the other largest element in reform, were interested solely in the reduction of taxes. But each of these groups could not work together for long without friction, for their objects necessarily interfered with each other. If the moral reformers had their way, taxes went up, and the economic reformers were angry. If the taxes were reduced enough to satisfy the business men, the improvements which the social workers were urging were not carried out. Tammany Hall did not care how high taxes were, and it was not interested in general improvement of living conditions. It was intensely interested in getting large numbers of people jobs at the expense of the business men and in permitting large numbers of people to indulge in their fancies at the expense of the moralists.

Theodore Roosevelt, who was appointed Police Commissioner

by Mayor Strong, recognized this difficulty. He said to his friend Eggleston: "The difficulty seems to be inherent in the conditions. If a reform administration honestly endeavors to carry out reform, it makes an end of itself at the end of its term and insures the return of Tammany to power. If a reform administration fails or falters in carrying out the pledges of reform on which it was elected, it utterly loses the confidence and support of the reform forces, and that again means a triumph for Tammany at the next election." Senator Palmer defined the situation in a more picturesque manner: "A reformer," he said, "is one who tries to stand a pyramid upon its apex; martyr is the title given his remains by his friends."

Tammany Hall workers were always tireless, because there was something in it for them personally in the way of money and prestige, but those whose interests were good government soon grew weary and discouraged at spending such a large share of their seventy-odd years against such overwhelming obstacles. The only hope there seemed to be was that every so often, when Tammany's workers got too gay, they could be jailed or put out of their jobs, depending upon the gravity of their offence and the industry of prosecuting attorneys.

The very zeal of the reformers was against them. Roosevelt, for example, was young, ambitious, and filled with a large sense of his own righteousness. He enforced the Sunday closing law vigorously, and the result was that he was a terror to pinochle players in the back rooms of saloons. The small joys began to disappear from daily life, and their place was taken by that abstract ghost, the Law, which, try as hard as they could, people who liked sex, beer, and cards could neither see, taste, nor touch.

While the people were thus gravitating back toward Tammany Hall, as an inveterate drunkard returns to his liquor, Richard Croker returned from the race tracks of England and his estate, Wantage, Berkshire. Both his health and his political position had improved in the interim, for the simple pleasures of a country gentleman in the counties of England were less disturbing than the hectic atmosphere of the smoke-filled office in Fourteenth Street, and the sachems of Tammany Hall had discovered in his absence that it was difficult to win victories without his guiding hand. The Tammany historian, Mrs.

Euphemia Vale Blake, felt that she had coined a phrase when she compared his arrival to the return of Napoleon from Elba.

Napoleon's generals, however, were disgruntled, for some of them felt that their leader had left them in a lurch, and had forced them to grapple with a problem which he could not handle himself. New leaders were beginning to arise in various districts, and they hoped to obtain the power that Croker enjoyed. Tim Sullivan was now a personage; John F. Carroll and John C. Sheehan, who had been Croker's assistants, were tired of the responsibility without authority which he gave them. There was general dissatisfaction. But as soon as the squat man with the scrubby beard appeared in Tammany Hall, those who had been talking most against him grew silent. They feared the snap of his tight jaw. He told them briefly that he had heard that there were complaints and grievances. He asked them to state their grievances and to voice their complaints, and no one dared to do so. Then he told them that Tammany Hall had a good chance to win the coming election of 1897 if they went to work instead of spending their time complaining. He ordered them to get back to their districts and work, and he threatened that unless they did so, he would replace each one of them with men who would.

The district leaders imitated in their own districts the arbitrary manners of Croker, but as soon as they got inside Tammany Hall, they were obedient, even abject. They fawned upon Croker, and they smiled the weak smile of subservience. They begged for what they wanted rather than demanded it, for Croker's anger was terrifying, and his power was unlimited. And after they had left Tammany Hall, the district leaders went back to their districts and told their own subordinates what they had said to Croker, how they had put it to him straight, and that he had come around to their way of thinking.

The "return from Elba" occurred in the summer of 1897. John C. Sheehan had been put in charge of Tammany Hall by Croker during the disastrous campaign of 1896. On the steamship *New York*, which was bringing the Boss back to the City in the summer of 1897, there was another distinguished passenger, W. T. Stead, the editor of the London *Review of Reviews*. Mr. Croker and Mr. Stead discussed New York politics during the voyage, and Mr. Stead wrote an account of the interview which he published in his magazine in October, 1897. Stead admitted that he had patched up Croker's language in places, but he insisted that the ideas were the ideas of the Boss of New York. Croker told him some interesting things concerning Tammany Hall:

"After a long and interesting conversation upon the merits and demerits of the Tammany dynasty, I had ventured to sum up the whole matter in one searching question," wrote Stead.

"'Mr. Croker,' I said, 'for nearly thirty years you have been up to the neck in the rough-and-tumble of New York politics. For nearly twenty years you have been supreme Boss of Tammany. You are now out of politics, contemplating a serene old age in the rural delights of your Berkshire seat. You can therefore speak dispassionately upon the events of your career. Looking back over the whole of these thirty years, is there any single act or deed which, now in the light of your experience, you regret having done or that you now feel you wish you had left undone?'

Cartoon by T. E. Powers.   © N. Y. Evening World.

"THE SQUIRE BIDS EDWARD VII GOOD-BY."

"The Boss paused. He removed from his lips his cigar of Brobdingnag, and half closed his eyes for a moment.

"Then with calm deliberate emphasis he replied—

"'No, sir. Not one! I do not remember ever having done anything that I ought not to have done. For I have done only good all my life.' . . .

"'And what is the rule?' I asked, somewhat curious to know the Boss's theory of the Universe. 'What is the underlying fundamental law of the Universe?'

"'Sir,' said Mr. Croker, speaking with quiet gravity, 'the law is that although wrong-doing may endure for a season, right must in the long run come to the top. Human nature is not built so that roguery can last. Honest men must come to their own, no matter what the odds against them. There is nothing surer than that. Lying, calumny, thieving may have their day, but they will pass. Nothing can last but truth.'

"'Really, Mr. Croker,' I exclaimed, 'what an optimist you are! I have not found so great faith, no, not in Israel,' I said, laughing.

"'That's right,' he replied. 'If you put ten honest men into an assembly with ninety thieves, human nature is such that the ten honest men will boss the ninety thieves. They must do it. It is the law of the world. All evil, whether lying or thieving, by its nature cannot last. Honest John Kelly, who was Boss before me, when I first came into politics before he was Boss, always used to tell me that, "Never mind the odds against you if you are in the right. Being in the right is more than odds. Keep hammering away and you are sure to win." And I have always found it so. . . .'

"'. . . and Tammany is coming out on top once more. It's bound to, for Tammany is honest and Tammany is true. And you have only got to go on being honest and true to come out on top—not every time, for we have our reverses; but on the whole, Tammany has come out on top most of the time. . . .'

"And then I thought that the Boss was playing it rather low down upon the innocent and confiding stranger. But his countenance was imperturbable, and I do not believe that he was saying a word which in some way or other he had not first convinced himself was gospel truth. . . .

"Sects may come and sects may go, but Rome goes on for

ever. And what Rome is in its immutability and its authority
that is Tammany Hall among its rivals. Mr. Croker is a kind of
mundane Pope, with the executive committee as his College of
Cardinals. To him the new era began with the overthrow of
Boss Tweed in 1871. Cardinal Manning once said to me, 'The
Council of Trent, that was the real Reformation.' So Mr. Croker
always dates the beginning of the true Tammany in the overthrow of the Tweed Ring. . . ."

Then Croker told Stead something really significant concerning the basis of Tammany's power as opposed to the weakness
of its reform opponents:

"'What is the one fact which all you English notice first of
anything in our country? Why, it is that that very crowd of
which we are speaking, the minority of cultured leisured citizens, will not touch political work—no, not with their little
finger. All your high principles will not induce a mugwump to
take more than a fitful interest in an occasional election. The
silk stocking cannot be got to take a serious hand continuously
in political work. They admit it themselves. Every one knows it
is so. Why, then, when mugwump principles won't even make
mugwumps work, do you expect the same lofty motives to be
sufficient to interest the masses in politics?'

"'And so,' I said, 'you need to bribe them with spoils?'

"'And so,' he replied, 'we need to bribe them with spoils. Call
it so if you like. Spoils vary in different countries. Here they
take the shape of offices. But you must have an incentive to
interest men in the hard daily work of politics, and when you
have our crowd you have got to do it in one way, the only way
that appeals to them. I admit it is not the best way. Think
what New York is and what the people of New York are. One
half, more than one half, are of foreign birth. We have thousands upon thousands of men who are alien born, who have no
ties connecting them with the city or the State. They do not
speak our language, they do not know our laws, they are the raw
material with which we have to build up the State. How are you
to do it on mugwump methods? I tell you it cannot be done.' . . .

"'There is no denying the service which Tammany has
rendered to the Republic. There is no such organization for
taking hold of the untrained friendless man and converting him

into a citizen. Who else would do it if we did not? Think of the hundreds of thousands of foreigners dumped into our city. They are too old to go to school. There is not a mugwump in the city who would shake hands with them. They are alone, ignorant strangers, a prey to all manner of anarchical and wild notions. Except to their employer they have no value until they get a vote.'

"'And then they are of value to Tammany?' I said, laughing.

"'Yes,' said Mr. Croker, imperturbably; 'and then they are of value to Tammany. And Tammany looks after them for the sake of their vote, grafts them upon the Republic, makes citizens of them in short; and although you may not like our motives or our methods, what other agency is there by which so long a row could have been hoed so quickly or so well? If we go down into the gutter it is because there are men in the gutter, and you have got to go down where they are if you are to do anything with them.'

"'And so,' I said, 'Tammany is a great digestive apparatus, fed with all manner of coarse, indigestible food, that would give a finer stomach sudden death. But Tammany's stomach is strong; nothing is too rough for Tammany's gastric juice, and so you build up the body politic out of material——'

"'That but for us would have remained undigested and indigestible—a menace to the State, a peril to society. You may carp at our motives and criticise our methods—we do not complain. All that we say is we have done the work, and we deserve more recognition for that than we have yet received.'"

On the day of his arrival in New York a group of men who were paving a street near the dock recognized Croker, took off their caps, and stood uncovered until he passed.

The campaign to which Richard Croker was returning was an exciting one. Henry George, the protagonist of the Single Tax, was the radical candidate for Mayor. Seth Low, former Mayor of Brooklyn and one-time president of Columbia University, was the reform candidate. The Republican candidate was Benjamin F. Tracy, the law partner of Thomas C. Platt's son, for Platt refused to join the Low reform forces, preferring defeat with a staunch Republican to victory with another reformer.

Tammany Hall did not choose its candidate for Mayor in 1897 until Richard Croker returned to New York and told the leaders who it was to be. The stakes were high in that election of 1897, for the Legislature had passed the act consolidating the boroughs of Manhattan, Brooklyn, Richmond, Queens, and the Bronx into the City of Greater New York. The act had also increased the Mayor's term of office to four years. The spoils of victory would be colossal, and it was no wonder that Croker was weaned from his retirement. The Republican Legislature had passed these acts under the impression that a Republican had a good chance of election that year, and the Legislature had increased the Mayor's term so that a Republican Mayor might be kept in office for four years. It was up to Croker to win these spoils and that long term for Tammany Hall.

Tammany Hall was the scene of excitement. Who the candidate would be was the question. He had to be a strict Tammany organization man, and yet he had to be a man who would attract the voters. At first it was rumoured that Croker himself would be the first Mayor of Greater New York. When W. T. Stead asked him on board the ship whether he would be the candidate, he answered that he had not quite made up his mind. He then went on to say that he had had enough of responsibility in the past twenty-five years, and that he was quite certain that if he were Mayor of Greater New York, he would be in his grave before the term of office expired. Croker added that he did not like the new charter, and that "no mortal man—no, not even an angel from heaven—could govern the city successfully under that charter, and I don't care to die for the chance of making a failure." Stead then quoted Macaulay to Croker:

> "To every man upon the earth
> Death cometh soon or late.
> And how can man die better
> Than facing dreadful odds
> For the ashes of his fathers
> And the temples of his gods?"

"'That is all very well,' said Croker, 'if I could do any good. But I don't see that I can, or that anybody can, under this charter. I have had a very rough, hard life, and I want to rest a few years after all the turmoil. I have got a little country place in Berkshire where I have a few horses—and I am very fond of horses. What I would like best of all would be to go back to Berkshire and spend the next few years quietly with my horses in the open air, and with my family at home, and let somebody else swing New York.'

"'Natural,' I said, 'but not the highest, is it?'

"Mr. Croker replied with sudden energy: 'I have not made up my mind. I cannot possibly make up my mind till I know how the situation stands in New York. That I am going to find out. When I know the facts, I shall make up my mind. And I would have you understand,' he said, speaking in a tone very foreign to his usual quiet, unemphatic way, 'that whatever way I decide it will be my own decision and nobody's else. I take no stock in the protestations of men who have been compelled against their wishes, etc., to accept office. Never. If I accept this or anything else it is because I wish to have it. If I did not wish for it, no power on earth could make me accept it. I never have been driven to accept anything against my wish, and I never will.'"

This would seem to indicate that Richard Croker was seriously considering running for the office of the first Mayor of Greater New York. Whether he felt that his chances of election would not be great in spite of all the efforts and frauds that his friends the district leaders could commit, or whether he did not fancy the strict confinement in the Mayor's chair, a confinement that might have kept him from the race tracks and that would certainly have kept him from his "little country place in Berkshire," we do not know. If he did not run for the office himself, the only alternative was the candidacy of a man who would obey his orders completely. Perhaps that would be better. A man to do the speech-making—Croker was never fond of speeches—and a man to sign the vast number of papers a Mayor of New York must sign, also a man who would pay strict attention to cables from Newmarket and Berkshire, was what Croker wanted. He found such a man in an obscure judge, Robert A. Van Wyck.

Van Wyck was unknown to the people of New York, and that was something of an advantage. The newspapers could have printed too much about Richard Croker personally and politically to please Richard Croker the man if he had run for Mayor of Greater New York. No one could say anything about Van Wyck, because there was nothing to say, except that he had been a loyal Tammany Hall man for some years, and that he had been an inconspicuous judge. The *World* had offered a reward to the person who could name in advance Croker's choice as candidate for Mayor, which choice would be promptly ratified by the Tammany convention. The day after the convention was held, the *World* said: "This reward has not been earned by anybody. Among the multitudinous responses, in which almost every possible Tammany candidate was named, there was not one which held the name of Judge Robert A. Van Wyck."

A statement concerning Van Wyck's nomination which illustrates vividly Richard Croker's methods as a leader was given out in December, 1901, by either John C. Sheehan or his friends. Sheehan, it will be remembered, was placed in charge of Tammany Hall by Richard Croker upon the occasion of his resignation. The statement read in part:

"Croker on his arrival declared that he was out of politics and went to the Murray Hill Hotel. He referred all inquirers to Sheehan. In the meantime, not a day passed that Sheehan was not warned by one or more Tammany leaders that Croker was seeking to bring about his downfall. These leaders told Sheehan that they had known Croker longer than he, and that he was not to be trusted.

"At the second interview between Croker and Sheehan possible nominees for Mayor were considered. Sheehan had in mind the nomination of a man like William Sohmer, ex-Mayor Grant, Charles H. Knox, Amos J. Cummings, Charles W. Dayton, or Delos McCurdy. These names were submitted to Mr. Croker by Sheehan. In discussing them Croker said:

"'Sohmer won't do; he's a German, and you can't trust a German; Grant is not the man; labor would not support him because he was opposed to Bryan. Knox is too ministerial; besides, his connection with the Standard Oil Company would kill him. Nobody would have anything to do with Dayton. Cummings isn't the kind of a man. John, have you thought about Van Wyck?'

"'No,' replied Mr. Sheehan, 'I never thought of Van Wyck.'

"'He might do,' said Mr. Croker. 'He comes from an old Knickerbocker family, and that would bring in the Dutch and German votes. But I'm out, John. I have no particular interest, and all I want to do is to get a good man for the organization.'

"'I don't believe that Van Wyck is a big enough man,' said Mr. Sheehan. 'I like Van Wyck, but I don't think he is a vote getter.'

"On the evening before the City Convention Croker, Sheehan, and a number of others met at the Murray Hill Hotel. Croker said during the dinner: 'Well, John, you'll soon have your hands full. The convention is to-morrow, and you haven't got any candidate yet. When did you see Van Wyck?'

"Sheehan replied that he had not seen Van Wyck in three weeks. Croker said that he had not seen him for a long time. Then Croker said that nothing could be said against Van Wyck, and Sheehan replied that he knew nothing against him except his arrest at the French ball some years before and Mr. Sheehan said that that would not last three days in the campaign.

"'Suppose you see Van Wyck and get him up here to-night,' Mr. Croker said. 'Do you know Delos McCurdy? I can't recall him.'

"'I know him well,' said Sheehan, 'and if we should nominate him there is no doubt that you would have a candidate as big as Tracy or Low.'

"That night at 11 o'clock Sheehan took Van Wyck to Croker's room. He had tried to find McCurdy, but could not do so. He had no difficulty in finding Van Wyck. Croker talked to Van Wyck and told him he was considering him as a candidate for Mayor. He said that Sheehan took no stock in any attacks that might be made on Van Wyck. Croker said that he was out, but that every man ought to be true to the organization, and in his heart he wanted to see Sheehan successful as the leader of Tammany Hall.

"At that interview with Van Wyck many promises were demanded from him, and they were given cheerfully. One of the men who was present said: 'After that evening I had less respect for 'Bob' Van Wyck than I had had before.' . . ."

Meanwhile, Sheehan saw Delos McCurdy and begged him to accept the nomination, but McCurdy refused absolutely be-

HIS GRACE, THE DUKE OF TAMMANY
Richard Croker, Commander-in-Chief of the Ancient and Dishonorable
Company of Ward Heelers.

cause of previous business engagements. Sheehan spoke to Croker on the telephone, and told him that McCurdy had refused the nomination. Croker said that the best thing to do was to nominate Van Wyck.

"When Van Wyck's name was presented to the Executive Committee," the statement went on, "it had the effect of a wet blanket. No member of the Executive Committee spoke for some time. Finally, James McCartney, then the leader of the north half of the Thirty-fourth Assembly District, arose in the rear of the hall and said:

"'Mr. Sheehan, is this nomination you've made your own selection, and in your judgment is it the best that could be made?' Sheehan's reply was: 'If I didn't think so, I wouldn't present the name.'

"Some time afterward Sheehan learned that Croker had gone to Grant and told him that Sheehan had prevented his nomination for Mayor. Then Sheehan began to suspect that Croker was trying to knock him out. Mr. Croker did not turn in much money to Tammany Hall. The total amount of his contributions was $2,500 from a large corporation, and $250 from a member of the judiciary. The total amount collected by Sheehan and turned over to John McQuade, the Treasurer of Tammany Hall, was $260,000, and at the end of the canvass McQuade had $50,000 in the treasury—a thing which had never happened before in the history of the organization.

"Having secured the nomination of a man absolutely subservient to him for Mayor, Croker now came out into the open. Two weeks after the city convention, and before the county convention, Daniel F. McMahon and Timothy D. Sullivan waited on Sheehan at Tammany Hall and announced that they were a committee to urge him to invite Croker to come to Tammany Hall. Mindful of the promise Croker had extracted from him to protect him from just this thing earlier in the year, Sheehan told the committee that he wouldn't. Then they said that there had been a meeting at the Murray Hill Hotel and almost all of the leaders were there, and they had decided that Croker ought to go to the hall. Sheehan hurried down to Croker's office, and told him what had happened. Croker said that some of the leaders had called on him and asked him to go to the hall, but that he wanted to do just what Mr. Sheehan wanted. Sheehan's eyes were beginning to open by this time, but he was absolutely helpless because the Croker ticket had been nominated and its success was assured. However, he went back to Tammany Hall and wrote a letter inviting Croker to the headquarters. That same afternoon he was informed that Delmour and Sheehy had approached every district leader in New York County and invited them to a conference. Twenty-two refused to go. One said, 'You ought to put bells on Croker's ears and send him back to England,' when he was invited. Croker has never forgiven that man. . . ."[1]

During the vituperative campaign of 1897 Richard Croker was vigorously denounced. His association on the race tracks of England with Edward VII, then Prince of Wales, was brought up at public meetings and in the newspapers. One speaker said of Croker: "He spends his time flocking with the lecherous sons of a rotten aristocracy." "The crowd," reported the *Sun*, "was beside itself." It was also said of Croker that he had made a deal with his fine English friends to keep the Irish out of politics in New York, for there were no Irish names on the Tammany ticket in prominent places that year.

During the campaign the Tammany District Attorney, Asa Bird Gardiner, got considerable notoriety when he remarked in the course of a political speech, "To Hell with Reform."

In the middle of the campaign Henry George died. He had been counted upon by the reformers of the Seth Low group to gain many Democratic votes and thus cause the election of their candidate over Van Wyck. His son, who was then thirty-five years old, took his father's place as a candidate of the radical group, but he was not his father, and the Democrats got some of the votes which would have been cast by personal admirers of the Single Tax advocate.

Van Wyck was elected by a plurality of 85,000 votes, and Tammany was restored to complete power over Greater New York for four years.

New York on election night, 1897, was an amazing spectacle. Men and women from the Tenderloin paraded through the

---

[1] New York *Times*, December 23, 1901.

streets, carrying toy tigers and shouting the refrain of "Well, well, Reform has gone to Hell!" Some men wore cardboard placards in their hats, reading, "I told you so!" "Painted women," wrote a *World* reporter, "forgot old sores and greeted each other with frenzied enthusiasm. 'We did not do a thing to reform, did we?' these ladies with the purchased complexions asked each other, and then they went in and had drinks on it." The pass word was "Wide open," and strangers invited each other to have a drink on the great victory. "There was a woman in a green plush dress that suggested a sofa bought on the installment plan. She told the passers-by that she 'could drink with any lady, but God knows she was no tank,' and there was a girl who shrieked, and said she was not afraid of Chapman [a police captain] now, and—'to hell with reform!'" A band near the Haymarket played "A Hot Time in the Old Town." Phalanxes of men blowing horns and chanting "Well, well, well, Reform has gone to Hell!" pushed their way in snake-dance formations through the packed streets. In the Haymarket there were cheers at each bulletin of election returns and roars of "What's the matter with Van Wyck?" followed by the assurance, "He's all right!" "Then two or three people began to plunk banjos, and a cushiony young person said it was just like heaven to hear a banjo again." "You kin do a twirl wid me rag," one man said to another, "but yer bring her back, see?—or I'll step on yer face, an' dat's no pipe dream." Champagne ran naughtily over the brims of the glasses.

George Washington Plunkitt was sitting with a different group that election night. Until ten o'clock he and Croker and "Big Tim" Sullivan and Charlie Murphy and John Carroll sat in the committee room of Tammany Hall receiving the returns. When they saw that Van Wyck was elected by a big majority, Plunkitt asked "the crowd to go across the street for a little celebration." "A lot of small politicians followed us, expectin' to see magnums of champagne opened. The waiters in the restaurant expected it, too, and you never saw a more disgusted lot of waiters when they got our orders. Here's the orders: Croker, vichy and bicarbonate of soda; Carroll, seltzer lemonade; Sullivan, apollinaris; Murphy, vichy; Plunkitt, ditto. Before midnight we were all in bed, and next mornin' we were up bright and early attendin' to business, while other men were nursin' swelled heads. Is there anything the matter with temperance as a pure business proposition?"[1]

So, three years after the Lexow revelations of prostitutes and police captains, bartenders and storekeepers had startled New York into a spasm of righteous wrath, Tammany Hall was more powerful than it had ever been in its entire career.

Richard Croker went to Lakewood with his new mayor, Van Wyck, and every Tammany Hall man of importance followed the court. It was there, during the six weeks after the beginning of December, 1897, that every office in the gift of the City was apportioned to the faithful followers. The trains were crowded with politicians; there was an almost infinite line of black derbies and brown cigars in the Pullman cars. The Lakewood Hotel, where Richard Croker was staying, was crowded with men who paid their respects to him and demanded favours of him. Croker walked up and down the corridor of the hotel with the men he wished to consult, while the rest remained at a respectful distance and watched the Boss until they were called into the presence. In the evening dress suits were compulsory, for Croker had lived part of the year in England, where, as George Ade once remarked, "their idea of a gentleman is a man who continues to wear evening clothes after he has worn out his underclothes." George Washington Plunkitt recorded that there were dire results from this sudden transformation of Tammany Hall men into gentlemen.

"Puttin' on style don't pay in politics," Plunkitt remarked emphatically. "The people won't stand for it. If you've got an achin' for style sit down on it till you have made your pile and landed a Supreme Court Justiceship with a fourteen-year term at $17,500 a year, or some job of that kind. Then you've got about all you can get out of politics, and you can afford to wear a dress-suit all day and sleep in it all night if you have a mind to. But, before you have caught onto your life meal-ticket, be simple. Live like your neighbors even if you have the means to live better. Make the poorest man in your district feel that he is your equal, or even a bit superior to you.

"Above all things, avoid a dress-suit. You have no idea of the harm that dress-suits have done in politics. They are not so

[1]*Plunkitt of Tammany Hall*, pp. 148–149.

fatal to young politicians as civil service reform and drink, but they have scores of victims. I will mention one sad case. After the big Tammany victory in 1897, Richard Croker went down to Lakewood to make up the slate of offices for Mayor Van Wyck to distribute. All the district leaders and many more Tammany men went down there, too, to pick up anything good that was goin.' There was nothin' but dress-suits at dinner at Lakewood, and Croker wouldn't let any Tammany men go to dinner without them. Well, a bright young West Side politician, who held a three-thousand-dollar job in one of the departments, went to Lakewood to ask Croker for something better. He wore a dress-suit for the first time in his life. It was his undoin'. He got stuck on himself. He thought he looked too beautiful for anything, and when he came home he was a changed man. As soon as he got to his house every evenin' he put on that dress-suit and set around in it until bedtime. That didn't satisfy him long. He wanted others to see how beautiful he was in a dress-suit; so he joined dancin' clubs and began goin' to all the balls that was given in town. Soon he began to neglect his family. Then he took to drinkin' and didn't pay any attention to his political work in the district. The end came in less than a year. He was dismissed from the department and went to the dogs. The other day I met him rigged out almost like a hobo, but he still had a dress-suit vest on. When I asked him what he was doin', he said: 'Nothin' at present, but I got a promise of a job enrollin' voters at Citizens' Union headquarters.' Yes, a dress-suit had brought him that low! . . .

"Now, nobody ever saw me puttin' on any style. I'm the same Plunkitt I was when I entered politics forty years ago. That is why the people have confidence in me. If I went into the stylish business, even I, Plunkitt, might be thrown down in the district. That was shown pretty clearly in the senatorial fight last year. A day before election, my enemies circulated a report that I had ordered a $10,000 automobile and a $125 dress-suit. I sent out contradictions as fast as I could, but I wasn't able to stamp out the infamous slander before the votin' was over, and I suffered some at the polls. The people wouldn't have minded much if I had been accused of robbin' the city treasury, for they're used to slanders of that kind in campaigns, but the automobile and the dress-suit were too much for them.

"Another thing that people won't stand for is showin' off your learnin'. That's just puttin' on style in another way. If you're makin' speeches in a campaign, talk the language the people talk. Don't try to show how the situation is by quotin' Shakespeare. Shakespeare was all right in his way, but he didn't know anything about Fifteenth District politics. If you know Latin and Greek and have a hankerin' to work them off on somebody, hire a stranger to come to your house and listen to you for a couple of hours; then go out and talk the language of the Fifteenth to the people. I know it's an awful temptation, the hankerin' to show off your learnin'. I've felt it myself, but I always resist it. I know the awful consequences."[1]

Richard Croker in his later years as Boss of Tammany Hall had acquired "an achin' for style." He had, as we have seen, made his pile, and he could afford it, but he was now also in a position to dictate to his associates, who did not have to be told just what kind of a dress tie to wear, for they watched him carefully at the Democratic Club in Fifth Avenue, which had replaced Tammany Hall as the social meeting place of the organization's leaders. There, in the evenings, Richard Croker sat silently with a few friends in evening clothes, and those who wished to speak with him approached his chair if the moment seemed auspicious. A *Tribune* reporter once watched at the door of the Democratic Club. He reported: "Four out of every five men that walk up the steps and enter the club stop at the door and give a nervous hitch at their hats or neckties. Then they turn to the colored doorman and say in a subdued voice, 'Is he in?' It is unnecessary to say that 'he' is always Squire Croker. The doorman has become accustomed to this use of the pronoun and always answers without asking who 'he' is."

When Croker attended a Democratic State Convention in 1898, a large crowd of enthusiasts met his train and cheered him. The police cleared a path for Croker, and his friend, John F. Carroll, walked before him elbowing out of the way the curious who broke through the police cordon. After he was seated in his carriage, Croker raised his hat in response to the cheers, and the crowd ran behind as if it were following a prima donna on the way from a triumph.

[1] *Plunkitt of Tammany Hall*, pp. 93–99.

The adulation of Richard Croker which pervaded the atmosphere wherever he was present during the last years of the 1800's moved William Allen White to the following peroration:

"And all this homage, all this boot-licking, to a mild-mannered, soft-voiced, sad-faced, green-eyed chunk of a man who talks slowly that he may peg in his 'seens' and his 'saws,' his 'dones' and his 'dids' where they belong, who has a loggy wit, who cares neither for books, nor music, nor theatrical performances, nor good wine, nor a dinner, nor the society of his kind! All this blind obedience by men of brains and some rudimentary culture to a dull, emotionless, prosimian hulk of bone and sinew—a sort of human megatherium, who has come crashing up from the swamps splashed with the slime of pre-Adamite wickedness! And now he sits on a throne and disposes a sort of jungle justice, while civilization knocks its knees together in stupid, terrified adulation!"[1]

Croker's nature was something of that of the orang-outang; his appearance was also somewhat similar: the short, thick, broad chest and shoulders, and the legs in proportion, the firm jaw, the sharp and at the same time appealing eyes, expressing an aggression that was pathetic because its possessor found it so necessary to be extreme. His glare was particularly that of the orang-outang, and in it there was expressed great contempt for the fear which it aroused. His friend Mayor Hugh J. Grant when he was testifying before the Fassett Committee denied that when he first knew Croker he was intimate with him, or even "extremely friendly," saying: "Mr. Croker is a peculiar man in that way; you know him a long time before you become what you call friendly with him."

A dinner commemorating Thomas Jefferson was held in New York in 1899. It was to be a brilliant Democratic function replete with oratory and effulgence. All the leading Democrats were to be present, but at the last moment Richard Croker ordered every Democratic State Senator to remain in Albany and attend to legislative business. None appeared at the dinner.

After Van Wyck was elected, Richard Croker filled the City's offices with deserving Democrats, and then he prepared to leave

[1] *McClure's Magazine*, Vol. XVI, p. 317, 1901.

for Europe. The City's expenses increased tremendously, and the Mazet Committee reported that "it would seem as if a consistent effort were being made to find out how two or more men could be made to do the work of one." The cry of "Wide Open" which had rung through New York on election night as a variation on the theme, "Well, well, Reform has gone to Hell," was answered promptly by Croker, and Van Wyck did his bidding. Captain William S. Devery, whose favourite answer to the charges brought up by the Lexow Committee against the police was, "Touchin' on and appertainin' to that matter, I disremember," was appointed Chief of Police. The town became wilder than ever, and it was during the four years of the Van Wyck régime that the things took place that we have already quoted from the report of the Mazet Committee, which investigated the period toward its end.

On February 9, 1898, after the new administration was installed in the City, the leaders of Tammany Hall gave a dinner at the Hotel Savoy for their chief. The cost was said to be $40 a plate. Mr. Croker was presented with a large loving cup. But harmony did not prevail throughout the evening. When Croker arose to reply to the speech of presentation which was made by the silver-tongued orator, Senator Thomas F. Grady, he departed from his formal, prepared address, and praised John C. Sheehan, who was to be in charge of Tammany Hall during Croker's absence abroad. Ex-Register John Reilly had the temerity to shout the point of information: "Who made Mr. Sheehan leader?" There was a silence. Croker was astounded at this sign of incipient treason. "Those in the majority," he mumbled. Then Surrogate Frank T. Fitzgerald dared to say as he rose in his seat: "We do not want Mr. Sheehan as leader." Croker became embarrassed and played with his napkin. Sheehan grew red in the face. Croker then recovered and said that he had not forced Sheehan on his district leaders, and that if he did not remain loyal to his friends Sheehan would be put out. Alderman Nicholas T. Brown shouted at this moment: "We do not want Mr. Sheehan for leader. He was never selected by the majority." This was too much. Croker did not deign to reply any more. Instead he praised County Clerk Henry D. Purroy for his unswerving loyalty to Tammany Hall.

These were small but important signs of discontent with the

dictatorship. They came to nothing at the moment, but several leaders had dared to stand up at a testimonial dinner to the chief and deny his infallibility and question his motives. And they had not been struck dead. It was a bad precedent. Some men thought that Richard Croker had become too tyrannical, and, what was worse, began to say so. There had been talk among the rank and file of Tammany Hall that dinners at $40 a plate to which only a few were invited indicated that the Boss was drawing away from his people. And there had been another annoying indication of this attitude on the part of Richard Croker. After Van Wyck was elected Mayor, "Big Tim" Sullivan and his followers held a magnificent parade, and the joyous Bowery victors planned to serenade their chief, Croker, who was staying at the Murray Hill Hotel. At the head of the column rode "Big Tim" Sullivan on a charger. A squad of mounted district leaders followed, and then the infantry, armed with brooms, yelled and screamed through the streets. These men were members of the Sullivan Association, the Elmwood Athletic Club, the Palm Pleasure Association, the Chop Suey Social Club, and the Bowling Green Wheelmen. They were followed by two floats, on one of which was the largest tiger obtainable, surrounded by Bowery Indians in appropriate war paint. On the other float were two children, representing Columbia and Uncle Sam. When the magnificent procession reached the Murray Hill Hotel, the men shouted for Croker, but their chief was nowhere to be seen, and they looked around for someone to review them. They had to be satisfied with Thomas S. Brennan, who took off his hat and bowed. The master of ceremonies had rushed into the hotel before the serenaders arrived. He saw Croker, but he rushed out again, and it was noted that he did not look particularly pleased. Mayor-elect Van Wyck, who had been seen at the Hoffman House a few minutes before "Big Tim" Sullivan on his charger arrived in the neighbourhood, suddenly, but efficiently, disappeared.

Croker, it was said, was ill, but there were also indications that he feared the rapid rise of "Big Tim" who was now in such a powerful position that Croker had to call on him, instead of issuing a royal summons. It was even said that "Big Tim" aspired to the leadership. And it was Sullivan who remarked in public apropos of Croker's departure for Europe: "For considerations touching on his own health, Mr. Croker transferred his court from Lakewood to Wantage."

Signs of revolt, however, did not prevent the leading politicians and administrators of New York City from crowding on to the pier and into the stateroom on the various occasions during these years when Richard Croker sailed for Europe. The crowd was so dense that some could not approach the stateroom, and they climbed on the rail and looked into the port holes, until the ship's officers ordered them away. The stateroom itself was filled to suffocation with large floral offerings. Chief of Police Devery sent a large horseshoe, and Commissioner Scannell, who had been in prison with Croker, sent a horse made entirely of roses. The Board of Governors of the Democratic Club sent a mass of red roses with an arch and a blue silk flag on which was gilded the word "Godspeed." "Al" Adams, the policy king, and Frank Farrell, the pool-room king, were there, and so were "Big Tim" Sullivan and Chief of Police Devery. In the crowd were judges, commissioners, the District Attorney, lawyers, gamblers, and small politicians.

Upon one occasion Croker was accompanied down the bay by his brother-in-law, Dr. William T. Jenkins. The police boat *Patrol* preceded the Cunard steamer through the Narrows, and when the steamer reached the lower bay of New York, the *Patrol* fired a salute of twenty-one guns. "Why, that's the President's salute," remarked Mr. Croker to the doctor with a smile.

IX

After Croker's great triumph in the election of Robert A. Van Wyck, New York experienced a period of rule by an absentee landlord, for Croker spent the next few years of his political career in England, Ireland, and on ocean steamers. Government by cable, was what some of the newspapers chose to call it, for whenever problems of great political importance arose, nothing was done until word was received from Croker. Meanwhile, his subordinates who held city offices and did the City's work were making hay rapidly, for no one could tell when, if ever, would come such perfect days.

The Police Department under the domination of Bill Devery

chartered vice and controlled graft. The docks were rented to the American Ice Company exclusively. The streets were regarded as sources of profit rather than as public highways. There was "a hot time in the old town "during those four years. When the newspapers clamoured against the picturesque outrages of Chief of Police Devery, Mayor Van Wyck stated publicly that "Devery is the best chief of police New York ever had."

Devery, whatever his faults and his virtues, was always news for the newspapers, and, like Barnum, he took it all as pleasing and valuable advertisement. Devery had thirty-six large scrapbooks of his press clippings. His office was a pump in front of a saloon on the corner of Eighth Avenue and Twenty-eighth Street, where for more than five years he was in the habit of standing every night from about nine o'clock until two or three the next morning, transacting his own business with his gambling associates, and the City's business with the police. When he was asked whether he knew that the saloon in back of his pump was keeping open after closing hours, he answered that he saw men going in and out, but that he did not know it was a saloon. Devery once remarked, "Providence made me Chief of Police," but he also said in one of his later speeches, "I carried my father's dinner pail when he was laying the bricks of Tammany Hall." When a Republican legislature removed Devery as Chief of Police by abolishing that office, Mayor Van Wyck, at the cabled order of Richard Croker, appointed him Deputy Police Commissioner, with even greater powers than he had enjoyed before.

It was one of the new Deputy Commissioner's duties to preside at the trial of charges against policemen, and he presided in extraordinary fashion. He told one patrolman: "When you're caught with the goods on you and you can't get away with it, you want to stand up with nerve and take your medicine. You don't know nothin' then. No matter under what circumstances, a man doesn't want to know nothin' when he's caught with the goods on him. You tell your lady to tip you off next time. Always get tipped off. You don't want to go blind to these things hereafter." Another policeman was suspected by Devery of being drunk, and he ordered him to open his mouth and blow his breath in the Deputy Commissioner's face. The policeman refused. "That is right, my man," said Devery, dismissing the case, "keep your mouth shut all the time. If you do that you won't get into trouble here." Policeman John Marrinan was brought before Deputy Commissioner Devery upon the charge of having a soiled uniform. The following conversation took place:

"Devery—Well, what yer got to say to that?

"Marrinan—I had a woman prisoner the night before who was very dirty and she soiled my clothing.

"Devery—Did she dress you in the mornin'?

"Marrinan—No, but she was a very unclean woman and——

"Devery—Unclean, you call her unclean! No matter how dirty she was she was cleaner than you—you—you——

"Marrinan—I don't think so, sir.

*   *   *   *   *

"Marrinan—Now, now——

"Devery—Now! now! Just spit it out. You're a bum. Clear out of here, and keep away from me. I'll fine you fifteen days' pay. Now go, you, you dirty bum you, and see if you can get that fine remitted. Go on, you bum, you loafer, you ——."[1]

The newspapers refused to publish the rest of Devery's remarks.

After he had captured New York City in the election of 1897, Croker tried to win the State by electing Mayor Van Wyck's brother, Augustus, Governor of New York in 1898. The Republican candidate was Colonel Theodore Roosevelt. Croker tried to prevent the nomination of Roosevelt by the Republicans, because he feared the popularity of the man who had just returned from the Spanish-American War as a hero and was still enjoying the *reclame* of his uniform. The Republicans had decided to make Roosevelt their candidate, and Chauncey M. Depew was requested to make the nominating speech at the State Convention. Depew was then president of the New York Central Railroad. After Croker's death, Depew told the following story:

"One day before the convention met, Senator Patrick McCarren of Brooklyn came into my office and said, 'I have a mes-

[1] *Ten Months of Tammany*, p. 34.

sage for you which, personally, I am ashamed to deliver. Mr. Croker has sent me to say to you that if you make that speech nominating Colonel Roosevelt in the Republican convention he will resent it on your railroad.' I said: 'Senator McCarren, I have done my best to make every man in the employ of the railroad a citizen with the same rights as any man in any other business. So far I have·succeeded, and it is so understood among railroad men that they can have their political conviction just the same as other men, and I know Mr. Croker's power and the injury he can do the road. You can say to him that I am amazed at such a message coming from a man I have always found to be a square fighter, as this is a blow below the belt. I am going to make that speech, but before I make it I shall resign as president and director of the New York Central Railroad. And when I put Mr. Roosevelt in nomination before the convention of the State of New York I will then say why I resigned.' Mr. Mc-Carren replied that it would beat the ticket, and I replied I knew it would, but it would vindicate my manhood. Senator McCarren returned in a short time and said: 'Mr. Croker wishes you to forget that message. His own words were: "It is withdrawn. I was very badly advised."'[1]

To have one brother in New York City and the other in Albany would have simplified matters considerably for Croker, and he could have gone back to his country place in England and his horses with the feeling that his affairs were in the hands of trustees who would look after his interests, but the public did not see the situation from Croker's point of view, and Augustus Van Wyck was defeated.

It was in this election of 1898 that Croker made a serious blunder. He refused a renomination to Supreme Court Justice Daly, because the judge had not appointed men whom Croker wanted appointed to subordinate offices in his courtroom. "Justice Daly," said Croker, "was elected by Tammany Hall after he was discovered by Tammany Hall, and Tammany Hall had a right to expect proper consideration at his hands." Reformers were aroused, and they held a large mass meeting in Carnegie Hall on the evening of October 21, 1898. Croker was denounced, and his autocratic, tyrannical powers were de-

[1]New York *Herald*, May 1, 1922.

scribed. W. Bourke Cockran, who had been a loyal Tammany man for years, and one of the organization's favourite "silver-tongued orators," made a long and stirring speech against his former boss, with whom he had quarrelled a few years before. Some said the quarrel was due to real-estate transactions, and some said that Mr. Cockran wanted to be United States Senator from New York and that Mr. Croker would not permit it. In speaking of Croker's powers, Cockran told the Carnegie Hall audience, "By an interview he can send the stock of a corporation soaring above that mysterious line known as par, or sinking below those gloomy levels which evoke spectres of bankruptcy and liquidation." "If he sought social success," said Cockran, "he has nominations to bestow upon the politically ambitious who could further his designs; and, if he were refused an invitation which he coveted, the person who disappointed him might find an engine house established in his back yard." "Indeed, as we survey the extent of his powers and the manner in which they have been exercised, I believe he would be justified in saying with Lord Clive: 'Considering my opportunities, I am amazed at my own moderation.'" If the judiciary fell under Croker's control, Mr. Cockran pointed out, no man in New York would be safe from his displeasure, for at least there was still recourse to the courts in the pursuit of life, liberty, and happiness. It was this same orator who, less than ten years before, when he was a close associate of Mr. Croker's, said before the Fassett Committee: "Tammany Hall has no leaders; those who are generally supposed to be leaders are really followers, among whom I include myself."

It was Croker's truculent domination that had cost Tammany Hall the election of 1898, for Roosevelt was elected only by a narrow majority of 17,000. Mayor Van Wyck's administration, however, thanks to the Republican Legislature of a few years before, still had three years of plenty, and the City remained under the complete control of the Boss. In the following year, 1899, the Mazet Investigation took place, and Croker was forced to disclose much more by his refusals to answer questions than he cared to disclose. Again the City was emotionally aroused, but nothing could be done about it until the election of 1901, when Croker returned from Europe once more to lead Tammany Hall to victory.

John F. Carroll, who was Croker's trusted assistant, visited the Squire of Wantage on his Berkshire estate during the summer of 1901. Carroll was noted for his aggressive silence, and when he returned to New York from the significant visit, newspaper reporters who asked him questions received odd replies.

"Will Richard Croker return this month?" a reporter asked. Carroll leaned back, studied his gold match box for a while, and inquired: "Anything else?" "A newspaper reported you as saying that Croker will not return for the campaign if he thinks his presence here will be unnecessary. Did you say that?" Carroll, after long thought: "I don't think I did. Do you?" Then followed this colloquy: Q. "Then I can say that Croker will return?" A. "You can say what you wish." Q. "Did you bring any message from Mr. Croker?" A. "Who said so?" Q. "Will you give out any information at all about your trip to Wantage?" A. "What information?" During one campaign a reporter said to Carroll: "Good-morning; it is a fine day, isn't it?" "Is it?" asked Carroll. "Of course," replied the reporter, pointing to the cloudless sky. "Then, why did you ask me?" Carroll inquired suspiciously. District leaders who did not have as much use for Carroll as Croker did found the best joke of the year in the following description of John F. Carroll in *The Brown Book*, the official biographical record of New York's city officials: "He thoroughly enjoys social life and is popular in the large circle of acquaintances in which he moves."

Croker realized that the reputation of Tammany Hall was blemished once more by the tarnish of prostitution and the stains of muddy business transactions. He needed a reputation, and he chose as his candidate for Mayor, Edward M. Shepard, a reputable Brooklyn lawyer. The reformers had nominated Seth Low, and Croker required a reformer to fight a reformer. Shepard had been an ardent advocate of civil service reform and ballot reform, and he had also been an ardent opponent of the methods of Tammany Hall. With William J. Gaynor he had been instrumental in sending the Democratic Boss of Coney Island, John Y. McCane, to jail for stuffing ballot boxes with illegal votes. Seth Low and his associates brought out Shepard's former denunciations of Tammany Hall, and they demanded to know what, if elected, Mr. Shepard intended to do about

RICHARD CROKER

Devery and red lights. Shepard said nothing in reply except that he took back nothing that he had formerly said, and that he would give the City an honest administration.

In this campaign of 1901, Croker was fighting another fight besides the mayoralty election, and that was the growing revolt in Tammany Hall against his autocratic power. He was also fighting the increasing power of "Big Tim" Sullivan and his associates.

Signs of revolt against the complete domination of the Old Man were now even more prevalent, and men grew less afraid as they saw that their boldness was effective. Slowly, but certainly, several men in Tammany Hall began to realize that this squat, thick man, who could get into such a rage when he was crossed, was not a god. And the god who was becoming a man again was somewhat frightened at finding himself questioned. The possibility of defeat began slowly to dawn upon his mind, and he made certain panicky efforts to avoid the inevitable. Croker had not been an early riser. Now he got up at five o'clock in the morning and spent much of his time walking up and down the empty corridors of the Democratic Club, where none but the sweepers observed his meditations. "Big Tim" Sullivan brazenly told newspaper reporters, "Croker ain't the whole thing."

A demonstration of the strength of the anti-Croker forces came in the primary election fight for the position of district leader in the Second District. Patrick Divver was Croker's friend and candidate for district leader, and he was opposed by Tom Foley, friend and candidate of "Big Tim" Sullivan. Sullivan had warned Croker shortly before that the Tammany vice investigating committee must not tamper with Sullivan's Bowery district, and the vice committee did not do so. Now he came out in open revolt and supported Foley. The contest was a sharp one. Both Foley and Divver catered to the Japanese vote, the Chinese vote, the Jewish vote, and the Italian vote in the polyglot district in which they lived. The Italian vote was large, and both men attended all the Italian funerals and christenings they could find, and they also kept a close watch on marriages. Each one had a reporter in the Italian district who traced marriages, and Foley, in order to get the better of Divver, hired a man to remain at the marriage bureau in City

Hall and telephone whenever an Italian couple from the district came to get married. Foley then had a number of presents ready and he rushed to the City Hall as soon as his worker telephoned to him, gave the bride a ring or a watch or a piece of silver, and offered his congratulations. When Divver went to the home of the bride, he found that Foley had been ahead of him. Toward the end of the campaign, Divver also stationed a man at the marriage bureau, and then there were foot races and fist fights to determine who could reach his leader first with the good news. Sometimes they were hot rivals for philanthropy at funerals. Upon one occasion they both received the news of an Italian labourer's death at the same time. Each district leader went to his favourite undertaker and took him to the house of the deceased. They met in front of the house, and there was a fight. After discussion, Divver's undertaker was selected, but Foley had more carriages at the funeral, and he impressed the Italian voters by paying the widow's rent for a month and sending her half a ton of coal and a barrel of flour. The Hebrew vote in the district was almost as large as the Italian vote, and upon the occasion of an important Baxter Street wedding, spies were employed by both Foley and Divver to find out what each intended to give as a present. Foley heard that Divver intended to give a set of silver. He bought an exact duplicate of Divver's silver set and added a silver tea service. George Washington Plunkitt remarked of an East Side district leader: "He eats corned beef and kosher meat with equal nonchalance, and it's all the same to him whether he takes off his hat in the church or pulls it down over his ears in the synagogue."

Sullivan's man Foley won the election, and Sullivan was in a stronger position in Tammany Hall than he had ever been. Croker was no longer able to dictate to him. It was said that "Big Tim" Sullivan sent men from other parts of the City into Foley's district to vote many times, and the Foley adherents claimed that Divver's men enrolled the names of men found on tombstones in Calvary and Greenwood cemeteries. Mr. Foley was noted among his followers for running what one of them described as "the swellest gin-mill below de line," the line being Fourteenth Street. At the corner of Centre and Franklin streets Tom Foley's saloon was located, and inside the brass shone as brightly and the glasses glistened as resplendently as in the most fashionable Broadway cafés. The floor was clean in all kinds of weather, and the free-lunch counter was piled with attractive delicacies.

Others of Croker's friends besides Paddy Divver were defeated in the primary elections of 1901, and his return from Europe was not so happy as on previous occasions.

The mayoralty campaign of 1901 was lively. William Travers Jerome, who was the reform candidate for the office of District Attorney, supplied most of the diversion, for Seth Low was a dignified, but dull, personality. Devery, whose *penchant* for nicknames amounted to genius, called the president of Columbia University "Little Eva." "Big Tim" Sullivan remarked of Jerome, "Why, that fellow couldn't strike a blow that would knock a hole through a pound of butter." In his speeches, however, Jerome struck many powerful blows against prostitution and political graft on the East Side, and it was his personal campaign that aroused the people. Tammany Hall sent out masses of campaign propaganda, even indulging for the occasion in poetry, which, it was said, was judged by Croker himself before it was printed. There was also a song writer and a ballad singer on the Tammany Hall staff. The Seth Low campaign managers sent throughout the City on posters and stereopticons the following opinion:

"Tammany's waste makes New York's want,
But
Croker's Wantage makes New York's wastage."

Seth Low was elected, and Tammany Hall went out of power again.

Once more Tammany Hall had been defeated by a complete investigation of its crimes, and this time Croker's domination was seriously damaged, though his influence remained great. Croker once told Chauncey M. Depew when Depew asked him how he managed to retain his power in the face of combinations against him in Tammany Hall: "Yes, there are combinations constantly being formed, but when the conspirators or rebels reach as many as five somebody always gives them away, and then I have no trouble." But two serious defeats were more harmful to his power than conspiracy. Croker himself was being exhibited before the public as the hateful source of all corruption, and his personality was becoming a hindrance to Tammany Hall rather than an asset. An anti-Croker League was formed in New York, which in its open letter to Croker charged that he had nominated Van Wyck only after receiving the assurance that he would be obeyed and had told Van Wyck bluntly that he needed money and that there was much to be made out of the administration of the City's affairs.

"We charge," said the open letter, "to your unscrupulous greed the development of the system of organized official blackmail which honeycombs the Police Department. Your trusted and confidential lieutenants, headed by that illiterate ruffian Devery, are the leading spirits in the coalition between the police and the vicious elements of the city. The tribute collected from the profits of shame and of illegal gambling did not stick to the fingers of wardmen. The major portion of it went 'higher up,' to the 'top,' to 'John Doe,' and when we reach the top and find the genuine 'John Doe' we recognize your features, and there is no case of mistaken identity about it, either.

"Because you needed money to support yourself in leading the life of a profligate absentee landlord you had your confidential friends appoint chiefs of departments, to act as your agents in perverting the public interests to subserve your private interests. To enrich you they bargained away public favors to the highest bidders. All of them were engaged in a conspiracy 'to make money' at the expense of the taxpayers."

When Croker was asked by newspaper reporters what he had to say to this statement, he answered: "Nothing at all. I have heard of it, but I have not seen it and do not want to see it."

At another farewell dinner at the Democratic Club Croker once more announced his permanent retirement from Tammany Hall and from politics. He made a twenty-three-minute speech, the longest of his career, and he reminded his admirers that he had to his credit fifteen victories and two defeats in the seventeen years of his leadership of Tammany Hall. He announced his successor, Lewis Nixon, and paid tribute to his capabilities;

"ALL IS LOST—SAVE WANTAGE"

"'Appertainin' to and touchin' on' the election of Tuesday"

Nixon had been an efficient shipbuilder and engineer. Among the guests were all the men prominent in Tammany Hall, some of the leading newspaper editors of the City, ex-mayors, Croker's two sons, state Senators, and judges. Croker was presented with a chest of silver service three feet by four feet. On the following day he sailed for Europe. Again the dock was crowded with politicians and officeholders, and again the stateroom was filled with enormous bouquets of flowers. "I am out of politics, and now I am going to win the Derby," Croker told reporters.

That ambition occupied the next six years of Richard Croker's life, and it seemed more difficult to accomplish than a New York election. When Croker first began to race horses in England in 1896 he was regarded as an usurper. Perhaps the kind of politics which he played was considered in Great Britain the same as being in trade. This attitude made him angry and determined. He had purchased a stock farm in America at Richfield Springs, and he later bought "Yorkville Belle" for $24,000, "Fairy" for $10,000, "Red Banner" for $15,000, and "Dobbins" for $20,000. He had also offered $50,000 for the famous brood mare "Thora" and $30,000 for the filly "Helen Nichols." Then he bought an interest in one of the most famous stud farms in the United States, the Belle Mead farm, paying, it was said, $250,000 for a half interest, and at the same time he purchased the famous "Longstreet" for $30,000. It was said by some that Croker paid too much for his horses, and there were men who boasted with delight of their ability to get the better of the Boss of Tammany Hall in a horse deal. When he transferred his turf activities to England, Croker had horses in training at Newmarket, but he was requested by the stewards to remove them. Croker then purchased a stud farm at Glencairn, Ireland. He devoted much time to the training of his horses, and in 1907 his horse "Orby" won the Derby at the long odds of 100 to 9. "Orby" also won the Irish Derby and the Curragh and Baldoyle Derby. Whereupon Croker received the freedom of Dublin, but he did not receive the customary invitation from King Edward to the "Derby Dinner," an omission which was said to be unprecedented.

Croker's æsthetic interests also extended to bulldogs, and he purchased for $5,000 the famous prize bulldog, "Rodney

Stone," one of the ugliest and therefore rarest of his species. "Rodney Stone," who was a boon to cartoonists, for they seldom failed to place him somewhere in the vicinity of Croker on his throne, won many prizes at dog shows, and Croker ordered a life-size bronze statue of the dog to be made out of the medals which he had won. At Glencairn there were also oil paintings of every horse bred at the stud who had won an important race. Croker's sons, Richard, Jr., and Frank, also bred bulldogs and won numerous prizes for their entries. When his sons, Richard, Jr., and Herbert, were in college at Cornell University, the newspapers reported that they had with them in their rooms the two prize bulldogs of their father's collection, "Rodney Stone" and "Bromley Crib." Extravagant stories about the way the Croker boys lived at Cornell, surrounded by horses and hounds, caused them much annoyance and made their father furious. Farmers from the country districts near Ithaca drove into town after work for the express purpose of looking at the Croker pets, and they refused to believe that the animals had been left with their father.

Town Topics had this to say concerning the change of habits and the change of habitat of the Boss of Tammany Hall:

"Mr. Richard Welstead Croker. How much sweeter to the tongue and more filling to the mouth than plain Dick Croker. Once this eminent retired capitalist and politician was only Croker. Indeed, the philosophers of the engine-house and the corner grocery may have had the impudence to call him Dicky, or even Old Croke. But power brings its responsibilities and has a chastening effect even upon nomenclature. To the severe simplicity of the Hon. Richard Croker and Mr. Croker has now succeeded the more florid style of Richard Welstead Croker. Mr. Croker found a middle name in Ireland, and I daresay he will pick up another the next time he visits that lovely parent of Tammany. There is something boldly baronial about Welstead. It suggests an abbey, and a castle, and a park full of red deer and beautiful little pigs, the parlor pets of Welstead's ancestors. But I am afraid the name is too literary for Croker's constituents. It suggests Charles Dudley Warner or Richard Harding Davis. I presume, in a year or two, we shall hear of Mr. Welstead-Croker or Mr. R. Welstead Crokaire. When a statesman of Mr. Croker's abilities begins monkeying with his name, you can never tell where he will stop. Fortunately Mr. Croker is able to support even the most luxurious and lofty name in proper style."

After his retirement, which was permanent, except that he frequently gave advice by cable, Croker spent most of his time at his stud farm in Ireland or on the race courses of England. People who saw him at Glencairn spoke of his leaning on a fence for hours, watching his cattle graze and saying nothing. It was also said that he showed real surprise for one of the few times in his life when he discovered Egypt. Two of Croker's sons died in 1905. Frank Croker died from injuries received in a collision while driving his racing automobile along the shore at Palm Beach. A few months later Herbert Croker was found dead in the compartment of a railroad train between Emporia and Newton, Kansas. A coroner's jury attributed the death to narcotic poisoning caused by smoking opium. In memory of these sons Croker built a chapel on his estate at Glencairn.

For some years Richard Croker had been estranged from his wife, and several of his children took their mother's side in the disagreement. Mrs. Croker, to whom Croker was married in 1873, had been Miss Elizabeth Frazer. Mrs. Croker was interested in the Catholic Church and its charities, and she was embarrassed considerably by the notoriety which her husband's political position brought to the family. It hurt her particularly when the newspapers called her husband a thief. Even before Croker's retirement from politics, he separated from his wife, and lived at the Democratic Club. After his retirement Croker scarcely saw his wife, who spent much of her time in the south of France with her daughter Florence, who married an Italian count, and her daughter Ethel, who married a riding master and divorced him soon afterward. When the war broke out in 1914, Mrs. Croker was in the Austrian Tyrol, where she died in September of that year. The body was sent to New York, and Croker returned there for the funeral, which was also attended by the leading friends of the former Boss of Tammany Hall.

A few weeks after the funeral Richard Croker, who was then seventy-three years old, married Miss Bula Benton Edmondson, who was twenty-three years old at the time. Miss Edmondson was said to be a direct descendant of Sequoyah, the Cherokee Indian chief who was credited with the invention of the Cherokee alphabet. Miss Edmondson's Indian name was given in the newspapers as "Kotaw Kaluntuchy." She studied singing, and she lectured, and it was said at the time of her marriage that her ambition was to portray to the white man the American Indian in his true light. The management of the New York Hippodrome told the *Herald* that Miss Edmondson had appeared at that theatre for five weeks during the summer previous to her marriage in a spectacle called "America," in which she in Indian costume rode across the stage on a horse and sang the national anthem in the Cherokee language.

Miss Edmondson first met Croker at the Democratic National Convention in Kansas City in 1900, and it was said that "he became interested in her zeal to make her people better understood." He met her again at dinner soon after he arrived in New York for his first wife's funeral. He asked her to marry him. The wedding took place at the home of Nathan Straus and was attended by none of Croker's family, but there was a sprinkling of Supreme Court justices. Croker's best men were Thomas F. Smith, Secretary of Tammany Hall, Andrew Freedman, his former business partner and political henchman, and Nathan Straus. The bride's hair was arranged in Indian style. She said to reporters: "I have been inspired by the example of Pocahontas, who did so much to make the English people understand our race. Then there was Saccawagea, the 'bird woman,' who piloted the Lewis and Clarke expedition 5,000 miles and made it a success. . . . I also find inspiration in Talahina, the Cherokee maiden, who helped Sam Houston to free Texas." "But," she added, "it is the dearest ambition of every Indian girl to win a chief, and," turning to Mr. Croker, "I have won the chief of men." It was noted by his friends that Mr. Croker was beginning to show signs of the feebleness of old age.

Croker and his bride left for Florida immediately after the wedding. "Didn't we have a time getting away from those photographers, though?" Mrs. Croker said to her husband as they were waiting for the train to leave the Pennsylvania Station. "Yes," he answered gruffly, "you've got to expect that in this land of liberty." "Will Mrs. Croker continue her work

on the subject of the Indians?" a reporter asked Croker.
"No," he answered bluntly, "unless she does it by herself."
"You're not interested in the Indians?" asked the reporter.
"Oh, I like to hear about them," answered the former chief of
Tammany Hall.

Croker spent most of his remaining years on his Irish estate
with his second wife. He returned to New York in 1920 to
answer the lawsuits brought against him by his children for
property which they alleged he owed them. The children sought
to have their father declared mentally unfit to administer his
affairs, but a Florida court declared him to be in full control of
his faculties. Just before returning to Ireland again, Croker
told newspaper men: "They say I am crazy because I won't
give them all my money. My son Richard had to admit on the
witness stand that I had given $150,000 to him to start him in
business. I have given to each of my other children $4,000 a
year for life. That was pretty mean, wasn't it? I am going to
try to forgive them." Croker, on the occasion of this last visit
to New York, attended the world series baseball game and took
great interest in the fact that pitchers had learned to curve a
ball so that it started in one direction and went in another.

During his last years Richard Croker was interested in the
efforts of Ireland to become a free state, and it was said that he
contributed money to the support of the cause. Even Tammany
Hall was now subordinate in his mind to the success of the
Irish movement, and he was interested in the Tammany victory
of 1921 only because of its possible effect on the Irish cause. He
arranged with his friend John Whalen to have cablegrams sent
to him with the election results on election night, and after the
election he dictated the following letter to Mrs. Croker:

"MY DEAR JOHN:
"Many thanks for your cables. I am delighted that Tam-
many had such a victory. It will have a splendid effect on the
Irish cause."

In the winter of 1922, Croker, who was then seventy-nine
years old, was ill with jaundice. He improved somewhat and
was wheeled to his stables to look at his beloved horses. On
April 29, 1922, he died in the presence of his wife and her

brother. He himself had superintended the erection of a vault on his estate, where he stipulated that he was to be buried, and he also requested that the bones of his Derby winner, "Orby," who was also buried at Glencairn, should be dug up and placed nearer his own.

The funeral services were held in the chapel Croker had built in his house, and the coffin bore a blanket of violets with a card inscribed "To Daddy from Bula."

Croker's estate was estimated to be worth more than $5,000,000, and it was left to his wife.

CHAPTER VII

MURPHY

I

WHEN Richard Croker made his last, final, and only authentic farewell speech after the disastrous election of 1901, he had, as we have seen, placed Lewis Nixon on his throne. In his speech Croker had urged the Tammany Hall district leaders to support Nixon as they had supported him, and he assured them that Nixon was a man such as they had never seen before, a man bigger even than the Democratic Party, which was the highest praise in his power to bestow.

In January, 1902, Lewis Nixon took charge of Tammany Hall. He had from the first indicated his independence and proclaimed his desire to change the methods of the Hall. After he had been Boss of Tammany Hall for about four months, Nixon sent telegrams to the district leaders requesting their presence in Tammany Hall on May 14, 1902, at four o'clock in the afternoon. When most of them had assembled, Nixon walked in and announced abruptly that he had sent in his resignation as chairman of the finance committee and leader of Tammany Hall. Michael C. Murphy began to make a speech in which he praised Mr. Nixon as "a splendid leader in whom the other leaders of Tammany had the utmost confidence." Nixon stopped him abruptly. "I do not want any vote of confidence," he announced. "I have decided to resign and my decision is absolute. My resignation will not be withdrawn under any circumstances. It is to go into effect immediately. I could not retain the leadership of Tammany Hall and at the same time retain my self-respect, and there is no political preferment that I would take in exchange for that. My resolution is unalterable. It will not be changed under any circumstances." The *Sun*, which reported the foregoing statement "as nearly as it could be remembered by the men who heard it,"

also reported that "Mr. Nixon's face was very red—redder than
its natural rosy hue—and he was very much excited, though
there was not a moment when he did not have complete control
of himself." Mr. Nixon went on to say that since he had taken
the leadership of Tammany Hall he had been hampered by a
"kitchen cabinet," headed by Croker's close friend and business associate, Andrew Freedman, and that, "Every important
act of mine has been cabled to England before it became effective." "Then a cablegram came from Wantage direct to me
to place certain men on the Board of Sachems, and when I
rebelled I found that at every turn I would be opposed by this
coterie of interferers." Many of the district leaders, Nixon told
them, got advice by cable from Croker before they carried out
Nixon's orders. Nixon then repeated to reporters that he could
not continue in his position and retain his self-respect, but he
refused to add to that statement any specific details.

When Nixon resigned, Tammany Hall came under the control
for a few months of a triumvirate, consisting of Charles F.
Murphy, Daniel F. McMahon, and Louis F. Haffen. "Bill"
Devery made the trio ridiculous by calling Murphy, McMahon,
and Haffen, "Sport," "Two-Spot," and "Joke," respectively.

The organization was now in a precarious condition, for
there were rivalries among the district leaders for the cloak of
Croker, and there was much manipulation for control in the
individual districts. "Big Tim" Sullivan and his relatives were
more powerful than ever on the Bowery; Devery, who had been
abandoned by Croker and Tammany Hall, was playing his own
private game of politics in a West Side section of the City;
various leaders were fighting for control of other districts. But,
in spite of all this dissension, a new strong man was gradually
gaining absolute power, and his name was Charles Francis
Murphy. Tammany Hall has never been controlled successfully
for long by more than one boss, and after a few months two
members of the triumvirate imperceptibly withdrew to the
background, while Murphy just as imperceptibly became the
acknowledged leader.

Charles Francis Murphy was born in New York City on
June 20, 1858. His father had seven other children. He lived
in the Gas House district, the habitat of active gangs, and, like
Croker, he became a leader among his associates because of his

physical strength. For a living, he worked at various periods of his youth as a "handy man" in "Barney" Curtin's saloon, as a labourer in Roach's shipyard, and in a wire factory. During his spare time he played catcher on the baseball team of his neighbourhood, known as the "Senators," composed of members of the Sylvan Social Club, which Murphy had organized. The baseball team was very successful and played to large crowds in vacant lots on Sundays for stakes of $100. Murphy was offered a job as a professional ball player, but he preferred to play politics, and he accepted as his first favour a job as driver on the "Blue Line" cross-town horse cars. His brother, later an alderman, brought him his dinner in a pail. Murphy saved $500, and he opened a saloon on Nineteenth Street near Avenue A; upstairs were the chambers of the Sylvan Social Club. Murphy sold a large glass of beer and a bowl of soup for five cents, and he steadfastly refused to serve women. The saloon soon became known to dock workers and longshoremen as "Charlie's place," and they patronized it regularly. The trophies which the "Senators" won in their baseball games were displayed back of the bar.

"Barney" Biglin, the Republican district leader of the Twentieth District, boasted that he and his three brothers could row better than any other four in New York City. Murphy organized a crew from the members of his Sylvan Social Club and challenged the boaster. The race was scheduled for a fine Sunday afternoon, and the course was along the East River from One Hundredth Street to One Hundred and Twenty-ninth Street. Large bets had been made, and the stakes were also large. A crowd gathered around the contestants. At the last moment, it was discovered that "Tecumseh," the stroke of Murphy's crew, was ill. Rumours spread that he had been drugged, and fist fights followed. While the excitement was going on, Murphy stepped into the place of "Tecumseh" and rowed stroke. The Sylvan boat won two out of three heats from the Biglin Republicans, and Murphy was the most popular man in his district. His friend Edward Hagan realized that this popularity could be turned to political use. Hagan was an assemblyman from the Eighteenth District. He had been turned down for a renomination by Tammany Hall, and he asked Murphy what he should do. Murphy, whose reputation as a tight-lipped man was already extensive, answered, "Run independent." Murphy managed his friend's campaign, and they beat Tammany Hall. Then, like so many of the men who started in opposition to Tammany Hall, he promised never to do it again, and went into the fold with the influence that naturally came from demonstrated ability.

Meanwhile, the saloon business had prospered, and by 1890 Murphy was the proprietor of four "handsome cafés," as the *Tammany Times* expressed it. The principal saloon at Twentieth Street and Second Avenue was also the headquarters of the Anawanda Club, a Tammany Hall district association that soon attained great local strength. Hagan was the leader of the district, and Murphy was his prime minister. Ballots at elections were still distributed in front of the polls by representatives of the parties, and at one election Republican ballots, with the name of the Tammany candidate for Congress, General Francis B. Spinola, were somehow put into the hands of Republican voters. Spinola was elected as a result of these irregular ballots, and Charlie Murphy was generally believed to be the original genius who had conceived the fraud, but nobody could prove it, for Murphy was tight-lipped, and he managed carefully to get the credit among his followers without the blame of the law.

In 1892 Hagan died, and on his deathbed he named Charlie Murphy his successor as district leader of the "Gas House District." Murphy was now thirty-four years old, popular in his district, noted for his silence and blessed for his charities. He stood against a lamp post on a Second Avenue corner every night at about nine o'clock, and anybody in the district who wished to see him called and discussed business or pleasure. Murphy gave $4,000 for the relief of sufferers from the blizzard of 1888, and he gave $1,500 to the mission maintained by Dr. William S. Rainsford, the rector of St. George's Protestant Episcopal Church, although Murphy himself was a Catholic. Murphy also managed to get many jobs for the people in his neighbourhood.

When Van Wyck was elected Mayor, and Tammany Hall came into its own in the fullest sense of the term, Murphy's reward for regularity was an appointment as one of the four dock commissioners of New York. This was one of the most profitable gifts in the power of Van Wyck and Croker to bestow,

for millions of dollars were to be spent on improvements, and
there were ice companies and other organizations that were
willing to pay for extraordinary privileges. The dock commissioners had wide powers, and Murphy was the treasurer. This
was the only official position Charles F. Murphy ever held, and
he was proud of the title, for in after years men who wished
to ingratiate themselves with him always called him "Commissioner." One of Murphy's associate dock commissioners was
Mr. J. Sergeant Cram, a graduate of Harvard and a member of
a rich family. It was J. Sergeant Cram who was generally
credited with having taught Charlie Murphy to wear a dress-
suit, and they remained firm friends during Murphy's entire
lifetime.

In 1901, the year of the great Tammany defeat after the
scandals of the Van Wyck administration, Charles F. Murphy
organized the New York Contracting & Trucking Company,
and in the year 1902 he had succeeded to the leadership of
Tammany Hall. The New York Contracting & Trucking Company leased docks from the City and made 5,000 per cent. on its
investment. It also received the contracts for excavating the
site of the Pennsylvania Station and for the improvement of
the New York, New Haven & Hartford Railroad. When Murphy left the office of dock commissioner, he was said to be
worth $1,000,000. He purchased a dignified estate at Good
Ground, Long Island, where he built a nine-hole golf course,
and in town his special refuge was Delmonico's restaurant.
Here on the second floor was what the newspapers called "The
Scarlet Room of Mystery." Every day when he was in town the
Tammany leader had lunch in this room. Those he wanted
to see especially were asked there; those who wanted to see
him met him at Tammany Hall. A large mirror in a gilt frame
hung on the north wall of the Scarlet Room. A thick red rug
covered the floor. A heavy mahogany armchair with red plush
upholstery was Murphy's seat at the head of a mahogany table,
and smaller chairs were ranged around the sides. The legs of
the table were carved with four tigers' paws. The *Evening Post*,
which was always a conservative paper, remarked of this room
on the occasion of Murphy's death: "Nearly every important
financier in the city is said to have entered it at one time or
another." Other visitors were prospective candidates for the

offices of governor and mayor and prominent contractors. "Phil" Donohue, one of Murphy's boyhood friends, always stood outside the door.

II

Murphy's first political campaigns were not easy victories. As we have seen, Croker left Tammany Hall in a state of dissension and disruption. He did not seem to realize that Tammany Hall's leadership was a growth and not an hereditary position. "Big Tim" Sullivan, who was the most powerful individual in Tammany Hall next to Croker, did realize this, and, since he did not want to be the Boss himself, he threw his influence toward Murphy, because Murphy was a good friend of the Bowery and of Sullivan, and because Murphy was a silent, forceful executive. There were others, however, who did not accept Mr. Murphy so thoroughly, and one of these was "Bill" Devery.

In the last days of Croker's reign, when the election of 1901 was causing trouble to Tammany Hall, Croker and his associates began to realize that Devery was a disgrace to them rather than an asset. His antics were amusing, but the alliance of the Deputy Commissioner of Police with vice and gambling was not profitable propaganda, and Tammany Hall lost votes because of Devery. Devery soon began to express his opinion of his Tammany associates openly, and he told a reporter in June, 1902, that Croker was trying to run Tammany Hall by the wireless telegraph system, that McMahon and Haffen "ought to be over skimming milk for Croker," and that "it would take a bigger man than what Charlie Murphy is to keep Tammany moving." In the spring and summer of 1902 Devery began his fight for the Tammany Hall leadership of the Ninth Assembly District. He had been removed from the Police Department when Seth Low's reform administration took office, and though he had a fortune of more than half a million dollars when he retired from his post, he determined to remain in politics in spite of the opposition of his former Tammany supporters. After Devery announced his candidacy for district leader against Frank J. Goodwin, who was supported actively by Croker's former assistant, John C. Sheehan, and by Tammany Hall, he took up his stand at the pump on Twenty-eighth

Street and Eighth Avenue and distributed dimes and nickels
to the children. While contemplating the riotous effect of his
own largess, Devery told newspaper reporters, "Say, you can't
do nothin' with the people unless you do somethin' for 'em."
He promised that if he was elected the district would have a
recreation pier for the young people to dance on in the evenings
and a free continuous vaudeville show. As summer approached,
he gave forty-pound chunks of ice to everybody in the Ninth
District who applied; the ice was distributed at three different
places in his district at six o'clock in the morning. It was said
that the bills for Devery's generosity were paid by the gambling combine of New York, who wanted him to be a power in
Tammany Hall and eventually to return to the Police Department.

On July 30, 1902, Devery gave a large outing for the women
and children of his district, and it was estimated that ten thousand of them, many with baby carriages, attended. The steamboats *Tolchester* and *Chrystal Stream*, and the barges *Susquehanna*, *Charles S. Spear*, *William Myers*, *William J. Haskett*,
Walter Sands, and *Coxsackle*, and the tugboat *Gilbert M. Edgett*,
were Devery's fleet for the occasion. The boats, carrying the
women and children, six physicians and six nurses, lifesavers,
William S. Devery, and some of his assistants, sailed up the
Hudson River soon after nine o'clock in the morning.
There were forty-five musicians on board, and 6,000 pounds
of candy and 1,500 quarts of ice cream were distributed,
as well as sandwiches, pies, soft drinks, and 1,500 nursing bottles
of milk for the small babies. An opera troupe under the direction of a Mr. Blumenthal had been sent on board from Arverne,
Long Island, to sing and dance for the guests. Mrs. Devery
and her daughters received on board the principal barge.
As the fleet made its way back to the City that night fireworks
were sent up from the decks of the two centre barges. Devery
told the women that he hoped that they had had a good time,
that he knew they had not come to hear a speech, but if they
had husbands and brothers and fathers, he would appreciate it
if they would induce them to vote for the man who did things
for the people. Then he distributed twenty-five-cent pieces to
the children, promised more outings, and left for his political
headquarters, The Pump.

Variety shows from noon to midnight were also part of Devery's election programme, and his activities as an impresario led one newspaper to call him William Shakespeare Devery. Addressing the French Club of his district, Devery said: "Do youse suppose that Lafayette would have refused to do people of this district favors if they had elected him? Lafayette was a gentleman. Sheehan and Goodwin ain't no Lafayettes. Pin that on your coat." Devery varied his campaign by attacking the trusts as heartless oppressors of the people, and when an engine passed along Eleventh Avenue where he was speaking, he remarked, "Here comes one of yer trusts." One of his campaign circulars said: "A liberal reward will be paid to any one who will produce proofs that Sheehan ever lent a helping hand to a distressed family in the IXth District or anywhere else. When a nickel drops into Sheehan's pocket it goes there to stay. One is reminded of the old hymn:

> "'Farewell, vain world, I fain would go,
> And join the other here below.'"

Shortly before the primary election in September Devery gave a barbecue on an empty lot in his district. It was said that twenty thousand glasses of beer were given away that hot summer day on the dusty lot. Men scrambled over each other to reach the refreshments. The beer was brought up in kegs, and the drivers of the brewery wagons wore red-white-and-blue rosettes, and the wagons were draped with Devery banners. Each keg was marked "Special Devery Brew." Fifteen bartenders served the large crowd, and butchers cut bullocks to make sandwiches. Devery had ordered that no beer should be given to children, but a *Sun* reporter saw small bodies crawling between the legs of the men in order to get where the beer was distributed. The police were forced to drive back with pieces of rubber hose some of the pushing crowd. Devery made a speech in which he attacked among others the Rev. Dr. Paddock, who in one of his sermons the day before had called Devery a demagogue. "He can't say a word against me as Chief of Police," Devery said, "but I can say this of him: That in the trial of Captain Herlihy this Rev. Dr. Paddock swore that he had been in the house of prostitution for six hours. Perhaps his watch stopped——" "Bill, he's a ——," a man in the crowd cried out. "That won't do," Devery said. Then he assured the audience. "He apologizes for the word." "How many people were in his church when he made this sermon?" Devery asked. "About forty. And how many of you are there here to-day?" " 'Leven millions," shouted the woman who would interrupt. "Five thousand," Devery went on. Then Devery attacked Sheehan for not employing people in the district on his contract jobs. "Mr. Devery," shouted the woman who would interrupt, "won't you throw us down a reporter or two? We're still hungry." After Devery finished his speech, he left, and the crowd broke loose in a wild attack on the remains of the beer and the bullocks. When night fell, men were sound asleep in the shadows of the dusty lot.

It was said that Devery spent $30,000 in his primary fight to become the Tammany leader of the Ninth District, and this was in addition to the money which was spent for the purchase of votes. Both sides, and especially the opposition to Devery, who needed fraud to counteract his generosity, introduced repeaters and people from other districts. Devery retaliated by buying the votes of the repeaters and floaters. Devery was elected, and a huge parade with fireworks and tin horns was held on the night of the election day, September 16, 1902. Devery smiled on 5,000 people from the balcony of the Four Corners Club, near his historic pump. Answering the call for a speech, Devery announced that he guessed his opponents knew there had been a primary that day, and he added that "Mr. Sheehan is as crooked as Pearl Street; Pearl Street hits Broadway twice, but Sheehan couldn't hit the peepul of this district but onct." There were thunderous cheers, and then Devery backed away bowing, sat down and gulped a glass of ginger ale. "Do?" he answered a reporter. "I ain't goin' to say what I'll do; I feel like takin' a long ramble."

After Devery was elected Tammany leader of the Ninth District, he was refused a seat in the State Democratic Convention "on account of the wholesale fraud and corruption at the primary election." When he heard the accusation that the gamblers of New York were backing him, Devery said: "They ain't no one behind me but Devery's shadow."

Devery attended a convention which was considering the

nomination of a Municipal Court judge. When William Dalton, leader of the Eleventh District, arose in convention and announced that all the delegates who wanted a drink could have as much as they wanted at the expense of the Eleventh District after the convention adjourned, Devery shouted, "That's not a fair deal! That's not on the level, and it's a cheap way to buy votes." When Devery was appealed to to support McLaughlin, he shouted, "And what do I get, a bit of wind pudding and a bunch of air sauce?" Meanwhile, someone sent word downstairs that Dalton was buying. A stepladder was raised to the end of the window, a bartender in an apron climbed up, holding a gallon can of beer and some glasses. Everybody laughed, and almost everybody started for the beer. Then Mr. Dalton offered to shoot dice with Devery for the right to name the Municipal Court judge, and when that was refused, he offered a game of "cutthroat euchre." Two more ballots were taken, but no agreement was reached. Devery, however, was defeated by the regular Tammany district leaders, controlled by Murphy, and his anger against the leader of Tammany Hall increased.

A mayoralty election was to take place in 1903, for the Republican State Legislature, having turned the City over to the Democrats for four years by raising the Mayor's term of office under the impression that Van Wyck would be defeated, reduced the term to two years again after Van Wyck's election. The result was that Seth Low, the reform candidate, had only a two-year term, and Tammany Hall enjoyed another opportunity to break into the City in 1903. This was Murphy's first mayoralty campaign. Devery announced himself as an independent anti-Tammany candidate for Mayor of New York, for he was very angry with Charles F. Murphy, because, even though he had been elected a district leader in the primary, he was not accepted in the councils of Tammany Hall and found that, for his large expenditure on clambakes and vaudeville shows, he had obtained a position without any power beyond his immediate neighbourhood. The emblem of Devery's campaign was The Pump, which appeared above his name on the ballot, and a dog named Pump was the mascot of the Devery Association.

Murphy chose as his first candidate for Mayor George B.

McClellan, who had been a popular Tammany Hall orator and a conspicuous Congressman for some years. McClellan had good manners, appeared to be a gentleman, and had received an education. He was the son of the general who fought with Lincoln so much during the Civil War. McClellan's background was of advantage to Tammany Hall, for Seth Low was the opposition candidate for reëlection, and Tammany also needed respectability as a contrast to the candidacy of Devery.

Seth Low's administration had been unpopular. There was a slight police scandal, due to inefficient management, and there was nothing picturesque about the efficiency of the other departments of the city government. Thomas C. Platt wrote in his autobiography:

"I know of nothing that occurred during the Low administration which should change the opinion I had concerning him in 1897. He came and went, and New York City is still the same old town, with the same old social and political problems, the same old grafters, the same body of office-holders, the same burden of debt and the same ratio of increase in the appropriations that it had when we were told that Mr. Low's election meant its emancipation from them all."

Platt, a party politician, also objected to the fact that Low had refused to turn out of office every Tammany Hall man who was working for the City when he entered the office of Mayor.

"The result was," Platt wrote sadly, "that instead of the devoutly wished for turning out of office of thousands of Tammany henchmen, which the people had a right to expect when they voted for Low, thousands upon thousands of them continued to hold jobs and labor incessantly for the machine in Fourteenth Street. . . . The result was that instead of Low and his running mates turning the 'Tammany rascals' out, an army of over forty thousand was permitted to retain place. And this army fought as one man successfully in 1903 to put Low out and McClellan in the Mayor's chair."

District Attorney Jerome said that the dissatisfaction with Seth Low's administration was due to the "unlovable personality

of the man himself." "Egotism, self-complacency, and constitutional timidity," he added, "are not the elements to make a
leader."

McClellan had a pleasing personality, and with all his other
attractions, he was a strict organization man. He had defended
Tammany Hall in its greatest hours of trial during the Van
Wyck administration; he had even defended Devery, and in a
speech he had called Mayor Van Wyck an "unswerving and
fearless Democrat." After the Mazet Investigation, he had declared that Tammany Hall had "nothing for which to apologize."

In order to strengthen his ticket, Murphy made advances to
two of the nominees of Seth Low's fusion party, Edward M.
Grout, Comptroller, and Charles V. Fornes, President of the
Board of Aldermen. Murphy weaned them away from their
reform associates by giving them Tammany Hall nominations.

Devery supplied the picturesque elements of the campaign.
He declared himself vaguely and generally in favour of municipal ownership and said that: "The working people is tired of
the divine right employer. They ain't strikin' for higher wages
or shorter hours. They are strikin' against this idee that to be
anybody or do anything you've got to have a letter from the
Almighty." He also favoured the establishment of a recreation
pier or a free bath along every half mile of the City's water-
front, the sale of beer after church hours on Sunday, and the
free conveyance of children on street cars to and from school.
"This is the occasion," Devery told his constituents, "when the
downtrod will rise in their might, an' when they do that you
kin bet that they'll make the Charlie Murphys and the Big and
Little Sullivans look like calico dogs stuffed with saloon sweep-
in's." "In the political graveyard there won't be anything more
interestin' than Murphy's sarcophagus," Devery remarked.
"It'll tell the story of a switchman that tried to sidetrack th'
Peepul's Consolidated Express and couldn't throw the switch
over. One of the lines on the stone will be, 'Devery done it.'"
On election day he predicted that there would be a deluge, and
that "Murphy's microbes will be takin' the elevators to the top
of the Flatiron Building before the deluge stops."

Murphy's orators retaliated with the statements that
Devery was making a deal with the Republicans under

Governor Benjamin B. Odell and that Devery and not Tammany had been responsible for the graft during the Van Wyck administration. These were dangerous statements, for they gave Devery the opportunities he wished. To the charge that he had met Odell and his associates at the Fifth Avenue Hotel, Devery said:

"'Why, at 11 o'clock last Thursday night I was sittin' in these very rooms enjoyin' a workin'-man's dinner in company with twenty honest workin'-men. We had two pigs' heads, and I ate the ears and swallowed the brains of both pigs. I am the workin'-men's friend and I ain't got any time these days to spend in any Fifth Avenue Hotel. Murphy had better find out what's goin' on up here before he smokes any more dope pills. You can trust a thief, but you can't trust a liar, and I ain't got no hesitancy in callin' him that outright.'"

"'And touchin' on and appertainin' to collectin' graft from dives and poolrooms,' Devery remarked of the second charge, 'if I'm the man that's doin' the boss collector act, tell Murphy that he'd better hurry up and send me around his hush money for that house not far from Twenty-seventh Street and Lexington Avenue, which they call the ——. Look up the plans and specifications of that buildin' and see if the owner's name don't begin with an M. I don't know who claims to own the house, but look up the real owner, the man who built it, on the files of plans and specifications. Tell Murphy that if I'm in the collectin' business I want to take in the money on that house. There's been more young girls ruined in that house than in any other place in the city. The trouble with that feller is that he's got a red light hangin' around his neck, and consequently he sees red in whatever direction he looks.'"

The New York *Tribune* took Devery's hint, looked up the ownership of the Borough Hotel, a Raines Law hotel on the southwest corner of Lexington Avenue and Twenty-seventh Street, and it was found that the owner was Charles F. Murphy, but that he had transferred it to another purchaser, whom the *Tribune* suspected of being a dummy for Murphy. Devery then added in his speeches a list of pool rooms in which Murphy

WILLIAM S. DEVERY

was financially interested. "Get all that's comin' to you is my motto," Devery said, "and I can't really afford to let my best customer go in without payin'." Then he insisted that when he was in the Police Department he had never got anything for himself, because all the graft went higher up. "They used to skin a bull and give away the hide, but I never got as much as the horns," Devery said. "When reform came into power," he added, "Charlie Murphy tried to brush the dust off his wings, so's they'd look lovely and white and he'd resemble an angel. But the mud's too thick to brush off, although it's somewhat hidden by the 'red light.'" Devery also maintained that Murphy owned the Empire, where a man had been killed, or, as he preferred to put it: "They were a little short of meat that day at the Empire, and they wanted chop suey. Murphy knows all about that place, because it was his place." Devery insisted that the lambs in Central Park made their way to the dinner table of the Boss of Brooklyn, Hugh McLaughlin, whom he called "Hugh Obelisk McLaughlin" who "used to play marbles with Cleopatry." He also attacked Murphy's record as Dock Commissioner, and in one of his speeches said: "I now propose that we get that Lehigh dock right over there as a recreation pier for the art gallery over there on those stones," pointing to a row of children who were sitting on a pile of paving stones and listening to the orator. "He's goin' through the bluff of being decent," Devery said of Murphy, "but look at his record in the old Dock Board! Does that look as if he's dyin' for his feller man? He's for Murphy, an' he ain't satisfied to use his hands. He wants to get in and use a steam shovel." "Charlie Murphy," Devery once said, "reminds me of one of them new amusements they have got down to Rockaway—a crook's cylinder, dark as a pocket inside and very smooth. They call it the Down and Out."

Murphy's interest in respectablity afforded Devery plenty of material for burlesque, and he frequently referred to the Tammany Boss as Sir Charles. "Since Charlie Murphy has got to running with J. Sergeant Cram, he's turned up his trousers at the bottom, and he's wearing glasses," Devery charged. "Instead of being a 'gas-house boy' and dressing like one, he goes over on Fifth Avenue every day. One of these days one of them panes of glass will fall out, and Charlie 'll have only one

pane of glass, like Cram, and then it'll be, 'Ah, there, chappie,'
and when you go to ask him for a job it'll be, 'Ah really cawn't
do it, old chappie, don't you know.' (Roars of laughter from the
sidewalk.)" He also promised if he was elected Mayor: "I will
take the middle piece out of J. Sergeant Cram's name and feed
it to my dog Pump." Devery was confident of the result of the
election. "Some time, even at a funeral," he said, "you have to
watch the fakir that peddles bad fruit, an' while I was thinkin'
of what was comin' to Murphy on Tuesday night next I couldn't
help but think of Codfish Russell, alias Sunny Jim. It's dollars
to rotten apples he'll be sellin' old Dowie stock in a soap mine
before the prophet gets out of this burg."

Devery's personal crusade against graft won him the admiration of Mrs. Carrie Nation, who visited Devery's headquarters
one day. Mrs. Nation had recently arrived in New York with
the intention of demolishing vice in the form of saloons and
gambling dens with the hatchet which she had wielded so power-
fully in the West. The crowd which saw Carrie Nation enter
Devery's headquarters demanded a speech. "I want to say,"
said Mrs. Nation, "that I approve of Mr. Devery's campaign.
(Loud applause.) He isn't a Republican or a Democrat or anything like that—he's a Prohibitionist." This tribute astounded
for a moment even "the best Chief of Police New York ever
had," and the crowd was bewildered at this statement concerning the man who had given them more free beer than any other
leader. There was a moment of anxiety—perhaps the eccentric
chief had really turned prohibitionist and would give away no
more beer? Then Mrs. Carrie Nation stepped up to the men in
the crowd and ordered them to throw away their "filthy cigarettes and cigars." The men, still dazed, obeyed. Mrs. Nation
pinned a small hatchet on Devery's lapel, and Devery gallantly
escorted her to her automobile.

There was some violence in this campaign of 1903. "Monk"
Eastman and his gang invaded Devery's district, voted on the
names of other men, and, as Devery put it, "then went back to
the East Side and murdered a couple of people and shot more."
A man named Harry Butler, who looked like Devery, came
out of a saloon and passed the crowd that was waiting for
Devery to appear in Murphy's own Tammany district. Someone pointed at Butler and shouted, "There's Devery, now."

Immediately twenty men sprang at Butler and pounded him.
He fell to the ground and was jumped on. Finally, he was able
to gasp that he was not Devery. Butler was patched up in the
corner drug store and taken home in a cab at the expense of his
apologetic assailants. Devery himself engaged in a few street
brawls, knocked down several men, and received some cuts and
bruises.

McClellan was elected Mayor, and Tammany Hall was in
full power in the City once more. After it was all over, Devery
remarked, "I spent my own money, and I had some fun."

There was joy in Tammany Hall and in the camp of "Big
Tim" Sullivan, for McClellan naturally appointed as his leading
associates in the government of the City the men designated by
Murphy and Sullivan, who were then in close alliance. Devery
was defeated for reëlection as district leader, and he retired
from politics to an expensive house on West End Avenue. But
he did not remain long in the neighbourhood, for it annoyed
him too much. "Up around there there are not so many children
and a whole lot more dogs," he said. "I never knew there were
so many breeds of dogs as you can see along West End Avenue
and on Riverside Drive." He moved to Far Rockaway, Long
Island, and gave as his reason: "I got tired of seein' dogs wear
sealskin pants on West End Avenue." "There's nothing in the
kid glove game," he concluded, "and as a man gets older he
gets more and more tired of the glad rags." Devery always carried his gold police badge, whistle, and book of rules in his
pocket, and he was fond of spending much time over his thirty-
six scrapbooks of press clippings which he had cross-indexed
elaborately. He died in 1919.

III

At the period when Murphy gained control of Tammany
Hall, the organization was actively engaged in catering to the
constant entertainment of its adherents. We have already seen
how Devery turned clam chowder into local votes, and he was
by no means the only patron of that art.

All during the summer and the fall of the early years of the
twentieth century the groves of College Point were hired
almost every week by one or another of the district associations

of Tammany Hall for their outings, chowders, clambakes, and
other similar festivities. Steamboats were hired to convey the
guests, who had paid five dollars apiece for their tickets if they
had money, or had paid five dollars apiece for the tickets of
those they wished to influence politically, if the latter had no
money. On board the boats roulette wheels, faro and poker
tables, dice, and other portable gambling appliances appeared
as soon as the hawsers were loosed. Some staterooms were set
aside for the distinguished guests, and in these "Big Tim"
Sullivan, "Silver Dollar" Smith, Patrick Divver, or John J.
O'Brien held special receptions with champagne and playing
cards. There was a bar where beer and whisky were handed out
to those who were gambling or taking the air.

When the groves were reached, some men rushed for the
water, others began to play baseball, and the more serious set up
tables among the trees and continued the faro, roulette, poker,
or pinochle games which had been interrupted by the necessity
for landing. A few sleight-of-hand artists started the notorious shell game or demonstrated their ability with loaded
dice, but this was dangerous, for when their victims were "put
wise" by their friends, the proprietors of the games usually had
their faces mutilated. This graphic description of one such incident appeared in the account in the New York *Times* of the
Patrick Divver Association outing at Witzell's Grove:

"'Ann Street Abe,' who is said to sell canes around the St.
Paul Building, appeared in the grove shortly after 4 o'clock
with a bunch of walking sticks. He soon laid these aside and
started a dice game, but a man named Goodheart discovered
that they were loaded, and broke Abe's nose with his fist. Then
they thought the cane peddler would die, but he was saved by
having two corks inserted in his nostrils."

Teams of nine fat men played baseball with teams of nine
lean men, and nine bachelors played against nine married men.
Thin men raced with thin men, and fat men raced with fat men,
while those of normal weight expressed their satisfaction
with shrieks of oafish laughter. Men splashed each other with
sea water and roared raucously. "Tom" Sharkey, "Kid" Mc-
Coy, "Joe" Bernstein, and "Terry" McGovern frequently

headed the procession at the outings of "Big Tim" Sullivan,
for he was the boxing czar as well as the leader of Tammany
Hall on the Bowery. Amateur bouts were organized for the entertainment of the crowds, while the gamblers steadily continued their absorbing games in the groves and looked up occasionally to watch a good punch. "Tom" Sharkey, drunk
with the admiration of his prowess, used to pass the gamblers'
tables, stop as if he were interested in placing a bet, and then
pound his fist on the tables until the money flew in all directions. His worshippers, who followed him from table to table,
howled their appreciation, while the gamblers and the players
tried to grin agreeably. At one moment Sharkey absent-
mindedly threw sixty champagne glasses at "Chuck" Connors
and "Goldbrick" Naylor. Through the groves, where barkers
were shouting, "The only straight gambling game here; it's
just the same as is played in our rooms in New York," wandered
slick young men who extracted watches from the pockets of the
intent gamblers and the patronizing Congressmen. In one
corner, the Chinese constituents quietly shuffled their fan-tan
counters.

"Big Tim" Sullivan and his friends engaged in quiet games of
poker in special rooms, where champagne was served to those
who liked it. It was not unusual for the leaders to lose or to
win more than a thousand dollars from each other during the
afternoon.

Clam fritters, beer, chowder, ice cream, and chicken were
served for dinner, and men rushed at the waiters and jumped
on tables in order to get their own estimates of their shares.

After the boats had carried the revellers back to the City
in the evening, the party ended with a torchlight procession
through the district where the association had its headquarters,
and fireworks proclaimed the glory of the local boss and the
grandeur of Tammany Hall.

Except what he may have lost in his private poker game, the
leader and his association usually made a profit by philanthropy, not only in prestige, but also in money, for it was the
duty of the secretary and treasurer of the club to see that
enough tickets had been sold at five dollars each to the saloon
keepers, the push-cart men, the storekeepers, the prostitutes,
and the gamblers of the district to pay for the clams, the steam-

boat, and the beer. It was also his duty to see to it that those who had dared to refuse to buy tickets did not have their licenses renewed by the City, or were raided by the police.

During the winter Tammany associations organized balls and beefsteak dinners for their friends in place of outings. It was the boast of each association that its members could eat more beefsteak, drink more beer, and consume more bread than any other similar association, and the figures were usually made public. The *World* announced on February 15, 1901: "Four and a half tons of beefsteak were consumed at the tenth annual dinner of the Mohican Club in the Grand Central Palace last night." More than 7,000 guests attended this affair, and many of them came as early as four o'clock in the afternoon in order to get seats near the rows of fifty-eight ranges used to broil the steaks. By six o'clock the hall was so crowded that the small tables had to be cleared, and the guests stood facing the one hundred and fifty attendants who each carried a pile two and a half feet high of attractive beefsteaks. Three hundred barrels of beer and two hundred gallons of ale were used on this occasion. The Chief of Police had a squad of men present to protect those who were carrying the beefsteaks from the eagerness of the guests, who stormed the railing of the ranges and yelled for more steaks. Commissioner of Corrections Lantry, who was in charge of the dinner, with the aid of other members of the Mohican Club, made up a flying wedge and cleared a path to the ranges, while the guests cheered his energy. Patrick Divver, a Tammany leader, when asked for statistics of beefsteaks, said: "I have eaten as high as fifteen—and I can do it again." Mr. O. H. P. Belmont consumed five.

"Big Tim" Sullivan gave a Christmas dinner to about five thousand men every year at his political headquarters, 207 Bowery. Turkey, goose, duck, mince pie, beer, and coffee were served to anybody who appeared. The diners were fed in relays of 250.

At the Tammany Hall balls the favourite songs of the period were sung. Some of those on the musical programme in the '90's and early 1900's were: "Columbus Was an Irishman," a schottische, "Huckleberry Doo," a polka Berlin, "Isle of Champagne" for the lancers, "Maud Marion," "Sunny Side of Thompson Street," and "Little Daughter Nell." A favourite

song played by Tammany bands and sung by Tammany voices
was concerned with one Roxana Dooley, and it began:

"Roxy's Irish as a boiled pertater,
    Her nose it is Connemara pug;
And when she dances in the big teayter
    She looks as Oriental as a rug."

The annual grand civic ball of the Lawrence Mulligan Association, the political club of "Big Tim" Sullivan's stepbrother, was thus described by George Kibbe Turner:

"That night—the eve of St. Patrick's Day—the streets of
the Tenderloin lie vacant of its women; the eyes of the city
detective force are focused on the great dancing-hall—stuffed
to the doors with painted women and lean-faced men. In the
center box, held in the name of a young Jewish friend, sits the
'Big Feller'—clear-skinned, fair-faced, and happy. Around him
sit the gathering of his business and political lieutenants, of
the heavy, moon-faced Irish type—the rulers of New York;
Larry Mulligan, his stepbrother, the head of this pleasing
association; Paddy Sullivan, his brother, the president of the
Hesper Club of gamblers; John Considine, business associate,
owner of the Metropole Hotel, where the 'wise ones' gather;
Big Tom Foley; and—an exception to the general look of rosy
prosperity—Little Tim, the lean little manager of the old
Third District and leader of the New York Board of Aldermen.
"The council unbends; it exchanges showers of confetti;
the 'Big Feller' smiles gayly upon the frail congregation below
him—the tenth short-lived generation of prostitutes he had
seen at gatherings like this since, more than twenty years ago,
he started his first Five Points assembly—he himself as fresh
now as then. In the rear of the box a judge of the General Sessions court sits modestly, decently, hat in hand. In the welter
on the slippery floor, another city judge, known to the upper
and under world alike as 'Freddy' Kernochan, leads through
the happy mazes of the grand march a thousand pimps and
thieves and prostitutes, to the blatant crying of the band:
"'Sullivan, Sullivan, a damned fine Irishman!'"[1]

---

[1] *McClure's Magazine*, Vol. XXXIII, 1909, p. 132.

This biting picture annoyed "Big Tim" Sullivan sufficiently to make him answer the implied charge with one of the few speeches of his career. On October 31, 1909, the "Big Feller" appeared before a large audience in Miner's Bowery Theatre, which he and Considine owned, and the tears rolled down his pink cheeks as he told of his past life and its blameless activity. It was the close of the political campaign of 1909, and every seat in Miner's Theatre was filled. Among those on the platform with "Big Tim" was William Sulzer, then a Tammany representative in Congress. "No introduction is needed for the next speaker," said Major George J. Kraus, the chairman; "I only need say that it is Big Tim." The applause was tremendous, and it was several minutes before "Big Tim," in a choking voice, could make himself heard. "I want you to bear with me," he said at last, "while I try to make a speech. I never made one in my life, but with the way things are going in this campaign, with vilification for everyone and the degrading of good men for the sake of a few offices, I want to make a speech." Then he consulted a paper which contained the charges that had been made against him in the campaign. First he took up the charge that he was many times a millionaire and had only a salary of $1,500 a year as a State Senator. He replied that his theatrical business, which had been in existence for thirteen years, made a profit the first year of $55,000 and had never fallen below that figure. The firm of Sullivan & Considine, he said, owned and controlled more theatres than any two men in the world, and that he was afraid to tell what the profits had been for fear his friends would be around in the morning to borrow money. "I am worth something," Sullivan said, "and there is no reason why I shouldn't be. I'm an average downtown boy, with a good, clear head, and it's always clear, for I don't drink or smoke. But I haven't changed my residence since I got my money, and I ain't going to. I was born among you, and I'm going to die among you." The sentiment met with approval.

"The trouble with the reformers is," "Big Tim" Sullivan said, "that they don't know our traditions down here. That's why they think because I've got a little money there must be something wrong, that I must be getting money in some crooked

"BIG TIM" SULLIVAN
(in center)

way or I wouldn't stay here. I'll tell you why I stay here.

"I was born in poverty, one of six children, four boys and two girls. The boys used to sleep in a three-quarters bed, not big enough for two, and the girls in a shakedown on the floor. Some nights there was enough to eat and some nights there wasn't. And our old mother used to sing to us at night and maybe it would be next day before we would think that she had been singing but that she had gone to bed without anything to eat.

"That's the kind of people we come from, and that is the kind of mothers that bore us down here. If we can help some boy or some father to another chance we are going to give it to them. The thieves we have down here ain't thieves from choice, they are thieves from necessity, and necessity don't know any law. They steal because they need a doctor for some dying one, or they steal because there ain't any bread in the house for the children."

The women wept and the men looked sad.

"There's something here written by a gentleman named Turner," Sullivan continued. "He's not so bad even if he has been writing horrible stuff, but I can't say as much for the people who have been paying him. I've been looking Turner up. He's got three children and a wife, and they might have been starving, and a man who has children starving will do anything.

"In an article he wrote last April about the Lawrence Mulligan ball he said that in the grand march the women were of questionable virtue and the men worse. I've got right here in my hand a list of one hundred couples in that march. It ain't no phony list, and the reporters can take it and look up the names and I'm here to say that they will find that every woman is a virtuous woman, and every man a decent man.

"Now we come to the last of all, the white slave talk. My God, they have put me in between thieves, and I'm not the first man who has been pilloried between thieves; I've been living here all my life and I never knew a man engaged in this business, and I won't stand for this; I am not going to say anything, but this man Turner had better keep out of this district.

"I've never professed to be more than the average man. I don't want you to think I'm very good, for I've done a lot of wrong things. I'm just an average man, but I've told you of that old mother of mine, what she did for me, and I want to say here before you all that there is no man on earth who believes in the virtue of women more than I do. . . .

"We do enough bad things, and when we do good things they hadn't ought to be distorted so they will seem bad. Fourteen years ago I began giving Christmas dinners and shoes away to the poor. Someone has said the Sullivans give the people a little turkey and a pair of shoes and rob them the rest of the year. As I'm the Sullivan that does this they must mean me, and I'm going to tell you how I got that idea of giving away shoes.

"It was way back in 1873 and a boy named Sullivan was goin' to the Elm Street school, and there was a Miss Murphy who was a teacher. This boy had an old pair of shoes, and one day she asked the boy to stay after school. He thought some other boy had done something and put it up to him and he was goin' to stand for it. So he said, 'Miss Murphy, if I've done anything let me know because I want to get away and sell papers,' and she told the boy he hadn't done nothing, and gave him an order. That order was to Timothy Brennan, brother of a big Tammany leader, and he gave me an order for a pair of shoes. I needed them shoes then, and I thought if I ever got any money I would give shoes to people who needed them, and I'm goin' to buy shoes for people just as long as I live. And all the people on earth can't stop me from doing what I think is right by calling me names."[1]

"Big Tim" Sullivan had not been in the theatrical business on the East Side of New York for thirteen years without learning something; his speech was a Bowery masterpiece of melodramatic construction. But it requires some dramatic criticism. We have seen from testimony that has always gone unanswered that "Big Tim" Sullivan and his associates were making money from gambling establishments and houses of prostitution. It will be remembered that a policeman testified that he was told not to touch certain places, and that he saw the "Big Feller" in the office of the Police Commissioner the next day. A few days later that policeman was retired. Chief of Police Devery's slip of the tongue, when he almost accepted

[1]New York *Herald*, November 1, 1909.

the statement that his friend Sullivan was interested in certain
houses of prostitution, will also be recalled. East Side theatricals
were profitable, but so also was a monopoly which made it
impossible for prize fights in Manhattan and upper New York
State to be held under any other auspices than those of "Big
Tim" Sullivan. It may have been true, as Sullivan pointed out,
that some thieves stole because "they need a doctor for some dying one," or because "there ain't any bread in the house for the
children." But thieves and gangsters repeated at elections not
because there was no bread in the house or because they had
dying ones, but because "Big Tim" Sullivan and his Tammany
Hall associates hired them for the purpose and protected them
the rest of the year. It was true that Sullivan did a great deal
of charity. It was estimated that he distributed more than
twenty-five thousand dollars a year to the poor of the Bowery,
and he was known to have started out at six o'clock in the
morning with gangs of men whom he wished to get jobs on public works. But the political profits of his district were estimated
at between seven and eight times as much as he gave away, and
he and his relatives got up just as early to lead the same gangs
of men or their companions on election day from polling place
to polling place in the endeavour to roll up large majorities for
Tammany Hall.

"Big Tim" Sullivan was the typical Tammany Hall district
leader with virtues that transcended most and powers that exceeded all. His simple personality was engaging, and it may be
said of him what the contemporary bard sang of a more ribald
aggressor, Jim Fisk:

"He may have done wrong but he thought he done right,
    And he always was good to the poor."

He was interested in politics on the Bowery; he was interested
in gambling; and it made him feel good to give away his money.
He knew many of the people on the Bowery, and everybody on
the Bowery knew him. Yet his view of his own position as leader
was sane and modest:

"Every community," he once said, "has to have some man
who can take the trouble to look for their public interest, while
they are earning their living, and it don't make any difference

whether he's tall, short, fat, lean or humpbacked and with only half his teeth, if he's willing to work harder than anyone else he's the fellow who will hold the job. They're not always grateful by any means and when they catch a man with a four-flush, no matter how good his excuse, 'skidoo,' back to the old home for his. And so after all there isn't much to it to be a leader. It's just plenty of work, keep your temper or throw it away, be on the level, and don't put on any airs, because God and the people hate a chesty man."

When he was a State Senator, Sullivan was the only Democrat for years who voted for the woman suffrage bill, and his reason was said to be that Miss Murphy, his school teacher, had once given him that pair of shoes when he needed them. He also thought that women would elevate politics, so he said. "A man can talk for hours," he was alleged to have remarked, "or days or weeks about his love for a woman, but until he begins to speak about the wedding ring and the priest she don't act particularly moved by his flow of words. Have you ever noticed that? It will be the same way with their votes." He forgot, perhaps, that most women are more interested in husbands than in traction problems.

While Sullivan was a State Senator, he sponsored two bills of importance to himself and to Tammany Hall. One was a bill making Columbus Day a legal holiday, and the other was the bill which still bears his name making the carrying of firearms without a license a penal offense. The first pleased Tammany's Italian constituency, and the other enabled the Senator and his associates to keep those same friends and their Jewish and Irish compatriots under control. Whenever a gangster who led repeaters, or an influential brothel keeper, grew obstreperous enough to prove inconvenient to the plans that were made in Tammany Hall, he could usually be found with a gun, or a gun could be planted upon his person, and he could be sent to the State prison under the Sullivan Law for a long enough time to keep him from being annoying. One of these men, "Big Jack" Zelig, found that the better part of discretion after the Sullivan Law was passed was to sew up all his pockets. He always travelled on his business expeditions thereafter with a henchman, who carried the gun and presented it, carefully wiped, at the proper time for the champion to do his work. The Sullivan Law prevented very little gunfire, because a person who wished to kill another did not trouble about the fact that he was also breaking another law. He wondered, if anything, how he was going to cover himself after the murder. But the Sullivan Law did prevent citizens from protecting themselves from thieves, and it probably made it more expensive for thieves and murderers to get guns in New York. But a five-cent ferry fare always carried them to the State of New Jersey. The Sullivan Law was, however, useful to Sullivan and to Tammany Hall, because it enabled them to control their gunmen friends when they should become their enemies.

Once Sullivan went as representative of New York to Congress. He had grown weary of Albany and the State Legislature after several terms there. The Republicans were in power, and the "graft was played out," as he was alleged to have expressed it. One of his friends remarked, "Why don't you go to Congress?" "Me in Congress?" Sullivan said. "To the itsey house with youse! Do you want to put me on the bum, like 'Tim' Campbell and Sulzer? Nit!" "But it's fine," his friend insisted. "Say, what is the graft over there?" Sullivan asked. The possibilities were explained to him. "How long does it take to get to Washington?" he asked. "Only five hours." "Sure?" he asked. A time-table was brought to him, and the fact was proved. "That ain't such a long time," Sullivan reflected. "Say, those guys that flag the Washington graft get famous and get to be the main squeeze at the White House if their gang is in, don't they? They are the whole cheese in national conventions. That ain't a bad lay. I will think it over. Maybe I will go down there and look the game over. It ain't a piker's game, and maybe I may take a stack and sit in." That was enough; "Big Tim's" campaign was started by his friends. When he was asked by a reporter whether it was true that he intended to go to Congress, Sullivan answered: "Who knows? It might be a grand game with the limit off. They pulled the blinders so tight at Albany that it got to be heavy going, and I pulled out. Maybe on a bigger track in faster company it would be worth while entering. I may take a hand. Who knows?" And then he walked off down the Bowery. Sullivan's hint that he was willing to go to Washington was all that was required for his certain election. He had to make no speeches. His campaign was even easier than that of Congressman "Tim" Campbell, who made one classic speech in his New York Tammany Irish district. His opponent was an Italian named Rinaldo. "Tim" Campbell's speech was:

"There is two bills before the country—the Mills bill and the McKinley bill. The Mills bill is for free trade with everything free; the McKinley bill is for protection with nothing free. Do you want everything free or do you want to pay for everything?

"Having thus disposed of the national issue I will now devote myself to the local issue which is the Dago Rinaldo. He is from Italy. I am from Ireland. Are you in favour of Italy or Ireland?

"Having thus disposed of the local issue and thanking you for your attention, I will now retire."

Congressman "Tim" Campbell was elected by a majority of more than 12,000. It was he who, when President Grover Cleveland objected that something he wanted done was contrary to the Constitution, retorted: "What the hell is the Constitution among friends?"

"Big Tim" Sullivan went to Congress for one term, but, though he was received at the White House and won the pinochle championship of Congress from Representative James McAndrews of Chicago, he did not like Washington, and he was seldom in his seat at roll call; he made no speeches. After one term he retired to the more ambitious fields of New York East Side politics. "There's nothing in this Congressman business," he told reporters. "They know 'em in Washington. The people down there use 'em as hitchin'-posts. Every time they see a Congressman on the street they tie their horses to him." Croker is said to have remarked once when he was asked to promote a young man to the office of Clerk of New York County: "He's a good boy, but that job requires brains and experience. He'll have to be satisfied with being a Congressman."

"Big Tim" Sullivan's interest in gambling was the leading interest of his life, next to Tammany Hall politics, which was always something of a gamble, with the paraphernalia sometimes

stacked against the opposition. Sullivan played for high stakes.
The story was told of one game that was taking place on the
special train en route to the Democratic National Convention
at St. Louis which nominated Alton B. Parker for the Presidency of the United States. Sullivan and some of his Tammany
friends were playing poker, and as they had no chips, twenty-
dollar bills were used instead. In one of the pots one twenty-
dollar bill was missing after the opening. "Somebody slipped,"
one of the players remarked. None would admit that he had
not put up his money. There was an argument for a moment,
and then "Big Tim," smiling, reached out, took the five twenty-
dollar bills, tore them gently into little pieces and tossed them
out of the train window. "There, boys," he said, "that puts a
stop to all argument; let's all put in again and there can't be
any misunderstanding."

Sullivan's literary tastes were representative of his character.
He could never understand why people read trash when they
could read such novels as those of Jack London and Dickens.
Les Miserables was one of his favourites, and he once said
that it was his firm belief that anyone who read *Three Weeks*
should get ten days.

In 1912 "Big Tim" Sullivan became insane. He suffered
from dementia præcox and delusions of persecution. His
estate, estimated at between two and three millions of
dollars, was placed officially in the care of a committee consisting of Lawrence Mulligan, Frank Farrell, Emanuel Blumen-
steil, and Patrick H. Sullivan, who were appointed in February, 1913, by Justice Hendrick, after it was determined that
Sullivan was incapable of managing his own affairs. Sullivan
was placed in a sanatorium, and then he was removed to a house
in Eastchester Road, Williamsbridge. He got some pleasure
from the game of eluding the guards who were hired to watch
him, and he continued to get enjoyment from card games.
Once he ran away from his guards and rushed in taxicabs along
Broadway and the Bowery, visiting his former haunts. On another occasion he was found wandering along the docks at the
Hudson River. In the summer of 1913, he took a trip to Europe
with his brother Patrick. Then he went back to the Eastchester
house.

In the first days of September, 1913, "Big Tim" Sullivan disappeared from his house, after he had tired out his four guards by playing cards with them all night. A body was found on the rails of the New York, New Haven & Hartford Railroad, close to the Westchester freight yards. The engineer reported that the man was dead before the cars passed over him. In the hatband of the man's hat was the name James H. McCluskey. The body was taken to the morgue, where it lay unidentified for fourteen days. Just before it was to be buried at the expense of the City, the policeman who was required by law to take a last look at all unidentified corpses, entered. He looked at the face and was said to have whispered: "It's Big Tim, God rest him." Men are still wondering just how "Big Tim" Sullivan met his death.

More than twenty-five thousand persons followed "Big Tim" Sullivan's body to the grave. Among the crowd were three United States Senators and a delegation of twenty members of the House of Representatives. Justices of the Supreme Court of New York and judges of every other court in the City were present. Mott Street, where the old St. Patrick's Cathedral stood, was swept and washed for the occasion. Charles F. Murphy and his candidate for Mayor, Edward E. McCall, marched side by side at the head of the honorary pallbearers. As the coffin was borne into the street from 207, The Bowery, a great blanket of roses was thrown over it by members of the Sullivan Association. "Sarsaparilla" Reilly, "Big Tim's" friend for thirty years, was the master of ceremonies. Monsignor Kearney, rector of the old St. Patrick's, stood at the door of the church, flanked on either side by altar boys and cross bearers. Monsignor Kearney, assisted by Father Facacci, Father Sheridan, Monsignor Murphy, Father Gaetano Aecesi, Father Curry, Father Daniel Quinn, and Father McGean, a Fire Department chaplain, celebrated a high requiem mass for "Big Tim" Sullivan's soul. A long line of carriages filled with mourners followed the hearse to Calvary.

IV

Charles F. Murphy had elected George B. McClellan Mayor of New York in 1903, but the term of office was only two years, and in 1905 he renominated McClellan. In that year William

Randolph Hearst entered New York City politics as the opponent of Tammany Hall and of Murphy. Hearst had organized the Municipal Ownership League as the party in opposition to the alliance which he alleged existed between the traction interests of New York and Tammany Hall. Hearst was the candidate of the Municipal Ownership League for Mayor, and a lively campaign followed, in which the Hearst newspapers attacked Murphy in picture and story. Murphy was caricatured dressed in the convict stripes which Hearst insisted he deserved because of his corrupt business activities. The election was close, and the unofficial figures gave McClellan a slight plurality over Hearst. William M. Ivins, the Republican candidate, was a negligible factor. Hearst insisted that frauds were committed, and that, among other things, many Hearst ballots had been thrown into the river. He demanded a recount, which was granted, and it was said that Tammany printed additional ballots and placed them in the ballot boxes for the recount. McClellan was finally officially declared elected by 3,478 votes.

Hearst attacked Murphy all through the year. Then the Democratic State Convention met in 1906 to nominate a candidate for Governor, and Murphy controlled the Convention. There were rumours of a deal between Hearst and Murphy, which everybody thought impossible because of the attitude of the Hearst newspapers in the previous year. Murphy, however, compelled a reluctant convention to nominate William Randolph Hearst for Governor on the Tammany Hall ticket. By forcing the unit rule of voting, according to which delegates had to vote in blocs by districts, and by tactics which the Tammany Senator Thomas F. Grady later characterized as "the dirtiest day's work of my life," Hearst was nominated. Charles E. Hughes, who had just finished a skillful and penetrating investigation of the insurance companies of New York, was the Republican candidate, and he defeated Hearst. It was rumoured that, after nominating Hearst, Murphy did not work anxiously and actively for his election, and the Boss of Brooklyn, Senator Patrick McCarren, openly worked with the up-state Democrats against the election of Hearst.

Murphy's support of Hearst caused an estrangement between him and his Mayor, McClellan. McClellan was supposed to have the support in Tammany Hall of the powerful Sullivan family. Just before his nomination for Governor, Hearst had sent a telegram to the Indianapolis *Star* in which he called Tim Sullivan a "keeper of dives and lord protector of crooks and criminals," and George B. McClellan an "election thief." Murphy's name was conspicuous by its absence in Hearst's telegram. Murphy also had his troubles with the Democrats of Brooklyn, who were led by Hugh McLaughlin and Patrick McCarren. The slogan of the Brooklyn Democrats was "The Tiger Shall Not Cross The Bridge." Richard Croker paused in his contemplation of his horses and added to Murphy's troubles by sending a cable to Senator McCarren in which he denounced Murphy's alliance with Hearst.

In addition to all his other difficulties investigations were held into the official conduct of Murphy's borough presidents, John F. Ahearn, of Manhattan, Louis F. Haffen, of the Bronx, and Joseph Bermel of Queens. The investigations, which concerned the condition of New York City's streets and contract work, resulted in the removal of Borough Presidents Ahearn and Haffen and the resignation of Borough President Bermel. It was said that the charges against these Tammany Hall men were stimulated by Mayor McClellan, who was in a position to know their misdeeds, and thorough investigations were conducted by John Purroy Mitchel, who received the fame during those investigations which finally made him Mayor of New York. Tammany men were worried, and they needed a scapegoat. William Dalton, Commissioner of Public Works under Borough President Ahearn, was chosen for that rôle, but he was reluctant to assume it. His testimony gives an insight into the methods of some politicians during the first ten years of Murphy's control.

"Will you first briefly describe to us the circumstances which led up to the severance of your connection with the Borough President's Office?" John Purroy Mitchel asked William Dalton.

"Well, the first intimation I had was about a week before I was removed. The Borough President sent for me and said: 'William, I have very bad news for you.' I said, 'What is it?' 'I hate to tell you.' 'Well,' I said, 'by your looks it would seem to me as though I had bad news for you. What is the trouble?' 'Well,' he said, 'you have read in the paper about this investigation, you know something of it.' 'Yes.' He said, 'Something has to be done; something must be done at once to help me out in this matter.' 'What do you want done?' I said to him. 'Well,' he said, 'I have been talking with some people, friends of yours, friends of mine, and we came to the conclusion that the only way to save me from being removed by the Governor was for you to resign.' I said, 'Resign for what reason other than those you give me—any charges against me? Have I neglected my duties in any way?' 'No, no.' 'Have I been absent, have I taken a vacation of more than a week or ten days at the outside in the three years and four months I have been with you?' 'No, there is nothing to that, William; there is no charges at all, but something has got to be done to save me; you don't want me to get out?' I said, 'I want anybody to get out if they are guilty, not an innocent man. Now, if you will show me any reason, one wrong act that I have done since I have been in office, it will be a pleasure for me to step out to help you out, step out of the office.' He said, 'No, I can't. Now,' he said, 'you have been in business, you have been in business for a good many years,' and then he asked me what business I was in. I told him I had been in the carpenter business years ago and I had been in the wholesale slaughtering business. 'Now,' he said, 'we have talked that over and we thought the nice way to do would be for you to resign, with the understanding that you were going in business; there will be no charges against you at all.' I said, 'How would that help you by my getting out if you are not going to prefer some charges?' 'Well,' he said, 'there may be some little things I would have to say, I found some little defects in your office, which would be an excuse for me getting you out, afterwards.' 'Now,' I said, 'I can't do that, I won't do it.' He said, 'Now, all right,' he says, 'I have got to protect myself.' He said, 'Now you better make up your mind in a day or two.' I went in and saw him in a day or two days after. He said, 'I understand from some friends that you are not going to resign.' I said, 'That is correct.' 'Now, why do you act that way? Now you and I have known one another for years; we are both leaders. Why do you act that way? Why don't you come in and help me? Do you see anything in looking at it this way and having me as an enemy?' I said, 'Do you see anything in having me as an enemy to you?' He said, 'This won't last long; we want to get a good man in there. When I say a good man,' he says, 'I mean a man who don't belong to the organization [Tammany Hall], who the public will take up and the newspapers make a great time and say, "Ahearn is doing the proper thing," and after a little while it will quiet down and you can come back again.' I said, 'No, I won't come back.' Then he went a little further and made this proposition to me. He said, 'You work hard over there, you put in many hours in laborious work; you are in your office a great many hours; I have often told you you stay there too long. Now,' he said, 'supposing that something was put in your way which would make up for at least your salary and more than your salary and you had nothing at all to do, wouldn't that be better for you?' 'No.' He says, 'Now, I will show you how we can help you out. Here is supplies given out every day, and here is one big job; here is a poor fellow,' he said, 'and I am very sorry to say he is not going to last long, and you can come in when he dies; you get his share of the profits of that plumbing business.' 'Who is that?' I said. 'Mr. Ryder, who is to-day very ill, if not dead. You can get his share.' I said, 'Mr. Ahearn, I have been in politics a good many years; I am almost as poor a man to-day, I believe I am, as when I went in. I had a good business when I went in; I never wanted to come in your department; I was asked by the organization to come in. I knew you; I felt as though I wouldn't have any power; I knew you never had any executive ability yourself and there wouldn't be any chance there for me at all to do anything more than sit in the office.' He said, 'You know that ain't so.' I said, 'It was so in Livingston's case most of the time,' but he said, 'You and I are district leaders; we are district leaders. You don't suppose I would treat you that way.' I said that should not make any difference. Well, however, I left him then. He said, 'Will you resign?' I said, 'No.' 'Well, if you do not I will have to ask Mr. Davis to send you a little letter.' 'What kind of a letter?' 'Your removal.' I said, 'It will be far more pleasure to be removed than to resign under those circumstances. . . .'

"I do not know as I mentioned it in my testimony, when he spoke about if I did not resign he would remove me, I said,

'Why take me? Are there any charges?' He said, 'No.'
'Why don't you take somebody who had charge of this work
and remove them?' His reply was, 'You don't want me to
go down to the bottom and take somebody, do you?' I said,
'I want you to take whoever is guilty.' Then he got this crying fit on again, was so sorry for me and all that sort of thing,
the saddest thing of his life, and he asked me, 'Won't you resign to please me?' And I says, 'No, I won't resign.' He was
so sorry for me."[1]

William Dalton received his letter of removal from the office
of Commissioner of Public Works the same evening of the day
of his final conversation with Borough President Ahearn, with
the message that "the President said he hoped there would not
be any hard feelings over the matter." Another reason why it
was expedient for the politicians to remove Dalton was indicated in another part of his testimony. He was too zealous
in his inspection of the work that was being done on the City's
public works:

"Now, just how far did you exercise authority in directing the
work of either Mr. Scannell or Mr. Olney?" Dalton was asked.

"You are speaking of the street repairs?" he inquired.

"Yes, entirely now of the streets."

"Not very far, for the reason that shortly after I was appointed to the department I was sent for by Mr. Ahearn, and
he said: 'You have been off on some work to-day?' 'Yes.'
'Well, now, you don't want to go out on this work; you want
to stay in the office; don't bother with this thing; you stay in
the office; let somebody else attend to that business.' I felt,
having a horse and wagon the city was paying for, I ought to
use it; I ought to be out; I told him that; I said: 'I think, as
Commissioner of Public Works, I ought to be on this work.
Now, if I have been stepping on somebody's ground and hurt-
ing somebody, tell me and I will get out and resign from the
department.' 'No, no, William, there is nothing like that;
you stay in the office and you attend to that work.' This happened, I think, on two or three occasions. . . . Well, I don't
know whether he thought perhaps it ought to be left to the chief

---

[1]Ahearn Investigation, Vol. II, pp. 1044–1047, 1081.

engineer; that he was more competent to inspect, or what the trouble or cause was, but I was ordered to stay in my office. I said: 'I have a horse and wagon.' He said: 'You use them as you go home at night, or as you come down in the morning, or something like that.' As I say, that happened on two or three occasions; that happened on Broadway, this wood block. . . . I said: 'A boy getting $6 a week can attend to my office work.'"[1]

The naïveté of the Commissioner of Public Works seems to have caused Tammany Hall considerable embarrassment.

In spite of the enmity of his candidate for Mayor, the opposition of Brooklyn and the investigations into city affairs, Charles F. Murphy was quietly increasing his power, not only in New York City, but throughout the State, and his silent manipulations of delegates, conventions, district leaders, and candidates, together with his deals with Hearst and the Republicans, enabled him gradually to control the politics of New York State as no other Tammany Hall leader had ever succeeded in doing. He had finally conciliated the Brooklyn Democrats, and these together with the regular Tammany Hall Democrats managed to be the dominators of the state conventions. The convention of 1906 at Buffalo, where, in the face of tremendous opposition, Murphy forced the nomination of William Randolph Hearst for Governor, showed his power, and he was respected for that power, whatever Democrats may have felt about the deed. Theodore Roosevelt testified that it was the general impression in New York State, after that convention of 1906, that Charles F. Murphy was the dominant factor in the politics of New York State.

Roosevelt also maintained that Murphy was in corrupt alliance with William Barnes, Jr., the successor of Thomas C. Platt as the Republican Boss of New York State. Mr. Barnes, who controlled Albany at the time when Murphy controlled New York City, was characterized in the following manner by the Bayne Legislative Investigating Committee:

"He testified before us that he had taken an active part in politics from early life, and that he had entered upon this career

---

[1] Ahearn Investigation, Vol. II, pp. 1068-1069.

'*for the purpose of obtaining honest elections in Albany and ele-vating politics.*' We regret to say that the evidence before us showed that Mr. Barnes's efforts in these particulars had re-sulted in dismal failure. Elections are not honest in Albany, and politics are not elevated. The most conspicuous beneficiary of graft, public extravagance and raiding of the municipal treasury, we find from the evidence, to be Mr. William Barnes, Jr., himself, as the owner of the majority of the stock of the Journal Company."[1]

In a statement that he gave to the newspapers Roosevelt said:

"Now, no doubt, Mr. Barnes and Mr. Murphy would like to have everything all the time, but they are perfectly willing each to take half instead of the whole, but we don't care any-thing about dividing the state equally between them, instead of giving it all to one. What we intend to do is to take it from both and we intend to take the nation from both."

Roosevelt's intentions were good, but the job was too big even for him. Governor Hughes fought hard during his ad-ministration to get a direct primary bill passed, by which the people would nominate their candidates directly instead of turn-ing that right over to state conventions dominated by bosses. But Tammany Hall, under Murphy, acted in conjunction with the Republicans, dominated by Barnes, and Hughes's bill was defeated. Barnes and Murphy were willing to coöperate to any extent for the defeat of direct primaries, which might lessen the organization control that was so essential to their efficient existence.

In 1910 Murphy chose John A. Dix as his candidate for Governor. Roosevelt said in a speech later:

"Mr. Barnes' machine was openly for the defeat of the Re-publican candidate and the election of Mr. Murphy's tool, Mr. Dix. The Republican machine in 1910 did its level best in securing Tammany control of the State. . . . When I speak of the bi-partisan combine I mean such things as these."

---

[1] *Barnes vs. Roosevelt*, Vol. I, p. 76.

John A. Dix was elected Governor. In the previous year, 1909, Murphy had succeeded in electing Judge William J. Gaynor Mayor of New York, in spite of the opposition candidacy of William Randolph Hearst, who had again broken with Murphy, but this was not a very valuable victory, for Gaynor was an independent person of unusual integrity, and Tammany Hall had lost in the election to the reform fusion movement the offices of Comptroller, President of the Board of Aldermen, and several borough presidents.

"This brood of Democrats coming in with Dix could have taught refined larceny to envious convicts," wrote John A. Hennessy. The first duty of the Democrats who controlled the State in 1910 was the election of a United States Senator. Murphy's choice was John C. Sheehan, but there was a group of Independent Democrats, headed by Franklin D. Roosevelt, who opposed Sheehan as United States Senator. These, working with some Republicans, were able to hold up the nomination, and the Legislature sat in a deadlock for about two weeks. William Loeb, Jr., Theodore Roosevelt's private secretary, testified in the Barnes-Roosevelt libel suit that he had had a conversation with William Barnes, Jr., in the offices of the bankers, J. S. Bache & Company: "I said to him that some Independents—some representatives of the Franklin Roosevelt Democrats in the Legislature, had been to me and asked me to find out from Mr. Barnes whether Mr. Barnes would not support an independent Democrat upon whom they could agree. Mr. Barnes said that he could not do it, because his arrangement with Mr. Murphy was that he was not to interfere in Mr. Murphy's plans about the senatorship." However, Mr. Murphy's plans about the senatorship were interfered with, and the independents refused to nominate Sheehan. Finally, after attempts at deals and attempts at counter deals, and ballots by day and ballots by night, both sides compromised and nominated James J. O'Gorman as Senator from New York. No one won and no one lost, except, perhaps, Mr. O'Gorman.

There was other business going on besides the election of Senators, however, among the Democrats whom Murphy had placed in Albany. The Tammany politicians had gone in heavily for contracting as a business during the early years of the twentieth century, and the control of the State was profitable for the contractors and their associates. John Aloysius Hennessy, who investigated conditions under Murphy's man, Governor Dix, wrote:

"Barbers became specialists in roadwork and were thought more of if they did their inspection work at home. Election district workers became State deputies of one thing or another. A gentleman, by profession a dentist, in Herkimer County, was put in charge of State roads there. A gentleman, by profession the village bootblack and peanut vendor in Norwich, Chenango County, became road inspector, he having taken the earlier precaution to get six relatives from Italy on the poll list. A gentleman, whose knowledge of assignation houses overshadowed his other business qualifications, was kidnapped from the obscurity of his native town to tell farmers—at $10 a day and expenses—how to raise crops. A man whose knowledge of oysters, lobsters, and clams was gained in road houses while he was building political fences, took charge of the coast fisheries of the State. A gentleman, unfortunate victim of drugs, took charge of a State hospital for the insane. A gentleman whose only known crime was larceny, to which he had pleaded guilty, became the confidential agent of a great State department. A man who uncautiously hung his overcoat in the Aldermanic room of the New York City Hall one day and lost a roll of $2,000 hurriedly slipped by him into an outside pocket, was employed to show certain contractors how their work could best be done with profit to themselves and others. One man thus interviewed took things so literally that he canceled an order for several thousand bags of cement on a rather small job and made so bad a mess of it that it took all the suavity of his most immediate political leader to get him the money on his contract.

"It was an era of thought in the Democratic Party. State Hospital officials discovered and called for newly-patented articles. Another political scientist discovered that the useless waste product of a certain Democratic paper mill would make a good covering for roads as a dust layer. Certain gentlemen interested in up-State schools, who ever believed in agile thinking, found that prison-made desks and chairs, good enough for New York City schools, lacked height and breadth, and, curiously enough, private manufacturers, with foresight amounting to genius, stood ready to supply the exact kind wanted. The prison shoe industry went down as the private sales went up. This was due in part to the esthetic demands from State institutions for varying styles. Blankets made in State institutions lost all sense of economy and cost more than superior goods made by union labor. Even office boys of Democratic parentage were ambitious to share in the recrudescence of their famous party, and one of them stamped the O. K. of the Governor on many big accounts against the State, thus permitting the Chief Executive to attend to those social duties which required him to pay $100 a dozen for napkins and to acquire a line of thermos bottles sufficient to strain the manufacturing facilities of a modest plant."[1]

Meanwhile, in the City, prostitution, gambling, and the liquor business were going merrily on their illegal way with the protection of the politicians and the police. In the early morning of July 16, 1912, Herman Rosenthal was shot down and killed in front of the Hotel Metropole in Forty-Third Street near Broadway. The murder proved to be a dramatic culmination of the system of police graft which was sanctioned by the politicians of Tammany Hall. Rosenthal had been one of New York's most eminent gamblers, and when he quarrelled with his competitors and with Police Lieutenant Charles Becker, he threatened to expose the extortions of Becker. He made affidavits which were published in the newspapers, and he had an appointment with District Attorney Whitman for the day after his murder, when he was to make a complete exposure. A few days before his murder Rosenthal had visited the office of the New York *World* and had dictated a statement in the course of which he said:

"There is only one man in the world can call me off, that is the big fellow, 'Big Tim' Sullivan, and he is as honest as the day is long, and I know he is in sympathy with me. He don't want to see anybody else hurt, and I don't want to hurt anybody. My fight is with the police. It is purely personal with me. I

[1]*What's the Matter with New York*, by John A. Hennessy, pp. 17-19.

am making no crusade and my friends know all about it. I am not going to hurt anybody else, and if I can't go through with this without bringing anybody else in I'll quit. But I am going to try to go through with it myself. The others will come in of their own free will before the thing is through.

"The police know that I think more of 'Big Tim' Sullivan than I do of anybody else alive. They know that the only way they can hurt me is by trying to involve him with me— by trying to show that he is, or was, my partner in the gambling business. They know this is not true—that it is a dirty lie. He is not and never was interested with me to the extent of a penny. I hope that his name will not be brought out in this connection.

"Tim Sullivan and myself have been friends for many years. I knew him as a boy. I would lay down my life for him, and on more than one occasion he proved his friendship for me. I believe that I could get anything he's got, and if I need money I can go to him for it and he will give it to me or get it for me. It is purely a matter of friendship, and he never expects to make a nickel profit out of it. He is the only man that could call me off, and he has told me that he believes I am doing right in trying to protect myself and my home."

Rosenthal said that he opened a gambling house with Police Lieutenant Becker as a partner. He needed money, and he went to his good friend "Big Tim" Sullivan to borrow $2,000: "'Big Tim' didn't have the cash, so he signed a note for $2,000 for me and I got the money. The loan was out of pure friendship." When Rosenthal quarrelled with his police partner, Becker, Becker tried to stop his intention to expose Becker by telling the newspapers that Rosenthal had been going about town "showing the note of an East Side politician."

"I never showed the note around town or to anybody except in the course of business," Rosenthal told the *World*. "Becker, as a partner in my business, knew of the existence of the note, and the only reason he did know of it was because he was my partner. Becker thought that by bringing the note into the controversy he could have me called off. He knows I would do anything that Sullivan wanted me to do, and would lose my life rather than do this friend a wrong. But I won't be called off by any such bluff. I borrowed the money. It was a legitimate transaction and there is no discredit attached to it."

Rosenthal did lose his life, and it was in the same year that "Big Tim" Sullivan began to suffer from insanity, with delusions of persecution.

Everybody in the graft system continued to make money except the prostitutes. Mrs. Mary Goode testified in 1912 before the Curran Committee, and she gave much information concerning the state of her trade during the Murphy régime:

"Did you women who got together in an effort to get away from the Police Department, make any estimate as to the number of prostitutes in New York?" Mary Goode was asked.

"Well, we think there is about 35,000. Of course, that takes in a number of girls who are working in the stores, who earn little and have to get out on the streets at night."

"You have no accurate way of getting estimates?"

"No. We just start by multiplying the number of flats and the number of girls in the house. And the girls in the stores. There is a lot of girls in the stores, you know, who are earning only four or five dollars."

"What about since you have been up in the Tenderloin, or since you have been back in New York this fall? There have been some raids, haven't there, up there?"

"Oh, yes."

"What kind of houses, mostly?"

"Well, all the big houses that the citizens would notice, and know are running, Inspector Dwyer has closed with a great flourish. They have broken down the doors with axes and crowbars and thrown the girls out into the streets, and then an officer is there, and the girl comes after her clothes and they say, 'You have got to go and see the Inspector.' She does not go, of course, because she is too frightened. They come in there warmly clad, warm underclothes, food, liquor and cigars. And the rest of us are thrown in the street. They stay there for weeks and weeks. If they fancy a picture, it disappears. If they fancy a tapestry, it goes. Nobody can ever see when it goes, but it goes. But what can a woman do? Who is going to believe her or take her word? Every additional power given those people enforces their power over us. . . ."

"Well, don't you think that the Mayor and the Police Commissioner can stop the men from taking money from your class of women?"

"Never," Mrs. Goode answered. "There is not a Mayor living can stop the police from taking money, and there is not a District Attorney can stop it either. Never."

"What is the matter with the police?"

"Well, I don't know. That Becker pocketbook, you know."

"The Becker pocketbook?"

"They want your life now. The Night Court at night. They were gotten up, for those women, and when the Mayor stopped the raids, there was no need for the magistrates to sit after twelve o'clock. Now, they will come along and raid your house along about theatre closing. That is the time, you know, the plain clothes man comes around with a great hurrah, and hundreds of people around. If he is too early, or a little bit early, and he can reach the Night Court, he drives you round in the wagon, and he waits until the Night Court closes. Then he takes you back to the station house that controls your precinct where you live. $100 to bail you out at night. $100 for the bondsman. Just to get you out that night. Just one bond, Mr. Buckner. Not the bond the next day. That $100 is split up with that Lieutenant and that bondsman. Whether with the officers that make your arrest, I don't know, but that Lieutenant behind that desk and that bondsman gets that $100. Why should it take $100 to take a woman out of jail? I have shown you it is the Becker pocketbook. Haven't they all gone mad in the last few months? Who has heard of $100 to bail a woman out until Rosenthal was killed? Who has heard it since this suit?"

"The prices seem to be going up?"

"They are making a fortune," said Mrs. Goode. "Little old Sol Wolf, when he said to me, 'Don't tell him you paid me the $25'—he would have to split up with Skelly."

"What is it you women want?"

"We want to be put under a committee. We don't care whether we are segregated or not. We always choose places where there are no families or children. We always go there of our own accord. Nobody has to ask us. In return for that, we will help you with the street walkers, we will help you with the noise and disorder; we will tell you about young girls on the street who are working for pimps; and every pimp makes a thief out of every girl he has. They have to be a thief on the street."

"What do you mean by that?"

"They have to pick their man's pocket, and to take every cent he has got, if they take him to a room. That is the street girl. There is not a street girl in the City of New York to-day, Mr. Buckner, that is not a thief. If they are put into the houses they will be taken care of. If they are diseased they will be found out. They will be reported. If they are thieves, they will be reported. If they are under age, they will be reported. There is no graft, there is no exposure and scandal of the police. There was the Rosenthal case. Now it is me, and there will be another. People are not going to stand any more jobs. The worm has turned this time. They are not going to stand any more jobbing. They have stopped that all. Now, you gentlemen have had committees all over the country, vice committees, you have had police officers, you have had everybody after the men who have lived off the earnings of the women. Have you accomplished anything? You never can accomplish a thing until we help you. We are the ones that can cure that evil."

"What do you mean by that?"

"What we call the pimps. The man who lives off the earnings of the girls. In this city to-day there are hundreds, more than that—thousands of girls that are glad to get rid of a pimp, but they are frightened to death. If it can be left to me, in my house, if there is any girl in my house and there is a man takes her earnings and abuses her, I can hand him to you. I can give him to you. He don't dare touch me."

"In talking to your various girls from time to time, have you run across the trail of the pimp vice often?"

"Well, I will recite you, this June, when I left. I took $19 in one week away from one girl. I said, 'Rose, I am not going to give you this money to take home to your pimp. You must start a bank account on Monday.' We all have a superstition if we put money away on Monday, we will earn it through the week. That is the superstition. She said, 'All right.' I saved her $19. I moved Monday. I said, 'Rose, I will give you your money to-day.' She said, 'Don't give me my money to-day. He would murder me if he knew I was opening a bank account or keeping money I did not give to him.'

"She came to the St. Paul Hotel to my room every day about two o'clock for three or four dollars when she could not make money on the street. She was arrested and sent away for five days. When she came out she was so frightened she was afraid to solicit much. She did not bring much money home, and he beat her and sent her away. She had $5 left of the $19 that she took from me that day. That is all she had. He threw her out because she could not make more money. That is one sample.

"I had a little girl up there the two weeks I was uptown. Little May. She was an Irish girl and had an Italian pimp. I said, 'How happy you would be with your baby if you could give up that man and be with your baby.' She said, 'I would be murdered. He has six brothers.'

"Now we are the ones that can correct that, and you never will stamp that evil out, Mr. Buckner, until we stamp it."

"Are there any considerable number of pimps in town?"

"Every girl in town has got a pimp. They may be a few of them working. Of course, there are a few, but I want to tell you one thing, gentlemen, I don't think you will find an American or an Irishman a pimp in this whole City of New York."

"They don't run that way?"

"No, sir; there is not an Irishman nor an American pimp to-day in this city. They are Italians and Jews, every one of them. . . ."

"Well, have you been friendly with the Jewish women who run disorderly houses, and with the Jewish men who own disorderly houses or not?"

"Well, I wasn't very friendly in Fifty-eighth Street, because they insisted in going on the street and soliciting at night. They solicited some of the friends of the Paulist Fathers and it destroyed our neighborhood. You know, you take a Jewish woman and it becomes a dull day, why she is wild, and she won't wait for trade to come back again. She goes right straight to solicit the people. . . ."

"Now, what has been your observation, experience, or from talking with other women of your profession, with reference to whether the officers, since they have been ordered by the Mayor not to go in the rooms with women, continuing to do so in order to get the evidence?"

"Well, is there any man so simple in this room to think that an officer comes in my house and he does not take a girl to the room? Is there any man within sound of my voice so simple as that? That he thinks he does not take a girl to the room? Gentlemen, there is not an officer ever goes into a house who does not take a girl to a room."

"After he gets there does he decline intercourse?"

"Stays there at his own inconvenience." [sic]

"Does he decline intercourse?"

"Certainly not."

"I used to wonder about that when I was in the District Attorney's office," said Emory R. Buckner, the examining counsel. "The affidavits invariably say that the said Sadie so and so exposed her person, and then he offered her $1 and declined and left. And it has been that practice that the Mayor has——"

Mrs. Goode interrupted: "It is not so, Mr. Buckner."

Buckner, continuing: "That the Mayor has very properly objected to. Now, what is the truth? Do they decline it or not?"

"Never, never."

"If they do decline, what would be the effect? What would you know at once?"

"We would know then that they were officers."

"And you could move out before the warrant comes?"

"The minute they pay their money and do not stay, and the girl comes out and says, 'That man did not stay, he just gave us the money,' every one of us would pack up and be out of that house in an hour. . . ."

"Now, there is another point entirely outside from the pimp situation, that is, the men who are living on the earnings of women individually. What about the men who are getting into the business of keeping houses of prostitution?"

"Well, they are foreigners and they are down on the East Side, but they are gradually coming up."

"Gradually coming up?"

"Yes."

"Is that business on the increase or on the decrease?"

"Oh, on the increase. . . ."

"What is the character of houses mostly that the men own?"

"Well, those are common dollar houses."

"What is that?"

"Common dollar houses, where there are French girls and all of that."

"Are those the names that you mentioned a while ago as being in the trust?"

"Oh, yes, sir. Everywheres you see Maas' beer wagon you may know they belong to the trust. Almost all of them. There is white slavery. Maas sells his beer, his cousin is the physician, and he collects the money. Is that white slavery? Is that a trust?" demanded Mary Goode.

"Now, in some of the literature I have been reading in cases on this subject, in Chicago and other places, I read of telephone houses. What is the telephone house in your business or profession?"

"Well, that is a call house."

"A call house?"

"That is another thing could be rectified. There are twenty or thirty girls in a call house. . . . Some woman or some man some blocks away telephones that she wants a light-haired girl or a dark-haired girl at such an hour. She does not know whether that girl is clean or not. She does not know it at all. If all of those houses are under a committee, a vice committee, every one of those girls in every one of those houses would be examined."

"Don't you think if you had a vice committee that the members of the vice committee might collect the graft, the same way as the police collect it?"

"No. They would be too afraid to do that. And we know when we are right. We know when we don't have to pay graft, and we know when we do have to pay it."

"What is the object of these call houses?"

"You cannot get evidence against them. There don't appear to be a law that covers a call house. They don't take them in, but some other house telephones for the girl, and the girl goes there. There don't seem to be any law to cover that, and they can't do anything with a call house."

"Are those on the increase or decrease in this city?"

"Just now they are on the increase, because there are so

few houses doing any business. So many of the houses are out, and they are hungry and starving, they have to do something."

"You never sold liquor."

"Any kind of a drink I never sold."

"So I heard. While we are on the subject, why did you never sell beer in your disorderly apartment?"

"Well, it was a one dollar house, and a two dollar house. In order to run a respectable house at that price you can't have drunken men, because it would ruin you."

"What do you call a respectable house of prostitution?" asked Alderman Dowling, a Tammany man, and a member of the investigating committee.

"Well, a respectable house can be run, for instance, by a woman who only lets gentlemen in. She never lets gunmen in nor convicts in."

"How are you going to tell a gunman from a convict?" asked Alderman Dowling.

"They won't be in the house very long before you find out," Mary Goode answered.

"How do you find out?"

"By their conversation, by their manner."

"Is that what you call a respectable disorderly house?"

"Yes, sir. It is a curious title, but it is a respectable disorderly house. . . ."

"Mr. Buckner—I think that is the distinction, Mr. Alderman, that the Mayor [Gaynor] makes in his outward order of decency philosophy."

"Alderman Dowling—I don't think the Mayor ever said anything about respectable disorderly houses, where a gunman hangs up his tools and uses language like a gentleman. I don't think the Mayor ever said that."[1]

It was after the murder of Rosenthal that the Curran Committee of the Board of Aldermen investigated the Police Department, and it was before that committee that Mrs. Mary Goode gave her picture of prostitution in New York in the time of the Tammany Boss whom some men jocularly called Charles the First.

---

[1] Curran Investigation, Vol. III, pp. 2167, 2175, 2186–2191.

V

Murphy, having gained what Croker had not been able to gain, and what no other Tammany Boss had been able to gain, the control of New York State, went to the Democratic National Convention in 1912 with the delegation from New York in his hand. It was said that he tried, in alliance with the financiers Thomas Fortune Ryan and August Belmont, to jam through the nomination of Champ Clark for President of the United States. But William Jennings Bryan, who finally realized that his nomination for President was impossible, bitterly denounced with all his oratorical powers the deal between Tammany Hall and the financiers. He was able to hold the convention and to defeat Murphy and his allies. Then, with the aid of other men, Bryan forced the nomination of Woodrow Wilson.

In that same year, 1912, Murphy had to nominate a Governor of New York. John A. Dix had proved too obviously complacent, and the newspapers clamoured for the defeat of his renomination. Murphy liked Dix, for Dix did as he was told, and that quality was Murphy's ideal of statesmanship. But he realized that it would be difficult to win with Dix. Oscar S. Straus was the candidate for Governor of Theodore Roosevelt's new Progressive Party, and Job E. Hedges was the Republican nominee. Both were honourable men. Murphy needed a candidate who would be loyal to him and striking enough to the popular imagination to win votes. He then made what he afterward termed "the greatest mistake of my life," in the nomination of William Sulzer for Governor.

William Sulzer had been one of Tammany Hall's leading orators for many years. With Bourke Cockran and Thomas F. Grady, he did the speech-making for the organization during the 'nineties, and during the Croker period Sulzer was one of the most popular men in Tammany Hall. The *Tammany Times* reported his selection by the ladies on a secret ballot as the most attractive gentleman present at the Press Club Fair. Sulzer was six feet tall and weighed 185 pounds. His features were rugged and his figure ungainly. He had been compared to Abraham Lincoln and to Henry Clay, and he himself did all that lay within his power of mimicry to live up to the comparison. For many years Sulzer had represented a New York district in Congress, on a Tammany Hall nomination, and while in Washington he appeared at a banquet dressed in an exact reproduction of the style and dress of Henry Clay. "It is said that Mr. Sulzer imagines," wrote the Jacksonville *Times Union* in December, 1903, "he very much resembles that distinguished statesman and makes a study of posing, running his fingers through his hair, assuming a languid manner, and all other little peculiar characteristics of the immortal Henry." But art in Tammany Hall had always been relatively unrewarded, for the men used for actors and orators had never received the respect or the remuneration paid to contractors and asphalt manufacturers. With the possible exception of A. Oakey Hall, who, as we have seen, worked under rather exceptional conditions, the showmen of Tammany Hall were never its millionaires. George Washington Plunkitt gave this advice:

"We've got some orators in Tammany Hall, but they're chiefly ornamental. You never heard of Charlie Murphy delivering a speech, did you? Or Richard Croker, or John Kelly, or any other man who has been a real power in the organization? Look at the thirty-six district leaders of Tammany Hall to-day. How many of them travel on their tongues? Maybe one or two, and they don't count when business is doin' at Tammany Hall. The men who rule have practised keepin' their tongues still, not exercisin' them. So you want to drop the orator idea unless you mean to go into politics just to perform the sky-rocket act."[1]

And Alfred Henry Lewis's Boss, Big John Kennedy, reminded his protégé: "Cheers are nothin' but a breeze; an' as for a crowd, no matter who you are, there would always be a bigger turn-out to see you hanged than to shake your mitt."

There are many samples of the oratory of William Sulzer in the seven large scrapbooks of newspaper clippings and the bound volumes of his speeches presented by him to the New York Public Library. One of these is the following speech on prohibition, for in his later career Sulzer was a prohibitionist in public:

[1] *Plunkitt of Tammany Hall*, p. 13.

"When they ask you why I am for prohibition," Sulzer told the Prohibition Convention at Pittsburgh in 1916, "you tell them that if the people were to save the money the indulgence in strong drink costs annually, and the same were utilized for public purposes, it would develop our great water powers and give us light, heat, and power free of cost; that it would build the best dirt roads since the days of the Cæsars; that it would erect the most beautiful public buildings the eye of man has ever witnessed—all poems in stone—challenging the admiration of every lover of the beautiful; that it would dig the deepest and the widest canals ever constructed on earth; that it would rear to heaven the most magnificent schoolhouses for the children of women ever modelled by the genius of man; and that beyond all, and above all, it would make our people sober and industrious and efficient, and capable of producing in every avenue of trade, every channel of commerce, and every line of human endeavor more than 20 per cent. of what they now produce, and hence to that extent increase the earning and saving capacity of our workers. . . .

"Tell them that I say no State, and no country, can long endure half wet and half dry, half drunk and half sober, and that all friends of good government should be with us in the fight to make the State sober, to banish forever the saloons from our country. . . .

"Tell them that if I were asked to sum up in a single word the cause on earth of more than seven-tenths of all the woes and all the wants; of all the fears and all the tears; of all the trials and all the troubles; of all the ghouls and all the ghosts; of all the crimes and all the criminals; of all the groans of helpless men, and all the griefs of weeping women, and all the heart pangs of sad-faced children, I should sum it all up in that short word—R-U-M—RUM—which menaces the progress of the race, and challenges the advance of civilization."

He got the nomination he was seeking at that time.

After Tammany Hall nominated him, William Sulzer was elected Governor of New York in 1912. During the campaign he had designated himself broadly as a man of the people, and he carried out that pose immediately after his election. He rechristened the Executive Mansion at Albany "The People's

House," and he invited the public to attend the legislative reception which followed his inauguration. The inauguration itself was the height of ostentatious simplicity. The usual parade was omitted. At a dinner given in his honour by the Lotos Club soon after his inauguration, Sulzer said in the course of his speech:

"I have little vanity. I want no glory—no credit for doing my duty—no future preferment—and when the office the people gave me goes back to the people—to whom it belongs—to give to some other man—I say again, and I say advisedly—I want to retire from the misrepresentations and the disappointments of political life—to a little farm, by the side of the road, and be the friend of man."

When he began to exercise the functions of Governor of New York, Sulzer continued to remember that he resembled both Abraham Lincoln and Henry Clay. And Abraham Lincoln had been President of the United States for two terms, and Henry Clay was suggested for that office many times. Then, too, a New Jersey Democrat had just been elected President of the United States by virtue of his vigorous defiance of the political bosses who had aided to make him Governor of New Jersey. The example of Woodrow Wilson must have entered the mind of William Sulzer often; and William Sulzer was ambitious, and he loved the sound of his own voice. But Woodrow Wilson had come straight from a university to fight the bosses after he had used them, and William Sulzer had come straight from Tammany Hall, where he had been used by the bosses for years. It was the fatal defect in the comparison, and it was part of Sulzer's tragedy that he never seemed to realize it.

In the week between Christmas Day, 1912, and New Year's Day, 1913, Sulzer, at the request of Murphy, spent an afternoon at Delmonico's with the Boss. "His attitude was very friendly and confidential," Sulzer said some months later. "He said he was my friend; that he knew of my financial condition and wished to help me out. As he went on I was amazed at his knowledge of my intimate personal affairs. To my astonishment he informed me that he knew that I was heavily in debt. Then he offered me money to pay my debts and have enough left to take things easy while Governor. . . . He said that this was really a party matter and that the money he would give me was party money; that I had been a popular candidate easily elected and for less money than any other candidate in his recollection. He said that nobody would know anything about it; that I could pay what I owed and go to Albany feeling easy financially. He then asked me how much I needed, to whom I owed it, and other personal questions."

But Sulzer did not wish "to be tied hard and fast as governor in advance," and he declined Mr. Murphy's kind offer, saying that he was paying off his debts gradually, and that his creditors were his friends and would not press him; "that I was economical, that I would try to get along on my salary as governor." Murphy remarked that the organization did not want to see Sulzer hampered financially while he was Governor, and that he would allow the Governor whatever he needed over his salary for his living expenses. Sulzer refused again, and then Murphy said:"If you need money at any time let me know and you can have what you want. We cleaned up a lot of money on your campaign. I can afford to let you have what you want and never miss it."

Governor Sulzer did not see Mr. Murphy again until a month after his inauguration as Governor. Then he went to New York City and met Murphy in the house of Judge Edward E. McCall. After dinner they discussed various appointments in the Governor's gift, and Murphy urged Sulzer to appoint as Public Service Commissioner Murphy's friend John Galvin. Sulzer wished to appoint one of his own reputable friends, Henry Morgenthau, George Foster Peabody, or Colonel John Temple Graves, but Murphy would not consent to any of these gentlemen. Then they discussed the new subway contracts, and finally they compromised on the appointment of their host Judge Edward E. McCall as Public Service Commissioner. Murphy also insisted, according to Sulzer, on the appointment to the Public Service Commission of his political lieutenant in Albany, Patrick E. McCabe. Murphy also wished "The" McManus, a prominent Tammany Hall district leader, to be made Commissioner of Labour, and James E. Gaffney, who was said to be a partner of Murphy's in the contracting business, to be State Highway Commissioner.

"This is the same Gaffney," Sulzer said in the interview with James Creelman in which he disclosed the cause of his differences with Murphy, "who, only a few months afterwards, on September 4, 1913, in undisputed testimony before the Supreme Court at Nyack, was shown to have demanded and received $30,000 in money (refusing to take a check) from one of the aqueduct contractors, nominally for 'advice.' This is the man who Murphy demanded should be put in a position where he would superintend and control the spending of sixty-five millions of the money of the state in road contracts."

Governor Sulzer did not meet Mr. Murphy again until they both happened to be in Washington for the inauguration of President Wilson. Murphy had suggested that he keep in touch with the Governor by long-distance telephone to Albany from Tammany Hall and from his estate at Good Ground, which Murphy had been in the habit of doing for some years with his governors. But Sulzer said that he told Murphy he did not wish to talk with him over the telephone. "Well, then," Murphy answered, "if I have anything to say to you I will send you word through some friend, or by Mr. Delaney, or someone in the Legislature." "That will do," Sulzer said he answered.

When they met at the Shoreham Hotel in Washington, Murphy followed Sulzer into the hall, as he was leaving a conference of Democratic Senators. He asked for the assurance that his friend "Jim" Gaffney would be appointed State Highway Commissioner. Murphy remarked that he was anxious to get away to Hot Springs, which was Murphy's favourite resort in the later years of his life, but he wanted that appointment settled before he went away for his vacation. He told Sulzer that if he appointed Gaffney, he could have his way in some other matters of legislation and appointments. "I told him that in my opinion it would be a mistake to appoint Mr. Gaffney," Sulzer told Creelman. Murphy said: "I want you to appoint Gaffney. It is an organization matter. I will appreciate it." Sulzer said he would think it over. "I want to go slow and get the very best man I can find for that position," he said he told Murphy; "I would rather be slow about the appointment than be sorry." "If you don't appoint Gaffney you WILL be sorry," Murphy answered. "Mr. Murphy finally said, 'I am for Gaff-

WILLIAM   SULZER

ney. The organization demands his appointment and I want you to do it.' I replied, 'I will make no promise about it.' He said: 'It will be Gaffney or war.'"

At a later conversation in his own house Murphy dictated appointments to Sulzer, told him that he controlled the Legislature absolutely, and that, unless Sulzer did as Murphy wished, none of the legislation which Sulzer was interested in would pass, and that he would make Sulzer's administration the "laughing stock of the state." He also threatened to discredit Sulzer personally. At another interview after the Jefferson banquet at the Hotel Waldorf on April 13, 1913, Murphy repeated his demands. At that time State Senator Stilwell was being tried for accepting a bribe. Sulzer asked Murphy what he intended to do about Stilwell. "'Stand by him, of course,' replied Mr. Murphy. 'Stilwell will be acquitted. It will be only a three-day wonder. How do you expect a senator to live on $1,500 a year? That is only chicken feed.'"

Sulzer told James Creelman that after this interview he went home disheartened. The fight for the people, the battle for civic virtue, seemed hopeless. In the depths of his despair he wrote out his resignation as Governor of the State of New York, but then that seemed cowardly, and he tore up the resignation he had written out.[1]

Murphy and Sulzer had now severed diplomatic relations. Meanwhile, Sulzer had appointed John A. Hennessy to investigate corruption in all the departments of the state government. Hennessy found enough to startle Murphy. Hennessy estimated that the State got thirty cents of value for every dollar spent on its roads, and that: "As these cases develop the electors of New York State will learn that the political organization, so-called Democratic, captained by Charles F. Murphy in New York City, by William H. Fitzpatrick in Buffalo, and by William H. Kelley in Syracuse, is organized to loot the treasury and regards every honest man as its enemy." Upon another occasion, Mr. Hennessy was quoted as saying: "Sulzer is absolutely crazy, and if they don't put him out they will have to establish a regency."[2]

[1] The account of Sulzer's relations with Murphy given above is taken from Sulzer's interview with James Creelman in the *Evening Mail*, October 20, 1913.

[2] *Current Opinion*, Vol. LV, p. 402, December, 1913.

Sulzer's pet measure was a direct primary bill. He felt that it would help him with the people, and that it would also help the people to govern; thus his ambition and his sense of righteousness would both be served. But Murphy's pet hate was a direct primary bill, and in this hatred he was joined by William Barnes, Jr., the Republican State Boss. We have already noted Charles E. Hughes's failure to obtain the passage of such a measure. When the Legislature, which was controlled by Murphy for the Democrats and Barnes for the Republicans, refused to pass a direct primary bill, Sulzer called an extraordinary session. The extraordinary session refused to do any of the things the Governor had called it to do, and instead did exactly as it was told by Murphy, who remained close to the telephone at his Good Ground estate, and called the floor leaders twice a day. While Murphy was answering and using his telephone, and playing golf in his spare time, Sulzer was fretting in Albany and was able to do nothing with the recalcitrant Legislature. The legislators refused to pass the regular appropriation bills that were needed to keep the state government running, and they refused the regular fund usually allowed the Governor for investigation purposes. From their point of view, Sulzer and his associate Hennessy had already done far too much investigating. It even refused to appropriate money for the state prisons, because Murphy wanted a friend of his appointed superintendent of prisons, and Sulzer refused to make the appointment. The New York Central Railroad transported prisoners to Sing Sing on credit for the State, with the hope that its bills would somehow be paid sometime by Sulzer's efforts. The state government was completely paralyzed, because Murphy refused to permit his henchmen to do anything for Sulzer's administration. The Legislature even refused to adjourn, for if it had adjourned, Sulzer could have made *ad interim* appointments. During the hot summer months a few members sat and kept the session going, while most of the legislators remained in the country.

The Speaker of the New York State Assembly at this time was Alfred E. Smith, and the leader of the Democratic majority in the State Senate was Robert F. Wagner. Murphy held conferences with these men and with the leaders of Tammany Hall. Meanwhile, Sulzer was making speeches throughout the State in favour of his direct primary bill and in denunciation of the bosses. He likened Murphy to Tweed. In one speech at the Opera House in Corning, New York, Sulzer said:

"The bosses say they will beat me. I have heard that before. . . . They say they will destroy me, but I tell them that no man can destroy me but William Sulzer. [Applause.] I care very little about the political future and less about personal consequences. I shall go on doing my duty to the people as God gives me the light to see the right. [Applause.] . . .

"All I want to be is honest. [A voice: "You're right."] All I want to do is to keep the faith; all I desire is to tell the truth. I want to make good. [Applause.] When I am dead and buried the only monument I want is to have the people say in their hearts—'Well done, Bill.' [Great applause.]"

According to Sulzer's speeches, his was a holy crusade, and he was fond of quoting poetry to prove it. "Now is the time for us to act," he said at the end of one speech, and then he added:

> "Once to every man and nation
> Comes the moment to decide,
> In the strife of truth with falsehood,
> For the good or evil side;
> Some great cause, God's new Messiah,
> Giving each the bloom or blight,
> Parts the goats upon the left hand,
> And the sheep upon the right,
> And the choice goes by forever,
> 'Twixt the darkness and the light."

Then the forces of darkness gathered together, and the order suddenly came from Good Ground for the Assembly to impeach William Sulzer. But the effort was a strenuous one for the Democratic leaders Smith, Wagner, and Aaron J. Levy. First the absent members of the Assembly had to be brought to Albany, and that was difficult in midsummer. Murphy, however, was determined, and men were dragged from their retreats in the Catskills and from their camps in the Adirondacks as well as from their contracting business in New York City to record their votes as Murphy wished them recorded. Tele-

grams were sent throughout the State to bring absent legislators to Albany, and deputy sergeants at arms hurried through
Albany with summonses to Assemblymen who were in the City
to be present at their desks.

The Assembly met in night session on August 12, 1913.
Crowds of people entered, until the galleries could hold no more.
On a roll call the opponents of Sulzer succeeded in mustering
only sixty-six votes, ten less than the required majority. Telegraph and telephone messages were sent to thirty absent Democrats. Wild rumours flew about Albany. One was that Governor
Sulzer's friends intended to take possession of the Assembly
chamber and to adjourn the session before it could act, and another rumour said that if the Governor was impeached, he
would call out the state militia, of which he was Commander in
Chief by virtue of his office, and retain that office by military
force. Meanwhile, Charles F. Murphy sat all day long just a
few feet from the telephone in his house at 317 East 17th Street.
He had come in from his country estate, although it was
summer, and although he liked golf. He abandoned his office
in Tammany Hall for the privacy of his own house telephone,
and every few minutes during the day he talked with Tammany's representatives in Albany.

The Assembly continued in session all through the night of
August 13th. Many of the members placed their heads on their
desks and slept, while the majority leader, Aaron J. Levy, spoke
in favour of the Governor's impeachment. Some of the Assemblymen brought newspapers and read at their desks what
they themselves had said and done a few hours before.

Finally, enough members were mustered at Albany to pass
the impeachment resolutions. After the final roll call on the
impeachment, members fell back in their chairs and slept, while
Speaker Alfred E. Smith pounded with his gavel in the effort
to wake them.

"A number of the members, I take it, are asleep in their
chairs," Smith shouted. "Members will please answer when
their names are called." Smith whacked on his desk with his
gavel, and newly awakened members thumped on their desks
with their fists in order to arouse their colleagues. Then the
Assembly took up the Blauvelt short election bill.

A month before the impeachment proceedings against him

were passed, William Sulzer was suddenly sued for breach of promise of marriage by Miss Mignon Hopkins, a saleswoman in the Wanamaker store in Philadelphia. Miss Hopkins in her affidavit maintained that William Sulzer had proposed marriage to her in 1903 and that she had accepted him, but that at his request the engagement was kept secret because its announcement might have interfered with his political career. When the news reached her in 1908 that Mr. Sulzer had married, she said, she was amazed "and heartbroken." Miss Hopkins sued for breach of promise and a settlement was made. Five years later, however, after Governor Sulzer had fallen out with Tammany Hall, Miss Hopkins suddenly remembered that his failure to marry her had "ruined her happiness, caused her much sorrow, and been a great grief, affecting her health and marring her whole life." She sued again for breach of promise, and she asked for a commensurate sum of money damages from Governor Sulzer, whom she designated in her affidavit as "a man of wealth and great influence in his state." One of the fellow boarders in the boarding house where Miss Mignon Hopkins resided told a reporter: "As far as I could see, Miss Hopkins did not carry a broken heart around this house. She seemed in a particularly happy mood last fall on the morning after the election. She chatted about the result in New York and seemed to have followed that contest closely. Then she burst out with the exclamation: 'Just think! My dearest friend has been elected Governor of New York.'"[1]

The impeachment charges against Governor Sulzer were: that he had not returned a complete account of his campaign fund contributions when he was a candidate for Governor, omitting some checks which he had received; that he had used those checks and others to gamble on the New York Stock Exchange, instead of for his legitimate campaign expenses; that he had urged witnesses not to tell the truth before the Frawley Committee of the State Senate which was appointed to investigate his campaign contributions; that he had promised to sign a bill appropriating $800,000 for roads in Essex County, in which Assemblyman S. G. Prime, Jr., was interested, if Assemblyman Prime would vote for certain legislation in

[1]New York *Times*, July 2, 1913.

which Sulzer was interested; that he had threatened Thaddeus C. Sweet, member of the Assembly from Oswego, that if Sweet did not vote for legislation Sulzer wished passed, the Governor would veto a bill appropriating money for the construction of a bridge in Oswego County; and that he had tried to affect the trend of the stocks he was speculating in by having legislation passed concerning the New York Stock Exchange.

When Sulzer became the candidate of the Democratic Party for Governor of the State of New York, he called upon several millionaires whom he knew and asked that they contribute to his campaign fund. While he was a Congressman, William Sulzer had spoken vigorously in favour of the repeal of the treaty between the United States and Russia because of the treatment of the Jews in Russia. This won him the admiration of several bankers in New York whose racial heritage caused them to sympathize with their Hebrew brethren. Among these were Jacob H. Schiff, Henry Morgenthau, Abram I. Elkus, and Herbert H. Lehman. When Sulzer was being considered as a candidate for Governor, Herbert H. Lehman, of the banking firm of Lehman Brothers, who was not at that time personally acquainted with Mr. Sulzer, wrote to the prospective candidate:

June 24, 1912.

Hon. WILLIAM SULZER,
No. 115 Broadway,
City.

MY DEAR MR. SULZER:

May I take the liberty of offering my aid in your possible effort to obtain the gubernatorial nomination this autumn? It seems both by your record and your personality that you are the logical Democratic candidate, and it would give me great pleasure to do what little I can to help you in securing the nomination.

It appears to me that while you, personally, are of course widely known throughout the State, the actual work which you have accomplished in Congress during the past many years is not as yet thoroughly appreciated. While I have followed your career closely, I frankly confess that I did not realize until very recently the large number of important movements with which you have been connected and which you have brought to successful issues. Would it not be possible and wise, before the next State convention, to bring before the voters your full record of accomplishments?

I fear that I have neither the time nor the experience to do very much practical work, but I should be very glad, if you would permit it, to help defray the expenses of such a campaign of publicity.

Very sincerely yours,
HERBERT H. LEHMAN.[1]

Mr. Sulzer consented, and Mr. Lehman had printed and distributed at his expense more than 50,000 copies of a collection of the speeches of William Sulzer. Mr. Lehman also gave Mr. Sulzer $5,000 in bills of $500 and $1,000 denominations, and Mr. Lehman testified that he contributed in all more than $12,000 toward Sulzer's success. John B. Stanchfield asked Mr. Lehman at the impeachment trial: "Now when you gave him then the $5,000 in bills, did you not mean by it to aid him in effecting a publicity of his campaign for Governor?" "Not by any means," Mr. Lehman answered. "What did you mean by it?" he was asked. "I gave him $5,000 unconditionally," Mr. Lehman said, "I knew that he was a man of straitened circumstances; I did not care what he did with his money, whether he paid his rent, or bought himself clothes, or paid for his office or any other expenses which he might incur."[2]

Jacob H. Schiff, of the firm of Kuhn, Loeb & Company, testified at the impeachment trial:

"Governor Sulzer came to my office and he discussed the general political situation. He said he was gratified that he was going to have my support. I asked him whether there was anything special I could do for him, and he said, 'Are you going to contribute to my campaign fund?' I said, 'Yes, I shall be willing to do so,' and he said, 'How much will you contribute?' I said, '$2,500.' He replied 'Can you make it any more?' I then

---

[1] *Proceedings of the Court for Trial of Impeachments The People of the State of New York By the Assembly Thereof Against William Sulzer, as Governor*, Vol. II, pp. 1116–1117. Hereafter this document will be referred to as Sulzer Impeachment Proceedings.

[2] Sulzer Impeachment Proceedings, Vol. II, p. 1127.

said to him 'No, that is about as much as I care to give you.'
Then he said, 'All right, please make your check to the order of
Louis A. Sarecky'—I believe is the name. That was the conver-
sation I had with him."[1]

Sulzer also asked Allan A. Ryan, the son of Thomas Fortune
Ryan, to contribute to his campaign fund. Sulzer had known
Thomas Fortune Ryan for many years, while Mr. Ryan was
running street railways and while Mr. Sulzer was employed in
Congress. The elder Ryan was in Europe at the time of Sulzer's
candidacy. Ignatius V. McGlone, private secretary to Thomas
Fortune Ryan, testified at the Sulzer trial:

"Tell us the conversation that you had with him at that
time?" asked John B. Stanchfield.

"I went to see him at 115 Broadway; he spoke about his
campaign. I said some things to him. I said I did not think there
was any question about his election. That he was sure to be
elected, and he said no, he wanted to make a personal campaign.
I said that inasmuch as he was nominated by the organization,
the organization ought to give him the money, and he said no,
that he needed certain money. . . . He said to me that he needed
some money. I told him I could not give it to him without
consulting with somebody else. He said he was going out on a
campaign tour. I said I would see him when he came back but in
the meantime I would have to talk with somebody else before
I gave him anything. I spoke to somebody else about it, and we
agreed to give him a certain sum of money, which I gave him.
That is all I know about it. . . ."

"Had there been anything said between you at that interview with regard to the amount that he wanted from you or
from Mr. Ryan, for his campaign?"

"Yes, sir. . . . That he wanted $7,500, or as much more as he
could get."

"After you left Governor Sulzer, did you see Allan Ryan?"

"I saw him the same afternoon, as I recall. . . ."

"When did you see Governor Sulzer again?"

"The next day. . . . At his office, 115 Broadway."

---

[1]Sulzer Impeachment Proceedings, Vol. I, pp. 485–486.

"Was there anyone present at the time of your interview with him?"

"Nobody. . . ."

"What was your talk with him upon this second occasion?"

"Simply went in to see him, and I handed him some money."

"How much?"

"$10,000."

"In what denomination?"

"$1,000 bills."

"Tell us the conversation."

"There was no conversation to speak of. I simply went in to see him. It was about two o'clock in the afternoon I think. I handed him the money. He counted it and put it in his pocket and thanked me, and said if he was elected Governor, and for any reason I should ever happen to be in Albany, he would be glad to see me, and asked me to remember him to Mr. Allan Ryan. That was the end of the conversation, and I went out."

"Did you have any further talk with him later?"

"I sent him a telegram of congratulations election night."[1]

Mr. Allan A. Ryan testified:

"Now, with reference to his becoming a candidate of the Democratic party for Governor on the morning of the 3rd of October, 1912, when did you next see him?"

"About December 12th. . . ."

"Did you see him before election at all?"

"Not to speak with."

"Did you have any personal communication with him at all before election?"

"Only by telephone. . . . About the middle of October. . . ."

"You may answer; give the substance now of that conversation."

"I can now recollect one or two sentences, exact sentences of the conversation."

"Give those."

"He said in these words, 'Tell your father I am the same old Bill.'"[2]

---

[1]Sulzer Impeachment Proceedings, Vol. II, pp. 1043–1050.

[2]Ibid., pp. 1031–1041.

Senator Edgar T. Brackett, of the counsel for the impeachment managers, in summing up the case against Sulzer said:

"Can you imagine Paul telephoning to Gamaliel that he was 'the same old Saul [*sic*],' and 'can't you make it more than $7,500?' 'Tell your father I'm the same old Bill.' Ah! What a flood of light streams from that single bit of evidence, that stands here undenied—true. 'The same old Bill' who, through the years, had been rendering Ryan valuable services, while loudly professing to be the enemy of all trust magnates. 'The same old Bill,' who wanted to continue the relation at 'the same old rate'—$7,500, and 'as much more as I can get' per —yes, 'the same old Bill' in every way."[1]

Sulzer had once said on the floor of the House of Representatives:

"These gigantic combinations called trusts constitute, in my judgment, the greatest and gravest menace at the present time to our democratic institutions. . . . They levy tribute, like robber barons of old, on every man, woman, and child in the Republic. They blight the poor man's home, darken the hearthside of his children, cloud the star of youth's legitimate hope and destroy equal opportunity. They control State and national legislation, escape taxation, and evade the just burdens of the Government. . . . Their tyrannical power, rapid growth, and centralization of wealth is the marvel of recent times and the saddest commentary the future historian will make on our legislative history. They practically own, run, and control the Government and defy prosecution for violation of law. If their power of concentration and centralization is not speedily checked, and they go on for another quarter of a century like they have in the past few years, I believe our free institutions will be destroyed, and instead of a government of the people, by the people, and for the people, we will have a government of the trusts, by the trusts, and for the trusts."

But that was in 1900, and by 1913, although such a government had by no means perished from the earth, Mr. Sulzer had met

---

[1]Sulzer Impeachment Proceedings, Vol. II, p. 1510.

and become intimate with Thomas Fortune Ryan and had discovered that he wasn't such a bad fellow even if he did control a few trusts. And Mr. Ryan found that Mr. Sulzer, though he spoke awfully and thunderously in public in his best Lincolnian manner, was not bigoted in the parlour. Perhaps the $10,000 in bills was intended for the purpose of providing that government of the people, by the people, and for the people might not become too energetic. Senator Edgar T. Brackett remarked of William Sulzer: "For a real friend of the common people, hating everything that looks like a trust, I must say that he absorbed a reasonable amount of trust money for one campaign, when he got $10,000 from Thomas F. Ryan, a gentleman popularly supposed to have some connection with a trust or two, and $2,500 from Jacob H. Schiff, who is surely not entirely removed from the trust influences himself."

In 1903, William Sulzer told the House of Representatives:

"Last spring, Mr. Chairman, I visited Cuba, and was greatly impressed with all I saw during my sojourn there. . . . Cuba is the land of perpetual flowers, of stately royal palms, the Bohemia of the dreamer, generous in tropical fruits, the home of the painter and the poet, the paradise of all the islands of the sea—one long, harmonious, brilliant, indescribable mental melody.

"The climate so dreamy, and so salubrious; the indescribable beauty of the magnificent scenery—odoriferous forever and a day with enchanting and entrancing perfumes; her vast undeveloped resources; the richness of the soil; her quaint towns and cities and villages resplendent in subdued colors of pale pink and lemon yellow and baby blue—remindful of the Orient."[1]

Hugh J. Reilly, a contractor of New York and Havana, testified at the trial of Governor Sulzer:

"Do you know Governor Sulzer?"
"Yes."
"Did you loan him any money in 1912?"

[1]Sulzer Scrap Books, Vol. III, p. 18. New York Public Library Collections.

"Yes, sir. . . ."

"In what amounts? What was the total amount of the moneys so loaned by you to Governor Sulzer?"

"$26,500."

"Has any part of that money so loaned by you to Governor Sulzer been repaid?"

"No, sir. . . ."

Cross-examination by Mr. Stanchfield:

"Mr. Reilly, are you the same Mr. Hugh J. Reilly who was interested in the years 1906, 1907, 1908, 1909, 1910, 1911, or 1912, in what is known as the Cienfuegos contract in the island of Cuba?"

"Yes, sir."

"That contract, generally speaking, was for the construction of a system of water works on the island of Cuba at the city of Cienfuegos, was it not?"

"Yes, sir. . . ."

"Now, that contract at one time was revoked or rescinded by the Cuban authorities, was it not?"

"Yes, sir."

"And you sought its reinstatement? . . . You sought to have it reinstated?"

"Yes, sir. . . ."

"Did you go to Washington and enlist the services of Congressman Sulzer to aid you in the reinstatement of that contract?"

Objected to on the grounds that it was irrelevant and immaterial.

"The President—Sustained. . . ."

"And at that time, did Governor Sulzer, then Congressman Sulzer, write letters for you to the President of the United States in regard to the restoration of that contract?"

"Mr. Hinman—I make the same objection on the same ground."

"The President—Same ruling."

"Was there, in the summer of 1912, an instalment paid to you or the corporation in which you were interested, for the balance due upon the work of constructing those water works at the city of Cienfuegos, the sum of upwards of half a million of dollars?"

"Mr. Hinman—I make the same objection on the same grounds."

"The President—Same ruling."

"You made those loans, did you not, in bills, in currency?"

"Cash."

"Well, I say in currency?"

"Yes, sir. . . ."

"In other words, you would send to your bank and get bills and let him have them?"

"Yes, sir."

"Was anyone present at the time except you and the Governor?"

"No, sir."

"Mr. Stanchfield—That is all, sir."[1]

The New York *Times* printed the following article in its issue of August 23, 1913:

"William Sulzer, when a Congressman, was the confidential friend, adviser, and associate of a Cuban contracting firm which is charged before the Supreme Court in this State with having defrauded one of its partners. It is also charged by a responsible firm of lawyers in this city with having by fraudulent representations induced the State Department to force the Cuban Government into recognizing a claim which it did not wish to recognize.

"At the time these things were done Mr. Sulzer was a member of the committees of the House having to do with Cuban affairs, those on Foreign Relations and Military Affairs, and when the principal offense was committed he was Chairman of that committee having to do with it directly—the Committee on Foreign Affairs.

"Yesterday Justice Weeks of the Supreme Court made permanent a temporary injunction obtained from Justice Gavegan in the litigation described in the NEW YORK TIMES of July 27 between the assignee of Senator Jose Antonio Frias of Cuba and Hugh J. Reilly, a contractor of New York and Havana. At that time an affidavit by a Roman Catholic Bishop,

---

[1]Sulzer Impeachment Proceedings, Vol. II, pp. 1292-1296.

Bonaventure F. Broderick, was printed in THE TIMES in which he said there were insinuations that 'a considerable sum of money collected from the Cuban government through the assistance of the United States Government was used to reward the services of a lawyer prominently connected with the Government of Cuba, and another considerable sum was paid to a well-known American legislator for his services for securing the efficient intervention of the United States Department of State in collecting this claim from Cuba."

Louis M. Josephthal, senior member of the firm of Josephthal, Lochheim & Company, bankers, and naval aide on the military staff of Governor Sulzer, testified at the Sulzer trial. He said that he took up Governor Sulzer's stocks when Sulzer could not afford to pay for them, and that he paid $26,000 for the stocks. When Commander Josephthal, Governor Sulzer, and Mrs. Sulzer went to Gettysburg to attend a celebration, this incident took place: "Mrs. Sulzer informed me that she owned certain stocks on which her husband had borrowed money, and I interrupted her and stated that I would rather discuss this matter with her husband. Thereupon that same evening William Sulzer requested me to take up the account." Commander Josephthal was cross-examined as follows by John B. Stanchfield:

"Commander, are you a member of the Stock Exchange?"
"Yes, sir."
"Do you recall during the winter of 1913, that various bills were introduced in the Legislature affecting, from the Exchange standpoint, injuriously the Stock Exchange?"
"Yes, sir."
"There were bills of various kinds there; one to incorporate the Stock Exchange, another to double the taxation upon transfers of stock, and quite a number of bills affecting the Stock Exchange?"
"Yes, sir."
"Did the Stock Exchange take any action with reference to the appointment of a committee to oppose the passage of the legislation embraced in those bills?"
"Yes, sir. . . ."

"Were you a member of that committee?"

"I was not. . . ."

"Were you with them when they met?"

"I happened to be up here at one time on naval militia matters."

"Did you note or observe their appearance then?"

"I couldn't help seeing the men, while I was lunching at the Ten Eyck Hotel . . ."

"Were you at any time before the Governor with reference to any of these Stock Exchange measures?"

"No, sir."

"Either in a personal capacity or representing in any way the interests of the Stock Exchange?"

"The Governor——"

"No, no. Just answer my question, please?"

"I am going to answer it in a fair way. At one time the Governor asked my opinion about the $4 tax, and I gave it to him."

"Was your opinion in favor of a tax or against it? . . ."

"It was against the tax."

"Are you in any way related to, or connected with, the Guggenheims?"

"Yes, sir. . . ."

"Are the Guggenheims largely interested in the control of the Smelters stock that you took up? . . . Those 200 Smelters that you had, those 200 shares of the ordinary or common stock of the American Smelting & Refining Company, was it not?"

"Yes, sir."

"And that concern is a so-called Guggenheim concern, is it not?"

"Yes, sir."[1]

A mass of testimony was taken to prove Sulzer's dealings with financiers and on the Stock Exchange, but it all only tended to prove what everybody knew, but which Sulzer had forgotten, that those who live in glass houses should not throw stones. Louis Marshall, Sulzer's leading attorney, made an extraordinarily sound defense for the Governor on the grounds

[1] Sulzer Impeachment Proceedings, Vol. II, pp. 1142–1144.

that whatever Sulzer had done was done before he was elected Governor, and that therefore he was not liable to impeachment for acts committed when he was not Governor of the State of New York. This was a solid technical argument, but it was also argued that campaign fund matters are related to the office of Governor, and offenses committed in this respect can only be committed before a man is elected to the office he later holds.

"Though the Psalmist," said Mr. Marshall, summing up for Governor Sulzer, "when he said in his haste, that all men were liars, was somewhat inaccurate, or else mankind has greatly improved since the utterance of this striking passage, yet even in our day, if the telling of a lie, whether of the black or white variety, were once recognized as ground for impeachment, there would be many vacancies in office to be filled."

In the last analysis all that the impeachers had against William Sulzer was that he had omitted some sums from his campaign statements, and that he had used those sums for his personal expenses. The men who gave them to him supported him by testifying that he was entitled to use them for whatever purpose he wished. But Murphy, on the other end of the telephone between Albany and New York, was credited with the statement that he wanted that —— —— ——, etc., out of there, and Murphy's political allies and personal friends took advantage for that purpose of an act which many of them had probably committed before and which many of them would no doubt commit again.

Sulzer realized how he had been trapped, and there was evidence that he was willing at the last moment to come to terms with Murphy. Allan A. Ryan testified at the trial that Sulzer tried to persuade him to go to Washington to see Senator Elihu Root, who was one of Thomas Fortune Ryan's lawyers, and to urge Root to persuade William Barnes, Jr., the Republican Boss of New York State, to order the Republican members of the State Legislature to vote against the impeachment of Sulzer. Mr. Ryan also testified that Governor Sulzer urged him to see De Lancey Nicoll, who was another of Thomas Fortune Ryan's lawyers, and who was also a close friend and political adviser of Charles F. Murphy, and to ask Mr. Nicoll if he

MINOR
IN
NEW YORK WORLD

© 1913 BY
PRESS PUBLISHING CO.

"Tammany's ENEMIES have to be honest"

would speak to Murphy about dropping the impeachment proceedings. Allan A. Ryan's testimony read:

"He wanted me to have Mr. Nicoll persuade Mr. Murphy
to endeavor to call off his inquiry by getting his following to vote
that the Court had no right, the Assembly had no right, to vote
his impeachment."

"There was more than that said, was there not?"

"No response."

"There was more than that said in the conversation, was
there not?"

"The President—If you recall anything, say so; and, if you
cannot recall any, say so."

"He said Mr. Nicoll could be the go-between."

"Yes. Won't you go right along and finish that conversation?"

"That he was willing to do whatever was right."

"That is, that who was willing to do whatever was right?"

"Mr. Sulzer. . . ."

"Did he specify in any particular what he would do as being
right, as you recall it?"

"No, sir. . . ."

"Did you, as a matter of fact, Mr. Ryan, see Mr. De Lancey
Nicoll?"

"No, sir. . . ."

"As a matter of fact, did you see Mr. Root?"

"No, sir. . . ."

"Now, it is a fact, is it not, common knowledge, that Senator
Root has been a long time your father's counsel?"

"Yes, sir."

"And Mr. De Lancey Nicoll had also been one of your
father's counsel, had he not?"

"Yes, sir."

"Now, in this last conversation to which I have been calling
your attention, in which you were requested to see Mr. Nicoll,
what reply, if any, did you make to Governor Sulzer?"

"I told him I would see what I could do, and I went out in
the country and forgot it."[1]

---

[1]Sulzer Impeachment Proceedings, Vol. II, pp. 1105–1107.

ROBINSON IN NEW YORK TRIBUNE

"For Not Playing the Game"

Sulzer had capitulated too late; he had showed Murphy his hand, and Murphy promptly destroyed the Governor. Judge Alton B. Parker, summing up the case against Sulzer, said: "Every disguise has been torn from his back, from the petticoat in which he trusted for safety to the armor of defiance in which he threatened to attack and expose a political leadership to which we have found him suing later for a merciful obliteration of his misdeeds, and offering the bribe of submission." On the other hand, D– Cady Herrick, of Sulzer's counsel, made the following significant statement before the Court: "The bringing of these impeachment proceedings are lamentable because of the object lesson of what may occur to any man in public life who dares stand and oppose the wishes of those who may know something about his private life and history not known to the general public."

On October 17, 1913, by a vote of 43 to 12 the Court of Impeachment voted to remove William Sulzer from the office of Governor of the State of New York. It was the first time in the history of the State that a Governor had been impeached, and its most important lesson was the power of a Tammany Boss's wrath. Governor Sulzer was impeached because Charles F. Murphy wished to avoid exposure of Tammany graft in the State government. Murphy also wished to make money for himself and his friends out of the State contracts. Sulzer's ambitions were for fame. Although, as we have seen, he used money when he needed it and could get it, if his interests had been entirely mercenary he could have made more money by playing Murphy's game than by fighting that game. Sulzer, however, never forgot for a moment that he resembled Henry Clay, and that he must behave a little like Lincoln. Murphy never forgot for a moment that he was Charles F. Murphy.

In a letter which he wrote to Theodore Roosevelt when the latter was being considered for the office of Governor of New York, Lemuel E. Quigg, Thomas C. Platt's lieutenant, wrote:

"You are a rare good fellow and you have got the American spirit, which, with the multitude, I greatly admire. You are dead honest, and I like that too; but in the great office to which you are being so certainly called, you have got to remember that nobody is ever surely right and nobody ever absolutely wrong. You have got to remember that compromise and adjustment are unfailingly necessary to all human progress."

After the impeachment of Sulzer a public demonstration was organized by some citizens of Albany to indicate their esteem for the deposed Governor. He was presented with a loving cup, which was engraved with the following inscription: "Presented to Hon. William Sulzer by citizens of Albany in Loving Remembrance of Duties Well Performed. A Martyr to the Cause of Honest Government, October 18th, 1913." It was raining when the crowd gathered outside the Executive Mansion and demanded a speech. The tall, lank form of William Sulzer appeared on the porch facing the grounds of the Mansion.

"They say they impeached me for taking my own money," he said. "I impeach the criminal conspirators, these looters and grafters, for stealing the taxpayers' money. That is what I never did. It is a long lane that has no turn. My day will come again. From Murphy's High Court of Infamy, I appeal to that higher court—the court of public opinion.

"'Let those who have failed take courage;
Tho' the enemy seems to have won,
Tho' his ranks are strong, if he be in the wrong,
The battle is not yet done;
For, sure as the morning follows
The darkest hour of night,
No question is ever settled
Until it is settled right.' (Cheers.)

"Yes, my friends, I know that the court of public opinion before long will reverse the judgment of Murphy's Court of Infamy. (Cheers.) Posterity will do me justice. Time sets all things right. I shall be patient.

"'Out of the night, that shelters me
Black as a pit, from pole to pole,
I thank whatever Fates there be
For my unconquerable soul.

"'In the fell clutch of circumstance
  I have not winced or cried aloud;
Beneath the bludgeonings of chance
  My head is bloody but not bowed.

"'However straight may be the gate,
  How charged with punishment the scroll,
I am the master of my fate,
  I am the captain of my soul.' (Loud cheering.)"

The lane, however, did not turn. Sulzer's day did not come again. And public opinion soon forgot him. He was a candidate for reëlection to the office of Governor, but he was defeated. He closed a campaign speech with the following adaptation of one of the stanzas in Kipling's "Recessional:"

"The tumult of the campaign dies,
  The Bosses and their tools depart;
Yet stands Thine ancient sacrifice,
  An humble and a contrite heart.
Lord God of Hosts, be with us yet;
Lest we forget, lest we forget!"

VI

The impeachment of Sulzer did not help Tammany Hall or Murphy in the next election. The publicity caused by the case indicated the dangerous power of Murphy more vividly than it did the misdeeds of Sulzer. Colonel Henry Watterson wrote an editorial in his newspaper, the Louisville *Courier-Journal*, in which he remarked that observant and thoughtful onlookers had long been of the belief that "the people of New York are incapable of self-government." "Even the scrub politicians," wrote Colonel Watterson, "who sometimes work into places of emolument and honor here are a trifle cleaner and less ravenous than the wolves who there prowl at all hours of the day and night between the purlieus of the great white way and the legislative red lights in the Capitol at Albany."

From Glencairn, Ireland, came a murmur of jealous discontent and a reflection of moral judgment. "The Hall will never win under Murphy's management," wrote Richard

Croker. "I hope some good man will get in and drive all them grafters-contractors out."

Murphy remained silent. He refused to take the public into his confidence, and he increased the popular sentiment against him by refusing a renomination for Mayor to Gaynor and nominating instead Edward E. McCall, who, Sulzer had said, was the emissary between Murphy and himself. Gaynor ran as an independent candidate and John Purroy Mitchel was nominated by the fusion party consisting of Republicans and anti-Tammany Democrats. The opposition to Tammany Hall was divided, as usual, and it looked hopeful for Murphy in spite of all that the newspapers had shouted about him. But Gaynor died, and his anti-Tammany support went to Mitchel, who needed only that additional support to win the election.

Tammany Hall was now in reduced circumstances, for it had lost its patronage in New York City and in New York County, and President Wilson, who owed nothing to Tammany, refused to give the organization anything. In 1914 Martin H. Glynn, who, as Lieutenant Governor, inherited Sulzer's office, was defeated for reëlection by Charles S. Whitman, the Republican candidate, who, as District Attorney of New York, had prosecuted Police Lieutenant Becker for the murder of "Big Tim" Sullivan's friend Rosenthal.

Although Tammany Hall was now deprived of offices, Tammany men were not poor, for the period of Murphy's reign was an era of unprecedented prosperity from hitherto unforeseen sources. Tammany Hall had changed considerably since the days of Croker. The rise of the large corporation had already influenced the sources of Tammany Hall's profit in Croker's last years of ownership, but corporations had become more powerful, more numerous, and more prosperous during the first fifteen years of the twentieth century than ever before in the history of the United States. And in the twentieth century the leaders of Tammany Hall were in the contracting business or were interested in water, gas, electricity, or railroads rather than prostitution, liquor, gambling, or extortion; for it was Murphy's great and lasting contribution to the philosophy of Tammany Hall that he taught the organization that more money can be made by a legal contract than by petty blackmail.

Tammany Hall, accordingly, grew outwardly more respectable. Even the nickname for the Monday before election day, which had been known during the blatant Croker period as "Dough Day," was changed to "Paraphernalia Day" during the campaign of Dix for Governor. The Corrupt Practices Act had made the use of money at the polls more dangerous, and it was thought wiser as well as more in keeping with the advance in dignity of the organization to change the name of "Dough Day." Besides, stationery as well as money was given out, and also some posters and badges.

Lincoln Steffens once wrote:

"If Tammany could be incorporated, and all its earnings, both legitimate and illegitimate, gathered up and paid over in dividends, the stockholders would get more than the New York Central bond and stockholders, more than the Standard Oil stockholders, and the controlling clique would wield a power equal to that of the United States Steel Company. Tammany, when in control of New York, takes out of the city unbelievable millions of dollars a year."

Although the Hall, as it was sometimes called under Murphy's régime, was highly respectable in its pretensions, there were certain indicative reversions to type. It was not above, for instance, using repeaters at the polls when occasion urgently demanded it. Police Commissioner Bingham estimated in 1909 that there were then from 30,000 to 50,000 illegal votes cast by Tammany Hall. George H. Gonzales, alias "Nigger George," left New York in October, 1909, because the election bureau deputies were seeking him on a charge of procuring false registration of twenty-two men from a certain house in Pearl Street. As late as 1921, Joseph Shalleck, campaign manager for James J. Hines, a Tammany district leader who was then fighting Murphy for control of Murphy's own Tammany district, was blackjacked, beaten, and shot in the chest in a polling booth at Seventeenth Street, within two hundred feet of Charles F. Murphy's city residence. Shalleck had gone to the polling place to investigate rumours of fraud, and when he saw the poll list, he noticed improper erasures.

"I told the Chairman that someone would go to jail for this," Shalleck said in the hospital. "At that, someone behind me struck me on the jaw with a blackjack, knocking me to the floor, and half a dozen of those clustered in the polling place, including a policeman in uniform, set upon me. They struck and kicked me repeatedly as I lay on the floor, helpless. There were three women in the polling place who had been acting as officials. They ran out screaming, and the man who led the assault slammed the door after them. Once the women were out and the door was closed so that no one outside could hear what was going on, they set upon me harder than ever. They beat me unmercifully, though I was down and was outnumbered more than six to one."

The Hines men, who arrived at the polling place, rescued Shalleck and another anti-Murphy man, Lynch, and while they were doing so, someone fired a pistol. The bullet cut a long furrow across Shalleck's breast. After he got outside the polling place, Shalleck said, the policeman who had been participating in the fight knocked him down with his club, kicked him in the ribs, and said: "I'll teach any —— —— —— friend of Hines to come down in Charlie Murphy's district and tell 'em how to run things." Tammany policemen were always so intensely loyal.

James J. Hines and Charles F. Murphy had been the best of friends until they quarrelled over a big business deal. Hines was instrumental in persuading Murphy to enter into a business enterprise with Louis N. Hartog. Louis N. Hartog wished to sell malt dextrine to the British government during the war. For this purpose he needed a regular supply of large quantities of glucose. He went to his friend James J. Hines, then a Tammany Hall district leader and close friend of Charles F. Murphy. Mr. Hines spoke to Mr. Murphy about Mr. Hartog's glucose business, and he suggested that there was considerable money to be made in it. Murphy and his personal attorney, Arthur J. Baldwin, called on Hartog and inspected the plant. "Who do we know in the Corn Products Company?" Hartog quoted Murphy as asking Baldwin. It was necessary to get the required supply of glucose from the Corn Products Company. "Mr. Baldwin said that Morgan J. O'Brien was counsel to Mr.

Bedford, President of the company," Hartog testified. "'I know him pretty well,' Mr. Murphy said. Mr. Baldwin went to the telephone and arranged for an appointment with Mr. O'Brien for the next day."

Soon afterward, Murphy's personal attorney, Baldwin, called on Hartog again, and this conversation took place, according to Hartog: "What do you propose to pay Mr. Murphy for getting you glucose?" Mr. Hartog said that Mr. Baldwin asked him. "I suggested 15 per cent. and Mr. Baldwin said he ought to get 20 per cent. I said, 'All right.'" It was later decided that it would be profitable for everybody concerned if Mr. Murphy became Mr. Hartog's partner in the business.

Murphy and Baldwin called on the official of the Corn Products Company. "Hartog said that Baldwin told him that the Corn Products people wanted Murphy to do certain favours for them in consideration of a better supply of glucose." "He told me," Hartog testified, "that the Corn Products people were interested in the Staten Island garbage plant and wanted Mr. Murphy to do something with the Mayor to make him go back on a campaign pledge. They also wanted him to look after some Health Department violations. Baldwin said he had seen Murphy and that Murphy had agreed to do what they wanted." Then Baldwin insisted, according to Hartog, that Murphy's profits should be increased by one cent a pound, and this was the reason Hartog said that Baldwin gave for the increase: "There are so many things that they wanted Murphy to do for them that it is necessary to accumulate a fund." When Hartog protested that such an arrangement would take away too much of his own profits, and when he asked why it was essential "to establish a fund in that way," Mr. Baldwin, he said, answered: "You want too much detail. We're used to doing business with people with a nod of the head. If you want glucose, that's the way you've got to do it." When the details of the formation of the corporation were being arranged, Hartog testified that Baldwin told him that he and Mr. Murphy had not yet decided the exact form the company should take. "Mr. Murphy," Baldwin told Hartog, "wanted to be in a position to say that he isn't connected with it if anything comes up."[1]

[1] Information of Murphy-Hartog relationship from New York *Times*, April 18, 1923.

CHARLES F. MURPHY
A photograph taken the year he died.

Murphy's profits from the glucose deal were said to be $5,000 a day. He was worried. Hines testified: "Mr. Murphy told me that the business was making too much money and that as leader of Tammany Hall he couldn't afford to stay in. I told him I had heard of men wanting to get out of businesses that were not making money, but that it was the first time that I had heard of anyone wanting to get out of a business making money. He said he would have to get out. I told him I had often heard it said he was making too much money, but that I could not tell them that he was getting out of a business that was making money." But another reason was also given for Murphy's wish to withdraw from a profitable business. He discovered that the excess profits tax would require him to pay to the government 80 per cent. of his profits.

Murphy had invested $125,000 in Hartog's business, and he wished to withdraw that money. Hartog refused to consent, and Murphy sued him. John A. ("Fishhooks") McCarthy, a contractor and a political associate of Murphy's, was accused of threatening Hartog that he would "hound him to death," if he refused to do what Murphy wished. Assistant District Attorney James E. Smith was also accused of threatening to prosecute Hartog for alleged sugar hoarding, for arson, and to tell his wife of alleged relations with another woman. Baldwin was accused of threatening that he would cut off Hartog's glucose supply, and Murphy himself was alleged to have threatened that he would have the Police Department and the Internal Revenue Collector investigate Hartog on criminal charges.

Murphy, Baldwin, McCarthy, Smith, and Ernest B. Waldon, Vice-president of the Corn Products Company, were indicted on these charges by the Extraordinary Grand Jury on June 20, 1920. Justice Robert F. Wagner, who, as the *Times* put it, "happened to be presiding in Part One at the time," dismissed the indictments on June 18, 1921, on the grounds that "the evidence before the Grand Jury was insufficient in law or fact to authorize or sustain the indictment."

When he was trying to persuade Hartog to do as Murphy wished, John A. ("Fishhooks") McCarthy was alleged to have said: "You will have to settle or go out of business. No man can live in New York and be on the outs with Murphy." "I guess you are confusing this with Russia, and I am going to live in New York," Hartog said he replied.

Hartog received no more glucose after his quarrel with Murphy, and he sued Murphy for $10,000,000, charging him with a conspiracy to prevent him from fulfilling his orders for malt dextrine with the British government, which wished it to make beer for its soldiers. It was claimed that Murphy's influence with the administration at Washington would enable him to overcome all difficulties of obtaining privileges during war time. Max D. Steuer, attorney for Hartog, asked Murphy on the witness stand: "The administration at Washington was Democratic in 1918, wasn't it?" "Was it?" Murphy asked with a look of surprise. "Perhaps it was," he added, after the titter in the courtroom had died down. "It wasn't to me though," he continued, "I didn't get much out of it." "But wasn't it Democratic?" asked Mr. Steuer. "Well," replied Murphy, "they called it that." Mr. Murphy was never an admirer of Woodrow Wilson's independent tactics.

Murphy as a witness was taciturn and self-controlled. He answered only questions of fact and gave non-committal replies concerning the extent of his influence. In summing up before the jury Mr. Steuer said: "Men crawl on their bellies in the dust for him. They have, and they will as long as he is in power. Yet the men who grovel at his feet now would be the first to step on him if he lost that power. Oh, it's all right to be modest in the court-room, but go up to Fourteenth Street and see the 'Czar' at his desk and you are dealing with a different individual." "Now the divine right of Fourteenth Street," said Mr. Steuer, "divides up the glucose of the country and says, 'You can have no more except through me—and the first 750 barrels you shall get free by the grace of me, Arthur J. Baldwin.' And this, gentlemen, was in the year 1918, when men were battling that liberty might retain a foothold in the world." "Do they really control everything and everybody?" asked Mr. Steuer. "Is there no soul in the citizenry of New York? Do the tentacles of Fourteenth Street reach so far that we are all crushed?"

Mr. Conboy, Murphy's attorney, told the jury that Murphy had decided to leave the glucose business because he thought that Hartog was a war profiteer. "When he made up his mind," said Mr. Conboy, "and set his jaw you might as well try to push over the rock of Gibraltar as to change his mind. Ask those who sat in the Syracuse convention when he made up his mind who was to be the Democratic nominee for Governor of New York." The case of Murphy and Hartog was finally settled privately out of court. But New York had enjoyed another opportunity to see something of the backstairs life of its rulers.

When John Purroy Mitchel was elected Mayor of New York, Murphy and William Randolph Hearst were enemies again, and the Hearst newspapers were attacking Murphy furiously. But in 1917 Murphy, who knew when it was the better part of discretion to swallow his pride, supported Hearst's candidate for Mayor, John F. Hylan. It was said that Murphy's friend, Alfred E. Smith, who was then Sheriff of New York, wished the nomination for Mayor, but Murphy decided that Hylan's support in Brooklyn together with the Hearst influence and the influence of the Hearst newspapers was too powerful to resist, and he urged Smith to become President of the Board of Aldermen instead, with a view to making him Governor of New York eventually.

Hylan was elected by a large majority in 1917, and in 1921 he was reëlected. By that time Murphy and Hearst had once more become political enemies. Hylan had managed to remain friendly with Hearst and with Murphy, for Hearst demanded practically no patronage from the Mayor, and therefore Tammany men were supplied with jobs.

In the following year, 1918, Murphy supported Alfred E. Smith for the office of Governor. Hearst was also a candidate for the nomination, but Smith received it and was elected Governor. Because of his delicate, but complete, control of New York State, Murphy was able to become an important influence once more in the national politics of the Democratic Party. His influence had disappeared during the ascendancy of Woodrow Wilson, who did not recognize Tammany Hall.

In 1920 Murphy was instrumental in forcing the nomination of James M. Cox for President of the United States, and in 1922, Murphy gained Smith a renomination as Governor of New York in spite of Mr. Hearst's aspirations. It was Murphy's intention to make Alfred E. Smith President of the United

States, and it was with this end in view that the convention of the Democratic Party was scheduled to be held in New York City in 1924. Murphy was exceedingly busy during the first months of 1924 making plans for the nomination of Governor Smith.

On the morning of April 25, 1924, Murphy had a serious attack of acute indigestion, from which he had suffered for some years. His doctor found him in the bathroom of his home suffering great pain. That same day Murphy died.

Sixty thousand people, the newspapers estimated, lined the streets while the body of Charles F. Murphy was carried to St. Patrick's Cathedral for a high requiem mass. Every pew in the Cathedral was crowded, and hundreds of people stood in the passageways. Governor Smith, Mayor Hylan, Bernard M. Baruch, J. Sergeant Cram, Ambassador Gerard, United States Senator Copeland, several judges, and some Tammany district leaders were among the honorary pallbearers.

The value of Charles F. Murphy's estate was estimated at more than two millions of dollars.

At one of the Tammany Hall Fourth of July celebrations, a newspaper man noticed that Charles F. Murphy was not joining in the singing.

"What's the matter with the Boss, can't he sing?" the reporter whispered to Thomas F. Smith, Secretary of Tammany Hall.

"Sure he can. Why, the Chief used to sing with a quartette in his younger days," answered Mr. Smith. "He can yodel some, take it from me."

"Why didn't he join in 'The Star-Spangled Banner,' then?" asked the reporter.

"Perhaps," said Mr. Smith, "he didn't want to commit himself."

THE END

BIBLIOGRAPHY

BIBLIOGRAPHY

(This is not a complete bibliography of Tammany Hall. It is merely a list of the books, pamphlets, magazine articles, and newspapers which were used as a basis for the material in this book. It is not a complete list of those works consulted, but merely a complete list of those from which material was used for quotations or suggestions.)

ADAMS, CHARLES F., JR., and HENRY ADAMS. *Chapters of Erie and Other Essays*. New York, 1886.

Address of the Grand Council of the Tammany Society, or Columbian Order, upon the Subject of Their Recent Decision Relative to the Political Use of Tammany Hall, February 4th, 1853. New York, 1853.

ALEXANDER, DEALVA STANDWOOD. *A Political History of the State of New York*, 4 volumes: Title of Volume IV, *Four Famous New Yorkers*. New York, 1906, 1923.

BARNARD, GEORGE G. *Charges Against Justice George G. Barnard, and Testimony Thereunder, before the Judiciary Committee of the Assembly*, Albany, New York, 1872.

BARNARD, GEORGE G. *Proceedings of the Court of Impeachment in the Matter of George G. Barnard, A Justice of the Supreme Court of the State of New York*, 3 volumes. Albany, New York, 1874.

Barnes vs. Roosevelt, Supreme Court Appellate Division, William Barnes against Theodore Roosevelt. Case on Appeal, 4 volumes.

BINGHAM, GENERAL THEODORE A. *The Girl That Disappears. The Real Facts About the White Slave Traffic*. Boston, 1911.

BINGHAM, GENERAL THEODORE A. *Policing Our Lawless Cities, Hampton's Magazine*, Vol. XXIII, No. 3, September, 1909, pp. 289–300.

BLAKE, E. VALE. *History of the Tammany Society from Its Organization to the Present Time, 1901*. New York, 1901.

BREEN, MATTHEW P. *Thirty Years of New York Politics Up-to-Date*. New York, 1899.

BRUMMER, SIDNEY DAVID, Ph. D. *Political History of New York State During the Period of the Civil War*. Columbia University Studies in History, Economics and Public Law, Vol. XXXIX, No. 2. New York, 1911.

BRYCE, JAMES. *The American Commonwealth*, first edition, 3 volumes. London, 1888.

BYRDSALL, F. *The History of the Loco-Foco or Equal Rights Party, Its Movements, Conventions and Proceedings, With Short Characteristic Sketches of Its Prominent Men*. New York, 1842.

CABEEN, FRANCIS VON A. *The Society of the Sons of Saint Tammany of Philadelphia, Pennsylvania Magazine of History and Biography*, Vols. XXV and XXVI, 1901, 1902.

Civic Bibliography for Greater New York, Edited by James Bronson Reynolds for the New York Research Council. New York Charities Publication Committee. Russell Sage Foundation, 1911.

CLARK, CHARLES, C. P., M. D. *The "Machine" Abolished and the People Restored to Power by the Organization of All the People on the Lines of Party Organization.* New York.

CLINTON, HENRY L. *Speech of Henry L. Clinton, Esq., to the Jury, on the Trial of A. Oakey Hall, Mayor of the City of New York, in the Court of General Sessions for the County of New York. Delivered March 1, 1872.*

COLBY, BAINBRIDGE. *Tammany—Past and Present, Speech of Bainbridge Colby Delivered at Anti-Tammany Fusion Mass-Meeting at Cooper Union, New York City, October 20, 1913.* Issued by Citizens' Municipal Committee New York.

COLER, BIRD S. *Commercialism in Politics, The Independent,* Vol. LIII, pp. 2561–2564, 1901.

CRAPSEY, E. *The Nether Side of New York; or, the Vice, Crime and Poverty of the Great Metropolis.* New York, 1872.

CROKER, RICHARD. *Some Things Richard Croker Has Said and Done.* Published by the City Club of New York, July, 1901.

CURTIS, GEORGE WILLIAM. *Orations and Addresses,* 2 volumes. New York, 1894.

DAVENPORT, JOHN I. *The Election and Naturalization Frauds in New York City, 1860–1870.* New York, 1894.

DAVIS, ELMER. *History of the New York "Times."* New York, 1921.

DEMOCRAT (Pseudonym). *(From the New York "Times," January 3, 1896.) Is Reconstruction of the Democratic Party of the City of New York Practicable?* A Pamphlet.

Documents of the Board of Aldermen, New York City, Vol. XXI, Part II, No. 55; Vol. XXVIII, Document No. 1, *Annual Message of His Honor the Mayor, Fernando Wood, January 7, 1861.*

DOUGLAS, GEORGE WILLIAM. *The Many-Sided Roosevelt, An Anecdotal Biography,* New York, 1907.

DUER, WILLIAM A. *Reminiscences of an Old Yorker.* New York, 1867.

EDWARDS, E. J. *Tammany, McClure's Magazine,* Vol. IV, 1894–1895.

EDWARDS, E. J. *Chapters in the History of Tammany, McClure's Magazine,* Vol. V.

Election Frauds. *House of Representatives, 40th Congress, 3d Session. Report No. 41. New York Election Frauds. The Reports of Committees of the House of Representatives. 1869, Vol. II, 40th Congress, 3d Session.*

Fassett Investigation. *Testimony Taken before the Senate Committee on Cities, Pursuant to Resolution Adopted January 20, 1890,* 5 volumes.

FLAGG, JARED. *Flagg's Flats,* New York, 1909.

FORD, JAMES L. *Forty-Odd Years in the Literary Shop.* New York, 1921.

FRANCIS, JOHN W., M. D. *Reminiscences of Samuel Latham Mitchill, M. D., LL. D.,* New York, 1859.

GARDNER, CHARLES W. *The Doctor and the Devil, or Midnight Adventures of Dr. Parkhurst,* New York, 1894.

GAYNOR, WILLIAM J. *Some of Mayor Gaynor's Letters and Speeches.* New York, 1913.

GENUNG, ABRAM POLHEMUS. *The Frauds of the New York City Government Exposed. Sketches of the Members of the Ring and Their Confederates.* New York, 1871.

GODKIN, EDWIN LAWRENCE, *Problems of Modern Democracy, Political and Economic Essays.* New York, 1897.

GOSNELL, HAROLD F. *Boss Platt and His New York Machine, A Study of the Political Leadership of Thomas C. Platt, Theodore Roosevelt and Others.* Chicago, 1924.

GOVER, WILLIAM C. *The Tammany Hall Democracy of the City of New York, and the General Committee for 1875.* New York, 1875.

HALL, A. OAKEY. Scrapbooks of newspaper clippings relating to A. Oakey Hall. Fourteen volumes, New York Public Library Collections.

HAMILTON, ALEXANDER. *The Works of Alexander Hamilton,* Vol. VI. New York, 1851.

Harper's Weekly, Vol. XXI, p. 284, 1877, *William M. Tweed, Romance of His Flight and Exile.*

HEADLEY, J. T. *The Great Riots of New York, 1712 to 1873.* New York, 1873.

HEATON, JOHN L. *The Story of a Page, Thirty Years of Public Service and Public Discussion in the Editorial Columns of the New York "World."* New York, 1913.

HENNESSEY, JOHN A. *What's the Matter with New York? A Story of the Waste of Millions.* New York, 1916.

HIBERNICUS. *"What Brings So Many Irish To America!"* A Pamphlet, New York, 1845.

HICKEY, JOHN J. *Our Police Guardians, History of the Police Department of the City of New York Compiled and Written by Officer "787" John J. Hickey, Retired.* New York, 1925.

HODDER, ALFRED. *A Fight for the City.* New York, 1903.

HOME, RUFUS. *The Story of Tammany, Harper's Magazine, 1872.*

HORTON, R. G. *A Brief Memorial of the Origin and Earlier History of the Tammany Society, or Columbian Order.* New York, 1867.

HUDSON, WILLIAM C. *Random Recollections of an Old Political Reporter.* New York, 1911.

IVINS, WILLIAM M. *Machine Politics and Money in Elections in New York City,* New York, 1887.

KERNAN, J. FRANK ("Florry"). *Reminiscences of the Old Fire Laddies and Volunteer Fire Departments of New York and Brooklyn.* New York, 1885.

KILROE, EDWIN P. *Saint Tammany and the Origin of the Society of Tammany or Columbian Order in the City of New York.* New York, 1913.

KNEELAND, GEORGE J. *Commercialized Prostitution in New York City. Publication of the Bureau of Social Hygiene.* New York, 1913.

Know Nothing: A Poem, for Natives and Aliens. By the author of "Nebraska." Boston, 1854.

LEWIS, ALFRED HENRY. *The Apaches of New York.* Chicago and New York, 1912.

LEWIS, ALFRED HENRY. *The Boss and How He Came to Rule New York*. New York, 1903.
LEWIS, ALFRED HENRY. *Confessions of a Detective*. New York, 1906.
LEWIS, ALFRED HENRY. *Richard Croker*. New York, 1901.
Lexow Investigation. *Report and Proceedings of the Senate Committee Appointed to Investigate the Police Department of the City of New York.* 5 volumes. Albany, New York, 1895.
LINN, WILLIAM, D. D. *The Blessings of America. A Sermon, Preached in the Middle Dutch Church, on the Fourth of July, 1791, Being theAnniversary of the Independence of America: At the Request of the Tammany Society, or Columbian Order.* New York, 1791.
McLAUGHLIN, J. FAIRFAX. *The Life and Times of John Kelly, Tribune of the People.* New York, 1885.
MACLEOD, DONALD. *Biography of Hon. Fernando Wood, Mayor of the City of New York.* New York, 1856.
McMASTER, JOHN BACH. *With the Fathers, Studies in the History of the United States,* New York, 1896.
MATTHEWS, FRANKLIN. *"Wide-Open" New York, Harper's Weekly,* Vol. XLII, pp. 1045-1046. October 22, 1898.
Mazet Investigation. *Investigation of Offices and Departments of the City of New York by a Special Committee of the Assembly, Hon. Robert Mazet Chairman. Report of Counsel, December 22, 1899.*
Mazet Investigation. *Report of the Special Committee of the Assembly Appointed to Investigate the Public Offices and Departments of the City of New York and of the Counties Therein Included.* 5 volumes. Albany, 1900.
MERRIAM, CHARLES EDWARD. *The American Party System.* New York, 1922.
MERRIAM, CHARLES EDWARD. *American Political Ideas, Studies in the Development of American Political Thought, 1865-1917.* New York, 1920.
Morrissey, John. *John Morrissey, His Life, Battles and Wrangles, from His Birth in Ireland Until He Died a State Senator.* New York, 1881.
Moss, FRANK. *The American Metropolis from Knickerbocker Days to the Present Time, New York City Life in All Its Various Phases.* 3 volumes. New York, 1897.
MUNRO, WILLIAM BENNETT. *Personality in Politics, Reformers, Bosses and Leaders, What They Do and How They Do It,* New York, 1924.
MYERS, GUSTAVUS. *History of Public Franchises in New York City.*
MYERS, GUSTAVUS. *History of Tammany Hall,* New York, 1901, revised edition, 1917.
Mysteries, The, and Miseries of the Great Metropolis with Some Adventures in the Country: Being the Disguises and Surprises of a New-York Journalist. New York, 1874.
"New Tammany," The. Interesting Biographical Sketches of Its Leaders. Reprinted from the New York "Evening Post." 1890.
New York City Council of Political Reform. Five Reports, By Dexter A. Hawkins. New York, 1873.
New York City. Police Department. Stenographer's Minutes Special Committee of the Board of Aldermen of the City of New York Appointed to Investigate

the City's Police Department. Pursuant to Resolution Dated August 5th, 1912. 6 volumes. (Curran Investigation.)

NEVINS, ALLAN. *The "Evening Post." A Century of Journalism.* New York, 1922.

O'BRIEN, FRANK M. *The Story of the "Sun."* New York, 1918.

ORTH, SAMUEL P. *The Boss and the Machine, A Chronicle of the Politicians and Party Organization. Yale University Press,* 1919.

ORTH, SAMUEL P. *Five American Politicians.* Cleveland, 1906.

OSTROGORSKI, M. *Democracy and the Organization of Political Parties,* two volumes. New York, 1902.

PARKHURST, REV. CHARLES H. *My Forty Years in New York.* New York, 1923.

PARKHURST, REV. CHARLES H. *Our Fight with Tammany.* New York, 1895.

PECK, HARRY THURSTON. *Twenty Years of the Republic, 1885-1905.* New York, 1906.

PINCHOT, AMOS. *A Letter to the County Chairman and Other Chairmen.* A Pamphlet (n.d.).

PLATT, THOMAS COLLIER. *The Autobiography of Thomas Collier Platt,* Compiled and Edited by Louis J. Lang. New York, 1910.

Political Mission of Tammany Hall, The. A Tract for the Times. 1892.

Proceedings of a Select Committee of the Senate of the State of New York, Appointed to Investigate Various Departments of the Government of the City of New York. Senate Document No. 38, Documents of the Senate of the State of New York, 88th Session, 1865. Vol. II.

Report and Proceedings of the Senate Committee Appointed to Investigate the Police Department of the City of New York, 5 volumes. Albany, 1895. (Lexow Investigation.)

Report of the Special Committee of the Assembly Appointed to Investigate the Public Offices and Departments of the City of New York and of the Counties Therein Included, 5 volumes. Albany, 1900. (Mazet Investigation.)

Report of the Special Committee on the Subject of the Fourth Ward Contested Election. Board of Aldermen, Document No. 13, September 17th, 1849. New York, 1849.

Report of the Special Committee of the Board of Aldermen Appointed to Investigate the "Ring" Frauds, Together with the Testimony Elicited During the Investigation. Board of Aldermen, January 4, 1878, Document No. 8, New York, 1878. (Tweed Ring Investigation.)

RIORDAN, WILLIAM L. *Plunkitt of Tammany Hall, A Series of Very Plain Talks on Very Practical Politics, Delivered by Ex-Senator George Washington Plunkitt, the Tammany Philosopher, from His Rostrum—the New York County Court-House Bootblack Stand—and Recorded by William L. Riordan.* New York, 1905.

ROOSEVELT, THEODORE. *American Ideals,* New York, 1897.

ROOSEVELT, THEODORE, *Autobiography.* New York, 1913.

SHERMAN, P. TECUMSEH. *Inside the Machine, Two Years in the Board of Aldermen, 1898-1899.* New York, 1901.

SMITH, MATTHEW HALE. *Sunshine and Shadow in New York.* Hartford, 1869.

SMITH, THOMAS E. V. *Political Parties and Their Places of Meeting in New York City,* New York, 1893.

Social Evil in New York City, The, A Study of Law Enforcement by the Research Committee of the Committee of Fourteen. New York, 1910.

Social Evil, The, With Special Reference to Conditions Existing in the City of New York. A Report Prepared (in 1902) *under the Direction of the Committee of Fifteen.* Second edition, revised, with new material, New York, 1912.

STEAD, W. T. *Mr. Richard Croker and Greater New York. Review of Reviews* (English), Vol. XVI, pp. 341–355.

STEFFENS, LINCOLN. *The Shame of the Cities.* New York, 1904.

STEFFENS, LINCOLN. *The Struggle for Self-Government.* New York. 1906.

Sulzer, William. *Proceedings of the Court for the Trial of Impeachments, The People of the State of New York by the Assembly Thereof Against William Sulzer, as Governor,* 2 volumes. Albany, 1913.

Sulzer, William. *Scrapbooks compiled by William Sulzer during his official life, and presented by his body-guard, Emil Kovarik, to the New York Public Library (1902–1906),* 7 volumes.

Sulzer, William. *Speeches. Miscellaneous Collection Presented to the New York Public Library by William Sulzer.*

Swartwout, Samuel. *Report of the Committee of Investigation on the Subject of the Defalcations of Samuel Swartwout and Others. 25th Congress, 3d Session, House of Representatives.* 1839.

Tammany Hall, Souvenir of the Inauguration of Cleveland and Stevenson, Washington, D. C., March 4th, 1893.

Tammany Society; or Columbian Order, Celebration at Tammany Hall, on Saturday, July 4, 1863. New York, 1863.

Tammany Society; or Columbian Order. Celebration of the Ninety-Fourth Anniversary of American Independence, at Tammany Hall, Monday, July 4, 1870. New York, 1870.

Tammany Times, The, Vols. I–VI, 1893–1896.

Ten Months of Tammany. Published by the City Club of New York, A. Pamphlet. 1901.

Testimony Relating to the Great Election Frauds of 1838, Taken in the Recorder's Court, New York, in October, 1840. A Pamphlet published by the New York *Evening Post.*

Testimony Taken Before the Senate Committee on Cities, Pursuant to Resolution Adopted January 20, 1890, 5 volumes. (Fassett Investigation.)

THOMAS, SAMUEL BELL. *The Boss, or the Governor, the Truth about the Greatest Political Conspiracy in the History of America,* New York, 1914.

TILDEN, SAMUEL J. *Letters and Literary Memorials of Samuel J. Tilden. Edited by John Bigelow, LL.D.,* 2 volumes. New York, 1908.

Tilden, Samuel J., Life of, by John Bigelow, 2 volumes, New York, 1895.

TOWNSEND, JOHN D. *New York in Bondage.* New York, 1901.

Triumph of Reform, The. A History of the Great Political Revolution, November 6, 1894. New York, 1895.

TURNER, GEORGE KIBBE. *Tammany's Control of New York by Professional Criminals. McClure's Magazine,* Vol. XXXIII, No. 2, June, 1909, pp. 117–134.

Tweed Ring Investigation. *Report of the Special Committee of the Board of*

Aldermen Appointed to Investigate the "Ring" Frauds, Together with the Testimony Elicited During the Investigation. Board of Aldermen, *January 4, 1878, Document No. 8,* New York, 1878.

Tweed, William M., *Romance of His Flight and Exile. Harper's Weekly,* Vol. XXI, 1877, p. 284.

Wallabout Prison Ship Series. Account of the Interment of the Remains of American Patriots, Who Perished on Board the British Prison Ships During the American Revolution. New York, 1865.

Walsh, Mike. *Sketches of the Speeches and Writings of Michael Walsh: Including His Poems and Correspondence.* Compiled by a Committee of the Spartan Association. New York, 1843.

Walsh, Mike. *The Subterranean.* A New York weekly, 1845.

WATERMAN, WILLIAM RANDALL. *Frances Wright,* New York, 1924.

WHITE, ANDREW DICKSON. *Autobiography,* two volumes. New York, 1905.

WHITE, WILLIAM ALLEN. *Croker. McClure's Magazine,* Vol. XVI, p. 317. 1901.

Wholesale Corruption! Sale of Situations in Fourth Ward Schools. Report of the Committee Appointed by the Board of Education. Published by the Citizens' Association of New York.

WILKES, GEORGE. *The Mysteries of the Tombs. A Journal of Thirty Days' Imprisonment in the New York City Prison; For Libel.* New York, 1844.

WILLIAMS, TALCOTT. *Tammany Hall.* Essay in *Historic New York, Being the Second Series of the Half Moon Papers.* New York, 1899.

WINGATE, CHARLES F. *An Episode in Municipal Government. The Tweed Ring. North American Review,* Vol. CXIX, p. 359; Vol. CXX, p. 119; Vol. CXXI, p. 113.

Wood, Fernando. *A Biography of Fernando Wood, A History of the Forgeries, Perjuries, and Other Crimes of Our "Model" Mayor.* A Pamphlet by Abijah Ingraham, not signed.

Wood, Fernando. *A Condensed Biography of a Candidate for Speaker! Fernando Wood, His Forgeries and Other Crimes.*

Wood, Fernando. *Annual Message of His Honor the Mayor, Fernando Wood, January 7, 1861. Documents of the Board of Aldermen, Part I, January to July 1861, Vol. XXVIII, Document No. 1.*

Wood, Fernando. *Memorial Addresses on the Life and Character of Fernando Wood, Delivered in the House of Representatives, February 28, 1881.*

Wood, Fernando. *Oration Delivered by Hon. Fernando Wood, on the Anniversary of Washington's Birthday, February 22, 1862, at Scranton, Pa.* New York, 1862.

WRIGHT, FRANCES. *What Is the Matter? A Political Address as Delivered in Masonic Hall, October 28th, 1838.* New York. Published for the Author. 1838.

NEWSPAPERS

New York *Times,* New York *Tribune,* the *Sun,* the *World,* the *Evening Post,* the *Morning Courier and Enquirer,* the *Evening Journal,* New York *American,* New York *Herald.* Various dates.

INDEX

INDEX

Abortionists, a source of graft for police and politicians, 375.

Adams, Charles Francis, comments on corruption of state legislatures, 178, 178.

Allen, Theodore, testifies as to method of obtaining fraudulent naturalization, 135.

American Commonwealth, The, author is sued by A. Oakey Hall for libel, 274–75.

Americus Club, its luxurious home, 196.

Ames, Fisher, comments on Colonel Alexander McGillivray, 14.

Anti-Croker forces, demonstration of their strength, 471; League is formed in New York, 474; its open letter to Croker, 474.

Anti-foreign sentiment, preached by the Know Nothings, 74–75.

Astor, John Jacob, a member of Boss Tweed's "whitewashing" committee, 207.

Aycrigg, Benjamin, secures collection of bones of Revolutionary War martyrs, 28.

Augusta *Sentinel,* speculates on whereabouts of Tweed, 247.

Baby farmers, a source of graft for police and politicians, 375.

Baker, Abraham, testifies to false registration and voting, 150.

Baker, Gardiner, curator of the Tammany Museum, 15.

Ballots, their printing and distribution paid for by the political parties, 31.

Barber, A. D., is described by Boss Tweed, 179.

Barnard, George G., one of Mayor Fernando Wood's counsel, 88; judge of the Supreme Court, 103, 113; character and early life, 124; habits and language on the bench, 126 ff.; his part in fraudulent naturalization, 134; issues injunctions at request of Fisk, Gould, Drew, and Tweed, 178; grants injunction preventing Comptroller Connolly from functioning, 222; grants bail to Boss Tweed, 235.

"Barnburners," Tammany faction opposed to monopolies, excessive rents, and extension of slavery, 70.

Barnum, P. T., secures Tammany Museum collections, 16.

Bartlett, Willard, one of Boss Tweed's counsel, 237.

Bartlett, William O., one of Boss Tweed's counsel, 235.

Bayard, Senator, considers Alexander Hamilton's proposed anti-Tammany organization impracticable, 24; predicts end of Tammany's system, 25.

Bayne Legislative Investigating Committee, characterizes William Barnes, Jr., as beneficiary of graft, 516.

Beach, William H., comments on Judge George G. Barnard, 127.

Bedford, Judge Gunning, refuses bail to Boss Tweed, 233.

Beecher, Henry Ward, comments on Tweed régime, 206.

Behrman, Dr. Morris, comments on conduct of pimps in Allen and Rivington streets, 401.

Belmont, August, chairman of Tammany meeting, 208.

Bennett, James Gordon, comments on Tweed wedding gifts, 193.

Bingham, Gen. Theodore A., comments on conduct of political leaders, 357; comments on wonderful "underground" telegraph in the Police Dept., 370; writes concerning the relations of Tammany Hall and the pimps of the East Side, 402.

Birdseye, Lucien, testifies to Judge George G. Barnard's language on the bench, 126.

"Bismarck of New York, The." *See under* Kelly, "Honest John."

Bisset, James B., signs notice of Tammany funeral procession for Alexander Hamilton, 26.

Black Horse Cavalry, is described by Boss Tweed, 174; its method, 177.

Black Rabbit, The, 409.

Blake, Mrs. Euphemia Vale, comments on Chief Tammany's visit to Peru, 3; comment on Creeks' visit to New York, 14.

Bloodgood, John M., dispenses necessities bought with money extorted from defendants in his court, 44.

Blossom Club, its building, 196.

Board of Aldermen, known as "The Forty Thieves," 70; Boss Tweed's comment on their honesty, 108.

Board of Aldermen Committee, investigation sheds light on methods of the Tweed Ring, 253; majority report, 269.

Board of Assistant Aldermen, profits from passing Third Avenue Railroad Company franchise, 71.

Board of Education, evidence of corruption under Tweed Ring, 109.

Board of Supervisors, its power somewhat similar to that of the Board of Estimate, 110; is abolished, 111.

Boeck, Maximilian, testifies on obtaining fraudulent naturalization, 137.

Boole, Francis I. A., head of the Health Department, 153.

Booth Committee, reports on increase of City's debt during Tweed régime, 160.

Bracket, Senator Edgar T., sums up the case against William Sulzer, 544.

Breen, Matthew P., account of Supreme Court examination of candidates for the bar, 128; estimates number of the "Shiny Hat Brigade," 170.

Brennan, Sheriff Matthew T., arrests Boss Tweed, 233.

Broderick, David C., urges Michael Walsh to commit suicide, 53.

Brown, E. D., a member of Boss Tweed's "whitewashing" committee, 207.

Bryant, Cornelius O'Brien, describes Tweed's escape from jail, 245.

Bryant, William Cullen, criticizes Fanny Wright, 41.

Bryce, James, is sued for libel by A. Oakey Hall, 274–75.

Burns, Big Tom, fights John Morrissey, 68.

577